Communications
in Computer and Information Science   1395

More information about this series at http://www.springer.com/series/7899

Pradeep Kumar Singh · Gennady Veselov ·
Valeriy Vyatkin · Anton Pljonkin ·
Juan Manuel Dodero · Yugal Kumar (Eds.)

Futuristic Trends in Network and Communication Technologies

Third International Conference, FTNCT 2020
Taganrog, Russia, October 14–16, 2020
Revised Selected Papers, Part I

 Springer

Editors
Pradeep Kumar Singh ⓘ
ABES Engineering College
Ghaziabad, India

Gennady Veselov ⓘ
Southern Federal University
Rostov-on-Don, Russia

Valeriy Vyatkin ⓘ
Luleå University of Technology
Luleå, Sweden

Anton Pljonkin ⓘ
Southern Federal University
Rostov-on-Don, Russia

Juan Manuel Dodero ⓘ
University of Cádiz
Cádiz, Spain

Yugal Kumar ⓘ
Jaypee Institute of Information Technology
Waknaghat, India

ISSN 1865-0929   ISSN 1865-0937 (electronic)
Communications in Computer and Information Science
ISBN 978-981-16-1479-8   ISBN 978-981-16-1480-4 (eBook)
https://doi.org/10.1007/978-981-16-1480-4

This Springer imprint is published by the registered company Springer Nature Singapore Pte Ltd.
The registered company address is: 152 Beach Road, #21-01/04 Gateway East, Singapore 189721, Singapore

Preface

The Third International Conference on Futuristic Trends in Networks and Computing Technologies (FTNCT 2020) provided a single platform for researchers from different domains of Networks and Computing Technologies to showcase their research ideas. The four main technical tracks of the conference were: Network and Computing Technologies, Wireless Networks and Internet of Things (IoT), Futuristic Computing Technologies and Communication Technologies, and Security and Privacy. The conference was planned as an annual ongoing event. We are sure about its growth and quality year after year. The 3rd International Conference on Futuristic Trends in Networks and Computing Technologies (FTNCT 2020) was hosted by Southern Federal University, Russia, during October 14–16, 2020. The conference had several academic partners such as: Jaypee University of Information Technology, Waknaghat, India, University of Buenos Aires, Argentina, University of Cádiz, Spain, Manipal University Jaipur, India, University of Informatics Sciences, Cuba, Luleå University of Technology, Sweden, Institute of Control Sciences of Russian Academy of Sciences, Russia, University of Málaga, Spain, Technical University of Košice, Slovakia, University of Havana, Cuba, IAC Education, India, and SETIT, University of Sfax, Tunisia. These 12 organizations were the academic collaborators for FTNCT 2020.

We are highly thankful to our valuable authors for their contributions and to our Technical Program Committee for their immense support and motivation towards making the third version of FTNCT a grand success. We are also grateful to our keynote speakers: Dr. Valeriy Vyatkin, Aalto University, Helsinki, Finland; Dr. Sheng-Lung Peng, National Dong Hwa University, Taiwan; Dr. Arpan Kumar Kar, IIT Delhi, India; Dr. Sanjay Sood, Assoc. Director, C-DAC Mohali, India; Dr. Maheshkumar Kolekar, IIT Patna, India; Dr. Sergei Kulik, Lomonosov Moscow State University, Moscow, Russia; Dr. Sudeep Tanwar, Nirma University, India; Dr. Pradeep Kumar, University of KwaZulu-Natal, South Africa; Dr. Vivek Sehgal, Jaypee University of Information Technology, Waknaghat, Solan, HP, India; and Dr. Yugal Kumar from Jaypee University of Information Technology, Waknaghat, Solan, HP, India. We thank them for sharing their technical talks and enlightening the delegates of the conference.

The Conference Inauguration took place in the presence of the Rector, Southern Federal University, the Director of the Institute of Computer Technologies and Information Security, and the Head of the Department of Information Security of Telecommunication Systems from SFU, Russia, other guests, and media persons. We are thankful to Dr. Yuriy Zachinyaev for organizing the conference in such a nice way.

The organizing committee would like to express their special thanks to Prof. Konstantin Rumyantsev for his guidance and support from time to time.

We express our sincere gratitude to our publication partner, Springer CCIS Series, for believing in us. We are thankful to Ms. Kamiya Khatter, Associate Editor, and Mr. Amin Mobasheri, Editor, Springer CCIS Series, for extending their help from time to time in the preparation of these proceedings.

October 2020

Pradeep Kumar Singh
Gennady Veselov
Valeriy Vyatkin
Anton Pljonkin
Juan Manuel Dodero
Yugal Kumar

Organization

Honorary Chairs

Gennady Veselov	Southern Federal University, Russia
Juan Manuel Dodero	University of Cádiz, Spain
Valeriy Vyatkin	Luleå University of Technology, Sweden
Sandeep Joshi	Manipal University Jaipur, India
Juan José Domínguez Jiménez	University of Cádiz, Spain
Hernán D. Merlino	University of Buenos Aires, Argentina
Bharat Bhargava	Purdue University, USA
Pao-Ann Hsiung	National Chung Cheng University, Taiwan
Wei-Chiang Hong	Oriental Institute of Technology, Taipei, Taiwan
Raúl Saroka	University of Buenos Aires, Argentina
Roman Meshcheryakov	Institute of Control Sciences of Russian Academy of Sciences, Russia
Miriam Nicado García	University of Havana, Cuba
Walter Baluja García	University of Informatics Sciences, Cuba
Iakov Korovin	Southern Federal University, Russia
Vladimir Kureychik	Southern Federal University, Russia
Konstantin Rumyantsev	Southern Federal University, Russia
Mikhail Karyakin	Southern Federal University, Russia
Evgeny Abramov	Southern Federal University, Russia
Ján Labun	Technical University of Košice, Slovakia
Pavol Kurdel	Technical University of Košice, Slovakia
José Francisco Chicano García	University of Málaga, Spain

Principal General Chairs

Yuriy Zachinyaev	Southern Federal University, Russia
Konstantin Rumyantsev	Southern Federal University, Russia

Executive General Chairs

Anton Pljonkin	Southern Federal University, Russia
Pradeep Kumar Singh	Jaypee University of Information Technology, India

Organizing Chairs

Alexey Samoilov	Southern Federal University, Russia
Abhijit Sen	Computer Science and Information Technology, Kwantlen Polytechnic University, Canada
Maria Ganzha	Warsaw University of Technology, Poland
Marcin Paprzycki	Systems Research Institute, Polish Academy of Sciences, Warsaw, Poland

Publication Chairs

Jitender Kumar Chhabra	Department of Computer Engineering, NIT Kurukshetra, India
Narottam Chand Kaushal	NIT Hamirpur, India
Sanjay Sood	C-DAC Mohali, India

Publicity Chairs

Ioan-Cosmin Mihai	"Alexandru Ioan Cuza" Police Academy, Romania
Pelin Angin	Purdue University, USA
Sudeep Tanwar	Nirma University, India

Organizing Secretaries

Yugal Kumar	Jaypee University of Information Technology, India
Sudhanshu Tyagi	Thapar Institute of Engg. & Technology, Patiala, India

Academic Collaborators

University of Buenos Aires, Argentina

University of Cádiz, Spain

MANIPAL UNIVERSITY
JAIPUR

Manipal University Jaipur, India

University of Informatics Sciences, Cuba

Luleå University of Technology, Sweden

Institute of Control Sciences of Russian Academy of Sciences, Russia

UNIVERSIDAD DE MÁLAGA

University of Málaga, Spain

Technical University of Košice, Slovakia

University of Havana, Cuba

JUIT, Waknaghat, India   SETIT, Tunisia

Organized By

Southern Federal University, Russia

Other Supporters of FTNCT 2020: Conference Alerts as technical promoters, IAC Education, India, Easy Chair, and many more.

Contents – Part I

Communication Technologies, Security and Privacy

Futuristic Computing Technologies

Contents – Part II

Wireless Networks and Internet of Things (IoT)

Communication Technologies, Security and Privacy

Medchain: Securing Electronic Medical Records with a Peer to Peer Networks and Distributed File System

H. L. Gururaj[1(✉)], B. Goutham[1], V. Janhavi[1], K. C. Suhas[2], and M. N. Manu[3]

[1] Vidyavardhaka College of Engineering, Mysuru, India
{goutham.b,janhavi.v}@vvce.ac.in
[2] Channabasaveshwara Institute of Technology, Tumkur, India
suhas@cittumkur.org
[3] SJB Institute of Technology, Bengaluru, India

Abstract. Though the advances in technology have changed every aspect of our lives, it has barely budged the way we think about our medical records being stored across various platforms. This electronic document talks about the problem that has always existed in the medical field but has failed to be solved; Privacy in the current electronic medical record systems. This paper discusses the failure of traditional medical record systems in terms of security and sustenance to ease of use and provides a possible solution to use today's technology to address the disadvantages.

Keywords: EHR · Health · Privacy · Medical · Records · Security · IPFS · Bigchaindb · RFID · dApp · Distributed systems · EAS

1 Introduction

The amount of digital data over the last few years have increased exponentially to the point where it doubles every year and completely changing how we live every day. This shows that there is no doubt that the oil of the future economy is data. Large scale companies require more and more data as machine learning algorithms become more robust. Social media sectors are already facing the backlash for selling data. In coming days, large scale corporates and big companies may pay to get their hands on our data, as data is valuable and intrinsically [1].

Today, actualizing and upgrading their electronic health record systems posed as a major challenge to hospitals and health systems [2]. The theme of this document is to safely store health related documents and for the purpose of a maintaining the single version of the truth. A most probable solution is to convert to a decentralized application. The many other organizations such as hospitals, doctors, laboratories and other health insurers can record transactions and serve their purpose, on the distributed ledger, by requesting permission to access a patient's record. Electronic health records can be stored and shared securely by building a platform and creating a distributed access with a verification unit which will completely replace the present centralized intermediaries Hence providing the solution to current health record problems.

© Springer Nature Singapore Pte Ltd. 2021
P. K. Singh et al. (Eds.): FTNCT 2020, CCIS 1395, pp. 3–16, 2021.
https://doi.org/10.1007/978-981-16-1480-4_1

2 Traditional Electronic Health Record Systems

From past certain few years there is a limitations in the level of care which health professionals can provide, this because of the non availability for the complete and accurate data of health records. This paper ignores the existence of non-electronic and only considers existing Electronic Health Records (EHR). An electronic health record (EHR) is a record of details patient's medical health like physical examination, history, investigations and treatment stored in a digital format. The is a different Record Management Software for every hospital. Some use a cloud service provider, some store data locally in their databases and some store the data in a format compliant with insurance agencies. The user's data is on a server that belongs to the hospital or is rented by the hospital most of the time [3].

2.1 Major Problems Caused by This Model [4]

- Fragmentation of the patient's medical information. Movement of patients between various providers leads to the loss of their past records. The data will be scattered among various organization. Which results in fragmentation of the patients medical information across the hospitals, medical related apps and among other medical practitioners.
- Transferring of records from one medical organization to another is a big challenge. Patients will not be able to get the complete access to their health records, Therefore patients face a lot of problem of undergoing the same test for multiple times in different organization.
- Inability for accessing of important information under emergency condition.
- Leaking of data from hospitals that sell the patient data to companies that benefit from patient's information.
- Data manipulation can be done by hospital authorities.
- Restricted access to medical data of patients.

3 Statistics

Figure 1 shows the statistics of health care data breaches from October 2009, which is obtained from the office of the department of health and human service. About 500 or more breaches of data is included in the statistics. OCR still investigates the cases and even the closed cases are also included in the statistics. From the record we can clearly say that from past nine years there is a upward trend in data breaches. According to the records 2017 has been viewed as the most data breaches than any other year. Health breaches cases of 2181 has been registered between the year of 2019 to 2017. These breaches were consisting of 500 plus records which ended in the exposure or theft up to 176,709,305 health record, which is almost 54.25% of USA population.

For Large healthcare data breach statistics showed in Fig. 2 and Fig. 3. These statistics show that, hacking is the main reason for healthcare data breaches, even though nowadays health care sector are much more improvised in detecting breaching. The decreased hacking incidents in the last few years is probably due to the organization's

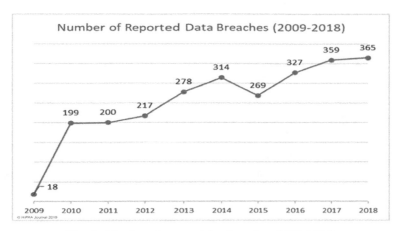

Fig. 1. Number of reported data breaches (2009–2018)

inability to quickly detect malware infections and hacking incidents. Most of the hacking incidents took place between years 2014 and 2017 occurred for many years months or also sometimes, years, before they were detected.

Healthcare organizations are doing well at identifying internal breaches and they are reporting these breaches, in time, to the Office for Civil Rights. Although hacking is presently reported as a main cause of breaches, Health care records or confidential information's unauthorized access are taking place regularly.

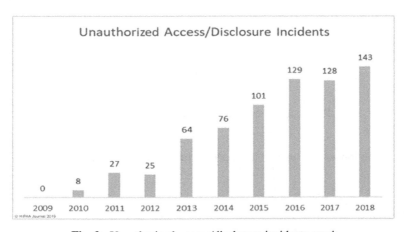

Fig. 2. Unauthorized access/disclosure incidents graph

No incident that has occurred can be treated lightly as the impact of each incident as seen in Table 1 [3] must be dealt with seriously. Data breach and impractise in the medical field is the latent issue that we need to address at the earliest.

With the ever greed in the race towards developing technology, the rise in better systems and better ways to breach security arises. The development of electronic medical

Table 1. Largest healthcare data breaches

Name of covered entity	Year	Covered entity type	Individuals affected	Type of breach
Anthem Inc.	2015	Health Plan	78,800,000	Hacking/IT Incident
Premera Blue Cross	2015	Health Plan	11,000,000	Hacking/IT Incident
Excellus Health Plan Inc.	2015	Health Plan	10,000,000	Hacking/IT Incident
Science Applications International Corporation	2011	Business Associate	4,900,000	Loss
University of California, Los Angeles Health	2015	Healthcare Provider	4,500,000	Hacking/IT Incident
Community Health Systems Professional Services Corporations	2014	Business Associate	4,500,000	Hacking/IT Incident
Advocate Medical Group	2013	Healthcare Provider	4,029,530	Theft
Medical Informatics Engineering	2015	Business Associate	3,900,000	Hacking/IT Incident
Banner Health	2016	Healthcare Provider	3,620,000	Hacking/IT Incident
Newkirk Products, Inc	2016	Business Associate	3,466,120	Hacking/IT Incident

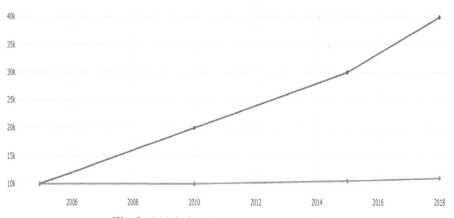

Fig. 3. Rise in breaches vs Improvements in EHRs

records can no longer be stagnant and needs a revolutionary improvement to challenge today's needs [5].

4 Strategy

As shown in Fig. 5, the number of breaches seems to be increasing or at least the possibilities of another huge data breach but the improvement needed to combat such risks in EHRs have completely been stagnated. The use of latest technologies to combat latest risks is an ideal option.

4.1 IPFS – Inter Planatary File System

Traditional Client-Server architecture based applications come with a lot of disadvantages. Traffic congestion is one of the major problems. Problems can occur when a huge number of similar clients send requests to the common server. The P2P network fastness is absent in the paradigm of Client-Server classic. Customer requests cannot be met when the servers go down. But the resources of P2P network are divided across many nodes of the network. A Client Server system also comes with a very high expense as the security, robustness and clients increase and hence the server needs to scale up [6].

Medical records are hence chosen to not be stored in a Client Server model. The idea of storing all the records in a single location not only compromises the security aspect of the application but also increases the cost to set up a server to serve multiple requests to store and fetch files of variable sizes. Hence we choose to use IPFS.

In HTTP, a single computer downloads a file at a time, without involving many computers for getting a different piece. This P2P method will save 60% of band cost, with video delivery.

Large volume of data distribution, with high efficiency can be achieved using IPFS. Zero duplication leads to massive savings in storage. The webpage will have only 100days of lifespan which is not good enough, as the main medium of our age cannot be so fragile. All types of your files is stored by IPFS and it makes the work easy to perform the resilient network for mirroring of data.

IPFS is currently the first vision of the open and flat web. The IPFS delivers the technology which makes that vision, a reality.

Offline, intermittent connections, natural disasters, developing world, are all trivial when compared to the interplanetary networking. The networks used today mostly belong to the 20th Century. The creation of diversely resilient networks is powered by IPFS. With or without Internet backbone connectivity, IPFS enables persistent availability.

IPFS has a very unique way to store the files that is provided. A unique fingerprint is given to each file and all the blocks within it, called a cryptographic hash. Next IPFS makes sure that there are no duplicate files receding in the network, rather than finding duplicates with merely each file's name, IPFS checks for the content and removes duplicate content. To improve efficiency, IPFS nodes only store content, that it is interested in and a little indexing information about the files that are being stored. Now when a file is requested from the IPFS a query with the hash is sent which is unique to each content of the file within a network.

IPFS is hence the best way to store the medical records for its security, P2P system and low cost to set up a node. Medchain uses the ipfs-http-client library which exposes multiple APIs to interact with the IPFS.

4.2 BigchainDB

In block chain characteristics, bigchain DB is like a characteristics, consisting of low latency, high throughput, powerful query functionality built-in asset support, decentralized control and immutable data storage. Developers are allowed in Bigchain DB for usage of block chain proof-of-concepts, platforms and application with a blockchain database.

BigchainDB starts with a bigdata distributed-database and rather than trying to enhance blockchain technology, it adds blockchain characteristics.

- Decentralization – For P2P network common point of control through a federation of voting node is not made.
- Immutability – The data which is stored once is just not tamper-resistant but even cannot be detected or changed.
- Byzantine Fault Tolerant – If arbitrary faults are faced by one third of the network, The other part of the network will come to action on the next block.
- Customizable – Design a completely custom private network with transactions, custom assets, transparency and permissions.
- Open Source – Any developer will be able to build the own application on top of it.
- Query – Write and run MongoDB query to search the content of all stored transactions, assets and metadata.
- Native Support for Multiassets – Any asset token, or currency can be used, due to absence of a native currency.
- Low Latency – A global network takes about a second to come to consensus on a new block, i.e., transactions happen extremely fast.

The IPFS exposes a cryptographic hash to refer the files that are stored in its system. Anybody who can access to his hashes have a possibility to access the file from the IPFS network. Medchain therefore required a system to store and record these assets in an immutable system. BigchainDB is the optimal solution. The hashes once generated are stored in BigchainDB and recorded as assets with the owners of each file via their public keys and signed using their private keys.

4.3 MongoDB

As Medchain is an end to end application, there exists data which needs to be securely stored but cannot use a decentralized system or blockchain. For example, an authentication system needs the username and password to be stored, but a blockchain or IPFS cannot be used because of the toll it takes on the user interface of the application. It was therefore required for a substitute storage solution for all other local information and to store each account's cryptic public key. Hence MongoDB was the obvious choice, they come with the following characteristics [7].

- Dynamic schema: Flexibility will be given to change the data schema without any changes in the existing data
- Scalabilty: MongoDB is horizontally scalable, which helps scale your business and reduce the workload with ease.
- Manageability: The database is fairly user-friendly since doesn't require a database administrator. Both the administrator and the developer can use this.
- Speed: For simple queries performance speed is high.
- Flexibility: Their will be a provision for addition of new fields and column without causing problem to the performance to the existing rows or applications.

4.4 RFID

RFID or Radio Frequency Identification System is a identification based technology system. The RFID helps identify objects just through the tags attached to them. They do not require any light of sight between the tags and the tag reader. The only thing that is necessary is a radio communication between the tag and the reader.

There are three main components of a RFID system: a RFID tag, a reader and a processor that receives the reader input and processes the data.

RFID tags are best suited to be linked with individual patients and a reader can be installed and set up with a doctor. The patient can carry the tag rather than a bulky and fragile medical file and trust Medchain to handle all the data linked with the patient.

4.5 Tendermint

The tendermint core is a byzantine-fault tolerant state machine replication system or a blockchain for short. The Tendermint Core is a application platform of the blockchain. Tendermint provides the equivalent of a database, or a web-server, or supporting libraries for blockchain applications which can be written in any programming languages. Tendermint serves blockchain applications, just like a web-server serving web applications.

Tendermint Core performs Byzantine Fault Tolerant (BFT) State Machine Replication (SMR) for arbitrary deterministic, finite state machines.

Even if up to 1/3 of the machines fail in arbitrary ways Tendermint can work. Also, every non-faulty machine sees the same transaction log and computes the same state. A fundamental problem in distributed systems is having secure and consistent replication. It plays a critical role in the fault tolerance of a broad range of applications.

The of two important technical components of Tendermint are- A blockchain consensus and a engine generic application interface. The Tendermint Core, or the blockchain consensus engine, ensures that the same transactions are recorded on every machine in order. The application interface, called the Application BlockChain Interface (ABCI), allows the transactions to be processed in any programming languages. Medchain does not directly interact with the Tendermint Core but uses the driver provided by BigchainDB to do the same.

5 Architecture and Implementation

The idea is to make Medchain a web application rather than the traditional native windows application because it is easy to set up and runs on any system which can run a browser. Figure 4 Shows the architecture of Medchain, the medchain symbol depicts the API which interacts with various elements of the architecture. Medchain is mainly built using the MERN stack.

The MERN stack consists of Express, MongoDB, Node.js and React/Redux. The most popular stack of technologies MERN stack is one of that can be used for building a modern single-page web applications, while keeping in mind the success of React in the frontend and of Node.js on the backend.

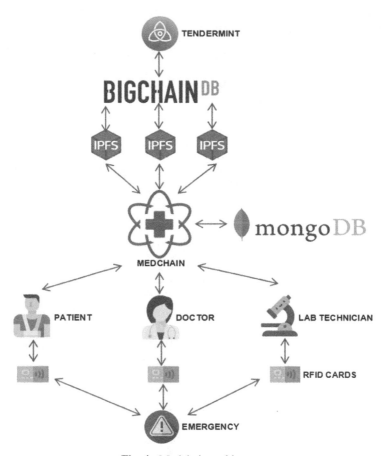

Fig. 4. Medchain architecture

The application mainly follows a particular flow, that patient, the doctor, the lap technician and any other third party can access Medchian. Once inside, any party has the ability to add records and connect it to a patient. The patient then has the ability to give permission to any party that needs the access. The patients can also store important emergency information which can be accessed via RFID cards.

The Medchain API interacts with MongoDB using mongoose to store non-sensitive information. Mongoose is an Object Data Modeling (ODM) library for MongoDB and Node.js. Mongoose can be used to translate between objects in code and the representation of those objects in MongoDB. It also manages relationships between data and provides schema validations. Mongoose exposes various APIs to make it easy to interact with mongodb. Many functions like find(), updateOne(), etc., can be used via mongoose. The application uses three models: File, Transaction and User to interact with the particular collections on Mongodb.

Medchain also uses Express to make RESTful APIs. Express is a unopinionated, fast, minimalist web framework for Node.js. Express and other nodejs packages are installed via npm or Node Packages Manager. Express is also installed the same way.

But mainly, express is a flexible Node.js web application and a minimal framework that provides a robust set of features for web and mobile applications. With a ocean of HTTP middleware and utility methods, express is capable of creating robust APIs that are quick and easily. Without obscuring Node.js features, Express provides a thin layer of fundamental web application features.

Medchain API interacts with the IPFS using ipfs-http-client. This is basically a client library for the IPFS HTTP API, implemented in JavaScript. This client library implements the interface-ipfs-core enabling applications to change between an embedded js-ipfs node and any remote IPFS node without having to change the code. In addition, this client library implements a set of utility functions. The two major functions that are used are ipfs.add () and ipfs.get () which are mainly used to store the files that is passed from react and served on Node.js via express and axis. The add function uses the file that is obtained using formidable, a Node.js library to handle files that are sent over an API. These files are then published to IPFS which returns the hash as a result. This hash Is then used to get the file using the ipfs.get() to obtain the file.

Medchain interacts with Tendermint via BigchainDB. BigchanDB is used in Node.js using the js-bigchaindb-driver. The main operations that are involved in Medchain and BigchainDB are the file information and the transactions. The file part keeps in check the file and the owner of the file. The public key is used to verify the file information and the private key is used to sign the asset. In the same way Medchain also records transactions and records them as an asset after getting signed from the owner of the transaction.

The patient obviously cannot expect to interact with Medchain during emergencies and hence are required of a system to overcome this. RDIF provides a viable solution where the important information is stored on MongoDB and the scanner can scan the IDs and process the information.

Finally, the application uses React for the front-end single page application. JavaScript library for building user interfaces is React. React makes it painless to create interactive User Interfaces. Medchain is completely built on React and hence has a robust architecture. The front-end interacts with Medchain API to use all its functions via axis.

6   Results

The users can be generally divided into patients and Doctors/Lab technicians.

Figure 5 shows the login page for Patients, which requires the patients phone number.

Figure 6 and 7 contain the registration portals of the patient and the doctor/lab technician respectively. The new patient is required to register by entering their name, phone number and a password, while the doctor/lab technician can register by entering name, username and password as their credential

Figure 7 shows the Dashboard of a user, containing the number of files presenting in the users account and the number of transactions that have been made with respect to any file belonging to the user.

The Patient or the Doctor can add files into the patient's account as shown in Fig. 8. The doctor can enter the patients number to let the platform know which patient is to receive the files.

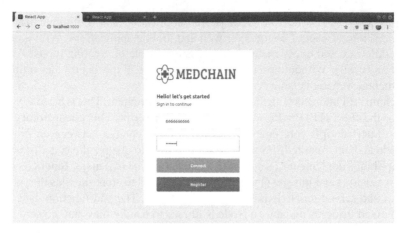

Fig. 5. Login page

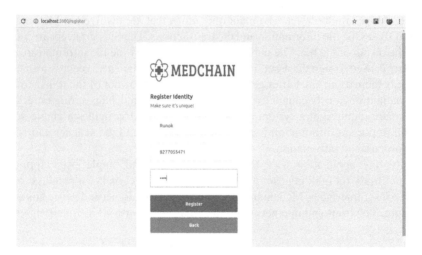

Fig. 6. Patient registration page

The uploaded files will be displayed in the window as shown in Fig. 9 and the number of Files in the patients dashboard gets increased accordingly. The transaction count increases in both the patient's and the doctor's dashboard.

The doctor cannot view any of the patient's files untill the patient permit the doctor to view a file. As shown in Fig. 10 the patient has to enter the user name of the doctor/lab technician to give them access to the file selected.

Figure 11 contains the updated dashboard of the doctor which shows the increase in the number of files and transactions. The doctor now also has the permission to view the patients file.

Figure 12 shows the list of nodes that the user's node is connected to, in a network. The location and ip of each connected node is also displayed.

List of Files:

Fig. 7. New dashboard

Fig. 8. Add files to a patient

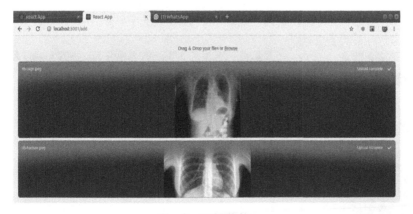

Fig. 9. Upload files

Fig. 10. Permit ThirdParty

Fig. 11. Updated dashboard

Fig. 12. New dashboard

7 Conclusion

The current EHR systems have major drawbacks due to the possibilities of fragmentation of data, manipulation of data, data leaks and inability to access vital information in cases of emergencies. This traditional system of EHRs can be challenged by using the latest technologies to combat the latest risks.

The use of IPFS in Medchain increases security and reduces expenses due to the low cost for setting the node. BigChainDB acts like a database with all of Blockchain's abilities making it easy for developers to deploy blockchain proof-of-concepts, platforms and applications with a blockchain database, support a wide range of use cases. The use of Tendermint makes Medchain less affected to machine failures. Tendermint works even if up to 1/3 of the machines fail in arbitrary ways.

By using medchain the fragmentation of data is avoided, privacy and security can be maintained efficiently. The patients will be have complete access and control over their data and will also have the capability to provide access to various users, hence improving data security.

In case of emergencies the risk of inability to access information is irradicated as the RFID cards carried by patients can be scanned by any medical practitioner, which will let them easily acquire the vital information about the patient's health. This will eradicate the problems of the current Electronic Health Record (EHR) systems. By digitizing health records and empowering users countless industry problems can be reduced.

References

1. Nigania, J.: Data is Gold: The Most Valuable Commodity, house of bots, 15 May 2018
2. Menachemi, N., Collum, T.H.: Benefits and drawbacks of electronic health record systems. Risk Manag. Healthc. Policy. **4**, 47–55 (2011). https://doi.org/10.2147/RMHP.S12985I
3. Aickin, M.: Patient-centered research from electronic medical records. Perm. J. **15**(4), 89–91 (2011)
4. O'Connor, S.: Pros and Cons of Electronic Health Records, Advanced Data Systems Corporation, 6 February 2017
5. HIPAA Journal, Healthcare Data Breach Statistics. ESDS, Advantages and Disadvantages of Client application server, 7 January 2011
6. Xplenty: The SQL vs NoSQL Difference: MySQL vs MongoDB, Medium, 2, 28 September 28, 2
7. Ruder, D.B.: Malpractice Claims Analysis Confirms Risks in EHRs. February 9, 2014 - Patton McGinley
8. Steward, M.: Electronic Medical Records Privacy, Confidentiality, Liability
9. Nakamoto, S.: Bitcoin: A Peer-to-Peer Electronic Cash System.
10. Benaloh, J., Chase, M., Horvitz, E., Lauter, K.: Patient controlled encryption: ensuring privacy of electronic medical records. In: Proceeding CCSW '09 Proceedings of the 2009 ACM workshop on Cloud computing security. Chicago, Illinois, USA, 13 November 2009
11. Wei, W.-Q., et al.: Impact of data fragmentation across healthcare centers on the accuracy of a high-throughput clinical phenotyping algorithm for specifying subjects with type 2 diabetes mellitus. J. Am. Med. Inform. Assoc. **19**(2), 219–224 (2012).Accessed 16 Jan 2012
12. Crosby, M., Nachiappan, Pattanayak, P., Verma, S., Kalyanaraman, V.: BlockChain Technology Beyond Bitcoin.

13. Alhadhrami, Z., Alghfeli, S.A.M., Abedlla, J.A., Shuaib, K.: Introducing blockchains for healthcare, 11 January 2018
14. Manoj, A., Ashwin, A., Nagarajath, S.M., Gururaj, H.L.: Decentralized E-Voting in crucial network using blockchain technology. Adv. Appl. Math. Sci. **18**(9), 843–850 (2019)

Secure IoT Framework Through FSIE Approach

Challa Madhavi Latha[(✉)] and K. L. S. Soujanya

CMR College of Engineering & Technology, Kandlakoya, Hyderabad, India

Abstract. Internet of Things (IoT) is one of the significant technologies, which interconnects and interrelate computing objects that transforms the information over the network. The digital and physical world is merged together and enables the communication with real time data. Nowadays, it is comprehensively affecting daily activities of human in both academic and industrial domains. Moreover, it aims to create a new intelligent era of IoT by integrating the smart objects with physical objects. However, IoT undergoes various challenging security issues, such as complexity of environment, constrained resources, scalability etc. To overcome these issues, many researchers developed efficient security solutions in various IoT frameworks, which focuses on ease of development, deployment and maintenance of IoT applications. In this paper, an IoT framework is mainly targeting to simplify the IoT application implementation and emphasizes the security mechanisms related to authentication, authorization, confidentiality, non-repudiation, privacy and availability. Moreover, the proposed framework named as Framework for Secure IoT Environment (FSIE) is compared with security architectures of AWS IoT, Azure IoT suite, Brillo/Weave (three) IoT frameworks. The comparative analysis is done by taking five parameters, which are computational complexity, communication complexity, mobility, scalability and quality of service. The new framework FSIE is providing security and privacy in terms of scalability and flexibility. It is also proved that it is more efficient than the other frameworks chosen.

Keywords: Internet of Things · Security · Authentication · Access control · Communication cost · Computational cost

1 Introduction

In the present scenario the physical world is transformed to smart world, in which Internet of Things (IoT) plays an outstanding role in all aspects for human beings. IoT makes the objects smarter than ever, which consists of sensors, chips embedded with physical objects and actuators (Al-Fuqaha et al. 2015). These are used to form network (Singh et al. 2019a) and transform the huge data among them and other components without intervention of human (Singh et al. 2018). IoT contributes considerably to enrich and enhance human comforts through many applications, which cover various sectors such as smart grids, smart cities, smart automobiles, smart homes, healthcare, industrial environment, entertainment etc.

However, application development in IoT is facing many challenges due to high complexity of computation, lack of communication and guidelines to implement novel

© Springer Nature Singapore Pte Ltd. 2021
P. K. Singh et al. (Eds.): FTNCT 2020, CCIS 1395, pp. 17–29, 2021.
https://doi.org/10.1007/978-981-16-1480-4_2

approaches and frameworks, ambiguity in several programming languages and compatibility of communication protocols (Derhamy et al. 2015). Further, it leads to handle both hardware and software requirements as well as infrastructure management by the developers (Fremantle and Scott 2017). To overcome these challenges several IoT programming frameworks are introduced, which mainly focuses on ease of development, deployment and maintenance of IoT applications.

In this paper, the comparative analysis of security features of selected frameworks and proposed framework is presented. The selected IoT frameworks are AWS IoT Amazon (2017), Azure IoT suite (Azure 2017), Brillo/Weave (Google. Brillo 2017). The selection was done based on reputation of software industries, number of developed applications, usage of framework and popularity. The main objective of this paper is focused on methods and models to ensure security and privacy services of the proposed FSIE approach and compare with the existing frameworks.

1.1 Motivation

Though the IoT systems have been used in various contexts, the resultant of smart devices, services of networks and information are creating unexpected problems (Zhang et al. 2017; Singh et al. 2019b). The central security (Madhavi et al. 2020) coordination is one of the solutions to address the issue of security for different contexts. However, this also presents few disadvantages, such as over usage of networks due to huge number of inter connected smart devices may lead to vulnerable attacks, various attacks are prone by limited capacity of smart devices. To overcome the above disadvantages, the proposed framework provides authentication, authorization, confidentiality, non-repudiation, privacy, and availability.

The paper consists of different parts. Section 2 describes Background of work. In Sect. 3, proposed framework which provides the services against the vulnerable attacks is described. Section 4 gives the Comparisons of security solutions and Security characteristics of AWS IoT, Azure IoT suite, Brillo/Weave and proposed FSIE framework. Section 5 enumerates summary and discussion of the results. Finally Sect. 6 reports the conclusion.

2   Background of This Work

The IoT environment is growing very rapidly among internet connected devices, ranging from simple sensors to complex servers (Rios and Lopez 2011). The existing IoT frameworks have been developed for the purpose of exchanging data among connected IoT devices (such as smart locks, smart bulbs, alarm clocks, vending machines, electronic appliances, IP cameras etc.,) without intervention of human actions. These allow remote control mechanism for IoT objects in network. The IoT framework covers the structure of IoT elements, which consists of protocols, set of rules and regulations that establish the technique to transform and process the secure data among all involved parties (users, IoT devices, servers) (Sheng et al. 2013). Moreover, it supports the IoT application implementation and simplifies the infrastructure protocols (Hunkeler et al. 2008). However, to maintain the secure IoT framework and protection from malicious attacks there is a need to provide the following services (Kumar and Patel 2014).

Authentication: it is a process of verifying the identification of authorized users and devices in a connected network environment and also it verifies the unauthorized persons and manipulation of devices. This process would be based on username and password, finger prints, scanning face or retina etc., and does work with connected devices. In IoT environment, the object, server and user's authentication is mandatory. According to the user's request the server is verifying security mechanisms provided by the IoT devices.

- Authorization: It is permitting the information to user or server or smart device in the IoT environment. The permission has been considered with appropriate identity of users, server and smart devices. This can allow the user, once the authentication is done.
- Confidentiality: It protects the smart objects and transformed information from the unauthorized access. It addresses the needful perceptions such as the mechanism of access control and smart device authentication process to ensure the authorized entities in IoT environment (Cooper 2017).
- Non repudiation: It is used to solve the data ownership problem in IoT environment. The data transmission among the nodes such as users, server and smart devices, are successful and they cannot deny other node's messages.
- Privacy: It ensures the data transmission among the IoT devices, users and server is confidential. In other words, without the knowledge of authorized entities the data cannot transfer to other nodes and it permits the transformation or sharing the information by the willingness of entity. In the IoT environment privacy supports the scalability by using various techniques like innovative enforcement techniques (Vikas 2015).
- Availability: The authorized users only get the access to the resources they required. It ensures the information reliability and recoverability in IoT environment. In the distributed environment of IoT, the plenty of data has been generated by entities, so the continuous assurance of data transmission takes place among the entities. Moreover, it is responsible for the malicious attacks and ensures the data availability and services availability in distributed IoT environment.

IoT framework security consists of techniques in order to ensure the guarantee the protection of data from various attacks such as leakage of data, infection of computer systems, fear to pay by card, monitored by unauthorized people etc. (Mahmoud et al.

Table 1. Various mechanisms for security services

Security services	Mechanism
1. Authentication	Message authentication code, digital signatures
2. Authorization	Passwords, PIN, security cards, hardware keys, fingerprint, pattern recognition (retina, face, voice)
3. Confidentiality	Symmetric key and public key encryption
4. Non repudiation	Digital signature, certificate authority
5. Privacy	K- anonymity, zero knowledge proof
6. Availability	Firewalls, intrusion prevention and detection, access control

2018; Narges et al. 2020). Several cryptographic techniques has been developed to ensure the security services and to deal with various attacks (Microsoft 2017) (Table 1).

3   Proposed Framework

Framework for Secure IoT Environment (FSIE) is a novel approach, which is responsible to provide the security in the aspects such as authentication, authorization, confidentiality, non- repudiation, privacy and availability.

3.1   Authentication

The single sign-in mechanism has been applied for the authentication procedure of users to interact with various IoT devices. Device authentication is necessary to transform data from various IoT devices. Various authentication procedures such as public key infrastructure, multichannel security (MCS), no spoofing and no-blocking channel (NSB) etc. are in use. The traditional authentication frameworks are very complex to manage smart devices like sensor nodes. Recently, MCS and NSB authentication protocols are more popular for out-of-band channels such as message passing, emails, face to face and call conversations. The MCS and NSB security protocols are maintaining protection among the network nodes. It is difficult for attackers to do eavesdropping, delay, manipulation, spoofing and blocking messages over the network by using these (MCS and NSB) security protocols. If the user has a smart phone registered with email and sim, then it is very simple to transform data between smart device and the IoT service provider by using public key. When smart devices are fixed in user's environment along with IP address, public key infrastructure becomes more complex and too ambiguous for smart devices. In this situation, the user and service provider cannot exchange their data, public keys and IP addresses securely. However, to solve such kind of problems the MCS protocols has been implemented. In this protocol the exchange of keys is applied by the following algorithm.

Algorithm for Authentication
Input: SDID, SDIP, SDPK, SPUQNonce
1. Message_A(SDID, SDIP, SDPK, SPUQNonce)
2. ACK_A(SPID, SPIP, SPPK, SDUQNonce, SPUQNonce)
3. Hash_MessSP()
   {
   SDres=Hash(SDID, SDIP, SDPK, SPUQNonce, SPID, SPIP, SPPK, SDUQNonce)
   Return(SDres)
   }
4. Hash_MessSD()
   {
   SDHash=Hash(SDID, SDIP, SDPK, SPUQNonce, SPID, SPIP, SPPK, SDUQNonce)
   }
5. Boolean b= ((SDHash == SDres)? "Yes": "No")

Step 1 explains the send message to smart device from service provider. Step 2 describes sending an acknowledgement to service provider from smart device. Step 3 can do hash function for Message_A and ACK_A generated by service provider, the output is sent to smart device. Step 4 does hash function for Message_A and ACK_A generated by Smart device. Step 5 return true when the smart device hash value and service provider hash values are same otherwise false through NSB. Figure 1 shows the exchange of messages among smart devices and service providers in which service provider and smart devices generate hash functions and NSB compares both the hash functions and generates the Boolean value.

3.2 Authorization

The user could get access rights on particular data, which is done by mechanism called as access control system (ACS) for example, role based access control, and policy based access control. ACS is useful to provide protection of data and privacy and it also supports to maintain user's data.

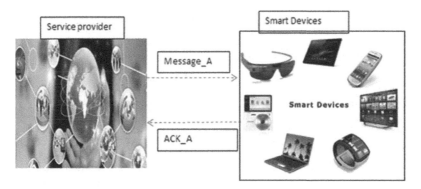

Fig. 1. Exchange messages among smart devices and service providers

Algorithm for Authorization
1. User_Req(RP) // user request to get access of smart IoT device
   {
   Authentication_ process()
   if (RP==identified) //Check authentication
     User=Authorized //User will get access
   else
     User = unauthorized //No access
   }
2. RP = Recognition pattern (PIN, Password, finger print, scan face, voice, retina etc.,)

Authorization algorithm checks the user privileges based on the authentication procedure. The above authorization algorithm provides the user access in the form of Boolean value. If the device generated hash value and the service provider generated hash value both are equal then the user could get access through NSB channel. Moreover it will not allow unauthorized users; therefore it assures the data privacy, easy access, auditing and manage data.

3.3 Confidentiality

Confidentiality has been approached through various encryption algorithms such as public key and private key mechanisms. Data encryption is a typical mechanism to ensure the confidentiality. In this paper confidentiality has been achieved through the following encryption and decryption algorithms (Fig. 2).

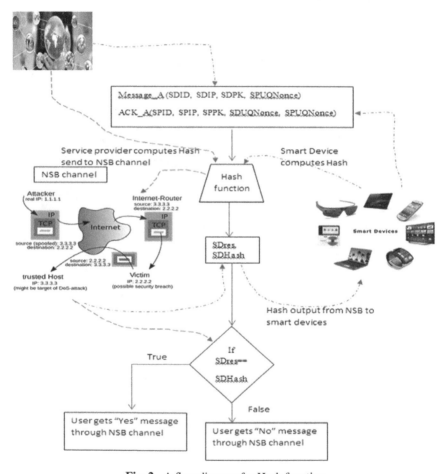

Fig. 2. A flow diagram for Hash function

Note: SDID: Smart device ID, SDIP: Smart device IP address, SDPK: Smart device Public Key, SPUQNonce: Unique nonce pseudo random number generated by service provider, SPID: Service provider ID, SPIP: Service provider IP address, SPPK: Service provider public key, SDUQNonce: Unique nonce pseudo random number generated by smart device.

Algorithm for Encryption process

Encry_process(N,p,q1,q2, PlTxt)
{

$(f, g) \leftarrow R f X g$

$f \quad f_p^{-1} \equiv 1 (mod\ p)$

$f \quad f_{q1}^{-1} \equiv 1 \ (mod\ q1)$

$g \quad g_{q1}^{-1} \equiv 1 \ (mod\ q1)$

$h1 = \left(p, f_{q1}^{-1}, g\right)_{q1}$

$h2 \leftarrow_R R_{q2}$

$PP^{-1} \equiv 1 \ (mod\ q1)$

$G = P^{-1} g_{q1}^{-1})q1$

$(r1, r2) \leftarrow R$

CiTxt $= (c1, c2) = ([r1\ h1 + r2]_{q1}, [r1\ h2 + r2 + PlTxt]_{q2})$
}

Algorithm for Decryption process

Dec_process(c1,c2)
{

$s = (f, c1)q1 \equiv p \quad g \quad r1 + f \quad r2\ (mod)q1$

$\left(s, f_{p1}^{-1}\right)_p \equiv f_{p1}^{-1}(p \ g \ r1 + f \ r2) \equiv r2(mod\ p)$

$s = p \ g \ r1 + f \ r2$

$r1 = \left(G \ (s - f \ r2)\right)_{q1} \left(\equiv P^{-1} g_{q1}^{-1} (p \ g \ r1 + f \ r2 - f \ r2)(mod\ q1)\right)$

PlTxt $= (c2 - r1 \ h2 - r2)_{q2}$
}

Encry_process() uses 5 parameters, in which 4 parameters N, p, q1, q2, where q1 and q2 consists of twin primes such that q1 + 2 = q2 ≈ q (Baocang et al. 2018) last one considered as plain text. Set $(f, g) \leftarrow RfXg$ and also compute inverses of f and g. f_p^{-1}, f_{q1}^{-1} and g_{q1}^{-1}, then compute h1 and h2 public keys and 3 tuple secrete key f, f^{-1}, G.

Cipher text could be processed to decryption, in which 's' should be compute first.

The D-NTRU cryptography algorithm is more secured because it produces the secret random polynomials f and g. Moreover the cipher text is divided into two parts such as c1 and c2, c1 is the first part, which is used to transfer shared key (r1 and r2), the second part c2 is encrypted by a one- time pad like encryption function.

3.4 Non Repudiation

Non repudiation is a process of assurance of data transmission between smart device and service provider. If both parties are authenticated then the data transmission should be allowed no one can stop the transmission. The following algorithm has been used in this framework to identify the user access.

Algorithm for Non repudiation
NRep(sender,receiver)
{
if(User_Req(RP))
EtEDataAgg() //then transmission allowed
}

3.5 Privacy

The smart objects and IoT servers could get communication through the infrastructure components of communication. One of the main challenges in communication is to enable the connection of smart objects or devices to the internet without any data lose or attacks (Yang et al. 2017). Moreover, it is dealing with connectivity as well as collection and sharing data to reach the goal. Therefore, smart technologies are playing a key role in privacy of data. However, according to the entity of user whose privacy has been threatened, the privacy problems classified into two categories (Rios and Lopez 2011). One is user centric problem, which comes from the ability of smart devices to detect the user presence and collect the sensitive data. Therefore, it is related to spy or surveillance of anyone or anything to trace. The second problem is network centric, which is related to the external attacks. The attacker, who wants to monitor the elements by the network, for instance, traffic analysis attacks. To solve the privacy problems the end-to-end encryption (Madhavi and Soujanya 2018, 2019) process for data aggregation has been used in this paper.

Algorithm for end-to-end encryption process for data aggregation
EtEDataAgg()
{
ND= read(SD); //Read data from smart device
Encry_process();
For(i=IP_N; i<(End_N) ; i=next_N)
{
If(i ==authorized)
Send(ND) // send data to nearby node
Else
Continue; //Change path and skip to another node
}
}

3.6 Availability

The availability of data has been classified into three categories; those are autonomy, pervasiveness and ubiquity.

Autonomy. It is responsible to independent control on own devices, in which all nodes react smartly and deliver the actions based on independent decision making.

Pervasiveness. The status of nodes always should be in running mode and accessible. Therefore, the nodes accessibility is increased rapidly.

Ubiquity. From anywhere each node has to respond and accessible, it is considered to everywhere or globally accessible nodes.

The availability has been achieved by connecting the devices through internet. If the smart devices, gateways and servers always connected to the internet then the availability of device and data could be possible as shown in the Fig. 3.

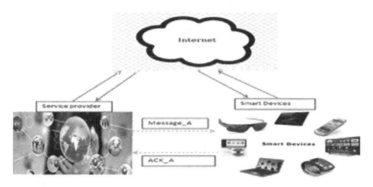

Fig. 3. Availability of devices and communication channels

4 Comparative Analysis and Results

The proposed framework has been compared with three selected frameworks (AWS IoT, Azure IoT suite, Brillo/Weave) (Table 2).

Table 2. Security characteristics of AWSIoT, Azure IoT suite, Brillo/Weave and FSIE frameworks.

Security characteristics	AWS IoT	Azure IoT suite	Brillo/Weave	FSIE
Access control	IAM roles, sand boxing, rules engine	Access control rules for Azure IoT hub	Sandboxing: UID, GID, ACL, SELinux,	FSIE IoT Access control rules and active directory policies, 16 x 16 s-box
Cryptography	128 bit AES, other primitives	Multiple cryptography primitives	Full disk encryption of Linux kernel	128 bit IAES, multiple primitives
Communication	SSL/TLS	TLS/DTLS	SSL/TLS	SSL/TLS
Authentication	X.509 certificate	X.509 certificate	OAuth 2.0, TEE	X.509 certificate, public/private key signature

In order to compare the selected frameworks with proposed framework five parameters has been taken, such as computational complexity (CC), communication complexity (Comm), mobility (MoB), scalability (SCA), quality of service (QoS). MatLab Simulation tool has been used to get the performance of proposed framework.

Table 3. Comparison of security solutions in various frameworks.

Security services	Various Frameworks	CC	Comm	MoB	SCA	QoS
Authentication	AWS IoT	+	+	*	*	*
	Azure IoT suite	*	*	−	*	*
	Brillo/Weave	*	*	* *	* *	* *
	FSIE	*	*	* *	* *	* *
Authorization	AWS IoT	*	*	*	*	*
	Azure IoT suite	*	*	−	*	*
	Brillo/Weave	*	*	* *	* *	* *
	FSIE	*	*	* *	* *	* *
Confidentiality	AWS IoT	* *	* *	* *	* *	* *
	Azure IoT suite	*	*	+	*	*
	Brillo/Weave	*	*	*	*	*
	FSIE	* *	*	* *	* *	* *
Non-repudiation	AWS IoT	*	*	*	*	*
	Azure IoT suite	*	*	+	*	*
	Brillo/Weave	*	*	*	*	*
	FSIE	*	*	*	*	*
Privacy:	AWS IoT	*	*	*	*	*
	Azure IoT suite	* *	* *	*	*	*
	Brillo/Weave	+	+	*	*	*
	FSIE	*	*	* *	* *	* *
Availability	AWS IoT	*	*	**	**	*
	Azure IoT suite	*	*	*	*	*
	Brillo/Weave	+	+	*	*	*
	FSIE	*	*	* *	* *	* *

Note: the representation of symbols: Poor: −, Average: +, Good: *, Very Good: **

5 Results and Discussion

As shown in Table 3 the comparison of security solutions in selected IoT frameworks with proposed IoT framework reveals authentication, authorization, confidentiality and non-repudiation services are efficient in terms of CC, Comm, SCA, QoS security solutions in all the frameworks except Azure IoT suit in terms of MoB. The reason for this is Azure IoT suite has device identity management to manage direct connection with Azure IoT hub and authentication of devices (Mahmoud et al. 2018). Therefore, the mobility of devices performance is less in this context. Privacy and availability services' performance is average in the framework of Brillo/Weave in terms of CC and Comm security solutions. The main reason for this is the Brillo/Weave framework can implement exclusively remote and android based operating systems, which is always connecting to the public google cloud (Mahmoud et al. 2018). The proposed framework FSIE is found to be more efficient in CC, Comm, SCA, QoS security solutions and services.

6 Conclusion

The intelligent world is emergent rapidly nowadays, where all the smart things, users, servers are connecting to the internet. The significance of proposing particular IoT infrastructure and protocols has been shifted to identify and support IoT frameworks in order to implement application platforms. The present comparative analysis has covered commercial frameworks and platforms. Moreover, it supports to develop client and industrial based IoT applications. The selected frameworks such as AWT IoT, Azure IoT suite, Brillo/Weave, are following various approaches in order to identify cloud applications by using distributed data sources. In this paper, the proposed FSIE framework has been compared with commercial frameworks based on the security services and solutions. The results support the FSIE framework in CC, Comm, SCA, QoS security solutions when compared to selected frameworks. In addition to this the proposed framework has various security features and resistance from IoT attacks and issues.

The present study uses only five parameters, which are described in Table 3, for the comparison of selected framework with the proposed framework. Moreover, the simulation was done using only MATLAB. As a part of future study more parameters can be used for the study. Real time study can be performed on various applications.

References

Al-Fuqaha, A., Guizani, M., Mohammadi, M., Aledhari, M., Ayyash, M.: Internet of things: a survey on enabling technologies, protocols, and applications. IEEE Commun. Surveys Tutorials 17(4), 2347–76 (2015)

Amazon. AWS authorization. https://docs.aws.amazon.com/iot/latest/developerguide/authorization.html. Accessed 11 Apr 2017

Amazon. Aws IoT framework. https://aws.amazon.com/iot. Accessed 11 Apr 2017

Amazon. Components of AWS IoT framework. https://aws.amazon.com/iot/how-it-works/. Accessed 11 Apr 2017

Amazon. Signature version 4 signing process. https://docs.aws.amazon.com/general/latest/gr/signature-version-4.html. Accessed 11 Apr 2017

Amazon. X.509 certificates. https://docs.aws.amazon.com/iot/latest/developerguide/x509-certs.html. Accessed 11 Apr 2017

Azure, M.: Azure IoT protocol gateway. https://azure.microsoft.com/en-us/documentation/articles/iot-hub-protocol-gateway/. Accessed 11 Apr 2017

Azure, M.: Internet of things security from the ground up. https://azure.microsoft.com/en-us/doc umentation/articles/iot-hub-security-ground-up/. Accessed 11 Apr 2017

Borgohain, T., Kumar, U., Sanyal, S.: Survey of security and privacy issues of internet of things. arXiv:150102211 (2015)

Bouij-Pasquier, I., El Kalam, A.A., Ouahman, A.A., De Montfort, M.: A security framework for internet of things. In: Reiter, M., Naccache, D. (eds.) CANS 2015. LNCS, vol. 9476, pp. 19–31. Springer, Cham (2015). https://doi.org/10.1007/978-3-319-26823-1_2

Cooper, D.: Internet X.509 public key infrastructure certificate and certificate revocation list (CRL) profile. https://tools.ietf.org/html/rfc5280. Accessed 11 Apr 2017

Derhamy, H., Eliasson, J., Delsing, J., Priller, P.: A survey of commercial frameworks for the internet of things. In: 2015 IEEE 20th Conference on Emerging Technologies & Factory Automation (ETFA), pp. 1–8. IEEE (2015)

Fremantle, P., Scott, P.: A survey of secure middleware for the internet of things. Peer J. Comput. Sci. **3**, e114 (2017)

Google. Brillo. https://developers.google.com/brillo/. Accessed 11 Apr 2017

Google. Weave. https://developers.google.com/weave/. Accessed 11 Apr 2017

Hunkeler, U., Truong, H.L., Stanford-Clark, A.: MQTT-SA publish/subscribe protocolfor wireless sensor networks. In: 3rd international conference on Communication Systems Software and Middleware and Workshops, COMSWARE 2008, pp. 791–798 (2008)

Kumar, J.S., Patel, D.R.: A survey on internet of things: security and privacy issues. Int. J. Comput. Appl. **90**(11) (2014)

Challa, M.L., Soujanya, K.L.S.: End-to-end device authentication through OSDA approach. Int. J. Comput. Sci. Inf. Secur. **17**(4), 129–142 (2019)

Challa, M.L., Soujanya, K.L.S.: Enhancing end-to-end device security of internet of things using dynamic cryptographic algorithm. Int. J. Civil Eng. Technol. (IJCIET) **9**(9), 408–415 (2018)

Challa, M.L., Soujanya, K.L.S., Amulya, C.D.: Remote Monitoring and Maintenance of Patients via IoT Healthcare Security and Interoperability approach, Cybernetics, Cognition & Machine Learning Applications proceedings of ICCMLA 2019. Springer (2020). https://doi.org/10.1007/ 978-981-15-1632-0. Series ISSN 2524-7565, Hardcover ISBN 978-981-15-1631-3, eBook ISBN 978-981-15-1632-0

Ammar, M., Russello, G., Crispo, B.: Internet of Things: a survey on the security of IoT frameworks. J. Inf. Secur. Appl. **38**, 8–27 (2017). https://doi.org/10.1016/j.jisa.2017.11.002

Microsoft. Operational security assurance. https://www.microsoft.com/en-us/SDL/OperationalS ecurityAssurance. Accessed 11 Apr 2017

Microsoft. Power bi. https://powerbi.microsoft.com. Accessed 11 Apr 2017

Microsoft: Security development lifecycle. https://www.microsoft.com/en-us/sdl/default.aspx. Accessed 11 Apr 2017

Nezhad, N.Y., Malhi, A., Framling, K.: Security in product lifecycle of IoT devices: a survey. J. Comput. Netw. Appl. (2020, in press). https://doi.org/10.1016/j.jnca.2020.102779

Rios, R., Lopez, J.: Analysis of location privacy solutions in wireless sensor networks, IET Commun. **5**, 2518–2532 (2011). https://doi.org/10.1049/iet-com.2010.0825

Sheng, Z., Yang, S., Yu, Y., Vasilakos, A.V., McCann, J.A., Leung, K.K.: A survey on the ietf protocol suite for the internet of things: standards, challenges, and opportunities. IEEE Wirel. Commun. **20**(6), 91–98 (2013)

Singh, P., Kar, A.K., Singh, Y., Kolekar, M.H., Tanwar, S.: Recent Innovations in Computing, vol. 597. Springer, Cham (2019a). https://doi.org/10.1007/978-981-15-8297-4. ISBN 978-3-030-29406-9

Singh, P.K., Paprzycki, M., Bhargava, B., Chhabra, J.K., Kaushal, N.C., Kumar, Y. (eds.): FTNCT 2018. CCIS, vol. 958. Springer, Singapore (2019). https://doi.org/10.1007/978-981-13-3804-5

Singh, P.K., Sood, S., Kumar, Y., Paprzycki, M., Pljonkin, A., Hong, W.-C. (eds.): FTNCT 2019. CCIS, vol. 1206. Springer, Singapore (2020). https://doi.org/10.1007/978-981-15-4451-4

Vikas, B.: Internet of Things (IoT): a survey on privacy issues and security (2015)

Yang, Y., Wu, L., Yin, G., Li, L., Zhao, H.: A survey on security and privacy issues in internet-of-things. IEEE Internet Things J. (2017)

Zhang, K., Ni, J., Yang, K., Liang, X., Ren, J., Shen, X.S.: Security and privacy in smart city applications: challenges and solutions. IEEE Commun. Mag. **55**(1), 122–129 (2017). https://doi.org/10.1109/MCOM.2017.1600267CM

Software Fault Prediction Using Machine Learning Models and Comparative Analysis

Manpreet Singh$^{(\boxtimes)}$ and Jitender Kumar Chhabra$^{(\boxtimes)}$

Computer Engineering Department, National Institute of Technology, Kurukshetra 136119, India

Abstract. Software Testing is an important phase of Software Development Life cycle. Effective software testing helps in identifying faulty modules, but this process becomes very time consuming, especially for large /complex software. Moreover early identification of error prone modules can be useful in producing better quality software. Hence software fault prediction has gained significant attention of the researchers in the recent years. Mainly two types of techniques are being used for it: statistical methods and Machine learning models, out of which recent trend is more inclined towards machine Learning based techniques. Identification of faulty modules is a binary classification problem and machine learning models such as Decision Tree and its variants, Random Forest and Support Vector Machine, are best suited for the fault prediction. This paper attempts to predict software faults using four different classification models. Further, the performance evaluation of these models is also carried out in this paper using accuracy, Precision, Recall, F1-Score and execution time of over 12 datasets, extracted from one of the most commonly used PROMISE repository. Based on these performance metrics comparison of applied four models is done and our comparative analysis indicates that in most of the cases Support Vector Machine model is able to predict software faults more efficiently than the rest in terms of accuracy as well as execution time

1 Introduction

Software testing is an important phase of Software Development Life Cycle (SDLC). More than 50% cost and effort of software development consumed by testing phase [1]. As software development is a human intensive task, developing a software without faults is nearly impossible. It necessitates the adequate testing and regular maintenance to ensure software quality. In large organizations software testing becomes more costly as well as time consuming as software size and complexity increase. Through manual testing it is impossible to detect each and every bug in software code. Further changes in requirements lead to change in the software code, which can lead to more bugs because of dependency of modules on each other. So, regression testing is also needed. It means additional time, effort and cost needed to handle the software testing phase.

To reduce software testing effort, cost and time, software fault prediction techniques are used [2]. These techniques can detect faulty modules of the software in early stages and make software testers' task easy. Mainly two types of techniques are used for software fault prediction: statistical methods [3] and machine learning methods [3]. Recently

P. K. Singh et al. (Eds.): FTNCT 2020, CCIS 1395, pp. 30–45, 2021.
https://doi.org/10.1007/978-981-16-1480-4_3

researchers are focusing more on machine learning methods for software fault predictions because these techniques can help in early detection of the faulty modules before the actual failure An accurate estimate of faulty modules will help the testers to test rigorously the identified modules and correct such modules at an early stage. Classification of modules as faulty and healthy is a binary classification problem and many binary classification methods like Decision Tree, Random Forest and Support Vector Machine can be used for this purpose. There are no authentic studies available about which classification model will perform better for different datasets. So, a comparative analysis is needed of various machine learning classification models for software fault prediction. This paper carries out the accuracy and time comparison of four machine learning methods: Gini-Index based Decision Tree, Entropy based Decision Tree, Random Forest and Support Vector Machine to predict software faults based on software metrics [3–5].For out experimentation we have used twelve software datasets. All datasets used in this research paper are taken from PROMISE repository [6]. Most of datasets in this repository are NASA's open source projects. Rest of this paper is organized as follows. Second section provides discussion about previous research done in this area. Third section explains the machine learning classification modes used for our experimentation and mapping of our problem to these four models: Entropy based Decision Tree, Gini-Index based Decision Tree, Random Forest and Standard Support Vector Machine (SVM) [3, 4]. Fourth section is about results and discussions where details about accuracy, Precision, Recall, F1-Score and time complexity of these four models are reported.

2 Literature Review

Considerable amount of research has been done in software fault prediction research area. Ilona Bluemke [7] explained many object oriented metrics which are useful to train machine learning models for fault prediction. He explained class metrics, metrics derived from class diagram and sequence diagram which are helpful to create dataset for fault prediction models. Harald Altinger, Sebastian Siegl, Yanja Dajsuren and Franz Wotawa [8] created dataset in their research to train machine learning models for fault prediction. They extracted code level metrics, class level metric, change metrics and model metrics to create dataset. This dataset is created from real time automobile industry project. In [9] authors explained software metrics for fault prediction using Machine Learning. They have used PROMISE repository datasets. Same repository is used in our research. This is free repository on which anyone can share fault prediction datasets. In [10] Sinan Eski and Feza Buzluca studied about structural change type and class level metrics for software fault prediction machine learning models. To verify their approach they have done case study on three open source projects JFreeChat, Yari and UCDector.Yusuke Takahashi and Naoya Nitta [11] proposed composite Refactoring for Decoupling multiple classes to reduce software complexity.

In their research Fikret Aktaş and Feza Buzluca [12] explained learning based approach for Object Oriented Systems to differentiate buggy and healthy classes.

In [4] authors have done comparison of two versions of decision trees one based on Entropy and Information gain. This algorithm also called ID3 also used In our experimentation. Second is based on Gain Ratio also called C4.5. Çağıl Biray and Feza Buzluca

[1] in their research trained Decision Tree model for bug prediction of Ericsson Turkey large software. Based on software code metrics extracted from github version control history. Choudhary [21] has applied Random Forest, KNN and Decision Tree algorithms on already existing change metrics and new change metrics proposed by him. Results show that models gives better performance when applied on new change metrics proposed by him. Singh, [22] has applied CART (Classification and Regression Tree), C4.5 (Decision Tree), PART and compared the performance. Results shows that C4.5 (Decision Tree) has performed better in case of within-project than the other rule based classifiers.

Shanthini. A and Chandrasekaran. RM [3] trained standard SVM and bagged SVM model for software fault prediction and compared their results. Bagged SVM was developed by them and gives better results than standard SVM. Chen [24] applied One class Support Vector Machine (SVM) on eight data sets taken from PROMISE repository and results are compared with Naïve Bayes (NB) and NB with log filter (NB + log). Results shows that one Class SVM performs better than other two models.

In [5] Cerrada, Mariela, Grover Zurita, Diego Cabrera, René-Vinicio Sánchez, Mariano Artés, and Chuan Li trained Random Forest machine learning model for Fault diagnosis in spur gears to achieve good performance. Bennin in [23] created new oversampling technique called Mahakil and five machine learning models (Decision Tree, SVM, Random Forest, KNN,NNET) are trained using Mahakil. Results show that proposed approach improves the performance of machine learning models.

3   Methodology

In this section the Machine learning algorithms used in our comparative study are explained For better understanding, this sections provides the details how these algorithms are adapted for the problem of defect prediction. Basically machine learning models are used for two types: classification and regression. As fault prediction is a binary classification problem, we have considered four commonly used machine learning classification models: Entropy Based Decision Tree, Gini-Index based Decision Tree, Random Forest and Support Vector Machine. Dataset used to apply these models contains n attributes out of which $n - 1$ are software metrics and one target attribute. Target attribute contains binary values (0, 1).

$$Target\ Attribute = \begin{cases} 0,\ healthy\ module; \\ 1,\ Faulty\ Module; \end{cases} \quad (1)$$

After training models based on software metrics, target attribute is predicted by models. After prediction of target attribute, values are compared with the correct values of the target attribute. Depending upon correctly predicted values, accuracy is calculated of each model which is explained in Sect. 3.1. Classification models used in our comparative study are explained as under.

3.1   Classification Methods

Following four supervised learning classification algorithms, used by us for our experimentation, are explained in this section.

Decision Tree

Decision Tree classifier is a supervised learning technique widely used in many practical machine learning problems. Decision Tree is basically an acyclic connected graph structure and each internal node of this tree represents a condition. Based on the current node condition, suitable branch will be selected by the prediction model to move to next node [4]. Model follows this process until leaf node reached. Leaf nodes provide the classification results (target attribute value). As attributes increase in input dataset depth of Decision tree will increase. If input dataset has n attributes then decision tree will have $n - 1$ levels because out of n attributes, $n - 1$ attributes will be used to create a decision tree and one attribute will be the target attribute. Each level of the decision tree represents one attribute and most relevant attribute will be the root of decision tree and so on. There are many criteria to build decision tree like Entropy Based decision Tree, Gain Ratio Based Decision Tree and Gini-Index based Decision Tree classifier etc. We have used two variants of Decision Trees for our research, which are explained as under.

Entropy Based Decision Tree

To build a Decision tree based on entropy, algorithm computes as fault prediction is binary classification problem as fault prediction is binary classification problem information gain of each attribute except the target attribute and then attribute with highest information gain will be selected as root node of the Decision Tree. Attribute with higher information gain splits data more efficiently. After selecting the root node, algorithm finds the second best attribute from dataset which will be placed at the second level of the decision tree by the algorithm and so on. Algorithms will repeat this process until all $n - 1$ attributes are covered. Information gain will be calculated by using following Eq. (2) [4].

$$IG(S, X) = E(S) - E(S|X) \tag{2}$$

Here E(S) is the entropy of sample dataset and E(S|X) is the sum of entropies after dividing dataset into m different classes based on X attribute. Entropy can be calculated by using formula of Eq. (3) [4].

$$E(S) = \sum_{i=1}^{n} -\left(p_i log_2 p_i\right) \tag{3}$$

Where:
p_i is probability of ith class and $E(S)$ is entropy of sample dataset S.

Gini-Index Based Decision Tree

In this method, Decision Tree is built by calculating the gini Index of all $n - 1$ attributes. Gini Index value varies between 0 and 1. Lowest gini index valued attribute is selected by the algorithm as root node in Decision Tree. This process will be repeated by the algorithm until all $n - 1$ attributes are added to Decision Tree. Attribute with lowest gini index will be on top in Decision Tree because gini index measures the degree of wrong classification of randomly chosen attribute. Gini index of an attribute can be calculated by using Eq. (4) [4].

$$Gini = 1 - \sum_{i=1}^{n} (p_i)^2 \tag{4}$$

Where:
p_i is the probability of an object being classified into particular class.

Random Forest
A group of Decision Trees created by selecting random attributes from main set of attributes is called Random Forest. Each individual Decision Tree in the Random Forest used to predict class of input data and class with most votes will become the resultant class of input data by Random Forest model. To predict software modules weather faulty or not, Input data is the metrics extracted from software code. Main steps of the Random Forest algorithm are given below [5]:-

1. Multiple subsets of attributes from original set of attributes with replacement are created.
2. Each subset is selected one by one from group of subsets and Decision Tree is built.
3. The class predicted by majority of the Decision Trees is considered as output of the model.

It is a type of ensemble learning. This model is a combination of several models and always improves accuracy of the prediction model but it increases the time complexity of the prediction model because a group of models needs to run on same record for prediction. We created a group of 60 decision trees to create Random Forest model for our experimentation.

SVM
Support Vector Machine (SVM) is a supervised machine learning method. It can be used for both regression and classification problems but it is more suitable for classification problems [3]. As our fault prediction is also a binary classification problem. So, SVM can be used for this problem. Basic idea behind SVM is finding the hyper-plane that differentiates two classes very well in n dimensional space. In our case space will be $n - 1$ dimensional, because out of n attributes $n - 1$ attributes will be used to train our model and remaining one attribute will be our target attribute. Suppose there is a problem to divide data into two classes (binary classification) based on values of two attributes. In this situation algorithm creates two dimensional planes and tries to find best possible hyper-plane in two dimensional spaces. It can be shown by two dimensional graph where one attribute is on X-axis and other on Y-axis of graph. Hyper-plane is the line dividing the points into two classes. This can be shown as two dimensional graphs as follows:

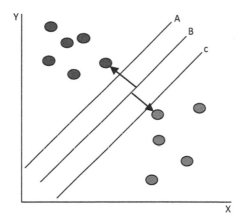

Fig 1 Classes differentiated by Hyper Planes (Color figure online)

In Fig. 1 red dots are in class-1 and green dots are in class-2 and there are 3 hyper planes A, B and C to separate these classes. Line B is best suitable line because it maximizes the distance from closest point of both classes from hyper plane.

4 Results and Discussion

This section of the paper discusses about experimentation setup, datasets used and comparison of results generated by the four machine learning classification algorithms explained in third section. We used the sklearn python library to implement the algorithms: Decision Tree classifier with gini-index as classification criteria, Decision Tree

Table 1. Datasets used in our experimentation

DataSet	Shape (rows, cols)	Total attributes	Total tuples
Ar1	(121, 30)	30	121
Ar3	(63, 30)	30	63
Ar4	(107, 30)	30	107
Ar5	(36, 30)	30	36
Ar6	(101, 30)	30	101
Cm1_req	(89, 9)	9	89
Kc1_class_level_Binary	(145, 95)	95	145
Kc1_class_level_top5	(145, 95)	95	145
Kc2	(522, 22)	22	522
Kc3	(458, 40)	40	458
Mc2	(161, 40)	40	161
Mw1	(403, 38)	38	403

classifier with entropy as classification criteria, Random Forest and Support Vector Machine.. These four models are tested on twelve datasets, downloaded from PROMISE repository [6, 13]. Datasets used in our experimentation are tabulated in Table 1. First row contains the name of each dataset third row contains the number of software metrics and fourth row contains the number of modules in each dataset.

After running these four models on given datasets in Table 1. Accuracy, Precision, Recall, F1-Score and Running Time of each algorithm is calculated. Then comparison of accuracy, Precision, Recall, F1-Score and running time of each algorithm on given datasets is done in this section to find out best model. Subsect. 4.1. Explains methods of computation of accuracy, Precision, Recall and F1-Score and its comparison for all four algorithms. Subsect. 4.2. Explains execution time comparison of four algorithms.

4.1 Accuracy, Precision, Recall and F1-Score Analysis

In this section after running these four models on given twelve datasets percentage accuracy, Precision, Recall and F1-Score of each algorithm on each dataset is calculated and then compared with each other. Each dataset is divided into 70% and 30% ratio. 70% dataset is used to train models and 30% dataset is used for verification and to calculate accuracy, Precision, Recall and F1-Score after prediction. Accuracy, Precision, Recall and F1-Score of model can be calculated by using following formulas used by many other researchers [14–19].

$$Accuracy(\%) = \frac{\# \ of \ correctly \ predicted}{(\# \ of \ correct \ predicted + \# \ of \ wrong \ predicted)} * 100 \qquad (5)$$

$$Precision = \frac{tp}{tp + fp} \qquad (6)$$

$$Recall = \frac{tp}{tp + fn} \qquad (7)$$

$$F1_{Score} = \frac{2 * tp}{2 * tp + fp + fn} \qquad (8)$$

After running all four models on 12 datasets accuracy, Precision, Recall and F1-Score lists of each model are generated which are listed in Table 2, Table 3 and Table 4. Comparison graphs of Accuracy, Precision, Recall and F1-Score are shown in Fig. 2, Fig. 3, Fig. 4 and Fig. 5 respectively.

From Table 2 it can be concluded that Ar1, Kc1_class_level_top5, Kc3 and Mw1 has good results of accuracy for all four algorithms whereas Ar4 and Mc2 datasets prediction accuracy is poor. In case of Ar1, Mw1 Random Forest and SVM gives better results than Decision Tree. In case of Ar5 Entropy based Decision Tree gives best results, Random Forest and Gini-Index based Decision Tree gives moderate results and SVM's performance is poor. In case of Cm1_req all four algorithms give average results but SVM and Random Forest performs slightly better than Decision Tree. In case of Kc1_class_level_Binary Decision Tree's performance is moderate whereas Random Forest and SVM gives poor results.

Table 2. Accuracies of all four algorithms

DataSet	Accuracy entropy	Accuracy Gini	Accuracy RF	Accuracy SVM
Ar1	89.18	89.18	94.59	97.29
Ar3	84.21	84.21	84.21	89.47
Ar4	69.69	66.66	81.81	87.87
Ar5	90.90	81.81	81.81	72.72
Ar6	80.64	80.64	87.09	87.09
Cm1_req	70.37	70.37	81.48	81.48
Kc1_class_level_Binary	72.72	70.45	61.36	56.81
Kc1_class_level_top5	88.63	88.63	97.72	97.72
Kc2	98.08	98.08	97.45	96.17
Kc3	85.50	87.68	89.13	87.68
Mc2	65.30	71.42	69.38	67.34
Mw1	88.42	88.42	93.38	93.38

Table 3. Precisions of all four algorithms

DataSet	Precision entropy	Precision Gini	Precision RF	Precision SVM
Ar1	0.87	0.94	0.95	0.95
Ar3	0.87	0.87	0.87	0.80
Ar4	0.79	0.86	0.76	0.77
Ar5	0.93	0.89	0.82	0.53
Ar6	0.81	0.81	0.91	0.76
Cm1_req	0.70	0.70	0.79	0.79
Kc1_class_level_Binary	0.73	0.71	0.67	0.61
Kc1_class_level_top5	0.95	0.95	0.95	0.96
Kc2	0.98	0.98	0.97	0.96
Kc3	0.77	0.85	0.77	0.77
Mc2	0.66	0.72	0.77	0.78
Mw1	0.88	0.88	0.91	0.87

From Table 3 it can be concluded that In case of Mw1, Ar1, Ar3, Kc2, Kc1_class_level_top5 and Ar6 all four algorithms give very good results which are closer to 1. In case of Ar4 Gini-Index based Decision Tree gives good results but other three performs moderate. In case of Ar5 SVM gives poor results but other three gives good results. For Mc2, Kc1_class_level_Binary and Cm1_req all four algorithms give moderate results.

Table 4. Recalls of all four algorithms

DataSet	Recall entropy	Recall Gini	Recall RF	Recall SVM
Ar1	0.84	0.89	0.95	0.97
Ar3	0.84	0.84	0.84	0.89
Ar4	0.70	0.67	0.79	0.88
Ar5	0.91	0.82	0.82	0.73
Ar6	0.81	0.81	0.90	0.87
Cm1_req	0.70	0.70	0.81	0.81
Kc1_class_level_Binary	0.73	0.70	0.66	0.57
Kc1_class_level_top5	0.89	0.89	0.95	0.98
Kc2	0.98	0.98	0.97	0.96
Kc3	0.86	0.88	0.88	0.88
Mc2	0.65	0.71	0.73	0.67
Mw1	0.88	0.88	0.93	0.93

From Table 4 it can be concluded that In case of Ar1, Ar3, Kc2, Kc3 and Kc1_class_level_top5 all four algorithms give good results but Random Forest and SVM performs slightly better than Decision Tree. In case of AR4 SVM gives good results whereas Gini-Index based Decision Tree gives worst results and rest two performs moderate. In case of Ar5 Entropy based Decision Tree gives best results. In case of Mc2 results are poor and for Kc1_class_level_Binary SVM gives worst results.

From Table 5 it can be concluded that in case of Ar1, Ar3, Ar6, Kc2, Kc2 and Mw1 all four algorithms' results are good. In case of Mc2 SVM and Entropy based Decision Tree gives worst results and other two gives average results. In case of Kc1_class_leve_Binary SVM gives poor results whereas other three gives moderate results. In case of Cm1_req all four algorithms give moderate results.

Figure 2 shows the comparison graph of accuracy of all four algorithms on twelve datasets tabulated in Table 2. Green line (second column of Table 2) shows the performance of Decision Tree algorithm using entropy as classification criteria. This performance is similar to the blue line (third column of Table 2) in most of the datasets, which shows the performance of Decision Tree classifier using Gini-Index as classification criteria. In some cases Decision Tree using entropy performs slightly better and vice-versa.but in most of the cases performance of both algorithms is similar. Red line (forth column of Table 2) represents the performance of Random Forest classifier algorithm which is clearly better than both Decision Tree classifier using entropy and Decision Tree classifier using Gini-Index except some exceptions. Yellow line (fifth column of Table 2) shows the performance of standard Support Vector Machine algorithm which

Table 5. F1-Scores of all four algorithms

DataSet	F1-Score entropy	F1-Score Gini	F1-Score RF	F1-Score SVM
Ar1	0.86	0.92	0.95	0.96
Ar3	0.86	0.86	0.86	0.85
Ar4	0.74	0.72	0.77	0.82
Ar5	0.91	0.83	0.82	0.61
Ar6	0.81	0.81	0.88	0.81
Cm1_req	0.70	0.70	0.80	0.80
Kc1_class_level_Binary	0.72	0.70	0.64	0.47
Kc1_class_level_top5	0.92	0.92	0.95	0.97
Kc2	0.98	0.98	0.97	0.96
Kc3	0.81	0.86	0.82	0.82
Mc2	0.65	0.72	0.70	0.58
Mw1	0.88	0.88	0.92	0.90

clearly generates best results in most of the cases. So, based on accuracy list of Table 2 we can conclude that Random forest and Support Vector Machine give better accuracy than both types of decision tree models.

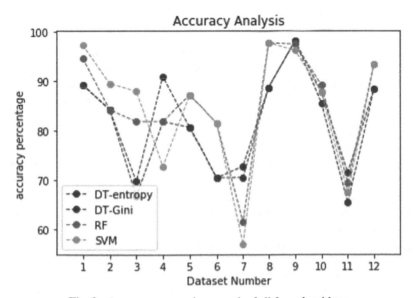

Fig. 2. Accuracy comparison graph of all four algorithms

Figure 3 shows the comparison of Precision of all four algorithms on twelve datasets. Precision is calculated by Eq. (5). Yellow Line (fifth Column of Table 3) shows the performance of SVM which is very poor in some cases but good in maximum cases. Red line (forth column of Table 3) shows the performance of Random Forest which is good for all datasets except dataset-7 (Kc1_class_level_top5) where it gives moderate results. Green line (second Column of Table 3) and blue line (third column of Table 3) gives almost similar results but Random Forest gives better results then both type of Decision Trees in most of the cases.

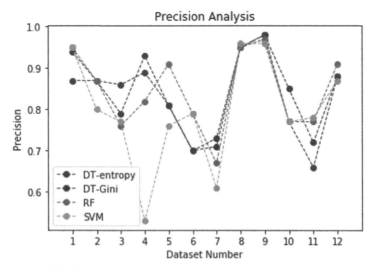

Fig. 3. Precision comparison graph of all four algorithms

Figure 4 shows the comparison of Recall of all four algorithms on twelve datasets taken for our experimentation. Recall is calculated by Eq. (6). It is clear from graph that SVM gives best results in most of the cases except dataset-7 (Kc1_class_level_Binary) where it gives worst results. SVM's performance is shown by yellow line in this graph (fifth column in Table 4). Red line (forth column in Table 4) shows the performance of Random Forest which is second best after SVM but in some cases it performs better then SVM like in dataset-5 (Ar6). Green Line (second column in Table 4) and blue line (third column in Table 4) shows the performance of Entropy based Decision Tree and Gini-Index based Decision Tree. It is clear from the graph that both type of decision tree performs almost similar except some cases where Gini-Index based Decision Tree gives slightly better performance but Random Forest and SVM outperforms both types of Decision Tree algorithms.

Figure 5 shows the comparison of F1-Score of all four algorithms on twelve datasets taken for our experimentation. Yellow Line (fifth column of Table 5) shows the performance of SVM which is very poor in case of dataset-4 (Ar5), dataset-7 (Kc1_class_level_binary) and dataset-11 (kc3). For rest of the cases performance of SVM is good. Red line (fourth column of Table 5) shows the performance of Random Forest which generates best results for most of the cases except dataset-7 where Decision Tree out performs it. Green line (second column of Table 5) and blue line (third column of Table 5) shows performance of entropy based Decision Tree and Gini-Index

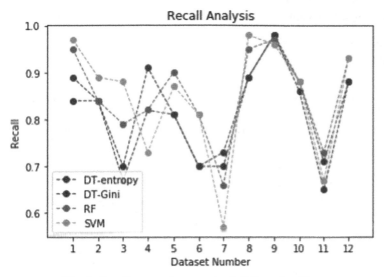

Fig. 4. Recall comparison graph of all four algorithms

based Decision Tree. It is clear from the graph that both type of decision trees gives almost similar results but Random Forests gives slightly better results than both type of Decision Trees.

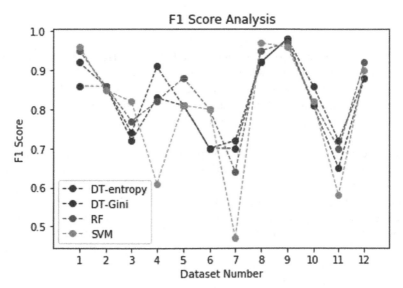

Fig. 5. F1-Score comparison graph of all four algorithms

4.2 Running Time Analysis

In this section, execution time of all four models on twelve datasets is reported, as tabulated in Table 6.

Table 6. List of running times of trained algorithms on twelve datasets

DataSet	Decision Tree entropy (ms)	Decision Tree Gini-Index (ms)	Random Forest (ms)	SVM (ms)
Ar1	0.005	0.015	0.076	<0.01
Ar3	0.015	0.015	0.078	<0.01
Ar4	<0.01	<0.01	0.076	<0.01
Ar5	<0.01	<0.01	0.071	<0.01
Ar6	<0.01	<0.01	0.074	<0.01
Cm1_req	<0.01	<0.01	0.078	<0.01
Kc1_class_level_Binary	<0.01	<0.01	0.078	<0.01
Kc1_class_level_top5	<0.01	<0.01	0.079	<0.01
Kc2	<0.01	<0.01	0.078	<0.01
Kc3	<0.01	<0.01	0.095	<0.01
Mc2	<0.01	<0.01	0.093	<0.01
Mw1	<0.01	0.015	0.093	0.015

It is clear from the table SVM, Entropy based Decision Tree and Gini-Index based Decision Tree generates results within 0.01 ms except Ar1, Ar3 where Decision Tree takes more time than SVM. Random Forest takes more time than other three algorithms for all datasets because it generates group of Decision Trees. We can conclude from Table 6 that Random Forest is worst algorithm if there is no compromise with execution time of algorithms.

Figure 6 represents the running time comparison graph of all four algorithms. X-axis of the graph shows the datasets (first row of Table 3) and Y-axis shows the running time of algorithms in milliseconds. Red line (forth row of Table 3) represents the running time of Random forest which is clearly least efficient algorithm in terms of execution time. Rest all three algorithms performance is similar because blue (second row of Table 3), yellow (third row of Table 3) and green lines (fifth row of Table 3) overlap one another in most of the cases except some cases where performances are slightly different. Execution time of the random forest algorithm increase more than other 3 algorithms which degrades the performance of Random Forest.

From Table 3 in Subsects. 4.1 it is clear that if only accuracy is the model performance measurement criteria then any of Random Forest and Support Vector Machine can be chosen, as. Both of these algorithms give similar results and are better than both type of decision trees. If Precision of F1-Score is the model performance measurement criteria then Random Forest outperforms rest three. On the other hand if Recall is measurement

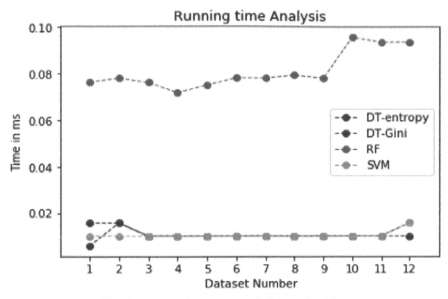

Fig. 6. Running time analysis of all four algorithms

criteria then SVM or Random Forest anyone can be chosen. But if running time is the only criteria to measure algorithm performance then any model except Random Forest can be chosen based on results discussed in Subsect. 4.2. Both factors are important for the software fault-prediction problem, and hence Support Vector Machine is the best choice, as its accuracy is better or similar to the other three and execution time is also better or similar to rest of the three alternates. Identifying faulty modules has got its practical applications in software industry during preventive maintenance, where the maintenance team can improve the reliability and quality of the potentially faulty modules and avoid the future failures in such modules.

5 Conclusion

The goal of this paper is to analyze the performance of various machine learning models for fault prediction. In this paper four machine learning models: Entropy based Decision Tree, Gini-Index based Decision Tree, Random Forest and Support Vector Machine are applied on twelve datasets taken from PROMISE repository for fault prediction. After applying these models different metrics Accuracy, Precision, Recall, F1-Score and running time of each algorithm is calculated and compared. From result and discussion section it can be concluded that if Accuracy is the only performance measurement criteria then Random Forest and Support Vector Machine both can be used for fault prediction. In case of Precision and F1-Score Random Forest outperforms other three algorithms. If Recall is measurement metric then SVM and Random Forest both gives good results and can be chosen any one for fault prediction. On the other hand if running time of algorithm is also important then SVM is the clear choice because Random forest gives worst performance of running time. Both types of Decision Tree models have good running time but SVM outperforms these two models in case of other metrics like Accuracy, Precision, Recall and F1-Score. So, in the end it can be concluded that if only Accuracy, Precision, Recall and F1-score matters then Random Forest and SVM both are good models and any one can be chosen for fault prediction but if Running time is also important factor then SVM is the obvious choice because Random Forest gives worst running time performance. Comparison can be done with outer models like Neural Network and Genetic Algorithm.

References

1. Aziz, S.R., Khan, T., Nadeem, A.: Experimental validation of inheritance metrics' impact on software fault prediction. IEEE Access **7**. 85262–85275 (2019)
2. Bareja, K., Singhal, A.: A review of estimation techniques to reduce testing efforts in software development. In: 2015 Fifth International Conference on Advanced Computing & Communication Technologies, pp. 541–546. IEEE (2015)
3. Shanthini, A., Chandrasekaran, R.M.: Analyzing the effect of bagged ensemble approach for software fault prediction in class level and package level metrics. In: International Conference on Information Communication and Embedded Systems (ICICES), pp. 1–5 (2014)
4. Hssina, B., Merbouha, A., Ezzikouri, H., Erritali, M.: A comparative study of decision tree ID3 and C4. 5. Int. J. Adv. Comput. Sci. Appl. **4**(2), 13–19 (2014)
5. Cerrada, M., Zurita, G., Cabrera, D., Sánchez, R.-V., Artés, M., Li, C.: Fault diagnosis in spur gears based on genetic algorithm and random forest. Mech. Syst. Signal Process. **70**, 87–103 (2016)
6. Boetticher, G., Menzies, T., Ostrand, T.: PROMISE Repository of Empirical Software Engineering Data. West Virginia University, Department of Computer Science (2007)
7. Bluemke, I.: Object oriented metrics useful in the prediction of class testing complexity. In: Proceedings of IEEE Euromicro Conference, Workshop on Component Based Software Engineering, pp. 130–136 (2001)
8. Altinger, H., Siegl, S., Dajsuren, Y., Wotawa, F.: A novel industry grade dataset for fault prediction based on model-driven developed automotive embedded software. In: 2015 IEEE/ACM 12th Working Conference on Mining Software Repositories, pp. 494–497. IEEE (2015)
9. Karim, S., Warnars, H.L.H.S., Gaol, F.L., Abdurachman, E., Soewito, B.: Software metrics for fault prediction using machine learning approaches: a literature review with PROMISE repository dataset. In: 2017 IEEE International Conference on Cybernetics and Computational Intelligence (CyberneticsCom), pp. 19–23. IEEE (2017)
10. Eski, S., Buzluca, F.: An empirical study on object-oriented metrics and software evolution in order to reduce testing costs by predicting change-prone classes. In: 2011 IEEE Fourth International Conference on Software Testing, Verification and Validation Workshops, pp. 566–571. IEEE (2011)
11. Takahashi, Y., Nitta, N.: Composite refactoring for decoupling multiple classes. In: 2016 IEEE 23rd International Conference on Software Analysis, Evolution, and Reengineering (SANER), vol. 1, pp. 594–598. IEEE (2016)
12. Aktaş, F., Buzluca, F.: a learning-based bug predicition method for object-oriented systems. In: 2018 IEEE/ACIS 17th International Conference on Computer and Information Science (ICIS), pp. 217–223. IEEE (2018)
13. https://tunedit.org/repo/PROMISE/DefectPrediction.
14. Antoniol, G., Canfora, G., Casazza, G., De Lucia, A., Merlo, E.: Recovering traceability links between code and documentation. IEEE Trans. Software Eng. **28**(10), 970–983 (2002)

15. Lucia, A.D., Fasano, F., Oliveto, R., Tortora, G.: Recovering traceability links in software artifact management systems using information retrieval methods. ACM Trans. Softw. Eng. Methodol. **16**(4), 13–63 (2007)
16. Bavota, G., Lucia, A.D., Oliveto, R., Tortora, G.: Enhancing software artifact traceability recovery processes with link count information, pp. 163–182. Inf. Softw. Technol. J. (2014)
17. Nishikawa, K., Oshima, K., Washizaki, H., Mibe, R., Fukazawa, Y.: Recovering transitive traceability links among software artifacts. ICSME, Bremen, Germany, pp. 576–580. IEEE (2015)
18. De Lucia, A., Di Penta, M., Oliveto, R., Panichella, A., Panichella, S.: Improving IR-based traceability recovery using smoothing filters. In: Proceedings of the 19th International Conference on Program Comprehension, pp. 21–30. IEEE (2011)
19. Diaz, D., Bavota, G., Marcus, A., Oliveto, R., Takahashi, S., De Lucia, A.: Using Code Ownership to Improve IR-Based Traceability Link Recovery, ICPC 2013. CA, USA, IEEE, San Francisco (2013)
20. https://loose.utt.ro/iplasma/iplasma.zip
21. Choudhary, G.R., Kumar, S., Kumar, K., Mishra, A., Catal, C.: Empirical analysis of change metrics for software fault prediction. Comput. Electr. Eng. **67**. 15–24 (2018)
22. Singh, P.: Comprehensive model for software fault prediction. In: 2017 International Conference on Inventive Computing and Informatics (ICICI), pp. 1103–1108. IEEE (2017)
23. Bennin, K.E., Keung, J., Phannachitta, P., Monden, A., Mensah, S.: Mahakil: diversity based oversampling approach to alleviate the class imbalance issue in software defect prediction. IEEE Trans. Softw. Eng. **44**(6), 534–550 (2017)
24. Chen, L.I.N., Fang, B.I.N., Shang, Z.: Software fault prediction based on one-class SVM. In: 2016 International Conference on Machine Learning and Cybernetics (ICMLC), vol. 2, pp. 1003–1008. IEEE (2016)

Detecting Fraudulent Transactions Using a Machine Learning Algorithm

S. L. Belyakov$^{(\boxtimes)}$, S. M. Karpov, and E. F. Zalilov

Southern Federal University, Nekrasovsky. 44, Rostov-on-Don 347928, Russia
{belyakov,karpov,zalilov}@sfedu.ru

Abstract. This study is dedicated to the problem of rapid detection of fraudulent financial transactions. Current approaches to monitoring and detection of fraud in banking transactions were analyzed. The problem of the most reliable recognition of classes of financial transactions using unbalanced data was considered. The problem of choosing the best classifier among ensemble algorithms was investigated. Specifically, these are algorithms of a Random Forest, Adaptive Boosting, and Decision Trees bagging. Methods of solving the problem of unbalanced data samples were analyzed. It was suggested to use the random undersampling algorithm to create balanced subsets of ensemble algorithm estimators. The results of experimental comparison of the selected methods are presented.

Keywords: Machine learning · Fraudulent financial transaction · Unbalanced data · Random undersampling

1 Introduction

Remote banking technologies are widely used in the modern banking system [1]. As in any other sphere of monetary circulation, they are the object of interest on the part of attackers. Fraudulent activities are carried out openly and are conducted as completely legal financial transactions. This happens due to the imperfection of user protection systems, phishing, social engineering, etc. A common way to detect fraud is to examine the data of committed transactions. By analyzing transaction attributes (time, amount, account numbers, purpose, etc.) one can find cases that are not typical of standard behavior models of transaction participants or models of transactions.

In this work the concept of "fraudulent" or "dishonest" transaction will reflect open, illegal financial transactions carried out with the aim of embezzlement or legalization of funds [2]. The term "legitimate" or "honest" transaction refers to all other financial transactions that are performed without malicious intent and do not fall under the definition of fraudulent financial transaction.

In practice, in order to detect the cases of fraud described above, software systems for monitoring financial transactions called anti-fraud systems are used [3]. Sets of

This research was financially supported by the RFBR grant 19-07-00074.

© Springer Nature Singapore Pte Ltd. 2021
P. K. Singh et al. (Eds.): FTNCT 2020, CCIS 1395, pp. 46–55, 2021.
https://doi.org/10.1007/978-981-16-1480-4_4

rules, logical conditions and machine learning (ML) models are used as algorithms for detecting suspicious transactions [4].

In this work a more efficient algorithm for classifying fraudulent transactions is determined by experimental analysis. The experiment is based on a set of real data about fraudulent transactions. A distinctive feature of the machine learning models design in this work is the consideration of data unbalance. Since fraud cases are rare in relation to all transactions, there is almost always a preponderance of the class of legitimate transactions over dishonest ones. When using machine learning models, this creates certain difficulties, since standard ML algorithms work inefficiently in conditions of unbalanced data distribution in classes [5]. To solve this problem algorithms are used to create an oversampling or undersampling [6].

2 Well-Known Approaches to Solve the Problem

To solve the described problem, various approaches are used that differ in the applied ML models and algorithms for changing the distribution of classes in samples [7]. Two approaches are used to change class ratios in data sets [7]. The first approach is to build oversampling. Oversampling – a sample formed from the original data set by increasing the size of the minority class by creating synthetic points that do not duplicate existing objects. The second approach involves the creation of undersampling. Undersampling – a sample formed from the original data set by reducing the size of the majority class. Combining classification algorithms with algorithms for changing the class ratio generates models that produce different results. Classifiers are currently used in conjunction with algorithms for creating a balanced undersampling [7]. Such an approach implies a reduction in the majority class up to a 1:1 ratio with the minority class. Further, the obtained data set is divided into training and test sets and the classifier is trained. However, the use of undersampling, although it gives high recognition rates for the minority class, often leads to unacceptable loss of majority class data, as a result, it is almost not recognized [7]. This is only effective when you need to recognize only one class from the original sample.

A combination of classifiers and algorithms for creating a balanced oversampling is also used. This approach involves an increase in the minority class by creating synthetic points without duplicating objects [7]. It is known that oversampling algorithms increase the probability of overtraining the model, increase the runtime of the algorithm and thus increase the computing power requirements.

In practice, ML models are used together with combined methods for creating a balanced sample. For example, there is an algorithm that uses the SMOTE (Synthetic Minority Oversampling Technique) method of synthetic resampling to create an oversampling, with the subsequent removal of instances of the class using the ENN (Edited Nearest Neighbors) algorithm. In fact, after obtaining a balanced dataset by creating synthetic instances of a class, any such instance with a class label other than at least two of its three closest neighbors is deleted. The disadvantage of the described approach is that the sample is created with a class ratio of 1:1, which cannot ensure the efficient operation of classifiers, since the optimal distribution does not always correspond to such a ratio. The optimal distribution is the ratio of classes in the training sample which provides the best indicators of accuracy in predicting the target class.

3 Proposed Approach

The specificity of fraud detection is that cases of illegal financial activity are extremely rare [7]. In other words, information about fraud is naturally unbalanced data. Therefore, the problem of creating a large and balanced sample will always be relevant. That is why the use of ensemble classifiers together with algorithms for creating a balanced sample is proposed as a model of ML. An ensemble is a unification of several "weak" single classifiers, referred to as learners of the ensemble, into one strong. Different approaches are used for this purpose. One of them is called bagging. The essence of bagging is the parallel training of weak learners independently from each other followed by the combination of their forecasts on the basis of averaging. Another approach is called boosting. It provides for the training of learners in a consistently adaptive way, i.e. each subsequent learner learns from the mistakes of the previous one.

The key feature of the proposed approach is to create an undersampling not for the entire classifier, but for each learner of the ensemble separately.

In the framework of the problem, we compare the results of the predictions of the following algorithms:

- balanced random forest;
- adaptive boosting with a random undersampling;
- balanced bagging.

As the source data we used a credit card fraud data set, which reflects the specifics of any transactions in remote banking systems and is suitable for demonstrating the operation of machine learning models within the framework of our problem.

Note that in the presented data, the distribution of fraudulent and honest transactions is extremely uneven. Thus, out of 284,807 transactions, only 492 transactions are fraudulent. To evaluate the operation of the machine learning model, we use the metrics of Recall, Precision, and harmonic mean of completeness and accuracy ($F1$) [9]. $F1$ is a target metric because its value reflects the accuracy of recognizing both a class of legitimate transactions and fraudulent ones. The Area Under Curve under the Receiver Operating Characteristic curve, denoted as the ROC-AUC criterion, is also another means of estimation. The graph of the ROC-curve displays the dependence of two values: a part of predicted fraudulent transactions among all fraudulent transactions (traditionally referred to as "true positive rate", further marked on the charts as TPR-metric) and a part of honest transactions predicted as fraudulent from all honest transactions (traditionally referred to as "false positive rate", further marked on the charts as FPR-metric), which allows more detailed assessment of the recognition of honest financial transactions.

4 Conditions for Conducting an Experimental Study

Ready-made solutions from the *imblearn* library were used to compare the selected ensemble methods:

- *BalancedRandomForestClassifier* (balanced random forest);

- *RUSBoostClassifier* (adaptive boosting with random undersampling);
- *BalancedBaggingClassifier* (balanced bagging).

The methodology for comparing the selected methods includes the following steps:

1. data preparation. Scaling the *"time"* and *"amount"* attributes in the source data set;
2. creating a test and training samples in the ratio of 20% and 80% of the original data, respectively;
3. selecting optimized parameters and preparing a dictionary;
4. searching for hyperparameters by value grid:
5. training the classifier model;
6. prediction based on a training sample;
7. prediction on a test sample;
8. calculating *Recall, Precision, F1, ROC-AUC* values;
9. plotting and output of *ROC*-curve graphs for the obtained predictions.

To improve the accuracy of the investigated algorithms, the selection of the parameters for each model was performed by searching for the best parameters in the grid, which is a predefined set of possible values.

5 Balanced Random Forest

A balanced random forest combines the method of undersampling for the majority class and the concept of an ensemble classifier, artificially changing the distribution of classes so that the classes are represented equally in each decision tree. Table 1 shows the result of this algorithm.

Table 1. Metric values for the balanced random forest algorithm.

№	Metrics	Training sample	Test sample
1	F1	79.71%	80.2%
2	Precision	76.89%	77.89%
3	Recall	82.74%	82.65%
4	ROC-AUC	91.35%	91.31%

Table 2 presents configuration parameters of the model for which the above-described metrics were obtained.

As the results of the model operation show, there are almost equal recognition rates for both the class of legitimate transactions and fraudulent ones at the level of ~80%. Meanwhile, the value of the ROC-AUC criterion equal to 91.31% indicates that the model is very good at recognizing fraudulent transactions and makes few mistakes when recognizing legitimate transactions, as illustrated by the graph in Fig. 1.

Table 2. Model parameters for the Balanced Random Forest algorithm.

Description	Parameter	Value
Number of the ensemble learners	n_estimators	80
Depth of decision trees	max_depth	3
Number of used features	max_features	Log2
Purity assessment criteria	criterion	Entropy
Class distribution in a subset	sampling_strategy	0.17

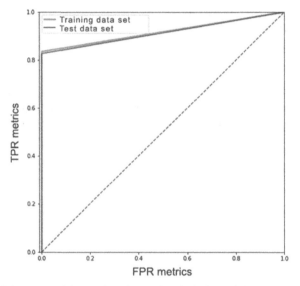

Fig. 1. ROC-curves of the random forest algorithm for training and test data sets.

The ROC-curve graph, as well as the AUC-area analysis, clearly demonstrates that the percentage of legitimate transactions classified incorrectly is less than 1% of all honest transactions in the test sample.

It is also worth noting that during the search for parameters in the grid of values, the best ratio of transaction classes turned out to be 0.17. That is, the class of fraudulent transactions amounted to 17% of the number of instances of the class of honest transactions in the subsets used to train decision trees. Recall that in the original sample, this value was 0.173%. This confirms the above-mentioned claims that the balance in the 1:1 ratio often does not reflect the essence of dependencies in the data.

6 Adaptive Boosting with a Random Undersampling

RUSBoostClassifier is a classic ensemble algorithm *ADABoost*, in which the ensemble learners are sequentially trained in an adaptive way, i.e. each subsequent learner learns from the incorrectly predicted objects of the previous one. A distinctive feature of the *RUSBoostClassifier* algorithm is the application of the random undersampling method at each iteration of the algorithm, which randomly removes instances of the majority class. Combining the basic algorithms into an ensemble allows to overcome the problem of information loss when using random undersampling in classic way, since missing instances of the majority class in one iteration will be present in another. Table 3 and Fig. 2 show the result of the experiment.

Table 3. Values of metrics of the *RUSBoostClassifier* algorithm.

№	Metrics	Training sample	Test sample
1	F1	83.66%	81.28%
2	Precision	81.64%	85.39%
3	Recall	85.78%	77.55%
4	ROC-AUC	92.88%	88.76%

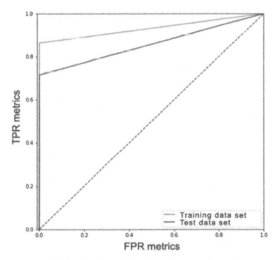

Fig. 2. ROC-curves of adaptive boosting algorithm for training and test data sets.

Table 4 presents configuration parameters of the model for which the above-described metrics were obtained.

The results show that there is a slight overtraining, since the model has deteriorated the accuracy of its predictions when working with independent data. Meanwhile, there is an improvement in the *Precision* indicator to the level of 85.39% relative to the previous model. The value of the *ROC-AUC* criterion also decreased to 88.76%. Metrics *F1* and *Recall* decreased and amounted to 81.28% and 77.55%, respectively.

Table 4. Model parameters for the *RUSBoostClassifier* algorithm.

Description	Parameter	Value
Number of the ensemble learners	n_estimators	100
Depth of decision trees	max_depth	3
Learning rate	learning_rate	0.6
Boosting algorithm	algorithm	SAMME.R
Distribution of classes in the sample	sampling_strategy	0.17

ROC-curve graphs show good results in recognizing true fraudulent transactions. The value of erroneous recognition of the honest transactions class also remained at the level of ~1%, which is an excellent indicator.

Let's add that based on the results of searching for the best parameters in the grid, the value of the class distribution parameter was also 0.17%.

7   Balanced Bagging

Balanced bagging is an ensemble algorithm that combines the idea of creating bootstrap samples with an algorithm for changing the class distribution, followed by training the ML model on each such subset of data. An average value of the results of each sample is the final prediction. Thus, the basic algorithms, learning from different samples, get different results and thereby compensate for emissions in the data (since subsets are formed randomly) and generally reduce the risk of prediction errors relative to any single result. Table 5 and Fig. 3 show the result of the algorithm operation.

Table 5. Metric values for the *BalancedBaggingClassifier* algorithm.

№	Metrics	Training sample	Test sample
1	F1	85.09%	85.09%
2	Precision	78.13%	77.06%
3	Recall	93.40%	85.71%
4	ROC-AUC	96.68%	92.84%

Table 6 presents configuration parameters of the model for which the above-described metrics were obtained.

Table 6. Model parameters for the *BalancedBaggingClassifier* algorithm.

Description	Parameter	Value
Number of the ensemble learners	n_estimators	100
Number of samples for learners training	max_samples	0.6
Number of features for learners training	max_features	0.2
The use of patterns in samples with replacement	bootstrap	True
Distribution of classes in the sample	sampling_strategy	0.17

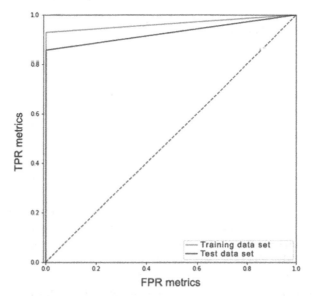

Fig. 3. *ROC*-curves of the balanced bagging algorithm for training and test data sets.

8 Discussion of Results

The comparison results in the following numerical data (Table 7).

Table 7. Values of ensemble algorithm metrics.

№	Metrics	Balanced random forest	Balanced adaptive boosting	Balanced bagging
1	F1	80.2%	81.28%	85.09%
2	Precision	77.89%	85.39%	77.06%
3	Recall	82.65%	77.55%	85.71%
4	ROC-AUC	91.31%	88.76%	92.84%

The adaptive boosting algorithm showed the worst results for predicting absolute fraudulent transactions of 77.55% (*Recall* metric) and at the same time the highest *Precision* metric of 85.39%. In comparison with the balanced random forest algorithm, this algorithm demonstrates an increase in accuracy for the *Precision* metric by ~7.5%, while a decrease in accuracy for the *Recall* metric is shown by almost 5%. Thus, there is a decrease in the number of false recognitions of the honest transaction class with a decrease in the number of correctly predicted fraudulent transactions. There is also a slight increase in *F1* accuracy by 1.08%. In comparison with the balanced bagging algorithm for adaptive boosting, there is a lag in the *Recall* and *F1* indicators by 8.16% and 3.81%, respectively.

The balanced bagging algorithm shows the best value of the *F1* metric among all test participants – 85.09%. It is also worth noting that in comparison with the balanced random forest method, there is an increase in the value of the *Recall* metric by 3.06%, with a slight decrease in the results for the *Precision* metric by 0.83%.

Thus, based on the obtained numerical data, we can conclude that for the problem of efficient transaction recognition, the balanced bagging algorithm of decision trees is the most preferred among all participants in the comparison.

9   Conclusion

The experimental study compared balanced ensemble algorithms for solving the problem of transaction recognition. The proposed method demonstrated good recognition rates for both classes of transactions. Thus, the percentage of true fraudulent transactions correctly recognized by the model from among all cases of fraud is 85.71%. The percentage of true fraudulent transactions out of all transactions predicted to be fraudulent is 77.06%. Harmonic mean, reflecting the relationship between the values described above, is 85.09%. Also, the *ROC*-curve graph showed that the percentage of incorrectly recognized honest transactions is less than 1%.

The result demonstrates that using ensemble algorithms together with a random undersampling allows one to get good prediction results on highly unbalanced data. Moreover, the use of such a sample specifically for subsets of ensembles learners allows one to use all the advantages of this method: to avoid the problem of data loss and get good prediction results. This approach can also be used in other binary classification problems where there is an uneven distribution of classes.

References

1. Sinigaglia, F., Carbone, R., Costa, G., Zannone, N.: A survey on multi-factor authentication for online banking in the wild. Comput. Secur. **95**, 0167–4048 (2020)
2. Robert, J., Edward, P., David, C.: Risk analysis, security surveys and insurance. In: Robert, J., Edward, P., David, C. (eds.) Introduction to Security, 10th edn, pp. 137–168. Butterworth-Heinemann (2019)
3. Bănărescu, A.: Detecting and preventing fraud with data analytics. Procedia Econ. Fin. **32**, 1827–1836 (2015)
4. Domashova, J., Kulaev, M.: Technology of forecasting potentially unstable credit organizations based on machine learning methods. Proc. Comput. Sci. **169**, 767–772 (2020)

5. Lavrov, I., Domashova, J.: Constructor of compositions of machine learning models for solving classification problems. Proc. Comput. Sci. **169**, 780–786 (2020)
6. Douzas, G., Bacao, F., Last, F.: Improving imbalanced learning through a heuristic oversampling method based on k-means and SMOTE. Inf. Sci. **465**, 1–20 (2018)
7. García, S., Zhang, Z., Altalhi, A., Alshomrani, S., Herrera, F.: Dynamic ensemble selection for multi-class imbalanced datasets. Inf. Sci. **445–446**, 22–37 (2018)
8. Brandon, N., Valeriya, V.: Illegal insider trading: commission and SEC detection. J. Corporate Fin. **58**, 247–269 (2019)
9. Portugal, I., Alencar, P., Cowan, D.: The use of machine learning algorithms in recommender systems: a systematic review. Expert Syst. Appl. **97**, 205–227 (2018)

Updated Analysis of Detection Methods for Phishing Attacks

Antonio Hernández Dominguez[(✉)] [iD] and Walter Baluja García[(✉)] [iD]

Universidad de las Ciencias Informáticas (UCI), 19370 Havana, Cuba
{ahdominguez,walterb}@uci.cu

Abstract. Phishing attacks use social engineering and some technical tricks to obtain users' personal identity data, account credentials and details of your bank cards to impersonate users on the network. Organizations are not immune to these attacks, so they should implement an orderly phishing detection plan, with the aim of reducing risks from direct exposure. Phishing is perpetrated in various telematic services such as email, web, social networks and instant messaging, among others. This paper brings an updated study of the main existing mechanisms for the detection of phishing. Additionally, the most effective solutions in the literature will be highlighted, matching solutions for different services will be identified and the most effective solutions will be featured, with the aim of applying these approaches in future integrated solutions for the detection of phishing attacks.

Keywords: Phishing · Phishing detection · Machine learning

1 Introduction

At the same time, the development and penetration of information and communication technologies (ICT) and the need for security of the information generated, stored, exchanged and processed are increasing. Global trends reveal an exponential growth of malignant actions aimed on putting information security at risk. The Internet Security Threat Report [1], issued by the US multinational corporation Symantec, shows how in recent years, the simplest tactics and most innovative computer criminals have achieved unprecedented results in the global threat landscape.

Phishing attacks are one of the most common among social engineering attacks [2]. Because the human is a determining factor, phishing has focused on social networks [3] and also on short text messaging or SMS (smishing) [4]. Other variants of this attack include email scams targeting specific individuals, organizations or companies (spear phishing) [5], email fraud targeting executives (whaling) [5], phishing through redirecting users to a fake site (pharming) [5], phishing through voice service (vishing) [5] and phishing based on the Uniform Resource Locator (malicious URL), contained in quick response codes or QR (QRishing) [6].

According to the Anti-Phishing Working Group (APWG), a total of 164,772 websites dedicated to phishing were reported in the first quarter of 2020, a 2% increase over the previous quarter [7]. Although there has been a decrease in these kinds of attacks using

© Springer Nature Singapore Pte Ltd. 2021
P. K. Singh et al. (Eds.): FTNCT 2020, CCIS 1395, pp. 56–67, 2021.
https://doi.org/10.1007/978-981-16-1480-4_5

email in the period from 2015 to 2019, these attacks remain a major threat to data networks [8].

Another aspect to note is that vishing attacks have been detected mainly in the financial sector, as well as phishing in social networks has increased considerably since 2016, due to the usefulness of user profiles for phishers [9]. Given the prevalence of these attacks, considerable research has been conducted on these issues. The preceding review papers [10, 11] have focused on studying and classifying the most significant detection techniques by scenario.

However, this paper will provide a comprehensive and up-to-date analysis of existing solution approaches. In the specific case of automated methods (algorithms, models, frameworks, among others), their effectiveness will be compared in terms of the **ACCURACY** of detection (relationship between correct predictions and total predictions) [12]. As part of the comparison, the most widely proposed methods and those with the best accuracy will be identified. In addition, the main features and the datasets used to extract these features will be listed, in order to determine which ones would be most suitable to be applied in the development of integrated solutions for phishing detection.

2   Phishing Detection Approaches

Various methods have been proposed internationally to detect phishing attacks. As can be noted in Fig. 1, the analysis of the paper [10] allows these solutions to be gathered into two main groups: conventional and automated.

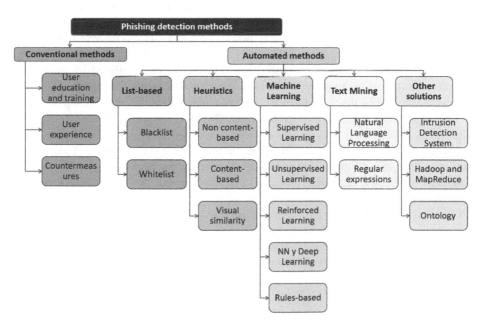

Fig. 1. Most widely proposed methods for detecting phishing attacks.

According to the literature, among the conventional methods there are solutions aimed at training users to detect this kind of attack. In addition, online communities such as Anti-Phishing (APWG, PhishTank, Symantec, and others) have been created to monitor and report on recent phishing activities [13]. The next sections will conduct an analysis (according to attacked service) of automated methods of detection.

2.1 Web Phishing Detection

Web phishing attacks encourage user interaction with fake websites. The main objective is to steal users' confidential information from the web. As a major web security concern, phishing has attracted the attention of many researchers and professionals. Despite the great attention it has received over the years, no definitive solution has been found. While recent solutions perform reasonably well, they require a large amount of training data and are not useful detecting phishing attacks against new targets [14].

According to the analyzed literature, lists-based approaches are proposed, such as blacklisting [15] and whitelisting [16]. Solutions using heuristics [17] were also found. Natural Language Processing techniques [18] evidence the use of Text Mining as an approach for phishing detection. The Hadoop framework and the MapReduce model [19] have been tested as another solution.

Table 1 shows a comparison of the main automated methods used in web phishing detection. Those related to URL, visual similarity and website content stand out for their effectiveness and frequency of use. These are obtained by processing and analyzing various sources of phishing data available on the web. From the above comparison, it is concluded that all the analyzed methods, with the exception of those based on lists, have similar accuracy offering values above 90%. Among the most widely used methods with higher accuracy are Decision Trees [20], heuristic methods based on visual similarity and the Naive Bayesian Classifier [21].

Among the most representative phishing datasets are those offered by the online communities Anti - Phishing PhishTank [19] and APWG [22], the University of California Irvine Machine Learning Repository (UCI Machine Learning) [23], the top 500 sites according to Alexa Internet [24] and the Open Directory Project (DMoz) [16]. On the other hand, in the proposed solutions the use of isolated methods predominates, such as blacklists [25], whitelists [26], heuristic methods based on content [27] and visual similarity [28], as well as machine learning algorithms: Support Vector Machine [29], Random Forest [30], Gradient Boosting [14], Fuzzy Logic [31] and Deep Learning algorithms [23].

Blacklists and whitelists are generally used in combined approaches [32]. In addition, some methodologies are proposed to increase detection efficiency levels by combining various machine learning [33] and text mining algorithms [34]. For instance, the Recurrent Convolutional Neural Network proposed by Adebowale [35].

Table 1. Comparison of the most used web phishing detection methods.

Method	Algorithm	Feature	Paper	Accuracy
List-based				
Whitelist	Designed by the author	URL-based	9	47–83%
Blacklist	Designed by the author	URL-based	18	78–90%
Heuristics				
Visual similarity	Designed by the author	URL lexical, content-based	10	80–99,60%
Machine learning				
Supervised learning	Decision trees	URL-based, content-based, certificate-based	26	81,98–99,64%
	Random Forest	URL-based, content-based, certificate-based	25	81,98–98,86%
	Boosting	URL-based, content-based, certificate-based	12	83,03–97,30%
	Naive Bayesian classifier	URL-based, visual similarity of the website, certificate-based	17	44–99,55%
	Support vector machine	URL-based, content-based, certificate-based	18	80,78–99,55%
Neural networks and deep learning	Neural networks	URL-based, content-based, certificate-based	10	87,14–97,42%
	Convolutional neural networks	based on URL domain, certificate-based	6	88,77–99%
Text mining				
Natural language processing	Term Frequency - Inverse Document Frequency	URL-based, content-based, certificate-based	5	89,4–97%

2.2   URL Phishing Detection

Illegal URLs are generally disguised as legitimate ones by phishing attackers [36]. These attacks are a particular case of web phishing, discussed before. The difference in detection methods is mainly about the features used to classify, which in this case are reinforced by URL-based ones. These attacks are not only developed through the Web, since a URL can be incorporated into the content of an e-mail, a message shared through a social network or through instant messaging, among others, hence the used features are different.

Typically, machine learning techniques are widely used to identify anomalous patterns in URLs as signs of phishing. However, adversaries may have enough knowledge and motivation to bypass URL classification algorithms by creating text combinations that evade classification algorithms [37]. Hence the importance of correct selection of the classifier when designing the detection method. According to the bibliography, list-based approaches are proposed, such as blacklists [13] and whitelists [11]. In addition, the heuristic method based on content was proposed by Huang [38]. Table 2 shows a comparison of the most commonly used automated methods for URL-based phishing detection.

Table 2. Comparison of the most used URL phishing detection methods.

Method	Algorithm	Feature	Paper	Accuracy
Machine learning				
Supervised learning	Decision trees	URL lexical, based on URL domain	9	68,2–99,14%
	Random forest	URL lexical, based on URL domain	10	86,9–99,5%
	Naive Bayesian classifier	URL lexical, based on redirection	8	64,6–99,8%
	Support vector machine	URL lexical, based on redirection	8	64,23–96,78%
	Logistic regression	URL lexical, based on URL domain, based on redirection, certificate-based	8	81,50–99,56%
Neural networks and deep learning	Neural networks	URL lexical, based on URL domain	7	93,17–99,3%
	Convolutional neural networks	URL lexical, based on URL domain	3	95,97–99,63%

From the table above, it can be concluded that the Naive Bayes Classifier and the Artificial Neural Networks must be the most effective methods for URL-based phishing detection, especially if combined with deep learning techniques such as Convolutional Neural Networks. It also outlined that Logistic Regression methods, Random Forests and Decision Trees have excellent accuracy values. The same datasets used on the web [36] are proposed for the case of URL-based phishing, as an observation highlights, to a greater extent, the data offered by the online community OpenPhish [38]. Also 45% of the URL-based approaches propose a combination of various ML algorithms [39] with blacklists or heuristic models [38]. Similar to the web, there are mixed proposals such as Recurrent Convolutional Neural Networks [38].

2.3 Email Phishing Detection

Email Phishing refers to an attacker using a fake message to trick the recipient into returning information such as an account password to a designated destination. Additionally, it may be used to trick recipients into entering special web pages, which are usually disguised as genuine, such as a bank's site, to convince users to enter sensitive information such as a credit card or bank card number and password [40]. Filtering through databases such as blacklists [13] and whitelists [41] are examples of the use of this kind of methods. Also, with the usage of heuristic methods acceptable results have been obtained, specifically with the non-content based approaches presented by Bikov [13]. With regard to Text Mining, Natural Language Processing techniques [42] have been used to detect phishing based on the message content. Among the most commonly used techniques for the extraction of lexical features to be used in phishing detection are Term Frequency - Inverse Document Frequency (TF-IDF) [43] and Distributed Memory Model of Paragraph Vectors (PV-DM) [44]. On the other hand, Intrusion Detection Systems (IDS) [13], configured to detect phishing, are examples of other emerging solutions used today. Table 3 shows a comparison of the most widely used automated methods for detecting phishing in email.

Table 3. Comparison of the most used email phishing detection methods.

Methods	Algorithm	Feature	Paper	Accuracy
Heuristics				
Not content-based	Designed by the author	Generic, sender, recipient	5	95–98,79%
Machine learning				
Supervised learning	Decision trees	Generic, sender, content	7	92,98–98,11%
	Random forest	Generic, sender, recipient, content	7	95,05–98.87%
	Support vector machine	Generic, sender, content	9	75–98%
	K-Nearest neighbors	Recipient, sender, content, attachments	3	92,46–96%
Neural networks and deep learning	Multi-layer perceptron	Recipient, content	3	91,05–96,44%
	Recurrent neural networks	Recipient, content: subject	3	96–97,38%

The features that have been used the most are related to the *sender* and the *content of the message*. The latter are very interesting for research, mainly for those attacks that redirect users to fake websites, since in this case, by including at least a URL in the message content, the methods described in Sects. 2.1 and 2.2 could be applied. As conclusion, it has to be said that Artificial Neural Networks represent the most effective method for the detection of phishing in email. With Convolutional and Recurrent Neural Networks, accuracy results over 97% are obtained.

However, by combining the methods described above, the accuracy must be increased by 2 percentage units, according to the model Recurrent Convolutional Neuronal Networks, proposed by Fang [40]. Natural Language Processing techniques, non-content based Heuristic Methods, Random Forests and Decision Trees [43] also stand out, with accuracy values above 98%. Among the most used datasets, in the case of e-mail, are Apache SpamAssassin [45], Enron [46], Nazario's [47] and APWG [43]. Some solutions have used the methods independently [48] and in other cases combined methods have been proposed, looking for better results in classification. In the case of hybrid approaches, blacklists have been proposed to be combined with machine learning [45] and text mining algorithms [42].

2.4 Phishing Detection on Social Networks

In recent years, Online Social Networking (OSN) has become popular. The interaction between users facilitated by this service can lead to phishing attacks. Phishing detection systems in social networks vary in robustness, but show a marked similarity in the detection techniques employed. Table 4 shows a comparison of the most widely used automated methods of phishing detection on social networks.

Some examples of these techniques are list-based [3], content-based heuristic methods, such as the proactive filtering and discovery solution proposed by Fang [49], and ML-based classifiers. Blacklists are considered to be one of the most widely used techniques in this field [3]. The features associated with the *published content* and the *URL* within the *content* are the most interesting to this research. Due to the existence of URL-based features, the methods described in Sects. 2.1, 2.2 and 2.3 can be applied. As a consideration, unlike the previous cases, no effective proposals were found to detect phishing on social networks using Neural Networks. The methods of best accuracy found were Decision Trees, the Hadoop framework using the MapReduce model and the Support Vector Machine. The datasets offered by the OpenPhish [50] online community are frequently used. In the case of social networks, only blacklists [50] are used independently for the detection of phishing attacks, the rest of the papers shows combined proposals for ML algorithms [51], for whitelists with blacklists [3], as well as the combination of the latter with heuristic methods [49].

2.5 Discussion

Table 5 shows a comparison of the most effective phishing detection methods according to the above sections. The accuracy values reflected are the maximum values found for each method. In cases where no accuracy value is defined, it is because the methods are not effective enough to be considered for that service attacks.

Table 4. Comparison of the most used phishing detection methods on social networks.

Method	Algorithm	Feature	Paper	Accuracy
List-based				
Whitelist	Designed by the author	Content: URL	1	98%
Blacklist	Designed by the author	Content: URL	2	86,41%
Heuristics				
Content-based	Designed by the author	Content: text, URL	1	93,86%
Machine learning				
Supervised learning	Decision trees	Content: text, URL	1	99,10%
	Random forest	User profile	2	71–92%
	Naive Bayesian classifier	Content: text, URL, user profile	3	38–95%
	Support vector machine	Content: URL	1	99,00%
	K-Nearest neighbors	User profile	1	80,00%
	Logistic regression	Content: text, URL	3	67–97%
Others	Hadoop/MapReduce	Content: URL	1	99,00%

Table 5. Comparison of the most effective phishing detection approaches.

Method	Web	URL	Email	Social network
Blacklist	90,00%	No	No	No
Whitelist	No	No	No	98,00%
Heuristic methods visual similarity approach	99,60%	No	No	No
Heuristic methods non-content based approach	No	No	98,79%	No
Decision trees	99,64%	99,14%	98,11%	99,10%
Boosting	No	99,60%	No	No
Naive Bayesian classifier	98,55%	99,80%	93,27%	95,00%
Logistic regression	No	99,56%	No	97,00%
Random forest	98,86%	99,50%	98,87%	92,00%
Support vector machine	99,55%	96,78%	98,00%	99,00%
K-Nearest neighbors	99,10%	No	No	No
Convolutional neural networks	99,00%	99,63%	97,20%	No
Recurrent convolutional neuronal networks	No	No	99,85%	No
Natural language processing	No	No	98,89%	No
Hadoop using MapReduce	No	No	No	99,00%

After performing the analysis of the phishing detection methods, in each of the services, it has been determined that the Decision Trees and the Support Vector Machine are the most effective and proposed methods to detect phishing in the analyzed services attacks. Table 5 shows that Convolutional Neural Networks, the Naive Bayes Classifier and the Random Forests stand out for their frequency of use and effectiveness.

In general, when designing integrated solutions, machine learning methods represent an essential element to be taken into account, due to the levels of effectiveness achieved after applying them to more specific problems. Artificial neural networks are among the most accurate. Likewise, when various machine learning methods are combined, accuracy values are further increased. Therefore, as part of the design of new comprehensive approaches, those combined methods that offer the best results should be selected. The most common features used to detect phishing are *content-based*, especially *text-based* and *URL-based*. On the other hand, due to the exponential growth in the use of mobile devices [22], phishers are currently taking advantage of hardware limitations and user attitudes when using these devices, which are equipped with applications that consume various services over the Internet. Hence, phishing attacks are developed through these services. Nowadays, the detection of phishing attacks in mobile devices is an interesting topic that will be analyzed in future scientific works.

3 Conclusions

This paper sets out the key ideas from a systematic review of phishing detection methods in email, web and social network services. The kinds of attacks and the main existing solution proposals were analyzed, highlighting the models and the algorithms involved. Although training and education of users are usually very effective measures, these must be combined with technical ones, given the growing innovative trend of attackers and the diversity of attack.

On the other hand, the methods or mechanisms proposed in the literature for technical solutions are valid for each telematic service individually. Important lacks persist, such as the absence of proposals for integral solutions to face these risks with a systemic approach and from the network management point of view. Automated methods, and specifically those of Machine Learning (Random Forest, Decision Trees and the Support Vector Machine) stand out for their effectiveness and the number of proposals found. Deep Learning techniques have not been sufficiently exploited in phishing detection, so these algorithms are a novel method to be explored deeply in future research. Therefore, these methods are the most suitable for the development of comprehensive solutions. In the near future, an integrated and systemic solution will be proposed that can be used regardless of the service where the attack is performed.

References

1. Symantec: Internet Security Threat Report 2019 (2019)
2. Sumner, A., Yuan, X.: Mitigating phishing attacks: an overview. In: Proceedings of the 2019 ACM Southeast Conference, Kennesaw, GA, USA, pp. 72–77. ACM (2019)

3. Yassein, M.B., Aljawarneh, S., Wahsheh, Y.A.: Survey of online social networks threats and solutions. In: 2019 IEEE Jordan International Joint Conference on Electrical Engineering and Information Technology (JEEIT), pp. 375–380 (2019)
4. Balim, C., Gunal, E.S.: Automatic detection of smishing attacks by machine learning methods. In: 2019 1st International Informatics and Software Engineering Conference (UBMYK), pp. 1–3 (2019)
5. Moul, K.A.: Avoid phishing traps. In: Proceedings of the 2019 ACM SIGUCCS Annual Conference, New Orleans, LA, USA, pp. 199–208. ACM (2019)
6. Chorghe, S.P., Shekokar, N.: A survey on anti-phishing techniques in mobile phones. In: 2016 International Conference on Inventive Computation Technologies (ICICT), pp. 1–5 (2016)
7. APWG: Phishing Activity Trends Report - 1st Quarter 2020, San Francisco, USA (2020)
8. APWG: Phishing Activity Trends Report - 2015–2019, San Francisco, USA (2019)
9. Sfakianakis, A., Douligeris, C., Marinos, L., Lourenço, M., Raghimi, O.: ENISA Threat Landscape Report 2018: 15 Top Cyberthreats and Trends, vol. 10 (2019)
10. Qabajeh, I., Thabtah, F., Chiclana, F.: A recent review of conventional vs automated cyber security anti-phishing techniques. Comput. Sci. Rev. **29**, 44–55 (2018). https://doi.org/10.1016/j.cosrev.2018.05.003
11. Althobaiti, K., Rummani, G., Vaniea, K.: A review of human- and computer-facing URL phishing features. In: 2019 IEEE European Symposium on Security and Privacy Workshops (EuroS&PW), pp. 182–191 (2019)
12. Tyagi, I., Shad, J., Sharma, S., Gaur, S., Kaur, G.: A novel machine learning approach to detect phishing websites. In: 2018 5th International Conference on Signal Processing and Integrated Networks (SPIN), pp. 425–430 (2018)
13. Bikov, T.D., Iliev, T.B., Mihaylov, G.Y., Stoyanov, I.S.: Phishing in depth – modern methods of detection and risk mitigation. In: 2019 42nd International Convention on Information and Communication Technology, Electronics and Microelectronics (MIPRO), pp. 447–450 (2019)
14. Marchal, S., Saari, K., Singh, N., Asokan, N.: Know your phish: novel techniques for detecting phishing sites and their targets. In: 2016 IEEE 36th International Conference on Distributed Computing Systems (ICDCS), pp. 323–333 (2016)
15. Bell, S., Komisarczuk, P.: An analysis of phishing blacklists: Google safe browsing, OpenPhish, and PhishTank. In: Proceedings of the Australasian Computer Science Week Multiconference, Melbourne, VIC, Australia, p. 11. ACM (2020)
16. Pham, C., Nguyen, L.A.T., Tran, N.H., Huh, E., Hong, C.S.: Phishing-aware: a neuro-fuzzy approach for anti-phishing on fog networks. IEEE Trans. Netw. Service Manag. **15**(3), 1076–1089 (2018). https://doi.org/10.1109/TNSM.2018.2831197
17. Nathezhtha, T., Sangeetha, D., Vaidehi, V.: WC-PAD: web crawling based phishing attack detection. In: 2019 International Carnahan Conference on Security Technology (ICCST), pp. 1–6 (2019)
18. Zuraiq, A.A., Alkasassbeh, M.: Review: phishing detection approaches. In: 2019 2nd International Conference on new Trends in Computing Sciences (ICTCS), pp. 1–6 (2019)
19. Dou, Z., Khalil, I., Khreishah, A., Al-Fuqaha, A., Guizani, M.: Systematization of knowledge (SoK): a systematic review of software-based web phishing detection. IEEE Commun. Surv. Tutor. **19**(4), 2797–2819 (2017). https://doi.org/10.1109/COMST.2017.2752087
20. Cuzzocrea, A., Martinelli, F., Mercaldo, F.: A machine-learning framework for supporting intelligent web-phishing detection and analysis. In: Proceedings of the 23rd International Database Applications & Engineering Symposium, Athens, Greece, pp. 1–3. ACM (2019)
21. Latif, R.M.A., Umer, M., Tariq, T., Farhan, M., Rizwan, O., Ali, G.: A smart methodology for analyzing secure e-banking and e-commerce websites. In: 2019 16th International Bhurban Conference on Applied Sciences and Technology (IBCAST), pp. 589–596 (2019)

22. Sharma, H., Meenakshi, E., Bhatia, S.K.: A comparative analysis and awareness survey of phishing detection tools. In: 2017 2nd IEEE International Conference on Recent Trends in Electronics, Information & Communication Technology (RTEICT), pp. 1437–1442 (2017)

23. Vrbančič, G., Fister, I., Podgorelec, V.: Swarm intelligence approaches for parameter setting of deep learning neural network: case study on phishing websites classification. In: Proceedings of the 8th International Conference on Web Intelligence, Mining and Semantics, Novi Sad, Serbia, pp. 1–8. ACM (2018)

24. Haruta, S., Asahina, H., Sasase, I.: Visual similarity-based phishing detection scheme using image and CSS with target website finder. In: GLOBECOM 2017 - 2017 IEEE Global Communications Conference, pp. 1–6 (2017)

25. Oest, A., Safaei, Y., Doupé, A., Ahn, G., Wardman, B., Tyers, K.: PhishFarm: a scalable framework for measuring the effectiveness of evasion techniques against browser phishing blacklists. In: 2019 IEEE Symposium on Security and Privacy, pp. 1344–1361 (2019)

26. Shyni, C.E., Sundar, A.D., Ebby, G.S.E.: Phishing detection in websites using parse tree validation. In: 2018 Recent Advances on Engineering, Technology and Computational Sciences (RAETCS), pp. 1–4 (2018)

27. Park, A.J., Quadari, R.N., Tsang, H.H.: Phishing website detection framework through web scraping and data mining. In: 2017 8th IEEE Annual Information Technology, Electronics and Mobile Communication Conference (IEMCON), pp. 680–684 (2017)

28. Wang, Y., Duncan, I.: a novel method to prevent phishing by using OCR technology. In: 2019 International Conference on Cyber Security and Protection of Digital Services (Cyber Security), pp. 1–5 (2019)

29. Patil, P., Rane, R., Bhalekar, M.: Detecting spam and phishing mails using SVM and obfuscation URL detection algorithm. In: 2017 International Conference on Inventive Systems and Control (ICISC), pp. 1–4 (2017)

30. Alswailem, A., Alabdullah, B., Alrumayh, N., Alsedrani, A.: Detecting phishing websites using machine learning. In: 2019 2nd International Conference on Computer Applications & Information Security (ICCAIS), pp. 1–6 (2019)

31. Barraclough, P., Sexton, G.: Phishing website detection fuzzy system modelling. In: 2015 Science and Information Conference (SAI), pp. 1384–1386 (2015)

32. Geng, G., Yan, Z., Lee, J., Jin, X., Liu, D.: An efficient antiphishing method to secure econsume. IEEE Consum. Electron. Mag. **8**(6), 42–46 (2019). https://doi.org/10.1109/MCE.2019.2928585

33. Abdelhamid, N., Thabtah, F., Abdel-Jaber, H.: Phishing detection: a recent intelligent machine learning comparison based on models content and features. In: 2017 IEEE International Conference on Intelligence and Security Informatics (ISI), pp. 72–77 (2017)

34. Yadollahi, M.M., Shoeleh, F., Serkani, E., Madani, A., Gharaee, H.: An adaptive machine learning based approach for phishing detection using hybrid features. In: 2019 5th International Conference on Web Research (ICWR), pp. 281–286 (2019)

35. Adebowale, M.A., Lwin, K.T., Hossain, M.A.: Deep learning with convolutional neural network and long short-term memory for phishing detection. In: 2019 13th International Conference on Software, Knowledge, Information Management and Applications (SKIMA), pp. 1–8 (2019)

36. Zhu, E., Chen, Y., Ye, C., Li, X., Liu, F.: OFS-NN: an effective phishing websites detection model based on optimal feature selection and neural network. IEEE Access **7**, 73271–73284 (2019). https://doi.org/10.1109/ACCESS.2019.2920655

37. AlEroud, A., Karabatis, G.: Bypassing detection of URL-based phishing attacks using generative adversarial deep neural networks. In: Proceedings of the Sixth International Workshop on Security and Privacy Analytics, New Orleans, USA, pp. 53–60. ACM (2020)

38. Huang, Y., Yang, Q., Qin, J., Wen, W.: Phishing URL detection via CNN and attention-based hierarchical RNN. In: 2019 18th IEEE International Conference on Trust, Security And Privacy In Computing And Communications/13th IEEE International Conference On Big Data Science And Engineering (TrustCom/BigDataSE), pp. 112–119 (2019)
39. Huang, Y., Qin, J., Wen, W.: Phishing URL detection via capsule-based neural network. In: 2019 IEEE 13th International Conference on Anti-counterfeiting, Security, and Identification (ASID), pp. 22–26 (2019)
40. Fang, Y., Zhang, C., Huang, C., Liu, L., Yang, Y.: Phishing email detection using improved RCNN model with multilevel vectors and attention mechanism. IEEE Access 7, 56329–56340 (2019). https://doi.org/10.1109/ACCESS.2019.2913705
41. Pongchanchai, N., Visoottiviseth, V., Ou, K., Yamai, N., Kitagawa, N.: Countermeasure against spoofed e-mails using display name as a user authenticator. In: 2018 Seventh ICT International Student Project Conference (ICT-ISPC), pp. 1–6 (2018)
42. Bagui, S., Nandi, D., Bagui, S., White, R.J.: Classifying phishing email using machine learning and deep learning. In: 2019 International Conference on Cyber Security and Protection of Digital Services (Cyber Security), pp. 1–2 (2019)
43. Park, G., Rayz, J.: Ontological detection of phishing emails. In: 2018 IEEE International Conference on Systems, Man, and Cybernetics (SMC), pp. 2858–2863 (2018)
44. Douzi, S., Amar, M., Ouahidi, B.E.: Advanced phishing filter using autoencoder and denoising autoencoder. In: Proceedings of the International Conference on Big Data and Internet of Thing, London, United Kingdom, pp. 125–129. ACM (2017)
45. Form, L.M., Chiew, K.L., Sze, S.N., Tiong, W.K.: Phishing email detection technique by using hybrid features. In: 2015 9th International Conference on IT in Asia, pp. 1–5 (2015)
46. Xiujuan, W., Chenxi, Z., Kangfeng, Z., Haoyang, T., Yuanrui, T.: Detecting spear-phishing emails based on authentication. In: 2019 IEEE 4th International Conference on Computer and Communication Systems (ICCCS), pp. 450–456 (2019)
47. Verma, R., Rai, N.: Phish-IDetector: message-ID based automatic phishing detection. In: 2015 12th International Joint Conference on e-Business and Telecommunications (ICETE), pp. 427–434 (2015)
48. Bhadane, A., Mane, S.B.: Detecting lateral spear phishing attacks in organisations. IET Inf. Secur. 13(2), 133–140 (2019). https://doi.org/10.1049/iet-ifs.2018.5090
49. Fang, L., Bailing, W., Junheng, H., Yushan, S., Yuliang, W.: A proactive discovery and filtering solution on phishing websites. In: 2015 IEEE International Conference on Big Data (Big Data), pp. 2348–2355 (2015)
50. Bell, S., Komisarczuk, P.: Measuring the effectiveness of Twitter's URL shortener (t.co) at protecting users from phishing and malware attacks. In: Proceedings of the Australasian Computer Science Week Multiconference, Melbourne, Australia, p. 11. ACM (2020)
51. Al-Janabi, M., Quincey, E.D., Andras, P.: Using supervised machine learning algorithms to detect suspicious URLs in online social networks. In: Proceedings of the 2017 IEEE/ACM International Conference on Advances in Social Networks Analysis and Mining 2017, Sydney, Australia, pp. 1104–1111. ACM (2017)

Criterion of Blockchain Vulnerability to Majority Attack Based on Hashing Power Distribution Assessment

Alexey Busygin$^{(\boxtimes)}$ and Maxim Kalinin

Peter the Great St.Petersburg Polytechnic University, St.Petersburg, Russia
{a.busygin,max}@ibks.spbstu.ru

Abstract. A blockchain distributed ledger is an actively developed technology that goes beyond its original cryptocurrency application and integrates to IoT, smart manufacturing, smart cities, logistics and more. Therefore, the blockchain security is of the current interest. The article considers a blockchain security issue caused by imbalanced hashing power distribution between nodes: the majority attack. The majority attack (the 51% attack) is a technique which intends to fork the blockchain in order to cancel confirmed transactions and violate data integrity. Despite the attack cost, it has become frequent in current blockchains. The existing security mechanisms against the majority attack have significant weaknesses and limitations. This paper proposes a novel criterion of the blockchain vulnerability to the majority attack. The criterion allows to detect vulnerable states of the distributed ledger based on hashing power distribution assessment. The blockchain hashing power time series are constructed and analyzed in order to evaluate the portion of total hashing power that is controlled by attacker. This estimate is used as a foundation of the proposed criterion. The criterion may be used to in conjunction with other security mechanisms to enhance protection of distributed ledgers in vulnerable states.

Keywords: Distributed ledger · Blockchain · Majority attack · 51% attack · Vulnerability criterion · Hashing power

1 Introduction

A blockchain distributed leger technology is attracting massive attention of business, engineering and scientific communities. Potential advantages of the technology, such as an absence of trusted intermediaries, transparency and verifiability of ledger operation, fault tolerance, have resulted in vast numbers of research projects since the October 2008—the date of the Bitcoin blockchain concepts publication. Various blockchain use cases outside of the financial industry have been identified, for example notary services, rights management, government services, Internet infrastructure and IoT [1]. The recent papers present blockchain applications in health care [2], microgrids [3], logistics and supply chain [4], Industry 4.0 and industrial IoT [5], smart cities [6] and more.

© Springer Nature Singapore Pte Ltd. 2021
P. K. Singh et al. (Eds.): FTNCT 2020, CCIS 1395, pp. 68–77, 2021.
https://doi.org/10.1007/978-981-16-1480-4_6

A central component of the distributed ledger is a consensus algorithm that is used by all participants to reach a consistent agreement on a current state of the ledger. This paper is focused on distributed ledgers utilizing the Proof-of-Work based consensus. Although a number of alternative consensus algorithms have been proposed, the Proof-of-Work based distributed ledgers are still of current interest. The reason is that the other commonly used consensus algorithms have the following constraints.

The Proof-of-Stake is a relatively new approach for which several security issues have not been formally discussed or addressed [7]. Furthermore, the Proof-of-Stake based consensus algorithms are based on cryptocurrency concepts that may not exist in some application domains (for example in IoT communications) or may not have a legal status under some jurisdictions.

The Proof-of-Authority approach security is heavily relied on trusted participants (authorities). Additionally, the Proof-of-Authority based consensus algorithms lack decentralization due to a limited number of authorities. That introduces a single point of failure, where attackers know exactly what to attack.

The Byzantine Fault Tolerance (BFT) based consensus algorithms (pBFT [8] and other) are susceptible to Sybil attacks and have a limited scalability caused by intensive message transmission overhead [9].

Although the Proof-of-Work based distributed ledgers have several advantages over alternative approaches, there are common scalability and security issues that should be solved. The scalability issues are addressed by increasing block size and frequency [10], introducing sidechains [11], off-chain transactions [12], sharding [13], replacing the blockchain with a directed acyclic graph [14] and reducing the need for long term data storage [15].

This article considers the most common security issue of the Proof-of-Work based distributed ledgers—the majority attack (51% attack). We propose a criterion allowing to perform a real time evaluation of a blockchain distributed ledger vulnerability to the majority attack. In Sect. 2 we briefly describe the Proof-of-Work based blockchain distributed ledgers and the majority attack. Section 3 provides an analysis of the current majority attack mitigation efforts in the Proof-of-Work based distributed ledgers. In Sect. 4 a blockchain vulnerability criterion is presented. The proposed criterion is evaluated in Sect. 5. Finally, we conclude the paper in Sect. 6.

2 Background

A typical blockchain is illustrated in Fig. 1. A distributed ledger data is represented as sequence (chain) of objects called blocks. When a new portion of data should be added to distributed ledger, it is packed into a new block which is appended to the chain. Each block b_i is composed of the following values:

- $h_i = \mathcal{H}(b_{i-1})$ is a value of cryptographic hash function $\mathcal{H}$ calculated over the previous block and defining a position of the block in the chain
- a block creation timestamp t_i
- a nonce r_i, which is explained bellow
- data d_i (for example, a sequence of transactions)

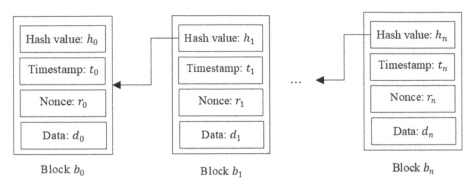

Fig. 1. Example of a blockchain

In order to append a new block b_{n+1} to the chain, a nonce r_{n+1} have to be found that satisfies the following condition:

$$\mathcal{H}(b_{n+1}(r_{n+1})) \leq h_{max} \qquad (1)$$

The value h_{max} is called target. The lower the target, the more "difficult" it is to generate a new block b_{n+1}. The found value r_{n+1} satisfying the condition 1 may be thought as a proof of work.

Condition (1) serves two purposes. Firstly, it reduces the probability that multiple conflicting blocks will be generated simultaneously. Secondly, used in conjunction with hash chaining, it provides the central security property of the blockchain: a modification of block b_{n-z} requires subsequent modifications of blocks $b_{n-z+1}, \ldots, b_n$ (confirmation blocks) and the "difficulty" of such alterations grows along with the value of the block depth z.

Any node of a distributed ledger may propose its own, possibly invalid, blockchain version. The Proof-of-Work based consensus algorithms are used to choose a single valid blockchain version from all the proposed. A blockchain that is contributed with maximum hashing "work" is chosen as valid (for example the longest blockchain). The security of the Proof-of-Work approach is based on assumption that hashing power is distributed equally between all nodes. Therefore, as long as the majority of nodes is honest, dishonest nodes will not be able to generate a blockchain that will be accepted as valid.

The majority attack (51% attack) is a technique that is used to force the honest nodes to accept an alternative blockchain as valid instead of the current one. An attacker privately generates the alternative blockchain. If the attacker controls more than a half of a distributed ledger hashing power, the privately generated blockchain will eventually involve more hashing "work" than the current one. Hence, when published it will substitute the current blockchain. This technique may be utilized for performing double spending or deleting arbitrary records from a ledger.

The majority attack is possible in practice because hashing power is not equally distributed between all the nodes. For example, currently more than a half of the Bitcoin hashing power is controlled by only five mining pools [16]. Since the April 2018 the following distributed ledgers have been successfully attacked: Bitcoin Gold, Verge, Ethereum Classic and other [17].

3 Related Work

The majority attack has been firstly analyzed in [18]. The probability of successful attack has been evaluated:

$$
P = \begin{cases} 1 - \sum\limits_{i=0}^{z} \frac{\lambda^i e^{-\lambda}}{i!} \left(1 - \left(\frac{q}{p}\right)^{z-i}\right), & q < \frac{1}{2} \\ 1, & q \geq \frac{1}{2} \end{cases} \tag{2}
$$

Here p is probability that an honest node finds the next block, $q = 1 - p$ is probability that the attacker finds the next block, z is a depth of the first block to be altered (number of confirmations), λ is an expected value of the attacker's progress:

$$
\lambda = z \frac{q}{p} \tag{3}
$$

The Eq. (2) formalizes security properties of a distributed ledger at some value of q. For example, it shows that an attacker with $q = 0.25$ is highly unlikely to alter the block with $z = 5$ confirmations. The probability of the attacker's success is less than 0.1%. The Eq. (2) may also potentially be applied for a real time estimation of a distributed ledger vulnerability to the majority attack, however it is not used for that purpose in practice, because it is not defined how to assess the current q value.

One of the proposed approaches to protection against the majority attack is to obstruct an attacker to acquire a significant portion of a distributed ledger hashing power. One possible solution is a development of mechanisms that reduce the effectiveness of dedicated hardware utilization for the Proof-of-Work computation. The paper [19] discusses an ASIC-resistance of employing multiple hash functions in the Proof-of-Work computation. A number of bandwidth hard hash functions is proposed as ASIC-resistant [20]. This approach may be used to counter a single attacker, however is inefficient in the case of collusion of multiple nodes with a significant summary hashing power.

A blockchain checkpointing techniques are discussed in [21]. The proposed techniques are either heavily relied on trusted participants and inherit the limitations of the Proof-of-Authority distributed ledgers, or delegate checkpointing to another distributed ledger that assumed to be secure by definition.

The main limitations of an advanced protection techniques against the majority attack are discussed in [22]. The paper shows that all the evaluated security techniques fail to provide enough protection against the majority attack:

- The penalty system for delayed block submission always fail to protect when an attacker controls more than a half of distributed ledger hashing power and significantly increases transaction confirmation period in some cases.
- The addition of a notary node and quorum concepts introduces the limitations of the Proof-of-Authority and the BFT based distributed ledgers.

- Merged mining technique is just an approach to increase the attacking cost by merging hashing power of multiple distributed ledgers, and it does not provide an effective solution.

The analysis presented in this section shows all the currently proposed security techniques have significant weaknesses and limitations.

4 Distributed Ledger Vulnerability Criterion

The main idea behind the proposed criterion follows: when the majority attack begins, the attacker stops working on the current blockchain and invests all the controlled hashing power to privately generated alternative blockchain. That results in decrease of total hashing power involved in generation of the current blockchain. Figure 2 shows that after the beginning of the majority attack at time t_A the hashing power falls from H_0 to H_A. Therefore, ΔH is the hashing power controlled by the attacker.

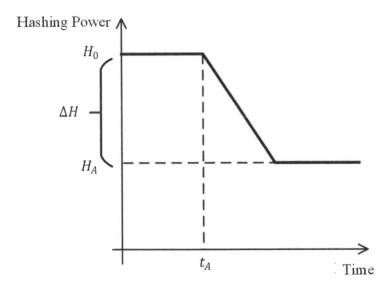

Fig. 2. Decrease of the blockchain hashing power after the start of the attack

Then the probability that the attacker finds the next block may be defined as follows:

$$q = \frac{\Delta H}{H_0} \tag{4}$$

The decrease of hashing power affects the rate at which news blocks are generated in the current blockchain. By analyzing new block generation statistics, we may detect the attack.

Firstly, the total hashing power of the distributed ledger should be estimated. Assuming that all values of n-bit hash function $\mathcal{H}$ are uniformly distributed, the probability of successful generation of a new block on the first trial is the following:

$$p = \frac{h_{max} + 1}{2^n} \tag{5}$$

The number of trials that should be performed in order to generate a new block have geometric distribution. The expected value is the following:

$$M = \frac{2^n}{h_{max} + 1} \tag{6}$$

Therefore, the hashing power involved in a block b_i generation may be assessed with the following equation:

$$H_i(k) = \frac{Mk}{t_i - t_{i-k}} \tag{7}$$

Here k is a number of blocks preceding the block b_i, which are used for average calculation, t_i and t_{i-k} represent time of the block b_i and the block b_{i-k} creation accordingly.

All values required for H_i calculation are available from the current blockchain. t_i and t_{i-k} values may be taken from the current blockchain timestamps, or measured independently with local clock, when the block is firstly observed.

The Eq. (7) is used to construct time series $\{H_i\}$. The total hashing power of the distributed ledger for the observed period w may be evaluated as follows:

$$H_0 = \max_{H_i \in w}(H_i) \tag{8}$$

The hashing power controlled by the attacker at the moment of a block b_i generation may be assessed with the next equation:

$$\Delta H = H_0 - H_i \tag{9}$$

Finally, (8) and (9) allow us to evaluate the probability q that the attacker finds the next block:

$$q = \frac{\Delta H + H_{covert}}{H_0} \tag{10}$$

Here we have extended (4) with H_{covert} parameter, where H_{covert} is a hashing power of the attacker that is kept in secret and has not ever been involved in generation of the current blockchain. H_{covert} may be defined, for example, by an attacker model. For distributed ledgers with a substantial total hashing power H_{covert} value may be negligible.

By applying (10) to (2) the we derive the following vulnerability criterion: the blockchain is vulnerable to the majority attack if the probability value computed according to (2) and (10) is higher than the threshold P_{max}.

The false negative error probability of the proposed criterion is calculated as follows.

$$P_{II} = \sum_{i=k}^{s} \left(C_{i-1}^{k-1} \left(1 - \frac{1}{M}\right)^{i-k} \frac{1}{M}^{k}\right), \quad s = \frac{H_A k M}{\hat{p} H_0}. \tag{11}$$

Here $\hat{p}$ is the value of p (hashing power of the honest nodes) for which the attack success probability is equal to P_{max}.

Similarly, the false positive error probability of the proposed criterion follows:

$$P_I = 1 - \sum_{i=k}^{s}\left(C_{i-1}^{k-1}\left(1 - \frac{1}{M}\right)^{i-k}\frac{1}{M}^k\right), \quad s = \frac{kM}{\hat{p}}. \tag{12}$$

The proposed criterion evaluation is presented in the following section.

5 Experimental Results

In order to evaluate the proposed criterion, the majority attack simulation has been performed. The simulation parameters are provided below:

- total hashing power of the distributed ledger: about 800 hash/s
- honest nodes' hashing power: about 400 hash/s
- dishonest nodes' (attacker's) hashing power: about 400 hash/s
- $H_{covert} = 0$
- target: $h_{max} = 2^{242} - 1$
- observer period size: $\#w = 100$

Figure 3 shows the results of real time assessment of hashing power involved in generation of the current blockchain of the simulated distributed ledger. The blue colored line shows the actual hashing power and the yellow colored line shows the estimate value calculated according to (6) for $k = 20$. Figure 3 shows that the majority attack starts after generation of block 51.

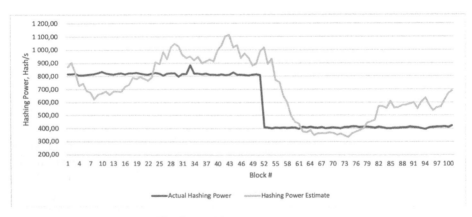

Fig. 3. Hashing power assessment

Figure 4 shows the attack success probability estimate, calculated according to (2) and (10). The probability P of the successful attack outcome increases after the block #54 generation and exceeds the threshold $P_{max} = 0.1$ after the block #55.

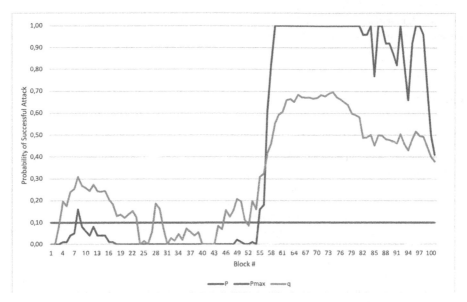

Fig. 4. Probability of successful attack

The grey line shows q—the estimate of the total blockchain hashing power portion that is controlled by the attacker.

The obtained experimental results confirm that the proposed criterion may be used to detect vulnerable states of a blockchain distributed ledger. The attack detection lag is close to $k/2$, where k is the number of previous blocks used in H_i calculation. The lag may be reduced in flavor of increased number false positives.

6   Conclusion

A formal criterion of the Proof-of-Work based distributed ledger vulnerability to the majority is presented in the article. A majority attack simulation has been performed. The simulation results confirm the applicability of the proposed criterion for detection of vulnerable states of distributed ledger.

The criterion may be used to in conjunction with other security mechanisms to enhance protection of distributed ledgers in vulnerable states. For example, when a vulnerable state is detected, an additional block verification procedure (BFT or Proof-of-Authority) may be enabled for a consensus algorithm. When the probability of successful attack falls below the threshold, the additional verification is disabled. Such an approach allows to mitigate the attack along with limiting period when BFT or Proof-of-Authority drawbacks are taken place.

The applicability of the proposed criterion is limited to distributed ledgers where the attacker is not able to gain a significant portion of total hashing power without a collusion with other nodes. This assumption is correct for the distributed ledgers with a substantial total hashing power.

Acknowledgements. The reported study was funded as the part of the State Task for Basic Research (code of theme: 0784-2020-0026); suppl. Agreement to the Agreement for the financial support No. 075-03-2020-158/2, 17.03.2020 (internal No. 075-GZ/SCH4575/784/2).

References

1. Nofer, M., Gomber, P., Hinz, O., Schiereck, D.: Blockchain. Bus. Inf Syst. Eng. **59**(3), 183–187 (2017)
2. Kuo, T., Kim, H., Ohno-Machado, L.: Blockchain distributed ledger technologies for biomedical and health care applications. J. Am. Med. Inform. Assoc. **24**(6), 1211–1220 (2017)
3. Goranović, A., Meisel, M., Fotiadis, L., Wilker, S., Treytl, A., Sauter, T.: Blockchain applications in microgrids an overview of current projects and concepts. In: 43rd Annual Conference of the IEEE Industrial Electronics Society, pp. 6153–6158. IEEE (2017)
4. Dujak, D., Sajter, D.: Blockchain applications in supply chain. In: Kawa, A., Maryniak, A. (eds.) SMART Supply Network. E, pp. 21–46. Springer, Cham (2019). https://doi.org/10.1007/978-3-319-91668-2_2
5. Alladi, T., Chamola, V., Parizi, R.M., Choo, K.-K.R.: Blockchain applications for industry 4.0 and industrial IoT: a review. IEEE Access **7**, 176935–176951 (2019)
6. Li, S.: Application of blockchain technology in smart city infrastructure. In 2018 IEEE International Conference on Smart Internet of Things, pp. 276–2766. IEEE (2018)
7. Nguyen, C.T., Hoang, D.T., Nguyen, D.N., Niyato, D., Nguyen, H.T., Dutkiewicz, E.: Proof-of-stake consensus mechanisms for future blockchain networks: fundamentals, applications and opportunities. IEEE Access **7**, 85727–85745 (2019)
8. Castro, M., Liskov, B.: Practical byzantine fault tolerance. In: OSDI, vol. 99, pp. 173–186 (1999)
9. Vukolić, M.: The quest for scalable blockchain fabric: proof-of-work vs. BFT replication. In: Camenisch, J., Kesdoğan, D. (eds.) iNetSec 2015. LNCS, vol. 9591, pp. 112–125. Springer, Cham (2016). https://doi.org/10.1007/978-3-319-39028-4_9
10. Croman, K., et al.: On scaling decentralized blockchains. In: Clark, J., Meiklejohn, S., Ryan, P., Wallach, D., Brenner, M., Rohloff, K. (eds.) International Conference on Financial Cryptography and Data Security 2016, LNCS, vol. 9604, pp. 106–125. Springer, Berlin, Heidelberg (2016). https://doi.org/10.1007/978-3-662-53357-4_8
11. Singh, A., Click, K., Parizi, R.M., Zhang, Q., Dehghantanha, A., Choo, K.-K.R.: Sidechain technologies in blockchain networks: an examination and state-of-the-art review. J. Netw. Comput. Appl. **149**, 102471 (2020)
12. Poon, J., Dryja, T.: The bitcoin lightning network: Scalable off-chain instant payments. https://lightning.network/lightning-network-paper.pdf. Accessed 18 Aug 2020
13. Luu, L., Narayanan, V., Zheng, C., Baweja, K., Gilbert, S., Saxena, P.: A secure sharding protocol for open blockchains. In: Proceedings of the 2016 ACM SIGSAC Conference on Computer and Communications Security, pp. 17–30. ACM, New York (2016)
14. Popov, S.: The tangle. https://assets.ctfassets.net/r1dr6vzfxhev/2t4uxvsIqk0EUau6g2sw0g/45eae33637ca92f85dd9f4a3a218e1ec/iota1_4_3.pdf. Accessed 18 Aug 2020
15. Bruce, J.: The Mini-Blockchain Scheme. https://cryptonite.info/files/mbc-scheme-rev3.pdf. Accessed 18 Aug 2020
16. Bitcoin.com Hashrate Distribution. https://www.blockchain.com/charts/pools. Accessed 18 Aug 2020
17. Komodo's Blockchain Security Service Brochure. https://komodoplatform.com/wp-content/uploads/2019/02/Komodo-Blockchain-Security-Service-Brochure.pdf. Accessed 18 Aug 2020

18. Nakamoto, S.: Bitcoin: A Peer-to-Peer Electronic Cash System. https://bitcoin.org/bitcoin.pdf. Accessed 18 Aug 2020
19. Cho, H.: ASIC-resistance of multi-hash proof-of-work mechanisms for blockchain consensus protocols. IEEE Access **6**, 66210–66222 (2018)
20. Ren, L., Devadas, S.: Bandwidth hard functions for ASIC resistance. In: Kalai, Y., Reyzin, L. (eds.) TCC 2017. LNCS, vol. 10677, pp. 466–492. Springer, Cham (2017). https://doi.org/10.1007/978-3-319-70500-2_16
21. Karakostas, D., Kiayias, A.: Securing Proof-of-Work Ledgers via Checkpointing. https://eprint.iacr.org/2020/173.pdf. Accessed 18 Aug 2020
22. Sayeed, S., Marco-Gisbert, H.: Assessing blockchain consensus and security mechanisms against the 51% attack. Appl. Sci. **9**(9), 1788 (2019)

A Panacea to Soft Computing Approach for Sinkhole Attack Classification in a Wireless Sensor Networks Environment

Kenneth E. Nwankwo[1], Shafi'i Mohammad Abdulhamid[2], Joseph A. Ojeniyi[3], Sanjay Misra[2(✉)], Jonathan Oluranti[2], and Ravin Ahuja[3]

[1] Federal University of Technology Minna, Minna, Nigeria
[2] Covenant University, Ota, Nigeria
shafii.abdulhamid@futminna.edu.ng, {Sanjay.misra,
jonathan.oluranti}@covenantuniversity.edu.ng
[3] Shri Vishwakarma Skill University, Gurgaon, India
ojeniyija@futminna.edu.ng

Abstract. Small sensor nodes with the capability to sense and process data make up a wireless sensor network (WSN). This environment has limitations of low energy, low computational power and simple routing protocols; making is susceptible to attacks such as sinkhole attack. This attack happens when the enemy node in the network camouflages as a genuine node nearest to the base station, thereby have information sent by a source node to another destination node travel through it, giving it chance to alter, drop or delay information from reaching to the base station as intended. In our paper, the research developed a sinkhole detection technique, an enhancement of ant colony optimization by including a hash table in the ant colony optimization technique to advance sinkhole attack detection and reduce false alarm rate in a wireless sensor network. An increase in the detection rate of 96% was achieved and result out performed other related research works when compared and further research discussed.

Keywords: Ant colony optimization · Swarm intelligence · Sinkhole detection · Wireless sensor network

1 Introduction

Wireless sensor network (WSN) contains a varied size of arranged interconnected nodes that forms cells for information dissemination (transceiver). WSN is a profoundly used system with application in numerous territories such as social insurance tracking, territory checking world and it environ sensing its observation likewise. Information received via sensors are managed by the cells. WSN utilization within a domain can either be genuine or rather without assurance [1]. The idea behind WSNs can be said to amount to its defenceless nature against numerous security dangers of various sorts and reason. With the straight forward idea of their directing strategies, security serves as the best test as they are increasingly defenceless to different system threat or exploits, of which

© Springer Nature Singapore Pte Ltd. 2021
P. K. Singh et al. (Eds.): FTNCT 2020, CCIS 1395, pp. 78–87, 2021.
https://doi.org/10.1007/978-981-16-1480-4_7

can lead to sinkhole exploit in a corporation, priority forwarding, wormhole exploits, hello-distributed attack, Sybil-attack, node replication exploit, as well as black hole [2]. Sinkhole attack is considerable as it can prompt each other attack referenced previously. Figure 1 shows a run of the mill WSN system and all it contains.

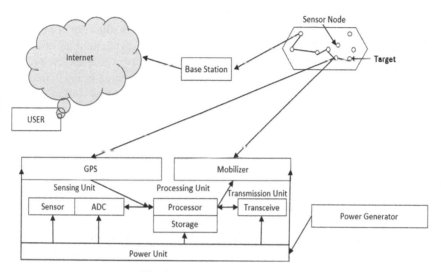

Fig. 1. Node sensor architecture

The military, as well as restorative exploration, are known commonly to utilize the functionality of sensor networks for the evaluation purpose, inclusive are threat tracing, conflict spots-review, as well as trespasser, acknowledge, WSN regularly explores threatening as well as the remote destination. Along these lines, there is a firm prerequisite for guaranteeing the distinguishing of data and recognizing readings. In detached circumstances, an interloper not only can tune in the correspondence, yet besides, the gatecrasher can get or meddle with the exchanged messages. Along these lines, various estimations, and shows don't work in hostile conditions without adequate wellbeing estimates set up. Thusly, security winds up as one of the most significant concerns while organizing security shows in resources constrained to work in WSNs. A piece of the employments of WSNs is for combat area observation, clinical administration applications, nature watching, keen home, and vehicular exceptionally designated frameworks VANETs.

An improved Ant Colony Optimization (ACO) proffered in this study through the incorporation of a hash table in the typical ACO order to improve detection rate (DR) as well as decrease false alert rate (FAR) in Sinkhole Attack Detection. The key contributions of this study are hereby highlighted or outlined:

- Design an "Enhanced Ant-Colony Optimization Tech (EACO)" used for sinkhole attack detection.
- Develop an EACO using DR and FAR.
- Evaluate the EACO comparatively with existing results in previous literature.

2 Related Works

For over a decade, research on prevention as well as forestalling Sinkhole Attack have been in steady peace, here is a brief review of some of the recent works. [1] presented a parameter evaluation used by ACS to get high values for throughput, best energy usage as well as a lag period which leads to an optimal process of packet routing was attained.

Authors [2] achieved optimal detection through a detection algorithm opined. This was made possible from the communications obtained by aggregation algorithm data for discovering the exploit that emerges from Body Area Network (BAN) as a result of sinkhole attack. In [3] authors deploy an (ESPO) to modify flocking is associated with a collection of algorithms that functions with cohesion, partitioning as well as alignment that exists in the collection of nodes within WSN deployed in a sizeable instance in order to forestall sinkhole attacker.

Authors [4] applied an enhanced ACS algorithm motivated from an alternate of ACO the remote as well as local update enhancements for discovery as well as exploitation improvement path with effective packet loss depletion while improving the efficiency of sensor edge energy. Authors in [5] employ COOJA as a simulator, with consideration of ACO-pheromone vanishing mechanism and ACO critical protection allocation for the effective balancing of edge interactions as well as speed management. Furthermore, in order to mislead an intruder, enhanced (KMT) method with Ant Colony optimization was explored to state a route in other to achieve safe as well as improve packet transmission ingress the nodes and egressing the cell and vice versa.

Authors [6] presented an enhanced ACO algorithm solving the challenges associated with traffic drop experienced when nodes communication traffic is in excess of its capacity. The research evaluation help in juxtaposing EACS with Cost Aware Ant Routing (SC) algorithm potentials as well as the strength of Efficient Ant Based Routing (EEABR) algorithm of which the presented model was planned for implementation in a WSN that is static.

There are several other works available in the literature on ant colony optimization problem [12–15]. We have not considered them for detailed explanation due to several reasons, including not much related and space issue due to conference paper.

2.1 Findings from Literature

Literature has revealed that different methodology such as the cryptographic, swarm intelligence [7] and machine learning [8] have been employed to address detection of sinkhole attack.

Minimal tradeoff is experienced in swarm intelligence as against all other methods as reviewed in the literature, based on the fact the WSN still remain fragile field that requires lots of attention in terms of energy utilization management, overhead computation management as well as package monitoring. The outperformance of ACO, swarm intelligence algorithm against others of such family algorithm in addressing challenges in various fields like the Travel Salesman Problem (TSP) have proved its prospect for success in its application. Furthermore, the reviewed literature points out gaps such as the need for novel technique, enhancement of existing techniques and addressing false alarm rate reduction in quest or an improved detection rate as well as reduced FAR in WSN.

3 Research Methodology

This study is composed of two major phases, formulation of the problem, planning as well as design. The implementation was achieved through simulation in NS-3.30.1.

An attacker edge was introduced into the network in order to determine the havoc incurred. Furthermore, an evaluation was carried out based on performance. A flow chart of EACO is Fig. 2.

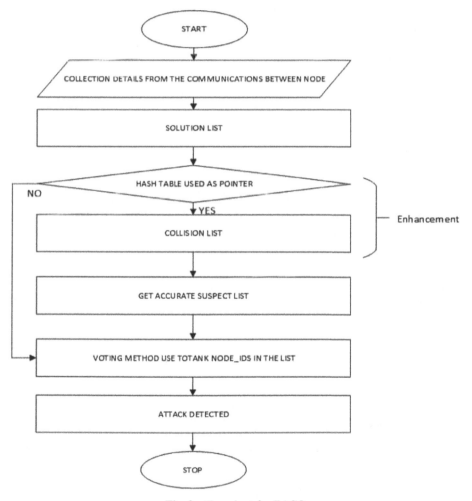

Fig. 2. Flowchart for EACO

A solution list is generated based on the interaction of nodes in a wireless sensor network serving as a pointer In the record is a hash collision is stored as collision list which builds up as a suspect list circulated between communicating edge to track an attacker after signing and voting against the existing ACO with the functionality of transmitting solution list unto suspect list (Table 1).

Table 1. Pseudo code for EACO

```
Procedure code EACO ( )
{
Input n, α , β , ρ
set the ant colony configuration
set the initial pheromone and heuristic value
get ant colony optimization system based on the calculated cost matrix
i = 1
while (I <= n)
{              r = 1
While ( r <= i)
{
Reset the ants
Build ant s' solution
Assume d(N)
// hash table implementation
if (h[d(N)]=0) { t=t+1 h[d(N)]=t and SL[t]= N //SL-Solution List
return TRUE}
if (h[d(N)] ? 0 and SL[h[d(N)] ] = N) then return FALSE if h[d(N)] ? 0 and SL[h[d(N)]
] ? N { if N ? CL {cl = cl+1
//CL-Collision List
CL[cl] = N
return TRUE
}else return FALSE
initiate local search
Update path best for i
Update pheromones
r = r + 1
}
Choose  path best for i
i = i + 1
}
}
```

4 Results and Discussion

Table 2 depicts the various parameters used in simulation with 300 edges.

Table 2. Parameters of simulation

Parameter	Description
Platform	Mac OS Catalina
Deployment area	700×300 m^2
Network topology	tree
Network size	250 nodes
Attacker node numbers	50
Simulation total time	1900 s
Traffic type	CBR/UDP
Packet size	512 bytes
Packet transmission rate	25 Kbps
Routing protocol	AODV
Medium access control type	IEEE 802.11
Communication range of sensor node	25 m
Communication range of cluster head	50 m

4.1 Simulation

The simulation was based on a normal flow, sinkhole attackers and EACO technique as outlined in the described scenario of WSN:

- Normal flow scenario: comprising 300 edges sending to and from the base station as well as negligible latency in packet ratio and communication of end-to-end node.
- Sinkhole attack scenario: variation in parameter was tracked, in this scenario which comprise of 200 edges as well as 50 attacker edges.
- EACO Implementation scenario: parameter variation was noted under WSN attack based on the simulation. The following were computed; An end to end latency (in ns), detection rate (DR), Packet delivery ratio (PDR), through put (in kps) as well as FA/FPR.

Figure 3 depicts influence on end to end latency which defines the period of packet getting to the base station for a normal flow, at point a sinkhole is compromised and after the implementation of EACO given as 70.06 ms, 736.66 and 153.46 ms respectively.

- Figure 4 depicts influence of packet delivery ratio which defines ratio to packet value ingress base station and origination from a remote edge. The output of normal flow

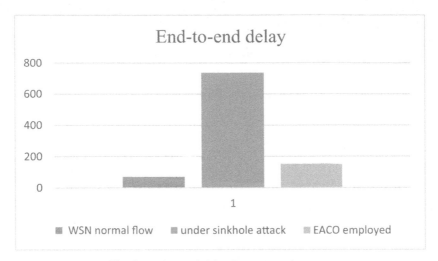

Fig. 3. End to end delay(latency) performance

WSN PDR ratio, sinkhole under attack and EACO implement method are 0.93, 0.46 and 0.9 respectively with a clearly notable performance in regards to PDR.

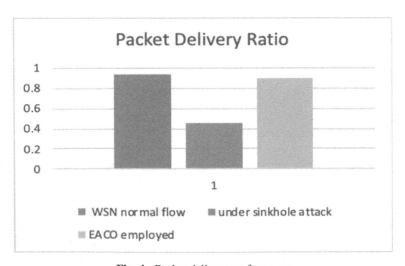

Fig. 4. Packet delivery performance

• Figure 5 depicts impact of throughput which defines transmitted bits value in unit time with a network expressed in (kps), the WSN normal flow, sinkhole under attack and EACO implementation results are 9.2 kps, 4.25 kps and 8.72 kps respectively with 94.32% improvement experienced under EACO.

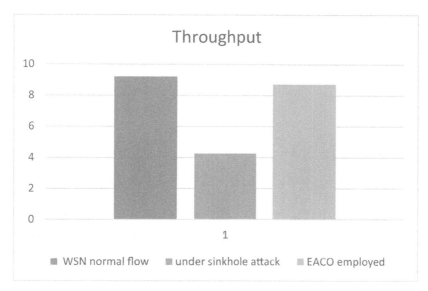

Fig. 5. Network performance

Furthermore, the simulation achieved the following: in our detection technique

I.   48 TP real attacks (attacker nodes) legitimate node (false positive) node of 2, legitimate nodes (True Negative) 198 and false negative (attacker mistaken as legitimate node) 2.

II. A total 200 legitimate node, 50 sinkhole attack node that was deployed in our study simulation achieved 96% and 1.0% respectively for DR and FPR

4.2   Performance Evaluation

A benchmark analysis in terms of performance comparison against some related literature was carried out as presented in Table 3 as well as Fig. 6 with an indication of distinct performance of our study against benchmark technique.

Table 3. Accuracy comparison

Authors	DR (%)	False alarm (%)
[10]	95	1.25
[11]	87.062	10.648
[9]	53	18
[2]	90	10
Our technique	96	1.0

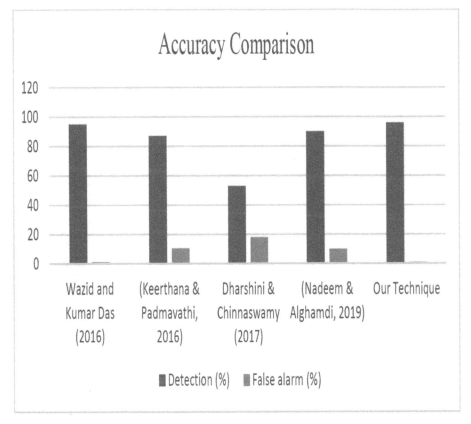

Fig. 6. Accuracy comparison

5　Conclusion and Future Work

A hash table was integrated into Ant Colony Optimization technique which serves as our design in enhancing performance in terms of time reduction in addressing an attacker alongside indexing which builds an accurate suspect list thereby addressing also false alarm associated with detection of the attacker. Secondly an optimal detection rate of 96% was achieved in our enhanced ant colony optimization method in regards to WSN. Furthermore, future research will look into security enhancement based on encryption of sensors as security protocols are given preference in WSN to aid addressing energy depletion, operational period lagging as well as detection enhancement.

References

1. Nasir, H.J.A., Ku-Mahamud, K.R., Kamioka, E.: Parameter adaptation for ant colony system in wireless sensor network. J. Inf. Commun. Technol. **18**(2), 167–182 (2019)
2. Nadeem, A., Alghamdi, T.G.: Detection algorithm for sinkhole attack in body area sensor networks using local information. IJ Netw. Secur. **21**(4), 670–679 (2019)

3. Nithiyanandam, N., Latha, P.: Artificial bee colony based sinkhole detection in wireless sensor networks. J. Ambient Intell. Humaniz. Comput. 0123456789 (2019)
4. Nasir, H.J.A., Ku-Mahamud, K.R., Kamioka, E.: Enhanced ant colony system for reducing packet loss in wireless sensor network. Int. J. Grid Distrib. Comput. 11(1), 81–88 (2018)
5. Iwendi, C., Zhang, Z., Du, X.: ACO based key management routing mechanism for WSN security and data collection. In: Proceedings of IEEE International Conference on Industrial Technology, vol. 2018, pp. 1935–1939 (2018)
6. Abdul, N.H.J., Ku-Mahamud, K.R., Kamioka, E.: Enhanced ant-based routing for improving performance of wireless sensor network. Int. J. Commun. Netw. Inf. Secur. 9(3), 386–392 (2017)
7. Kasliwal, B., Bhatia, S., Saini, S., Thaseen, I.S., Kumar, C.A.: A hybrid anomaly detection model using G-LDA. In: Souvenir 2014 IEEE International Advance Computing Conference, IACC 2014, pp. 288–293 (2014)
8. Sun, X., Yan, B., Zhang, X., Rong, C.: An integrated intrusion detection model of cluster-based wireless sensor network. PLoS ONE 10(10), 1–6 (2015)
9. Dharshini, T.N., Chinnaswamy, C.N.: Swarm Intelligence Technique for Sinkhole Attack Detection in Wireless Sensor Network - Performance Comparison of the Algorithms, no. 4, pp. 647–656 (2017)
10. Wazid, M., Das, A.K., Kumari, S., Khan, M.K.: Design of sinkhole node detection mechanism for hierarchical wireless sensor networks. Secur. Commun. Netw. 9(17), 4596–4614 (2016)
11. Keerthana, G., Padmavathi, G.: Detecting sinkhole attack in wireless sensor network using enhanced particle swarm optimization technique. Int. J. Secur. Appl. 10(3), 41–54 (2016)
12. Alfa, A., Misra, S., Ahmed, K., Arogundade, O., Ahuja, R.: Metaheuristic-based intelligent solutions searching algorithms of ant colony optimization and back. In: Singh, P.K., Pawłowski, W., Tanwar, S., Kumar, N., Rodrigues, J.J.P.C., Obaidat, M.S. (eds.) gation in Neural Networks. In *Proceedings of First International Conference on Computing, Communications,*. LNNS, vol. 121, pp. 95–106. Springer, Singapore (2020). https://doi.org/10.1007/978-981-15-3369-3_8
13. Crawford, B., Soto, R., Johnson, F., Misra, S., Paredes, F., Olguín, E.: Software project scheduling using the hyper-cube ant colony optimization algorithm. Tech. Gaz. 22(5), 1171–1178 (2015)
14. Adubi, S.A., Misra, S.: A comparative study on the ant colony optimization algorithms. In: 2014 11th International Conference on Electronics, Computer and Computation (ICECCO), pp. 1–4. IEEE, September 2014
15. Soto, R., et al.: Autonomous tuning for constraint programming via arti. In: Gervasi, O., et al. (eds.) ICCSA 2015. LNCS, vol. 9155, pp. 159–171. Springer, Cham (2015). https://doi.org/10.1007/978-3-319-21404-7_12

Predicting Destructive Malicious Impacts on the Subject of Critical Information Infrastructure

Elena A. Maksimova[1]([⊠]) [iD] and Vladimir V. Baranov[2]

[1] Volgograd State University, Volgograd, Russia
maksimova@volsu.ru
[2] South-Russian State Polytechnic University named after M. I. Platov Novotscherkassk, Novocherkassk, Russia

Abstract. The security of a subject of critical information infrastructure (CII) is one of the key issues of its life support. The current approach (legal and regulatory) regulates solutions to this issue without taking into account the influence of the violator, which can have a destructive effect on the subject of CII. This, in our opinion, leads to significant errors in the analysis of information security of the CII subject, therefore, reduces the effectiveness of declared information security tools for CII objects. The purpose of this work is to develop a model of an information security violator taking into account the parameter "potential of the violator". At the same time, the activity of the violator is considered in the space of its implementation of destructive effects on the objects of CII. The proposed model for assessing the capabilities of the violator to implement destructive effects on the subject of critical information infrastructure is implemented in the module "categorizing the attacker" of the cognitive model "Assessment of information security of the subject of CII". The proposed model allows us to assess the level of information security under destructive influences and to predict changes in malicious actions on CII objects in dynamics.

Keywords: Violator · Subject · Object · Critical information infrastructure · Category · Model · Cognitive map · Potential · Information security · Destructive malicious actions

1 Introduction

A special place in the social infrastructure of any state is occupied by objects of critical information infrastructure (CII). Violation of the functioning of such objects can be destructive, accompanied by human casualties. Therefore, measures to counteract malicious attacks (MA) on them should fully cover the threats and vulnerabilities of information security (IS). In this case, the forecasting of the MA should be complex and comprehensive in relation to a specific object.

One of the key issues in the forecasting process MA the formation of a model of a potential attacker who can cause significant damage and lead to destructive consequences.

© Springer Nature Singapore Pte Ltd. 2021
P. K. Singh et al. (Eds.): FTNCT 2020, CCIS 1395, pp. 88–99, 2021.
https://doi.org/10.1007/978-981-16-1480-4_8

2   Problem Statement

In the process of modeling the actions of an attacker, for example, descriptive models of networks and attackers are considered as the basis [1], structured description based on trees [2], object-oriented discrete event modeling [3], regulatory modeling [4], and others.

However, when building a security system for a subject of critical information infrastructure (SCII), an algorithm of actions is used, which is prescribed in legal acts [5] and does not take into account the "strength" of destructive influences as one of the significant indicators of a potential violator. Thus, the purpose of the study is to build a model for assessing the capabilities of violators to implement destructive impacts on critical information infrastructure objects as an element of a comprehensive, regulatory model for assessing information security of the SCII.

3   Analysis of Methods of Analysis and Assessment of Destructive Impact on Cii Objects

The first mention of the intruder (malefactor) model in the Russian Federation refers to the guidance document of the state technical Commission of Russia in 1992 [6]. It established the term and its explanation as an "abstract description". In the future, the definition was fixed and clarified in the state standards. A serious step in the regulatory consolidation of the attacker model was the release in 2008 of the FSTEC methodological document "Methodology for determining threats to information security in information systems" dated February 14, 2008 and approved in 2015 methodological recommendations [7]. In these documents, the regulators have identified a consistent behavior in the development of the model of the attacker. Despite the difference in the number of groups of attackers in the methods, this division is interconnected and can be conditionally correlated.

Alternative methods and approaches to the issue related to the development of the intruder model are offered by a number of scientists. So, in 2007, Boyarintsev A.V., Nichikov A.V., Redkin V. B. when considering the General approach to the development of models of violators [8] described a methodology that assumes four approaches to this issue. The first approach described was a method called "pessimism position", that is, assuming that the attacker is as prepared as possible to implement the threat. The second approach is the "position of optimism", according to which assumptions are made based on the best possible scenario. The third is the "position of realism", where experts put forward the most likely model. The fourth is the "position of justified pessimism", characterized in that the characteristics of the attacker are not absolute, but they are not underestimated.

In 2010, Spivak A. I. when describing the methodology for evaluating the effectiveness of the attacker [9] proposed an additional tool for the descriptive part of the intruder model. The methodology introduced the concept of the value of destructive impact. This value was mathematically an increment of the probability of threat realization after the attacker's influence. The introduction of the value of destructive impact considered a new aspect in the development of the attacker model. However, this value was relevant only if there was limited knowledge or complete ignorance about the activities of the violator. This did not allow the method to be applied in practice in some cases of real-time interaction.

In 2012, V. G. Zhukov, M. N. Zhukova, and A. p. Stefarov, when describing the model of an access rights violator in automated systems [10], proposed a method for constructing an attacker model that combined the main OSI/ISO and TCP/IP network models at that time. It was based on a classification of the offender's exposure levels. These levels were: level of technical channels, the application layer of the Protocol stack TCP/IP, the transport layer of the Protocol stack TCP/IP network layer Protocol stack TCP/IP, the link layer of the Protocol stack TCP/IP, the physical layer of the Protocol stack TCP/IP, the level of malicious activity, the level of eavesdropping devices, the level of information security system. Based on these levels, seven categories of attackers are proposed. Based on the impact levels and categories of attackers, a table of current security threats was compiled. One of the main advantages of this approach is that the model took into account the offender's awareness indicator and its technical means. However, the presented model, due to the strict category-level ratio, did not consider the possible relationship of categories and their joint action. The model made it possible not to involve information security specialists at the pre-project survey stage, which could lead to losing sight of specific threats.

In 2013, Ishcheinov V. Ya., Chudinov S. M. when assessing the risk of exposure to the object of Informatization [8] considered a mathematical approach to substantiating the attacker model from the point of view of the fuzzy sets apparatus. The functional threat model used, consisting of the threat source function and the threat functions themselves over time, eventually allowed us to create a field for the distribution of risk indicators, where each row corresponded to a specific model, and the maximum value in the row was the maximum risk for the actions of a specific offender. The undoubted advantage of this approach was the direct calculation of risks for the model and visibility by presenting the final values in the form of a table. However, the estimation based on fuzzy sets (intervals) was highly dependent on the preliminary assessment of the expert group, which under certain conditions could be inaccurate.

In 2017, Savchenko S. O. and Kapchuk N. V., describing the algorithm for constructing the violator model [11], used the methods and concepts of game theory. The description of the security intruder was presented as a one-way zero-sum matrix game. In this model, there are two players-the offender and the defender. They know everything about the opponent's actions, but they can't cooperate. The model is supplemented with elements of probability theory and graph theory. The model almost fully describes the behavior of "players" and allows you to fairly accurately assess the security of the system. But the condition of full knowledge of the opponent's actions, as well as the opposite condition in the methodology of A. I. Spivak in 2010, does not allow us to consider situations that contradict this condition, for example, the situation of covert influence on the system [8].

In 2018, Gafizov RM and Akhmatzoda sh. a. when developing a model of a wireless network intruder [12] introduce the motives of the attacker into consideration and classify the violators. Depending on their motivation they have identified four groups of violators.

The introduction of the concept of motivation in the algorithm for considering the attacker's model leads to more accurate hypotheses about possible actions of the intruder. However, the model does not consider possible levels of access for an attacker in the system, namely, the gradation of possible unreliable employees or violators by technical or logical access. This does not allow you to properly evaluate its (the attacker's) capabilities.

The approaches to model development and assessment of intentional destructive impacts, despite their certain importance, do not describe fully the behavior pattern and actions of the offender in any simple and straightforward indicator, convenient for further applications in assessment or design of protective measures. The method proposed below uses the strengths of existing algorithms, fills in gaps and removes a number of assumptions that limit functionality during development, as well as introduces a reasonable quantitative value that characterizes the level of destructive impact of the intruder on the system.

4 Methodology and Discussion

SCII is a complex, multi-component system [13–15]. It can be considered from the point of view of different approaches. For example, when conducting a comprehensive assessment of the isii, an assessment of the security of ISI objects is taken into account, which, in turn, can be considered as economic systems [16].

Another indicator when analyzing the functioning of the SCII is reliability. In [17], mathematical support for analyzing the reliability of network information systems is proposed. The complex provision of information security SCII also an example of a sociotechnical system, since here the most important management decisions are made by a person. [18] The factors indicated in [18] make it difficult to analyze and build formal models that take into account the specifics of the STS. Thus, taking into account the features of weakly formalized processes occurring in sociotechnical systems, in particular in the system of assessment of information security, it was decided to use methods of cognitive modeling.

When considering the issues related to the use of cognitive modeling of destructive malicious impacts in the assessment of IBS, we relied on the views of N. p. Sadovnikova And N. P. Zhidkova [19], who note the importance of determining the optimal requirements for indicators that characterize the quality of decisions and the need to take into account the complex nature of their relationships based on existing state Standards and norms (in our case, the requirements of regulators). To obtain a forecast of the situation development, the method of impulse processes [20], which belongs to the category of dynamic methods, was used.

The main sources of risks in activity of subjects of SCII for the construction of a cognitive model submitted in accordance with the RF Government Decree of February 8, 2018 No. 127 "On approval of Rules for categorization of objects of critical informational infrastructure of the Russian Federation and the list of indicators of criteria of significance of the objects of critical informational infrastructure of the Russian Federation and their values (with amendments of 13 April 2019) [21].

In addition, the target vertex V13 "Information security of the CII subject" was introduced into the cognitive model. Based on the results of the work, it will assess the impact of destructive malicious influence on the information security system.

In the course of modeling, a cognitive map is constructed for assessing the IS of a CII subject under destructive influences. For a more in-depth analysis of the model, an algorithm is built in the form of a weighted digraph for the effect of changes in the values of one vertex on the values of other vertices.

This algorithm is based on the idea of a pulse process, proposed by F. S. Roberts. Its essence is that an external perturbation is introduced to a certain vertex of the analyzed graph.

Algorithm development of a pulse process can be represented as a matrix equation:

$$V(t) = V(orig) + P0 * (I + A + A2 + \cdots + At)$$

where: V(orig)-vector of initial States; P0-initial pulse; A is the adjacency matrix, I is a unit matrix of size n*n.

As a result of this algorithm, a quantitative assessment of the IS SCII obtained. To translate it into a qualitative one, it is proposed to use the scale of qualitative assessment of the level of information security CII.

The assessment of destructive malicious impact is implemented in the attacker categorization module in the model of cognitive assessment of information security CII in case of destructive impacts.

To implement this assessment, the following methodology is proposed.

By destructive impact, we will understand the result of threat implementation, which leads to adverse and destructive consequences for the subject of critical information infrastructure. A subjective source of destructive influence is an IB violator. The purpose of the impact, including may be-violation of the functioning of CII facilities or infrastructure serving it that has access to CII facilities (deliberate threats to information security) [5]. In this case, the offender's achievability of the result will depend on a number of indicators. The combination of these indicators provides the category of an is violator.

Thus, when modeling the actions of an is violator, a formalized model is built that takes into account the parameters (potential) of the violator in the space of their implementations of destructive effects on the objects of CII. The result of modeling here is a five-level model of access to information and (or) components of CII objects by the violator of is at the level of physical access (PhL); logical access (LogL), competence (C) of the violator; equipment (A) of the violator; motivation (M) of the violator. We define access levels according to [22].

The capabilities of the violator at the designated levels of access to information and (or) to the components of CII objects determine the basic potential (Pt_{BASE}) that the violator of the is has on the subject of CII. The basic potential is used to build a model of is threats in terms of assessing the probability of their implementation. The assessment of the preliminary basic potential of the violator is made on the basis of numerical values of the levels of competence and equipment.

Based on the above, we present a five-level model of access to information and (or) components of CII objects by an is violator in the form of:

$$\text{Php:}[x]/\text{Log:}[x]/C:[x]/A:[x]//M:[x],$$

where [x] is the value of the corresponding parameter.

The proposed method is based on an assessment of the value of the coefficient of destructive malicious influence, which is carried out in two stages.

At the first stage, the attacker's category is determined by building a model. The intruder model on a CII object is a formal description of a potential intruder based on the five characteristics presented above.

The set of features determines the basic potential of the attacker when the object is exposed to the CUE. To evaluate it, first, based on the numerical values and the level of competence of the attacker, it is necessary to determine the preliminary basic potential.

The preliminary baseline potential of an attacker ($PREL\_Pt_{BASE}$) is calculated as:

$$\text{quan\_}[PREL_{Pt_{BASE}}] = \text{quan\_C:}[x] + \text{quan\_A:}[x].$$

As a result, we have

$$(\text{quan\_}[PREL\_Pt_{BASE}] \geq 8) \Rightarrow \left(\text{qual\_}[PREL_{Pt_{BASE}}] := \text{HIGH}\right) \text{V}$$

$$\text{V}(\text{quan\_}[PREL\_Pt_{BASE}] \geq 5)\text{V}(\text{quan\_}[PREL\_Pt_{BASE}] < 8) \Rightarrow$$
$$\left(\text{qual\_}[PREL_{Pt_{BASE}}] := \text{AVERAGE}\right)\text{V}$$

$$\text{V}(\text{quan\_}[PREL\_Pt_{BASE}] \geq 3)\text{V}(\text{quan\_}[PREL\_Pt_{BASE}] < 5) \Rightarrow$$
$$\left(\text{qual\_}[PREL_{Pt_{BASE}}] := \text{LOW}\right)\text{V}$$

$$\text{V}(\text{quan\_}[PREL\_Pt_{BASE}] < 3) \Rightarrow \left(\text{qual\_}[PREL_{Pt_{BASE}}] := \text{ABSENT}\right).$$

The final adjustment $\text{qual\_}PREL\_Pt_{BASE}$ is made according to the following rules:

$$(\text{qual\_M: }[x] := \text{AVERAGE}) \Rightarrow (\text{qual\_}Pt_{BASE} := + \text{qual\_}PREL\_Pt_{BASE}),$$
$$(\text{qual\_M: }[x] := \text{ABSENT}) \Rightarrow (\text{qual\_}Pt_{BASE} := - \text{qual\_}PREL\_Pt_{BASE}),$$
$$(\text{qual\_M: }[x] = \text{HIGH}) \Rightarrow (\text{qual\_}Pt_{BASE} := \text{qual\_}PREL\_Pt_{BASE}).$$

Here, the "+" sign means going to the next level (from a low or medium transition to a step higher), the "−" sign means going to the next level (from a medium or high transition to a step lower).

To assess the coefficient of destructive malicious influence, we will consider three types of CII objects [5]: Information system (IS), Information and telecommunications system (ITS), Automated control system (ACS).

For each object, we define 3 possible hazard categories for destructive malicious actions, where 1 – the most dangerous level of malfunction, 3 – the least dangerous level of malfunction.

For each type of object, the coefficient of destructive malicious impact is calculated.

In the case of simultaneous impact on the object of CII of several attackers (a variant of the impact of "many to one" or "many to many"), situations are possible:

1. A group consisting of n attackers performs a coordinated destructive action on 1 CII object.
2. A group consisting of n intruders performs a non-coordinated destructive impact on 1 CII object.
3. A coordinated destructive impact on 1 CII object is performed by a group consisting of n intruders and a non-coordinated destructive impact on 1 CII object by a group consisting of m intruders.
4. A group consisting of n attackers performs a coordinated destructive impact on k CII objects.
5. A group consisting of n intruders Performs a non-coordinated destructive impact on k CII objects.
6. A coordinated destructive impact on k CII objects is performed by a group consisting of n intruders and a non-coordinated destructive impact on 1 CII object By a group consisting of m intruders.

To describe the rules that are used to evaluate the coefficient of destructive malicious influence on the subject of CII, we introduce the notation;

N_CIN - N of CII objects that are subject to destructive malicious attacks,

M_SV - M attackers affect the subject of the CUE,

V[a] - type of interaction between attackers. Here

$$a = \begin{cases} 1, \text{ if destructive malicious actions are subjectively coordinated} \\ 0, \text{ if destructive malicious actions are not subjectively coordinated.} \end{cases}$$

Thus, the rules for evaluating the coefficient of destructive malicious actions on the subject of the CII for working in each of the indicated situations can be presented in the following form.

Situation 1 is characterized by the following: [1]_CII, [n]_SV, V_[1]. Therefore, we have:

Rule 1 for evaluating the coefficient of destructive malicious actions on the subject of CII:

$$(\text{quan}_{Pt_{BASE}}[1, 1]|(([1]\_CII \wedge ([n]\_SV) \wedge (V\_[1]))) \Rightarrow (\text{quan}_{Pt_{BASE}}$$
$$:= \prod_{i=1.n} \text{quan}\_Pt_{BASE}[i]. \tag{1}$$

Situation 2 is characterized by the following: [1]_CII, [n]_SV, V_[0]. Therefore, we have:

Rule 2 for evaluating the coefficient of destructive malicious actions on the subject of CII:

$$(\text{quan}\_Pt_{BASE}[1, 0]|(([1]\_CII) \wedge ([n]\_SV) \wedge (V\_[0])) \Rightarrow (\text{quan}\_Pt_{BASE}$$
$$:= \text{quan}\_Pt_{BASE} := \text{quan}\_Pt_{BASE}[\text{max}\_\text{weight}[i]]. \tag{2}$$

Here $\text{quan}\_Pt_{BASE}[max\_weight[i]]$ – is a quantitative assessment of the attacker's potential, which has the maximum quantitative assessment for the indicator with the maximum weight coefficient.

Situation 3 is characterized by the following: [1]_CII, [n]_SV и V_[1], и [m]_SV и V_[0]. Therefore, we have:

Rule 3 for evaluating the coefficient of destructive malicious actions on the subject of CII:

$$(\text{quan}\_Pt_{BASE}|(([1]\_CII) \wedge (([n]\_SV) \wedge (V\_[1])) \wedge (([m]\_SV) \wedge (V\_[0]))$$

$$\Rightarrow \text{quan}\_Pt_{BASE} := \max\left(\prod_{i=1}^{n} \text{quan}_{Pt_{BASE}}[i], \text{quan}\_Pt_{BASE}[\max\_weight[i]]\right). \tag{3}$$

Situation 4 is characterized by the following: [k]_CII, [n]_SV, V_[1]. Therefore, we have:

Rule 4 for evaluating the coefficient of destructive malicious actions on the subject of CII:

$$(\text{quan}\_Pt_{BASE}[k, 1]| \bigvee_{j=1}^{k} (([j, k]\_CII) \wedge ([j, s]\_SV) \wedge (V\_[1])))$$

$$\Rightarrow (\text{quan}\_Pt_{BASE} := \prod_{i=1.n} \text{quan}\_Pt_{BASE}[j, i], \tag{4}$$

where j is the number of the CII object and s is the number of intruders affecting the j-th CII object.

In the formula (4) $\text{quan}\_Pt_{BASE}[j, i]$ is calculated according to rule 1 for destructive malicious actions for each object of the CII.

Situation 5 is characterized by the following: [k]_CII, [n]_SV, V_[0]. Therefore, we have:

Rule 5 for evaluating the coefficient of destructive malicious actions on the subject of CII:

$$(\text{quan}\_Pt_{BASE}[L, 0]| \bigvee_{j=1}^{k} (([j, k]\_CII) \wedge ([j, s]\_SV) \wedge (V\_[0])))$$

$$\Rightarrow (\text{quan}_{Pt_{BASE}}[j] := := \max_{i=1.n} \text{quan}\_Pt_{BASE}[j, i] \tag{5}$$

Here $\text{quan}\_Pt_{BASE}[j, i]$ is calculated according to rule 1 for destructive malicious actions on each CII object.

Situation 6 is characterized by the following: [k]_CII, [n]_SV и V_[1], и [m]_SV и V_[0]. Therefore, we have:

Rule 6 for evaluating the coefficient of destructive malicious actions on the subject of CII:

$$(\text{quan } Pt_{BASE}[k, 1]|([k, j]CII \wedge j, nSV \wedge V1 \wedge lj = 1j, lCII \wedge j, mSV \wedge V0 \Rightarrow \text{quan\_PtBASE}$$

$$:= \text{quan\_PtBASE}, 1 * \text{quan\_PtBASE}[l, 0]. \tag{6}$$

Here $\text{quan}\_Pt_{BASE}[k, 1]$ is calculated by rule 4, $\text{quan}\_Pt_{BASE}[l, 0]$ - by rule 5.

The use of rules when building a cognitive model will allow to predict the many potential scenarios when building the model of malicious destructive influences and to quantify each situation as a ratio, destructive malicious actions to the object CII.

5 Experiment

Study health cognitive assessment model of information security SCII in destructive malicious effects was conducted on the results of studies of changes of information security subject CII. The study is based on the results of the study of changes in the information security of the subject CII. Studies were conducted for various types of destructive effects on the CII objects. This corresponds to the study of vertex V9 behavior in a cognitive model. If the research results indicate that the information security of a CII subject is at a low level, then you should select recommendations for improving the level of information security.

The study of the efficiency of the proposed model was performed in the course of solving the following tasks:

Experiment No. 1: Study of the impact of destructive actions of a low-potential violator on the assessment of the IS of a CII subject consisting of an is object with 1 category of significance.

Experiment No. 2: Study of the impact of destructive effects of the offender without capacity and with a high potential for evaluation IS subject SCII, consisting of object – is with 3 level of importance and ACS – 2 categories of significance caused by destructive actions in the infrastructure.

Experiment No. 3: Study of the influence of destructive influences offenders with high, medium and low potentials for evaluation IS subject CII consisting of: IS 2 categories of importance, ITS – 1 category, and ACS – 3 categories of significance caused by destructive actions in the infrastructure.

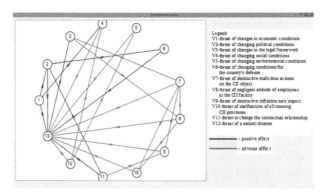

Fig. 1. Constructed cognitive map of the subject's IS assessment CII (screen copy).

During the experimental study, a cognitive map was constructed (see Fig. 1).

The results of the software package for the tasks to be solved are shown in Figs. 2, 3 and 4.

The diagram of vertex placement relative to pulse processes is shown in Fig. 5.

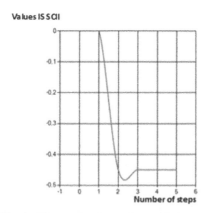

Fig. 2. The result of experiment № 1 (on-screen copy).

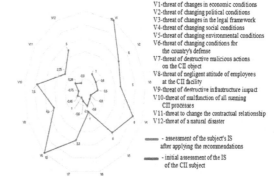

Fig. 3. Result of experiment №2 (screen copy).

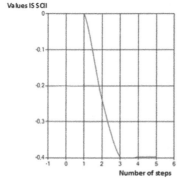

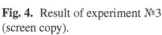

Fig. 4. Result of experiment №3 (screen copy).

V1-threat of changes in economic conditions
V2-threat of changing political conditions
V3-threat of changes in the legal framework
V4-threat of changing social conditions
V5-threat of changing environmental conditions
V6-threat of changing conditions for
      the country's defense
V7-threat of destructive malicious actions
      on the CII object
V8-threat of negligent attitude of employees
      at the CII facility
V9-threat of destructive infrastructure impact
V10-threat of malfunction of all running
      CII processes
V11-threat to change the contractual relationship
V12-threat of a natural disaster

━━ - assessment of the subject's IS
      after applying the recommendations
━━ - initial assessment of the IS
      of the CII subject

Fig. 5. Diagram of vertex placement relative to pulse processes.

6   Conclusions

Thus, in the course of the conducted research, it was possible to assess the IS of SCII under destructive influences. The developed software package made it possible to categorize the attacker, build a cognitive map of the CI subject's IS assessment, simulate the destructive effects of the attacker through various source nodes, build experimental graphs, and provide recommendations for improving the subject's is level of critical information.

Acknowledgments. The reported study was funded by Russian Ministry of Science (Information security, project № 3).

References

1. Yuill, J., et al.: Intrusion-detection for incident-response, using a military battlefield-intelligence process. Comput. Netw. **34**(4), 671–697 (2000)
2. Dawkins, J., Campbeil, C., Hale, J.: Modeling network attacks: extending the attack tree paradigm. In: Workshop on Statistical and Machine Learning Techniques in Computer Intrusion Detection, Johns Hopkins University (2002)
3. Chi, S.-D., Park, J., Jung, K.-C., Lee, J.-S.: Network security modeling and cyber attack simulation methodology. In: Varadharajan, V., Mu, Y. (eds.) ACISP 2001. LNCS, vol. 2119, pp. 320–333. Springer, Heidelberg (2001). https://doi.org/10.1007/3-540-47719-5_26
4. Model of threats and security violators of personal data processed in mass communications of the Russian Federation. Moscow (2010). https://minsvyaz.ru/common/upload/publication/1410084of.pdf. Accessed 06 Oct 2020
5. Federal law "on the security of critical information infrastructure of the Russian Federation" dated 26.07.2017 N 187-FZ (latest version) (2017). https://www.consultant.ru/document/cons_doc_LAW_220885. Accessed 05 June 2020
6. State Technical Commission of Russia. Guidance document. Protection against unauthorized access to information. Terms and definitions. Military Publishing House, Moscow (1992)
7. FSS guidelines "on the development of regulatory legal acts defining threats to the security of personal data relevant to the processing of personal data in information systems of personal data used in the implementation of relevant activities" dated March 31, No. 149/7/2/6-432. Approved by the FSS (2015)
8. Boyarintsev, A.V., Nichikov, A.V., Redkin, V.B.: General approach to the development of models of violators. Security Systems, no. 4, pp. 50–53 (2007)
9. Spivak, A.I.: Evaluating the effectiveness of an attacker's attacks in the process of building its model. Scientific and technical Bulletin of the Saint Petersburg state University of information technologies, mechanics and optics, no. 2, pp. 108–112 (2010)
10. Zhukov, V.G., Zhukova, M.N., Stepanov, A.P.: Model of access rights violator in an automated system. Software products and systems, no. 2, pp. 45–54 (2012)
11. Savchenko, S.O., Kapchuk, N.V.: Algorithm for constructing the intruder model in the information security system using game theory. Dynamics of systems, mechanisms and machines, no. 4, pp. 84–49 (2017)
12. Khafizov, R.M., Ahmadzade, S.A.: Development of a model of a wireless network. Innovations in science, no. 2, pp. 10–12 (2018)
13. Maksimova, E.A.: Study of algorithms for secure transmission of data between the objects of critical information infrastructure. In a Collection of papers of the XXIII plenary FUMO IN IB and all-Russian scientific conference "Fundamental problems of information security in the age of digital transformation" (INFOBEZOPASNOST 2019). Reports of the XXIII Plenum of the FUMO IN the IB and the all-Russian scientific conference. Editor: V. I. Petrenko, pp. 157–163 (2019)
14. Maksimova, E.A., Shahverdiev, A.S.: Management of operation of objects of critical information infrastructure. Management of large systems. Materials of the XVI all-Russian school-conference of young scientists, pp. 392–397 (2019)
15. Maximova, E.A., Baranov, V.V., Lauta, O.S.: Analysis of the model of information support of processes and systems in the implementation of multi-agent intellectual interaction. Devices and systems. Management, monitoring, diagnostics, no. 4, pp. 32–41 (2019)
16. Tishchenko, E.N.: Analysis of security of economic information systems. Monograph: M-vo obrazovaniya ROS. Confederations. Growth. State economy. UN-t, 191 p. (2018)
17. Gromov, Yu.Y., Eliseev, A.I., Minin, Yu.V., Sumin, V.I.: Reliability analysis in network information systems. Bulletin the Voronezh Institute of the Federal penitentiary service of Russia, vol. 1, pp. 33–41 (2018)

18. Azhmukhamedov, I.M.: Management of weakly formalized sociotechnical systems based on fuzzy cognitive modeling (on the example of integrated information security systems). Dissertation for the degree of doctor of technical Sciences, Astrakhan (2014)
19. Sadovnikova, N.P., Zhidkova, N.P.: Selection of territorial development strategies based on cognitive analysis and scenario modeling. In Internet-Vestnik VolgSASU, no. 7, vol. 21, pp. 4–10 (2012)
20. Roberts, F.S.: Discrete mathematical models with applications to social, biological and environmental problems. In TRANS. from English. Nauka, Moscow, 496 p. (1986)
21. "On approval of Rules for categorization of objects of critical informational infrastructure of the Russian Federation and the list of indicators of criteria of significance of the objects of critical informational infrastructure of the Russian Federation and their meanings (as amended on April 13 (2019)
22. Drobotun, E.B., Tsvetkov, O.V.: Building a model of information security threats in an automated system for managing critical objects based on scenarios of intruder actions//Software products and systems. Publishing house: ZAO research Institute "Contor program system" (Tver), no. 3, pp. 42–50 (2016)

The Formation of Legal Measures to Counter Information Security Incidents in the Use and Application of Cyber-Physical Systems

Vlada M. Zhernova[1]([⊠]) [iD] and Aleksey V. Minbaleev[1,2] [iD]

[1] Federal State Autonomous Educational Institution of Higher Education "South Ural State University (National Research University)", Chelyabinsk, Russia
zhernovavm@susu.ru, alexmin@bk.ru
[2] Kutafin Moscow State Law University, Moscow, Russia

Abstract. The development of the legal framework for ensuring information security of cyber-physical systems in recent years is associated with their widespread use and equipment of industries and households. Various kinds of cyber attacks on cyber-physical systems bring benefits to the attackers in the form of data whose distribution is limited, as well as in the form of the failure of such systems. The article provides statistics on the most common attacks on cyber-physical information systems, as well as the consequences faced by a household or organization. The main stage of the research is the analysis of existing norms of legal regulation of the development and operation of cyber-physical systems. This analysis is the foundation for creating criteria on the basis of which a model for the development of legal support of information security in the field of the functioning of cyber-physical systems can be formed. The result of the research is a formed set of legal measures, the implementation of which will reduce both the number of attacks and the consequences of such attacks on cyber-physical systems.

Keywords: Information security incidents · Legal regulation · Cyber-physical systems · Cyber-attack

1 Introduction

Cyber-physical systems have firmly entered the life of mankind. On the one hand, scientists are trying to define this high-tech phenomenon, in order, for example, to clarify the existing and future normative documents governing activities related to cyber-physical systems. But on the other hand, recently, the opinion is gaining momentum that cyber-physical systems do not need definition, since it is a rather complex multi-component object and the formation of a conceptual apparatus in this case may be meaningless. Indeed, the subject area of cyber-physical systems can include multi-level objects, such as, for example, household appliances or self-driving car or medical devices, etc. Definition of the concept - compilation of a glossary - the formation of definitions as one of the main actions in the development of the regulatory framework in this case will be ineffective. It is much more important to form a classification of the objects that

© Springer Nature Singapore Pte Ltd. 2021
P. K. Singh et al. (Eds.): FTNCT 2020, CCIS 1395, pp. 100–110, 2021.
https://doi.org/10.1007/978-981-16-1480-4_9

make up the cyber-physical system, which will later serve as the basis for the creation of comprehensive legislation in the field of cyber-physical systems.

2 Elements of Legal Regulation Model

The cyber physical system (CPS) has a complex structure, and consist of three levels [1]: the physical, the software and the network layer. This determines the model of the cyber-physical system. At the physical level, the system includes devices, components of sensors. It would be logical to include the environment at the physical level, although the environment is not part of the object of legal relations in this case, but it can affect the operation of the system as a whole. According to researches [2], the environment also can be an object of cyber attacks. In addition, it is possible to include the physical essence of a cyber-physical system, since this physical object is the result of the labor of a person or organization, even if using automatic or automated production. The next level includes a data transmission network, represented by various data transmission technologies using appropriate protocols. At the moment, the correct implementation and operation of the system at this level determines the work of the entire CPS as a whole. The third level is represented by software that collects and analyzes the information received from the first level through the second.

Such a complex organization of the investigated object can be the reason for the emergence of some types of vulnerabilities characteristic of such groups of objects as information systems, distributed databases, the Internet, etc. This also leads to the possibility of implementing a variety of relevant threats. Information security incidents are becoming an integral part of the functioning of cyber-physical systems [3]. Often, cyber components are targeted by attackers, i.e. part of the CPS, responsible for receiving and transmitting data (various interfaces), as well as processing and storing information. It is this part of the CPS that it will be considered, meaning the object of the cyber attack [4].

In the past two years, Russia has adopted a number of strategic documents aimed at regulating artificial intelligence technologies, including CPS, such as, for example, the Concept for the development of regulation of relations in the field of artificial intelligence technologies and robotics [5].

Certain issues related to the design, use and decommissioning, ensuring the safety of CPS components are today regulated within the framework of both information legislation and the norms of other branches of legislation. So, the CPS is subject to general requirements for information systems and information technologies, which are imposed by the Federal Law "On information, information technology and information protection" (hereinafter – Law on Information) [6], the Civil Code of the Russian Federation [7], the Criminal Code of the Russian Federation [8], the Code of the Russian Federation on Administrative Offenses [9], the Federal Law "On Commercial Secrets" [10], the Federal Law "On Personal Data" [11], etc. These are, in particular:

- provisions on the legal status of the owner, proprietor, operator of the information system, the owner of information contained in the databases of the information system;

- provisions on the legal regime of information contained in the CPS (norms on open information and information of limited access, a ban on the dissemination of certain types of information through the CPS;
- provisions on legal liability for violation of legislation in terms of the CPS.

In terms of the development of legislation in the field of CPS, its design, use and decommissioning, ensuring the safety of components, the following current vectors of development can be distinguished:

- it seems that the CPS is an object of civil law relations, as a set of objects of civil circulation - computer programs, patents for a useful model, databases, etc.
- CPS as an object of increased danger, which in case of undeclared behavior can cause harm and damage to property, the environment and human life and health.
- formation of the representation of cyber-physical systems as a subject of legal relations.

Probably, with the widespread use of new technologies, such as Internet of Things, artificial intelligence, data mining, etc., civil legislation in general and in the field of CPS in particular will be replenished with new objects and legal norms that will correspond to today's progressive realities. The purpose of the article is to form a model of legal regulation of relations arising in the field of CPS to prevent cyber attacks, as well as to minimize their consequences.

During the forming a legal regulation model, it is necessary to take into account not only the peculiarities of the composition of the object, but also the essential characteristics of the subjects who enter into relations regarding the CPS and their components. Such subjects, in addition to traditional subjects of information systems, such as owners, users, end customers, developers of both the physical essence of the system and software, as well as providers of the data transmission network (they can be called as "positive" subjects), include: persons who can be sources of information security incidents, and, consequently, the "authors" of cyber attacks [12] on cyber-physical systems (they can be called as "negative" subjects). It is worth considering that "positive" actors can also become a source of an incident through unintentional actions due to the lack of necessary competencies, or act with intent ("offended" employees, insiders).

All these individuals and organizations interact with each other through cyber-physical systems, and within the framework of such interaction, the information security triad should be guaranteed, which consists in ensuring the integrity, confidentiality and availability of information.

Thus, there are several types of cyber hackers which can be ranked according to the degree of access to the physical, network and software components of the cyber-physical system [13]. In addition to the fact that intruders can be classified according to the degree of access to objects, it is necessary to consider the capabilities of the intruder with respect to the cyber-physical system. So, it is possible to use for an attack those components that are in the public domain or already known vulnerabilities, or the intruder has the mental and material resources to search for new vulnerabilities and implement previously unpermitted attacks.

In addition to the fact that we have determined the composition of the CPS and its subjects, it is also necessary to define the essential properties of the system, which could concretize the requirements for the norms being formed in relation to the sphere of cyber-physical systems.

3 Essential Characteristics of Cyber-Physical Systems

Not all cyber-physical systems are attractive to attackers, but those that have certain properties, such as: accumulation of a large amount of important information, the ability to have an impact (including negative) on the environment, etc. etc. Undoubtedly, in order to form the norms governing the relations that arise during the development, operation and liquidation of CPS, it is necessary that the CPS as a result of its activities could perform legally significant actions. Legally significant actions in relation to the CPS can be understood as such actions as:

- accumulation of information about personal data subjects,
- harm to human health while performing their functions, or in case of failure, damage to property, things with which the CFS interacts, etc.

As noted in the Concept of Regulation of Artificial Intelligence Technologies and Robotics, the issue of introducing regulatory restrictions for the use of artificial intelligence (AI) technologies can be considered if the source of the above risk is the delegation of legally significant decisions to systems with AI, which can lead to the infliction of corresponding harm, and not just the fact of their application in these areas[14]. Since AI technologies can be components of the CPS, this statement is also applicable to the CPS.

It is such systems, the mismanagement of which can harm human health and property, become targets for cyber attacks. Therefore, in order to predict the probability of a cyber attack on various types of cyber-physical systems, it is necessary to determine what may be legally significant actions, the implementation of which is possible by cyber-physical systems. It is possible to determine that systems that are significant in the following spheres of human life have a particular danger in the implementation of cyber attacks:

- social sphere (damage to human life and health during the implementation, including cyber attacks, ensuring human life)
- the economic sphere (damage to various objects that have economic value for the constituent entities of the Russian Federation or the state as a whole, during the implementation, including cyber attacks)
- environmental sphere (damage to the environment during the implementation, including cyber attacks)

In order to form a basis for the formation of a regulatory framework for regulating CPS, the scientists claim [15] that cyber-physical and robotic systems must have autonomy. Perhaps it is worth agreeing with this opinion, since the lack of control over the actions of the CPS allows attackers to find inherent vulnerabilities and implement threats.

The autonomy of the CPS can be achieved through special information technologies that allow the CPS to act as follows:

- according to an algorithm that will produce a predictable result in advance (standard programs that have an algorithm with conditions and branches)
- by a special mechanism that will produce an unknown result in advance - AI and neural networks that make decisions based on the data received; may differ from, of course, the outcome of human decision-making.

For the possibility of forming and developing the regulatory legal framework in relation to the CPS, taking into account the fact that we do not consider the CPS as an object of civil rights, it is necessary that the actions of the system were performed as decisions made by the system. The nature of decision making by the software part of the CPS is also diverse - it can be a program code, an algorithm, a self-learning system, a neural network, an error in an algorithm, a cyber attack, etc.

Considering the so-called the autonomy and significance of actions, and, consequently, the consequences, the question arises of classifying CPS as objects of increased danger or recognizing CPS as a source of increased danger. The Civil Code of the Russian Federation [16] indicates that legal entities and citizens whose activities are associated with an increased danger to others are obliged to compensate for harm caused by a source of increased danger, if they do not prove that the harm arose as a result of force majeure or intent endured. Thus, it is necessary to determine the scope of responsibility of each subject in relation to actions related to the CPS. Further in the article, this issue will be given attention.

In addition, "the source of increased danger" definition is given in legal documents [17]: any activity, the implementation of which creates an increased likelihood of harm due to the impossibility of full control over it by humans, as well as activities for the use, transporting, storage of items, substances and other production facilities with the same properties. Thus, the assignment of a CPS to an object that is a source of increased danger is necessary in view of such a property as autonomy.

In the case that certain types of CPS are recognized as a source of increased danger, it is necessary to formulate requirements for the protection of such objects. Moreover, the legislation "On the Security of the Critical Information Infrastructure of the Russian Federation" already quite successfully regulates relations in the field of ensuring the security of the critical information infrastructure of the Russian Federation in order to ensure its stable functioning when carrying out against its computer attacks.

The basic principles of critical information infrastructure regulation can also be translated into the regulation of activities related to CPS:

- legality;
- continuity and complexity of security
- the priority of preventing computer attacks.

4 Responsibility as an Element of the Legal Regulation Model

Legal liability for acts related to the operation of the CPS can minimize the undesirable consequences of the introduction of artificial intelligent and cyber-physical systems [18].

An extremely responsible attitude is required from the developers, designers and manufacturers of cyber-physical systems. Responsibility should be aimed at forming a responsible attitude to the performance of their duties by the subject in the information sphere. It is possible to develop a system of incentives from the state for quotas and a reduction in sanctions if the system is recognized as highly invulnerable.

In addition to the introduction of responsibility for the development of the CPS, it is necessary to provide for responsibility for improper maintenance and support of systems. In addition, it should be considered that users, by their intentional or unintentional actions, can also lead to undesirable consequences of the CPS operation.

To be held accountable for the "actions" of robots and artificial intelligence systems, it must be in causal relationship with the actions or inaction of developers, manufacturers and other entities who had the opportunity and are obliged to foresee and avoid the negative consequences of the robot's functioning [19].

The existing legislation in the field of CPS is aimed only at protecting computer systems, and information in it (in case it is personal data or information of limited access). It is necessary to revise and introduce new norms in the legislation, which would be aimed at protecting not only the computer component, but also all components of the cyber-physical system.

Thus, the lack of a regulatory framework adequate for new technologies at the moment is to some extent a factor holding back the development of cyber-physical systems.

Administrative measures such as product certification and licensing of activities for the development and production of components and cyber-physical systems, as well as the requirement to install "black boxes" in cyber-physical devices, which will subsequently allow to establish the degree of the culpability of the user, software, manufacturer or third party.

The development of insurance institutions will help reduce the negative effect of cyber attacks. At the moment, the lack of special provisions on this matter makes it almost impossible to insure in the field of cyber-physical systems.

It is believed that the existence of a concluded contract of insurance of liability for causing harm may be a key condition for the release of some types of robots or AI systems into circulation.

Thus, in the sphere of using CPS, it makes sense to develop an insurance system to compensate for damage, including after the implementation of cyber threats. You can add a characteristic - an indicator of system trust, based on previous data, manufacturer feedback, the degree of possibility of an attack and the presence of potential vulnerabilities. So, based on the assessment, the consumer will be able to independently choose the manufacturer and component, and the manufacturer will do everything to raise his assessment. The rating system should take into account the risks of "positive" subjects, determine the amount of damage, etc.

5   Classification of Cyberattacks Relevant to the Cyber-Physical System

The essential features of CPS lead to the fact that the possibility of implementing a cyber attack increases. The CPS consists of a very large number of different devices, has autonomy and is often characterized by the absence of manual control and monitoring. It is worth noting that the essential features that distinguish CPS from IS and contribute to an increase in the risks of cyber attacks:

- remote location of system elements
- system autonomy
- large groups of devices
- lack of manual control and human supervision, etc.

Based on the theory of information systems security, the functioning of the CPS should ensure the triad of information security - confidentiality, integrity, availability. It is along these three vectors that cyber attacks are carried out:

- cyber attacks aimed at violating confidentiality, such as: cracking encryption, attacks on password, violation of access control policies. In general, CPS is not distinguished by stable encryption, since there are system limitations on the capacity of computing power and consumed electricity.
- cyber attacks aimed at violation of integrity. This type of cyber attacks can be divided according to the criterion of the end object, which is a target for attackers, namely, configuration integrity, data integrity, and code integrity can be violated. The risks of an integrity attack are very high. Thus, attacks of this type can affect several types of "positive" subjects. False data injection is an example of an integrity attack that affects both users and suppliers. The large amount of data coming from multiple sources makes it difficult to maintain the security and privacy of data on the network. Especially if the data, public or private, has multiple owners.
- cyber attacks aimed at disrupting accessibility - the most popular attack is DDoS. From a system performance perspective, ensuring security and privacy results in finer data detail. Additional control information is embedded in the data, and this can cause unacceptable delay in the transmission of information. User-centric access control approaches provide the user with flexibility in controlling access to their data stored in the system. In these approaches, access control policies can be configured to dynamically change based on some external information, such as user activity in social networks. Dynamically changing access control policies are expensive, but can have positive effects.

Since the cyber-physical system has a direct connection with the environment, the list of types of attacks can be supplemented with a type of attack on the environment, when the direct object of the attack is not the components of the CPS, but the disruption of work occurs indirectly. Such attacks include, for example, a sound attack [20], when vibration disrupts the operation of the system's mechanism, or a change in the electromagnetic field, temperature, etc.

Due to the complex composition of the CPS, any significant component of the system can become the target of an attack. For a cyber-physical system, the accuracy of measurements is important, on the basis of which decisions will then be made, i.e. it is necessary to protect the sensors.

Data from sensors must be stored for some time; data modification must not be allowed. By its nature, data in an intelligent network must be stored for a certain period of time. Long-term storage of data requires more powerful cryptographic solutions as the computational ability to crack cryptographic algorithms increases over time. In addition, user experience and privacy requirements can change over time. With this in mind, the system must be designed in such a way that there is room for changes in security and privacy measures for data that is stored for a long time.

Attacks on data transmission technologies are also widespread because of a number of organizational features of cyber-physical systems. Thus, the following common types of attacks can be distinguished:

- the most common type of attacks that disrupt the process of data transmission in the channel, especially with wireless communication. Since it is easier for an attacker to intercept wireless communication channels than authenticated networks. In the network and transport layers, denial of service (DDoS) attacks can reduce end-to-end communication performance.
- MQTT vulnerabilities. Message Queuing Telemetry Transport (MQTT) is a messaging protocol that has been in use for nearly two decades, mainly for industrial automation.
- data transfer using http or ftp. HTTP request smuggling is an attack in which an attacker intervenes in the processing of a sequence of HTTP requests that a web application receives from one or more users. Vulnerabilities associated with HTTP request smuggling are often critical, allowing an attacker to bypass security measures, gain unauthorized access to confidential data, and directly compromise the information of other users of the application.
- attacks on wi-fi or Bluetooth technologies. Given the limited use of Bluetooth in CPS devices, many attacks do not pose a threat, but the protocol itself was not designed with an emphasis on security, which could theoretically introduce new vulnerabilities.
- threats of LPWA protocols. A number of LPWA protocols try to solve at least some security problems, but they are simply not able to cope with the increased number of cyber threats in the area, for example, in the "smart city", when one of the threats is the exploitation of vulnerabilities in the LPWA protocols, such as overcrowding. Development of databases of protocols.
- threats of LPWAN protocols are complex cyberattacks on critical infrastructure by shutting down the system
- vulnerabilities of routers of smart systems and objects, etc.

Software disruption is also a common target for cybercriminals. There are two types of software:

- the first type refers to the software that ensures the functioning of the network of the cyber-physical system itself - the software is responsible for processing events,

logic. It is developed in low-level programming languages and is responsible for the functioning of the lower layers of the OSI network model.
- the second type of software refers to the software that is responsible for interactive interaction with the user through the command language. It is usually used for external or remote control of devices.

Since the user often cannot influence the choice of software for working with smart devices, and is tied to a single option, it will be correct to know about the vulnerabilities of such software. In addition, the user must also adhere to the instructions for working with the CPS, so as not to entail undesirable consequences with his actions.

Legal protection is usually an ex post facto defense, since it is aimed not only at organizing the process of interaction with respect to CPS, but at punishing intruders. Liability measures are not always preventive measures. If an accident or natural disaster occurs, then legal protection loses its meaning in the form in which it is now present. Here organizational protection begins to play a major role, and if it was done correctly, then the losses for the CPS and the owner and other subjects are minimal.

On the one hand, the state is engaged in ensuring security - the formation of safety standards, the implementation of which is mandatory, on the other hand, the organization itself or the owner of the CPS, or its tenant - through the formation of stable organizational protection. Thus, organizational protection includes, but is not limited to:

- simulation of security threats
- assessment of CPS vulnerabilities
- designing a robust architecture for threat processing

6 Conclusion

To regulate the CPS, it is necessary to have a comprehensive key document aimed at strategic planning for the development of the design, implementation and operation of the CPS, which will include the following points:

- Determination of the degree of importance of the used CPS, its characteristics, essential properties;
- Based on the categorization according to the above criteria, it is possible to form an insurance policy in relation to the activities of the CPS
- Based on the analysis of the most typical threats for various components of the CPS, a certification and licensing policy should be introduced, possibly with respect to not the entire system, but its significant components
- The development of "soft" forms of regulation should be supported: the adoption and use of documents on the standardization of voluntary use, codes of ethical rules, standards of self-regulatory organizations and other instruments [14]
- Already existing and operated CPS should undergo a periodic security audit, which will assess the security of key elements of the industrial network infrastructure from possible malicious internal and external influences.
- As for artificial intelligence [22] it is possible to introduce an experimental legal regime in a separate territory in the development and operation of CFS.

A balance must be struck between legal requirements and organizational measures so as not to stifle the development and implementation of cyber-physical systems, but also to secure the operation of such a system.

Acknowledgment. The reported study was funded by Grants Council of the President of the Russian Federation according to the research project № МД-2209.2020.6 "Development of the system of legal means of ensuring cybersecurity in the Russian Federation".

References

1. Rehman, S.U., Allgaier, C., Gruhn, V.: Security requirements engineering: a framework for cyber-physical systems. In: 2018 International Conference on Frontiers of Information Technology (FIT), Islamabad, Pakistan, pp. 315–320 (2018)
2. Kadosh, N., Frid, A., Housh, M.: Detecting cyber-physical attacks in water distribution systems: one-class classifier approach. J. Water Resour. Plann. Manag. **146**(8), 04020060 (2020). https://doi.org/10.1061/(ASCE)WR.1943-5452.0001259
3. Ogie, R.I.: Cyber security incidents on critical infrastructure and industrial networks. In: ICCAE 2017: Proceedings of the 9th International Conference on Computer and Automation Engineering, pp. 254–258 (2017). https://doi.org/10.1145/3057039.3057076
4. Singha, A., Jainb, A.: Study of cyber attacks on cyber-physical system. In: 3rd International Conference on Advances in Internet of Things and Connected Technologies (ICIoTCT) (2018). https://doi.org/10.2139/ssrn.3170288. https://www.researchgate.net/publication/325 330593_Study_of_Cyber_Attacks_on_Cyber-Physical_System. Accessed 10 Aug 2020
5. Order of the Government of the Russian Federation of 08.19.2020 № 2129-r "On approval of the Concept for the development of regulation of relations in the field of artificial intelligence and robotics technologies until 2024"
6. The State Duma of the Russian Federation. Federal Law of the Russian Federation "On Information, Information Technologies and Information Protection" (July 27, 2006 № 149-FZ), Moscow, Russia (2006)
7. The State Duma of the Russian Federation. The civil code of the Russian Federation (part four) (December 18, 2006 № 230-FZ), Moscow, Russia (2006)
8. The State Duma of the Russian Federation. The Criminal Code of the Russian Federation. (June 13, 1996 № 63-FZ), Moscow, Russia (1996)
9. The State Duma of the Russian Federation. The Code of the Russian Federation on Administrative Offenses (December 30, 2001 № 195-FZ), Moscow, Russia (2001)
10. The State Duma of the Russian Federation. On Commercial Secrets (July 29, 2004 № 98-FZ), Moscow, Russia (2004)
11. The State Duma of the Russian Federation. On personal data (July 27, 2006 № 152-FZ), Moscow, Russia (2006)
12. Bou-Harb, E.: A brief survey of security approaches for cyber-physical systems. In: 8th IFIP International Conference on New Technologies, Mobility and Security (NTMS), pp. 1–5. IEEE (2016)
13. Santosa, E., et al.: Modeling insider threat types in cyber organizations. In: 2017 IEEE International Symposium on Technologies for Homeland Security (HST) (2017). https://doi.org/10.1109/THS.2017.7943445
14. The concept of regulation of artificial intelligence and robotics technologies in Russian Federation until 2023

15. Ansari, F.: Strategy Paper of the Research, Development & Innovation Expert Group: Priority Research Areas & Measures to Support the Austrian Research Landscape in the Context of Industry 4.0. The Association Industry 4.0, Austria, pp. 26–29 (2018)
16. Russian Federation. The civil code of the Russian Federation (part four) (December 18, 2006 № 230-FZ). Moscow, Russia (2006)
17. Resolution of the Plenum of the Supreme Court of the Russian Federation, p. 17
18. Models of legal regulation of the creation, use and distribution of robots and systems with artificial intelligence. Ed. Naumov, V.B., p. 67. NP-Print, Saint Petersburg (2019)
19. Arkhipov, V.V., Naumov, V.B.: Artificial intelligence and autonomous devices in the context of law: on the development of the first law on robotics in Russia. In: Proceedings of SPIIRAS, vol. 6, no. 55, pp. 46–62 (2017)
20. Civil law norms on robotics: resolution of the European Parliament. https://www.europarl.eur opa.eu/legislative-train/theme-area-of-justice-and-fundamental-rights/file-civil-law-rules-on-robotics. Accessed 10 Aug 2020
21. McNicholas, J.B., Kettani, H.: Consideration of insider based collusion attacks on cyber systems international. J. Soc. Sci. Humanit. **9**(2) (2019). https://doi.org/10.18178/ijssh.2019. 9.2.986
22. The State Duma of the Russian Federation. Federal Law of the Russian Federation "On conducting an experiment to establish special regulation in order to create the necessary conditions for the development and implementation of artificial intelligence technologies in a constituent entity of the Russian Federation – a city of federal significance Moscow and amending". (April 28, 2020 № 123-FZ), Moscow, Russia (2020)

Human-Robot Collaboration in the Society of the Future: A Survey on the Challenges and the Barriers

Rinat Galin$^{(\boxtimes)}$ and Mark Mamchenko$^{(\boxtimes)}$

V. A. Trapeznikov Institute of Control Sciences of Russian Academy of Sciences, Profsoyuznaya Street 65, 117342 Moscow, Russia

Abstract. The robotization of industries and daily life activities had long been transformed from innovation and curiosity to reality. The use of collaborative robots (cobots) has now become widespread, capable of safely working together with a human in a single working space and increasing the efficiency of work in professions that are cannot be automated easily so far. The researchers and economists are making optimistic projections of increasing the rate of adoption of robots and cobots both in industries and in everyday human activities. However, there are difficulties and problems on the way to mass robotization, and construction of the socio-cyber-physical environment, including fear and distrust of robots, differences in the attitude towards robots in different countries and social groups, incomprehension of the relevance of robotization, etc. In addition, there are well-known problems, that are still under discussion and have no ready solutions. In this article we consider the current state of affairs in the sphere of deployment of cobots in the world and Russia, consider optimistic forecasts of the process of robotization, but also form a list of known and potential problems and negative factors, that could potentially hamper the implementation of plans for mass robotization and cobotization of industries and society, and provide our common vision of the solution of these problems.

Keywords: Robotics · Collaborative robot · Cobot · Robotization · Future of robotics

1 Introduction

Robotization initially involved delegating heavy and hazardous work to robots, resulting in increased productivity and reduced number of accidents [1]. However, due to the rapid development of cyber-physical systems and technologies, the focus of robotic deployment has now shifted significantly – from specialized industrial robots to collaborative and social ones (social robots are a special case of human-robot collaboration). That meant that the introduction of robots into all spheres of human life and activity instead of the robotization of industries production in currently on the agenda.

Given the rapid increase in the intensity of robotization, a new type of society – a social robotized society united by a single cyber-physical environment – is being formed.

© Springer Nature Singapore Pte Ltd. 2021
P. K. Singh et al. (Eds.): FTNCT 2020, CCIS 1395, pp. 111–122, 2021.
https://doi.org/10.1007/978-981-16-1480-4_10

In the new "robosociety", where people live side by side with robots since they are born, a robot would be considered not just as an extension of human capabilities or a kind of entertainment, but as a full-fledged unit of the socio-cyber-physical environment.

Many researchers make optimistic predictions about the timing of building such a society. It should be noted, however, that the practice often makes adjustments to such forecasts, and unforeseen obstacles and challenges may arise on the way to the progress. The purpose of this work is to assess the current state of deployment of cobots in the world and in Russia, as well as to analyze the circumstances and events (including the unlikely ones), that could potentially prevent the further introduction of collaborative robots into the society.

2 Cobots, and Their Differences from Industrial and Service Robotics

Traditionally, among the diversity of all robots, it is common to distinguish three main classes: industrial robots, collaborative robots, and service robots [2]. Despite the apparent similarities, cobots differ from industrial and service robotics, e.g.:

1. Unlike industrial robots, service robots are not used in production [3], and unlike cobots, they do not necessarily imply the ability to work with humans, as they can both operate autonomous and be remotely controlled.
2. Industrial robots are used in manufacturing, rarely imply collaborative work with humans, and are essentially automatically controlled, reprogrammable multipurpose manipulators [4], whereas a collaborative robot can be used not only in production and necessarily involves interactive work with a human. The functionality of cobots and industrial robots differs too. In particular, cobots are more accurate and less error-prone than industrial robots, but their movements are slower due to the HRI safety requirements, and their working space is smaller. Collaborative robots can be programmed easier and faster, but have a less carrying capacity [5]. There is also a number of other specific differences between cobots and industrial robots. A qualitative comparison of cobots and industrial robots is presented in Table 1.

Table 1. A qualitative comparison of cobots and industrial robots.

Characteristics	Industrial robots	Cobots
Installation type (usually)	Fixed [6]	Mobile [6]
Type of tasks performed	Repeatable only [6]	Repeatable and non-repeating [6]
Tasks changes	Rarely [6]	Frequently [6]

(continued)

Table 1. (*continued*)

Characteristics	Industrial robots	Cobots
Interaction with worker	Only during programming [6]	Frequently and safe [6]
Profitable at small-lot and single-lot production	No [6]	Yes [6]
Size available	Small or big [6]	Small only [6]
Speed of operation	From slow to fast [6]	Slow only [6] (limited due to HRI safety standards)
Price	Lower [5]	Higher [5]
Operation accuracy	Lower [5]	Higher [5]
Load capacity	Higher [5]	Lower [5]
Programmability	More complicated and time-consuming [5]	Easier and faster [5]
Service (time and cost)	More [5]	Less [5]
Weight of robot	Higher [5]	Lower [5]
Safety and external forces sensors	Usually missing [5]	Organic [5]
Operation space available	More [5]	Less [5]

3   The Current State of the Introduction and Use of Cobots in the World and in Russia

3.1   Cobots in the World

Currently, collaborative robots are being successfully implemented in industry, particularly in small-scale manufacturing and repairing facilities. Cobots are also actively used in other areas, including health, services, education, and agriculture. Special cases include the use of cobots in precision farming, medical operations and the rehabilitation of disabled persons [7].

According, to IFR estimations, there were 11,000 cobots for 400,000 industrial robots in 2017, and 14,000 cobots for 423,000 industrial robots in 2018 (the ratio decreased from 35.4 to 29.2 times) [8]. Thus, the total number of cobots in 2018 increased by 27.3 per cent compared to 2017, while the total number of industrial robots increased by only 5.75%.

Considering the projected increase in the number of operational industrial robots of 465,000 in 2020 and 522,000 in 2021 (according to IFR data) [4, 8], as well as the growth of deployed service and collaborative robotics, the number of operating cobots could be more than 20,000 worldwide already by the end of 2020.

The global market dynamics of cobots is also favorable: the total turnover in this area has increased by almost 50% from less than $400 million in 2017 to about $600 million in 2018 [6]. In 2019, the global cobot market exceeded the value of $1 billion [9].

Cobots are so much valued, that many companies involved in the development and production of industrial robots are now producing specialized models of their robots that ensure the safety of the person working in the vicinity of the robot. In fact, this "industrial cobot" is a hybrid of a cobot and an industrial robot, i.e. it has a functionality of an industrial robot with cobot's level of safety [10].

3.2 Cobots in Russia

The market of collaborative robotics in Russia is in its initial stage of development. We failed to find exact data on the cobot's market. However, we believe that the current state of the cobots' market in Russia is similar to the state of the market of industrial robots, therefore we provide data on the market of industrial robots.

It suffices to note that the values of total sales of industrial robots in Russia are not in thousands, but in hundreds of units (713 robots in 2017, 1007 – in 2018), and the market size of industrial robots is small compared to the world (from 2 billion rubles in 2017 to 3 billion rubles in 2018). In addition, the ratio of industrial robots to employees in 2018 was only five robots per 10,000 employees of industrial enterprises, while the global average was 99 robots per 10,000 employees [11].

Industrial proportions in 2015–2017 shows, that out of 1,622 industrial robots sold in Russia, 508 (31.3%) were purchased by the auto industry companies; these companies purchased 40%, 7.2% and 36.7% of all the sold industrial robots in 2015, 2016 and 2017 accordingly. Thus, despite the sharp decline in 2016, the auto industry is one of the main customers of industrial robots in Russia, forming 30–40% of the total demand [4]. Overall, in 2018, industrial robots were used in the following sectors: 39% - automobile industry, 16% - mechanical engineering, 4% - food industry, 2% - R&D and education, 1% - chemical and petrochemical industries, 5% - other industries, 32% - no data avaliable [12].

Thus, the Russian market is really in the early stages of development, the main reason is the low profitability of the production and use of industrial robots in Russia. [4, 13]. Currently, the Russian market is in a classic vicious circle: in order to increase the number of produced and operated industrial robots in Russia, it was necessary to ensure the profitability of their production and to reduce the cost of their acquisition, installation and maintenance, and that's only possible if there's a significant increase in demand for these robots. In turn, the demand will increase only when the acquisition, installation and operation of the robots is profitable for business and enterprises.

4   Robots and Cobots in the Society of the Future: A Positive Vision

According to Barclays Research estimates, the total market of cobots would already exceed $3.1 billion that by the end of 2020 with a sustained growth to $9.7 billion by 2025 [14]. According to MarketsAndMarkets, investments in the global cobot market will reach $12.5 billion by 2025. Market share will increase due to the need for enterprises to automate their processes, as well as to the growing workforce deficit [15].

The coronavirus pandemic had given a new impetus to industrial robotization. An enterprise with many robots and few people is more resilient to external influences, and able to function more effectively, for example, under total quarantine. Overall, robots are projected to replace up to one fifth of all jobs by 2030 [16].

In addition, the active introduction of robots and cobots, according to some researchers, corresponds to the main current trends in the world, namely:

1. Reduction of impact on environment through improved use and distribution of resources, technical upgrades, introduction of energy-saving and closed-loop production technologies [17].
2. Increasing the duration of employment of older workers – by delegating the physical work to cobots,
3. Improving the competitiveness of industries, enterprises, and economy of the country (countries) as a whole within Industry 4.0 – through massive robotization of labour, reducing the cost of production and labour, and increasing its added value, increasing efficiency, quality and flexibility of production [6, 18].
4. Improvement of the safety of remaining staff by delegating hazardous work to robots [18].

In general, a positive vision of the prospects for robotization, as well as introduction and use of cobots can be described by the phrase in the article [19]: "Smart and skilled operators collaborate with robots and are aided by machines, advanced human-machine interaction technologies and adaptive automation".

5   Pessimism and Skepticism About the Robots and Cobots: Challenges and Possible Solutions

Despite the generally positive attitude towards the robotization of mankind and technological processes, it should be noted, that realistic prognosis for the use of robots and cobots in in future also implies the consideration of some other factors, including:

- diversity in perception of robots among different population groups and even whole countries;
- different current and future rates of robotization and cobotization in different countries;
- too optimistic a priori view on the prospects for the introduction of robots and cobots;
- resistance to robotization in the workplaces;
- fear of robots for no reason;
- unpredictable or underestimated factors with a huge negative influence (the so-called "black swans"), etc.

In this section we will try to describe why these factors may have a negative impact on the future world-wide deployment of robots and cobots.

5.1   The Perception of Robots

We offer the analysis of the results of a number of sociological studies, revealing the attitude of different population groups of different countries towards robotization and robots. Please note that the pool of studies analyzed in this paper can be considered neither as the only true, nor as a complete one. A comprehensive analysis of the worldwide perception of robots and cobots is not the purpose of this study.

USA. A poll of visitors of the Minnesota State Fair showed that slightly more than half of respondents (55%) felt uncomfortable about the automated robotic surgery, with the vast majority of respondents mistakenly thinking, that autonomous robotic surgery is already underway. However, the trust of medical AI is much greater: most respondents are willing to trust AI services for medical imaging analysis and providing diagnoses [20].

European Union Countries. T. Gnambs and M. Appel analyzed data from the Eurobarometer project, which presents the results of surveys of 80,396 respondents from 27 European countries on critical issues of public life [21]. The overall result of the study is as follows:

- the attitude toward robots has changed to the worst within five years, from 2014 to 2017;
- the attitude toward robotic assistants has become significantly more negative (which means exactly the negative shift of the attitude towards the cobots);
- in 2017 Europeans became more skeptical about autonomous unmanned vehicles and the use of robots in medical operations (than in 2014);
- the perception of robots performing tasks in the workplace (as in 2014) is more positive than of the robots in other fields and spheres;
- men treat robots better; women treat them worse;
- the better education, the better attitude towards the robots;
- the attitude of the office workers toward robots is better in comparison with the perception of robots by the workers, people of physical labor jobs or unemployed persons;
- countries with older populations treat robots better (older societies were more interested to receive "robotic" assistance);
- North Europeans treat robots much better, than the southerners do.

Thus, the general attitude of Europeans towards robots declined in 2017 compared to 2014. EU citizens are willing to accept robots as long as they remain an abstract concept, but do not welcome them in their daily lives if the robots gain a definite, clearly defined and irreplaceable function or have a direct impact on their lives. The worst perception of robots has been demonstrated by the workers and the unemployed with a low level of education. This can be explained by the fact, that these people may be the first to be fired because of the robotization of monotonous physical labor [21].

In addition, analysis of Eurobarometer 82.4 (2014) data by T. Hinks showed that people's fear of robots is not entirely independent, but is correlated with low life satisfaction, fears of loneliness, unemployment, loss of physical and psychological health, or other deep phobias. Moreover, an inverse relationship has been revealed, when people who fear robots report their dissatisfaction with life. Residents of the former USSR countries that have joined the EU, as well as southern countries of the European Union, are more scared of robots. More experienced (and therefore older) workers fear the robots more, in comparison with the 15–30-aged workers [22]. The polls of citizens in different countries of the EU show other interesting patterns and features.

Germany. People fear most of all the loss of control and the robots controlling the humans. The Germans believe that robots will be dangerous when they become smarter than the humans. The author, Anna-Lisa Vollmer, suggests that such opinions may be related to the age of a person or the influence of religion [23].

United Kingdom. A survey of visitors of the Royal Society Summer Science Exhibition 2019 (Royal Society, London) by D. A. Robb et al. revealed different attitudes towards robots of different generations. For example, Generation Y appreciates, that robots will perform dangerous work, more than Generation X. And Generation Z advocates that robots should handle even more dangerous work. The X-generation is more confident (in comparison with the Z generation representatives) that the next 10–15 years human work will prevail over the work of the robots. Therefore, a younger generation is more optimistic about the robots [24]. In addition, A. Rossi et al. made social survey of students, staff and visitors of the schools and departments of the University of Hertfordshire revealed the attitudes towards errors made by the robots. Respondents considered the robot's serious errors as the actions that carry serious consequences (this includes harm and death to people and animals, unauthorized disclosure of personal data, and damage or destruction of property). Robot's minor errors were defined as those that do not lead to significant consequences, but to the inconvenience of using a robot (Making incorrect purchases, obstructing the movement of people, etc.) [25].

Japan. In contrast to the fear of robots of the Germans, justified inter alia (supposedly) by the influence of religion [23], it is worth noting the following study [26] by J. Ito. The author claims that the high level of robotization in Japan and the virtual absence of fear of robots are a consequence of the Shinto religion and some influence of Buddhism. According to the author, Shinto and Buddhism do not imply a clear separation of human from the world in which he lives, compared to the anthropocentrism of the countries of the West, which are traditionally more strongly influenced by the Judeo-Christian monotheist faiths. This leads to a shift in the attitude towards a robot, to be treated no longer as an instrument, but as an equal (or almost equal) member of the new cyber-physical society.

5.2   Non-obvious Hindrances to the Deployment of Robots and Cobots

The "RoboLuddites". Human consciousness has a kind of conservatism. Skepticism about everything new and unfamiliar is a normal and predictable human reaction. As we have already shown in the previous sections, people in different countries may be skeptical about the intensive deployment of robotics. In addition, in some cases, the robotization and cobotization of workplaces (as a special case of the introduction of new technologies) will be meet the resistance of the workers and personnel [27, 28].

This reaction is also completely predictable. In the history of scientific and technological progress, such stories have happened before. It is enough to recall the Luddites [29] to understand, that such stories were mainly not related to resistance to the new technologies, but were a result of the lack of dialogue and misunderstanding between workers, the management of the enterprises, and the local or public authorities. It is the establishing of a dialogue and the provision of explanations that should be addressed during the active robotization of production and societies.

Massive Unemployment and Other Yet Unresolved Problems. It was much worse when companies and/or national authorities identify a problem that might arise from the introduction of new technologies (for example, during the process of robotization), but do not offer even an approximate solution. For example, the idea, that mass robotization of production will lead to the massive unemployment, is getting deeper and deeper inside the people's heads. Scientists, politicians and business people still argue and propose different solutions: basic income, taxes on robots, a single robot law, etc. It should not be assumed that this problem is of the distant future, because people are already aware of this problem, as well as of the absence of any agreed solution of this problem. This impasse only strengthens the fear of the citizens and the workers, and may increase the resistance to the process of robotization.

Conspiracy. After the uncontrolled growth of the level of mistrust and fear of the robots, people may start to act illogically, i.e.: create and disseminate rumors and conspiracy theories, create robotic dissident movements and engaging new followers. This is again a reflection of the lack of a dialogue between the general public, the workers, the authorities, the enterprises management (including robot integrators) and subject matter experts. It is also a sign of the absence, ineffectiveness or inflexibility of public education and awareness-raising activities. As a real example, we should note the widespread conspiracy theory that 5G cell towers allegedly contribute to the COVID-19 contamination [30]. In Russia, for example, this uncontrolled illogical fear of 5G and COVID-19 inspired the protesters to destroy a cellular communication antenna in the village of Nogir in the Republic of North Ossetia (Russia) [31], while there was not a single 5G tower in North Ossetia at that time.

Responsibility of Robots and the Human Factor. Human behavior, reactions and state at home and at the workplace are still considered unanticipated, and the problem of providing absolutely safe HRI is not yet fully solved. It is only a matter of time before new types and models of cobots would lead to unforeseen situations and accidents. The problem of the responsibility of the robot for causing damage to property, health and life, as well as for the other serious consequences, had not yet been solved in a unified manner both in Russia and in the world. It seems to be a problem of the distant future, but in fact it is not. In particular, according to one of the proposals, the developer should be held responsible for the accident due to the wrong actions of a fully autonomous UV; but if the driver even somehow controlled the vehicle, the accident would be his own fault. Other experts suggest that the liability for UV crashes should be primarily imposed on with the developer [32]. Another open problem sounds like this: who will be responsible for the consequences of AI's misdeeds and wrong actions [33] – the developer, the AI itself, or the operator who controlled it?

Inaccurate Predictions. In 1930 John Maynard Keynes wrote in his essay named "Economic Possibilities for our Grandchildren": "Three-hour shifts or a fifteen-hour week may put off the problem for a great while. For three hours a day is quite enough…" [34]. Working shifts now range from 7 to 8 h, and there are 35 to 40 working hours per week. The 100-years forecast will expire in 2030. It is unlikely that a reduction in working hours will be significant within the next 10 years [35]. Thus, this example reflects the dangerous nature of predictions when a certain trend is superimposed on the present situation, and the future is modelled mainly on the basis of this trend. Such predictions do not take into account the constant change in the situation as a result of the influence of the trend, and the myriad of other factors, including the unpredictable or underestimated events with unexpectedly significant impact. We will try to present our vision and examples of these factors in the following subsection.

The "black swans". It is difficult to forecast these factors, and it is even more difficult to predict their impact on the robotization process and the social perception of the robots. Examples of such factors can be provided by:

- spontaneous anti-robot and anti-AI demonstrations in response to an accident with UV in which several people died;
- massive negative reaction to inappropriate social robot's statements and actions due to the use of incorrect machine learning samples (or learning through interaction with users on the Internet);
- urgent discontinuation of the production of the certain model of a cobot due to several consistent accidents causing deaths of the operators as a result of incorrect security settings and the errors during the stage of design;
- phasing-out a service robot whose appearance was positively assessed by the developers and the focus-groups, but did not find demand by the mass user.

6   Conclusion

Robotization is one of the world's key trends to be reckoned with. The massive deployment of the robots in the production would allow the enterprises and economies to remain competitive, and develop vigorously by creating new products and services with high added value and reduced costs. In addition, the process of robotization has long been seen not only as a means of automating work in factories, instead robots are increasingly "penetrating" into people's daily activities. In our view, sooner or later in the future robots and artificial intelligence systems will replace humans in their workplaces. Cobots, service and social robots used in everyday activities will be "merged" into a single type of robot capable of acting autonomously, being remotely controlled by a human, and work in collaboration with people.

Despite this, the steps towards "robosociety" will be uneven, primarily due to the different rates of robotization in the world, different perception of the robots in different countries and even different groups of people, as well as the diversity of the assessments of the relevance of robotization and cobotization among the leaders of different enterprises and countries. In addition, robotization will continue to pose new challenges, including those related to human psychology. In this regard, we would like to point out the obvious fact that the challenges encountered can and should be addressed as soon as possible. The authorities of the countries, the leaders of the enterprises and robot integrators, as well as the specialists of the robot communities should not only talk about the inevitable robotization and the "bright future", but also do the following:

- respond quickly to emerging problems, address them and/or adjust the plans of robotization;
- actively engage in advocacy and education to address fears and mistrust of the robots, resistance to the process of robotization, as well as dispel myths and conspiracy theories;
- establish and maintain a broad-based dialogue with the public in the sphere of robotization, showing and proving them their personal benefits form robotization of the production and their daily routine;
- organize, hold and support trainings in robotics, exhibitions and other public events in order to give people the experience of interaction with robots, etc.

Humanity will have to go through a complex and at the same time miraculous stage of development on the way to mass robotization and cobotization of production and our daily life. We will be able to draw conclusions about this period of history only decades later, and now we must accept that mass robotization is not a utopia or a distant future, but a reality that is happening right now. Only those countries and people who understand and accept this reality will be able not only to integrate more quickly into the new socio-cyber-physical environment, but also to gain a significant advantage and benefit over those who doubt that intelligent robots and AI systems are the future of mankind.

Acknowledgements. The reported study was partially funded by RFBR according to the research project No. 19–08-00331.

References

1. Galin, R.: Virtual test area for collaborative robotics (Virtual'naya poligonnaya baza dlya otrabotki vzaimodejstviya kollaborativnoj robototekhniki). In: Proceedings of the 5th International Scientific and Practical Conference "Virtual Modeling, Prototyping and Industrial Design", vol. 2, no. 5, 186–190. FBOU WU TGTU Publishing Centre, Tambov, Russia (2018)
2. Galin, R., Meshcheryakov, R.: Automation and robotics in the context of Industry 4.0: the shift to collaborative robots. In: IOP Conference Series: Materials Science and Engineering, vol. 537, no. 3, pp. 1–5. Institute of Physics Publishing, Krasnoyarsk, Russia (2019)
3. Paluch, S., Wirtz, J., Kunz, W. H.: Service robots and the future of service. In: Marketing Weiterdenken – Zukunftspfade für eine marktorientierte Unternehmensführung, pp. 1–21. Springer Gabler (2020). Paluchetal_ServiceRobots_2019–12–07.pdf
4. Konyuhovskaya, A., Cyplenkova, V.: The Robotics Market: Threats and Opportunities for Russia (Rynok robototekhniki: Ugrozy i vozmozhnosti dlya Rossii), 1st edn. LitRes, Moscow (2020)
5. Matúšová, M., Bučányová, M., Hrušková E.: The future of industry with collaborative robots. In: MATEC Web of Conferences, vol. 299, pp. 1–6. EDP Sciences, Les Ulis, France (2019)

6. Knudsen, M., Kaivo-oja, J.: Collaborative robots: frontiers of current literature. In: Taşkın, H., Erden, C., Uygun, Ö. (eds.) Journal of Intelligent Systems: Theory and Applications, vol. 3, no. 2, pp. 13–20. Harun Taşkın, Turkey (2020)

7. Yuschenko, A.: Ergonomic problems of collaborative robotics. In: Lopota, A. (eds.) Robotics and Technical Cybernetics, vol. 7, no. 2, pp. 85–93. Russian State Scientific Center for Robotics and Technical Cybernetics (RTC), Saint-Petersburg, Russia (2019)

8. IFR World Robotics Presentation, 18th September 2019, Shanghai. https://ifr.org/downlo ads/press2018/IFR%20World%20Robotics%20Presentation%20-%2018%20Sept%202019. pdf. Accessed 15 Aug 2020

9. The Collaborative Robot Market Will Exceed US$11 Billion by 2030, Representing 29% of the Total Industrial Robot Market. https://www.abiresearch.com/press/collaborative-robot-mar ket-will-exceed-us11-billion-2030-representing-29-total-industrial-robot-market/. Accessed 15 Aug 2020

10. Pilat, Z., Klimasara, W., Pachuta, M., Słowikowski, M.: Rzeplińska-Rykała, K. (eds.) Some New Robotization Problems Related to the Introduction of Collaborative Robots into Industrial Practice. In. Journal of Automation, Mobile Robotics and Intelligent Systems, vol. 13, no. 4, pp. 91–97. ŁUKASIEWICZ - PIAP Institute, Warsaw, Poland (2020)

11. People in factories still fear robots. What is happening in the market of industrial robotization in Russia ("Lyudi na zavodah vse eshche boyatsya robotov". Chto proiskhodit na rynke promyshlennoj robotizacii v Rossii). https://rb.ru/longread/industrial-robotics/. Accessed 15 Aug 2020

12. Notes: Russian Market for Industrial Robotics, Alice Konyukhovskaya, NAURR (Konspekty: Rossijskij rynok promyshlennoj robototekhniki, Alisa Konyuhovskaya, NAURR). https://robotrends.ru/pub/1917/konspekty-rossiyskiy-rynok-promyshlennoy-rob ototehniki-alisa-konyuhovskaya-naurr. Accessed 15 Aug 2020

13. Most robots in Russia buy auto productions (Bol'she vsego robotov v Rossii poku- paet avtoprom). https://www.vedomosti.ru/technology/articles/2019/09/19/811579-bolshe- vsego-robot. Accessed 15 Aug 2020

14. Collaborative Robotics Market Value to Reach $9.7 Billion by 2025. https://tractica.omdia. com/newsroom/press-releases/collaborative-robotics-market-value-to-reach-9-7-billion-by- 2025/. Accessed 15 Aug 2020

15. Global Collaborative Robot or Cobot Market is Expected to Reach USD 12.5 Billion by 2025, Observing a CAGR of 50.0% during 2020–2025: VynZ Research. https://www.glo benewswire.com/news-release/2020/02/26/1991230/0/en/Global-Collaborative-Robot-or- Cobot-Market-is-Expected-to-Reach-USD-12-5-Billion-by-2025-Observing-a-CAGR-of- 50-0-during-2020-2025-VynZ-Research.html. Accessed 15 Aug 2020

16. Jobs lost, jobs gained: What the future of work will mean for jobs, skills, and wages. https://www.mckinsey.com/featured-insights/future-of-work/jobs-lost-jobs-gai ned-what-the-future-of-work-will-mean-for-jobs-skills-and-wages#. Accessed 15 Aug 2020

17. Huang, J., et al.: A case study in human–robot collaboration in the disassembly of press-fitted components. In: Maropoulos, P.G., et al. (eds.) Proceedings of the Institution of Mechanical Engineers, Part B: Journal of Engineering Manufacture, vol. 234, no. 3, pp. 654–664. SAGE Publishing, Newbury Park, CA, USA (2020)

18. Galin, R.R., Meshcheryakov, R.V.: Human-Robot Interaction Efficiency and Human-Robot Collaboration. In: Kravets, A.G. (ed.) Robotics: Industry 4.0 Issues & New Intelligent Control Paradigms. SSDC, vol. 272, pp. 55–63. Springer, Cham (2020). https://doi.org/10.1007/978- 3-030-37841-7_5

19. Mattson, S., Fast-Berglund, Å., Li, D., Thorvald, P.: In Dessouky, M., et al. (eds.) Forming a cognitive automation strategy for Operator 4.0 in complex assembly. In: Computers & Industrial Engineering, vol. 139, p. 15. Elsevier Ltd., Amsterdam, Netherlands (2020)

20. Stai, B., et al. Public perceptions of artificial intelligence and robotics in medicine. In: Smith, A.D., Landman, J., Sundaram, C., Clayman, R.V. (eds.) Journal of Endourology, vol. 34, no. 9, pp. 1–29. Mary Ann Liebert, Inc., NY, USA (2020)

21. Gnambs, T., Appel, M.: Are robots becoming unpopular? Changes in attitudes towards autonomous robotic systems in Europe. In: Guitton, M., et al. (eds.) Computers in Human Behavior, vol. 93, pp. 53–61. Elsevier Ltd., Amsterdam, Netherlands (2019)

22. Hinks, T.: Fear of Robots and Life Satisfaction. In: Sam Ge, S. (ed.) International Journal of Social Robotics, pp. 1–14. Springer Nature, London, UK (2020)

23. Vollmer, A.-L.: Fears of Intelligent Robots. In: Imai, M., Mutlu, B., et al. (eds.) HRI '18: Companion of the 2018 ACM/IEEE International Conference on Human-Robot Interaction, pp. 273–274. Association for Computing Machinery, NY, USA (2018)

24. Robb, D. A., et al.: Robots in the danger zone: exploring public perception through engagement. In: Imai, M., Mutlu, B. et al. (eds.) HRI '20: Proceedings of the 2020 ACM/IEEE International Conference on Human-Robot Interaction, pp. 93–102. Association for Computing Machinery, NY, USA (2020)

25. Rossi, A., Dautenhahn, K., Koay, K. L., Walters, M. L.: Human Perceptions of the Severity of Domestic Robot Errors. In: Kheddar, A., et al. (eds.) Proceedings of the Ninth International Conference on Social Robotics (ICSR 2017), p. 10. Springer International Publishing AG, Cham, Switzerland (2017)

26. Ito, J.: Why Westerners Fear Robots and the Japanese Do Not. In: Thompson, N., et al. (eds.) Wired Ideas, pp. 1–4. WIRED.com, Boone, IA, USA (2018)

27. Okiki, O.C., Durodolu, O.O.: Evaluating resistances to new technological experience by Librarians in Academic Environment. In: Hu, N. (eds.) Journal of Applied Information Science and Technology, vol. 10, no. 3, pp. 74–83. Center for Promoting Ideas (CPI), USA (2017)

28. Sorenson, J.: Robot sabotage: resisting technological transformations in the workplace. In: Whitmore, K. (ed.) AAA/CASCA Annual Meeting, pp. 1–28. Canadian Anthropology Society, Canada (2019)

29. Matthews, P., Greenspan, S.: Automation and Collaborative Robotics: A Guide to the Future of Work, 1st edn. Apress, Berkeley, CA, USA (2020)

30. Jolley, D., Paterson, J.: Pylons ablaze: examining the role of 5G COVID-19 conspiracy beliefs and support for violence. In: Gibson, S., Smith, L. (eds.) British Journal of Social Psychology, vol. 59, no. 3, pp. 628–640. John Wiley and Sons, Oxford, UK (2020)

31. A cellular mast burns in North Ossetia over '5G technology fears'. https://oc-media.org/a-cellular-mast-burns-in-north-ossetia-over-5g-technology-fears/. Accessed 15 Aug 2020

32. Jamjoom, A.A.B., Jamjoom, A.M.A., Marcus, H.J.: Exploring public opinion about liability and responsibility in surgical robotics. In: Venema, L., et al. (eds.) Nature Machine Intelligence, vol. 2, pp. 194–196. Nature Publishing Group, London, UK (2020)

33. Laptev, V.A.: Artificial intelligence and liability for its work (Ponyatie iskusstvennogo intellekta i yuridicheskaya otvetstvennost' za ego rabotu). In: Bogdanovskaya, I. et al. (eds.) Pravo. Zhurnal Vysshey Shkoly Ekonomiki, vol. 2, pp. 79–102. HSE Publishing House (Izdatel'skij dom VSHE), Moscow, Russia (2019)

34. Keynes, J.M.: Economic possibilities for our grandchildren. In: Essays in Persuasion. 1st edn. Palgrave Macmillan, London, UK (2010)

35. Zolotov, A.V.: K. Marx and J.M. Keynes about the reduction of working time: failed, but brilliant forecasts (Marks i Kejns o sokrashchenii rabochego vremeni: prognozy nesbyvshiesya, no genial'nye). In: Grudzinskij, A.O., et al. (eds.) The Bulletin of the N.I. Lobachevsky Nizhny Novgorod University. Serie: Social Sciences. (Vestnik Nizhegorodskogo universiteta im. N.I.Lobachevskogo. Seriya: Social'nye nauki), vol. 4, no. 40, pp. 27–35. N.I. Lobachevsky Nizhny Novgorod University publisher, Nizhny Novgorod, Russia (2015)

Analysis of Socio-political Content of Internet Resources Based on Hybrid Neural Network Technologies

Aleksey F. Rogachev[1,2]([⊠]) [iD] and Gennadiy A. Atamanov[3] [iD]

[1] Volgograd State Agrarian University, Volgograd, Russian Federation
[2] All-Russian Research Institute of Irrigated Agriculture, Volgograd, Russian Federation
[3] Volgograd State University, Volgograd, Russian Federation

Abstract. Countering sociocultural and cyber threats, as well as ideological extremism, requires identifying undesirable content of information sources, primarily the content of Internet resources. Significant volumes, as well as semantic and lexicological diversity of Internet content, make it necessary to improve artificial intelligence (AI) methods for neural network analysis in order to identify potential threats and undesirable content. The problem is complicated by the presence of "information garbage" in the studied content, which is a specific information noise. It can be solved using neural network technologies, including frequency preprocessing of text arrays, justification of the structure and construction of a subject-oriented database of text data bodies, justification and experimental study of the architecture of the hybrid ANN based on the vector representation of pre-formed dictionaries of terms. The authors substantiate a modified approach to neural network detection of explicit or latent socio-cultural and cyber threats contained in the information content of Internet resources. Thematic dictionaries used for neural network classification of texts are pre-formed based on computer analysis of the target Internet content. An ensemble of combined ANN is constructed based on a combination of convolutional, fully connected and recursive layers, aimed at identifying text content containing undesirable information, including sociotechnical and cyber threats. The degree of recognition of thematic texts is reached in the range of 0.79...0.85. As a result, we obtained a set of neural network assessments of typical RSS feeds based on the criteria of detected signs of explicit or latent socio-cultural and cyber threats.

Keywords: Socio-political content · ANN-technology · The task of classification

1 Introduction

One of the most important directions of the Strategy of scientific and technological development of the Russian Federation is "Countering man-made, ... Socio-cultural threats,

The reported study was funded by RFBR and EISR according to the research project № 20-011-31648.

P. K. Singh et al. (Eds.): FTNCT 2020, CCIS 1395, pp. 123–133, 2021.
https://doi.org/10.1007/978-981-16-1480-4_11

... and ideological extremism, as well as cyber threats and other sources of danger to society, the economy and the state". The legal basis for ensuring information security (IS) is the national IS Doctrine, approved on 06.12.2016, although, according to researchers, part of its methodological provisions is debatable [1]. The task of classifying content, including identifying its belonging to the target category in an exponentially increasing volume of information, is relevant for various socio-political spheres, including ensuring their information security [2]. The Substantiation of approaches and methods for researching the content of Internet content is devoted to publications of domestic and foreign scientists-political scientists, sociologists, philologists [3], who have created a number of ML-methods for analyzing the emotional color and tone of texts in the media on the Internet, including cognitive and interpretive decoding [4, 5].

Countering sociocultural and cyber threats and ideological extremism requires identifying undesirable content from information sources, primarily content from Internet resources. The significant volume, as well as semantic and lexicological diversity of Internet content makes it necessary to create new methods for its computer analysis in order to identify potential threats and undesirable content using artificial intelligence (AI) methods. This task can be solved using neural network technologies, including frequency preprocessing of text arrays, justification of the structure and construction of a subject-oriented database of text data bodies, justification and experimental study of the architecture and hyperparameters of a hybrid neural network based on the vector representation of pre-formed dictionaries of terms. The use of artificial neural networks (INN) is promising the possibilities of their successful application in the field of political technologies include analysis and generalization of opinion polls, prediction of rating dynamics, identification of significant factors, objective clustering of the electorate, and visualization of social dynamics of the population [6].

The fundamental principles of technologies for creating and training ins, including the formation of corpus of thematic articles, preprocessing of source data, architecture and hyperparameters of ins, are systematically described in the work [7], which considers technologies for analyzing text information, including symbols and structures that adapt the language, new definitions, and contexts [8]. ANN researchers note the wide possibilities of using neural network approaches for text processing in natural languages (NLP - Natural Language Processing) and artificial intelligence (AI) methods for detecting undesirable content [10–12].

One of the specific features of the task of identifying undesirable information containing socio-cultural and cyber threats is not only the identification of a set and contextual sequence of indicator terms based on thematic thesauri, but also the preliminary vector representation of terms in a multidimensional space to improve the effectiveness of their computer analysis. A possible variant of this representation, in contrast to the traditional "bag of words", are embeddings (eng. *Embedding - an attachment*), the dimension of space, the optimal volume and method of obtaining which, taking into account the architecture of the ins, represent a separate scientific and methodological task [13]. Thus, taking into account the socio-political orientation of the discourse of the problem being solved and its specifics, it is necessary to conduct research in the field of justification and construction of corpus of typical Internet content texts, methods of their frequency preprocessing and analysis using hybrid ins based on embeddings of selected dictionaries of terms.

2   Methods and Materials

The main purpose of this research is to develop a methodology and build an ANN for analyzing the socio-political content of Internet resources using hybrid neural network technologies.

The subgoal of the research is to solve the problems of NLP, using neural network AI methods, that arise when analyzing thematic content, using the example of identifying undesirable content of Internet resources of a socio-political profile. The results of an analytical review of the current state of neural network analysis, in relation to the problem of identifying thematic content on the example of identifying undesirable content and latent threats, allowed us to justify the main approaches to mathematical modeling, building ANN and their training.

Ensembles of ANN built in Python using specialized libraries - Keras, Scikit Learn, NLTK, Gensim, spaCy, NetworkX in the Google Collaboratory environment [9] were studied on the basis of formed corpus of thematic texts. The latter were downloaded from the Internet, and specially prepared for emulation of the subject area.

2.1   Language Model

The construction, configuration and selection of ANN hyperparameters for natural language processing, including the use of Russian-language "word2vec", was performed on the basis of methods and techniques of system analysis [14, 15]. The formation of a subject-oriented database of corpus of thematic texts was carried out by parsing Internet resources, primarily RSS feeds, which are a type of web channels that publish news in a format that is convenient for computer download. Markup of the corpus base for training the studied ins architectures was performed using the "one-hot-encoding" (OHE) format.

2.2   Architectural Solutions for Artificial Neural Networks

Combined architectures based on various types of layers and their combinations (recursive, LSTM with long-short-time memory, convolutional, etc.) were used to build hybrid ANN focused on text processing [14]. The concatenation of these layers was implemented using functional programming in Python. To ensure the stability of ANN learning processes, data regularization and normalization methods were used, as well as genetic algorithms for their structural and parametric optimization.

An experimental numerical study of the learning and functioning indicators of the developed ANN architectures was carried out according to the selected criteria of accuracy (loss, accuracy) and quality indicators (stability, lack of retraining, etc.). It was also planned to study fuzzy approaches [16].

3 Results and Discussion

The problem of classifying content, including identifying its belonging to target categories in an increasing volume of information, is relevant for various socio-political spheres, including science, for which today, from the point of view of ensuring information security, one of the significant problems is the exponential increase in the so-called "information garbage" and "information trash".

The authors interpret the concept of "information garbage" as broadly as possible. It is suggested that content components (fragments of texts and programs and/or texts and programs in General) that are unsuitable for objective and/or subjective reasons for use for their intended purpose should be included in this category.

Information junk refers to content components (fragments of texts and/or texts) that are usable, but are put out of use (subject to removal) for objective (unreliability, irrelevance, incorrectness) and/or subjective (rejection, misunderstanding, underestimation) reasons. Information garbage and information trash are increasingly becoming a scourge of science and the socio-cultural sphere as a whole. They pose a real threat to the intellectual sphere of society. Urgent measures and effective mechanisms are required to identify the content that contains them and then neutralize (block) the sources of such content, especially on the Internet.

During the research, hypotheses were put forward and experimentally tested for the possibility of selecting a hybrid architecture and ins hyperparameters to solve the problem of detecting latent socio-cultural and cyber threats, which are not always explicitly contained in the studied text bodies. The object of the study was a corpus of socio-political texts downloaded from available Internet resources, including RSS feeds containing information about explicit or latent socio-cultural and cyber threats, as well as about ideological extremism.

3.1 Working Hypothesis

The main stages of the study, providing verification of the formulated hypotheses, were the following.

1. Formation and marking of a subject-oriented database of corpus of thematic texts for teaching the studied ANN architectures.
2. Compilation of a frequency dictionary (thesaurus) of terms for the formed text bodies by the method of "tokenization".
3. Building a dictionary based on a statistical approach that normalizes the frequency of lexemes appearing in the document, taking into account the content in the rest of the body in the coordinates "Term Frequency—Inverse Document Frequency" (TF–IDF). The TF-IDF encoding method allows you to measure the relevance of a token in a document by the scaled frequency of appearance of the token in the document, normalized by the inverse scaled frequency of appearance of the token in the entire case.
4. Building embeddings based on the "word2vec" algorithm implemented in the Google Collaboratory cloud environment. A vector representation of words in a multidimensional space, in which words similar in meaning appear next to each other in a

vector space with a priori dimension of the order of 10…150, which will be selected experimentally.

3.2 Architectural and Software Solutions for Artificial Neural Networks

Justification and choice of architecture and hyperparameters for building a hybrid ANN that includes recursive (RNN/GRM/LSTM), convolutional (Conv1D) and fully connected (Dense) layers of neurons and their sequential and/or parallel combinations.

A combined architecture based on fully connected, convolutional, and recursive layers was adopted for the design of a subject-oriented ins. The latter were implemented using the LSTM architecture, the structure of the base element of which, the combination of which forms the intermediate layers [6], is shown in Fig. 1.

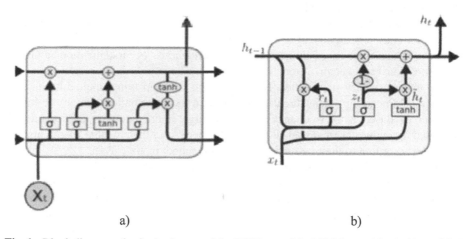

a)   b)

Fig. 1. Block diagram of a single element of the INN layer of the LSTM type a) basic; b) modified.

Each of the cells of the intermediate layer contains three interconnected filtes (input, intermediate and output), several neurons with the functions of activation of the sigmoid and hyperbolic tangent, as well as controlled adders that provide switching of transmitted signals. With all the advantages of such an ANN architecture - the ability to train temporally dependent data that is characteristic of NLP, its training takes a long time, which, depending on the volume of training and verification samples, can be tens of hours. To eliminate these shortcomings, a modified version of [6] recursive ins with memory can be used, as shown in Fig. 1 (b).

This structure has actually three inputs and outputs, whose mathematical interaction algorithm is described by a system of equations.

$$z_t = \sigma \left(W_z \bullet [h_{t-1}, x_t] \right)$$

$$\tau_t = \sigma \left(W_\tau \bullet [h_{t-1}, x_t] \right)$$

$$\widetilde{h}_t = tanh \left(W \bullet [\tau_t * h_{t-1}, x_t] \right) \tag{1}$$

$$h_t = (1 - z_t) * h_{t-1} + z_t * \tilde{h}_t,$$

where x_t is the input signal of each layer cell;

h_t and h_{t-1} - intermediate signals transmitted between identical elements-cells of the hidden ins layer;

σ - the sigmoidal activation function of neurons;

tanh - activation function in the form of a hyperbolic tangent.

Training ANN of this architecture with modified recursive layers takes significantly less time than with LSTM layers, which is especially important for automated selection of hyperparameters, for example, using genetic algorithms. After selecting the optimal architecture, building and compiling the ins in the Google Collaboratory environment, a series of numerical studies of the performance indicators of the developed ins for ML-classification of texts will be conducted.

Well-known NLP technologies of artificial neural networks include (1) structure justification and construction of a domain-specific text data structure, (2) frequency analysis, (3) construction of domain-specific dictionaries, (4) tokenization, and (5) multidimensional text vectorization.

The authors justify a modified NLP approach to identifying sociocultural and cyber threats, including latent threats, contained in the information content of Internet resources. Based on the frequency analysis of target Internet content, dictionaries of terms used for multi-class text analysis are pre-formed. After that, the text fragments are marked up according to their belonging to the corresponding six classes.

The software implementation of the ANN family was implemented using the built-in tools and libraries of Google Colaboratory. Technically, Google Coollaboratory is a dedicated service hosted in the cloud. This service provides high-performance access to computing resources via the browser and does not require additional configuration for use.

The developed ensemble of neural networks had the following structure. It included two types of blocks: invariant blocks designed for preprocessing texts that were identical for all the analyzed architectures, and variable blocks containing layers of neurons of different architectures. Text preprocessing units provided (1) loading text data, (2) splitting it into words, (3) creating dictionaries, (4) converting data to indexes, and (5) generating training and test samples [5].

To justify the choice of variable ANN blocks architectures, that are directly focused on the analysis of terms, phrases, and sequences of analyzed texts, layers of different types of neurons were analyzed. First of all, we studied modifications of recurrent layers that allows to remember the analyzed token sequences (CNN, LSTM, GRU). In addition, we considered one-dimensional convolutional layers (Conv1D) with variable window sizes and the number of convolution cores. Combinations of such powerful layers of neurons can contribute to the appearance of an undesirable phenomenon of retraining neural networks, so, for example, dropout layers were provided as a means of regularization.

Architecture of variable blocks developed by ANN that provide generalization and preliminary identification of various features and their combinations in the analyzed texts. This architecture included a combination of fully connected, convolutional, and/or recurrent layers..

Invariant blocks are modules that implement text classification directly. They contained data regularization and normalization layers, as well as a fully connected output layer. The number of output layer neurons corresponds to the number of recognized classes.

Activation functions of the recognition layer had the form "softmax" or "sigmoid" depending on the network architecture and the variant of the problem being solved. Recommendations are given for choosing hyperparameters for "loss", as well as the number of neurons and the activation function of the last recognition layer. When solving the problem of multiclass NLP-analysis for various architectures of hidden layers of hybrid ins, these parameters were invariant.

In the course of the research, callback layers were used to ensure that the network learning process of neural networks is interrupted when the quality of training deteriorates. This approach made it possible to preserve the optimal values of its trained weight coefficients of neurons selected in the process of training the neural network.

3.3 Analysis of the Quality of Built ANN

Further in the article, the indicators of the quality of ANN training, built in the course of the study, are presented.

The article goes on to describe the ANN architecture focused on multiple classification using the example of 6 text classes. The ANN architecture is based on fully connected layers with the "Relay" activation function and a 16-dimensional "embedding" word representation model with regularization via the "SpatialDropout1D" layer.

```
modelEm = Sequential()

modelEm.add(Embedding(maxWrdsCnt, 16, inp_lngth = xLn))

modelEm.add(SpatialDropout1D(0.2))

modelEm.add(Flatten())

modelEm.add(BatchNormalization())

modelEm.add(Dense(200, activation='relu'))

modelEm.add(Dropout(0.2))

modelEm.add(BatchNormalization())

modelEm.add(Dense(6, activation='sigmoid'))
```

It was experimentally established that text models of the "bag of words" type were characterized by simplicity and relatively high learning speed. However, further research required for reliable detection of hidden threats involved the use of more complex embedding models that implement the representation of tokens in an n-dimensional dense vector space [2].

Figure 2 shows the results obtained by training ANN of the architecture, described above.

The diagrams in Fig. 2 for verification and test samples show a relatively high learning rate even at 10…30 epochs, and classification accuracy of about 80%, which can be considered acceptable in the subject area under study. This allows us to recommend such

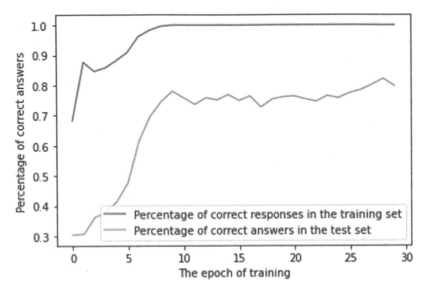

Fig. 2. ANN based on fully connected layers learning results

an architecture with the obtained values of hyperparameters for subsequent numerical experiments and selection of a more optimal neural network architecture.

Research has also been conducted for ANN with an architecture, based on LSTM layers with similar hyperparameters. Numerical experiments showed significantly higher learning time. This served as the basis for the study of the architecture based on the one-dimensional convolution "Conv1D" with hyperparameters. (20, 5, activation = 'relu')" in combination with the layer of neurons "MaxPooling1D".

Figure 3 shows the results of training ANN, architecture of which is based on layers of one-dimensional convolution.

Analysis of the diagram in Fig. 3 shows a slightly lower learning speed, compared to a network with only a fully connected architecture. The accuracy of classification in the test sample is also about 80%. At the same time, it becomes possible to select an additional hyperparameter for the size of the convolution window for texts of various contents, taking into account the presence and nature of "information garbage". This allows us to recommend such an architecture with the reduced values of hyperparameters for further numerical experiments.

Below is a snippet of the program code in Python 3.

```
modelECn = Sequential()
modelECn.add(Embedding(maxWrdsCunt, 10, inpt_lngth=xLn))
modelECn.add(SpatialDropout1D(0.2))
modelECn.add(BatchNormalization())
modelECn.add(Conv1D(20,5,activation='relu'))
modelECn.add(MaxPooling1D(2))
modelECn.add(Dropout(0.2))
modelECn.add(BatchNormalization())
modelECn.add(Flatten())
modelECn.add(Dense(6,activation='softmax'))
```

Consequently, a modified approach is justified and a software implementation of neural network detection of texts containing explicit or latent socio-cultural and cyber threats, as well as signs of ideological extremism contained in the information content of Internet resources, based on thematic dictionaries (thesauri) built on the basis of computer analysis of the target Internet content.

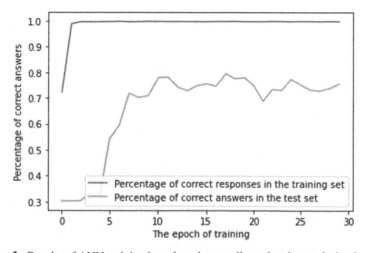

Fig. 3. Results of ANN training based on the one-dimensional convolution layer

The significance of the results obtained is determined by the proposed scientific and methodological approaches to the formation of thematic corpus of training and test texts and the construction of hybrid ANN based on a combination of fully connected, convolutional and recursive layers aimed at identifying specific socio-political threats in Internet content. The applied value of the results consists in the software implementation in Python of the proposed approach, the formation of problem-oriented dictionaries of terms and the resulting set of neural network assessments of a number of RSS channels based on the criteria for the presence of signs of socio-cultural and cyber threats and ideological extremism (explicit or latent).

4 Conclusions

The conducted research, including the formation of corpus of thematic texts and the construction of an ensemble of ins combined architecture allowed us to formulate the following conclusions.

The concept of "information garbage" as a specific content, the identification and elimination of which contributes to increasing the level of relevance of information selected for further analysis and research.

A preliminary corpus of texts containing both undesirable information, including socio-cultural and cyber threats, and "information garbage" was formed, which allowed us to obtain training, verification and testing samples for training created INN aimed at identifying undesirable content.

Despite the relatively low performance of recurrent layers within combined architectures, such ANN are left for further research, since they are supposed to be able to detect "hidden" threats contained in texts.

An ensemble of combined ins is constructed based on a combination of convolutional, fully connected and recursive layers aimed at identifying text content containing undesirable information, including sociotechnical and cyber threats. The degree of recognition of thematic texts is reached in the range of 0.79...0.85.

References

1. Atamanov, G.: Azbuka bezopasnosti. Methodology of information resource protection. Information Protection. Insider **2**(62), 8–13 (2015)
2. Atamanov, G.: Azbuka bezopasnosti. Methodology for ensuring information security of subjects of information relations. Inf. Prot Insid. **5**, 8–13 (2014)
3. Olyanitch, A., et al.: Cognitive development of semiotic data in computer-based communication (signs, concepts, discourse). Commun. Comput. Inf. Sci. **1084**, 109–121 (2019)
4. Polyakov, P., Kalinina, M., Pleshko, V.: Automatic object-oriented sentiment analysis by means of semantic templates and sentiment lexicon dictionaries. In: Proceedings of the 21st International Conference on Computational Linguistics Dialog–2015 **2**, 44–52 (2015)
5. Surkova, A., Chernobaev, I.: Comparison of neural network architectures in the task of automatic text classification In: Modern Informatization Problems in the Technological and Telecommunication Systems Analysis and Synthesis. In: MIP-2019'AS Proceedings of the XXIV-th International Open Science Conference, pp. 377–382 (2019)
6. Kyunghyun, Ch.: Learning Phrase Representations using RNN Encoder-Decoder for Statistical Machine Translation/[Electronic resource]. Access mode https://arxiv.org/abs/1406.1078 (2014)
7. Bengforth, B., Bilbro, R., Ojeda, T.: Applied text data analysis in Python. Machine learning and the creation of applications for natural language processing. - Saint Petersburg: Piter, 368 pp. (2019)
8. Google: Google Books Ngram Viewer, https://bit.ly/2GNlKtk (2013)
9. Keras: The Python Deep Learning library [Electronic resource]/Official website of the Keras library. https://www.keras.io/, 23 Apr 2019
10. Kim, Y., et al.: Character-aware neural language models. ArXiv Prepr. ArXiv1508.06615 (2015)

11. Tarasov, D.: Deep recurrent neural networks for multiple language aspect-based senti-ment analysis of user reviews In: Proceedings of the 21st International Conference on Computational Linguistics Dialog. **2**, 53–64 (2015)
12. LeCun, Y., Zhang, X.: Text understanding from scratch. Computer Science Department, arXiv: 1509.01626 (2016)
13. Gordeev, D.: Detecting state of aggression in sentences using CNN. Lect. Notes Comput. Sci. **9811**, 240–245 (2016)
14. Smirnova, O., Shishkov, V.: Choosing the topology of neural networks and their application for classification of short texts. Int. J. Open Inf. Technol. **4**, 8 (2016)
15. Chernobaev, I., Skorynin, S., Surkova, A.: Application of recurrent neural networks in the task of detecting insincere messages in online services. In: System Analysis in Design and Man-agement. Collection of Scientific Papers of the XXIII International Scientific and Practical Conference, pp. 403–412 (2019)
16. Rogachev, A.F.: Fuzzy set modeling of regional food security. In: Popkova, E.G., Ostrovskaya, V.N. (eds.) ISC 2017. AISC, vol. 726, pp. 774–782. Springer, Cham (2019). https://doi.org/10.1007/978-3-319-90835-9_89

Protection of Signals in the Video Stream of a Mobile Robotic Group Agent

Olga Shumskaya[1] ⓘ, Andrey Iskhakov[2(✉)] ⓘ, and Anastasia Iskhakova[2] ⓘ

[1] St. Petersburg Federal Research Center of the Russian Academy of Sciences (SPC RAS),
14-th line of V.I., 39, 199178 Saint-Petersburg, Russia
[2] V. A. Trapeznikov Institute of Control Sciences of Russian Academy of Sciences,
65 Profsoyuznaya street, Moscow 117997, Russia

Abstract. This article presents the results of a study on the current problem of creating new multi-agent robotic complexes with a protected network-centric control system. The main task of the work is to model and create algorithms for the processes of transmitting control signals and concealing them from third-party objects. The list of developments of interest also includes ways to investigate incidents in the implementation of these processes. The proposed approach for masking control signals makes it possible to transmit control signals between robots without revealing them, as well as the fact of their transmission. The paper describes the approach to hiding these signals in MJPEG frames of the video stream received through digital cameras installed on mobile robots. The achievements are based on the use of steganographic methods of data concealment, as well as the solutions proposed by the authors to minimize the consequences of distorting factors. Calculations and experiments have shown resistance to various attacks and high performance in signal transmission in the presence of distorting factors. At the same time, due to selected solutions, absolutely correct built-in data extraction is not a prerequisite for successful and efficient operation and interaction of robots. This approach could be useful for creation of secure mechanisms of data exchange between robotic agents in group systems.

Keywords: Multi-agent robotic system · Robot management · Information security · Steganographic protection of information · Digital watermark · Verification · Control systems

1 Introduction

The increased security risks, such as the ability to intercept information signals, the malicious imposition of instructions to robotics systems, and the lack of availability of critical intelligent devices, make it imperative to assess the use of known solutions to build secure robotics systems and develop new efficient and theoretically reasonable ones.

Today, the achievements of robotics find their application in the implementation of household, medical, transport, military and other tasks of human life. In particular,

P. K. Singh et al. (Eds.): FTNCT 2020, CCIS 1395, pp. 134–143, 2021.
https://doi.org/10.1007/978-981-16-1480-4_12

authors of [1, 2] have written that methods of group application of mobile robots show high efficiency in solving reconnaissance as well as tactical tasks.

When implementing group systems, it becomes a priority to solve the problem of forming secure mechanisms of inter-machine data exchange, when communications between robots are carried out in the uncontrolled territory zone. Robotics is the priority direction, but also differs in especially extreme conditions for the protected data exchange as every day there are more and more specific technologies to which the existing systems of protection cannot always adapt, according to [3].

The purpose of this work is to investigate an approach that allows to implement the masking of different signals in the video stream. Algorithmic provision with the use of digital watermark technology and results of its testing are described in detail in the article. It is possible to notice that by means of the given maintenance conditions for formation of the protected interaction between agents in conditions of impossibility of application of classical methods of cryptographic protection of the information are created.

2   Research Object Description

The subject of the research is the task of network-centric management of a group of mobile robots in the presence of an attacker who performs traffic analysis. The following prerequisites were used as a starting point:

- Performance of a target task is carried out by group of the mobile robots consisting of 2 subgroups - A1 and A2. The Attacker (group B) knows about only one of these subgroups - A1. The fact of presence of subgroup A2 should be hidden.
- The Attacker has full control over the traffic transmitted between the members of group A1. The use of cryptographic methods of information protection is unacceptable.
- The task is to provide the possibility of masking control signals from the participants of group A1 to the participants of group A2 by applying methods of digital steganography to the broadcast video stream generated by the elements of A1.

The general scheme of the target task is shown in Fig. 1. We pay attention that the drawing has private character, however the offered maintenance can be applied in a context of heterogeneous architectures of group management by mobile complexes of robotic systems.

The method proposed in this article is based on the use of video compression format MJPEG. This standard assumes that the video sequences are built on the basis of consecutive static frames of the JPEG format. Compression is performed individually for each frame. In this regard, we can talk about absolute independence in each image. Using MJPEG algorithm for video streaming does not require high performance of the mobile robot processor. This fact is especially important when performing network-centric tasks by Internet devices of things. However, it should be noted that there is a significant load on the wireless data transfer channels, which creates high requirements for network bandwidth.

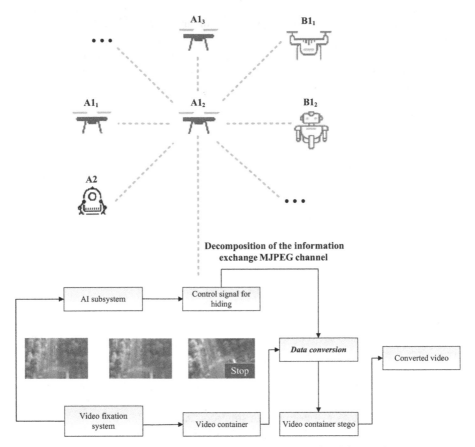

Fig. 1. Communication diagram between elements of multi-agent system

Of course, it should be noted that the use of MJPEG as well as any other codec for compression causes some distortions and artifacts in the video sequence, such as blockages and fields with combined colors, but with proper setting of encoding parameters on the camcorder such errors will be absolutely invisible. The distinctive feature of this compression method is that when analyzing the video stream, the subsystem of intelligent analysis requires with a certain periodicity to obtain the appropriate stop frames for further decoding and recognition of objects.

According to [4, 5] today methods of digital watermarks find their wide application in such specific container, as streaming video, formed by autonomous video devices.

3   Transmitted Control Signals Masking Based on DWT Use

In this work, an MJPEG video stream received from a group of mobile robots is used as a stego container. Resistance to attacks is achieved by embedding in the frequency domain of the image, namely in the discrete Fourier transform coefficients. It should be noted that all similar algorithms have common basic steps: generating DWT from initial information, inserting it into a Fourier image, checking for the presence of DWT in an image with a certain predetermined probability.

As noted in [6], there is also a unified parameter characterizing the power of embedding. In general, such algorithms are widely used in practice. Known work [7], which proposes a circular symmetric integration of the watermark. Fourier image elements form a ring in the middle range. The circular symmetry of the formed DWT provides resistance to a geometric attack of "image rotation". The authors considered two options for insertion: additive and multiplicative. In order to identify the presence / absence of a digital watermark, the authors suggest calculating the ratio between an assumed watermark and an image with a potential watermark. Using the threshold value, you can make a decision about the presence of DWT with a certain probability.

In [8] an additive insertion into discrete Fourier transform coefficients is discussed. Researchers form the DWT as a circle with an optimal insertion radius rather than as a ring, and all elements pick up values in set $\{0, 1\}$. To determine whether a DWT is present, the back-insert algorithm is used.

Known work [9], in which the space for masking secret information is determined only from the upper half of the Fourier image, whose values on the complex plane are placed within a circular region of a pre-defined width. Thus, when embedding and detecting DWT, the algorithm accepts 2 secret keys: the dimensions of the standard image to scale the original image and the limits of the radiuses enclosing the ring area.

To determine the presence of the estimated DWT in the image, it is necessary to calculate the variation of symmetrically placed items in the first and second quadrants within a circular area of a pre-defined width. In the works listed above, steganography is an independent method of ensuring information security. However, many papers suggest using steganography in conjunction with cryptography to achieve the best level of security. The works [10–15] have become quite famous, which indicates the popularity of this direction in the problem of information hiding.

4 Control Signal Masking Algorithm

4.1 Conversion of Signal to DWT

Input: Line that Contains Signal; Radii R_{min}, R_{max}, that Limit the Insertion Ring Width; Dimensions of DWT $M \times M$.

Output: Generated DWT.
For DWT Calculations, Use the Necessary Expression 1.

$$W(x, y) = \begin{cases} 0, R_{\max} < r < R_{\min}, \\ 1, R_{\min} < r < R_{\max} \end{cases}, \tag{1}$$

where R_{min} and R_{max} – boundaries of the ring region, $r = \sqrt{x^2 + y^2}$.

It should be noted, that to the DWT generation algorithm was added condition in case the message length is less than the DWT ring space capacity. In such case, random values are generated from the set $\{-1, 1\}$, which minimizes the possibility of creating a second such DWT.

4.2 DWT Integration Algorithm

Input: DWT ($M \times M$ pixels); image ($N \times N$ pixels); DWT force factor *a*.

Output: Stego-image (M $\times$ N pixels).
The formula to calculate the new amplitude value at the stage of embedding is presented in expression 2.

$$M'(x, y) = M(x, y) + \alpha M(x, y) W(x, y), \tag{2}$$

where $M(x,y)$ is the starting amplitude value of the coefficient of the discrete Fourier transform with coordinates (x,y).

4.3 DWT Detecting Algorithm

Input: Stego-image ($N \times N$ pixels); DWT ($M \times M$ pixels); DWT force factor *a*; threshold *T*.

Output: Decision of the existence of DWT.

1) Take the stego-image, convert to the YCbCr color model, apply discrete Fourier transform (F'' matrix).
2) Take the DWT, convert to a view $-1, 0, 1$ (matrix W).
3) For each item in checked scope:
   if $W(x,y) = 1$, then

   a) add to the total sum *Sum* the corresponding element $F(x,y)$;
   b) increase the positive element counter N_+ by one;
   c) add to the positive elements sum Sum_+ the corresponding $F(x,y)$ element;
   else

   a) add to the total sum *Sum* the corresponding element $F(x,y)$;
   b) increase the negative element counter N_- by one;
   c) add to the negative elements sum Sum_- the corresponding $F(x,y)$ element.

4) Calculate the correlation using the formula:

$$C_n = \left(\frac{\sum_{M' \in M'_+} M'(x, y)}{N_+} - \frac{\sum_{M' \in M'_-} M'(x, y)}{N_-} \right) \cdot \frac{N_+ + N_-}{\sum_{M' \in M'_\pm} \alpha M'(x, y)}, \tag{3}$$

where N_+ is the number of DWT elements that equal 1, N_- is the number of DWT elements that equal-1.9
5) When $C_n > T$, make the decision on the presence of verified DWT in the stego-image, otherwise the stego-image does not contain verified DWT.

Each convolutional layer extracts features from the image and simultaneously acts as a discriminator. It is worth noting that the convolutional layers in the residual blocks have no activation functions. This is necessary for the successful implementation of package normalization. A layer of packet normalization is necessary to reduce internal covariant shift, which increases convergence rate and allows higher learning ratios to be used. It is only after the normalization step that a nonlinear transformation occurs in the ReLU layers where rectified linear neurons are used.

5 Results of Experimental Studies

Photos of park area were taken as containers for transmitting information, as an example of an image of a similar landscape. The size of containers is 256 × 256, and the size of generated DWT is 128 × 128 pixels. The DWT size may match container's size, but in this case introduced distortion will be significant, and stability of the method will significantly decrease. There is no need to generate such a large DWT. In the case of a difference in size between DWT and container, watermark occupies container's central area so that the center of watermark and container coincide. Due to symmetry feature of watermark, hidden transmitted signals are resistant to a number of attacks.

The C_n threshold for all tests is 0.17. Radii: $R_1 = 13$, $R_2 = 41$. DWT force factor $a = 0.3$. The following DWTs are generated from secret lines:

1) 48 characters long (Fig. 2.a);
2) 77 characters long (Fig. 2.b);
3) 300 characters long (Fig. 2.c).

The largest DWT capacity reaches 2,300 characters.

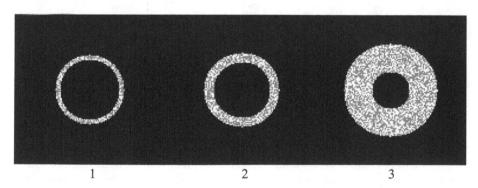

Fig. 2. Created DWT generated from secret line: (1) – 48 characters; (2) – 77 characters, (3) – 150 characters

Below, the experimental results are presented (Table 1): the image before and after embedding, the DWT of secret signal, the applied attack and the results of checking the DWT existence in the container.

Table 1. Table captions should be placed above the tables.

Initial image	DWT	Stego-image	Attack		Checked DWT	C_n	Has a verified DWT been found?
	-				a	0.047	No
	c		-		c	0.4370	Yes
					a	0.0007	No
	b		change of brightness	-40%	b	0.3972	Yes
				-20%		0.3120	
				+20%		0.3483	
				+40%		0.2317	
				-40%		0.3812	
			change of contrast	+40%		0.4281	
	c		turn on	3°	c	0.3690	Yes
				60°		0.0100	No
				180°		0.4917	Yes

As can be seen from the results of computational experiments with implementation of distortion of transmitted images with built-in (masked) control signal, distortion of brightness and/or contrast do not affect further signal recognition. In all cases of image parameter distortion, the value of C_n exceeded the threshold, including 40% dimming, i.e. significant distortion. Experiments were conducted with an "image rotation" attack to check the stability of the transmitted hidden signal. As previously noted, in view of the symmetry feature of watermark, the transmitted signal is resistant to many attacks, however, the image rotation is a significant distortion. The results showed that when the image is rotated by less than 15° or by an angle multiple of 90°, the detection of the control signal is successful. When rotating, for example, by 60°, it has already become impossible to determine the control signal.

As noted earlier, the advantage of the algorithm is the high the DWT capacity, containing more than 2,300 bits of information, while in the works considered in the review, the DWT capacity ranges from 80 [9] to 200 bits [8]. The proposed algorithm does not involve additional transformations, unlike [9], where the hash-function is used, and [10], where the log-polar mapping is used. The method [8] is not resistant to changes of brightness and contrast, and it is also designed for specific medical images (X-ray images, etc.) and the work does not provide parameters that adapt the algorithm for classical images. The algorithm [7] has low resistance to rotation when turning by more than 2°.

A distinctive feature of the presented algorithm is the adaptability of the DWT ring width, which allows reducing not only the degree of made distortions into stego-container, but also the time to form a watermark. In addition, it was decided not to process an entire embedding container, but only a part of it, the dimensions of which are twice the dimensions of the embedded DWT, which allows significantly reducing the time spent on the DFT and the IDFT.

In case of complete loss of image's content with a secret attachment due to certain attacks, methods of hidden transmission of control signals using digital watermarks are not enough. In such cases, additional measures should be applied specifically to protect the integrity of the container itself. From the above results, it can be concluded that the proposed method copes with the presented types of attacks as part of the task of hidden control signals transmission when container's content is partially lost.

6   Conclusion

Application of group approaches and network-centric operating modes in mobile robotics allows to increase speed and quality of executed operations, i.e. to raise efficiency. The main problem associated with the development of a protection system for such a network-centric coalition of mobile robots is the difference of this type of network from the classical means of computer technology and data networks. This problem makes it possible to understand the need to build new models of data exchange between robots in a group in an unfavorable environment with a security threat. Therefore, the creation of approaches to intelligent control of robotic systems should occur in conjunction with the development of methods that ensure the secure information exchange with one or more operators.

The proposed approach has been tested on vulnerabilities both to accidental distortions (unintentional errors, failures and distortions in data transmission) and to deliberate attacks by attackers. The results obtained confirm the stability of the proposed approach. The results of the analysis of the proposed methodological support also demonstrate undoubted advantages over similar solutions of classical steganography. In particular, using the proposed solutions from the receiving agent does not require completely error-free recognition of transmitted data, while in the application of classical algorithms errors in the recognition of even a few bits of information is unacceptable.

Comparative analysis showed that the proposed algorithm, in addition to resistance to natural and intentional attacks, is characterized by a high capacity of transmitted information, reduced time spent on stego-container pre-processing and digital watermark forming.

Formulated in this paper, the approach can be scaled to the formation of a set of techniques and algorithms for secure machine-to-machine data exchange in the environment of info-communications agents of group robotics with network-centric mode of operation.

Acknowledgment. The reported study was partially funded by RFBR, project numbers №19–01-00767, 19–08-00331 (Sects. 4.1 and 4.2).

References

1. Budko, P.A., Vinogradenko, A.M., Litvinkov, A.I.: Reconfiguration of communication channels at management of robotic complexes of the mixed groups. Izvestiya SFedU. Eng. Sci. **2**(187), 266–278 (2017)
2. Sigov, A.S., Nechaev, V.V., Baranyuk, V.V., Smirnova, O.S.: Approaches to forming of common information-control field of mixed robotics groupings. Modern Inform. Technol. IT-Educ. **1**, 146–151 (2016)
3. Zikratov, I.A., Kozlova, E.V., Zikratova, T.V.: The analysis of vulnerabilities of robotic complexes with Swarm intelligence. Sci. Tech. Messenger inf. Technol. Mech. Opt. **5**(87), 149–154 (2013)
4. Panyavaraporn, J., Horkaew, P.: DWT/DCT-based invisible digital watermarking scheme for video stream. In: 2018 10th International Conference on Knowledge and Smart Technology (KST), Chiang Mai, pp. 154–157 (2018). https://doi.org/10.1109/KST.2018.8426150
5. Ponnisathya, S., Ramakrishnan, S., Dhinakaran, S., Ashwanth, P. S., Dhamodharan, P.: CHAOTIC map based video watermarking using DWT and SVD. In: 2017 International Conference on Inventive Communication and Computational Technologies (ICICCT), Coimbatore, pp. 45–49 (2017). https://doi.org/10.1109/ICICCT.2017.7975156
6. Shumskaya, O.O., Budkov, V.: Comparative study of classification methods in digital image analysis. Inform. Comput. Eng. Control **72**(3), 121–134 (2018)
7. Solachidis, V., Pitas, I.: Circularly symmetric watermark embedding in 2-D DFT domain. IEEE Trans. Image Process. **10**, 1741–1753 (2011)
8. Poljicak, A., Mandic, L., Agic, D.: Discrete fourier transform-based watermarking method with an optimal implementation radius. J. Electron. Imaging **20**, 033008–1–033008–8 (2011)
9. Cedillo-Hernandez, M., Garcia-Ugalde, F., Nakano-Miyatake, M., Perez-Meana, H.: Robust watermarking method in DFT domain for effective management of medical imaging. SIViP **9**, 1163–1178 (2015)
10. Ridzon, R., Levicky, D.: Content protection in grayscale and color images based on robust digital watermarking. Telecommun. Syst. **52**, 1617–1631 (2013)
11. Gaata, M.T.: An efficient image watermarking approach based on Fourier transform. Int. J. Comput. Appl. **136**(9), 8–11 (2016)
12. Mandal, J.K., Khamrui, A.: A genetic algorithm based steganography in frequency domain (GASFD). In: International Conference on Communication and Industrial Application, pp. 1–4 (2011)

13. Bhattacharyya, D., Kim, T.-H.: Image data hiding technique using discrete fourier transformation. In: Kim, T.-H., Adeli, H., Robles, R.J., Balitanas, M. (eds.) UCMA 2011. CCIS, vol. 151, pp. 315–323. Springer, Heidelberg (2011). https://doi.org/10.1007/978-3-642-20998-7_39
14. Ronzhin, A.L., Yusupov, R.M.: Multimodal interfaces of autonomous mobile roboticcomplexes. Izvestiya SFedU. Engineering Sciences 1(162), 195–206 (2015)
15. Shumskaya, O.O., Iskhakova, A.O.: Application of digital watermarks in the problem of operating signal hidden transfer in multi-agent robotic system. In: Proceedings of the 2019 International Siberian Conference on Control and Communications (SIBCON) (2019). https://doi.org/10.1109/SIBCON.2019.8729669

Development of a Cyber-Resistant Platform for the Internet of Things Based on Dynamic Control Technology

Sergei Petrenko[1] (ORCID), Alexander Petrenko[2], Krystina A. Makoveichuk[3](✉) (ORCID), and Alexander Olifirov[3] (ORCID)

[1] Saint Petersburg Electrotechnical University "LETI", St. Petersburg, Russia
[2] MIREA - Russian Technological University, Moscow, Russia
aa_petrenkoa@guu.ru
[3] V.I. Vernadsky Crimean Federal University, Yalta, Russia

Abstract. The relevance of the development of a cyber-resistant platform for the Internet of things is explained by the need to ensure the required security and stability of the critical information infrastructure of the Russian Federation, and by the imperfection of the known models, methods, and means of collecting and processing data in IIoT/IoT networks based on wireless technologies. This article presents the main scientific and technical results of solving the mentioned problem based on the author's models and methods of the theory of similarity and dimensions of distributed computing, the domestic wireless protocol Logic InterNode Connection, LINCand the domestic OS FenixOS, intended for the collection and processing of telemetric data. The obtained scientific results allowed us to design a prototype of the domestic platform of the Internet of things with self-healing paths for receiving and transmitting data between smart devices in IIoT/IoT networks and systems in the face of growing security threats.

Keywords: Digital economy · Internet of things platform · IIoT/IoT · Cybersecurity · Cyber resilience · Similarity invariants · Dimensions · Control of similarity invariants · Big Data · Cloud computing · Wireless technologies

1 The Relevance of Research

According to IHS Markit's IoT Trend Watch, the number of connected IoT devices in the world will exceed 51 billion by 2021. First of all, an increase in their number will occur due to the need for remote control of equipment. The commercial and industrial sectors using building automation, industrial automation, and smart lighting are projected to account for about half of all connected devices between 2020 and 2030.

At the same time, the so-called hyper-convergence of modern digital transformation technologies comes to the fore here: the Internet of Things (IIoT/IoT), artificial intelligence (AI), cloud and fog computing (Cloud and Fog Computing) and, of course, the collection and processing of big data (Big Data).

© Springer Nature Singapore Pte Ltd. 2021
P. K. Singh et al. (Eds.): FTNCT 2020, CCIS 1395, pp. 144–154, 2021.
https://doi.org/10.1007/978-981-16-1480-4_13

The number of IIoT/IoT devices and related microelectronic components is currently increasing at a high rate. At the same time, the complexity of IoT platforms - many different finite elements (sensors, sensors, base stations, etc.), as well as the complexity of the behavior of these systems - algorithms, and ways of interaction between them - are also constantly growing. First, this concerns IIoT/IoT platforms for smart (smart) cyber systems: smart energy, smart city, and transport, smart home, etc.

To top it all off, these IIoT/IoT platforms and end devices support a variety of interworking formats, including long-range network formats.

In the aforementioned review, IHS Markit analysts highlight the following key factors and trends that will affect the development of IIoT/IoT soon.

1. Attractive possibilities of the Internet of Things have contributed to the emergence of a large number of duplicate and similar solutions based on wireless technologies Bluetooth, Wi-Fi, 5G, NB-IoT, LoRa, Sigfox, etc. Consolidation of communication and data processing standards is ahead, but in the near future, it will be fragmentation, and competition of IIoT/IoT solutions prevail.
2. A hybrid approach based on on-premises data centers and private clouds is gaining momentum because for enterprises in the digital economy such placement and associated data processing is a clear competitive advantage. More and more digital enterprises are expected to use both on-premises data centers and on-premises cloud services to manage their IT infrastructure.
3. Cellular IIoT IoT gateways for connecting to the Internet are used to organize and perform so-called edge or edge computing. At the same time, the cybersecurity issues of cellular IIoT/IoT gateways will require more attention.
4. The problem of cybersecurity is becoming one of the main problems for the formation and development of well-known IoT platforms: the risks for them will significantly increase. Despite the popularization of blockchain technology, it is not a panacea for building secure and trusted solutions. At the initial stages of IIoT/IoT platforms development, the blockchain will be involved in asset and smart contract management.
5. Most IIoT/IoT platforms are becoming more and more integrated: today there are more than 400 known developers and suppliers of such solutions. However, significant innovations and corresponding results will begin to appear when developers of IIoT/IoT applications master all the rich functionality of big data collection and processing technology.

Thus, the relevance of developing an Internet of Things (IIoT/IoT) platform with the required properties of cybersecurity and cyber resilience is explained by the need to build trusted distributed systems for collecting and processing data from a large number of so-called smart (SMART) devices, and the imperfection of known platforms based on widespread wireless communication technologies and management of SigFox, LoRaWaN, Strizh/Vaviot (XNB/Nb-Fi), NBIoT, etc. [10–12].

For example, the solutions of the Modern Radio Technologies company (www.strij. tech) - Strizh are based on the proprietary LPWAN XNB data transmission technology (formerly Marcato2) - is a modification of the French LPWAN technology SigFox. The mentioned technology is characterized by many significant limitations and has a narrow focus on the application. In particular, the impossibility of functioning without the Internet, low data transmission rate, limited volume of transmitted data, lack of a symmetric return channel, low cryptographic resistance of communication, and data channels. XNB technology is characterized by low energy efficiency and data transfer rate (data packet transmission time is about 6 s) [12].

Waviot solutions (https://waviot.ru/) (withdrawn from Modern Radio Technologies) are based on NB-Fi wireless data transmission technology, which in 2019 received the status of the first national communication standard for the Internet of Things IIoT/IoT. Data transmission technology - Nb-Fi has strong limitations and a narrow focus of the application, for example, a very low data transfer rate, an extremely small amount of useful data and a large amount of overhead data in a packet (overhead), the absence of symmetric return channel for any operation modes and devices, the impossibility building local systems without the Internet, weak crypto-protection of communication and data channels. The mentioned technology is characterized by low energy efficiency and data transfer rate (a packet is transmitted for about 6 s) [12].

Solutions of companies from the Lartech LoRa - Alliance (https://lar.tech/): Smartiko (https://smartiko.ru/), Net868 (https://net868.ru/), ER-telecom (https://iot-ertele com.ru/) and others, which are based on the American LoRaWan technology (Long Range Wide Area Networks). The mentioned technology was developed based on the LoRa modulation method of the Californian company Semtech, USA (https://www.sem tech.com/lora). The technology and related solutions belong to the broadband class, provide high rates of the communication channel budget (up to 168 dB). At the same time, the above-mentioned solutions irrationally use the allocated frequency band, use a large amount of service information in the packet (overhead). For these reasons, the number of end devices is limited. In this regard, the duration of the packet is long, which leads to lower energy efficiency and less frequent data transmission. A full return channel is not possible for stand-alone devices. There are no relay modes, they are characterized by weak noise immunity. LoRa Alliance solutions do not work without Internet access.

Note that in addition to the founders, IBM and Semtech, the LoRa Alliance also includes many well-known electronics manufacturers Cisco, Kerlink, IMST, Microchip Technology, as well as many leading telecom operators Bouygues Telecom, Inmarsat, SingTel, Proximus, Swisscom, etc. According to the LoRa Alliance, LoRaWAN networks are in operation in more than 15 countries around the world and are being tested in about 60 countries, the largest of which are deployed in the USA, the Netherlands, Belgium, France, Switzerland, and Australia, Finland, Italy, Germany, Denmark, and the Czech Republic.

Energomera's solution (https://www.energomera.ru/) is called an automated system for commercial metering of electricity (ASCME) based on ZigBee communication technology. Energomera is the largest manufacturer of electricity meters in Russia. It develops its automated system for commercial metering of electricity and has offices in large cities of Russia and the CIS. The dissemination of the data collection system is limited to the electricity market.

ZigBee communication technology is based on the automatic relay and signal routing, has a small radio signal range, the complexity of signal routing, and network configuration. Due to the peculiarities of the ZigBee protocol implementation, it is not possible to use stand-alone devices.

The solution of the domestic company RiA-Group (https://aura360.ru/) is called Aura360 based on its wireless communication protocol LINC (Logic InterNode Connection) [1–3, 5, 10]. The Aura360 data acquisition system uses all 7 (application) OSI layers and operates on top of the LINC protocol (currently released in version 3), which combines OSI layers 2 to 6. The system can use any available data transmission medium, including Ethernet, RS-485, GSM (GPRS, LTE, NB-IoT, etc.), and even LoRa. However, a narrow-band LPWAN radio channel of unlicensed bands was chosen as the physical environment of the "last mile", which refers to the implementation of the last mile to the so-called UNB systems. Ultra Narrow Band (UNB) has higher bandwidth and maximizes bandwidth efficiency. In the upper license-free range in Russia 868.7–869.2, up to 60 communication channels can be provided, in contrast to LoRaWAN with three channels, 125 kHz wide.

LINC communication technology can work on top of any existing data transmission channels, retaining all their inherent disadvantages, but when used in its pure form, it surpasses the characteristics of existing foreign and based on foreign, Internet of Things communication technologies - LoRaWAN, XNB (Strizh), NB-Fi (Vaviot), ZiNa (Fenix), SigFox, Zig-Bee, etc.

An important advantage is that the LINC v3 protocol has unique characteristics, a high level of cryptographic protection is the most versatile for any industrial and sectoral data transmission applications, and can work in any physical communication medium.

Thus, the advantages of Aura360 include:

- high communication parameters: range up to 15 km point-to-point (25 mW) or up to 100 km (using directional retransmission);
- constant two-way communication (half-duplex) even with stand-alone devices;
- full control of end devices (including autonomous ones);
- efficient use of the frequency range (UNB);
- point-to-point, point-to-multipoint connection;
- implementation of relay and broadcast command modes;
- optimization for devices with low computing resources;
- data transfer rate is not limited (according to transceiver specifications);
- the amount of transmitted data is not limited;
- the amount of data in a package is up to 256 bytes;
- up to 48000 devices per channel of the Base Station, up to 60 channels in the upper 868 MHz band;
- options for working without the Internet and cloud technologies in local systems;
- the ability to work on any platform and component base;
- organization of protection of communication channels based on the TLS 1.3 specification;
- independence from the sanctions policy of foreign states;
- work in a wide range of temperatures: $-60 + 80$ C.

2 Operating Systems for IIoT/IoT Platforms

A number of well-known companies are developing operating systems (OS) for the Internet of Things: Amazon Web Services (Amazon IoT), Arm Holdings with technology partners (OS Mbed), Kontiki (OS Contiki for a microcontroller), Phoenix Link (FenixOS) and etc. Also, most of the diversified large IT companies, including IBM, Microsoft, SAP, Oracle, Apple, Google, and others, conduct similar developments. At the same time, it should be noted the fragmentation and wide variety of system and application software, as well as IIoT computing devices. Let's comment on a number of known solutions.

Amazon Web Services (AWS) is an Internet of Things platform with the OS of the same name. The American company of the same name is developing its own Amazon IoT platform (from end devices to cloud systems): a number of solutions have been developed for the industrial and consumer segments of the Internet of Things. The features of these solutions include "binding" to the Amazon server infrastructure, integration with Amazon Web Services, and support for a limited list of hardware platforms (microcontrollers).

The open source OS-based ARM IoT platform Mbed is being developed by the UK-based ARM Holdings for the respective microcontroller-based devices. The Mbed code is distributed under the Apache 2.0 license. The development of this OS is carried out in the direction of supporting IIoT/IoT communication channels and adding server tools and APIs for integrating the solution platform on the Internet.

Contiki: The Open Source OS for the Internet of Things is a non-commercial open source operating system designed to manage a variety of IIoT/IoT devices with limited resources. The OS got its name in honor of the team of the famous Norwegian explorer-traveler Thor Heyerdahl, in 1947 to prove the hypothesis of the resettlement of the ancestors of the Polynesians from South America to the islands of the eastern part of the Pacific Ocean, which repeated their route on a replica of the 5th century raft. n. e. "Kon-Tiki". The Contiki OS project was initiated by the Swedish Institute of Computer Science (SICS) in 2006 and continues to this day. Contiki OS is written in C and runs on a variety of computing platforms and architectures, ranging from the TI MSP430 (with 2K bytes of RAM and 60K bytes of non-volatile flash memory) and Atmel AVR to earlier architectures. This operating system is relatively small in terms of source code and memory utilization. For example, to run and run Contiki OS with a graphical interface, no more than 30–40 Kbytes of RAM is required, in addition, the amount of memory can be adjusted for the tasks being solved.

Let's dwell on this OS in more detail, for which we list its features.

An event-driven (ED) core of the system that allocates processor time but not memory (designed for hardware without a memory management unit, MMU). For this reason, all processes run in the same address space. A compact scheduler that dispatches events to running processes. Events come in two flavors: asynchronous and synchronous. The former are similar to deferred procedural calls—they are queued by the kernel and passed to processes some time later. The latter initiate immediate scheduling of processes. Control returns back to the initiator process after the target process completes processing the event.

A polling mechanism, which is a high priority event that is triggered between asynchronous events. Typically used by processes that operate on hardware, for example, to check for device status updates. When a poll is scheduled, all processes where it is applied are called in priority order.

Preemptive Multitasking - Implemented as a library and can be linked as needed with applications that require this behavior.

The mechanism of protothreads, threads working with one common stack. It is written in the C programming language without using machine-oriented assembly code and requires only 2 bytes of memory to store states. This made it possible to significantly reduce the complexity of programs developed using the finite state machine paradigm, radically reduce the number of states and transitions, and reduce the amount of code.

A dynamic runtime linker that links, transports, and loads applications and services in the form of ELF object files, which is standard for many operating systems for personal computers and workstations, and is suitable even for WSN nodes.

The CTK (ContikiTool-Kit) providing graphical user interface primitives is designed to be highly modular to allow the same program to run on a wide variety of monitors, from graphical terminals, virtual displays like VNC to text-based (in a terminal window from Telnet).

A lightweight implementation of the uIP TCP/IP stack for communication with the Internet for systems with limited resources. Supports protocols: TCP, IP, ARP, SLIP, ICMP (ping) and Unicast UDP. The number of TCP connections is unlimited. The uIP code takes up several kilobytes in read-only memory and several hundred bytes in main memory. The stack also includes a web server and client, an SMTP client, Telnet and DNS servers, and PPP support is underway.

Contiki VNC-server that provides remote access to the system desktop from almost any OS via the Internet. It is a uVNC port, connects to CTK as a driver.

FenixLink is a domestic IIoT/IoT platform based on the original FenixOS for collecting and processing telemetry data. In this development, the main principles were:

- priority of efficiency in providing basic telematics processes and resources over functionality (not directly related to telematics) and a variety of tasks to be solved;
- limiting the number (variety) of processes;
- simplification of existing processes, including those necessary for solving telematics problems;
- microkernel as a type of operating system kernel;
- threads as a programming model;
- minimizing the need for middleware;
- algorithms for fast transition to hibernation (sleep mode);
- own process control algorithms.

Thus, FenixOS is a microkernel-based operating system as opposed to a monolithic Kernel-based OS. At the same time, the FenixOS core contains only the key components required for telematics systems for the Internet of Things. It uses algorithms to control operating system processes that minimize power consumption and hardware requirements, including algorithms:

- execution of processes;
- prioritizing the order of execution of processes;
- process planning and dispatching;
- allocating resources (available) to a process; and allocating resources between processes.

Note that FenixOS does not implement preemptive multitasking. Here "multitasking" is achieved by switching between processes - cooperative multitasking ("simulating" multitasking and multiprocessing), without "real" parallelization, unlike other known operating systems. The FenixOS kernel is written in the C programming language, which allows precise control of processes at a low level. FenixOS libraries and drivers support various communication standards, including LPWAN. Devices, the microcontroller of which operates on the basis of FenixOS, work with common communication formats, such as LoRa, XBN, NB-Fi, Sigfox, ZigBee, ZiNa, Fenix Link, PLC, LINC, etc. An API has also been developed to work with various applications and devices Internet of Things, IIoT/IoT.

3 "Certification" of Data Reception and Transmission Schemes

Today, the TCP/IP protocol stack is the standard for the interaction of typical digital platforms of the Digital Economy of the Russian Federation. The functions of networking in the stack are performed by the IP protocol (protocol versions v.4 and v.6. The transport layer protocols are UDP, TCP, and the modern SCTP standard [4–7]. As protocols of the lower layer IP can use almost all known standards, most often Ethernet, FrameRelay, ATM, PPP, MPLS, etc. are used as the link-layer protocols.

Due to the special position occupied by the TCP/IP stack, almost all modern application layer protocols are focused on using TCP or UDP as a transport protocol. These include, for example, Email (SMTP and POP), Domain Name System (DNS), WWW - World Wide Web (HTTP), File Transfer (FTP), Electronic Newsletter (NNTP), Microsoft Basic Networking Service (NetBIOS), Interoperability distributed databases (SQL * Net), etc.

A characteristic feature of the current protocol system is, firstly, the tendency to implement the functions of the session layer of the OSI model either by a protocol originally designed as a transport protocol, for example, TCP or SCTP or by an application layer protocol. In some cases, the functions of storing session information are even split between these protocols. Secondly, in the vast majority of cases, the functions of the 6th layer of the OSI model - data presentation - are inextricably integrated with the application layer protocol. This tendency is because, at the stage of development of most application-level protocols, the processing format of the data presentation layer was rigidly fixed. Third, a similar situation is observed with the combination of approximately equal in terms of the volume of a functional load of the physical and channel levels [8–10].

Thus, most often, the network protocol stack through which a message passes consists of four protocols:

- application protocol;
- transport layer protocol (TCP or UDP);
- IP protocol;
- one or more physical and link layer protocols.

Briefly, the essence of the proposed certification is that for the information graph of the data processing model of a network or IIoT/IoT system, a system of relationships between the dimensions of variables and constants is built as follows. Each operator of the model, containing computational operations and/or an assignment operator and having a homogeneous form concerning its arguments, is represented as a sum of functionals φ:

$$f_u(x_1, x_2, ..., x_n) = 0, \ u = 1, 2, \ldots, r, \quad \text{where} \tag{1}$$

$$f_u(x_1, x_2, ..., x_n) = \sum_{s=1}^{q} \varphi_{us}(x_1, x_2, ..., x_n) \text{and} \tag{2}$$

$$\varphi_{us}(x_1, x_2, ..., x_n) = \prod_{j=1}^{n} x_j^{\alpha_{jus}}. \tag{3}$$

In this case, the provisions of the theory of dimensions and similarity [10] make it possible to create a system of requirements for the dimensions of the quantities x_j, arising from the following considerations (the record $[X]$ means "the dimension of the quantity X"):

$$[\varphi_{us}(x_1, x_2, ..., x_n)] = [\varphi_{uq}(x_1, x_2, ..., x_n)], \tag{4}$$

$$\left[\prod_{j=1}^{n} x_j^{\alpha_{jus}}\right] = \left[\prod_{j=1}^{n} x_j^{\alpha_{juq}}\right], \tag{5}$$

$$\prod_{j=1}^{n} [x_j]^{\alpha_{jus}} = \prod_{j=1}^{n} [x_j]^{\alpha_{juq}}, \tag{6}$$

$$\prod_{j=1}^{n} [x_j]^{\alpha_{jus} - \alpha_{juq}} = 1, \tag{7}$$

and after taking the logarithm

$$\sum_{j=1}^{n} (\alpha_{jus} - \alpha_{juq}) \cdot \ln[x_j] = 0, \tag{8}$$

$$u = 1, 2, \ldots, r \,;\, s = 1, 2, \ldots, (q-1).$$

A necessary criterion for the semantic correctness of the data processing model of a network or IIoT/IoT system is the existence of a solution for system (8) in which none of the variables ($ln\ [x_j]$) is zero. Here, to solve this question, one can use trivial equivalent transformations of the equations of the system written in matrix form (Fig. 1).

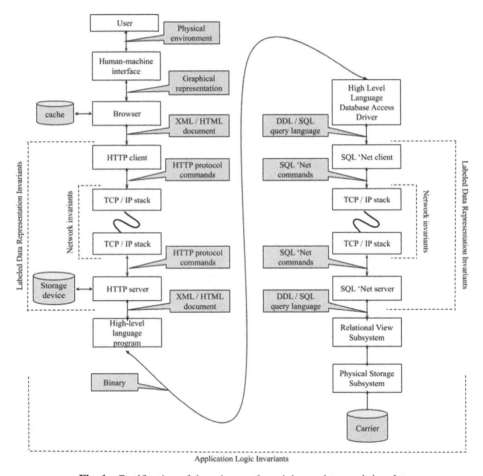

Fig. 1. Certification of the scheme of receiving and transmitting data

Thus, to construct an initial set of Eqs. (2) for each data processing model of a network or IIoT/IoT system, the following methodology is proposed:

– arbitrarily take a sample of realizations of the process described by the model;
– check the representativeness of the sample by covering all vertices of the control graph of the model;

- we will carry out the reduction of the control graph of the model to select computational operators from operators for checking conditions and organizing cycles;
- select from the sample all unique operators that meet the restrictions on the type of functional connection described above;
- select the variables and constants involved in the operators, assuming:
- the elements inside the array are of equal size,
- numerical constants in pairs of different sizes (determination of their belonging to certain classes will occur automatically at the stage of matching the dimension matrix)

Transitions of the control graph associated with the calculation of complex functional dependencies and corresponding to the subprograms call operators to complement system (2) with sets of formal parameter assignment operations. Such additional constraints will play a connecting role between the values of the main body of the algorithm and the values of subprograms. This step must be performed in the case of building a unified model of the functioning of a network or IIoT/IoT system.

4 Conclusions

The proposed certification of schemes for receiving and transmitting data in IIoT/IoT networks and systems based on the classical three-tier architecture and control systems for invariants and dimensions has many advantages. These include, first of all, high selectivity and, accordingly, the highest quality of detection of abnormal functioning and unauthorized actions. Developed by the principles of the systems approach, such a system provides the closest approximation of the required criterion of semantic correctness with the actual concept of semantic correctness.

The construction of an end-to-end system for identifying data processed in a computer system at various levels of the scheme for receiving and transmitting data in IIoT/IoT networks and systems can provide a high-quality and reliable system for backtracking errors or unauthorized influences. In this case, it becomes possible to unambiguously indicate the level of its initial impact and the object that was the point of application of the impact.

A single space of variables, or mapping schemes between variables of different levels, can make it possible to unambiguously determine the minimum set of data potentially damaged as a result of a security incident. Moreover, when using certain combinations of controlled invariants, it is possible to recover damaged data in real-time with a predetermined correcting capacity of the system.

The goal of finding the optimal set of similarity and dimension invariants for controlled schemes of receiving and transmitting data in IIoT/IoT networks and systems can be to maximize the correcting ability of similarity and dimension invariants. The value that is the initial optimization parameter can be either the amount of additionally transmitted information or the probability of successful self-recovery of data in the face of growing security threats.

Acknowledgement. This work was supported by the RFBR grant (No. 18–47-160011 p_a).

References

1. Barabanov, A.V., Markov, A.S., Tsirlov, V.L.: Methodological framework for analysis and synthesis of a set of secure software development controls. J. Theoret. Appl. Inf. Technol. **88**(1), 77–88 (2016)
2. Biryukov, D.N., Lomako, A.G. Approach to Building a Cyber Threat Prevention System. Problems of Information Security. Computer systems, Publishing house of Polytechnic University, vol. 2, pp. 13–19, St. Petersburg, Russia (2013)
3. Biryukov, D.N.: Cognitive-functional memory specification for simulation of purposeful behavior of cyber systems. Proc. SPIIRAS **3**(40), 55–76 (2015)
4. Biryukov, D.N., Lomako, A.G., Rostovtsev, Yu.G.: The appearance of anticipatory systems to prevent the risks of cyber threat realization. Proc. SPIIRAS **2**(39), 5–25, (2015). https://doi.org/10.15622/sp.39.1
5. Biryukov, D.N., Glukhov, A.P., Pilkevich, S.V., Sabirov, T. R.: Approach to the processing of knowledge in the memory of an intellectual system. Nat. Techn. Sci. (11), 455–466 (2015)
6. Biryukov, D.N., Rostovtsev, Y.G.: Approach to constructing a consistent theory of synthesis of scenarios of anticipatory behavior in a conflict. Proc. SPIIRAS. **1**(38), 94–111 (2015). https://doi.org/10.15622/sp.38.6
7. Vugrin, E.D., Turgeon, J.: Advancing cyber resilience analysis with performance-based metrics from infrastructure assessment. In: Cyber Behavior: Concepts, Methodologies, Tools, and Applications, Hershey, PA, pp. 2033-2055. IGI Global (2014)
8. Vugrin, E.D., Turgeon, J.: Advancing cyber resilience analysis with performance-based metrics from infrastructure assessment. In: Cyber Behavior: Concepts, Methodologies, Tools, and Applications, Hershey, PA, pp. 2033–2055. IGI Global (2014). https://doi.org/10.4018/jsse.2013010105
9. Florin, M.V., Linkov, I. (eds.): IRGC Resource Guide on Resilience. Lausanne: EPFL International Risk Governance Council (IRGC) (2016). https://doi.org/10.5075/epfl-irgc-262527
10. Sergei, P.: Cyber Resilience, ISBN: 978–87–7022–11–60 (Hardback) and 877–022–11–62 (Ebook) © 2019 River Publishers, River Publishers Series in Security and Digital Forensics, 1st ed. 2019, 492 p. 207 illus.
11. Petrenko, A.S., Petrenko, S.A., Makoveichuk, K.A., Chetyrbok, P.V.: Protection model of PCS of subway from attacks type «Wanna Cry», «Petya» and «Bad Rabbit. In: IoT, 2018 IEEE Conference of Russian Young Researchers in Electrical and Electronic Engineering (EIConRus), Moscow, Russia, pp. 945–949. IEEE (2018). https://doi.org/10.1109/EIConRus.2018.8317245
12. Petrenko, A.S., Petrenko, S.A., Makoveichuk, K.A., Chetyrbok, P.V.: The IIoT/IoT device control model based on narrow-band IoT (NB-IoT). In: 2018 IEEE Conference of Russian Young Researchers in Electrical and Electronic Engineering (EIConRus), Moscow, Russia, pp. 950–953 IEEE (2018). https://doi.org/10.1109/EIConRus.2018.8317246

An Efficient Authentication Scheme for Mobile Cloud Computing Using a Key Server

Sunil Mankotia$^{(\boxtimes)}$ (iD) and Manu Sood (iD)

Department of Computer Science, Himachal Pradesh University, Shimla, India

Abstract. In today's world, mobile devices and smartphones are used heavily and have become one of the essential requisites of everyday life. The development of several applications feasible for those devices has revealed that there is a huge demand for applications of mobile. A technology which aroused in the IT sector provides an opportunity to solve those issues, namely mobile computing and cloud computing. The modern mobile architecture integrates cloud computing and mobile technology to produce Mobile Cloud Computing (MCC). Processing, data storage, and computation accompanied by the applications are moved off the mobile device to be a robust centralized platform of computing that resides in the cloud. The significant risk of mobile cloud computing is securing remote applications and data from illegal access. There is a possibility of unauthorized access, which is accessed by third parties. Therefore the issue of security in mobile cloud computing becomes one of the major research areas. It is necessary to implement strict authentication controls in MCC. The proposed research work is an attempt for secure authentication in a mobile cloud by using a key server and AES-256 algorithm for cryptographic purposes.

Keywords: Smartphone · Authentication · Mobile cloud computing · AES-256

1 Introduction

The modern mobile architecture integrates cloud computing and mobile technology to produce Mobile Cloud Computing (MCC) [1]. Processing, data storage, and computation accompanied by the applications are moved off the mobile device to be a robust centralized platform of computing that resides in the cloud. The mobile cloud computing came into existence after the cloud computing concept. It has been enhancing the attention of people in business as a lucrative field that decreases the development and running costs of mobile users and mobile applications [2]. The capability to assess applications and data from anywhere and at any time with the reduced price is the essential advantage of mobile cloud computing. The main security problem on mobile cloud computing is securing remote applications and data from illegal access [3]. There is a possibility of unauthorized access, which is accessed by third party users, known as hackers. Therefore the issue of security in mobile cloud computing becomes one of the major research areas. Smartphones are getting smarter and are offering different applications and services over a wireless network to bring the world in front of the owner of the mobile phone

© Springer Nature Singapore Pte Ltd. 2021
P. K. Singh et al. (Eds.): FTNCT 2020, CCIS 1395, pp. 155–167, 2021.
https://doi.org/10.1007/978-981-16-1480-4_14

[4]. Mobile computing devices and smartphones are adopted worldwide. The developing familiarity of smartphones has allowed users to carry out their day to day tasks using these devices [5]. According to a study conducted by eMarketer, in India 73.9 million people were using mobile or smartphones for making payments until the end of the year 2018. The global market will achieve a new landmark in 2020 with over one billion people are expected to make payments using mobile devices [6]. Therefore it is essential to offer services of security, which includes integrity, confidentiality, and authentication between servers of financial institutions and mobile devices used by the customers, as their communication is through unprotected networks [7]. Moreover, privacy and security is a significant problem while storing sensitive information on the cloud. In case information is confidential and required to be secured, it would need some protection process.

This paper concentrates on the problem of secure authentication in the mobile cloud and proposes an efficient and reliable authentication scheme for mobile cloud computing. The proposed mechanism aims to encrypt all the credentials needed for accessing the cloud server before sending out to the cloud using the AES-256 algorithm. A Key Server is deployed in the cloud to generate a random key for encryption and decryption purposes. Every time a user wants to log in to the cloud, a session key is generated by the Key Server and forwarded to the cloud server and the user's mobile device. The credentials at the user end are encrypted using the same key and sent to the cloud server for authentication. At the server end, the encrypted parameters are decrypted using the same key, and values are matched with the database records. Depending upon the result, access is granted or denied to the user.

1.1 Objectives

Thus, the objectives for this work are described as follows:

1. To achieve High Secure Authentication (of users) in Mobile Cloud Computing.
2. To reduce the encryption time, decryption time and key generation time of transaction parameters than existing algorithms.

Hence, the main contribution of this paper is:

- It proposes an efficient and secure scheme for authentication of users in a mobile cloud using a key server.

2 Related Work

This section reviews recent research suggestions and approaches in different security issues of cloud computing. Information authentication in a mobile cloud over SaaS and PaaS layers has been provided by [8]. Authentication, session management with high security, logging of weblets to make a more secure framework are some of the elements which are closely linked with the security framework of mobile computing [9]. The unified cloud authenticator for mobile cloud computing environment is suggested for authentication [10]. Authentication of the user has been considered as very important to verify the originator of the file successfully. SEcret Key (SEK) to the user of the mobile is responsible for generating the authentication code message for the mobile client. In addition to these, the Trusted COprocessor (TCO) has created the incremental authentication code, and it also tends to send the code directly to the mobile client [11]. Some schemes have been developed to ensure secure authentication, such as cloud management using the HGAPSO algorithm [12]. Moreover, a secure authentication scheme with user anonymity in MCC [13] uses three entities Mobile User (MU), Foreign Agent (FA), and Home Agent (HA) for communication in three phases. An efficient and provably secure anonymous two-factor user authentication protocol for the mobile cloud computing environment not only provides mutual authentication between mobile devices and cloud computing but also fulfils the known security evaluation criteria. Also, Elliptic Curve Cryptography is used to reduce the computing cost for mobile devices [14]. An authentication scheme to provide novel security to the mobile cloud services against password attack in mobile cloud environment verifies the user and service provider without transmitting the password using the Zero-knowledge proof-based authentication protocol [15]. Knowledge-based, possession-based, and biometric-based approaches of user authentication are reviewed and assessment of the various authentication approaches have been done for a secure authentication process in cloud computing [16]. Suitable cryptography and secure authentication system for cloud computing include auto encryption and KEYs changing process in the cloud end. The procedure ensures extra security for data/files as well as prevents hackers from getting original files/data [17]. A Dual-Factor Authentication Protocol for MCC devices (D-FAP) aims at increasing authentication security by using multi-factors offloads computation to the cloud to reduce battery consumption results in mitigating various outsider and insider attacks [18]. An improved authentication and key agreement scheme for IoT-based cloud computing environment using automated security verification (ProVerif), BAN-logic verification, and informal security analysis is performed which proves that it is effective in resisting all kinds of known attacks [19].

In summary, most of the present 1approaches are using more than one cryptographic technique to secure data on the cloud, which is time-consuming and has specific other issues. Third-party is also involved in some schemes, which increases the chances of data leakage. But his type of security does not satisfy the current needs due to low-efficiency levels and some unanswered problems. The proposed scheme is an attempt to provide a higher level of protection in the Mobile Cloud.

3 Proposed Research Methodology

Cloud computing could deliver infrastructure, platform, and software as services that are made available to consumers. In industry level, these services are referred to as Infrastructure-as-a-Service (IaaS), Platform-as-a-Service (PaaS), and Software-as-a-Service (SaaS) accordingly. Many computing service providers such as Google, Microsoft, Yahoo, and IBM are deploying data centres in diverse locations around the world aimed to deliver cloud computing services [20]. Cloud computing has been widely recognized as the next-generation computing infrastructure. Cloud computing allows some advantages by enabling users to use the infrastructure, platforms, and software provided by cloud providers at a low cost. Additionally, cloud computing allows users to utilize resources in an on-demand fashion elastically. As a result, mobile applications could be rapidly provisioned and released with the least management efforts or service provider's interactions. With the rapid increase in the number mobile apps and the support of cloud computing for a variety of services for mobile users, mobile computing is introduced as an integration of cloud computing into the mobile environment. Mobile cloud computing evolves new types of services and facilitates mobile users to take full advantage of cloud computing. As cloud computing is achieving increased popularity, several concerns are being expressed about the security issues introduced in this cloud computing [21].

4 Proposed Authentication

The user authentication is the process where it is verified whether the log in process is executed by the correct user or not because by knowing the username and password, it is easy for a hacker to get access to the process without the knowledge of the user. The AES algorithm is deployed for encryption of parameters using the key provided by the proposed Key Server. In user authentication, the users log in to the cloud by using their data such as username and password. The username and password created as per the credentials entered to log in to the cloud server.

4.1 Proposed Architecture for Cloud and Key Server

Cloud Server and Key Server are implemented with the help of Java programming Language and deployed in the same cloud. The cloud server is used to store data and provide resources/services to the users. The login credentials of the users are also stored in a database of the cloud server based on which access is granted or denied. The key server is used to generate a random key of 256 bits and forward it to the cloud server and user's mobile phone, which is used for cryptographic purposes. This key is generated every time a user wants access to the cloud server.

4.2 AES-256 Encryption

AES is the most frequently used algorithm preferred for encryption. It is based on several substitutions, permutations, and linear transformations, and each is executed on the data blocks of 128 bits or 16 bytes. AES algorithm is highly preferred because no attack exists against the AES algorithm.

The AES Algorithm encrypts a 128-bit plaintext into a 128-bit ciphertext using a cipher key K of either 128,192 or 256 bits. The different key lengths employed for AES are referred to as AES-128, AES-192, and AES-256. The algorithm operates on bytes, and the block size for the input, output and key are represented by 32-bit words, i.e., 4 bytes [22]. The number of cryptographic rounds Nr depends on the actual key length used, as indicated in Table 1 for AES-128, AES-192, and AES-256.

Table 1. Input and Output Block size, Key lengths, and the number of cryptographic rounds N_r for AES encryption [22].

AES algorithm	Input/Output length Nb	Key length Nk	Number of rounds Nr
AES-128	4 Words	4 Words	10 rounds
AES-192	4 Words	6 Words	12 rounds
AES-256	4 Words	8 Words	14 rounds

Each round consists of four byte-oriented cryptographic transformations:

1. Byte Substitution
2. Shifting Rows
3. Mixing Data within a column
4. Addition of Round Key

AES Key Management. As is the case for DES, the AES is a symmetric block cipher cryptosystem that requires the secure distribution of the secret key between the sender and recipient. Table 2 indicates the length of the public key for the three AES key lengths. The entries also show the advantage of using a key exchange scheme based AES instead of Elliptic Curve Cryptography (ECC) and the RSA algorithm for the same level of security [22].

Table 2. Required RSA and Elliptic Curve Cryptography (ECC) key lengths for encryption of AES secret keys with equivalent security [22].

AES algorithm	AES key length	RSA key length	ECC key length
AES-128	128 bits	3072 bits	283 bits
AES-192	192 bits	7680 bits	409 bits
AES-256	256 bits	15360 bits	571 bits

Hence the AES algorithm remains the preferred encryption standard for government sectors, banks, and places where high-security systems are required around the world [23]. The AES also is known as Rijndael, is used for the security purpose of the stored information. AES is a systematic cipher that has been analyzed and used widely in various fields of data security. The symmetric key algorithm, AES, is used with a key length of 256 bits for providing protection.

4.3 Proposed Algorithms

In this section, the description of the proposed algorithms is presented. Two main algorithms support the security and authentication methods, which include user registration and user authentication algorithms. The detailed mechanism of the algorithms is explained below.

User Registration Algorithm. The user registration algorithm is designed to register the user who intends to use the proposed mobile wallet application "Frequent Region." This algorithm is for new users, i.e., who wants to register themselves. The user has to select a unique User ID uid and password pwd as per the rules mentioned in the user interface of the application. After this, the user has to fill up the registration form as per the specified fields. The output of this algorithm is the successful registration of new users, and their details are saved in the database of the cloud server using the AES256 encryption scheme. Existing users are directed to the user authentication process of the application.

Algorithm 1. User Registration

```
1. procedure: REGISTRATION_ACTIVITY
   Input: uid, pwd, mobnum, emailID, address
   Output: TRUE if REGISTRATION SUCCESSFUL, else
   FALSE
2.     if (new_user) then
3.        define uid,
4.           if (uid is unique)/* Compare uid with
   the table existing users in cloud server*/
5.              choose pwd /* pwd should consist of
   allowed parameters only*/
6.              else
7.              goto step 3
8.              end if
9.    fill registration details and submit
10.   Output TRUE, REGISTRATION SUCCESSFUL, save
   registration details in cloud server  /*
   AES256 is used for encryption of details */
11.     else
12.     Output FALSE
13.     Execute USER_AUTHENTICATION  /*Algorithm2*/
14. end if
```

User Authentication Algorithm. This algorithm is designed to accomplish the check the authenticity of the user trying to signing in. The inputs of this algorithm are uid and pwd selected by the user in the previous phase. The main aim of this algorithm is to allow access to the genuine user and to prevent the credentials of the user during transmission of the data to the cloud side. Session key k is generated by the Key Server and is simultaneously forwarded to the cloud server and to the user. Encryption of the login credentials is done with the key k, using Enc1() method at the user end, and decryption of the same is done at the cloud end using Dec1() method. Finally, the parameters obtained from the decryption are matched with the database, and the decision is taken accordingly.

Algorithm 2. User Authentication

```
1. procedure: USER_AUTHENTICATION
2. Input: uid, pwd
3. Output: TRUE if uid, pwd is authenticated;
   else FALSE.
4. Request sent to cloud server, which forwards
   the same to the key server for key generation.
5. The key server generates a random key k, and
   forwards it to cloud server and user's regis-
   tered mobile
6. Enc1() at user end using AES256 and key k to
   obtain ciphertext
7. The ciphertext is forwarded to cloud server
8. Dec1() at cloud end using AES256 with the same
   key k to get the plaintext
9. if (parameters matches)
10. login granted
11. else
12. Display error message "username or password
    is incorrect"
13. end if
```

4.4 Experimental Setup for Proposed Authentication Method

The experimentation and evaluation of the proposed design are validated using the Java platform. Java is one of the most widely accepted programming languages in use, particularly for client-server web applications with a reported nine million developers. Java could decrease the costs, impel innovation, and advance application services as the programming language of option for IoT (Internet of Things), enterprise architecture, and cloud computing. Android-based Mobile Payment Application is developed, and Cloud Server is implemented through Java. A Key Server is deployed in the same cloud for generation of a random key for the encryption purpose. Every time a user is provided with a unique session key for starting a session. A random key generation method is deployed for Key Server. AES algorithm with 256 bits of key length is used for encryption and decryption purposes. The exchange of information between these three entities is done through socket communication.

5   Results and Discussions

The proposed research method is evaluated in the Java platform, and the outputs are obtained. The present section represents the experimental results based on specific parameters and the comparisons with existing schemes.

5.1   Parameters Selected for Evaluation

There are specific performances to be evaluated to conclude the efficiency of the proposed authentication method. They are given by as follows.

Key Generation Time. Key generation time is the minimum amount of time required by proposed Key Server to generate a random key of size 256 bits in order to encrypt and decrypt the user credentials such as username and password. Every time the user login from his mobile phone, a unique key is generated by the Key Server. Simultaneously this unique key is sent to the cloud server and user's phone to perform the encryption and decryption.

Encryption Time. Encryption time is defined as the time taken to implement the encryption process. It is the total time taken to perform all the steps mentioned in the AES 256 encryption scheme. The operations involved in the AES-256 encryption scheme, i.e., the addition of round key, byte substitution, shift row, mix columns, etc. are completed during this time, and finally, the plaintext is converted to ciphertext.

Decryption Time. Decryption time is defined as the amount of time required for retrieving the original information from the encrypted parameters. It is the reverse process of encryption. In this process, the plaintext is obtained from the encrypted data (ciphertext).

Total Time Taken for Authentication. The total time taken to authenticate the users is the sum of key generation time, encryption time and decryption time. It is the total time taken to perform all the steps mentioned in the authentication processes.

5.2   Results with Comparison

Key Generation Time. Key generation time is the minimum amount of time required by the proposed Key Server to generate a random key of size 256 bits and to send it to the Cloud Server and to the user's mobile phone, in order to encrypt the user credentials such as username, password, etc. The key generation time for the existing scheme and the proposed scheme is given below in Table 3.

Table 3. Key Generation Time for existing and proposed schemes.

Key Generation Time (in ms)	
Existing algorithm	Proposed algorithm
6.5	4.2

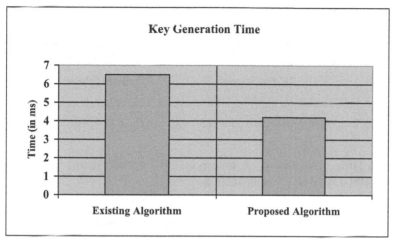

Fig. 1. Comparison of key generation time of the Existing and Proposed Schemes.

Figure 1 shows that the key generation time for the existing scheme is 6.5 ms, and that of the proposed scheme is reduced to 4.2 ms. It is an improvement of approximately 35% over the key generation time of the existing scheme proposed in [24]. There is a significant improvement over the existing scheme.

Encryption Time. The encryption time for the existing scheme and the proposed scheme is compared, and the values obtained are produced in Table 4 given below.

Table 4. Encryption time for the existing and proposed scheme.

Encryption Time (in ms)	
Existing scheme	Proposed scheme
10.2	8.2

The encryption time required for the existing scheme is 10.2 ms. The encryption time required for the proposed scheme is reduced to 8.2 ms. It shows that there is an improvement of approximately 20% in the encryption time of proposed model in comparison to the existing model. The comparison of the result obtained in the form of a graph is shown below in Fig. 2.

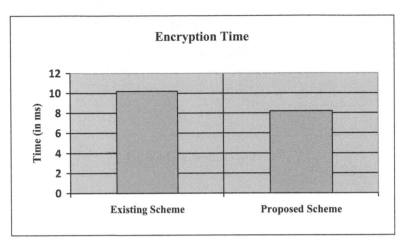

Fig. 2. Comparison of encryption time of Existing and Proposed Schemes.

Decryption Time. The decryption time required for the existing method and the proposed method is given below in Table 5.

Table 5. Decryption time for the existing and proposed scheme.

Decryption Time (in ms)	
Existing scheme	Proposed scheme
11.5	8.8

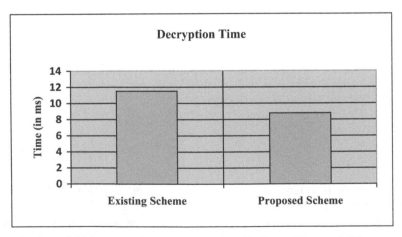

Fig. 3. Comparison of decryption time of the Existing and Proposed Schemes.

The decryption time for the existing method and the proposed method is compared, and the resultant graph is shown in Fig. 3. The decryption time of our model has been measured to be 8.8 ms in comparison to 11.5 ms of existing scheme. This shows an improvement of approximately 24%.

From the Figs. 1, 2 and 3 given above, it is evident that the key generation time, encryption time and decryption time required for the proposed method are significantly less when compared to the existing method and hence the process of the authentication is achieved in a reduced time interval and with an improved level of security. Thus, the superiority of the proposed research method is proved experimentally.

Total Time Taken for Authentication

The total time required by the existing method for the complete cryptographic process along with the proposed method is given below in Table 6. It is absolutely clear from this data that the method proposed in this research work has gained a significant upper hand as far as the time taken for the complete cryptographic process is concerned.

Table 6. Total Time taken for Authentication process by the existing and proposed scheme.

Total Time Taken(in ms)		
Parameters	Existing Scheme	Proposed Scheme
Key generation time	6.5	4.2
Encryption time	10.2	8.2
Decryption time	11.5	8.8
Total time taken	**28.2**	**21.2**

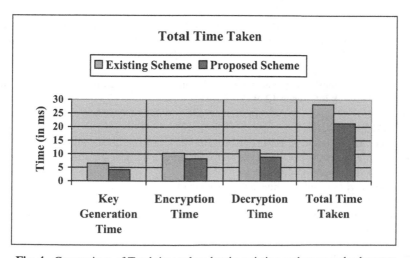

Fig. 4. Comparison of Total time taken by the existing and proposed schemes.

The data shows that there is an overall improvement of approximately 25% in the total time taken by the method proposed. This can be depicted in the form of a graph as shown in Fig. 4.

6 Conclusion and Future Scope

The present paper discussed various problems related to security in cloud computing, such as privacy, confidentiality, and integrity, and proposed a strategy for secure authentication. In Mobile Cloud Computing, data is stored in the public cloud, and everyone shares resources; therefore, security is always at risk. The proposed authentication scheme can be deployed in the public cloud environment to ensure a high level of protection. Moreover, the AES-256 algorithm is used with key management using a random key generator system and a well-developed architecture. This model can be deployed in various cloud computing platforms to get a more efficient way of authentication of users in Mobile Cloud. The security of user's data and time consumption are the significant factors of the present research, which makes it useful in real-time execution environment.The proposed scheme can be extended with the incorporation of Biometric based recognition techniques. Improvement in AES based encryption in the key generation using various Machine learning algorithms like Cuckoo Search Algorithm, Genetic Algorithm, etc., can be used to further optimize the evaluation of these algorithms.

References

1. Meshach, W.T.: Secured and efficient authentication scheme for mobile cloud. Int. J. Innovat. Eng. Technol. (IJIET) **2**(1), 1058–23169 (2013)
2. Cheung, L., Newport, C.: Provably secure ciphertext policy-ABE. In: Proceedings of the 14th ACM conference on Computer and Communications Security 2007, pp. 456–465 (2007)
3. Li, X.: Cloud computing: introduction, application and security from industry perspectives. Int. J. Comput. Sci. Network Secur. **11**(5), 224–228 (2012)
4. Chowdhury, R., De, D.: Secure Money Transaction in NFC Enabled Mobile Wallet Using Session Based Alternative Cryptographic Techniques. In: Chaki, N., Cortesi, A. (eds.) CISIM 2011. CCIS, vol. 245, pp. 314–323. Springer, Heidelberg (2011). https://doi.org/10.1007/978-3-642-27245-5_37
5. Yuksel, Z.: A comprehensive analysis of android security and proposed solutions. Int. J. Comput. Network Inf. Secur. **12**, 9–20 (2014)
6. eMarketer.   https://www.emarketer.com/content/global-mobile-payment-users-2019. Accessed 28 Oct 2020
7. Albasheer, M.O., Bashier, E.B.M.: Enhanced model for PKI certificate validation in the mobile banking. In: International Conference on Computing, Electrical and Electronic Engineering (ICCEEE) 2013, pp. 470–476 (2013)
8. Guha, V.: Review of information authentication in mobile cloud over SaaS and PaaS layers. Int. J. Adv. Comput. Res. 31 (2013)
9. Malik, S.: Privacy and security in mobile cloud computing: review. Int. J. Comput. Appl. **80**(11) (2013)
10. Donald, A.C.: A unified cloud authenticator for mobile cloud computing environment. Int. J. Comput. Appl. (2014)

11. Tayade, D.: Mobile cloud computing: issues, security, advantages, trends. Int. J. Comput. Sci. Inf. Technol. **5**(5), 6635–6639 (2014)
12. Selvarani, P., Suresh, A., Malarvizhi, N.: Secure and optimal authentication framework for cloud management using HGAPSO algorithm. Clust. Comput. **22**(2), 4007–4016 (2018). https://doi.org/10.1007/s10586-018-2609-x
13. Madhusudhan, R., Suvidha, K.S.: An enhanced secure authentication scheme with user anonymity in mobile cloud computing. In: International Conference on Public Key Infrastructure and its Applications (PKIA) 2017, Bangalore, pp. 17–22 (2017)
14. Jiaqing, M.: An efficient and provably secure anonymous user authentication and key agreement for mobile cloud computing. Wirel. Commun. Mob. Comput. 1–12 (2019)
15. Munivel, E.: New authentication scheme to secure against the phishing attack in the mobile cloud computing. Secur. Commun. Networks 1–11 (2019)
16. Sudha, S.: A survey on different authentication schemes in cloud computing environment. Int. J. Manage. IT Eng. **9**(1), 359–375 (2019)
17. Islam, S.J., Chaudhury, Z.H., Islam, S.: A simple and secured cryptography system of cloud computing. In: IEEE Canadian Conference of Electrical Computer Engineering (CCECE) (2019)
18. Abuarqoub, A.: D-FAP: dual-factor authentication protocol for mobile cloud connected devices. J. Sen. Actuator Networks 1–23 (2019)
19. Yicheng Yu, L.H.. A secure authentication and key agreement scheme for IoT-based cloud computing environment. Symmetry 1–16 (2020)
20. Beloglazov, A.: Energy-aware resource allocation heuristics for efficient management of data centers for cloud computing. Futur. Gener. Comput. Syst. **28**(5), 755–768 (2012)
21. Zissis, D.: Addressing cloud computing security issues. Futur. Gener. Comput. Syst. **28**(3), 583–592 (2012)
22. NIST: Data Encryption Standard (AES). Technical Report FIPS PUB 197. National Institute of Standards and Technology, Washington DC (2001)
23. Pancholi, V.R.: Enhancement of cloud computing security with secure data storage using AES. Int. J. Innov. Res. Sci. Technol. **2**(9) (2016)

Modelling Smart City Cyber-Physical Water Supply Systems: Vulnerabilities, Threats and Risks

Nikolai Fomin$^{(\boxtimes)}$ and Roman Meshcheryakov

V. A. Trapeznikov Institute of Control Sciences of Russian Academy of Sciences, Moscow 117997, Russia

Abstract. The article presents an approach to modeling the cyber-physical water supply system of a smart city. The shortcomings of control models are considered, and the list of vulnerabilities of the cyber-physical water supply system of a smart city based on scenario modeling is supplemented. The features of modeling the cyber-physical water supply system of a smart city were formed by a comprehensive threat analysis. The proposed approach makes it possible to generalize vulnerabilities, threats and create requirements for modeling scenarios of violation of the management of cyber-physical water supply systems in order to reduce potential risks. Based on a multi-criteria assessment, the optimal model for control the cyber-physical water supply system of a modern city was determined - a Digital water utility with a centralized data exchange system based on the state information system for water resources management. The results of the study were practically used in one of the largest water supply companies in Russia - the city of Saint Petersburg.

Keywords: Cyber-physical systems · Modeling of control systems · Smart city · Water supply systems · Modernization of control models · Cyber-physical water supply system of a smart city

1 Introduction

In recent years, the threat to critical water infrastructure has increased, as evidenced by the growing number of reported attacks on these systems. Preventive security mechanisms are often insufficient to detect and neutralize the actions of attackers in order to limit the potential damage from successful attacks. Ensuring the security of the functioning of the smart city's enabling cyber-physical systems is a complex task [1]. The resilience of cyber-physical systems of a smart city to potential intrusions and cyber threats is particularly relevant due to the increase in the number of equipment connected to the systems. In addition to the quantitative increase in equipment, the complexity of building the architecture of cyber-physical systems of a smart city is also due to the disparity of the integrated subsystems, as well as the individual characteristics of the architectures themselves. The problem of safe functioning and resource management of modern cities is particularly relevant. Urbanization imposes certain requirements for

© Springer Nature Singapore Pte Ltd. 2021
P. K. Singh et al. (Eds.): FTNCT 2020, CCIS 1395, pp. 168–180, 2021.
https://doi.org/10.1007/978-981-16-1480-4_15

improving resource management models [2]. By analyzing the existing trends in the functioning of cyber physical systems in modern cities, it is possible to identify a list of current vulnerabilities and threats and form an optimal management model.

2 Materials and Methods

Firstly, we will create a consolidated list of potential threats based on vulnerabilities for both digital and analog water utilities. Next, based on the hierarchy analysis method, we will conduct a multi-criteria assessment of possible alternatives to water management models in a modern city. To simplify the perception, we will divide the management alternatives into 4 categories, which will become the basis for choosing alternatives to management models based on the hierarchy analysis method.

3 Results

For ease of perception of the results obtained in the course of research, we group them into subsections:

- Assessment of control models of active water supply systems taking into account negative factors.
- Classification of potential vulnerabilities, threats and risks of functioning of cyber-physical water supply systems in a smart city.
- Modeling of scenarios of water supply system control failure.

3.1 Assessment of Control Models of Active Water Supply Systems Taking into Account Negative Factors

Formulate the main terms used in the study.

A threat to the security of a cyber-physical system is a set of conditions and factors that create a potential or actual danger of violating the security of the functioning of a cyber-physical system.

Vulnerability of the cyber-physical system - a lack (weakness) of the infrastructure, software (software-technical), software-hardware levels, as well as the influence of the human factor on the functioning of the cyber-physical system as a whole, which can be used to implement security threats.

Security risk of a cyber-physical system is the product of the probability of a threat to the functioning of a cyber-physical system by the size (magnitude) of the potential consequences.

Cyber-physical attacks on water infrastructure have increased with the number of connected equipment and water automation-transforming into smart water management. Identifying and neutralizing potential vulnerabilities is an important process that allows you to safely and effectively use the benefits of digital equipment in the smart city water supply industry [3]. One way is to improve algorithms for detecting cyber-physical attacks in water network management [4]. Which uses data analysis from infrastructure equipment, model-based detection mechanisms, and rule checking (Fig. 1).

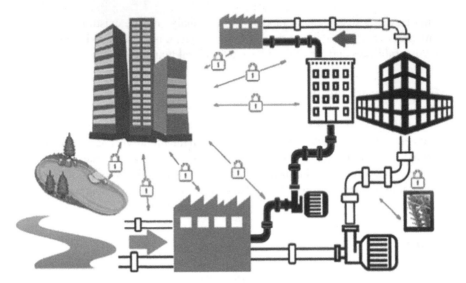

Fig. 1. Simulation of the functioning of the "digital water supply"

The digital water supply control model differs from the analog water supply control model. Digitalization of the industry has a positive impact on the level of development of water utilities, centralized data exchange via secure communication channels, and the ability to build both deterministic and stochastic models, which result in optimizing costs and improving the quality of services provided to consumers [5]. Often, the main problem of the transition to the management of a "digital water channel" is the lack of funding even to maintain the existence of an "analog water channel". The authors believe that this problem is a serious test and challenge for the modern world during the transition to digital format [6]. Smart city technology solutions must meet security requirements, including in the field of CPS water supply for Smart cities [7].

An important aspect is the procedure for detecting an attack on a cyber-physical water supply system. There are various mechanisms for integrated assessment of the state of systems, including the implementation of sustainable and safe remote monitoring. A set of measures to assess the state of the system at each time step contributes to the timely detection of certain attacks. The authors of [8] a numerically efficient algorithm for achieving stability and detecting attacks on remote monitoring systems has been developed. In [9] several traditional methods for detecting anomalies are considered and evaluated in the context of detecting attacks in water distribution systems. These algorithms were centrally trained across the feature space and compared with multi-stage detection methods that were developed to isolate both local and global anomalies. In addition, a new ensemble technique combining density-based and parametric algorithms was developed and tested in the applied environment. Traditional methods had comparable results with multi-stage systems, and when used in conjunction with a local anomaly detector, the effectiveness of these algorithms was significantly improved.

The infrastructure of water supply, distribution, and sanitation systems is socially significant. When modeling a water distribution system [10] a universal agent-based structure is used to evaluate the collective behavior of the control system during cyber-attacks launched against the implementation of this model. A real-time model of urban water cycle management is considered in [11], divided into water supply systems and urban drainage systems necessary for the functioning of urban society. Cyber-physical water supply system is presented as a technological complex for effective management of critical systems. Validation of the proposed approaches to managing the cyber-physical system was performed using virtual reality simulations based on MATLAB/SIMULINK and EPA-SWMM. Through modeling in these environments, a physical model of real objects and its digital counterpart (digital twin), water users and the environment were presented. The evaluation of information flows in the interaction of agents and management systems is carried out.

The work [12] is devoted to automatic detection of water losses in water distribution networks by dynamic analysis of time series associated with water consumption within the network, and the use of a classifier for wavelet detection of points of change to detect anomalies in the consumption structure. The wavelet point change method uses a continuous wavelet transform of time series (signals) to analyze how the frequency content of a signal changes over time. In the case of water distribution networks, the time series is associated with the streaming of water consumption data from automatic meter reading devices either at the level of individual consumers or at the level of the aggregated district area of the meter. The method of detecting wavelet points of change analyzes the provided time series to obtain its own knowledge about water consumption in normal conditions at the household level or throughout the territory, and then makes conclusions about water consumption in abnormal conditions.

A critical review of uncovered documented and malicious cybersecurity incidents in the water sector described in [13] also confirms the increased incidence of external interference. For each individual incident, the situation, response measures, remedial measures and lessons learned were compiled and described. The results of this review indicate an increase in the frequency, diversity and complexity of cyber threats in the water sector. While the emergence of new threats, such as ransomware or crypto jacking, has been detected, the recurrence of similar vulnerabilities and threats, such as insider threats, has also been evident, underscoring the need for an adaptive, cooperative, and comprehensive approach to water-based cyber defense.

3.2   Classification of Potential Vulnerabilities, Threats and Risks of Functioning of Cyber-Physical Water Supply Systems in a Smart City

The described vulnerabilities and threats will be the basis for building new models for managing active water supply systems. It is important to note that managing these risks will increase the level of strategic security of cities in management. When assessing the vulnerabilities of digital water channels, the degree of threat impact on the stability of the water management system, we suggest dividing it into several contours: *a) Operation of IoT and IIoT terminal equipment; b) Integration of the cyber-physical system with smart city systems; c) Data centralization in the unified information system of the country.*

This paper does not address the third circuit issues - the possibility of centralizing the exchange of information from several smart cities. Such systems of combining information from several cities and regions represent a higher-level system. The requirements for such systems will be described by the authors in the following scientific papers. Such large-scale systems require additional analysis of vulnerabilities and threats [14], comparison of architecture options for building cyber-physical water supply systems in smart cities [15], and improvement of security [16].

Based on the results of current and previous studies, the authors concluded that it is necessary to group the problems of managing cyber-physical water supply systems into several areas (aspects):

- limited water resources;
- increased wear and tear of water supply systems;
- increase in the urban population;
- degradation of water sources;
- lack of backup water sources;
- non-compliance of equipment at water treatment plants with modern types of pollution - both chemical and biological: antibiotics, micro plastics, biologically active bacteria.

Next look at each of these aspects in more detail. The created classification (Table 1) is a basic one, compiled by an expert method based on the vulnerabilities, threats and risk levels identified in previous studies. When conducting a comprehensive assessment of the security status of cyber-physical water supply systems in a smart city, it is necessary to take into account the features of the system architecture, data exchange, and hardware used both for the operation of systems and for preventing potential management threats [17].

Table 1. Basic classification of potential vulnerabilities, threats and risks of functioning of cyber-physical water supply systems in a smart city.

Vulnerability	Threats	Risk level
Group 1 - Infrastructure level (water supply systems, equipment, water supply sources)		
Use of outdated technologies to detect the degree of water pollution	Chemical infestations Biological infections Increasing morbidity of the population The decline in the quality of water supplied	Medium
High level of water infrastructure wear and tear	Failure of water supply networks Losses during transport The decline in the quality of water supplied Increasing morbidity of the population Chemical infestations Biological infections	Medium

(*continued*)

Table 1. (*continued*)

Vulnerability	Threats	Risk level
Lack of backup water supply sources	Emergency situation in a part of the city, district, and in the agglomeration as a whole The interruption in supply of water	Medium
Lack of fresh water storage facilities	Emergency situation in a part of the city, district, and in the agglomeration as a whole Water supply interruption (iodine deficiency) Poisoning of the population Failure of equipment and water treatment plants	Medium
Lack of network health monitoring systems	Losses during transport Chemical infestations Biological infections Unauthorized connections to the networks	High
Lack of main systems for monitoring the state of water supplied to the consumer	Losses during transport Chemical infestations Biological infections Unauthorized connections to the networks Poisoning of the population	High
Group 2 - Program level		
A program code of not declared possibilities of the software	Failure of systems and equipment Interception and corruption of data Remote monitoring and management of systems	Medium
Software injections	Failure of systems and equipment Interception and corruption of data Remote monitoring and management of systems	Medium
Accessibility from outside (a potential invasion of hackers)	Failure of systems and equipment Interception and corruption of data Remote monitoring and control of systems	Medium
Backdoors of imported software	Failure of systems and equipment Interception and corruption of data Remote monitoring and management of systems	High

(*continued*)

Table 1. (*continued*)

Vulnerability	Threats	Risk level
Group 3 - Hardware level (digital equipment)		
Availability for connecting hardware	Failure of systems and equipment Interception and corruption of data Remote monitoring and control of systems	Medium
Ability to intercept the signal, suppression, distortion	Failure of systems and equipment Interception and corruption of data Remote monitoring and control of systems	High
Accessibility from outside (a potential invasion of hackers)	Failure of systems and equipment Interception and corruption of data Remote monitoring and control of systems	High
Backdoors of imported hardware	Failure of systems and equipment Interception and corruption of data Remote monitoring and control of systems	High
Remote control of equipment	Failure of systems and equipment Interception and corruption of data Remote monitoring and control of systems	Medium
Group 4 - Human factor (human influence on the system)		
Incorrect actions of the staff	Emergency situation in a part of the city, district, and in the agglomeration as a whole Water supply interruption (iodine deficiency) Poisoning of the population Failure of equipment and water treatment plants	High
Deliberate negative actions of personnel on the functioning of systems (sabotage)	Emergency situation in a part of the city, district, and in the agglomeration as a whole Water supply interruption (iodine deficiency) Poisoning of the population Failure of equipment and water treatment plants	Medium

(*continued*)

Table 1. (*continued*)

Vulnerability	Threats	Risk level
Potential data leaks	The use of information for subversive purposes Remote monitoring and management of systems	Medium
Incorrect actions of the staff in case of an emergency (due to poor training)	Emergency situation in a part of the city, district, and in the agglomeration as a whole Water supply interruption (iodine deficiency) Poisoning of the population Failure of equipment and water treatment plants	High

3.3   Modeling of Scenarios of Water Supply System Control Failure

Modeling the stability of the functioning of cyber-physical systems of smart cities is an important aspect of management [18]. It is necessary to determine the optimal management model based on a multi-criteria assessment of possible management alternatives [19]. When building models, both the digital water channel and the analog water channel will be analyzed. This type of organization management of cyber-physical water supply systems in smart cities is also possible, due to the lack of automated management and control systems. To complete the study, each group is divided into subgroups and represents management alternatives. The General structure of the hierarchy analysis method can include several hierarchical levels with their own criteria [20].

The method consists of a set of the following steps:

a)   The first step is to structure the task as a hierarchical structure with several levels.
b)   At the second stage, the goal, evaluation criteria, and possible alternatives are formed.
c)   In the third stage, pairwise comparisons of elements of each level are performed.
d)   The importance coefficients for each level's elements are calculated. This checks the consistency of judgments.
e)   The combined weight coefficient is calculated and determined the best of the alternatives presented.

Problem statement: choose the optimal control model based on multi-criteria analysis using the analytic hierarchy process from the generated alternatives.

Goal: to identify which management model is more resilient to potential negative management threats.

Defining control alternatives:

a)   A digital water utility with a centralized data exchange system based on the state water management information system (A1).

b)   Digital water utility without a centralized data exchange system (A2).
c)   Analog water utility with improved (updated) infrastructure (A3).
d)   Analog water utility without infrastructure upgrade (A4).

Assessment criteria:

a)   Ability to detect chemical contamination at both water treatment plants and water
     supply networks (C1).
b)   Ability to detect biological contamination both at water treatment plants and water
     supply networks (C2).
c)   Operational control of potential unauthorized connections to networks and identifi-
     cation of water resources losses (C3).
d)   Ensuring water quality control at the consumer (C4).
e)   Stability of control systems to cyber-attacks (C5).
f)   System management level (C6).
g)   Centralization of data on water production and consumption (C7).

The described hierarchical model consisting of 7 criteria and 4 alternatives can be
presented visually (Fig. 2).

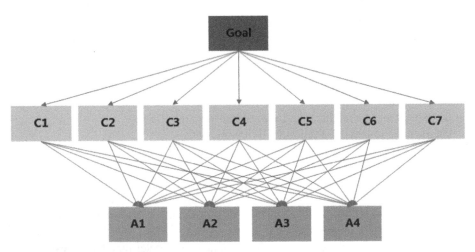

Fig. 2. The design of the model hierarchy

The matrix of paired comparisons represents the second level of the hierarchy. For
pairwise comparisons, we use a scale of relative importance from 1 to 9. For Example,
criterion C5 is significantly more important than criterion C2, so the number 3 is entered
in the corresponding cell; 1/3 is automatically entered in a cell that is symmetrical relative
to the diagonal, which corresponds to the opposite comparison. The basis for calculating
the relative importance of criteria is an expert assessment. The expert assessment of the
criteria is based on a survey of 5 groups of people with different profiles: specialists in
the field of water supply; specialists in the field of cyber security; specialists in the field

of Economics; civil servants; residents of several cities of different gender and age. The resulting values are rounded and shown in Table 2.

Table 2. The matrix of comparing the criteria.

Criteria	C1	C2	C3	C4	C5	C6	C7	Eigenvector	The vector of priorities
C1	1	1	3	2	4	4	3	2.25	0.27
C2	1	1	2	2	3	4	3	2.03	0.24
C3	0.33	0.5	1	1	1	3	3	1.06	0.13
C4	0.5	0.5	1.0	1	3	3	2	1.24	0.15
C5	0.25	0.33	1.0	0.33	1	1	2	0.66	0.08
C6	0.25	0.25	0.33	0.33	1	1	2	0.54	0.06
C7	0.33	0.33	0.5	0.5	0.5	0.5	1	0.64	0.08

After that, priority vectors were calculated, which are also shown in Table 2, the maximum eigenvalue λmax, the consistency index, and the consistency ratio. The maximum eigenvalue λmax is calculated using the matrix of paired comparisons as follows: stack each column of judgment, then the sum of the first multiplied by the value of the first components of the normalized vector of priorities, the sum of the second column on the second component, etc. then the resulting numbers are added together. The consistency index (CI) is determined using the following formula (1), where n is the number of elements to compare (the size of the matrix).

$$CI = (\lambda_{max} - n)/(n - 1) \tag{1}$$

Calculating the average value of the consistency index for the resulting matrix. Dividing the CI by the number corresponding to random consistency (RC), we get the consistency ratio (CR). For a matrix of size n = 7, random consistency $RC = 1.32$. Calculate the consistency ratio using the following formula (2):

$$CR = CI/RC \tag{2}$$

The consistency ratio of the resulting CR matrix = 0.09. The consistency level is considered acceptable when the CR is ≤ 0.1. if the consistency level exceeds 0.1, then a review of the judgments is necessary. This is not required in the current case.

After performing the calculations of the second level, we proceed to the third - a pairwise comparison of alternatives with each of the criteria [21]. We get seven matrices of judgments with dimension 7 × 4, since there are seven criteria at the second level and four control alternatives. The resulting matrices allow us to calculate the coefficients of importance of the corresponding elements of the hierarchical level. This was computed eigenvector matrix, and then normalized. As a result, the following priority vectors for each criterion were obtained, shown in Table 3.

Table 3. Priority vector for level 3.

Alternatives/criteria	C1	C2	C3	C4	C5	C6	C7
A1	0.47	0.47	0.54	0.53	0.56	0.54	0.55
A2	0.28	0.28	0.26	0.27	0.26	0.26	0.27
A3	0.16	0.16	0.12	0.14	0.12	0.12	0.13
A4	0.1	0.1	0.07	0.06	0.07	0.07	0.06

The maximum eigenvalue λ_{max} the consistency index, and the consistency ratio were also calculated to detect inconsistency of the obtained level 3 matrices. For a matrix of size n = 4, random consistency $RC = 0.9$. The consistency Ratio for level 3 pair comparison matrices was: according to the criterion C1 = 0.01; C2 = 0.01; C3 = 0.04; C4 = 0.07; C5 = 0.04; C6 = 0.04; C7 = 0.05. The resulting OS values correspond to the OS condition ≤ 0.1, and therefore no revision is required to improve consistency.

The best alternative is determined using the formula (3), where V_i is the quality weight of the i – th alternative; w_i the weight of the i-th criterion; V_i is the importance of the j-th alternative according to the i-th criterion.

$$V = \sum_{i=1}^{n} w_i V_i \qquad (3)$$

For each control method, we determine the weight coefficient and get the following values (Table 4).

Table 4. Calculated values of the weighting factors of the alternatives.

Alternatives	Weighting factor
A1	0.5
A2	0.27
A3	0.14
A4	0.08

The above calculations allow us to determine the weight coefficient of each control alternative according to the specified criteria and identify the optimal control model from them. In this case, the best indicator is the A1 control model based on digital control with a centralized data exchange system, the weight coefficient of which is = 0.5. The presented calculations became the basis for the practical implementation of the modernization of the management model in one of the largest cities in Russia - the city of Saint Petersburg. The population of the city is more than 5 million people.

4 Discussion

The results of the study suggest that modeling the functioning of cyber-physical systems of smart cities is important. Cases of external intrusions aimed at destabilizing the functioning of systems have become more frequent. The authors ' basic classification of potential vulnerabilities and threats to the functioning of cyber-physical water supply systems in smart cities allows us to summarize potential incidents.

Based on a multi-criteria assessment of possible alternatives for managing the cyber-physical water supply system of a modern city, the optimal management model was chosen - a Digital water utility with a centralized data exchange system based on the state information system for water resources management. Secure centralization of information makes it possible to increase the level of strategic security of cities and countries in General. The authors will design architectures for building a centralized system at the state level in the following studies. Features of the projected cyber-physical systems and existing cyber-physical water supply systems of cities will be taken into account.

5   Conclusion

The article presents an approach to modeling the cyber-physical water supply system of a Smart city. The shortcomings of management models are considered, and the list of vulnerabilities of the cyber-physical water supply system of a Smart city based on scenario modeling is supplemented. Thanks to a comprehensive threat analysis, the features of modeling the cyber-physical water supply system of a smart city were formed. The proposed approach makes it possible to generalize vulnerabilities, threats and create requirements for modeling scenarios of violation of the management of cyber-physical water supply systems in order to reduce potential risks. New models for managing active cyber-physical water supply systems in a smart city allow you to increase the level of management, reduce potential negative factors in providing water supply to the city, and can be applied by different cities. Based on a multi-criteria assessment, the optimal model for managing the cyber-physical water supply system of a modern city was determined - a Digital water utility with a centralized data exchange system based on the state information system for water resources management.

Data centralization in the unified information system of the country from several smart cities is not considered in this paper. Such systems of combining information from several cities and regions represent a higher-level system. The requirements for such systems will be described by the authors in the following scientific papers. Such large-scale systems require additional analysis of vulnerabilities and threats, and comparison of architecture options for building cyber-physical water supply systems in smart cities.

Acknowledgments. The reported study was partially funded by ICS RAS according to the state project.

References

1. Habibzadeh, H., et al.: A survey on cybersecurity, data privacy, and policy issues in cyber-physical system deployments in smart cities. Sustainable Cities Soc **50**, 101660 (2019)
2. Vasel-Be-Hagh, A., Ting, D.S.K. (eds.): Environmental Management of Air, Water, Agriculture, and Energy. CRC Press, Boca Raton (2020)

3. Yang, L., Elisa, N., Eliot, N.: Privacy and security aspects of E-government in smart cities. In: Smart Cities Cybersecurity and Privacy, pp. 89–102. Elsevier (2019)

4. Taormina, R., et al.: Battle of the attack detection algorithms: disclosing cyber attacks on water distribution networks (Article). J. Water Resour. Plann. Manage. **144**(8), 11 (2018). https://doi.org/10.1061/(asce)wr.1943-5452.0000969

5. Alilou, H., et al.: A cost-effective and efficient framework to determine water quality monitoring network locations. Sci. Total Environ. **624**, 283–293 (2018)

6. Shao, Q., et al.: Developing a sustainable urban-environmental quality evaluation system in China based on a hybrid model. Int. J. Environ. Res. Public Health **16**(8), 1434 (2019)

7. Camara, M., et al.: Economic and efficiency based optimisation of water quality monitoring network for land use impact assessment. Sci. Total Environ. 139800 ((2020))

8. Ge, X.H., Han, Q.L., Zhang, X.M., Ding, D.R., Yang, F.W.: Resilient and secure remote monitoring for a class of cyber-physical systems against attacks (Article). Inf. Sci. **512**, 1592–1605 (2020). https://doi.org/10.1016/j.ins.2019.10.057

9. Ramotsoela, D.T., Hancke, G.P., Abu-Mahfouz, A.M.: Attack detection in water distribution systems using machine learning. Hum.-centric Comput. Inf. Sci. **9**(1), 1–22 (2019). https://doi.org/10.1186/s13673-019-0175-8

10. Mishra, V.K., Palleti, V.R., Mathur, A.: A modeling framework for critical infrastructure and its application in detecting cyber-attacks on a water distribution system (Article). Int. J. Crit. Infrastruct. Prot. **26**, 19 (2019). https://doi.org/10.1016/j.ijcip.2019.05.001

11. Sun, C.C., Puig, V., Cembrano, G.: Real-time control of urban water cycle under cyber-physical systems framework (Article). Water **12**(2), 17 (2020). https://doi.org/10.3390/w12020406

12. Christodoulou, S.E., Kourti, E., Agathokleous, A.: Waterloss detection in water distribution networks using wavelet change-point detection. Water Resour. Manage **31**(3), 979–994 (2016). https://doi.org/10.1007/s11269-016-1558-5

13. Hassanzadeh, A., Rasekh, A., Galelli, S., Aghashahi, M., Taormina, R., Ostfeld, A., et al.: A review of cybersecurity incidents in the water sector (Review). J. Environ. Eng. **146**(5), 13 (2020). https://doi.org/10.1061/(asce)ee.1943-7870.0001686

14. Chow, R.: The last mile for IoT privacy. IEEE Secur. Priv. **15**(6), 73–76 (2017)

15. Kim, H., Ben-Othman, J.: Toward integrated virtual emotion system with AI applicability for secure CPS-enabled smart cities: ai-based research challenges and security issues. IEEE Network **34**(3), 30–36 (2020)

16. Zhao, L., et al.: Optimal edge resource allocation in IoT-based smart cities. IEEE Network **33**(2), 30–35 (2019)

17. Chatterjee, S., et al.: Prevention of cybercrimes in smart cities of India: from a citizen's perspective. Information Technology & People (2019).

18. Jan, S., Cohen, A., Oron, G.: Multi-objective optimization for solving water shortage issues in arid zones via the analytic hierarchy process (AHP): The Israeli case. Desalination and Water Treatment **188**, 10–19 (2020)

19. Carli, R., Dotoli, M., Pellegrino, R.: Multi-criteria decision-making for sustainable metropolitan cities assessment. J. Environ. Manage. **226**, 46–61 (2018)

20. Saaty, T.L., De Paola, P.: Rethinking design and urban planning for the cities of the future. Buildings **7**(3), 76 (2017)

21. Saaty, T.: Decision-making. Analytic hierarchy process. Radio and Svyaz. p. 278 (1993)

Software for Analyzing Security for Healthcare Organizations

Shamil G. Magomedov[✉]

MIREA - Russian Technological University, 78 Vernadsky Avenue, 119454 Moscow, Russia
magomedov_sh@mirea.ru

Abstract. Clinics, medical centers, other healthcare institutions are faced with a large amount of personal data of both employees and patients. Many documents fall into the category of medical confidentiality. Medical institutions are switching to electronic document management, electronic records or medical records of patients are being automated. Problems of optimizing registries and securing databases have become actual for healthcare. With the development of information technology, the transition of medical institutions to a new level of processing and storage of personal data has accelerated. Hacking the information infrastructure of a medical institution can cause colossal financial damage to medical institutions and companies, and, more importantly, pose a real threat to the health and life of patients. This work describes the process of assessing the security of the information infrastructure of healthcare institutions.

Keywords: DICOM · PACS · Security analysis · Medical data exchange

1 Introduction

The number of cyberattacks is growing exponentially every year. They are exposed to absolutely all areas that we encounter in our daily life. This is the banking sector, industrial enterprises, metro, energy, medicine and many others. Some attacks are to steal personal data of users (customers, employees, etc.), many of them cause reputational losses and the loss of a part of the service market, and others results in theft of company finances. This list can be enumerated indefinitely, since the motives of attackers can be completely different.

Some of the areas are more protected. Until recently, the state was only concerned about the financial sector, since the loss of money most strongly affected it. But the period since 2010 has shown that hackers can go even further and not stop there. Attacks on the energy sector and industrial enterprises, the purpose of which was to inflict a destructive effect on automatic process control systems (APCS), cryptographic influence on data and subsequent blackmail for the purpose of ransom, as well as spread over the network using viruses such as "network worms" endangered not only the target of the attackers, but also neighboring spheres interacting with it over the network. And successful blackmail is a reason to repeat the same influences.

© Springer Nature Singapore Pte Ltd. 2021
P. K. Singh et al. (Eds.): FTNCT 2020, CCIS 1395, pp. 181–189, 2021.
https://doi.org/10.1007/978-981-16-1480-4_16

Different states try to protect themselves from hackers in different ways and allocate huge funds for this. But first of all, this money goes to the financial and industrial sectors, leaving the medical sector unattended, although this is not correct. Because in addition to money, health and human lives are at stake. Exposure to surgical devices during surgery and their failure can lead to irreparable loss for the patient. The patient's life may be the price.

Consider the articles of reputable international publications and expert information security experts on the protection of the medical sector:

- According to a report by Cybersecurity Ventures, the number of ransomware attacks on healthcare organizations will quadruple from 2017 to 2020, and will grow to 5 times by 2021 [1].
- In the 2019 HIMSS Cybersecurity Survey, nearly 60% of hospitals and healthcare IT professionals in the US said email was the most prevalent point of infiltration. This includes phishing scams and other forms of email scams [2].
- HIPAA Magazine contains data from a vendor report that claims that healthcare email fraud has increased 473% in two years [3].
- According to a report analyzed by Health IT Security, 24% of US health workers have never received cybersecurity awareness training. This type of training aims to help users identify and respond to phishing scams, which initiate more than 90% of all cyber-attacks [4].
- More than 93% of healthcare organizations have experienced a data breach in the past three years, and 57% have had more than five data breaches in the same period of time [5].
- According to Lisa Rivera, a former federal attorney who currently advises healthcare professionals and medical device companies, four to seven percent of the healthcare IT budget is for cybersecurity, compared with about 15% for other sectors such as a financial industry [6].
- Research firm IT Gartner predicts that by 2020 more than 25% of cyberattacks in healthcare organizations will be connected to the Internet of Things (IoT). More specifically, from a medical point of view, these are wireless and implantable medical devices (IMDs) with wireless connectivity, such as defibrillators (ICDs), pacemakers, brain stimulators, insulin pumps, ear tubes and much more [7].
- Medical devices have an average of 6.2 vulnerabilities each; 60% of medical devices are at end-of-life, with no patches or available updates [7].

And this small number of articles already demonstrates that there is a serious security issue in this sector, not to mention that, for example, in the United States, the healthcare industry will collectively spend more than $65 billion on cybersecurity products and services over the five-year period from 2017 by 2021 [8], while the Russian Federation has allocated for this period only 28 billion rubles for the entire area of information security [9].

Now let's look at the consequences of this attitude towards information security in the medical sector.

- In 2016, the Presbyterian Medical Center in Hollywood, California, USA, was forced out of operation for four days by a ransomware for whom he paid a ransom of $ 17,000 [10].
- The 2017 WannaCry outbreak forced hundreds of UK NHS facilities to halt for several days, resulting in the cancellation of thousands of surgeries and the transfer of emergency patients from affected emergency centers [11].
- In 2019, Israeli researchers announced they had created a computer virus capable of adding tumors to computed tomography and MRI scans, malware designed to trick doctors into misdiagnosing high-profile patients [12].

These are examples that have been publicly available over the past 5 years, but it is very easy to follow from them how attacks are changing and what they can lead to.

2   Interfaces and Standards for Working with Medical Equipment

The problem of creating unified international standards for the exchange of medical data in different countries is resolved in different ways, for this reason there are many medical standards: ASTM, ASC X12, IEEE/MEDIX, NCPDP, HL7, DICOM, etc. As a rule, the standards are named groups/committees and other non-profit organizations that develop them.

Each standards development group has some specialization. So, ASC X12N deals with external standards for the exchange of electronic documents, ASTM E31.11 is for standards for the exchange of laboratory test data, IEEE P1157 is for medical data exchange standards (MEDIX), ACR/NEMA DICOM are standards related to the exchange of images, etc.

The most serious and rapidly developing standards find software and hardware support from such major manufacturers of medical equipment as Philips, Siemens, Acuson and others. In a number of countries, the issues of standardizing the exchange of medical data are being resolved quite globally. For example, in the United States in 1996, the American National Standards Institute (ANSI) approved the national standard for the exchange of medical data in electronic form HL7 (Health Level 7).

Among the most significant standards of medical informatics are HL7, DICOM, SNOMED, RCC. In addition to developing standards, the US government also took care of the development of a law.

This is how the Health Information Portability and Accountability Act (HIPAA) was passed in 1996 and the Health Information Technology for Economic and Clinical Health (HITECH) Act were passed in 2003. These laws require organizations dealing with health information to take certain privacy and security measures and inform patients when their privacy and security is at stake.

3   Vulnerability Analysis of Software Implementing DICOM Protocol

The general principles of network operation have been described many times, but the protection of specific medical protocols and equipment, which have their own characteristics, is poorly studied. This is especially true for software working with the widespread DICOM protocol and medical devices.

There are many different solutions on the market for scanning networks for vulnerabilities such as Rapid7, Nessus, OpenVAS. These systems have different prices from free (OpenVAS) to systems costing over $ 2500 per year (Rapid7, Nessus). A review and comparison of these systems can be found in the work [21].

If we consider information security in medical organizations, we will find many features in the form of PACS systems, which include DICOM servers and servers with medical information systems, etc. Of the scanners listed, these features are not fully taken into account only by the Nessus software. For the Nessus scanner, there is a module for detecting the presence of DICOM traffic outgoing from the host [22], which allows you to determine the presence of DICOM traffic, but not to determine the DICOM server, which does not help in testing for vulnerabilities.

Therefore, most of the security scanners mentioned in scientific articles cannot meet the requirements of the information security sphere in medical institutions, since they do not have modules for detecting vulnerabilities of PACS systems and servers of medical information systems. If you do not take into account these features when performing an information security audit, you may face the fact that hackers can take advantage of vulnerabilities specific to this area. The actions of hackers in this area can endanger not only the finances or reputation of a medical company but also the lives of patients.

Let's take a closer look at the DICOM (Digital Imaging and Communications in Medicine) data structure.

DICOM is a standard for processing, storing, printing and transmitting information in medical imaging systems. It includes file format description and network protocol. The network protocol uses TCP/IP at its core for communication between systems. Also, systems that support reading and writing DICOM files can exchange DICOM files with each other. The owner of the standard is the American organization National Electrical Manufacturers Association (NEMA). It is being developed by the DICOM standard committee, which consists of several working groups (WG).

DICOM allows the integration of scanners, servers, workstations, printers, and network equipment from many different manufacturers into a single PACS (picture archiving and communication system) system. The various devices are supplied with a document called the DICOM conformance statement, which describes how and what functions the supplied device performs.

DICOM files simultaneously contain both images and additional information about the observed patient. Patient and exam information cannot be separated from the image itself. This reduces the number of possible errors. The JPEG format is organized in a similar way, which can also have additional information describing the image in the file.

Any DICOM object consists of many attributes, such as the patient's name, identifier, examination date, etc. There is also one special attribute that contains the pixel data.

Thus, there is no separate header for the DICOM file - only a set of attributes, including the image data. The attributes in the standard are called tags, each tag is assigned its own number, consisting of two fields - the group number and the element number. For example, the tag with the number 0010, 0010 (tag numbers are written in hexadecimal notation) always contains data about the patient's full name. Each tag has a standard name. 0010, 0010 is called 'Patient's Name'. A list of all standardized tags can be found in the 6th section of the PS 3.6 standard: Data Dictionary [15].

3.1 Development of a Vulnerability Exploit for Open Source PACS Server dcm4chee

In many healthcare facilities, the PACS infrastructure is based on an open source project called dcm4chee [6]. The project is also accompanied by detailed installation and operating documentation, which explains its popularity. The openness and popularity of this and similar projects, as expected, makes cybercriminals and security researchers want to test its resistance to hacking.

In addition to encryption and protocol issues, you need to consider the properties of the server software that processes incoming messages. If there are no authorization mechanisms, then any attacker can view images of any patients using the DICOM protocol.

In particular, the study revealed that the dcm4che software package (which is a set of software and utilities for working with DICOM) has such a property. Dcm4che includes a DICOM server, programs for extracting and loading DICOM files, implements a DICOM server, has a client, and a web application to view the results. The web application implements an authorization mechanism, and to view the snapshots, you need to enter a username and password, however, an attacker can connect to the server via the DICOM protocol and retrieve other people's snapshots using the Query/Retrieve DICOM service.

After scanning the network and detecting a server with an open port 11112, which DICOM services use, and discovering that the host is using the dcm4chee server, you can try to apply an exploit to it to obtain the data. Using the Python programming language and libraries for DICOM interaction, it is possible to develop a script obtaining patients via direct request to dcm4che DICOM server, bypassing the web application where authorization and authentication procedures are implemented.

To interact with the DICOM server, we will use the utility findscu [6, 20] included in the package. The utility launch line looks like this:

```
usage: findscu [options] -c <aet>@<host>:<port> [dcmfile_in...]
```

Thus, the connection is determined by three parameters: aet, host, port. The AET parameter is the Application Entity Title value, in which it is customary to write a unique identifier for a DICOM device, consisting of uppercase letters and numbers. A default value for AET was discovered in the documentation: the string «DCM4CHEE». The «−c» switch in the program call means sending a C-FIND request using the DICOM protocol. In this case, you can also pass the «−m» option, which passes a filter for searching images by various parameters, such as patient name, image type, age, etc. It was found that not only literal values, but also patterns can be substituted into filter parameters: the «*» symbol means any substring.

Thus, the utility allows you to retrieve the results of studies of any patients from the default DICOM server with a secure web interface based on the dcm4che project.

The exploit is written in the python programming language and uses the third-party pynetdicom and pydicom libraries. At the first step, we try to find the DICOM server in the infrastructure, then we compose a request to receive all patients with the required data. In the second step, we send a request without the data required for user authentication to the detected DICOM server, which uses the dcm4chee software and get the result (Fig. 1).

```python
1  from pynetdicom import AE
2  from pydicom import Dataset
3  from pynetdicom.sop_class import VerificationSOPClass
4  from pydicom.uid import (
5      ImplicitVRLittleEndian, ExplicitVRLittleEndian, ExplicitVRBigEndian
6  )
7
8  ae = AE(ae_title='DCM4CHEE')
9  ae.add_requested_context(VerificationSOPClass, [
10     ImplicitVRLittleEndian,
11     ExplicitVRBigEndian
12 ])
13
14 print('Trying to associate with the DICOM server')
15 connection = ae.associate(HOST, 11112)
16
17 if connection.is_established:
18     print('Connection established')
19
20     # DICOM dataset with the wildcard value for a PatientId
21     query = Dataset()
22     query.PatientId = '*'
23     query.QueryRetrieveLevel = 'PATIENT'
24
25     # Issue a C-FIND request and get the result
26     result = connection.send_c_get(query, query_model='P')
27
```

Fig. 1. The code snipped written in Python implementing the exploit.

To protect against this exploit, you can use rules in IPS/IDS systems that will intercept Request/Receive packets to the dcm4chee PACS server and check the hash of the authorization data used in the request packet. Further, this rule will skip or reject this packet depending on the correspondence of the authorization data specified in the packet with the hash stored by the IPS/IDS system.

4   Scan Strategy on a Regular Basis

To ensure the safe operation of the health information infrastructure, a list of measures must be taken. In the work [16–19], recommendations were proposed for building a secure infrastructure, as well as the recommended configuration of a network segment containing PACS. However, the process of reconfiguring the current infrastructure is a long process that requires a lot of approvals and does not interfere with the daily work of the organization. In this regard, it is proposed to establish a continuous process of monitoring the infrastructure in order to timely identify potential information leaks. Below is an algorithm and flowchart for this process (Fig. 2).

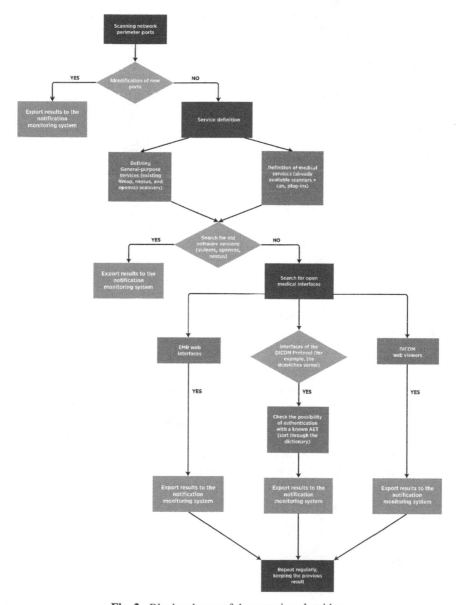

Fig. 2. Block-scheme of the scanning algorithm.

The security assessment process should be continuous, scanning should be regular (Fig. 3).

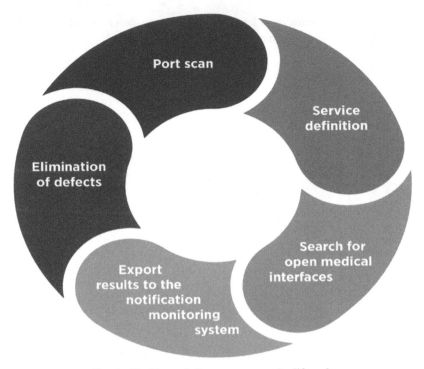

Fig. 3. Healthcare infrastructure security lifecycle.

5 Conclusion

Cyberattacks are increasingly common in the healthcare sector. As the number of networked medical devices increases, so does the need for information security professionals to understand and mitigate device security threats. Specific medical data is not specifically protected: using the example discussed in the article, you can write an exploit in a few lines of code that will allow you to get the data of all patients. In order to increase the level of security of the healthcare information infrastructure, it is necessary to actively identify open interfaces by scanning on a regular basis, as well as establish an ongoing infrastructure monitoring process in order to identify potential information leaks in a timely manner.

References

1. Cybersecurity CEO: Ransomware Attacks On Hospitals Predicted To Increase 5X By 2021. https://cybersecurityventures.com/cybersecurity-ceo-ransomware-attacks-on-hospitals-predicted-to-increase-5x-by-2021/
2. The real cybersecurity risk sits between the chair and keyboard. https://www.healthcareitnews.com/news/europe/risk-between-chair-and-keyboard
3. Healthcare Email Fraud Attacks Have Increased 473% in 2 Years https://www.hipaajournal.com/healthcare-email-fraud-attacks-have-increased-473-in-2-years/

4. Shojania K. G. et al. Making health care safer: a critical analysis of patient safety practices. Evid Rep Technol Assess (Summ). 43(1), 668 (2001)
5. Healthcare Data Breaches Costs Industry $4 Billion by Year's End, 2020 Will Be Worse Reports New Black Book Survey. https://blackbookmarketresearch.newswire.com/news/healthcare-data-breaches-costs-industry-4-billion-by-years-end-2020-21027640
6. Healthcare's number one financial issue is cybersecurity. https://www.healthcarefinancenews.com/news/healthcares-number-one-financial-issue-cybersecurity
7. Patient Insecurity: Explosion Of The Internet Of Medical Things. https://cybersecurityventures.com/patient-insecurity-explosion-of-the-internet-of-medical-things/
8. Healthcare Security $65 Billion Market. https://cybersecurityventures.com/healthcare-cybersecurity-report-2017/
9. The authorities are investing 28 billion in Russia's cyber security, without daring to triple this amount. https://cnews.ru/news/top/2020-01-03_vlasti_vkladyvayut_v_kiberbezopasnost
10. Ransomware Goes Hollywood. https://www.isaca.org/resources/news-and-trends/isaca-now-blog/2016/ransomware-goes-hollywood
11. WannaCry cyber-attack cost the NHS £92m as 19,000 appointments cancelled. https://www.telegraph.co.uk/technology/2018/10/11/wannacry-cyber-attack-cost-nhs-92m-19000-appointments-cancelled/
12. Health care's huge cybersecurity problem. https://www.theverge.com/2019/4/4/18293817/cybersecurity-hospitals-health-care-scan-simulation
13. Medical device regulations Author links open overlay panel Mounika Gudeppu, Swaroop Sawant, Chella Ganapathy Chockalingam, Prakash Srinivasan Timiri Shanmugam. Trends in Development of Medical Devices, pp. 135–152 (2020). https://www.sciencedirect.com/science/article/pii/B9780128209608000083
14. Singh, K., Selvam, P.: Medical device risk management. Trends in Development of Medical Devices, pp. 65–76 (2020). https://www.sciencedirect.com/science/article/pii/B9780128209608000058
15. Open Source Clinical Image and Object Management. https://www.dcm4che.org/
16. Magomedov, S.G.: Security analysis of computer networks and applications of the healthcare organizations information processes Cloud of Science, vol. 7 pp. 685–704 (2020)
17. Benssalah, M., Rhaskali, Y.: A secure DICOM image encryption scheme based on ECC, linear cryptography and chaos. In: 2020 1st International Conference on Communications, Control Systems and Signal Processing (CCSSP), pp. 131–136. IEEE (2020)
18. Mortajez, S., et al.: A novel chaotic encryption scheme based on efficient secret keys and confusion technique for confidential of DICOM images. Inf. Med. Unlocked, 100396 (2020)
19. Shini, S.G., Thomas, T., Chithraranjan, K.: Cloud based medical image exchange-security challenges. Procedia Eng. **38**, 3454–3461 (2012)
20. Dorgham, O., et al.: Enhancing the security of exchanging and storing DICOM medical images on the cloud. Int. J. Cloud Appl. Comput. (IJCAC) **8**(1), 154–172 (2018)
21. Roldán-Molina, G., Almache-Cueva, M., Silva-Rabadão, C., Yevseyeva, I., Basto-Fernandes, V.: A comparison of cybersecurity risk analysis tools. Procedia Comput. Sci. **121**, 568–575 (2017)
22. DICOM Protocol Detection. https://www.tenable.com/plugins/nnm/700400

Behavior-Based Assessment of Trust in a Cyber-Physical System

Alexander S. Basan[1], Elena S. Basan[1(✉)], Maria A. Lapina[2], and Vitalii G. Lapin[3]

[1] South Federal University, 2 Chekhov Street, Taganrog 347928, Russia
[2] North-Caucasus Federal University, 1 Pushkin Street, Stavropol 355017, Russia
[3] Stavropol Regional Clinical Consulting and Diagnostic Center,
304 Lenina Street, Stavropol 355000, Russia

Abstract. In this paper, we propose a method for assessing the stability of the CPS to attacks based on the analysis of changes in network node parameters. The main purpose of this work is to develop a methodology for evaluating the ability of the catch to demonstrate trusted behavior in the normal operation of the network and during attacks. One of the research tasks is to simulate the operation of the CPS, traffic flows, provided that the network nodes are moving. The analysis of existing CPS is carried out and the structure for further modeling is revealed. Routing protocols and data transfer protocols are analyzed. The existing modeling tools are studied, and their comparative analysis is carried out to identify a suitable CPS for the specified parameters. Nine network scenarios were modeled. Including normal mode, denial of service attack, and Sybil attack. The method of calculating node trust was studied, which further contributed to the detection of a malicious node in the system.

Keywords: Cyber-physical system · Information protection · Information systems

1 Introduction

Today, cyber-physical systems are being actively developed and used in modern society. These systems arose because of the fourth industrial revolution, which allowed the transition from automated production control systems to intelligent systems. Cyber-physical systems include the following key technologies: "Internet of Things", "Smart Cities", "Big Data", "Smart Manufacturing", "Artificial Intelligence" [1]. The use of such technologies poses new challenges to the field of information security, which is responsible for minimizing risks and information threats, ensuring the stable and reliable operation of information systems (which include cyber-physical systems).

The use of standard methods and means of information protection for cyber-physical systems cannot always give a positive result, this is due to the emergence of the following scientific problems. Firstly, methods and means of protection developed for typical information systems do not consider the risks associated with the influence of the information system on production and the facility with which the system works. Such objects

© Springer Nature Singapore Pte Ltd. 2021
P. K. Singh et al. (Eds.): FTNCT 2020, CCIS 1395, pp. 190–201, 2021.
https://doi.org/10.1007/978-981-16-1480-4_17

can be temperature, gas pressure, manufactured products, including crops (in the case of the Smart Greenhouse), as well as many other things, including the person himself [2]. In this case, we are talking about the fact that the implementation of an information threat to the temperature control sensor can lead not only to a leak or substitution of temperature data, but also to a change in the temperature in the room and, therefore, a disruption of the technological process, a threat to human life, etc. Secondly, when creating cyber-physical systems, technologies that differ from standard, typical ones can be used. These can be new communication protocols, applications, operating systems, network architectures, etc. In addition, as stated in the order adopted by the Government of the Russian Federation dated July 28, 2017 No. 1632, these may be "new production technologies; industrial internet; components of robotics and sensorics, heterogeneous communication technologies and terminal devices". The presence of new infrastructure solutions leads to the emergence of new vulnerabilities and threats to information security, which differ from those present in typical information systems. In this regard, standard methods, and approaches to ensuring information security will not be able to maintain the required level of protection. Third, since the architecture of cyber-physical systems can differ significantly from typical information systems the nodes of a cyber-physical system can be mobile, located outside the controlled area, communicate with each other directly - without an intermediary device, or have a direct access to the global network, then the placement of standard information security tools becomes difficult [3].

This paper proposes a method for assessing the resistance of CPS to attacks based on the analysis of changes in the parameters of network nodes. In this article, resistance to attacks means the presence of trusted behavior of network nodes it is the probability that a node exhibits behavior similar to neighboring network nodes and does not harm the rest of the network. A node's behavior is considered trusted when its parameters do not change significantly from the parameters of its neighbors. It is assumed that the effectiveness of the technique is achieved because the CPS is distributed and large-scale, the network nodes are in different areas and the attacker cannot attack more than 50% of the network nodes at the same time. One of the objectives of the study is to simulate the work of the FSC, traffic flows, provided that the nodes of the network are moving.

2 Related Works

In [4] it could be found a description of an framework based on the theory of non-cooperative games to assess the reliability of separate sensor nodes that make up the CPS. In this paper game-theoretic model which analyzes the ways of influence the reliability of CPS sensors was considered. In addition, the model is used to evaluate the equilibrium solution of the game according to Nash to obtain a criterion for the threshold of confidence. The trust threshold is the value that should be observed for a node in a cyber-physical system. In this work, the authors understand trust as the possibility of maintaining integrity, accessibility and confidentiality when communicating with the nodes. Multi-agent optimization can be used to calculate trust relationships. Each sensor, using a game theory approach, performs some specific function that is useful. To implement the approach, each sensor evaluates a utility function that determines the satisfaction of the sensor. Then, based on this value, which is obtained using the game approach, you can determine the degree of confidence of the sensor.

In [5], the authors propose a contextual trust scoring scheme for security of CPS which used wireless networks. The article discusses a set of rules that allows you to calculate the level of reliability of a node. To test this scheme, the authors realize a set of tests by simulation and the use of testbed which is based on the use of set of smartphones. Experimental results show that the CARE-CPS scheme can correctly assess the reliability of reporting devices in the CPS. There are three main functional blocks in the CARE-CPS schema, they are collection of the rules management, and trust evaluation. The data collection department is engaged in the process of collecting and submitting data to the policy department or the trust department. In the policy block, all important information will be used in rules. Various important information such as information about environment, and signal strength can be associated with these meter readings. The Policy Management Block analyzes important information and uses policies to determine if meters are deliberately reporting false readings or if current environmental conditions are causing these false meter readings. Let us consider an example if a meter reports incorrect data due to bad weather, then the reliability of that meter is reduced less. Also, reliability may decrease if weather conditions are normal, but the sensors give poor readings, this indicates a decrease in confidence.

Zikratova et al. [6] consider the problem of constructing protection mechanisms for a multi-agent robotic system against malicious robots. This article focuses on the mechanisms of "soft" defense or second line of defense. The authors build a system for ensuring security with the use of methods that are used in multi-agent computers (MAC). The authors claim the applicability of the Xudong method [7] and the Buddy Security Model (BSM) [8, 9] for MAC security, which are well aligned with the architecture of decentralized systems. In addition to this, they employ social control mechanisms such as trust and reputation controls to protect users. At the same time, to detect attacks, they only use the analysis of the reliability of the data transmitted by the robots they determine the correctness of the calculation of targets. The authors propose two algorithms for calculating the level of trust between nodes. The nodes form a score vector and generate an array of score targets. These estimates are formed in accordance with the reliability of the information and the distance to the target. Authors use Weibull-Gnedenko function to calculate reputation level. One of the drawbacks of the approach is its specification for a specific set of problems and areas of time. In addition, only one parameter is used, namely the distance to the target. If an attacker carries out several different active attacks that are not related to the accuracy and accuracy of the data, this system will not be able to detect it. Thus, it can be noted that the existing work on assessing trust in the CPS is aimed at assessing that the transmitted parameters are correct and correspond to the expected ones. The proposed method is more versatile and assesses not the fidelity of the parameters measured by the node, but the change in its own parameters in relation to other CPS nodes. In particular, the presented solutions evaluate the accuracy of the measurements, which reflects its behavior in the network.

3   Development of a Model of a Cyber-Physical System

3.1   Structural and Functional Characteristics of the Developed Model of a Cyber-Physical System

A system consisting of "sensor devices" has been created to conduct the research. These devices can be sensors used to measure specified parameters, mobile robots, sensor drones. The nodes can move. The nodes exchange information with each other directly. The mesh topology was chosen. Mesh network implementations allow full connectivity between nodes using a routing protocol. The movement of the nodes can be generated, and the nodes can be divided into zones. After creating nodes, you need to realize communication process among different network nodes. We could use as an agent special TCP connector to receive, send information and listening ports. The TCP connector is used for organized communication between separate nodes. Table 1 shows the parameters which were used during simulation.

Table 1. Parameters wich used during simulation

Parameter	Value
Number of network nodes	21
Time of experiment, s	50
The size of the transmitted packets	500
Trusted Host Transfer Interval	1,5
Attacker nodes transfer interval	0,5
Routing protocol	AODV
Data transfer protocol	TCP

Table 2 provides a comparative analysis of the routing protocols and identifies the most suitable one. As part of the study, the AODV protocol was selected as the most suitable for the given parameters. When creating the model, it was decided to use several protocols. At the transport level, UDP will be used to simulate the transmission of a video stream between nodes and an operator. For transmission of control commands, TCP protocol and for the same purposes, imitation of the MAVLink protocol. The MAVLink protocol is used to exchange messages between UAVs, and today there is little information about the traffic flows that are transmitted through this protocol.

Based on their analysis of the literature, an algorithm for the operation of the protocol is proposed in the framework of the study of traffic flows, which is shown in Fig. 1.

At the link level, the IEEE 802.11n standard is used, this is a version of the 802.11 standard. 802.11n uses frequency channels in the WiFi 2.4 GHz and 5 GHz frequency spectra. This standard is compatible with 11b/11a/11g. Messages.

Table 2. Analysis of routing protocols

Protocol	Network size	Route calculation method	Storing routes	Strategy	Advantages disadvantages
DSR	Small	Shortest path or next in the table	Route cache	Complete rewriting of routes	Many routes, impossible to listen
AODV	Different sizes	New shortest path	Route table	Full or partial rewriting of routes	Adapts to highly dynamic topologies
ZRP	Large	New shortest path	Route table	Periodic updating of routing tables	Discovers routes faster

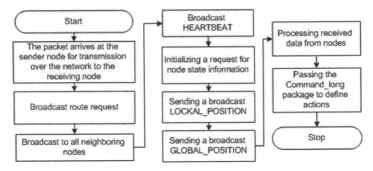

Fig. 1. MAVLink protocol simulation algorithm

3.2 Simulation of Attacks on CPS

In the work carried out, six variants of the network scenarios were simulated. Scenarios are described in Table 3.

During normal operation of a network consisting of 20 nodes, 0, 2, 4, 6, 8, 10, 12, 14, 16, 18 act as sources that transmit information via TCP to nodes to receivers No. 1, 3, 5, 7, 9, 11, 13, 15, 17, 19. The CBR application generates messages at intervals of 1.5 with a packet size of 500 bytes. When the network is operating normally, dropped packets may appear, but not in large numbers. During a Denial-of-Service attack, an UDP agent was created and connected to node # 2. Since the agent cannot generate traffic, a CBR application joins it and inclement malicious packets every 0.5 ms. Further, the receiver agent is similarly created, Null which is connected to the node # 3. Then UDP and Null agents are connected. In this attack, the attacker implements malicious packets into the communication process at a higher rate than trusted hosts.

In a Sibyl attack, the attacker poses as nodes and tries to capture the greatest influence over the network. It redirects packet routes to itself. Instead of sending packets along

Table 3. Modeling scenarios

Modeling type	The number network hosts and the number of attacker hosts								
	20	30	40	50	60	70	80	90	100
Normal mode, nodes are static	0	0	0	0	0	0	0	0	0
Normal mode, nodes are moving	0	0	0	0	0	0	0	0	0
Denial of Service Attack	5	10	15	20	25	30	35	45	50
Sibyl Attack	5	10	15	20	20	30	30	45	45

a valid and beneficial route, nodes send packets to an attacker. Two UDP agents have been created, which are attached to nodes # 0 and # 2, respectively; to generate traffic, two CBR applications and two Null receivers have been created, which are attached to nodes # 1 and # 3, respectively. Then UDP and Null agents are connected.

We realized this attack by making changes in files Aodv.h and Aodv.cc in the Ns2–35 modulation system to create a flooding attack which is send among of packets to victim and loaded it.

4   Methodology for Analyzing the Resistance of Nodes to Attacks by an Intruder

After analyzing the attacks, you can make the input that for the realization of many network attacks, which actively influence on network nodes, the attacker requires significant energy resources, for example: flooding attack, denial of service attack, Sibyl attack. To carry out these attacks, an attacker needs to send many packets, thus, a node must consume a large amount of energy, thus, its energy must be spent in proportion to the sent packets. Comparing the level of remaining energy Q (E) and the load of the node L (the total number of sent/received/forwarded packets in each period), one can see a proportional pattern [10]:

1) if a node has a maximum value of the level of remaining energy, then either the minimum value of the traffic load of the network node L or an average value must correspond to it,

$$\begin{cases} Q(E) = \max \\ L = \min, average \end{cases}$$

2) if a node has an average value of the level of remaining energy Q (E) - average, then it must correspond to the average load L, or the threshold value L,

$$\begin{cases} Q(E) = average \\ L = average, threshold \end{cases}$$

3) if the node has the minimum value of the remaining energy Q (E) - min, then it can correspond to the values of L from the minimum to the maximum.

$$\begin{cases} Q(E) = \min \\ \min < L < \max \end{cases}$$

If these conditions are met, the host could be considered as the trusted. If the level of remaining energy is higher than average, and the number of sent packets is higher, then most likely this node is malicious. To determine the resistance of a node to attacks, the parameters load L and remaining energy Q (E) are considered.

In order for a node to be considered resistant to attacks, it is necessary that the level of its remaining energy does not exceed the maximum specified energy level in the Emax network and is not significantly lower than that of neighboring nodes. At the same time, the level of workload of a node should not significantly exceed the level of workload of neighboring nodes and should not be below the minimum required level of workload. Both indicators should be considered at the same time. The low of the normal distribution could be used to represent the traffic load parameter L and the remaining energy Q (E) to calculate the trusted intervals and also the probability of the current value falling into the confidence interval.

$$L_i(t) \sim N(\overline{L}, \sigma_L^2), \tag{1}$$

$$Q(E)_i(t) = N(\overline{Q(E)}, \sigma_{Q(E)}^2) \tag{2}$$

where $\sigma_{Q(E)}$, σ_L – common for every host in a cluster; $\overline{L}$, $\overline{Q(E)}$ – the expected value for the load and remaining energy of the network host.

The use of this type of the probability distribution is connected with area of usage of such distribution especially for distributed service networks to estimate the number of messages over time, that is similar to our cases.

To find the confidence interval, you must first calculate the general average, for the following parameters: the remaining energy $\overline{Q(E)}$, $\overline{L}$ for the values remaining energy Q(E)i and workload Li for te cluster included in the cluster for each time interval:

$$\overline{Q(E)} = \left(\sum n_i Q(E)_i\right)/n, \tag{3}$$

$$\overline{L} = \left(\sum n_i L_i\right)/n. \tag{4}$$

Next, you need to calculate the D and the σ:

$$D_{Q(E)} = \left(\sum_i^N (Q(E)_i - \overline{Q(E)})^2\right)/n, \tag{5}$$

$$D_L = \left(\sum_i^N (L_i - \overline{L})^2\right)/n, \tag{6}$$

where n – is the sample size; $D_{Q(E)}$ – dispersion for remaining energy; D_L – variance for workload.

$$\sigma_{Q(E)} = \sqrt{D_{Q(E)}}, \tag{7}$$

$$\sigma_L = \sqrt{D_L}. \tag{8}$$

When determining the level of stability, it is important that the current values of the node do not go beyond the confidence interval, that is, the load of the node and the remaining energy do not exceed the permissible values. These values are calculated for the nodes of each cluster; accordingly, a selection of the current parameters of the nodes of one cluster is used. The central node calculates the bottom bmin and the top bmax the boundary of the trusted node for the load of the node and the remaining energy amin, amax by formulas:

$$a_{\min} = \overline{Q(E)} - t \cdot \sigma_{Q(E)}/\sqrt{n}, a_{max} = E_{max}, a_{min} < a_{max}, \tag{9}$$

$$b_{min} = L_{min}, \ b_{max} = \overline{L} + t \cdot \sigma_L/\sqrt{n}, \tag{10}$$

where $t * \sigma/\sqrt{n}$ – estimation accuracy; t – argument of the Laplace function; $\Phi(t) = \frac{\alpha}{2}$ – Laplace function; α – target reliability.

For remaining energy, the upper boundary of the interval is always Emax, since nodes can migrate from cluster to cluster and new nodes with the maximum remaining energy can appear, we should consider such factor to avoid an error of a first kind. The lower limit of the trusted interval was calculated only for the remaining energy parameter. Therefore, the lower bound for the traffic load parameter for the host is determined according to the necessary number of packets that node processed during a communication session. This is necessary so that the network node does not abandon its functions for transmitting packets to save energy. Next, we calculated likelihood that current values could be filled into trust interval:

$$P_{Q(E)}(a_{\min} < Q(E)_i < a_{max}) = \Phi\left(\frac{a_{max} - \overline{Q(E)}_s}{\sigma_{Q(E)s}}\right) - \Phi\left(\frac{a_{\min} - \overline{Q(E)}_s}{\sigma_{Q(E)s}}\right), \tag{11}$$

$$P_L(b_{\min} < L_i < b_{max}) = \Phi\left(\frac{b_{max} - \overline{L}_s}{\sigma_{L_s}}\right) - \Phi\left(\frac{b_{\min} - \overline{L}_s}{\sigma_{L_s}}\right), \tag{12}$$

where Φ – is the function of Laplace; $P_{Q(E)}$, P_L – the likelihood of hitting the host remaining energy and the host traffic level within the trusted interval.

To calculate the value of the standard deviation and expected value, we should take into account only the previous one L_{i-1}, $Q(E)_{i-1}$, current L_i, $Q(E)_i$ node values. So, for example, the level of remaining energy can decrease from 30 J to 2 J. In addition, the mathematical expectation will not give an exact value. If we take the value of adjacent intervals, then this will allow us to estimate whether the current value falls within the confidence interval without losing the accuracy of the calculation. To obtain the stability level of a node, you must use a combination of values $P_{Q(E)}$, P_L direct value of trust T_{cent} we use a special algorithm which is based on Bayes theorem:

$$T_{cent} = P(T_{cent}|P_{Q(E)}) * P(T_{cent}|P_L). \tag{13}$$

5 Analysis of Experimental Data

During the experiments, two parameters were changed: the total number of nodes and the number of attackers' nodes. The first series of experiments was carried out for the case when the network was operating normally, without attacks. 9 variants of the network were simulated, with a different number of nodes. During normal network operation, the level of resistance of a node to attacks tends to one, as shown in Fig. 3. Accordingly, this node can be considered trusted.

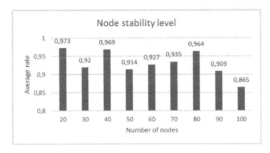

Fig. 3. During normal operation of the system, the level of resistance of the node to attacks tends to unity

Below are metrics for packets received/sent/forwarded and remaining energy during normal network operation, as shown in Fig. 4.

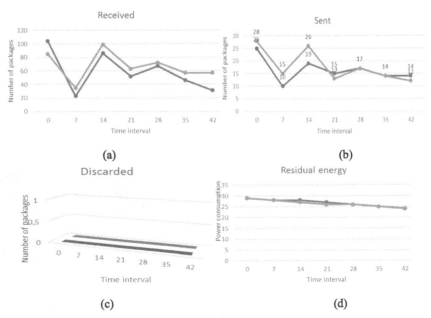

Fig.4. Analysis of experimental data during normal network operation (a) for received packets by node (b) for sent packets by node (c) for discarded packets (d) and for remaining energy

The second set of experiments was carried out for the case when a denial-of-service attack was implemented. 9 variants of the network were simulated with the possibility of promoting nodes. Thus, the level of traffic and the level of routing packets increased in the network since the attacker could be located at an inaccessible distance from the victim. Figure 5 shows the change in the parameters sent/received/dropped packets and remaining energy. The figure shows that there are significant changes for node 2, which implements attacks, and changes are observed in all parameters.

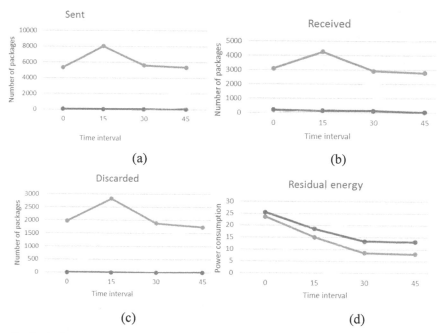

Fig. 5. Analysis of experimental data during a denial of service attack(a) for received packets by node (b) for sent packets by node (c) for discarded packets (d) and for remaining energy

At the same time, the level of trust in the network nodes decreased, that is, since the attack spreads to most of the network nodes, the level of the network's resistance to attacks decreases. Node 2 and 12 are malicious, and node 3 and 13 are trusted. You need to pay attention to the value of the probability $P_{Q\in}$ hitting the confidence interval of the current value of nodes 2, 12, 3, 13, calculated by the system when calculating the centralized value of trust in Table 4.

The table shows that the value for node 2 and 12 decreases. This situation means that the system detects nodes 2 and 12 as malicious. Table 5 shows the value of the probability of falling into the confidence interval of the load indicator PL for nodes 2, 12, 3, 13.

From Table 5 it can be seen that the level of resistance of a node to attacks at nodes 2 and 12 decreases to 0. At the same time, the level of trust of nodes 3 and 13 increases over time. When implementing the Sibyl attack, the overall level of resistance of network nodes to attacks also decreased, as can be seen from the Fig. 6.

Table 4. Probability of falling into the confidence interval of the remaining energy indicator $P_{Q\in}$

ID - node	Time interval, sec		
	15–29	30–44	45–59
12	0.52601363	0.238852068	0
2	0.731966849	0.969258091	0
3	0.74236144	0.621719522	0.68199999997609e−006
13	0.494457377	0.779350054	0.82275811

Table 5. Probability of falling into the confidence interval of the indicator workload P_L

ID - node	Time interval, sec		
	15–29	30–44	45–59
12	0.030166034	1.58099999997274e-006	0
2	0.03318886	0	0
3	0.991575814	0.999996268	1
13	0.829526234	1	1

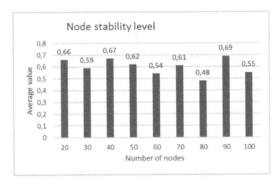

Fig. 6. Average level of nodes resistance to the Sibyl attack when the number of network nodes changes.

6 Conclusion

The analysis of the existing CPS is carried out and the structure for further modeling is revealed. The routing protocols and data transmission protocols are analyzed. The existing modeling tools were studied, and their comparative analysis was carried out to identify the CPS suitable for the given parameters. Nine network operation scenarios were simulated. Including normal mode, denial of service attack and Sibyl attack. The methodology for calculating the trust of nodes was studied, which later helped to identify a malicious node in the system. After conducting the analysis, it was revealed that an attacker requires a significant amount of energy resources to carry out attacks. During the simulation, trace files were obtained, with the help of which the operation of the network was studied. With the help of trace files, malicious nodes were identified by analyzing transmitted, received and dropped packets, the level of energy consumed and by calculating the probability of falling into the confidence interval. This work was supported by the RFBR grant 18–07-00212 "Development of a method and decision protocol for detecting anomalous node behavior in group control systems of autonomous mobile robots".

References

1. Valeev, S., Kondratyeva, N.: Safety system for cyber-physical systems based on self-learning multiagent system. In: 2018 Eleventh International Conference "Management of Large-Scale System Development" (MLSD), Moscow, Russia, 1–3 October 2018, pp. 1–3. https://doi.org/10.1109/iThings-GreenCom-CPSCom-SmartData.2016.140

2. Barrère, M., Hankin, C., Barboni, A., Zizzo, G., Boem, F., Maffeis, S., Parisini, Th.: CPS-MT: a real-time cyber-physical system monitoring tool for security research. In: 2018 IEEE 24th International Conference on Embedded and Real-Time Computing Systems and Applications (RTCSA), Hakodate, Japan, 28–31 August 2018, pp. 240–241. https://doi.org/10.1109/RTCSA.2018.00040

3. Chu, X., Tang, M., Huang, H., Zhan, L.: A security assessment scheme for interdependent cyber-physical power systems. In: 2017 IEEE/ACM 3rd International Workshop on Software Engineering for Smart Cyber-Physical Systems (SEsCPS), Buenos Aires, Argentina, pp. 22–25 (2017). https://doi.org/10.1109/SEsCPS.2017.5

4. Jithish, J., Sankaran, S., Achuthan, K.: Towards ensuring trustworthiness in cyber-physical systems: a game-theoretic approach. In: 2020 International Conference on Communication Systems & NETworkS (COMSNETS) (2020). https://doi.org/10.1109/COMSNETS48256.2020.9027362

5. Li, W., Jagtap, P., Zavala, L., Joshi, A., Finin, T.: CARE-CPS: context-aware trust evaluation for wireless networks in cyber-physical system using policies, Pisa, Italy, 6–8 June 2011, pp. 171–172. https://doi.org/10.1109/POLICY.2011.45

6. Zikratov, I.A., Zikratova, T.B., Lebedev, I.S., Gurtov, A.V.: Building a model of trust and reputation for the objects of multi-agent robotic systems with decentralized control. Sci. Tech. J. Inf. Technol. Mech. Optics 3(91), 30–38 (2014)

7. Xudong, G., Yiling, Y., Yinyuan, Y.: POM-a mobile agent security model against malicious hosts. In: Proceedings of the 4th International Conference on High Performance Computing in the Asia-Pacific Region, Beijing, China, pp. 1165–1166 (2000)

8. Karnik, N.M., Tripathi, A.R.: Security in the Ajanta mobile agent system. Softw. Pract. Exp. 31(4), 301–329 (2001)

9. Sander, T., Tschudin, C.F.: Protecting mobile agents against malicious hosts. In: Vigna, G. (ed.) Mobile Agents and Security. LNCS, vol. 1419, pp. 44–60. Springer, Heidelberg (1998). https://doi.org/10.1007/3-540-68671-1_4

10. Basan, E., Basan, A., Makarevich, O.: Probabilistic method for anomalies detection based on the analysis of cyber parameters in a group of mobile robots. Adv. Sci. Technol. Eng. Syst. 3(6), 281–288 (2018)

Futuristic Computing Technologies

Optimization of K-Nearest Neighbors for Classification

Kanika Joshi[1][(✉)], Shreya Jain[1], Sumit Kumar[1] (iD), and NiharRanjan Roy[2] (iD)

[1] Department of CSE, Amity School of Engineering and Technology,
Amity University Utter Pradesh Noida, Noida, India
[2] School of Engineering, GD Goenka University, Sohna Rural, Haryana, India

Abstract. KNN is one of the simplest algorithm used for classification of new data point. In this paper, another strategy of classification method is proposed by combining Class Confidence Weighted (CCW) KNN and Weighted KNN (WKNN) for enhancing the performance of KNN. Inspired from the classic KNN, the main idea being classifying test sample using the most frequent neighbors tag. The optimized KNN uses weights to classify test sample. The new technique is tested on four standard datasets. Results show the significant increment in accuracy in comparison with conventional KNN strategy.

Keywords: K-Nearest Neighbors · Class Confidence Weighted K-Nearest Neighbors · Weighted K-Nearest Neighbors

1 Introduction

In supervised learning, we are given a data set and already know what our correct output should look like, having the idea that there is a relationship between the input and the output. It is categorized into "regression" and "classification" problems. In a regression problem, we predict results which are continuous in nature, meaning that we are trying to map input variables to some continuous function. In a classification problem, we predict results which are discrete in nature.

One of the most popular supervised learning algorithms is K Nearest Neighbor (KNN). The main idea behind this algorithm is the closeness between the points [4]. The closer the points are they tend to fall in the same category. K-value plays a vital role in determining the class of the point as it is the measure of the number of points that should be considered depending upon their closeness with the given point whose class is to be determined. It is a powerful non parametric algorithm which bypasses the problem of probability densities completely [1, 9]. KNN is also termed as lazy learning algorithm as it does not learn from the train set it rather memorizes the train dataset. The selection of parameter k affects the performance of KNN [15]. Dudani was the first one to introduce distance weighted KNN rule and provided experimental results [2] where weights are defined in terms of distance. Each neighbor of test sample with its weight contributes in the final decision [1].

In this paper, an optimized algorithm is proposed so as to improve the accuracy rate of traditional KNN. The algorithm uses two weights which contribute in the final decision

P. K. Singh et al. (Eds.): FTNCT 2020, CCIS 1395, pp. 205–214, 2021.
https://doi.org/10.1007/978-981-16-1480-4_18

of classifying the test sample. The algorithm preprocesses the training set by evaluating the number of different categories present. Then the final classification is done by using this number count and by evaluating distance weights of the nearest samples. Finally, we do the comparative analysis of performance using three k values of classification algorithms.

The paper is organized as follows. Section 2 presents related work, working of Traditional KNN, WKNN and CCW KNN. The proposed work is presented in Sect. 3. The experimental results are addressed in Sect. 4. Finally, Sect. 5 concludes the paper.

2   Related Work

In the given section, we give a quick overview of works related to the modification of KNN.

Hamid Parvin et al. [1] using the formula given by S. Dudani proposed an algorithm which makes uses of parameter validity to find the class of test sample. The approach multiplies the distance weight and validity computed through data processing improved the performance of KNN significantly. S. Dudani [2] introduced weighted KNN by giving the formula to compute the weights of nearest neighbors. The weight of each neighbor was calculated using the distance that is between the test sample and the nearest neighbor which contributed in the final decision of classifying the test sample. Wei Liu et al. [3] introduced the probabilistic based weight in KNN for imbalanced data in order to optimize the performance of KNN. The approach proposed made use of likelihood weight which had a lot of significance in improving the performance of traditional KNN. The likelihood was computed by observing the number of times a class is present in the dataset. M. Bicego et al. [4] reinterpreted the weighted KNN by classifier combining approach, as a fixed combiner rule that is the sum rule. In this the formula of weights calculation given by S. Dudani was used in the sum rule. In [5], Xiuzhen Zhang et al. proposed an algorithm which emphasis on a new concept of assigning the rare class present in k neighbors. In this a new concept was introduced where the minority class present in k-neighbors could be assigned to the test sample. In [6] Jiangping Gou et al. proposed weighted KNN and dual weighted KNN which is the expansion of WKNN so as to reduce the sensitivity of selecting the nearest neighbors k value. The proposed approach gave a better performance in pattern classification when the performance is evaluated using twelve datasets.

2.1   K-Nearest Neighbor

KNN is a classification algorithm that works on no assumption theory that means it does not make assumptions about parameters. A sample is classified by voting of its neighbors, the class which is most common in its k neighbors [1].

If $k = 1$, the test sample is simply allocated the class of its single nearest neighbor. If $k > 1$, then the class which receives the maximum votes in k neighbors is assigned. The class $\bar{y}$ can be predicted using Eq. (1).

$$\bar{y} = \arg\max_{(c)} \left[\sum_{(i=0)}^{K} I_c(n_i) \right] \tag{1}$$

Where Ic(z) is the indicator function for class c −

$$I_c(z) = \begin{cases} 1, & \text{if } z \in \text{class } 0 \\ 0, & \text{otherwise} \end{cases}$$

2.2 Weighted KNN

Weighted KNN is an altered variant of KNN. The most straightforward strategy is to take the dominant part vote, yet this can be an issue if the closest neighbors fluctuate generally in their distances and the nearest neighbors indicate the class of test sample [11].

When $k > 1$, every neighbor has an associated weight with it which contributes in the final decision [1]. The weight W_{ni} can be assigned to nearest neighbors as the inverse of distance between the test sample and the neighbor. Weighted KNN assigns test sample $\bar{x}$ to that class $\bar{y}$ for which the sum of the weights of the representatives among the nearest neighbors is the greatest [2].

$$\bar{y} = \arg\max_c \left[\sum_{i=0}^{K} I_c(n_i) W_{ni} \right] \tag{2}$$

2.3 Class Confidence Weighted KNN

CCW makes use of probability of the given attributes values mainly class label [3, 5]. This likelihood computed contributes in the final decision of classifying the test sample. When $k = 1$, CCW KNN and KNN are equivalent. When $k > 1$, we compare the likelihood of each training sample.

Let c1 be the majority class and other being the minority. Likelihood of both the classes can be computed using Eq. (3) and (4). This is called as class confidence weight which contributes in the final decision of classifying the test point.

$$L_0 = \sum_{i=1}^{n} p(x_i | y_i = c_1) \tag{3}$$

$$L_1 = \sum_{i=1}^{n} p(x_i | y_i = c_2) \tag{4}$$

Then the class $\bar{y}$ of test sample is predicted using Eq. (5).

$$y = \arg\max_c \left[p(xi|yi) \sum_{i=0}^{K} I_c(n_i) \right] \tag{5}$$

Where $I_c(z)$ is the indicator of both the classes.

$$I_c(z) = \begin{cases} 1, & \text{if } z \in c_1 \\ 0, & \text{otherwise} \end{cases}$$

Where Ic(z) is the indicator function for class c −

$$I_c(z) = \begin{cases} 1, & \text{if } z \text{ class } 0 \\ 0, & \text{otherwise} \end{cases}$$

3 Proposed Work

In the given section we propose a hybrid approach obtained by combining two popular techniques discussed in previous sections namely: CCW and WKNN.

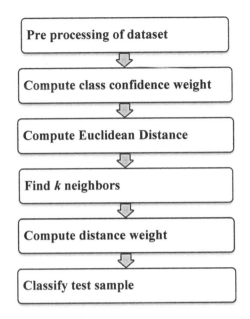

Fig. 1. Flowchart of proposed work

Figure 1 represents the flowchart of the hybrid algorithm which makes use of both weights: likelihood of classes referred to as W_{ni}^{CCW} as well as the weights computed through distances W_{ni}^{WKNN}. If $k = 1$ then the working of this algorithm is equivalent to KNN. When $k > 1$, both the weights contribute equally in the final decision of classifying the test sample into either class. The working methodology is explained in Algorithm 1.

Let L be a training set such that $-L = \{(x_i, y_i), i = 1, \ldots n\}$ where $\{x_i\}$ is the set of n training points and each is equipped with its label $\{y_i\}$.

Algorithm 1: CCW + WKNN.

Step 1: Let c_1 be the majority class present in y of training set L then the null hypothesis H_0 is defined as 'x_i belongs to class c_1'. Another class present in y of training set L be c_2 then an alternative hypothesis H1 can be defined as 'x_i belongs to class c_2' [3]. Likelihood of both the classes can be computed using Eq. (3) and (4).

Step 2: Let $\bar{x}$ is to be tested, then find euclidean distance of $\bar{x}$ from each train point in $L -$

$$\mathbf{d}(\mathbf{x_i}, \bar{\mathbf{x}}) = \left[\sum_{s=1}^{n} (\mathbf{x_{is}} - \bar{\mathbf{x}}_s)\right]^{1/2} \tag{6}$$

Step 3: Sort the distances and find $\{N_K\}$ which contains the k neighbors of test point —

$$N_K = \min_K \left[d\left(x_i, \bar{x} \right) \right] \tag{7}$$

Step 4: Calculate the weight of each neighbor referred to as W_{ni}^{WKNN} using Eq. (8).

$$W_{ni}^{WKNN} = \frac{1}{d(x_i, \bar{x})} \tag{8}$$

Step 5: Assign $\bar{y}$ the class to test sample as -

$$y = \arg \max_c \left[W_{ni}^{CCW} \sum_{i=0}^{K} I_c(n_i) W_{ni}^{WKNN} \right] \tag{9}$$

Where

$$W_{ni}^{CCW} = p(x_i | y_i) \tag{10}$$

And $I_c(Z)$ is the indicator of both the classes one at a time.

$$I_c(z) = \begin{cases} 1, & \text{if } z \in c_1 \\ 0, & \text{otherwise} \end{cases}$$

4 Experiments and Results

This section discusses the experimental results for the above mentioned algorithms.

4.1 Datasets

The hybrid algorithm is observed on four standard data sets, namely, Social Network Ads, Diabetes, Mall Customers and Breast Cancer whose description is given in Table 1. None of them had missing values.

In social Network Ads on the basis of three attributes the customer was classified in a category of purchasing a particular product or not. In diabetes dataset on the basis of eight attributes the patient was classified as a diabetic or non-diabetic patient. In Mall Customers on the basis of three features the genre was predicted (male or female). The text categorical data was converted into numerical category. In Breast Cancer 10 features were used to categorize the tissue diagnosed of the test sample.

Table 1. Description of dataset

	Instance	Features	Class
Social network ads	400	5	2
Diabetes	768	9	2
Mall customers	200	5	2
Breast cancer	569	32	2

4.2 Experimental Setup

For evaluating the results, the data sets were divided into two different sets- training set and the test set. For this purpose the size of training is set is kept 75% and test set is kept as 25% of the whole dataset. The results were recorded for three different k values i.e. 5, 6 and 7.

4.3 Performance Measures

There are different performance measures available to evaluate a Machine Learning algorithm. In this study three performance measures are taken into account namely, recall, precision and accuracy.

Accuracy is computed to evaluate the overall performance of classifier.

$$Accuracy = \left(\frac{TP + TN}{TP + TN + FT + FP} \right) *100 \tag{11}$$

Precision (positive predictive value) is the fraction of relevant document retrieval.

$$Precision = \frac{TP}{TP + FP} \tag{12}$$

Recall (or sensitivity) is defined as the number of positives returned by the model.

$$Recall = \frac{TP}{TP + FN} \tag{13}$$

Table 2. Comparison table for accuracy rate (%)

		KNN	*WKNN*	*CCW KNN*	*CCW + WKNN*
Social network ads	K = 5	69	77	79	82
	K = 6	66	77	77	82
	K = 7	75	80	80	82
Breast cancer	K = 5	91.608	91.608	90.909	91.608
	K = 6	88.811	92.300	92.307	92.308
	K = 7	90.209	92.307	91.608	92.308
Mall customers	K = 5	52	56	52	62
	K = 6	48	50	52	54
	K = 7	56.01	56.01	52	57.999
Diabetes	K = 5	75	75.521	77.6041	75.521
	K = 6	75	73.437	75.520	76.562
	K = 7	75	75.521	76.041	77.083

Table 3. Comparison table for precision and recall

	KNN		WKNN		CCW KNN		CCW + WKNN	
	Precision	Recall	Precision	Recall	Precision	Recall	Precision	Recall
Social network ads	0.7058	0.8135	0.7941	0.8571	0.9411	0.7901	0.8823	0.8571
Breast cancer	0.9111	0.9111	0.9555	0.9247	0.9666	0.8888	0.9666	0.9157
Mall customers	0.7692	0.5263	0.7307	0.558	0.7692	0.5263	0.8846	0.5897
Diabetes	0.8384	0.8014	0.8461	0.8540	0.9615	0.7668	0.9153	0.8677

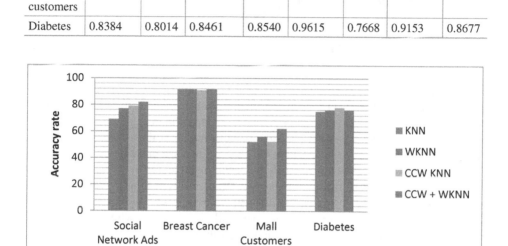

Fig. 2. Comparison chart for $k = 5$

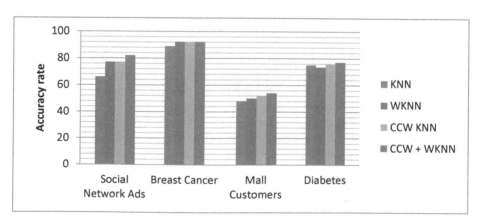

Fig. 3. Comparison chart for $k = 6$

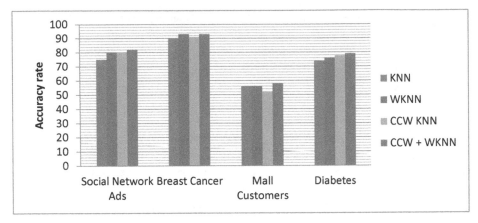

Fig. 4. Comparison chart for $k = 7$

Table 2 compares the performance of classification algorithms on the terms of accuracy rate computed by Eq. (11). The experiments show that the combination of CCW KNN and WKNN method significantly increases accuracy in most of the cases as compared to KNN. In some cases the accuracy of both the algorithms is same as seen in Table 2 when $k = 5$ for breast cancer but we can see increase in recall and precision of CCW + WKNN as compared to KNN for the same in Table 3.

Table 3 draws the performance comparison on the basis of other two factors recall and precision computed by using Eq. (12) and Eq. (13) respectively. The table shows that the quantity of positive class expectations that really have a place with a positive class and the quantity of positive class forecasts made out of every single positive model in the datasets utilized, both are most noteworthy for the proposed approach. Visualization of results is done through bar graphs in Fig. 2, Fig. 3 and Fig. 4. On each of these comparison charts, datasets are represented on x-axis and accuracy rate is plotted on y-axis.

In Fig. 2, the comparison is done for the algorithms when $k = 5$. It is seen that for breast cancer the performance measure gives almost the same value for KNN, WKNN and combination of CCW and WKNN and slightly lesser value for CCW KNN. For diabetes dataset the proposed approach gives higher plot as compared to KNN but lesser plot when compared to CCW KNN. For other two datasets the plot of the proposed approach is significantly higher as compared to other approaches.

In Fig. 3, the comparison is done for $k = 6$. CCW + WKNN give the higher plot as compared to other three algorithms for all datasets. But for breast cancer dataset, the plot for the three optimizations of KNN is almost equal but still greater than standard KNN.

In Fig. 4, the comparison is done for classification algorithms when $k = 7$. Through this figure it can be inferred that the proposed approach is giving the highest plot for all the datasets as compared to other three algorithms.

5   Conclusion

In this paper, we have proposed a hybrid approach, which is an improved version of KNN. The proposed algorithm is a combination of CCW and WKNN. The proposed algorithm makes use of two weights to classify a test sample. One is the likelihood and the other is the distance weight. Experiments were done on four standard datasets namely social network ads, breast cancer, mall customers and diabetes using different k values 5, 6 and 7 respectively. The comparison table shows improvement in the performance. The proposed work is compared against KNN, WKNN, CCW KNNN and the findings were tabulated. It was been observed that the hybrid approach to CCW KNN and WKNN algorithm gives higher value of accuracy on all the taken datasets at all the different k values than the existing algorithms. Hence, the proposed algorithm is the optimized version of the existing algorithm.

References

1. Parvin, H., Alizadeh, H., Minaei-Bidgoli, B.: MKNN: modified K-nearest neighbor. In: World Congress on Engineering and Computer Science, WCECS 2008 (2008)
2. Dudani, S.: The distance-weighted k-nearest neighbor rule. IEEE Trans. Syst. Man Cybern. **SMC-6**(4), 311–313 (1978)
3. Wei, L., Chawla, S.: Class Confidence Weighted KNN Algorithms for Imbalanced Data Sets. School of Information Technologies, University of Sydney
4. Bicego, M., Loog, M.: Weighted K-nearest neighbor revisited. In: 2016 23rd International Conference on Pattern Recognition (ICPR). IEEE (2016)
5. Zhang, X., Li, Y., Kotagiri, R., Wu, L., Tari, Z., Cheriet, M.: KRNN: k rare- class nearest neighbour classification. Pattern Recogn. **62**, 33–34 (2016)
6. Gou, J., Du, L., Zhang, Y., Xiong, T.: A new distance-weighted k- nearest neighbor classifier. J. Inf. Comput. Sci. **9**(6), 1429–1436 (2012)
7. Yang, X., et al.: Weighted k-nearest neighbor classification algorithm based on genetic algorithm. Telkomnika **11**(10), 6173–6178 (2013)
8. Darasay, B.V.: Nearest neighbor pattern recognition techniques. IEEE Computer Society Press, Las Alamitos
9. Duda, R.O., Hart, P.E., Stork, D.G.: Pattern classification. Wiley, Hoboken (2000)
10. Weinberger, K.Q., Blitzer, J., Saul, L.K.: Distance metric learning for large margin nearest neighbor classification. Advances in Neural Information Processing Systems (2006)
11. Zuo, W.M., et al.: Diagnosis of cardiac arrhythmia using kernel difference weighted KNN classifier. In: 2008 Computers in Cardiology. IEEE (2008)
12. Soucy, P., Mineau, G.W.: A simple KNN algorithm for text categorization. In: Proceedings 2001 IEEE International Conference on Data Mining. IEEE (2001)
13. Han, X., et al.: An optimized k-nearest neighbor algorithm for large scale hierarchical text classification. In: Joint ECML/PKDD PASCAL Workshop on Large-Scale Hierarchical Classification (2011)
14. Lubis, A., Lubis, M.: Optimization of distance formula in K-nearest neighbor method. Bull. Electr. Eng. Inf. **9**(1), 326–338 (2020)
15. Hand, D.J., Vinciotti, V.: Choosing k for two-class nearest neighbour classifiers with unbalanced classes. Pattern Recogn. Lett. **24**(9–10), 1555–1562 (2003)

16. Coomans, D., Massart, D.L.: Alternative k-nearest neighbour rules in supervised pattern recognition: Part 1. k-Nearestneighbour classification by using alternative voting rules. AnalyticaChimicaActa **136**, 15–27 (1982)
17. Wahid, A., Rao, A.C.S.: A distance-based outlier detection using particle swarm optimization technique. In: Fong, S., Akashe, S., Mahalle, P.N. (eds.) Information and Communication Technology for Competitive Strategies. LNNS, vol. 40, pp. 633–643. Springer, Singapore (2019). https://doi.org/10.1007/978-981-13-0586-3_62

Representing Autonomous Probabilistic Automata by Minimum Characteristic Polynomials over a Finite Field

Vjacheslav M. Zakharov[1](✉) (iD), Sergei V. Shalagin[1](✉) (iD),
and Bulat F. Eminov[2](✉) (iD)

[1] Kazan National Research Technical University named after A.N. Tupolev, Karl Marks St., 10,
420111 Kazan, Russia
[2] Simbirsoft Ltd., 420111 Kazan, Russia

Abstract. This paper proposes a method to represent a finite autonomous probabilistic automaton with a transition function defined by an ergodic stochastic matrix with rational elements, using the minimum characteristic polynomial over a finite field. The minimum polynomial constructed develops a Markovian sequence with a law that coincides with the pre-defined stochastic matrix of the automaton.

Keywords: Autonomous probabilistic automaton · Minimum-degree
polynomial · Stochastic matrix · Matrix representation accuracy · Finite field

1 Introduction

Works [1–3] present the methods and algorithms of constructing probabilistic automata [4, 5], based on the machinery of the $GF(2^n)$ finite fields theory [6]. Validity of using the approach [1–3] to synthesizing probabilistic automaton models is determined by the efficiency of finite fields arithmetic in the problems of digital data processing [7–9]. Constructing probabilistic models based on operations in finite fields allows representing the models by algebraic expressions (polynomials), as well as defining and promptly modifying the law of the sequences to be modelled by changing the coefficients of polynomials. In this approach, the problem of constructing polynomial models is solved by method [1] of computing the coefficients of polynomials over field $GF(2^n)$, based on the pre-defined ergodic stochastic matrices [10]. A challenging task in representing the automaton transformations of probabilistic sequences over field $GF(2^n)$ is the reduction of the field order (value of order 2^n of field $GF(2^n)$ in the said approach [1–3] depends on the order of the pre-defined stochastic matrices and on the accuracy of defining their elements).

Works [11, 12] propose the method of modelling and transforming Markovian chains (Markovian sequences) by minimum characteristic polynomials [9] over finite field $GF(q)$, $q \geq 2$, using Berlekamp-Massey algorithm (BMA) [13]. This method provides the solution of the problem related to representing stochastic matrices by minimum polynomials with a pre-defined accuracy. However, the matters are not adequately

© Springer Nature Singapore Pte Ltd. 2021
P. K. Singh et al. (Eds.): FTNCT 2020, CCIS 1395, pp. 215–224, 2021.
https://doi.org/10.1007/978-981-16-1480-4_19

investigated, regarding representing probabilistic automata defined by stochastic matrices, using minimum polynomials over finite field $GF(q)$. They include the problems of representing the probabilistic and the determinate transition functions of autonomous probabilistic automata [4, 5] by minimum polynomials over finite field $GF(q)$ with a pre-defined accuracy.

This study is aimed at solving the problem of representing autonomous probabilistic automata by minimum characteristic polynomials over field $GF(q)$, $q \geq 2$, with a pre-defined accuracy determined by the accuracy of defining the rational elements of ergodic stochastic matrices.

2 Problem Statement

Let us consider an autonomous probabilistic automaton (APA) appearing as [4, 5]

$$APA_1 = \left(S, \ \mu(s'/s), \ \bar{\pi}_0\right), \tag{1}$$

where $S = \{s_0, s_1, \ldots, s_{m-1}\}$ is a finite set of states; $\mu(s'/s)$ is the probabilistic automaton transition function defined by ergodic stochastic matrix $P_S = (p_{ij})$, $i, j = \overline{0, m-1}$, sized $m \times m$, determines the probability of the automaton transition to new state s', provided that it is in state s; and $\bar{\pi}_0$ is the m-sized vector of the initial distribution of the probabilities of Markovian chain states.

Autonomous probabilistic automaton equivalent to system (1) can be represented as [5]

$$APA_2 = \left(S, \ \hat{X}, \ \Delta(x, s) = s, \ \bar{\pi}_0\right), \tag{2}$$

where elements S, $\bar{\pi}_0$ are the same as in (1), $\hat{X}$ is a discrete random variable, $\hat{X} = \begin{pmatrix} x_0 \ x_1 \ \ldots \ x_{l-1} \\ p_0 \ p_1 \ \ldots \ p_{l-1} \end{pmatrix}$, taking the finite set of values $X = \{x_0, \ldots, x_{l-1}\}$ at the input of APA (1) with probabilities represented by a pre-defined stochastic vector $\bar{P} = \{p_0, \ldots, p_{l-1}\}$, $0 \leq p_j \leq 1$, $\sum_{i=0}^{l-1} p_i = 1$; and $\Delta(x, s)$ is the transition function defined by the table sized $m \times l$.

For the given elements $\left(\hat{X}, \Delta(x, s)\right)$ of the automaton (2), the stochastic matrix of the automaton (1) can be unambiguously set in the form of

$$P_S = \sum_{k=0}^{l-1} p_k M(x_k), \tag{3}$$

where $p_k, k = \overline{0, l-1}$ are elements of the stochastic vector $\bar{P} = \{p_0, \ldots, p_{l-1}\}$; $M(x_k)$, $k = \overline{0, l-1}$ is a simple matrix [4] sized $m \times m$, corresponding to the symbol x_k, with elements $\pi_{ij}(x_k) \in \{0, 1\}$; value l satisfies the relation $l \leq m^2 - m + 1$ [4]: in (3), the elements $\pi_{ij}(x_k), i, j = \overline{0, m-1}$ of a simple matrix $M(x_k), k = \overline{0, l-1}$, are determined by relation [14],

$$\pi_{ij}(x_k) = \begin{cases} 1, & \text{if } s_j = \Delta(x_k, s_i) \\ 0, & \text{else.} \end{cases} \tag{4}$$

Note that it is possible to generate implementations of Markovian sequences defined by the given ergodic stochastic matrices, using automaton (1). At a fixed length N of the implementation, the elements p_{ij} of the matrix $P_S = (p_{ij})$, $i,j = \overline{0, m-1}$ can be estimated by the obtained frequencies $p'_{ij} = \frac{a_{ij}}{a_i}$ [10], $i,j = \overline{0, m-1}$, where a_i is the number of occurrences of the state s_i in the implementation of length N, a_{ij} is the number of occurrences of pairs standing side-by-side in the states of s_i and s_j. Expected with a pre-defined authenticity, the accuracy of approximating matrix P_S by matrix $P' = \left(p'_{ij} = \frac{a_{ij}}{a_i}\right)$, $i,j = \overline{0, m-1}$, grows proportionally to the value of $\frac{1}{\sqrt{N}}$. We can assume that automaton (1) in modeling the implementation of a Markovian sequence of a given length N represents matrix P_S with an accuracy of at most $\frac{1}{\sqrt{N}}$.

Let us denote by the $\varphi = \{s_{i1}, \ldots, s_{iN}\}$ the implementation of the Markovian chain of length N, with symbols from alphabet S, $i = \overline{0, m-1}$, which has the following properties:

- for $\forall i = \overline{0, m-1}$ the letter s_i is included $a_i^{(\varphi)} \geq 1$ times in a sequence φ;
- the letter s_j ($j = \overline{0, m-1}$) follows $a_{ij}^{(\varphi)} \geq 0$ once s_i (we assume that s_{iN} follows s_i);
- the equalities are true

$$P_\varphi = \left(p_{ij}^{(\varphi)}\right) = \left(\frac{a_{ij}^{(\varphi)}}{a_i^{(\varphi)}}\right), a_i^{(\varphi)} = \sum_{j=0}^{m-1} a_{ij}^{(\varphi)} = \sum_{j=0}^{m-1} a_{ji}^{(\varphi)}, \sum_{i=0}^{m-1} a_i^{(\varphi)} = N.$$

(5)

Sequence φ is comparable to an ergodic stochastic matrix $P_\varphi = \left(p_{ij}^{(\varphi)}\right)$, $i,j = \overline{0, m-1}$, sized $m \times m$, where rational elements (relative frequencies) $p_{ij}^{(\varphi)} = \frac{a_{ij}^{(\varphi)}}{a_i^{(\varphi)}}$ satisfy relation (5) and the limiting vector [10] of the matrix P_φ is equal to.

$$\bar{\pi}_\varphi = \left(\pi_i^{(\varphi)} = \frac{a_i}{N}\right), i = \overline{0, m-1}.$$

(6)

Assume that value ε, $0 < \varepsilon < 1$ is associated with the length N of the sequence φ following the linear equation [15]:

$$N \geq N^*, N^* = max\left\{ \max_{\substack{i,j = \overline{0, t-1} \\ p_{ij}\pi_i \neq 0}} \left\{\frac{1}{(p_{ij}\pi_i)}\right\}, \max_{i,j=\overline{0,t-1}} \left\{\frac{(1+p_{ij}+\varepsilon)}{(\pi_i\varepsilon)}\right\}\right\}.$$

(7)

Let us note the result [15], which establishes the relationship of matrices P_S and P_φ.
Let us introduce a stochastic matrix in the form of P_φ sized $m \times m$, having properties (9), (10) and satisfying the following conditions.

$$|N - N^*| \leq m - 1;$$

(8)

$$\left|p_{ij}^{(\varphi)} - p_{ij}\right| \le \varepsilon, i, j = \overline{0, m - 1}; \tag{9}$$

$$p_{ij}^{(\varphi)} = \begin{cases} 0, & \text{if } p_{ij} = 0 \\ \delta > 0, & \text{if } p_{ij} > 0 \end{cases}; \tag{10}$$

$$\left|\pi_i^{(\varphi)} - \pi_i\right| \le \left(\frac{1}{N}\right) + \frac{\pi_i(N - N^*)}{N}. \tag{11}$$

where π_i, $i = \overline{0, m - 1}$, are the elements of the limit vector.

According to [15],

Theorem 1 [15]. For the P_S data, its limit vector $\bar{\pi}$, and the number ε, $0 < \varepsilon < 1$ there is a stochastic matrix P_φ sized $m \times m$ and satisfying conditions (5)–(11).

Further, to define automaton (1), we will use matrix P_φ satisfying conditions (5)–(11).

Let us introduce the following definitions. Sequence over field $GF(q)$ shall mean any function $u: Z \to GF(q)$ defined on the set Z of non-negative integers and taking values in the field $GF(q)$ [7]. Sequence $u = (u_i)$, $i \in Z$ is called linear recurrence sequence (LRS) of order $Z > 0$ over the field $GF(q)$, if there are constants $b_0, b_1, \ldots, b_{L-1} \in GF(q)$, such that $u(i + L) = \sum_{j=0}^{L-2} b_j \cdot u(i + j)$, $i \ge 0$ [7]. Polynomial

$$f(x) = x^L + \sum_{j=0}^{L-1} b_j \cdot x^j \tag{12}$$

is called the characteristic LRS polynomial [7].

The characteristic polynomial (12) of the LRS u, having the minimum degree, is its minimum polynomial [7].

We denote by u_N the LRS u of an arbitrary length N, where the length of LRS is the number of characters in LRS. We say that the polynomial $f(x)$ (12) generates a sequence u_N if u_N is a subsequence of some LRS with this characteristic polynomial.

In the function of sequences of u_N we consider Markovian sequences of a given length N with properties (5) and (6) (sequence of) defined by ergodic stochastic matrices P_φ.

The solvable problem of representing the minimal polynomial over the field $GF(q)$ of the given automaton (1) (an automaton (2) represented as an equivalent automaton (1)) is as follows. Let an automaton (1) with a matrix $P_S = P_\varphi = \left(\frac{a_{ij}}{a_i}\right)$, $i, j = \overline{0, m - 1}$ be given. It is required to construct the minimum polynomial (12) over the field $GF(q)$, $q \ge 2$, generating a sequence of u_N with a length N such that the ergodic stochastic matrix (notation $P_\varphi(u_N)$) constructed from this sequence coincides with the given matrix of the automaton (1), i.e. matrix $P_\varphi(u_N) = P_\varphi$.

3 Representing APA$_1$ as a Minimum Polynomial over a Field $GF(q)$

We will consider the solution of the problem of representing APA$_1$ by a minimum polynomial as the implementation of the following three stages.

Stage 1. Mapping matrix P_S into matrix P_φ.

Matrix $P_\varphi = \left(p_{ij}^{(\varphi)}\right)$, $i,j = \overline{0, m-1}$, can be set (calculated) on the basis of the matrix to define the automaton (1) $P_S = \left(p_{ij}\right)$, $i,j = \overline{0, m-1}$, given the system (1) according to the algorithm approximation of elements (denoted as AE) p_{ij} matrix P_S by rational elements $p_{ij}^{(\varphi)} = \dfrac{a_{ij}^{(\varphi)}}{a_i^{(\varphi)}}$ presented in [15].

At the input of the AE algorithm: matrix P_S with a size of $m \times m$; number ε, $0 < \varepsilon < 1$ and the number N^* calculated by the formula (7).

Output: ergodic stochastic matrix P_φ sized $m \times m$.

Computational complexity of the AE algorithm is determined by the estimate $O\left(m^4\right)$ [15].

Stage 2. Constructing set φ by a given matrix $P_\varphi = \left(p_{ij}^{(\varphi)}\right)$.

By matrix $P_\varphi = \left(p_{ij}^{(\varphi)}\right)$, we will construct sequence $\varphi = \{s_{i1}, s_{i2}, \ldots, s_{iN}\}$, in alphabet $S = \{s_0, s_1, \ldots, s_{m-1}\}$ with the law $P_\varphi = \left(p_{ij}^{(\varphi)}\right)$, in accordance with the algorithm (notation A_φ) [15] where the integral matrix $M_\varphi = \left(a_{ij}^{(\varphi)}\right)$ sized $m \times m$, $a_{ij}^{(\varphi)}$ - numerators of the elements $p_{ij}^{(\varphi)} = \dfrac{a_{ij}^{(\varphi)}}{a_i^{(\varphi)}}$ is regarded as the adjacency matrix of the euler-oriented graph [16] with m vertices $s_0, s_1, \ldots, s_{m-1}$. Exactly $a_{ij}^{(\varphi)}$ arcs lead from vertex s_i to vertex s_j, and by virtue of property (5) of each s_i vertex incident in exactly $a_i^{(\varphi)}$ incoming and $a_i^{(\varphi)}$ outgoing arcs. Algorithm A_φ implements the procedure of probabilistic traversal of a directed closed Euler chain. The starting vertex is determined by vector $\bar{\pi}_0$.

Stage 3. Using set φ to construct the minimum characteristic polynomial (12) according to the Berlekamp-Massey algorithm.

An effective algorithm for constructing the minimum characteristic polynomial according to a given u_N is Berlekamp-Massey algorithm (BMA) [13]. The following property of Berlekamp-Massey algorithm should be noted.

Theorem 2 [13]. Let a set of u_N with the length N from the field elements $GF(q)$ be specified. Then, using the sequence u_N, Berlekamp-Massey algorithm constructs a single minimum polynomial with degree L satisfying the condition.

$$2L \leq N.$$

Set φ with a length of N constructed in step 2 will be considered as set u_N. We encode the symbols of the alphabet S with the elements of field $GF(q)$, where $q > m$. According to the sequence u_N of length $(N+1)$ (it is taken into account that symbol s_{iN} follows symbol s_{i1}) we construct with the help of BMA the minimum polynomial of $f(x)$ with a degree L, where L is defined according to the statement:

Consequence 1 (from Theorem 2). The Berlekamp-Massey algorithm constructs from a sequence of u_N with a length $(N+1)$ specified by the law $P_\varphi(u_N)$ a single minimum characteristic polynomial (12) with a degree L satisfying the expression

$$L \leq \begin{cases} \dfrac{(N+1)}{2}, & \text{if } N - \text{even}; \\ \dfrac{((N+1)+1)}{2}, & \text{if } N - \text{odd}. \end{cases} \tag{13}$$

Example 1. Illustration of implementing Stages 1–3.

Stage 1. Mapping matrix P_S into matrix P_φ.

Given are matrix P_S (Fig. 1), number $\varepsilon = 0.05$, and vector $\bar{\pi} = (40/138; 28/138; 35/138; 35/138)$.

By AE algorithm, we are going to construct matrix P_φ (Fig. 2), where $N^* = 21$, $\bar{\pi}_\varphi = (6/21; 5/21; 5/21; 5/21)$, $\left| p_{ij}^{(\varphi)} - p_{ij} \right| \leq 0.05$, and $\left| \pi_i^{(\varphi)} - \pi_i \right| \leq 0.0352$, that is, conditions (5)–(11) are complied with.

$$P_S = \begin{pmatrix} 0.3 & 0 & 0.7 & 0 \\ 0 & 0.25 & 0 & 0.75 \\ 0 & 0.6 & 0 & 0.4 \\ 0.8 & 0 & 0.2 & 0 \end{pmatrix}.$$

Fig. 1. Matrix P_S

$$P_\varphi = \begin{pmatrix} 2/6 & 0 & 4/6 & 0 \\ 0 & 1/5 & 0 & 4/5 \\ 0 & 4/5 & 0 & 1/5 \\ 4/5 & 0 & 1/5 & 0 \end{pmatrix}.$$

Fig. 2. Matrix P_φ

Stage 2. Constructing sequence φ by a given matrix $P_\varphi = \left(p_{ij}^{(\varphi)} \right)$.

By matrix P_φ (Fig. 2), we will construct sequence φ, $N = 21$ long, in alphabet $S = \{s_0, s_1, s_2, s_3\}$ by algorithm A_φ [15] (by probabilistic bypass of the directed closed Euler chain by 21 arcs formed by pairs $(s_i\, s_j)$). A variation of the relevant sequence u_N, $N' = 21$ long, appears as.

$$u_N = s_1\, s_1\, s_3\, s_0\, s_2\, s_1\, s_3\, s_0\, s_2\, s_3\, s_2\, s_1\, s_3\, s_0\, s_2\, s_1\, s_3\, s_0\, s_0\, s_0\, s_2.$$

Stage 3. To code the states of set $S = \{s_0, s_1, s_2, s_3\}$, we are going to use field $GF(q)$, $q = 7$, in constructing the minimum polynomial by Berlekamp-Massey algorithm. BMA can be executed based on the software implementation of [17]. Minimum polynomial constructed by the above sequence u_N with the length of $N' = 21$ has the order of $L = 11$ and appears as:

$$f(x) = x^{11} - 4x^{10} - 2x^9 - 5x^8 - 5x^6 - 3x^5 - 3x^4 - x^3 - 6x^2 - 3x.$$

Based on the probabilistic algorithm, A_φ (Stage 2), we can build by the given matrix, $P_\varphi = \left(p_{ij}^{(\varphi)} \right)$, a certain set of sequences u_N with the predefined length, N^*, and in Stage 3, use the Berlekamp-Massey algorithm to construct the relevant set of minimal polynomials with the power determined by formula (13).

For instance, for the data from Example 1, another sequence, u_N, built in a similar manner appears as:

$$u_N = s_1\, s_3\, s_2\, s_1\, s_1\, s_3\, s_0\, s_0\, s_2\, s_3\, s_0\, s_2\, s_3\, s_0\, s_2\, s_1\, s_3\, s_0\, s_0\, s_2\, s_1,$$

and the relevant minimal polynomial has the power of $L = 11$ and appears as:

$$f(x) = x^{11} - 3x^{10} - x^8 - 2x^7 - 6x^6 - 6x^5 - 5x^4 - 4x^2 - 2x - 1.$$

Let us find the potency of a set of minimal characteristic polynomials being represented by automaton (1) defined by matrix $P_\varphi = \left(p_{ij}^{(\varphi)}\right)$.

Sequence u_N built by algorithm A_φ can be considered as a permutation of the S set elements with repetitions [18]. Number of different permutations of set S with repetitions is defined by function [18]

$$C_K(a_1, a_2, ..., a_m) = h = K!/(a_1! \cdot a_2! \cdot ... \cdot a_m!), \tag{14}$$

where $K = N^*$, $a_1, a_2, \ldots, a_m$ – a set of natural numbers, such that $\sum_{j=1}^{m} a_j = K$.

From Theorems 1 and 2 and from formula (14), it follows that the following statement is true:

Statement 1. Given set S, matrix $P_\varphi = \left(p_{ij}^{(\varphi)}\right)$ sized $m \times m$, and number N^*, the number of minimal characteristic polynomials (12) of power (13), representing matrix $P_\varphi = \left(p_{ij}^{(\varphi)}\right)$, is limited from above by the value of (14).

Example 2. Given set $S = \{s_0, s_1, s_2, s_3\}$, matrix P_φ (Fig. 2), and set $(a_1, a_2, a_3, a_4) = (6, 5, 5, 5)$, $K = 21$, then according to (14) h is equal to.

$$21!/(6! \cdot 5! \cdot 5! \cdot 5!).$$

4   Representing a Non-autonomous Probabilistic Automaton

Let us consider how to apply Stages 1–3 to solving the problem of representing a specific type of non-autonomous probabilistic automaton [4] by minimal polynomial. Suppose there is a given particular type of a non-autonomous probabilistic automaton [4] – Bernoulli automaton [4]

$$\left(S, \hat{X}, \{P(x_k)\}, \bar{\pi}_0\right), \tag{15}$$

where elements $S, \hat{X}, \bar{\pi}_0$, the same as in (2), $\{P(x_k)\}$, $k = \overline{0, l-1}$, are a set of ergodic stochastic matrices sized $m \times m$ and defining automaton transition function (15). In a similar manner, the transition function is also defined in general probabilistic automaton [4, 5]. In functioning automaton (15), matrix $P(x_k)$ is associated to input letter x_k, and this matrix defines the automaton transition into a new state.

Let us uniquely associate automaton (15) to automaton (1) by algorithm [4]. We will form ergodic stochastic matrix P_S sized $m \times m$ by the following rule [4]:

$$P_S = \sum_{k=0}^{l-1} p_k P(x_k), \tag{16}$$

where p_k, $k = \overline{0, l-1}$, are the elements of stochastic vector $\overline{P} = \{p_0, p_1, ..., p_{l-1}\}$.

Representing Bernoulli automaton (15) as automaton (1) with matrix (16) allows solving the problem of representing automaton (15) by minimal polynomial, implementing Stages 1–3 over the relevant automaton (1).

Let us list the following potential applications of solving the above problem.

Using the proposed method of representing autonomous probabilistic automata, we can use given stochastic matrices to build sequences over finite field $GF(q)$ from the class of Markovian sequences with a given "linear complexity" defined by the power of the minimal polynomial constructed.

Based on minimal polynomial, we can use the Berlekamp-Massey algorithm to construct a linear shift register [7, 17] consisting of at most $N/2$ q-ry bits and model/obtain the implementations of Markovian sequences of the given length N with a regularity defined by the given ergodic stochastic matrix P_φ with the accuracy of $1/N$.

Representing autonomous probabilistic automata on linear shift registers in accordance with the constructed minimal polynomials is relevant to the hardware implementation [1–3, 19–21] of Markovian sequence generators using the FPGA (field programmable gate array) technology [22].

Such generators are used in constructing special-purpose electronic devices in areas, such as signal processing in communications and control systems, statistical modeling, developing probability models to solve the information security problems, and performing the technical diagnostics of digital devices [7, 14, 21, 23, 24].

5 Conclusion

Problem of representing a finite autonomous probabilistic automaton appearing as (1) by minimum characteristic polynomial (12) over a finite field is solved as a problem of representing with a polynomial the ergodic stochastic matrix P_φ describing the predefined automaton. Solving the problem of representing the autonomous probabilistic automaton appearing as (2) by the minimum polynomial is reduced to constructing the equivalent automaton (1).

Implementing Markovian sequences on registers described by minimal characteristic polynomials allows improving the accuracy of representing the given regularity of Markov chain. It is shown that the known alternative models, (1) and (2), when modeling a MC of the given length, N, represent a stochastic matrix with an accuracy that does not exceed the value of $1/\sqrt{N}$.

References

1. Zakharov, V.M., Nurutdinov, Sh.R., Shalagin, S.V.: Polinomialnoye predstavleniye tsepey Markova nad polem Galua [Polynomial Representation of Markovian Chains over Galois Field]. In: Vestnik KGTU im. A.N. Tupoleva [Scientific Journal of Kazan National Research Technical University], no. 3, pp. 27–31 (2001). (in Russian)
2. Nurutdinov, Sh.R.: Osnovy teorii polinomialnykh modeley avtomatnykh preobrazovaniy nad polem Galua [Basics of the Theory of the Polynomial Models for Automaton Transformations over Galois Field]. Kazan University Press, Kazan (2005). 155 p. (in Russian)

3. Shalagin, S.V.: Realizatsiya tsifrovykh ustroystv v arkhitekture PLIS/FPGA pri ispolzovanii raspredelennykh vychisleniy v polyakh Galua. Monografiya [Implementinv Digital Devices in the FPGA Architecture in Using Distributed Computations in Galois Fields. Monograph]. KNITU-KAI University Press, Kazan (2016). 228 p. (in Russian)
4. Pospelov, D.A.: Veroyatnostnyye avtomaty [Probabilistic Automata]. Energiya, Moscow (1970). 88 p. (in Russian)
5. Bukharaev, R.G.: Osnovy teorii veroyatnostnykh avtomatov [Probabilistic Automata Theory]. Nauka, Moscow (1985). 287 p. (in Russian)
6. Lidl, R., Niederreiter, H.: Finite Fields (Encyclopedia of Mathematics and its Applications), 2nd edn. Cambridge Univ. Press, Cambridge (2008). 772 p. ISBN-10: 0521065674; ISBN-13: 978–0521065672
7. Alferov, A.P., Zubov, A.Yu., Kuzmin, A.S., Cheremushkin, A.V.: Osnovy kriptografii [Basics of Criptography]. Gelios ARV, Moscow (2002). 480 p. (in Russian)
8. Pesoshin, V.A., Kuznetsov, V.M., Shirshova, D.V.: Generators of the equiprobable pseudorandom nonmaximal-length sequences based on linear-feedback shift registers. Autom. Remote control 77(9), 1622–1631 (2016)
9. Gibadullin, R.F., Vershinin, I.S., Minyazev, R.S.: Development of load balancer and parallel database management module. In: Proceedings - 2018 International Conference on Industrial Engineering, Applications and Manufacturing, ICIEAM 2018. https://doi.org/10.1109/ICIEAM.2018.8728629. https://ieeexplore.ieee.org/document/8728629
10. Kemeny, J.G., Snell, J.L.: Finite Markov Cchains, p. 210. Van Nostrand, Princeton (1960)
11. Eminov, B.F.: Metod modelirovaniya sluchaynykh posledovatelnostey klassa neodnorodnykh tsepey Markova polinomami minimalnoy stepeni nad polem GF(q) [Method of Modelling Random Sequences Belonging to the Class of Non-Uniform Markovian Chains by Minimum-Degree Polynomials over Field GF(q)]. In: Sistemy upravleniya i informatsionnyye tekhnologii [Control Systems and Information Technology], vol. 4.1(30), 203–207. Nauchnaya kniga, Voronezh (2007). (in Russian)
12. Zakharov, V.M., Shalagin, S.V., Eminov, B.F.: Representing Lumped Markov Chains by Minimal Polynomials over Field GF(q). J. Phys. Conf. Ser. **1015**, 032033 (2018)
13. Massey, J.L.: Shift-register synthesis and BCH decoding. IEEE Trans. Inform. Theory **IT-15**, 122–127 (1969)
14. Levin, B.R., Schwartz, W.: Veroyatnostnyye modeli i metody v sistemakh svyazi i upravleniya [Probabilistic Models and Methods in Communication and Control Systems]. Radio i svyaz, Moscow (1985). 312 p. (in Russian)
15. Zacharov, V.M., Kuznetsov, S.E.: Complexity of the problem of approximation of stochastic matrix by rational elements. In: Budach, L., Bukharajev, R.G., Lupanov, O.B. (eds.) FCT 1987. LNCS, vol. 278, pp. 483–487. Springer, Heidelberg (1987). https://doi.org/10.1007/3-540-18740-5_106
16. Harary, F.: Graph Theory. Addison-Wesley, Reading (1969). 273 p.
17. Khusainov, R.N., Eminov, B.F., Galimov, M.D., Kryukov, A.I.: Development of a software implementation of the Berlekamp-Massey algorithm for the analysis and synthesis of binary recurrent sequences. Herald Technol. Univ. **18**(24), 89–91 (2015)
18. Bronstein, I.N., Semendyaev, K.A.: Spravochnik po matematike dlya inzhenerov i uchashchikhsya vtuzov [Mathematics Reference for Engineers and Technical College Students]. 13th edition, revised. Nauka, Moscow. Chief Editorial Board for Physical and Mathematical Literature (1986). 544 p. (in Russian)

19. Zakharov, V.M., Nurutdinov, Sh.R., Shalagin, S.V.: Metod modelirovaniya i preobrazovaniya funktsiy tsepey Markova v polyakh Galua i yego realizatsiya v basise PLIS [Method for Modeling and Transforming the Functions of Markov Chains, and Implementing It in the FPGA Basis]. In: Metody i sredstava obrabotki informatsii: tez.dokl. 2-y Vseross.nauch.konf. [Information Processing Methods and Tools: Proceedings of the 2nd Russian National Scientific Conference] on 5–7 October 2005, pp. 256–262. MSU, Moscow (2005). (in Russian)
20. Zakharov, V.M., Shalagin, S.V., Eminov, B.F.: Representing maximal pseudo-random sequences on the basis of non-linear vector-valued complication function over a finite field. In: 11th IEEE International Conference on Application of Information and Communication Technologies, AICT 2017 – Proceedings, 20–22 September 2017. Date Added to IEEE Xplore: 11 April 2019. https://doi.org/10.1109/ICAICT.2017.8687001
21. Kuznetsov, V.M., Pesoshin, V.A.: Generatory sluchaynykh i psevdosluchaynykh posledovatel-nostey na tsifrovykh elementakh zaderzhki: monographiya [Random and Pseudo-Random Sequence Generators on Digital Delay Units: Monograph]. Kazan State Tech. Univ. Press, Kazan (2013) 336 p. (in Russian)
22. Spartan-3 Generation FPGA User Guide, UG331 (v1.8)). https://www.xilinx.com/support/documentation/user_guides/ug331.pdf
23. Ivanova N.N.: Razrabotka optimalnykh algoritmov i ustroystv obrabotki markovskikh signalov v odnostupenchatoy SOK [Developing Optimal Algorithms and Devices to Process Markovian Signals in a Single-Stage RNS]. In: Ivanova, N.N. (ed.) Vestnik Chuvashskogo Universiteta [Chuvash University Herald], vol. 2, pp. 219–223 (2009)
24. Stolov, E.L.: Metody kompaktnogo testirovaniya tsifrovykh ustroystv [Compact Testing Methods for Digital Devices]. Kazan University Press, Kazan (1993). 116 p.

Analysis of Histopathological Images Using Machine Learning Techniques

Ratima Raj Singh[1]($\boxtimes$), Sumit Kumar[1]($\boxtimes$), Surbhi Vijh[2]($\boxtimes$), and Nihar Ranjan Roy[3]($\boxtimes$)

[1] Amity University, Noida, Uttar Pradesh, India
[2] KIET Group of Institution, Ghaziabad, Uttar Pradesh, India
[3] School of Engineering, GD Goenka University, Sohna Rural, Haryana, India

Abstract. According to a reports of WHO, one in 10 Indians is going to grow a lifetime of cancer and another in 15 will die from it because survival rates in India are low due to late detection. Indian Medical Council of research recently reported that total number of new cases is approximately expected to be 17.3 lakhs in 2020. It is predicted by experts that there will be a 500% increase in cancer incidence in India by 2025. There are many advanced methods and techniques of breast cancer diagnosis in modern medical science. Computer scientists and pathologist are working to use latest artificial intelligence (AI) techniques for improving the efficiency of diagnostic workflows in the analysis of pathological slides for diagnosis, prognosis, prevention and other significant clinical purposes. Histopathological images attained by biopsy is one of the refine imagining modality used to collect samples for the detection of breast cancer. This article discusses and summarizes the digital imaging methods for the identification of breast cancer in histopathological photographs and elaborates its future possibilities.

Keywords: Histopathological images · Healthcare · Machine learning

1 Introduction

Healthcare is one of today's fastest growing regions considered as the cornerstone of a complete global transformation. Artificial Intelligence (AI) is now helping to streamline hospital management, diagnose infectious diseases and personalize patient care [1]. It is used to predict ICU transfers, enhance clinical workflows and even identify the risk of a patient from hospital infections [2]. Machine learning and deep learning are the AI technologies which have different fundamental features and can be applied in different fields. Such methods have been developed drastically in recent years and the large constructive approach for the use of cancer medicine has been implemented [3]. Throughout the testing of complicated healthcare data, the use of sophisticated algorithms and software to simulate human cognition is a primary aim for AI applications. Structured and unstructured data are the types of healthcare data on which artificial techniques can be applied to give the optimum results. The main focus should be dealing with the study of the linkages between treatment approaches and the outcomes of patients [4].

© Springer Nature Singapore Pte Ltd. 2021
P. K. Singh et al. (Eds.): FTNCT 2020, CCIS 1395, pp. 225–233, 2021.
https://doi.org/10.1007/978-981-16-1480-4_20

People worldwide have become a chronic epidemic of breast cancer. The global cancer report 2020 states that the incidence of cancer in India increasing steadily [5]. According to WHO, 25.8 women in India per 100000 people for the prevalence of breast cancer. Based on the study conducted in 2017 almost 3, 50,000 women live with breast cancer if we consider the population of India is 1.3 billion in which half of them are females. By the beginning of 2020, it is expected that this will rise to staggering 18, 00,000.

Digital histopathology includes detailed examination of image content for diagnosis and treatment. But it is difficult to achieve accurate result because of color variation in the images [6]. Screening programs like Ultrasound, Computer Tomography (CT), X-ray, Positron Emission Tomography (PET), Mammogram and Magnetic Resonance imaging (MRI) is advised by doctors initially [7, 8]. A biopsy will be suggested by the medical experts, if some suspicions have found in the patient records. During biopsy the tiny tissue is extracted from the body of human and diverted to pathologists to examine those tissues by microscopes for the definite detection of cancer [8]. Thus, analysis of biopsy image is an effective method for detecting breast cancer. Histopathology is an examination process done by pathologist under microscope for studying the growth of malignant tumors, cancer [9].

1.1 Role of Machine Learning in Healthcare

Machine learning (ML) has an immense importance in healthcare and is also used in predicting diseases like cancer including breast cancer, prostate cancer, lung cancer and Alzheimer disease and cataract detection [10]. AI technologies such as profound learning, Natural language processing, Regulatory expert systems, Physical robots, robotic process are beneficial to make the task easy [11]. In machine learning, structured data are easy to categorize and easy to quantify whereas unstructured data is difficult to quantify and categorize [12, 13]. Machine Learning (ML) is an AI area in the field that develops algorithms to adapt to a new challenge without reprogramming. ML model learns to solve the problem directly with provided set of data by using the statistical method to identify patters without any human inference [14]. Machine learning is able to process the large data beyond the limits of human capacity and then reliably turn information into clinical insights that supports medical professionals preparing and delivering treatments [15, 16].

'Features' are the observed variables from the chunk of outcome variables called 'labels' which are mapped by the mathematical models based on ML algorithms [17]. Kaushal et al. [18] showed the computer-aided support systems (CAD) system which diagnose the breast cancer using histological images. Waring et al. [19] represents the work done on automated machine learning in healthcare and explore the barriers or gaps to using AutoML in healthcare. As a result, this paper shows that machine learning techniques improves the healthcare outcomes.

Convolutional neural networks (CNN) with hierarchical pattern detector layers have been very effective in the picture recognition problem. Vo et al. [20] proposed a new convolutional neural network (CNN) based multimodal disease risk prediction algorithm. To tackle the difficulty of missing data, they applied a latent factor model to rebuild the missing data and experiment their new CNN based algorithm on cerebral infraction disease. It gives the prediction accuracy of 94.8% which is faster than other CNN unimodal risk prediction algorithm. Dabeer et al. [21] stated that manual detection of a cancer cells results an error therefore, by computer aided mechanism detection the performance can be improved. In this paper, convolutional neural network is used for feature extraction and deep learning is used which gives accuracy up to 99.36%.

1.2 Digital Pathology

By elaborating the process of detection of cancer various techniques have been developed which are efficient enough to results in early and accurate detection. Digital pathology and image processing are the one of the techniques in detecting the breast cancer [22]. Images are extracted by the process called biopsy of the affected tissue and stained by H&E by the pathologist after acquiring the tissue affected by the tumour [23]. The malignant features are examined by the microscope by pathologist and those features in cellular structures are called nuclei [24] and then images captured by microscope are further used for developing computer aided detection system. Basically, the focus of histopathological images is on prediction of types of lesions whether it is benign or malignant tumor [25]. Earlier manual detection was in use but that comprises full of human error and time consuming. Medical image processing using machine learning gives more beneficial results as compare to the objective diagnosis done by human pathologist. Feature extraction plays a vital role in computer aided detection of breast cancer with histopathological images and it is challenging also to give accurate results. After the extraction of features the classification of tumor or legion is cancerous or non-cancerous is done by ML classifiers and also helps in diagnosis of cancer [26, 27]. Wang et al. [28] proposed a novel automate feature-based analysis scheme for classification of the histopathological images. This paper conclude that proposed segmentation method gives the appropriate results with classification accuracy.

Hekkler et al. [29] examined the 95 hematoxylin and eosin stained slide of lesion by pathologist and trained result histopathological images with Convolutional neural network (CNN) to aim the potential of deep learning for diagnosis of histopathologic melanoma Therefore, main goal is to identify the tumor in malignant or benign in nature. Zheng et al. [30] proposed a novel nucleus assisted feature extraction framework based on convolutional neural network for histological images and also stated a framework which gain a better classification performance for breast lesion than the compared state-of-arts methods.

2 Literature Survey

Rampun et al. [31] proposed a breast boundary and pectoral muscle segmentation method in mammograms. However, for correcting the over evaluated boundary a post processing technique is introduced. Gurcan et al. [32] represents the latest state of the art computer assisted diagnosis (CAD) technology for digitized histopathology and also evaluates the problems related to analysis of image technology for a specific histopathology. Bardau et al. [33] compared two approaches of machine learning, trained by Support Vector Machine and convolutional neural network (CNN). The accuracy rates are in between 96.15% and 98.33% for CNN with hand-crafted featured based classifier and 83.3% for multiclass classification in binary classification. Kott et al. [34] stated the state-of-art deep learning techniques for histopathological image detecting cancer and Gleason grading of prostrate biopsy specimens. The Convolutional Neural Network (CNN) is used to classify and randomization tests were used for hypothesis tests which gives excellent results. Sae et al. [35] studies the radiological and clinical pathological factors that could predict the reoccurrence of breast cancer surgeries by Cox proportional hazard model. M. Matsuda et al. [36] examined the importance of synthetic Magnetic resonance imaging (MRI) to predict the ki-67 status in breast cancer with estrogen receptor positive. El Benday et al. [37] proposed a model that classify the breast cancer subtypes by feature fusion on METABRIC dataset, namely clinical, gene expression, copy number abbreviation (CNA), copy number variation, histopathological images to improve performance. The highest accuracy of 83.36% is achieved for using Linear SVM, and 97.1% achieved for Pam50 subtyping. Gupta et al. [38] proposed a two-phase model for automatic classification which classifies benign and malignant samples on the basis of magnification. In this paper main focus is on deep learning approaches like Convolutional neural network (CNN) and two Machine learning approaches Linear Regression (LR) and Support vector machine (SVM). As a result, CNN + LR gives better performance than CNN + SVM for classification. Carvalho et al. [39] proposed a method which classify histopathological breast image into four classes – invasive carcinoma, situ carcinoma, normal tissue and benign legion by phylogenetic diversity index to characterized images for creating a model.

2.1 Comparative Analysis of Techniques

Machine Learning (ML) is an AI field of study that continues to develop algorithms that can learn the computer to adjust without reprogramming to a new issue. Awasthy et al. [40] applied an effective k-mean clustering for segmentation and gives a result of 91.1% accuracy by using SVM classifier for classification. Deep learning approaches are basically based Artificial Neural Network which have been applied to immense number of fields. Deep neural networks, deep belief networks, recurrent neural networks (RNN) and convolutional neural networks (CNN) are the deep learning architecture. Deep learning continues to show successful performance for clinical applications like classification of tumor tissue, legion detection, segmenting the organ and enhancement of the imaging. CNNs is a regularized representation of multilayer perceptron i.e. each neuron in one layer fully connected to each neuron of next layer in the network whereas RNN gives a formation of directed graph between the connected nodes. CNN is designed to learn spatial hierarchies by back propagation automatically and adaptively using multiple building blocks, such as convolutional layers, pooling layers and completely connected layers. Boosting Strategy with CNN gives better result in extracting useful features. Sebai et al. [41] proposed a robust and precise technique for automatically detection of mitosis from histological breast cancer slides using Mask RCNN detection and deep learning frame work. The 2012 CPR dataset and 2014 ICPR MITOS ATYPIA dataset are used for analysis. As a result, the highest f-score is achieved on 2012 ICPR dataset i.e. 0.863 by using mitosis detection and instance segmentation model trained on pixel level labels. Deep learning captures a lot of information, including patient data, health monitoring and insurance records, and uses its neural networks to deliver the best results (Table 1 and Fig. 1).

Table 1. Comparative analysis of techniques for histopathological images.

Author	Dataset	Technique	Performance
Sudarshan et al. [42]	BreakHis dataset contains 8000 microscopic biopsy images	MIL methods including APR, Diverse Density, MI-SVM, citation KNN, Non -parametric MIL, MILCNN	SVM based approaches perform better
Dundar et al. [43]	327 ROIs collected across 62 patient cases and tested with a sequestered set of 149 ROIs collected across 33 patient cases	Multiple Instance learning technique used	87.9% accuracy on entire test data
Tellez et al. [44]	Heterogeneous dataset of Hematoxylin and eosin histopathology image from 4 organs and 9 pathology laboratories	Convolutional neural network	Found out that any type of stain color augmentation i.e. HSV and HED transformation should always be used
Li et al. [45]	NIA malignant lymphoma dataset from IICBU Biological Image Repository and USCB breast cancer cell dataset	Illuminant Normalization Module and Spectral Normalization module	Generates stable and reliable color cues for stain normalization
Awasthy et al. [46]	USCB dataset	General classifier - ANN, GCNN, GLCM	Spectral imaging is one important challenge in histo-pathology
Hoffman et al. [47]	204 images, out of which 50 from OV samples, 52 from GBM, 55 from RCC1 and 47 from RCC2	Color normalization algorithm, k-mean, VB, EM clustering methods	Better than Global color normalization method
Khurd et al. [48]	25 H & E images of Gleason grade3 and 50 images for Gleason grade 4	Random forest, SVM classifier, k-mean clustering	RBF kernel and KNN perform relatively well in comparison of SPM kernel for classification
Yan et al. [49]	3771 breast cancer histopathological images to the scientific community	Hybrid convolutional and recurrent deep neural network	Average accuracy of 91.3%
Kausar et al. [50]	ICAR 2018 and BreakHis dataset	Deep convolutional neural network with wavelet decomposed images	ICAR 91% accuracy and on Breakhis dataset 95.85% multi-class accuracy
Sherafatian et al. [51]	miRNA expression dataset of breast cancer patients from TCGA dataset	Tree-based classification models	70% of balanced and normalized miRNA expression of TCGA

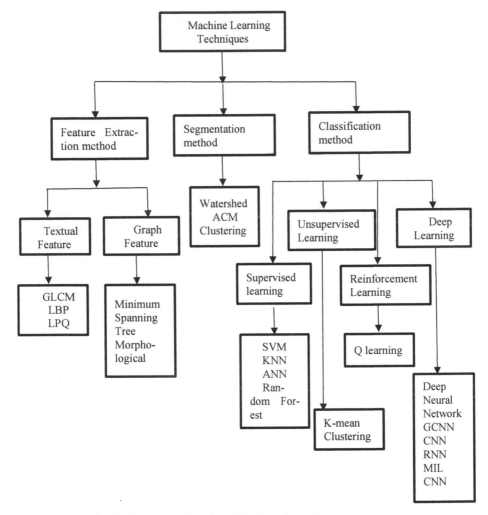

Fig. 1. Representation of machine learning techniques taxonomy.

3 Conclusion

The aim of this work to review the relevant techniques used for Histopathological image analysis for detection of breast cancer and classification and discussing the work related to color normalization methods which results in better quality of histopathological images. Histopathological slides gathered by biopsy which are indispensable in diagnosing the breast cancer in early stages. The machine-learning classification computational complexity based on deep knowledge increases with the number of layers. Massive amount of data helps to get better results in accuracy than limited raw data. However, for classification most used techniques are basic SVM but Cubic SVM, Radial SVM, Ensemble SVM which can diagnose the cancer more accurately. Many of the state of arts techniques focuses on deep learning approaches like CNN and RNN in classification stages to classify the histopathological images which gives good results and minimize the time complexity with cost of CAD system. The future work involves development of machine learning techniques for visualization and prediction using medical imaging.

References

1. Bayrak, E.A., Kirci, P.: Intelligent big data analytics in health. In: Early Detection of Neurological Disorders Using Machine Learning Systems, pp. 252–291. IGI Global (2019)
2. Ben-Israel, D., et al.: The impact of machine learning on patient care: a systematic review. Artif. Intell. Med. **103**, 101785 (2020)
3. Sechopoulos, I., Teuwen, J., Mann, R.: Artificial intelligence for breast cancer detection in mammography and digital breast tomosynthesis: state of the art. Sem. Cancer Biol. (2020)
4. Huang, S., Yang, J., Fong, S., Zhao, Q.: Artificial intelligence in cancer diagnosis and prognosis: opportunities and challenges. Cancer Lett. **471**, 61–71 (2020)
5. Sheth, D., Giger, M.L.: Artificial intelligence in the interpretation of breast cancer on MRI. J. Magn. Reson. Imaging **51**(5), 1310–1324 (2020)
6. Robertson, S., Azizpour, H., Smith, K., Hartman, J.: Digital image analysis in breast pathology—from image processing techniques to artificial intelligence. Transl. Res. **194**, 19–35 (2018)
7. Gupta, P., Garg, S.: Breast cancer prediction using varying parameters of machine learning models. Procedia Comput. Sci. **171**, 593–601 (2020)
8. Wishart, G.C., et al.: The accuracy of digital infrared imaging for breast cancer detection in women undergoing breast biopsy. Eur. J. Surg. Oncol. (EJSO) **36**(6), 535–540 (2010)
9. Mima, Y., Hizukuri, A., Nakayama, R.: Computerized classification scheme for distinguishing between benign and malignant masses by analyzing multiple MRI sequences with convolutional neural network. In: 15th International Workshop on Breast Imaging (IWBI2020), vol. 11513, p. 115131Z. International Society for Optics and Photonics, May 2020
10. Ferroni, P., Zanzotto, F.M., Riondino, S., Scarpato, N., Guadagni, F., Roselli, M.: Breast cancer prognosis using a machine learning approach. Cancers **11**(3), 328 (2019)
11. Yala, A., Lehman, C., Schuster, T., Portnoi, T., Barzilay, R.: A deep learning mammography-based model for improved breast cancer risk prediction. Radiology **292**(1), 60–66 (2019)
12. Esteva, A., et al.: A guide to deep learning in healthcare. Nat. Med. **25**(1), 24–29 (2019)
13. Hatton, C.M., Paton, L.W., McMillan, D., Cussens, J., Gilbody, S., Tiffin, P.A.: Predicting persistent depressive symptoms in older adults: a machine learning approach to personalised mental healthcare. J. Affect. Disord. **246**, 857–860 (2019)
14. Kulkarni, S., Seneviratne, N., Baig, M.S., Khan, A.H.A.: Artificial intelligence in medicine: where are we now? Acad. Radiol. **27**(1), 62–70 (2020)
15. Din, I.U., Guizani, M., Rodrigues, J.J., Hassan, S., Korotaev, V.V.: Machine learning in the Internet of Things: designed techniques for smart cities. Futur. Gener. Comput. Syst. **100**, 826–843 (2019)
16. Vijh, S., Sharma, S., Gaurav, P.: Brain tumor segmentation using Otsu embedded adaptive particle swarm optimization method and convolutional neural network. In: Hemanth, J., Bhatia, M., Geman, O. (eds.) Data Visualization and Knowledge Engineering. LNDECT, vol. 32, pp. 171–194. Springer, Cham (2020). https://doi.org/10.1007/978-3-030-25797-2_8
17. Mohan, S., Thirumalai, C., Srivastava, G.: Effective heart disease prediction using hybrid machine learning techniques. IEEE Access **7**, 81542–81554 (2019)
18. Kaushal, C., Bhat, S., Koundal, D., Singla, A.: Recent trends in computer assisted diagnosis (CAD) system for breast cancer diagnosis using histopathological images. IRBM **40**(4), 211–227 (2019)

19. Waring, J., Lindvall, C., Umeton, R.: Automated machine learning: Review of the state-of-the-art and opportunities for healthcare. Artif. Intell. Med. **104**, 101822 (2020)
20. Vo, D.M., Nguyen, N.Q., Lee, S.W.: Classification of breast cancer histology images using incremental boosting convolution networks. Inf. Sci. **482**, 123–138 (2019)
21. Dabeer, S., Khan, M.M., Islam, S.: Cancer diagnosis in histopathological image: CNN based approach. Inf. Med. Unlocked **16**, 100231 (2019)
22. Ahmed, Z., Mohamed, K., Zeeshan, S., Dong, X.: Artificial intelligence with multi-functional machine learning platform development for better healthcare and precision medicine. Database (2020)
23. Elter, M., Schulz-Wendtland, R., Wittenberg, T.: The prediction of breast cancer biopsy outcomes using two CAD approaches that both emphasize an intelligible decision process. Med. Phys. **34**(11), 4164–4172 (2007)
24. Madekivi, V., Boström, P., Karlsson, A., Aaltonen, R., Salminen, E.: Can a machine-learning model improve the prediction of nodal stage after a positive sentinel lymph node biopsy in breast cancer? Acta Oncol. **59**(6), 689–695 (2020)
25. Shen, L., Margolies, L.R., Rothstein, J.H., Fluder, E., McBride, R., Sieh, W.: Deep learning to improve breast cancer detection on screening mammography. Sci. Rep. **9**(1), 1–12 (2019)
26. Singh, A.K., Singla, R.: Different approaches of classification of brain tumor in MRI using gabor filters for feature extraction. In: Pant, M., Sharma, T., Verma, O., Singla, R., Sikander, A. (eds.) Soft Computing: Theories and Applications, pp. 1175–1188. Springer, Singapore (2020). https://doi.org/10.1007/978-981-15-0751-9_108
27. Vijh, S., Gaur, D., Kumar, S.: An intelligent lung tumor diagnosis system using whale optimization algorithm and support vector machine. Int. J. Syst. Assur. Eng. Manag. **11**(2), 374–384 (2019). https://doi.org/10.1007/s13198-019-00866-x
28. Wang, P., Xu, S., Li, Y., Wang, L., Song, Q.: Feature-based analysis of cell nuclei structure for classification of histopathological images. Digit. Signal Process. **78**, 152–162 (2018)
29. Hekler, A., et al.: Pathologist-level classification of histopathological melanoma images with deep neural networks. Eur. J. Cancer **115**, 79–83 (2019)
30. Zheng, Y., et al.: Feature extraction from histopathological images based on nucleus-guided convolutional neural network for breast lesion classification. Pattern Recogn. **71**, 14–25 (2017)
31. Rampun, A., Morrow, P.J., Scotney, B.W., Winder, J.: Fully automated breast boundary and pectoral muscle segmentation in mammograms. Artif. Intell. Med. **79**, 28–41 (2017)
32. Gurcan, M.N., Boucheron, L.E., Can, A., Madabhushi, A., Rajpoot, N.M., Yener, B.: Histopathological image analysis: a review. IEEE Rev. Biomed. Eng. **2**, 147–171 (2009)
33. Bardou, D., Zhang, K., Ahmad, S.M.: Classification of breast cancer based on histology images using convolutional neural networks. IEEE Access **6**, 24680–24693 (2018)
34. Kott, O., et al.: Development of a deep learning algorithm for the histopathologic diagnosis and gleason grading of prostate cancer biopsies: a pilot study. Eur. Urol. Focus (2019)
35. Chung, S.R., et al.: Prognostic factors predicting recurrence in invasive breast cancer: an analysis of radiological and clinicopathological factors. Asian J. Surg. **42**(5), 613–620 (2019)
36. Matsuda, M., et al.: Utility of synthetic MRI in predicting the Ki-67 status of oestrogen receptor-positive breast cancer: a feasibility study. Clin. Radiol. (2020)
37. El-Bendary, N., Belal, N.A.: A feature-fusion framework of clinical, genomics, and histopathological data for METABRIC breast cancer subtype classification. Appl. Soft Comput. **91** (2020)
38. Gupta, K., Chawla, N.: Analysis of histopathological images for prediction of breast cancer using traditional classifiers with pre-trained CNN. Procedia Comput. Sci. **167**, 878–889 (2020)
39. Carvalho, E.D., et al.: Breast cancer diagnosis from histopathological images using textural features and CBIR. Artif. Intell. Med. **105**, 101845 (2020)
40. Aswathy, M.A., Jagannath, M.: Performance analysis of segmentation algorithms for the detection of breast cancer. Procedia Comput. Sci. **167**, 666–676 (2020)

41. Sebai, M., Wang, X., Wang, T.: MaskMitosis: a deep learning framework for fully supervised, weakly supervised, and unsupervised mitosis detection in histopathology images. Med. Biol. Eng. Compu. **58**(7), 1603–1623 (2020). https://doi.org/10.1007/s11517-020-02175-z

42. Sudharshan, P.J., Petitjean, C., Spanhol, F., Oliveira, L.E., Heutte, L., Honeine, P.: Multiple instance learning for histopathological breast cancer image classification. Expert Syst. Appl. **117**, 103–111 (2019)

43. Dundar, M.M., et al.: Computerized classification of intraductal breast lesions using histopathological images. IEEE Trans. Biomed. Eng. **58**(7), 1977–1984 (2011)

44. Tellez, D., et al.: Quantifying the effects of data augmentation and stain color normalization in convolutional neural networks for computational pathology. Med. Image Anal. **58**, 101544 (2019)

45. Li, X., Plataniotis, K.N.: A complete color normalization approach to histopathology images using color cues computed from saturation-weighted statistics. IEEE Trans. Biomed. Eng. **62**(7), 1862–1873 (2015)

46. Aswathy, M.A., Jagannath, M.: Detection of breast cancer on digital histopathology images: present status and future possibilities. Inf. Med. Unlocked **8**, 74–79 (2017)

47. Hoffman, R.A., Kothari, S., Wang, M.D.: Comparison of normalization algorithms for cross-batch color segmentation of histopathological images. In 2014 36th Annual International Conference of the IEEE Engineering in Medicine and Biology Society, pp. 194–197. IEEE, August 2014

48. Khurd, P., et al.: Computer-aided Gleason grading of prostate cancer histopathological images using texton forests. In: 2010 IEEE International Symposium on Biomedical Imaging: From Nano to Macro, pp. 636–639. IEEE, April 2010

49. Yan, R., et al.: Breast cancer histopathological image classification using a hybrid deep neural network. Methods **173**, 52–60 (2020)

50. Kausar, T., Wang, M., Idrees, M., Lu, Y.: HWDCNN: Multi-class recognition in breast histopathology with Haar wavelet decomposed image based convolution neural network. Biocybern. Biomed. Eng. **39**(4), 967–982 (2019)

51. Sherafatian, M.: Tree-based machine learning algorithms identified minimal set of miRNA biomarkers for breast cancer diagnosis and molecular subtyping. Gene **677**, 111–118 (2018)

Exploiting an Ontology-Based Solution to Study Code Smells

Ivian Castellano Betancourt[1]([🖂]) [iD], Nemury Silega Martínez[1] [iD],
Manuel Noguera García[2] [iD], Olga Rojas Grass[1] [iD], and Osmar Capote Vázquez[3] [iD]

[1] University of Informatics Sciences, La Habana, Cuba
{ilcastellano,nsilega,yarisbel}@uci.cu
[2] University of Granada, Granada, Spain
mnoguera@ugr.es
[3] International University of Andalucía, Seville, Spain
osmar.capote@gmail.com

Abstract. Code smells (CS) are anomalies in the source code of software which may affect its structure and quality. They affect the maintainability of the systems because reduce reusability and make difficult the analysis of code. The coexistence of these errors causes architectural problems that hinder the maintenance process and evolution of the software, increasing future failures. CS usually rises due to the adoption of bad programming practices. Hence, the knowledge and skills of the developers and architects are crucial to avoid them. To address this issue, in this paper we introduce an ontology-based approach to represent and analyze the knowledge about CS. To develop the ontology, the well-known Protégé tool was used and a sound methodology for the development of ontologies was followed. This approach could be a useful instrument to enhance the knowledge of the software developers and architects. Finally, some evidences that proof the impact of the approach are presented.

Keywords: Code smell · Knowledge · Ontology

1 Introduction

Software quality is a key area for the software engineering. The ISO/IEC 25010 quality standard determine the quality characteristics of software that can be evaluated, including maintainability [1]. Maintainability is defined as the ability of a software product to be modified effectively and efficiently, for evolutionary, corrective, perfective or adaptive needs [1]. Software evolution and maintenance are costly tasks in software development. These costs increase as systems become larger and more complex [2].

A common concern that hinders the previous argument is the existence of structural problems in the source code, which were not sufficiently addressed in early stages of software development. These problems are often described as code smell (CS). This concept was attributed to Kent Beck in 1999 [3] and later, his conceptual framework was complemented by anomalies or bad "symptoms" at the level of software design.

© Springer Nature Singapore Pte Ltd. 2021
P. K. Singh et al. (Eds.): FTNCT 2020, CCIS 1395, pp. 234–246, 2021.
https://doi.org/10.1007/978-981-16-1480-4_21

CSs are structures in the source code, which, although they do not prevent the operation of software, however, indicate violations of the fundamental design principles due to the non-application of good practices. Consequently, they affect the maintainability of the systems. Additionally, CSs slow down software development and increase the risk of future errors or failures. These anomalies generally occur because the programmers and architects have insufficient knowledge about them or little experience in software development [4].

In order to know the knowledge about CSs of software developers and architects, a survey was applied to two Cuban software development companies. The types of CSs defined by Fowler [3] and Lanza [5] were taken into account in the survey. The survey yields that 47% of the participants have basic knowledge about CSs and recognize that CSs do not receive an appropriate treatment in the projects. This evidences that CSs are not adequately followed up due to the lack of preparation of the specialists involved.

Similarly, the most common types of code anomalies are identified. Furthermore, 100% of those surveyed affirm that good practices are not applied to reduce the occurrence of CSs in the projects. The low rate of exploitation of tools that support the detection of CSs was demonstrated; only 44% affirm that the SonarQube tool is used, and it was also verified that there were no trained specialists for the correct management of these CSs. The result of the survey demonstrates the need for alternatives to train software developers about the management of CSs.

Based on the previous results, a bibliographic search to identify alternatives to share and communicate knowledge was executed. An interesting alternative is the use of ontologies to represent and analyze knowledge about CSs [6, 7]. Therefore, the objective of this article is to introduce an ontology that allows representing the information about CSs. This ontology may be a useful instrument to train architects and programmers. In addition, it will enable the consistency checking of the information represented in the scientific bibliography with the aim of providing suitable technical support to the software development professionals involved in the software development.

This article has been structured as follows: in Section II the basic concepts of the research are presented, Section III describes the related works, in Section IV the ontology is developed to represent the concepts associated with the CSs, an evaluation of the ontology is shown in Section V. Finally, the conclusions and future works are presented.

2   Code Smell

CSs or types of CSs can degrade different aspects of the quality of software, such as reusability, comprehensibility and maintainability. Although a CS does not prevent the operation of the software, it could slow down its development or lead to the introduction of failures in next stages of the development process [8, 9]. CSs indicate violations of fundamental design principles due to the fact that good practices are not applied, these violations provoke a negative impact on software quality [10].

Mäntylä and Lassenius [11] describe different common problems during software development that could cause design and architectural problems [12]. It is suggested that there are large classes because they have a considerable number of lines of code due to different reasons which stand out: unnecessary repeated code, many methods which lead to low levels of abstraction, design and reuse. In addition, the existence of methods with an excessive list of parameters is another common problem which makes difficult to understand the code and increase the coupling.

In order to know the state of the art about CSs a literature review [3–5, 9, 13] was carried out. We identified a catalogue of CSs and classifications of these in terms of granularity and similarity. The search yields that the most popular CSs are those presented by Fowler and others [3] as well as Lanza and Marinescu [5].

On the other hand, Mäntylä and Lassenius [11, 14] define a set of categories or classifications that group the CSs in terms of the similarity that they could have among them. Furthermore, the CSs are classified according to their granularity or scope, which considers the structural and lexical levels [15].

3 Related Works

Several investigations have documented the benefits of identifying CSs in early stages of software. Some of these studies are analyzed below.

Paiva and others [16] introduce a study carried out on two software developed with Java language: MobileMedia and Health Watcher. JSpIRIT tool was used for the analysis with respect to three types of CS: God Class, God Method and Feature Envy. On the other hand, AlKharabsheh and others [13] describe a study carried out among six tools: iPlasma, Together, JDeodorant, PMD, DÉCOR. SourceForge was used to analyze systems developed in Java. Furthermore, Liu [17] discuss a study carried out among some CS detection tools, such as Checkstyle, Infusion, PMD, iPlasma, DECOR and others. Bastias and López [1, 15] describe the features of SonarQube to analyze several quality elements as well as to find technical threats of a software in terms of CSs [18].

The aforementioned approaches evidenced the effort of the scientific community to reduce bad effects of CSs. However, in these approaches some lacks were identified, such as: they address a reduced set of CS; some tools have a low detection rate of CS or only some categories of CSs are prioritized.

The representation of the concepts related to CSs is another dimension that demands the efforts of scientific community. The adoption of solutions to communicate and share the knowledge about CSs is key to capacitate software developers. An interesting alternative is the application of ontologies for the representation of CSs. For example, Garzás and Piattini [19] introduce an ontology that gather and structures the knowledge about design in object-oriented micro-architectures. They identify a set of relevant concepts such as good practices, bad smells, refactoring and patterns. Da Silva [20] proposes an ontology named ONTOCEAN, which is capable of representing the knowledge necessary to track CSs and evaluate its impact on software by activating reasoners on semantic rules. Luo, Hoss and Carver [21] proposed an ontological representation to formally describe the concepts of anti-patterns, CSs, refactoring and their relationships. This work could be useful in the reuse of concepts of the solution that is exposed in this article. In the same way, concepts from the ONTOCEAN ontology could be reused.

These works show the applicability of ontologies to represent the knowledge about CSs, although they only consider a minimum group of CSs and their impact on software quality. Furthermore, these approaches lack a detailed description of the domain discussed in this research to train engineers with insufficient knowledge. This motivates the proposal presented in Sect. 4.

3.1 Ontology

In the domain of computing an ontology is defined as: "*A formal and explicit description of the concepts in a domain of discourse, the properties of each concept that describe the features and attributes of the concept and the restrictions of the slots*" [7]. Ontology with a set of individual instances of classes constitutes a knowledge base [7]. In the scientific literature there are studies of solutions based on ontologies, suitable for sharing and communicating knowledge [6, 7, 22–24].

4 Ontology to Represent Knowledge About Code Smells

There are several languages to specify ontologies, such as: Ontolingua, XML Schema, RDF (Resource Description Framework), RDF Schema (or RDF-S), OWL. OWL is distinguished by significant features, such as a rich set of operators - e.g. intersection, union and negation. It is based on a logical model that allows defining the concepts as they are described. In addition, the possibility of using reasoners allows to automatically checking the consistency of the represented models. OWL is supported by Protégé, a widely used tool to build ontologies and as a general framework to represent knowledge [25]. The reasoner Pellet is used to make inferences in the Protégé and to check the formal logical properties as well as to validate the consistency of the ontology.

4.1 Methodology

The adoption of a sound methodology is a crucial factor to achieve ontology with high level of quality. We followed the methodology proposed by Alvarado [26], which is based on principles and good practices of the methodologies: Methontology [27] and Development of ontologies-101 [7], emphasizing the clear and concise determination of the requirements of the ontology to be built. The methodology includes five activities [26]: a) determination of the ontology requirements, b) reuse of ontologies, c) elaboration of the conceptual model, d) implementation and e) evaluation of the ontologies. The results after execute each activity are described below.

Determination of the Ontology Requirements
In Alvarado's methodology the following questions are defined:

- What domain will the ontology cover?
- What is the ontology going to be used for?
- What questions should the ontology answer?
- Who will use and maintain the ontology?

The answer to these questions is explained below.

What domain will ontology cover?
The review of the scientific literature allowed identifying a set of concepts related to the research. From these concepts, it is desired to model an ontology in which the main characteristics of CSs are represented, including their different types of classifications with the aim of grouping these into taxonomies that are easier to understand, design principles that may be affected or quality characteristics belonging to different quality standards, as well as architectural anomalies that could be reflected in classes and methods framed in the components of a system. In addition, the metrics used by different tools to identify these anomalies would be represented. Hence, some of the main classes that the ontology will model are: *TypeCodeSmell, ClassificationTypeCodeSmell, ArchitectureAnomaly, CodeCrowd, QualityCharacteristic, QualityStandard, DesignElement, ProgrammingLanguage, Tool, Metric, Component, System, Clazz* and *Method*.

What is ontology to be used for?
Since the ontology represents knowledge about CSs, it could be a useful instrument for training software developers and architects on the subject in order to carry out an adequate analysis and monitoring of CSs.

What questions ontology should answer?
The ontology should be able of answering the following questions:

- Q1: What is the classification of a code smell?
- Q2: What quality characteristics are affected by a code smell?
- Q3: What metrics can be used to identify a certain code smell?
- Q4: What tools can be used to identify a specific code smell?

Who will use and maintain the ontology?
The potential users of this ontology are developers and software architects. The administrators of the ontology will be responsible for its maintenance.

Reuse of Ontologies
As a second activity for ontological development, it should be verified if there are ontologies that can be reused. This activity was carried out in order to speed up the development of the solution.

In this research, the ONTOCEAN ontology [20], is taken as a reference, which coincides with elements addressed in the domain of the solution, for example, the concepts Clazz, Method and Metric. Likewise classes considered by Luo [21], such as Bloaters, Encapsulators and Dispensable were reused. Therefore, the classes mentioned above will be reused in the ontology presented.

The DAML[1] and DBpedia[2] repositories in which multiple domain ontologies are published were also reviewed. In the review it was determined that in these repositories

---

[1] Ontology Library (Online in: https://www.daml.org/ontologies/).

[2] Ontology Library (Online in: https://mappings.dbpedia.org/server/ontology/classes/).

there are not ontologies that respond to the domain, with the scope and requirements set forth in the research.

Elaboration of the Conceptual Model

From the concepts identified and explained in the requirements of the ontology, the conceptual model was elaborated making use of these concepts, as well as the relationships between them. Table 1 shows the identified concepts and Table 2 their relationship between each other.

Table 1. Concepts of the ontology.

Concept	Description
Type of code smell	This term is evaluated as a CS and it is a structural problem of a software that needs to be restructured to improve the quality [6, 7]
Classifications of code smell	Terms that group the CSs regarding the similarity that they could have between them
Code agglomeration	Group of CSs that are related to each other. The relationship between two CSs can be established, for example, through method calls or Inheritance [28]
Architectural anomaly	Symptom of architecture degradation of a software in its implementation through the progressive introduction of CSs [28]
Quality standard	International quality standards like ISO 25000 [1]
Quality characteristic	Quality characteristic that sets the quality standards for a software product [1]. For example Maintainability
Quality sub-characteristic	Quality sub-characteristics contained within the quality characteristics [1]. For example Reusability is sub-characteristic of Maintainability
Design element	Principles, good practices or design patterns. For example Coupling and Cohesion
Tool	Tools that are used for CS identification
Metric	Metrics used by tools to identify the CS
System	Software that could have architectural anomalies due to the occurrence of CSs
Component	Prepackaged piece of code that encapsulates some functionality exposed through standard interfaces in a system
Class	Is used in object-oriented programming to describe one or more objects. It serves as a template for instantiating, specific objects within a program
Method	A procedure or function in object-oriented programming
Programming language	Formal language that provides instructions that allow the programmer to write sequences to control the physical and logical behavior of a computer in order to produce various kinds of data

Table 2. Relationship between the concepts of the ontology.

Concept	Relationship	Concept
Type of code smell	affects	Design element
		Quality characteristic
		Quality sub-characteristic
Classifications of code smell	Classifies	Type of code smell
Code agglomeration	Are composed	Type of code smell
	Is located in	Component
	Causes	Architectural anomaly
Quality standard	contains	Quality characteristic
Quality characteristic	contains	Quality sub-characteristic
Tool	Identifies	Type of code smell
	Sopports	Programming language
	Uses	Metric
Metric	Can identifiy	Type of code smell
Component	Has	Method
		Class
System	Has	Component
	Use as technology	Programming language
Class	Has	Method

We studied the quality standard ISO 25000 which contains the quality characteristics and sub-characteristics of software that are affected by several CSs. Hence, some terms of ISO 25000 were included in the ontology.

Implementation

To implement the ontology, the popular tool Protégé (version 5.0) was used.

Classes, properties, restrictions and instances are the most important components in ontology. Figure 1 depicts a fragment of the 22 classes identified and modeled in Protégé. Classes in ontology are classified into primitive or defined. The primitive classes are those that have specified only necessary conditions for class membership, while the defined classes are those that specify necessary and sufficient conditions for class membership [29]. Figure 1 depicts class *Clazz* which contains five types of disjoint classes (red box).

After modeling the classes of the ontology, the properties were established. There are two types of properties: object property and data property. Object properties allow representing relationships between individuals.

Figure 2 shows a fragment of the 38 object properties represented in the developed ontology. For example, the property *isClassificationOf* relates an individual of the class *ClassificationTypeCodeSmell* to individuals of the class *TypeCodeSmell*; the property

Fig. 1. Ontology classes to represent code smells.

affectsQualityCharacteristic relates an individual of the *TypeCodeSmell* class to individuals of the *QualityCharacteristic* class; in turn, the property *canBeIdentifiedByMetric* relates an individual of the *TypeCodeSmell* class with individuals of the *Metric* class; likewise the property *canBeIdentifiedByTool* relates an individual of the *TypeCodeSmell* class with individuals of the *Tool* class.

Each object property has an inverse property. This indicates that if a property relates individual A to individual B, then its inverse property relates individual B to individual A. Figure 2 illustrates the inverse properties defined for the object properties mentioned above, for example, the property *isClassificationOf* is the inverse of *isClassifiedBy*, *affectsQualityCharacteristic* is the inverse of *isQualityCharacteristicAffectedBy*, *canBeIdentifiedByMetric* is the inverse of *allowIdentifyCodeSmell*, and *canBeIdentifiedByTool* is the inverse of *helpsToIdentifyCodeSmell*.

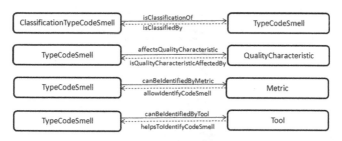

Fig. 2. Object properties of the ontology.

In order to make a better description of the concepts, some data properties were defined in the ontology. These properties have a domain and range which are shown in Table 3. These include the characteristics and scope of the metrics, the development center, the number of methods, number of lines of code, number of parameters of a method, the existence of temporary variables, switch statements or duplicate code in a class and type of granularity as a classification of CSs. In addition the attributes class name, method and system were identified, as well as the description of the classes represented in the ontology.

Table 3. Domain and range of data properties of the ontology.

Data property	Domain	Range
metricCharacteristic	Metric	String
isMetricScope	Metric	String
developmentCenter	System	String
hasNumberOfMethod	Clazz	Integer
hasNumberOfLinesOfCode		Integer
hasNumberOfParameter	Method	Integer
hasTemporaryField		Boolean
hasSwitchStatement	Clazz	Boolean
hasDuplicatedCode	Clazz	Boolean
typeOfGranularity	TypeCodeSmell	String
className	Clazz	String
methodName	Method	String
systemName	System	String
description		String

To demonstrate the applicability of the ontology to represent CSs, we described some concepts related to a software development project by means of the ontology. Figure 3 depicts individuals which are instances of the classes *ClasificationTypeCodeSmell* (blue box) and *TypeCodeSmell* (red box).

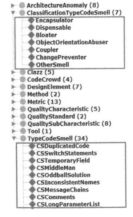

Fig. 3. Individuals represented in the ontology. (Color figure online)

5   Evaluation of the Ontology

By using the Pellet reasoner, Protégé allows to check the consistency of the ontology, automatically obtain the taxonomic classification and compute the inferred types. The consistency checking allows verifying that there are no contradictions in the ontology. For class taxonomy validation look at the relationship between each class and check the entire class hierarchy. The class inference verification determines the class to which each individual belongs [26].

During the design of the ontology, the conditions and properties as a formal system are verified through the use of the Pellet reasoner. Besides, compliance with the defined requirements is verified by answering the competence questions formulated in the first activity of the methodology previously explained. These questions are explained in the execution of the last activity of the methodology. The results are detailed below.

Evaluation of Ontology to Study Code Smells

The evaluation takes into account the questions defined in the activity of the methodology "*Determination of the ontology requirements*" explained in the previous section. Once the ontology is populated, the questions are verified by using the Pellet reasoner.

Q1: ¿What is the classification of a code smell?
Firstly, the individual *CSLargeClass* of the *TypeCodeSmell* class is selected in the Protégé; Fig. 4 illustrates how the reasoner infers knowledge from the selected individual and by means of the object property *isClassifiedBy* where it is obtained that the inferred classification is *Bloater* (red box).

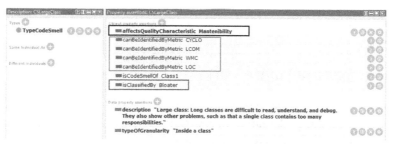

Fig. 4. Knowledge inferred for individual *CSLargeClass* from class *TypeCodeSmell*. (Color figure online)

Q2: ¿What quality characteristics are affected by a code smell?
Since a CS may affect one or more quality characteristics, when a *TypeCodeSmell* is selected several quality characteristics may be related through the property *affectsQualityCharacteristic*. In this case, Fig. 4 depicts that after selecting the individual *CSLargeClass*, an instance of the *TypeCodeSmell* class, by means of the object property *affectsQualityCharacteristic*, we can observe that the quality characteristic *Maintainability* is affected (black box).

Q3: ¿What metrics can be used to identify a code smell?
This information also can be consulted by selecting the specific instance of the class *Type-CodeSmell* and observing the values of the property *canBeIdentifiedByMetric*. For example, Fig. 4 shows that the individual *CSLargeClass canBeIdentifiedByMetric* CYCLO, LCOM, WMC and LOC (blue box).

P4: ¿What tools can be used to identify a specific code smell?
This information can be consulted by selecting an instance of the *TypeCodeSmell* class and observing the value of the property *canBeIdentifiedByTool*. For example, Fig. 5 depicts that *CSGodClass canBeIdentifiedByTool VComplex, inCode* and *JDeodorant* (red box).

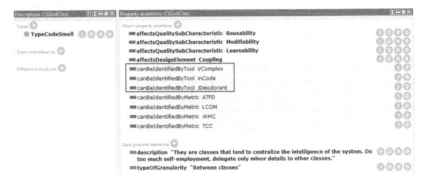

Fig. 5. Knowledge inferred for individual *CSGodClass* from class *TypeCodeSmell*. (Color figure online)

6   Conclusions and Future Works

The literature review allowed identify the most common types of CSs, identification tools as well as ontologies developed to represent relevant information about CSs. The application of a survey to software developers and architects, helped to know some issues related to the management of CSs during development of software projects. To tackle some of these issues introduced an ontological approach.

The ontology was developed following a sound methodology and It was implemented using the well-known tool Protégé. This ontology could be a useful instrument to train programmers and software architects since it represents a wide range of concepts related to CSs, such as other relevant concepts. To enhance the knowledge of programmers and software architects is a crucial step to adopt good programming practices and therefore avoid CSs undesirable effects. The developed ontology has a wide domain compared to the studied ontologies, making possible the detailed representation of each one of the identified concepts.

As future work, a method that includes the activities to use, maintain and extend the ontology will be developed. The solution will be validated through the application of a quasi-experiment to evaluate its impact to enhance the knowledge and skills of the software developers and architects involved in the management of CSs.

Acknowledgements. This research has been partially sponsored by VLIR-UOS Network University Cooperation Programme – Cuba.

References

1. López, J.V.: Auditoría Mantenibilidad Aplicaciones Según La ISO/IEC 25000 (2015)
2. April, A., Abran, A.: Software Maintenance Management: Evaluation and Continuous Improvement, vol. 67. Wiley, Chicester (2012)
3. Fowler, M., et al.: Refactoring: improving the design of existing code. Addison-Wesley Professional, Boston (1999)
4. Malavolta, A.: Análisis de detección de Code Smells para el lenguaje JavaScript (2018)
5. Lanza, M., Marinescu, R.: Object-Oriented Metrics In Practice: Using Software Metrics to Characterize, Evaluate, and Improve the Design of Object-Oriented Systems. Springer, Cham (2007)
6. Fernández Breis, J.T., Un entorno de integración de ontologías para el desarrollo de sistemas de gestión del conocimiento. Universidad de Murcia (2003)
7. Noy, N.F., McGuinness, D.L.: Ontology development 101: a guide to creating your first ontology. Stanford knowledge systems laboratory technical report KSL-01–05 (2001)
8. Yamashita, A. and L. Moonen. Do code smells reflect important maintainability aspects? In: 2012 28th IEEE International Conference on Software Maintenance (ICSM). IEEE (2012)
9. Alonso, M., Klaver, F.H.: Aplicación de un Proceso de Refactoring guiado por Escenarios de Modificabilidad y Code Smells (2016)
10. AlKharabsheh, K., et al.: Sobre el grado de acuerdo entre evaluadores en la detección de Design Smells, pp. 143–157. JISBD, Jornadas de Ingeniería del Software y Bases de Datos (2016)
11. Mäntylä, M.V., Lassenius, C.: Subjective evaluation of software evolvability using code smells: an empirical study. Empir. Softw. Eng. **11**(3), 395–431 (2006)
12. Aniche, M., et al.: Code smells for model-view-controller architectures. Empir. Softw. Eng. **23**(4), 2121–2157 (2018)
13. AlKharabsheh, K., et al.: Comparación de herramientas de Detección de Design Smells. JISBD (2016)
14. Mika, M., Vanhanen, J., Lassenius, C.: A taxonomy and an initial empirical study of bad smells in code. IEEE (2003)
15. Bastias, O.A.: Código con"mal olor": Un mapeo sistemático. Revista Cubana de Ciencias Informáticas **12**(4), 156–176 (2018)
16. Paiva, T., Damasceno, A., Figueiredo, E., Sant'Anna, C.: On the evaluation of code smells and detection tools. J. Software Eng. Res. Dev. **5**(1), 1–28 (2017). https://doi.org/10.1186/s40411-017-0041-1
17. Liu, X., Zhang, C.: The detection of code smell on software development: a mapping study. In: Proceedings. 5th Internation Conference on Machinery, Materials and Computing Technology (2017)
18. Ospina Delgado, J.P., Análisis de seguridad y calidad de aplicaciones (Sonarqube). (2015)

19. Garzás, J., Piattini, M.: An ontology for microarchitectural design knowledge. IEEE Softw. **22**(2), 28–33 (2005)
20. da Silva Carvalho, L.P., et al.: An ontology-based approach to analyzing the occurrence of code smells in software. In: ICEIS (2) (2017)
21. Luo, Y., Hoss, A., Carver, D.L.: An ontological identification of relationships between anti-patterns and code smells. In: 2010 IEEE Aerospace Conference. IEEE (2010)
22. Welty, C., Guarino, N.: Supporting ontological analysis of taxonomic relationships. Data Knowl. Eng. **39**(1), 51–74 (2001)
23. Beniaminov, E.M.: Ontology libraries on the web: status and prospects. Autom. Doc. Math. Linguist. **52**(3), 117–120 (2018). https://doi.org/10.3103/S0005105518030020
24. Saldarriaga Benjumea, J.D.: Ontologías para conceptualización de modelos de negocio (2018)
25. Fernández Hernández, A.: Modelo ontológico de recuperación de información para la toma de decisiones en gestión de proyectos (2016)
26. Alvarado, R.: Metodología para el desarrollo de ontologías. 2010. 28 noviembre 2018. https://es.slideshare.net/Iceman1976/metodologia-para-ontologias
27. Fernández-López, M., Gómez-Pérez, A., Juristo, N.: Methontology: from ontological art towards ontological engineering (1997)
28. Oizumi, W.N., Garcia, A.F., Colanzi, T.E., Ferreira, M., Staa, A.V.: On the relationship of code-anomaly agglomerations and architectural problems. J. Software Eng. Res. Dev. **3**(1), 1–22 (2015). https://doi.org/10.1186/s40411-015-0025-y
29. Horridge, M., et al.: A practical guide to building owl ontologies using protégé 4 and co-ode tools edition1. 2. The university of Manchester, 107 (2009)

Accelerating Stochastic Gradient Descent by Minibatching, Learning Rate Annealing and Momentum

Udai Bhan Trivedi[✉] and Priti Mishra

PSIT College of Higher Education, Kanpur 209305, India
udaibhantrivedi@gmail.com, bca@psit.ac.in

Abstract. In last five to ten years of history of machine learning, the prediction capacity of machine learning has been increases drastically. However, with this increase in data comes great responsibility. Online large scale Machine Learning requires dealing with algorithm complexity and architecture of system simultaneously. Stochastic gradient descent (SGD) does not use all data point of training sets in order to improve the present value of parameters. SGD in fact start changing the parameters value after reading the single training data point. Initialize the parameters at some value $w_0 \; \epsilon \; R^d$, and decrease the value of the empirical risk iteratively by sampling a random index ~ i_t uniformly from $\{1, , , n\}$ and then updating it. In this paper we also discussed how Minibatching, Learning Rate Annealing and Momentum help to accelerate stochastic gradient descent to convergence.

Keywords: Machine learning · Stochastic Gradient Descent (SGD) · Minibatching · Learning Rate Annealing and Momentum

1 Introduction

Large scale machine learning involves a huge amount of dataset for training purpose. Large data set in turn makes Gradient Descent Algorithm very expensive example data sets like Census data, Website traffic data. Stochastic Gradient Descent (SGD) defines a different way to optimize for large data sets which will allow scaling the algorithms [2, 3, 19].

Application of Gradient Decent algorithm to calculate linear regression.

$$\text{Hypothesis: } h_\theta(x) = \sum_{j=0}^{n} \theta_j x_j \tag{1}$$

$$\text{Cost function: } j_{train}(\theta) = \frac{1}{2m} \sum_{i=1}^{m} \left(h_\theta\left(x^{(i)}\right) - y^{(i)} \right)^2 \tag{2}$$

© Springer Nature Singapore Pte Ltd. 2021
P. K. Singh et al. (Eds.): FTNCT 2020, CCIS 1395, pp. 247–255, 2021.
https://doi.org/10.1007/978-981-16-1480-4_22

Repeat {

$$\theta_j := \theta_j - \alpha \frac{1}{m} \sum_{i=1}^{m} (h_\theta(x^{(i)}) - y^{(i)}) x_j^{(i)}$$

(3)

(for every $j = 0, \ldots, n$**)**

}

In the inner loop algorithm repeatedly updates the parameters θ. As large scale ML a large number of training set (m) this makes Gradient Descent very expensive, and takes a long time to converge. Especially disk I/O is typically a system bottleneck and this algorithm requires a *huge* number of reads [1, 4, 18] (Fig. 1).

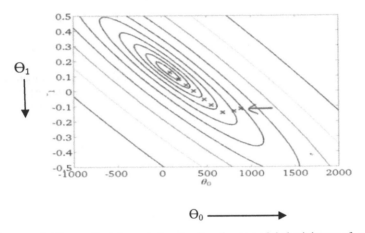

Fig. 1. Contour plot for gradient descent showing iteration to a global minimum of cost function

Stochastic Gradient Descent (SGD) looks only single example in one inner iteration and defines cost of error as mean of square error.

$$cost\left(\theta, (x^{(i)}, y^{(i)})\right) = \frac{1}{2}(h_\theta\left(x^{(i)}\right) - y^{(i)})^2$$

(4)

The overall cost function can now be re-written in the form

1. Randomly shuffle training example
2.

Repeat {
 for $i := 1, \ldots, m$
 {

$$\theta_j := \theta_j - \alpha(h_\theta(x^{(i)}) - y^{(i)}) x_j^{(i)}$$

(5)

 }   **(for every** $j = 0, \ldots, n$ **)**

}

The inner for loop adjust Θ_j by calculating cost of θ with respect to a specific one training example (x^i, y^i). The adjustment in parameters Θ_j keep on updating it in second, third …Until it gets to the end of the data. The algorithm repeats this procedure and takes multiple passes over the data (1 to 10 times).

The randomly shuffling at the start of algorithms will remove the problem of high bias data and speed up convergence a little bit. Although stochastic gradient descent is a lot like batch gradient descent, rather than waiting to sum up the gradient terms over all m examples, it progress in improving the parameters from first example itself. With stochastic gradient descent each iteration is much faster, but every iteration is fitting a single example [10, 11, 17] (Fig. 2).

Θ_1

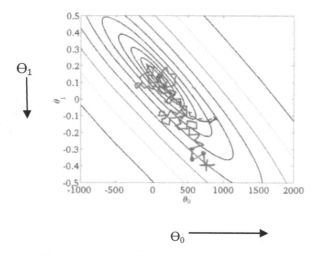

$\Theta_0 \longrightarrow$

Fig. 2. Contour plot for Stochastic Gradient Descent showing iteration to a global minimum

Stochastic Gradient Descent generally moves in the direction of the global minimum, but not always converges like batch gradient descent, but it ends up around some region close to the global minimum. This is not a problem as long as it close to the global minimum.

2   Background and Related Works

A Stochastic Gradient Descent emerges as one of the leading algorithm for large scale machine learning. The algorithm suffers the problem of convergence. These papers discuss the insight of impact of Minibatching, Learning Rate Annealing and Momentum on speed and convergence of algorithm. Some research paper dealing with Stochastic Gradient Decent has been reviewed.

A., Srivastava, Hinton, G.E., Krizhevsky, N.., Salakhutdinov, R & Sutskever, I. [2014] have discussed idea to randomly drop units from Neural Network during model building. This prevents units from co-adapting too much. Which will solve the over fitting problem and better than other methods of solving Overfitting like features drop, Early stopping etc.

L´eon Bottou, from NEC Labs America, Princeton NJ, USA [2010] has discussed computational complexity of large-scale data sets and underlying optimization algorithm in non-trivial ways. They also discussed stochastic gradient descent optimization algorithms and its performance for large-scale problems.

Rie Johnson, and Tong Zhang [2013] discussed the Stochastic gradient descent algorithm for large scale optimization and its drawback of slow convergence due to the inherent variance. To overcome this problem they introduce an explicit variance reduction method for stochastic gradient descent known as stochastic variance reduced gradient (SVRG). stochastic variance reduced gradient (SVRG) enjoys the same fast convergence rate as stochastic dual coordinate ascent (SDCA) and Stochastic Average Gradient (SAG) for smooth and strongly convex functions.

Tong Zhang from IBM T.J. Watson Research Center [2004] discussed Linear prediction methods, such as least squares for regression, logistic regression and support vector machines for classification. He also studies stochastic gradient descent (SGD) algorithms on regularized forms of linear prediction methods.

Mu Li, Tong Zhang, Yuqiang Chen, Alexander J. Smola [2014] established how to parallelize Stochastic gradient descent (SGD) employed minibatch training to reduce the communication cost and impact of batch size on convergence of SGD. They also establishes the fact that convergence rate does not slow down with increase minibatch size.

Moritz Hardt, Benjamin Rechty and Yoram Singerz [2016] established that parametric models trained by a stochastic gradient method (SGM) with few iterations had vanished generalization error and how convex cases gives insights for multiple epochs of stochastic gradient methods generalize well. They also gave new interpretation of common practices in neural networks in the non-convex case.

3 Mini Batch Gradient Descent

Mini-batch gradient descent (Minibatching) is an approach which can work faster than stochastic gradient descent. Instead of using one training data in each iteration, Mini Batch Gradient Decent use batch size (b) training data in each iteration. Typical batch size ranges from two to hundred training data to train the algorithm.

Mini-batch algorithm for batch size 100 and number of training example 10000 and number of features = n.

Repeat {
For i=1,100,200.--------------------,9900
{
$$\theta_j := \theta_j - \alpha \frac{1}{100} \sum_{k=i}^{i+b} (h_\theta(x^{(k)}) - y^{(k)})x_j^{(k)} \tag{6}$$
(for every $j = 0, \ldots, n$**)**
}
}

Compared to batch gradient descent Mini-batch gradient descent allows us to get through data in a much more efficient way. After every batch size (b) Minibatching improve parameters, this algorithm neither updates parameters after every train example nor have to wait until you cycled through all the data. Vectorized implementation of Minibatching partially parallelizes your computation and converges faster than Gradient Decent and Stochastic Gradient Decent (SGD) [5, 6].

4   Stochastic Gradient Descent Convergence

Stochastic gradient Descent generally moves in the direction of the global minimum, but not always converges like batch gradient descent, but it ends up around some region close to the global minimum. The tuning of learning rate alpha (α) become necessary if Stochastic Gradient Descent (SGD) does not shows decline (actually increasing) in cost function with numbers of iterations. Stochastic Gradient Descent cost function define as

$$cost\left(\theta, (x^{(i)}, y^{(i)})\right) = \frac{1}{2}(h_\theta\left(x^{(i)}\right) - y^{(i)})^2 \qquad (7)$$

This is half the squared error on a single example. While the algorithm is looking at the example (x^i, y^i), and before it has updated θ (Eq. 7) compute the cost of the example (cost (θ, (x^i, y^i))) which will gives an idea how well the hypothesis is working on the training example.

We can plot the costs averaged over the last 1000 training data set which will gives estimate of how well algorithms perform over last 1000 data sets [8, 9, 21] (Fig. 3).

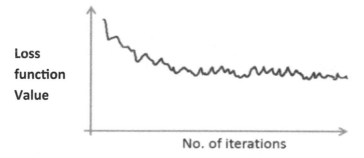

Loss function Value

No. of iterations

Fig. 3. Loss function value of Stochastic Gradient Descent v/s number of iteration

Algorithm may have convergence as (cost (θ, (x^i, y^i)) is going down with number of iterations. If we build the plot by taking smaller learning rate algorithm will get better final solution. This is because the parameter oscillates around the global minimum. A smaller learning rate shows smaller oscillations [10, 11] (Fig. 4).

If algorithm average over 5000 examples rather than 1000 examples the plot will become a smoother curve (Fig. 5).

Sometimes plot that shows cost is not decreasing at all. In such situation we need to increase to averaging over a larger number of examples to see general trend. Figure

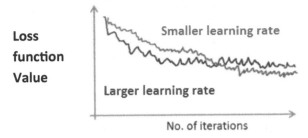

Fig. 4. Loss function value of Stochastic Gradient Descent v/s number of iteration with smaller and larger learning rate

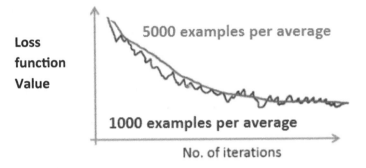

Fig. 5. Loss function value of Stochastic Gradient Descent v/s number of iteration with more (5000) example per average and less (1000) example per average

shows that blue line was too noisy, and that noise is ironed out by taking a greater number of data sets per average. it is also possible that it may not decrease, even with a large number. We need to try it with reducing learning rate (Fig. 6).

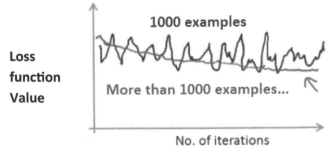

Fig. 6. Loss function value of Stochastic Gradient Descent v/s number of iteration with more (>1000) example per average and less (=1000) example per average

If plot shows the increasing trend then the algorithm may be displaying divergence. Should use a smaller learning rate Learning rate We saw that with stochastic gradient descent we get this wandering around the minimum In most implementations the learning rate is held constant However, if you want to converge to a minimum you can slowly decrease the learning rate over time [14, 20] (Fig. 7).

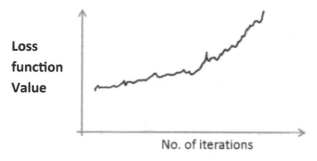

Fig. 7. Loss function value of Stochastic Gradient Descent v/s number of iteration shows the increasing trend

One of the method of calculating $\alpha = $ const1/(iteration Number + const2). Which means as the number of iterations increases with fix value of const1 and const2 the value of α will decrease and this will guarantee to converge [12, 15, 16] (Fig. 8).

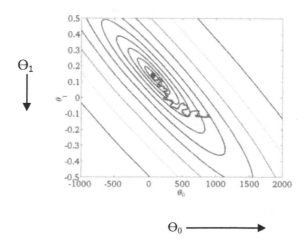

Fig. 8. Contour plot for Stochastic Gradient Descent showing iteration to a global minimum with decreasing learning rate

5   Stochastic Gradient Descent with Momentum Contour

During Gradient Descent, we use $\delta\Theta$ and δb to update our parameters Θ and b as

$$\Theta t = \Theta_{t-1} - \alpha * \delta L/\delta\Theta_{t-1} \tag{8}$$

$$bt = b_{t-1} - \alpha * \delta b_{t-1} \tag{9}$$

In Stochastic Gradient Decent momentum algorithm uses Exponential moving average of Θ values.

$$\Theta_t = \Theta_t - [\beta \times V_{t-1} + \alpha * \delta L(\Theta)/\delta\Theta t-1] \quad \text{with } v_1 = \Theta_1 \tag{10}$$

Where 'β' is called momentum parameter and its value lies between 0 and 1. Momentum parameter uses exponential weighted average to calculate the current value of parameters. For majority of application $\beta = 0.9$ will be use for calculation of parameters or any value between 0 and 1 which can smoothen the noise and converges to global minima.

6   Conclusion

Batch Gradient Descent performs expensive computations for datasets, which is not suited for large datasets generated online. Stochastic Gradient Descent removes expensive computations by performing one update at a time. This makes Stochastic Gradient Descent much faster and can be used to learn online. Stochastic Gradient Descent performs frequent updates with a high variance will leads to objective function fluctuate heavily. This fluctuation enables it to jump to new and potentially better local minima. On the other side, this complicates convergence to the global minimum, as Stochastic Gradient Descent will keep overshooting. However, this problem can be remove by slowly decrease the learning rate with number of iteration, algorithm shows the same convergence behaviour as batch gradient descent, and converging to a global minimum. Stochastic Gradient Decent can also utilize momentum (Eq. 10) in order to smoothen the noise and other fluctuation while converging to global minima.

References

1. Léon, B.: Large-scale machine learning with stochastic gradient descent. In: Proceedings of the 19th International Conference on Computational Statistics (COMPSTAT 2010), pp. 177–187. Springer, Paris, France, August 2010 (2010)
2. Mu, L., Tong, Z., Chen, Y., Smola, A.J.: Efficient mini-batch training for stochastic optimization. In: Proceedings of the 20th ACM SIGKDD International Conference on Knowledge Discovery and Data Mining, pp. 661–670. ACM (2014)
3. Benjamin, R., Christopher, R., Stephen, W., Feng, N.: HOGWILD!: a lock-free approach to parallelizing stochastic gradient descent. In: Advances in Neural Information Processing Systems, pp. 693–701 (2011)
4. Schraudolph, N., Jin, Y., Günter, S.: A stochastic quasi-newton method for online convex optimization. J. Machine Learn. Res. **2**, 428–435 (2007)

5. Shalev-Shwartz, S., Zhang, T.: Stochastic dual coordinate ascent methods for regularized loss. J. Mach. Learn. Res. **14**(1), 567–599 (2013)
6. Duchi, J., Hazan, E., Singer, Y.: Adaptive subgradient methods for online learning and stochastic optimization. J. Machine Learn. Res. **12**, 2121–2159 (2011)
7. Diederik, P.K., Jimmy, L.B.: Adam: a Method for stochastic optimization. In: International Conference on Learning Representations, pp. 1–13 (2015)
8. Darken, C., Chang, J., Moody, J.: Learning rate schedules for faster stochastic gradient search. In: Neural Networks for Signal Processing II Proceedings of the 1992 IEEE Workshop, (September), pp. 1–11 (1992)
9. Bottou, L.: Online algorithms and stochastic approximations. In: Saad, D. (ed.) Online Learning and Neural Networks, p. 247. Cambridge University Press, Cambridge (1998)
10. Hashemi, F.S., Ghosh, S., Pasupathy, R.: On adaptive sampling rules for stochastic recursions. In: Proceedings of the 2014 Winter Simulation Conference (WSC 2014), 2014, pp. 3959–3970 (2014)
11. Johnson, R., Zhang, T.: Accelerating stochastic gradient descent using predictive variance reduction. In: Advances in Neural Information Processing Systems 26, 2013, pp. 315–323. (2013)
12. Le Roux, N., Schmidt, M., Bach, F.R.: A stochastic gradient method with an exponential convergence rate for finite training sets. In: Advances in Neural Information Processing Systems 25, 2012, pp. 2663–2671 (2012)
13. Park, H., Amari, S., Fukumizu, K.: Adaptive natural gradient learning algorithms for various stochastic models, Neural Netw. **13**(2000), 755–764 (2018)
14. Mokhtari, A., Ribeiro, A.: RES: regularized stochastic BFGS algorithm. IEEE Trans. Signal Process. **62**(2014), 6089–6104 (2015)
15. Liu, H., Simonyan, K., Yang, Y.: DARTS: differentiable architecture search. In: International Conference on Learning Representations (ICLR) (2019a)
16. Singh, P., Paprzycki, M., Bhargava, B., Chhabra, J., Kaushal, N., Kumar, Y.: Futuristic Trends in Network and Communication Technologies. FTNCT 2018. Communications in Computer and Information Science, 958, pp. 3–509 (2018)
17. Singh, P.K., Bhargava, B.K., Paprzycki, M., Kaushal, N.C., Hong, W.C.: Handbook of Wireless Sensor Networks: Issues and Challenges in Current Scenario's, Advances in Intelligent Systems and Computing, Springer, Cham, Volume 1132, pp. 155–437 (2020)
18. Singh, P.K., Kar, A.K., Singh, Y., Kolekar, M.H., Tanwar, S.: Proceedings of ICRIC 2019, Recent Innovations in Computing, 2020, Lecture Notes in Electrical Engineering, vol. 597, pp. 3–920. Springer, Cham (2020)
19. Bista, R., Thapa, A.: Handbook of Wireless Sensor Networks: Issues and Challenges in Current Scenario's, Advances in Intelligent Systems and Computing, vol. 1132, pp. 239–259. Springer, Cham (2020)
20. Olson, R.S., Moore, J.H.: TPOT: a tree-based pipeline optimization tool for automating machine learning. In: Hutter, F., Kotthoff, L., Vanschoren, J. (eds.) Automated Machine Learning, The Springer Series on Challenges in Machine Learning. Springer, Cham (2019)
21. Ratner, A., Bach, S.H., Ehrenberg, H.Snorkel., et al.: rapid training data creation with weak supervision. The VLDB J. **29**, 709–730 (2020)
22. Singh, P., Sood, S., Kumar, Y., Paprzycki, M., Pljonkin, A., Hong, W.C.: Futuristic trends in network and computing technologies. Commun. Comput. Inf. Sci. **1206**, 1–660 (2019)
23. Singh, P.K., Arpan Kumar, K., Yashwant, Singh, M.H., Kolekar, S.T.: Recent Innovations in Computing, vol. 597. Springer, Switzerland (2019)
24. Singh, P.K., Panigrahi, B.K., Suryadevara, N.K., Sharma, S.K., Singh, A.K. (eds.) Proceedings of ICETIT 2019, Emerging Trends in Information Technology, Lecture Notes in Electrical Engineering (LNEE), Springer, Switzerland (2019)

An Ensemble Approach
of Multi-objective Differential Evolution
Based Benzene Detection

Veerawali Behal$^{(\boxtimes)}$ and Ramandeep Singh

Lovely Professional University, Punjab, India
ramandeep.singh@lpu.co.in

Abstract. Benzene is among the most common and menacing contaminant in the air that accelerate the rate of severe health issues among people. Presently, environmental sensor-based networks are utilized to monitor the quality of the air. The cost including numerous sensors with dynamic network sizes limit the operational and monitoring efficiency. In the proposed study, the advanced non-linear problem-solving principles of Adaptive Neuro-Fuzzy Inference System (ANFIS) and Differential Evolution (DE) algorithm is utilized to monitor the quality of the air and to predict the scale of C_6H_6 in the surrounding environment of the individual without installing or creating any sensor-based network. The concentration of C_6H_6 in the air is predicted by utilizing ANFIS through which evaluation of the relationship between several atmospheric gases is accomplished and DE is responsible to optimize the parameters of the ANFIS model for effective prediction accuracy. The prediction performance of the system is evaluated by calculating Accuracy, Coefficient of Determination (r^2), and Root Mean Squared Error (RMSE) on five publicly available datasets. To validate the experimental results of the proposed system, the calculated results are compared with several base-line and hybrid methods of machine learning. The calculated outcomes justify the suitability of building self-reliable cost-effective and time-sensitive air monitoring system for predicting the concentration of benzene in the air.

Keywords: An adaptive neuro-fuzzy inference system · Air quality · Benzene prediction · Machine learning · Differential evolution

1 Introduction

Contaminated air is one of the important cause of critical health issues. A "Global Burden of Disease" survey found that air quality has been one of the top ten environmental risks. The existence of inordinate levels of contaminants including gases such as Benzene (C_6H_6), Ozone (O_3), Sulfur Dioxide (SO_2), Carbon Dioxide (CO_2), Carbon Monoxide (CO), Methane (CH_4), Nitric Oxide (NO), Particulate Matter (PM), Nitrogen Dioxide (NO_2), and particles such as

© Springer Nature Singapore Pte Ltd. 2021
P. K. Singh et al. (Eds.): FTNCT 2020, CCIS 1395, pp. 256–275, 2021.
https://doi.org/10.1007/978-981-16-1480-4_23

dust, haze, and liquid droplets can lead to air pollution. A study conducted by World Health Organization confirmed that the ambient air was responsible for an expected 4.2 million premature deaths in 2016[1]. About 90% of the fatalities are registered from the low and middle-revenue countries. Another study conducted by the American Lung Association registered that over 40% of US population is at risk of serious diseases, such as cancer, cardiovascular disease, diabetes, and asthma[2].

The major factors of air emissions can typically be classified into four larger groups: traffic sources, stationary sources, regions and natural sources. Air pollution may be produced by transport vehicles [29]. Furthermore, stationary emissions can occur due to excessive discharge from various stationary sources such as petroleum refineries, trade companies, and factories etc. [35,36]. The aforementioned sources may emit tremendous quantities of air contaminants during manufacturing process of raw material or goods production. The amount of pollutants emitted by a community or country will contribute to higher rates of mortality or serious medical conditions [1,2].

Thus, Air quality control has now been one of the most suitable approach for controlling air emissions in both emerging and industrialized countries.

Related Work: In recent years, several methods have been developed to forecast air quality and estimate emissions rates. The regression techniques are most commonly utilized machine learning based approaches. Specific machine learning mathematical models were used in the proposed analysis to forecast emission rates from the atmosphere by analyzing the air level of PM (2.5) [5]. In article [6], authors have analyzed the atmosphere based on the grid and have identified the effect of the mesoscale wind form on toxic substances emitted from the source of slit. This research indicates that the wind exacerbates the aggregation of pollutants. In globally accepted model named THOR [7], multiple versions for various applications are used. The experiment was used for three days to forecast the atmosphere and the risk of pollutants.

In Article [22], the authors developed an air control system that could predict indoor PM levels using the artificial neural network (ANN). The environmental quality of the subway stations has been generally tracked. The authors assessed the interaction between the performance of the forecast and the depth of the station. The correlation has been calculated by the divergence. The authors calculate the amounts of pollutants in the environment using the Support Vector Regression (SVR) process [23]. The concentration of PM (2.5) from real-time measurements from the air quality monitoring system has been predicted. The authors recommended a hybrid approach: linear regression, neural network and random forest for the estimation of toxic contaminant concentrations. The findings revealed the efficiency of the prediction model for concentrations of PM (10).

---

[1] Source: https://www.who.int/en/news-room/actualitysheets/detail/encompassing (outside)-air-quality-and-wellbeing.

[2] Source: https://www.lung.org/about-us/media/officialstatements/2018-condition-of-the-air.html.

In article [25] the authors presented data mining strategies for estimating the concentration of atmospheric PM (10) and PM (2.5). By sensing impact importance, they evaluated the data's behavior. In order to evaluate PM (10) and PM (2.5) atmospheric levels, k-means clustering techniques were also developed along with Artificial Neural Networks (ANN). The PCA findings are transferred to ANN for the purpose of the forecast, and k-means is used to aggregate the findings for further review. For the estimation of air quality levels, the authors employed the random-forest approach in conjunction with differential evolution [26]. The method suggested improves the predicted efficiency and outperformed other cutting-edge models. In Article [27], the authors used a technique to predict air pollution levels based on Gradient Boosting and Hierarchic-Temporary-Memory neural networks (BHTMNN). However, the data pre-analysis analysis is carried out with multiple normalization and data mining techniques. BHTMNN has been tracking the emission prediction data which is related to pollutants like CO, NO, NO_2, SO_2 and Particulate Matter (PM). In addition, the Fuzzy Classification and Regression Tree (FCART) technique was introduced for classifying contaminants based upon its strength in the air.

Contribution: The Air Quality Index (AQI) is considered as an air quality measure ranging from 0 to 500. The air pollution calculation is based on the amount of AQI. The high value contributes to an expansion of the spectrum of pollution and well-being concern [3,4]. Specifically, an AQI rating of 40 is considered an appropriate dimension of air quality with limited risk for general health, while the AQI value above 300 represent the dangerous air quality. Six major air contamination gases namely, CO_2, O_3, CO, NO_2, CH_4, and PM are considered as an air toxins. Many factors such as temperature and humidity are also considered to ensure the efficacy of the proposed solution for air quality. The aims of the proposed solution for monitoring are as follows:

1. Calculate the association between pollution related parameters by utilizing an Adaptive Neuro-Fuzzy Inference System (ANFIS).
2. Analyze and forecast the interaction between the polluted characteristics of surrounding air using the computational decision analysis methodology in an optimized fashion.
3. Network performance optimization and evaluation with different performance metrics including (r_2), RMSE, and accuracy.
4. Optimization of ANFIS utilizing the Differential Evolution (DE) technique to increase overall system efficiency.

Research Motivation: The notion of air quality monitoring can be accomplished with optimal effectiveness by sophisticated artificial intelligence technologies such as machine learning and deep learning [37]. The tracking and real-time analysis of various air quality-oriented parameters is a crucial aspect of the system addressed. Maximum accuracy should often be obtained by government bodies in order to establish minimum air regulatory standards. With a view to integrating machine learning technologies into air quality monitoring, a range of study gaps have been found and have become the motivating aspect of current study.

1. Determination of AI based air quality criteria that have not been previously addressed by researchers. Developing strategies for decision-making is the need-of-hour.
2. Minimal work has been provided to ensure the continuous reporting of air quality levels and associated characteristics by government and control authorities, thus undermining public health.
3. Air quality-oriented metrics, such as atmospheric environment, temperature, and humidity, are sometimes neglected, as these are two of the main factors that can have an effect on air quality.
4. Eventually, minimal work has been done to measure air quality standards over environmental factors and criteria for successful decision-making by government agencies and citizens.

Article Structure: Rest of the article is organized into following sections. Section 2 addresses the proposed approach for air quality prediction. Section 3 validates the prediction efficiency of the framework by contrasting the predictions with multiple baseline and hybrid approaches. Finally, the article is concluded in Sect. 4 with some important insights.

2   Proposed Methodology

Recent studies have shown that the Artificial Neural Network (ANN) along with Fuzzy Inference Systems (FIS) have been the two most common non-linear machine learning algorithms. Such two approaches include the vast potential to treat nonlinear data with the ability to learn themselves and even to handle reliable data by estimated reasoning [33]. Neural Networks have capacity to tolerate failures, persistent learning, and adaptation of patterns. Neural networks are very convincing to demonstrate a range of true implementations, perhaps with a few limitations [24]. Fuzzy reasoning, though, can quantify derived outcomes in order to form inferences to overcome ambiguity. The fusion of these two approaches, commonly called ANFIS, is thus more effective in tackling complexity and data ambiguity [8].

2.1   Adaptive Neuro-Fuzzy Inference System (ANFIS)

ANFIS model is originally proposed by Jang [9] and can be used for a variety of domains [10]. By adopting the learning rules of the neural network, ANFIS is able to derive rules from sampled input data and even to adapts a neural-fuzzy controller to tackle these rules [30, 34]. The ANFIS also enables the system to adapt and automatically organize itself using tuning rules [11]. Figure 1 represents the five layered ANFIS architecture. Each layer contains several nodes that is represented by the node function.

Fuzzification (Layer 1): The former ANFIS layer is liable for the fuzzification task. Each node of this layer produces the membership grade for each fuzzy set. Each node is adaptive in nature in this layer and represented as:

$$M_j^1 = \zeta H_j(r) \tag{1}$$

where M_i^1 is the generalized Gaussian shaped membership function, r is regarded as the actual value given to the node j, and H_j is regarded as the linguistic tag which further links to the node.

Product Rule (Layer 2): By conducting an element-wise product operation, the second layer nodes pass a signal from the input to the next layer which is represented as follows:

$$M_j^2 = \zeta B_j(r) \times \zeta C_j(z), \; j = 1, 2 \tag{2}$$

Normalization (Layer 3): All nodes of this layer is having responsibility for computing a single firing strength rule ratio to average of all the firing strength rules as seen in Eq. (3). s_i' denotes the standardizing firing strength.

$$M_j^3 = s_j' = \frac{s_j}{s_1 + s_2} \; for \; j = 1, 2 \tag{3}$$

This layer is liable for the evaluation of the input for the final output by the jth rule. The parameters d_i, e_i, t_i are termed as consequent optimized variables. The fuzzification function of this layer is represented as follows:

$$N_j^4 = s_j' f_j = s_i'(d_j r + e_j z + t_j) \; for \; j = 1, 2 \tag{4}$$

Output Generation (Layer 5): The layer is named the output layer, the total of all the outputs in a defuzzification node is computed and the output as shown by Eq. (5):

$$M_j^5 = \sum s_i' f_i = \frac{\sum_j s_j f_j}{\sum_j s_j} \tag{5}$$

2.2 Differential Evolution (DE) Algorithm Based Network Optimization

Several optimization algorithms have been suggested by researchers for model optimization, such as Differential Evolutionary (DE), Particle Swarm Optimization (PSO), and Genetic Algorithms (GA). In the proposed air quality prediction method [12], an evolutionary DE algorithm is utilized to normalize the model parameters. Each of these methods is linked to parallel stochastic algorithms that are part of the swarm. These algorithms are all based on common techniques like crossover, mutation and population algorithm selection and function. In comparison with traditional basic processes [13,14], DE implements a particular method of mutation and selection to produce optimal outcomes by changing

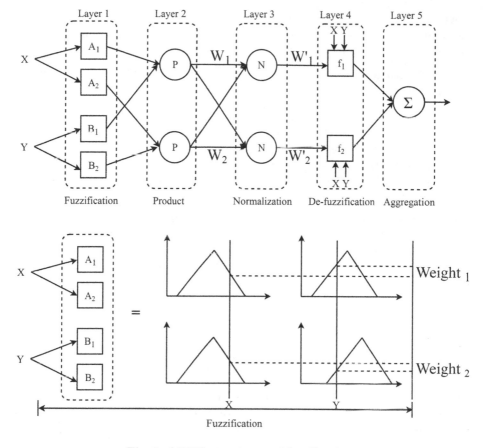

Fig. 1. ANFIS structure and fuzzification.

parameters and helps to monitor the current search status with the storage of existing knowledge in memory [15,16]. DE has a broad global presence that will lead to the best outcomes. GA and PSO, on the other hand, have huge amounts of parameters, which have a major impact on the results. The issue of improving the problems in actual applications is managed by a broad number of parameters. DE thus has stronger adjustment power.

Step 1. Initialization: In the first step of optimization, the population is derived which is used to give the input to the model. The population is constructed as $N \times D$ matrix. The element N is the number of vectors and D is the complete length of the chromosome. The procedure for the *ith* vector population generation is as follows:

$$Y_{j,k} = m[k] + rand * (i[k] - m[k]) \tag{6}$$

where, the total number of rows and matrix column is indicated by j and k. The rand term corresponds to the standard distribution of probability. The $i[k]$ is the upper limit and $m[k]$ is the lower limit of the kth column's respectively.

Step 2. Mutation: The mutant vectors are generated after initialization via mutation operation.

$$W_i = Y_{t_1} + F * (Y_{t_2} - Y_{t_3}) \tag{7}$$

where Wj is the mutant vector that is connected to a recent population with increasing target value Yj. F indicates an aspect of mutation. The variable $t_n \in 1, 2, ..., N$ indicates the random factor numbers and the value of these two factors are entirely separate from the other. The statistical unequality of random numbers is represented as $t_1 \neq t_2 \neq t_3 \neq j$.

Step 3. Crossover: Crossover is applied by DE following the mutation. Crossover methods are essentially responsible for creating population diversity. A crossover procedure between Y_j and W_j generates the trial vector V_j. The binomial operator is the most frequently used crossover operator. For each component, the crossover process is shown as follows:

$$V_{j,k} = \begin{cases} W_{j,k}, & \text{if } (rand(k) \leq D \text{ or } k = k_{rand}) \\ Y_{j,k}, & \text{otherwise} \end{cases}$$

where D indicates the crossover rate, and k_{rand} indicates the randomly chosen index within [1, E].

Step 4. Selection: The technique for selection is used to keep population size constant by determining the next generation target or test vectors. The single-to-one tournament selection process is defined as:

$$Y_j = \begin{cases} V_j, & \text{if } f(V_j) \leq f(r_i) \\ Y_j, & \text{otherwise} \end{cases}$$

where the objective function is indicated by f(r) which is required to be optimized.

2.3   Multi-objective Fitness Function

It should be noted that for some values of principle parameters there is a linear relation between the attributes. A multi-objective fitness function is designed to determine DE-ANFIS based regression. This reduces RMSE and therefore raises the (r_2). In order to calculate the result and feasibility of the prediction, fitness function is evaluated by using RMSE, (r^2), and accuracy metrics. Let the values of regression sum of squares, total sum of squares, and error sum of squares be SSR, SSTO, and SSE respectively. Mathematically, it is represented as

$$RMSE = \sqrt{\left(\frac{d_i - f_i}{n}\right)^2} \tag{8}$$

where d$_i$ is the actual value and f$_i$ is the predicted value using the ANFIS model.

$$r^2 = \frac{SSR}{SSTO} = 1 - \frac{SSE}{SSTO} \tag{9}$$

where $\overline{d}$ is the mean value of the actual value and $\overline{f}$ is mean value of the predicted value.

$$Accuracy = \left(\sum_i if \frac{|d_i - f_i|}{n} \leq \sigma \right) \tag{10}$$

where σ represents the accepted error rate which is taken as 0.1 in the presented study. The multiobjective optimization function can be treated as where σ represents the accepted error rate. The optimization function can be treated as

*MinimizeFit (RMSE, r^2, Accuracy) = $C_1 * RMSE - C_2 * r^2 + C_3 * Accuracy*

where C_1, C_2, $C_3 \in [0, 1]$ are the constants such that $C_1 + C_2 + C_3 = 1$. The values of $(0.3, 0.3, 0.4)$ are being used for (C_1, C_2, C_3).

2.4   ANFIS Parameter Tuning with DE

The optimistic ANFIS utilizes parameter tuning to minimize multi-objective fitness function by using DE. Figure 2 shows the standard flow of the prediction process. It will reduce the average error rate of generic ANFIS system training model. There exist two parameters which are required to be tuned: antecedent parameters and consequent parameters. Gaussian membership functions are defined as follows:

$$\mu_{A_i(x)} = \exp \left[- \left(\frac{x - d_i}{b_i} \right) 2c_i \right]$$

Fuzzy membership function has b_i as variance, d_i is the fuzzy membership function's centroid, and c_i can be tuned utilizing DE and is also considered as variance of the membership functions. The antecedent or predecessor variables are b_i, c_i, d_i and consequent or output variables are q_i, r_i, s_i. The systematic process of fuzzy system modeling includes optimal variables search process to accomplish the desired model. During estimation of the multiobjective optimization, besides the possible optimum points according to each target, there is a possibility of specific optimal points at all target points. This helps designers to pick a perfect location. Figure 3 depicts the overview of DE parameter tuning for fuzzy system estimation. Fuzzy model design involving the essential factors namely Fuzzy model choice, Input output variables, fuzzy structure with member function types having rules, model input output parameters, specification of antecedent and consequent functions and variables, specification of fuzzy consequent variables are based on fuzzy rules [28,32]. The initial population is generated and DE parameters are specified. Input and output variables according to DE are tuned, and FIS rules and fuzzy membership functions are formed. Each solution's RMSE is calculated and new better values are altered accordingly.

Furthermore, optimized parameter set for creating the fuzzy model is obtained. It helps to detect the concentration of benzene better while using the interdependence ratio between the pollutants the other pollutants concentrations are known.

2.5   ANFIS-DE Assisted Ensemble Approach for Benzene Prediction

Figure 4 demonstrates the complete process of the presented approach. The methodical development of the proposed DE optimizer based ANFIS model is addressed in Table 2. The interdependence relationship may be used to understand the level of various gases. The DE algorithm parameters are defined in Table 1.

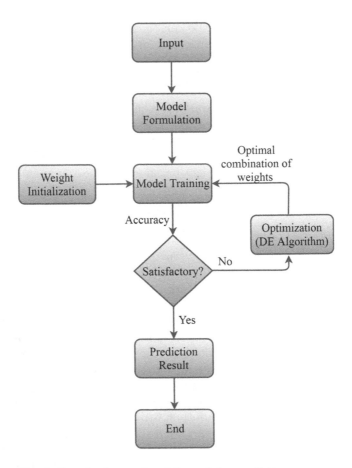

Fig. 2. Standard procedural flow of the prediction process.

Table 1. Parameters of DE algorithm

Dimensions	Size of the parameters
Size of population	20
Mutation	0.5
Crossover	0.9
Boundaries	12

Table 2. ANFIS-DE algorithm for benzene prediction

Algorithm 1: Benzene prediction utilizing ANFIS based DE Algorithm
Input: Training dataset values are inputted
Output: The set of FIS parameters are optimized for the scale prediction of benzene in the air
Step 1: Initial population generation and specification of the original DE algorithm parameters
Step 2: Membership functions are designed based on fuzzy principles for initial FIS architecture.
Step 3: The cumulative iterations at a given time instance δT.
Step 4: Input and output variables with DE to be tuned in a rule-based way.
Step 5: Fitness degree for every particle is determined
Step 6: Evaluation of the RMSE loss rate with new population-related equilibrium values
Step 7: Revising all the values based on prior populationAssessing the existing population-based values
Step 8: Revising the value of epoch for next time event $\delta T = t + 1$, where t is the instance of a specific time T slot
Step 9: Development of a fuzzy model with optimum parameters
Step 10: return optimized parameters and go to step 4

- The population is generated at the initial stage for the initial input and the DE optimizer parameters are defined.
- The FIS rules are designed by the use of membership functions after generating the input population. The variables for input and output are further balanced by combining DE parameters.

- The loss is computed for each sample solution, using the RMSE Loss Function. The values are fully realized to optimize the system's predicting potential by evaluating the error rate.
- Finally, a set of optimal parameters is established to form a fuzzy model which helps detect more precisely the benzene and its concentration.

3 Prediction Performance Evaluation

Three most common but high performance evaluation metrics, such as Accuracy, r^2, and RMSE are utilized to evaluate the performance of the proposed benzene prediction methodology.

3.1 Experimental Material and Resources

The proposed methodology is implemented by utilizing the CARET package in R-Studio (3.2.5). The configuration of the system is as follows: CPU: Intel Core i5 5th generation, Memory (RAM): 8 GB, GPU: Nvidia GeForce GT 710, GPU Memory: 2 GB. The proposed model is trained and the performance is evaluated by performing a k-fold cross-validation technique. Total 10-folds are used for training and testing purposes by dividing the dataset into 70:30 ratio. The 70% of the data is used for training purposes and 30% is used for validating and testing the performance of the system by dividing it into two parts 15:15. The best advantage of this technique is that it helps to remove the biasness of the system by performing training and testing operation on each fold. The prediction performance is evaluated on five publicly available datasets, namely, C_6H_6-B [17], Benzene PubChem [18], PetraVidnerova Sensors Scikit Test [19], AirBase The European air quality database cite air base [20], NACP Greenhouse Gases Multi-Source Data Compilation [21].

Performance Validation of the Proposed Study: Simulation Environment is based on real-world applications for experimental implementation. The cumulative system performance has been measured through air quality monitoring and prediction model. The online UCI and Kaggle data repository has been used to collect 5 intimidating data sets on air quality parameters. These include Air Quality Dataset of Benzene PubChem open chemistry databases with nearly 10832 instances[3], Air Quality Dataset of AirBase—the European air quality database with 12276 instances[4], Pollution Data from petravidnerova sensorsscikittes with 32645 data instances[5], Air Quality Data set from Nacp greenhouse gases multi-source data compilation with 118640 instances[6], and data from

---

[3] https://pubchem.ncbi.nlm.nih.gov/compound/benzene.

[4] Source: http://www.eea.europa.eu/data-and-maps/data/airbase-the-european-air-qualitydatabase-8.

[5] Source: https://github.com/PetraVidnerova/SensorsScikitTest/blob/master/data/C6H6-nrm-part5.test.csv.

[6] Source: https://daac.ornl.gov/NACP/guides/NACPGHGDataCompilation.html.

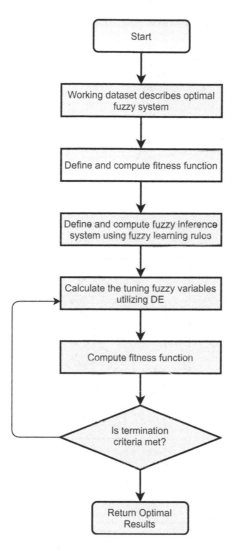

Fig. 3. DE fuzzy system.

national institute of standards and technology with 14876 instances[7]. Table 3 enlists the calculated outcomes of the proposed methodology based on different datasets. It records the prediction accuracy, the relationship between the parameters, and error values during training and testing periods of the proposed method on the datasets. The outcomes are further represented in Fig. 5 for easy and better understanding. The values and graph plots for accuracy, r^2, and RMSE for the selected datasets represent the prediction consistency and promising accuracy of the proposed methodology for both training and testing.

---

[7] https://www.nist.gov/file/36031.

Table 3. Performance validation on five datasets

Performance metrics	Accuracy		r^2		RMSE	
Dataset	Training	Testing	Training	Testing	Training	Testing
Benzene	99.8	98.6	0.98	0.94	2.2	1.3
AirBase	99.7	99.4	0.94	0.98	1.4	1.7
PetraVidnerova	98.6	98.9	0.91	0.93	1.2	1.0
NACP	98.9	98.6	0.94	0.97	2.0	2.3
C_6H_6-B	99.1	98.7	0.96	0.94	1.9	2.4

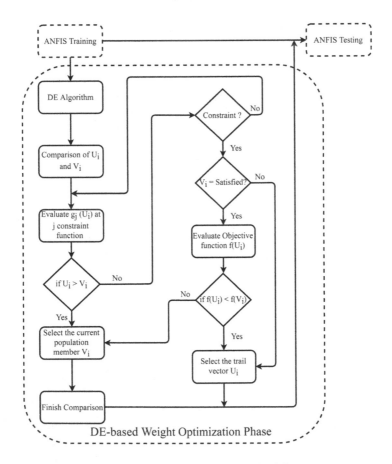

Fig. 4. Proposed prediction methodology.

Comparative Analysis of the Study: The performance of the proposed technique is validated by comparing the calculated outcomes with the selected baseline such as, k-Nearest Neighbor Regressor (k-NNR), Support Vector Regressor (SVR), Decision Tree Regressor (DTR), Artificial Neural Network (ANN),

Table 4. Accuracy

	Methods	Benzene	AirBase	PetraVidnerova	NACP	C_6H_6-B
Base-line techniques	k-NNR	88.1	88.8	89.1	90.6	90.3
	SVR	88.9	88.5	89.6	92.7	89.5
	DTR	89.6	90.7	92.1	93.3	91.2
	ANN	90.4	91.4	93.2	94.5	93.4
	SGDR	91.9	92.1	94.7	95.1	94.1
Ensemble technique	RFR	92.7	93.2	95.1	95.9	95.3
	ADABOOST	94.7	94.7	96.8	96.4	96.6
	GBDT	96.1	96.1	97.2	95.2	95.9
	ANFIS	95.1	96.4	97.6	97.1	96.8
	PROPOSED	**98.6**	**99.4**	**98.9**	**98.6**	**98.7**

Table 5. Coefficient of determination

	Methods	Benzene	AirBase	PetraVidnerova	NACP	C_6H_6-B
Base-line techniques	k-NNR	0.77	0.82	0.79	0.77	0.83
	SVR	0.78	0.84	0.80	0.79	0.85
	DTR	0.76	0.83	0.77	0.76	0.86
	ANN	0.80	0.85	0.80	0.78	0.88
	SGDR	0.81	0.87	0.82	0.80	0.89
Ensemble technique	RFR	0.83	0.89	0.85	0.82	0.90
	ADABOOST	0.85	0.90	0.87	0.83	0.91
	GBDT	0.87	0.91	0.89	0.85	0.93
	ANFIS	0.85	0.93	0.91	0.89	0.92
	PROPOSED	**0.94**	**0.98**	**0.93**	**0.97**	**0.94**

Table 6. RMSE

	Methods	Benzene	AirBase	PetraVidnerova	NACP	C_6H_6-B
Base-line techniques	k-NNR	4.2	5.9	3.9	3.2	5.2
	SVR	3.6	4.1	3.4	3.6	4.0
	DTR	5.2	5.3	2.8	4.1	4.2
	ANN	5.7	4.5	3.2	4.6	3.7
	SGDR	4.1	4.8	2.7	2.8	4.8
Ensemble technique	RFR	3.8	5.2	2.9	2.5	5.8
	ADABOOST	4.6	3.7	2.6	1.9	4.5
	GBDT	4.9	3.9	2.3	2.3	3.9
	ANFIS	3.9	2.8	2.1	2.6	4.9
	PROPOSED	**1.3**	**1.7**	**1.0**	**2.3**	**2.4**

Table 7. Time analysis (in sec)

	Methods	Benzene	AirBase	PetraVidnerova	NACP	C_6H_6-B
Base-line techniques	k-NNR	108.2	91.6	110.2	112.8	110.5
	SVR	94.3	87.3	96.7	104.2	89.8
	DTR	90.7	107.3	92.8	115.7	106.7
	ANN	95.4	114.9	113.4	109.2	105.3
	SGDR	114.5	110.6	103.6	97.2	101.9
Ensemble technique	RFR	107.2	105.8	108.8	98.5	99.3
	ADABOOST	85.6	95.7	97.3	94.8	97.4
	GBDT	104.8	93.8	95.4	101.5	98.2
	ANFIS	86.9	98.9	91.6	90.2	102.9
	PROPOSED	**75.6**	**75.4**	**76.7**	**80.3**	**76.3**

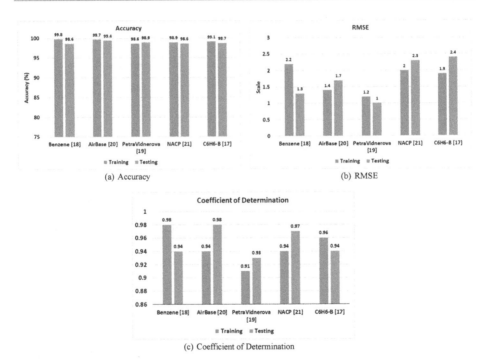

(a) Accuracy

(b) RMSE

(c) Coefficient of Determination

Fig. 5. Performance evaluation. (a) Accuracy, (b) RMSE, and (c) r^2

Stochastic Gradient Descent Regressor (SGDR) and ensemble approaches, namely Random Forest Regressor (RTR), AdaBoost, and Gradient Boosting Decision Tree (GBDT) for various selected datasets. Table 4 represents the prediction accuracy of the system, while r^2 and RMSE are listed in Table 5 and Table 6 which are further explained graphically in Fig. 6 a, b, c respectively. The plot of Fig. 6 (a) demonstrates that the proposed methodology has been more effective in the training and testing phase compared to selected baselines and

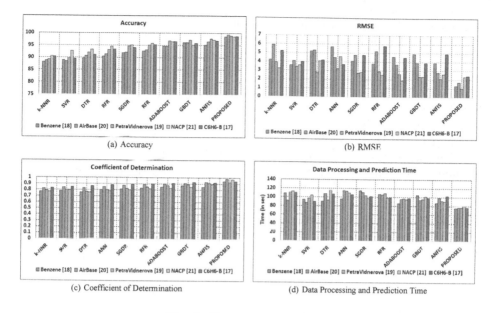

(a) Accuracy

(b) RMSE

(c) Coefficient of Determination

(d) Data Processing and Prediction Time

Fig. 6. Comparative analysis

ensemble techniques with minor variations. Figure 6 (b) indicates that less RMSE is obtained from the proposed methodology, which further illustrates a reduced error-rate predictive accuracy of the model. Figure 6 (c) illustrates the strength of the higher r^2 of the proposed methodology in the training and testing phase. Subsequently, the higher prediction accuracy represents the high coefficient of determination between predicted and the actual scale value with lower RMSE for both training and testing stages. The performed operations help to validate the utility of the proposed methodology for air quality monitoring and benzene prediction.

Data Processing and Prediction Time: Data preprocessing and prediction time performs an imperative role in real-time monitoring. Table 7 and Fig. 6 (d) shows that the proposed technique consumed less training time and less

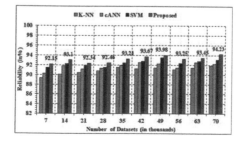

Fig. 7. Reliability analysis

testing time. Thus, the experimental results justify the utility of the proposed methodology for air monitoring in real-time.

3.2   Reliability Analysis

Reliability analysis is a critical measure to assess the overall reliability of the proposed model. The results are contrasted with the various decision-making models namely DTR, ANN, and SVR to determine the progress. Predictive decision modeling, as has already been mentioned, relies on the techniques of mathematical analysis and is thus substantially efficient. Figure 7 indicates that the proposed model is likely to obtain an overall reliability of 92.69% across datasets. In contrast to this, the DTR registered a reliability rate of 88.28%, ANN recorded a reliability rate of 89.21% and SVM recorded a reliability rate of 90.32%. Henceforth, the superior trend for the reliability study of the proposed predictive decision modeling demonstrates the efficacy of the air quality prediction system.

3.3   Stability Analysis

System reliability is a indicator of occurrence for evaluating the overall efficiency of the model. In other terms, it is used to measure the cumulative consistency of a wide number of datasets. In fact, the reliability of the system is calculated by the Average Absolute Shift (AAS). The magnitude of the AAS calculation varies between (0, 1) where the value 0 indicates the lowest stability and the value 1 indicates the highest stability. Figure 8 displays the findings for the proposed stability prediction model. This can be represented that the air quality prediction methodology provided obtains a minimal value of 0.58 and a maximum value of 0.87 for AAS, an average of about 0.74. On the basis of these findings, it is assumed that the current framework is extremely reliable for the study of broad databases for air pollution monitoring.

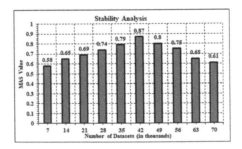

Fig. 8. Stability analysis

4   Conclusion

Due to the hazardous impact of benzene on health and the lack of infrastructure for sensors installation, machine learning based benzene prediction techniques perform an imperative role for measuring the quality of air. A novel ANFIS-DE based benzene prediction methodology has been proposed for benzene prediction. The performance of the proposed methodology is tested on five publically available air quality datasets. The comparative results demonstrate the effectiveness of prediction applicability over other comparative techniques. The high accuracy, low RMSE, high (r^2) with low data preprocessing and prediction time validated the prediction performance of the system. The calculated outcomes represent the efficacy of the proposed system for real-time benzene prediction. Therefore, we can conclude that the proposed methodology is proficient for continuous prediction of C_6H_6 which can be effectively utilized without including additional equipment.

References

1. Raaschou-Nielsen, O., et al.: Particulate matter air pollution components and risk for lung cancer. Environ. Int. **87**, 66–73 (2016)
2. Fecht, D., et al.: Spatial and temporal associations of road traffic noise and air pollution in London: implications for epidemiological studies. Environ. Int. **88**, 235–242 (2016)
3. Shooter, D., Brimblecombe, P.: Air quality indexing. Int. J. Environ. Pollut. **36**, 305–323 (2009). https://doi.org/10.1504/ijep.2009.021834. ISSN: 0957–4352
4. Raipure, S.: Calculating pollution in metropolitan cities using wireless sensor network. Int. J. Adv. Res. Comput. Sci. Manag. Stud. **2**(12), 293–296 (2014). ISSN: 2321–7782
5. Kleine Deters, J., Zalakeviciute, R., Gonzalez, M., Rybarczyk, Y.: Modeling PM2.5 urban pollution using machine learning and selected meteorological parameters (2017). Accepted 11 May 2017
6. Krishna, S., Lakshminarayanachari, K., Pandurangappa, C.: Mathematical modelling of air pollutants emitted from a line source with chemical reaction and mesoscale wind. Int. J. Sci. Eng. Res. **8**(5), 48 (2017)
7. Brandt, J., Christensen, J.H., Frohn, L.M., Zlatev, Z.: Operational air pollution forecast modelling using the THOR system. Department of Atmospheric Environment, National Environmental Research Institute (2002)
8. Jang, J.-S.: ANFIS: adaptive-network-based fuzzy inference system. IEEE Trans. Syst. Man Cybern. **23**(3), 665–685 (1993)
9. Lin, C.-T., Lee, C.G.: Neural Fuzzy Systems. Prentice-Hall Inc., Upper Saddle River (1996)
10. Moghaddamnia, A., Gousheh, M.G., Piri, J., Amin, S., Han, D.: Evaporation estimation using artificial neural networks and adaptive neuro-fuzzy inference system techniques. Adv. Water Resour. **32**(1), 88–97 (2009)
11. Liu, M., Ling, Y.Y.: Using fuzzy neural network approach to estimate contractors' markup. Build. Environ. **38**(11), 1303–1308 (2003)
12. Storn, R., Price, K.: Differential Evolution-A Simple and Efficient Adaptive Scheme for Global Optimization Over Continuous Spaces. ICSI, Berkeley (1995)

13. Sha, D.Y., Hsu, C.Y.: A new particle swarm optimization for the open shop scheduling problem. Comput. Oper. Res. **35**(10), 3243–3261 (2008)
14. El Ela, A.A.A., Abido, M.A., Spea, S.R.: Optimal power flow using differential evolution algorithm. Electr. Eng. **91**(2), 69–78 (2009)
15. Babu, B.V., Munawar, S.A.: Differential evolution strategies for optimal design of shell-and-tube heat exchangers. Chem. Eng. Sci. **62**(14), 3720–3739 (2007)
16. Khademi, M.H., Rahimpour, M.R., Jahanmiri, A.: Differential evolution (DE) strategy for optimization of hydrogen production, cyclohexanede hydrogenation and methanol synthesis in a hydrogen-perm selective membrane thermally coupled reactor. Int. J. Hydrog. Energy **35**(5), 1936–1950 (2010)
17. C_6H_6-B.csv national institute of standards and technology. https://www.nist.gov/file/36031. Accessed 17 Mar 2017
18. Benzene PubChem Open Chemistry Database. https://pubchem.ncbi.nlm.nih.gov/compound/benzene. Accessed 17 Mar 2017
19. C_6H_6-nrm-part5.test.csv petravidnerova sensors scikit test. https://github.com/PetraVidnerova/SensorsScikitTest/blob/master/data/C6H6-nrm-part5.test.csv. Accessed 17 Mar 2017
20. AirBase-The European Air Quality Database. http://www.eea.europa.eu/data-and-maps/data/airbase-the-european-air-qualitydatabase-8. Accessed 17 Mar 2017
21. Nacp Greenhouse Gases Multi-Data Compilation (2000–2009). https://daac.ornl.gov/NACP/guides/NACP_GHG_Data_Compilation.html. Accessed 17 Mar 2017
22. Park, S., et al.: Predicting PM10 concentration in Seoul metropolitan subway stations using artificial neural network (ANN). J. Hazard. Mater. **341**, 75–82 (2018)
23. Li, M., et al.: Prediction of PM2.5 concentration based on the similarity in air quality monitoring network. Build. Environ. **137**, 11–17 (2018)
24. Karatzas, K., et al.: Revisiting urban air quality forecasting: a regression approach. Vietnam J. Comput. Sci. **5**(2), 177–184 (2018)
25. Franceschi, F., Cobo, M., Figueredo, M.: Discovering relationships and forecasting PM10 and PM2. 5 concentrations in Bogotá, Colombia, using artificial neural networks, principal component analysis, and k-means clustering. Atmos. Pollut. Res. **9**(5), 912–922 (2018)
26. Kumar, D.: Evolving differential evolution method with random forest for prediction of air pollution. Procedia Comput. Sci. **132**, 824–833 (2018)
27. Sagayaraj, S., Vetrivelan, N.: Improving air quality management using gradient boosting based hierarchical temporal memory neural networks and fuzzy based classification based regression tree. Int. J. Eng. Technol. **2**, 12–17 (2018). https://doi.org/10.14419/ijet.v7i2.9.9229
28. Pannu, H.S., Singh, D., Malhi, A.K.: Improved particle swarm optimization based adaptive neuro-fuzzy inference system for benzene detection. CLEAN-Soil Air Water **46**(5), 1700162 (2018)
29. Pannu, H.S., et al.: Improved particle swarm optimization based adaptive neuro-fuzzy inference system for benzene detection. CLEAN-Soil Air Water **46**(5), 1700162 (2018)
30. Singh, P.K., Paprzycki, M., Bhargava, B., Chhabra, J.K., Kaushal, N.C., Kumar, Y. (eds.): FTNCT 2018. CCIS, vol. 958. Springer, Singapore (2019). https://doi.org/10.1007/978-981-13-3804-5
31. Singh, P.K., Bhargava, B.K., Paprzycki, M., Kaushal, N.C., Hong, W.-C. (eds.): Handbook of Wireless Sensor Networks: Issues and Challenges in Current Scenario's. AISC, vol. 1132. Springer, Cham (2020). https://doi.org/10.1007/978-3-030-40305-8

32. Muchtar, F., Al-Adhaileh, M.H., Alubady, R., Singh, P.K., Ambar, R., Stiawan, D.: Congestion control for named data networking-based wireless ad hoc network. In: Singh, P.K., Pawłowski, W., Tanwar, S., Kumar, N., Rodrigues, J.J.P.C., Obaidat, M.S. (eds.) Proceedings of First International Conference on Computing, Communications, and Cyber-Security (IC4S 2019). LNNS, vol. 121, pp. 121–138. Springer, Singapore (2020). https://doi.org/10.1007/978-981-15-3369-3_10

33. Reddy, C.S., Raju, K.V.S.N.: An improved fuzzy approach for COCOMO's effort estimation using gaussian membership function. J. Softw. 4(5), 452–459 (2009)

34. Zhang, T., et al.: Control of a novel synthetical index for the local indoor air quality by the artificial neural network and genetic algorithm. Sustain. Cities Soc. 51, 101714 (2019)

35. Zeinalnezhad, M., et al.: Air pollution prediction using semi-experimental regression model and adaptive neuro-fuzzy inference system. J. Clean. Prod. 261, 121218 (2020)

36. Al-Janabi, S., Mohammad, M., Al-Sultan, A.: A new method for prediction of air pollution based on intelligent computation. Soft Comput. 24(1), 661–680 (2019). https://doi.org/10.1007/s00500-019-04495-1

37. Fan, J., Knoch, U., Bond21, T.: Application of Rasch measurement theory in language assessment: using measurement to enhance language assessment research and practice. Pap. Lang. Test. Assess. 8(2), 117–142 (2019)

The Heartfelt and Thoughtful Rulers
of the World: AI Implementation in HR

Garima Vijh[1]([⊠]), Richa Sharma[1]([⊠]), and Swati Agrawal[2]([⊠])

[1] Amity University, Noida, Uttar Pradesh, India
garimavijh672@gmail.com, rsharma25@amity.edu
[2] Jaipuria University, Noida, Uttar Pradesh, India
swatiagrawal@japuria.ac.in

Abstract. The emerging technologies such as robotics, artificial intelligence, and machine learning are exponentially changing the work performance and showing transformation in various fields such as companies, shedding its light on medical, financial affairs, logistics, retail market, education, and human resource. The prevailing AI data-driven substantial IQ interactivity is moving towards the deeply challenged human traits, including emotional skills, establishing and maintaining interpersonal relationships, detecting the severity of anxiety as well as stress in mental health care, implanting empathy. The emerging bond between the physical world and digital technologies leads to a powerful creation of Emotion AI or affective computing agents that contribute to sensing, adapting, and interpreting the human emotions wellbeing at the workplace. The paper presents the proposed framework for the evolutionary stages of artificial intelligence in the business domain, specifically human resource management. The methodology attempts to examine the role of artificial Intelligence technologies in human resources practices. The statistical computation of proposed methodology is measured using T and Anova Test respectively.

Keywords: Artificial Intelligence (AI) · Human resource · Machine learning (ML) · Emotions · Organization

1 Introduction

Artificial Intelligence (AI) and Deep learning involve the development of an intelligent system that serves as a purpose in complex decision making in a rapidly dynamic environment [1, 2]. The advanced data-driven technologies have shown extreme variation and modification in competitive dimensions such as recruiting competent candidates at organizational settings, organizing complex logistics, handling traffic management systems, detecting patients, forecasting technological development, human resource, and now sneaking into organization's behavioral competencies [3, 4]. In the early 1950–70s, AI originated with the concept of generating models and computational algorithm building blocks that makes predictions and analyses the data through machines as intelligently as human minds [5]. AI is a superset of Machine learning that trains computers

© Springer Nature Singapore Pte Ltd. 2021
P. K. Singh et al. (Eds.): FTNCT 2020, CCIS 1395, pp. 276–287, 2021.
https://doi.org/10.1007/978-981-16-1480-4_24

by incorporating the information which provides the ability to function their behavior incoherent terms to socially intelligent human referred to as interpretability [6]. The investment of organization and industries are shifting towards AI and data analytics for growing business functionalities, employee's engagement, reducing the repetitive tasks, standardization, and computing metrics [7]. The demanding aspect of AI and technological advancement has already taken control over monotonous operational procedures that humans may find tedious and time taking [8]. The technological innovations determine two coined views as (i) optimistic (ii) pessimistic for human health and wellbeing. Automation enhanced flexibility, workplace efficiency, and productivity. To overcome the challenges of technological disruption, the positive impact that employees are learning the required necessary skill set for upgrading the shift from mechanical to thinking jobs, unskilled to skilled workers [9]. However, the negative impact of these disruptive tools is affecting the health – (mental, emotional, physical, and social) of workers across various sectors [10, 11].

According to Forbes, Augmented intelligence, another conceptualization of artificial intelligence emphasized on advancing human performance. AI and ML lead to innovation, creativity, building social and emotional skills in data-driven organizations [12]. Emotion plays a crucial role at different parameters such as decision making, emotional affinity, creation of innovative ideas, and task accomplishment [13, 14], but still, the human emotional moving process and feelings are neglected at more than 60% of organizations. Chara papoutsi et al. (2019) presented the correlation of working variables in an organization with emotions. The analysis concludes the positive relationship with mentioned factors as organizational engagement or commitment, conflict management strategies, job satisfaction/performance, workforce behavior, self-efficiency, and wellbeing (stress, happiness, anxiety). The observations determine that the skills of emotional intelligence are considered more predictive than IQ for measuring personal success and organizational efficiency. The hybrid of artificial intelligence (AI) understanding the concept of emotional and social skills allowing managers to mobilize towards thinking tasks such as analyzing, reasoning, problem-solving, decision making, flourishing creativity, and evaluating data or information resulting in a paradigm shift within the organization [16].

The integration of AI with robotics are meeting the vulnerabilities of human and moving towards new technical frontier-Emotional AI (Emotion recognition system). The global Emotion Detection and recognition market expected to reach a value of USD 45.48 million by 2025 [17]. Emotion AI or Affective Computing is an area of association between Cognitive intelligence and artificial intelligence to measure human emotion [18]. Health care and corporate wellness industries are seeing a plethora of benefits from the influx of technology and machine learning. This application is currently explored in human Resource Management (HRM), Customer relationship management (CRM), marketing, and entertainment. This paper is unfolding two sections - firstly, the impact of Artificial Intelligence transformation in the regular flow of human resource management. Secondly, the technological disruption challenges faced by the organization and HR managers in adopting AI.

2 Artificial Intelligence

In late 1956, John McCarthy introduced the conceptual theory of artificial intelligence for giving directions to develop the intelligent machine that behaves like a human [19]. Traditionally, AI refers to comprehensive technologies that allow the computer to perform the mechanical task that requires human cognition. Within the last decade, AI has grown tremendously, focusing on a subclass of algorithms (ML) that rely primarily on the availability of data for the prediction task [20]. The 60% of organizations have adopted modern technologies such as pattern recognition, deep learning for meeting the growing demands of the industry [21]. Human resource management is an essential resource for an organization in upgrading the strategic approach and practices for creating a healthy environment. The upcoming HRM functionalities are showing a paradigm shift from the administrative role of management towards autonomous workforce characteristics [22]. AI uses a different algorithm for training the network for the predictions of the various factors in an organization such as Talent acquisition, employee engagement, learning, and development [23]. The vital information and inferences can be obtained through applied AI techniques overcoming the challenges of the human Workforce. The AI tools and technologies would facilitate the emerging human to machine interaction, the logic building of functional enterprise model, and transformation in the wellbeing of employees [9]. The proposed framework represents the improved role of AI in human resource management and its functionalities. The designed flow is sliced into three phases (i) Mechanical (ii) Thinking (iii) emotional as shown in Fig. 1.

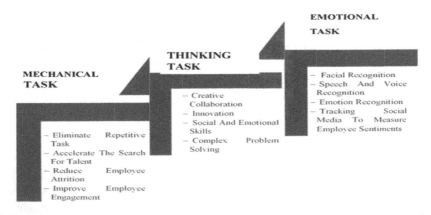

Fig. 1. Proposed Framework showing the emerging role of AI in Human Resource Management.

2.1 Mechanical Task

The widely available technologies today improving organizations by automating repetitive, standardized, and time-consuming tasks and providing assisted intelligence as in chatbots. The AI, Machine learning, and computer vision are significantly manifest the implications in human resource management from assets planning to recruitment and on-boarding process, sentiment analysis in interviews, and using chatbots for monitoring compliance [24]. AI-Based talent acquisition software evaluates an applicant's resume for the recruiting process, thereby allowing HR managers to spend more time analyzing only the eligible shortlisted candidates while eliminating unsuitable profiles for an existing job [25]. For instance, in terms of HR management, during recruitment, AI can assist HR in observing permutation & combinations of traits that the company is looking for respective candidates. Thus, the selection process can be accelerated, multi-focused, neutralized. The candidate's performance can be measured autonomously by adding sentiment analysis and computational linguistics [26]. Companies are deploying NLP/AI based bots answering transactional queries of candidates and employees, thereby providing more time to the teams to focus on other critical areas of work that require more of human intervention. The estimated abilities of the newly recruited candidate can not only be measured in terms of the organizational ROI in hiring, training, and remuneration, but also relating to the individual's ability to learn on the job, develop new skills, and his or her social contributions.

2.2 Thinking Task

The integration of AI with human intelligence leads to the formation of augmented intelligence for better business solutions and services involving creative and lateral thinking. The augmented intelligence saves a lot of time and amount in the investigation of information, thereby supporting expertise judgment and decisions [27]. In the year 2016, IBM Watson introduced the cognitive platform adding a significant contribution towards AI. The transformation to cognitive Computing collaborating human intelligence with a range of artificial intelligence techniques such as machine learning, natural language processing, image analysis, and the expert system is playing a differential role in organizations [28]. Cognitive augmentation improves customer services, personalized customer experience, learning experience by introducing new educational tools and customized programs for the employees and customers [29, 30].

In the same way, AI is reshaping and redefining the innovation process with the repetitive cycle of sense-think-and-act. AI trains the network by taking extensive input data, creates the knowledge base and provides the prediction analysis accurately. The Intelligent agents (IA) can be a machine (industrial and home robots, self-driving cars) or a software agent (chatbots, recommender systems). It takes the data input in the form of images, videos, sound, text for analyzation, and visualization using AI algorithms to delivers AI-powered solutions [31]. The unique human traits – such as emotional intelligence, creativity, persuasion, innovation, social skill– become more profitable by merging the co-existence of man and machine [16]. Accenture research on the impact of AI revealed that AI technologies would boost business productivity by 40% and can double the annual economic growth rate with the co-existence of man and machine by 2035.

2.3 Emotional Task

The companies are establishing the most advanced form of technologies relying on AI that act on their own and reach out to the unconscious level of information. We can also see algorithms autonomously take over decision making and selection processes. In this scenario, the intelligent system predicts the employee's performance by analysing the present situation, the selection of sub-objective by constructing the program based on experience and action. Chabot's and mobile apps would be able to understand the emotions efficiently and respond to the emotional aspect of individuals such as anger, irritation, frustration, and determining the stress levels in professionals as well in personal lives. The study of systems that can perceive, interpret, and incorporates emotion parameters referred to as Affective Computing or Artificial Emotional Intelligence. AI systems utilize data science and machine algorithms to understand the specific signatures of behaviour to determine emotions, build a group performance dashboard and optimization algorithms that provide suggestions at an organizational level. Emotional AI will be used to detect or diagnose the mental health of employees within the workplace to increase organization productivity. The future involves the creation of smart bracelets that can detect the human emotional states by utilizing data science, incorporation of sophisticated machine learning algorithms, and increasing adoption of bio-sensor, which can act as a game-changer in the business community. Nonetheless, emotionally designed agents will be implanted in the technologies that employees frequently use, running in the surroundings, making the tech communication more relevant, customized, and interactive.

3 Research Methodology

The primary and secondary data have been subsequently used for the purpose of study. A quantitative methodology is adopted with the help of structured questionnaires which are focused on HR employees and IT professional working in corporate sector. The random sampling method has been used for collection of data. The study conducted a primary data collection from around 50 professionals to understand AI implementation in human resource practice. In addition, extensive research have also conducted from secondary sources, such as journals, articles, publications and various database websites.

3.1 Objective of the Study

- To understand the perception of employees about AI.
- To identify the current AI technologies use in human resource practices.

3.2 Data Analysis and Interpretation:

The proposed study identifies the various AI technologies used by employees in IT sector and their perception towards AI technologies in HRM practices. The data was collected from 50 respondent on the basis of random sampling. The analysis of data is done by applying statistical tools such as percentages, T-test and Anova Test. The graphical representation of demographics on basis of percentage is shown in Fig. 2. The statistical analysis result are presented in Table 5, 6, and 7.

3.3 Cronbach's Alpha Reliability Test

Cronbach's Alpha is used to assess the internal consistency or reliability of the questionnaire that is made of multiple Likert type scale. The formula of Cronbach's Alpha is shown in Eq. (1).The test revealed the reliability score of 0.88, hence the questionnaire found to be reliable.

$$\alpha = \frac{N.\overline{C}}{\overline{V} + (N-1).\overline{C}} \tag{1}$$

Where, N is the number of items, $\bar{c}$ stand for average covariance between item-pairs, $\bar{v}$ stands for average variance (Table 1). The demographics of the respondent are given in Tables 2, 3 and 4.

Table 1. Cronbach's alpha reliability test

Cronbach's Alpha	N of items
0.8810012890	50

3.4 Demographics

Table 2. Statistical analysis on the basis of Age (%)

Age	Percentage
22–25 years	11.43
26–30 years	77.17
31–40 years	8.57
Above 40 years	2.86

Table 3. Statistical analysis on the basis of Gender (%)

Gender	Percentage
Male	88.57
Female	11.53

3.5 T-Test

T- Test is used to determine whether there is a significant difference between the means of two groups. A p-value less than 0.05 (typically ≤ 0.05) is statistically significant. A p-value higher than 0.05 (> 0.05) is not statistically significant.

Interpretation: The findings revealed that there is significant difference between perceptions on AI technologies with the gender of employees.

Table 4. Statistical analysis on the basis of Work Experience (%)

Work experience	Percentage
1–5 years	62.86
6–10 years	28.57
11–15 years	2.86
16–20 years	5.71

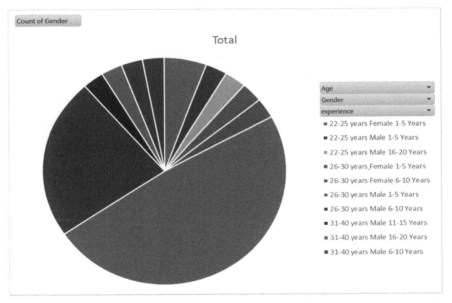

Fig. 2. Graphical representation of Demographics Factors like Age, gender and working experience.

Table 5. Gender wise perception of the employees regarding adoption of AI technologies in Human Resource Practices- T test

HR practices	Talent acquisition	On boarding	Learning and development	Compensation management	Health and safety
P values	$2.29*10^{-18}$	$6.67*10^{-18}$	$1.68*10^{-19}$	$1.52*10^{-18}$	$1.97*10^{-17}$

3.6 Anova Test

ANOVA is used to determine where there are any statistically significant difference between the means of three or more independent groups. ANOVA checks the impact of one or more factors by comparing the means of different samples. This test produces a P value whether relationship is significant or not. If P values are greater than 0.05 it reveals that there is no significant difference and if P value is less than 0.05 than there is significant difference between mean.

Table 6. Age wise perception of the employees regarding adoption of AI technologies in Human Resource practices- ANOVA Test

HR practice/Age	Sum-sq.	Mean-sq.	F	P(>F)
Talent acquisition	10.659259	3.553086	2.638805	0.07
On boarding	7.513300	2.389065	1.973986	0.06
Learning and development	2.941005	0.980335	0.748498	0.53
Compensation management	11.052910	3.684303	3.215602	0.06
Health and safety	7.589418	2.529806	2.047822	0.12

Interpretation: In Table 6, the findings revealed that there is no significant difference between the age group and their perception towards AI technologies in HR practices.

Table 7. Education wise perception of the employees regarding adoption of AI technologies in Human resource Practices-ANOVA Test

HR practice/Education	Sum-sq.	Mean-sq.	F	P(>F)
Talent acquisition	7.572414	3.786207	2.702769	0.082
On boarding	7.513300	3.756650	3.233925	0.06
Learning and Development	1.404926	0.702463	0.533458	0.59
Compensation Management	7.164532	3.582266	2.908945	0.069
Health and safety	5.651232	2.825616	2.247319	0.12

Interpretation: The findings shows that there is no significant difference between the education and their perception towards AI technologies in HR practices in Table 7.

The graphical representation in Fig. 3 shows AI powdered technologies used by the employees at workplace and Fig. 4 shows the challenges faced by the business leaders while implementing AI technologies.

* Likert scale is used where 1 = strongly Disagree, 2 = Disagree, 3 = Neutral, 4 = Agree and 5 = strongly Disagree.

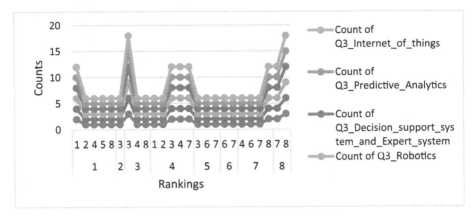

Fig. 3. Rankings are given to AI powdered Technologies used by the employees.

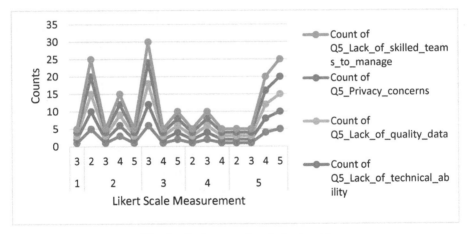

Fig. 4. Challenges when deploying AI

4   Challenges When Deploying AI

(i) Need for sufficiently large Dataset (quality, quantity, Labelling): AI learning requires a massive amount of data. Thus, HR should be able to understand the quality of necessary information needed to be taken from the employee's in various formats such as text, image, video, and audio for authentic learning of network. Nowadays, a system utilizing machine learning or deep learning performs supervised, unsupervised, and reinforcement techniques for categorizing the patterns. The challenge in growing business demand is to obtain an abundant knowledge base or dataset.

(ii) Creating Trust: AI is still like the "black box" for some people ending up with prediction without any validation. In many cases, an individual wanted to know "How" the algorithm came to its decisions and existence according to different applications. However, The lack of Explainability represents massive blockade in adopting and implementing AI. The factual findings with legal repercussions are essential for business decisions for improved performance.

(iii)   Need for experts to train the system: There are many myths concerning artificial intelligence, varying from the mundane task requiring in house data science to smart robots ending humanity. HR managers require not only a deep understanding of AI technologies but also need a strategic approach, particular objectives, identifying KPI's, and tracking ROI. Additionally, it is also necessary to find well-trained experts to implement the AI solution.

(iv)   Integration Complexity: Companies need to have structured data information to have the right kind of input mechanism that will empower AI algorithms. An organization required to be adaptable for accommodating new team models, new business models, and new workflows across all teams and departments. Companies evaluate the customizable and commercial off-shelf AI applications before deciding to build solutions from the ground because current AI solutions for HR are specially designed, confined, and singularly focused.

(v)   Security and Privacy implication: Digital data involves the fundamental risk issue as it contains the personal data such as medical records, facial recognition, the emotional health state of employees, financial data of the company. AI developers, Data scientist, and policymakers need to identify vulnerabilities and consider innovative, proactive strategies to protect data.

5   Conclusion

The epidemic growth toward specialized AI system in the organization has a dramatic impact on Human resource management. The disruptive technology alters the way of business operations by taking over manual, repetitive and administrative roles and allowing professionals to learn, unlearn and re-learn. The organization are successfully integrated the semi-automated process that gathers, normalize and screen the data in talent acquisition, performance analysis, retention rate to move towards automated systems. In the near future, AI will augment HR roles and their capabilities that will lead to a collaborative environment with the co-existence of human and machine. The fusion of Artificial Intelligence (AI) and human resources (HR) practices will make healthy lifestyle in organization because these applications can analyze, predict and diagnose to make quality decisions. In a nutshell, HR professionals of the future need to act on the data at the fingertip, developing interpretable models and an explainable effect that win over the confidence of Key decision-makers.

References

1. Kaplan, A., Haenlein, M.: Digital transformation and disruption: on big data, blockchain, artificial intelligence, and other things (2019)
2. Iansiti, M., Lakhani, K.R.: Competing in the age of AI. Harv. Bus. Rev. **98**(1), 60–67 (2020)
3. von Krogh, G.: Artificial intelligence in organizations: new opportunities for phenomenon-based theorizing. Academy of Management Discoveries (2018)

4. PR Newswire. New virtual human technology from talespin leverages VR and AI for teaching "Soft Skills." (2019)

5. Kaplan, A., Haenlein, M.: Siri, Siri, in my hand: who's the fairest in the land? on the interpretations, illustrations, and implications of artificial intelligence. Bus. Horiz. **62**(1), 15–25 (2019)

6. Verbraeken, J., Wolting, M., Katzy, J., Kloppenburg, J., Verbelen, T., Rellermeyer, J.S.: A survey on distributed machine learning. ACM Comput. Surv. **53**(2), 1–33 (2020). https://doi.org/10.1145/3377454

7. Pandey, S., Khaskel, P.: Application of AI in human resource management and gen Y" s reaction. Int. J. Recent Technol. Eng. (IJRTE) (2019). ISSN: 2277–3878

8. George, G., Thomas, M.R.: Integration of artificial intelligence in human resource. Int. J. Innovative Technol. Exploring Eng. (IJITEE) (2019). ISSN: 2278–3075

9. Soni, N., Sharma, E.K., Singh, N., Kapoor, A.: Impact of artificial intelligence on businesses: from research, innovation, market deployment to future shifts in business models. arXiv preprint arXiv:1905.02092 (2019)

10. Salo, M., Pirkkalainen, H., Koskelainen, T.: Technostress and social networking services: Explaining users' concentration, sleep, identity, and social relation problems. Inf. Syst. J. **29**(2), 408–435 (2019)

11. Pirkkalainen, H., Salo, M., Tarafdar, M., Makkonen, M.: Deliberate or instinctive? proactive and reactive coping for technostress. J. Manag. Inf. Syst. **36**(4), 1179–1212 (2019). https://doi.org/10.1080/07421222.2019.1661092

12. Huang, M.H., Rust, R., Maksimovic, V.: The feeling economy: managing in the next generation of artificial intelligence (AI). Calif. Manag. Rev. **61**(4), 43–65 (2019)

13. Brackett, M.: Permission to feel: unlocking the power of emotions to help our kids, ourselves, and our society thrive. Celadon Books (2019)

14. Austin, D.: Windmills of your mind: understanding the neurobiology of emotion. Wake Forest Law Rev. **54**(4), 931–972 (2019)

15. Papoutsi, C., Drigas, A., Skianis, C.: Emotional intelligence as an important asset for HR in organizations: attitudes and working variables. Int. J. Adv. Corp. Learn. **12**(2), 21–35 (2019). https://doi.org/10.3991/ijac.v12i2.9620

16. Sousa, M.J., Wilks, D.: Sustainable skills for the world of work in the digital age. Syst. Res. Behav. Sci. **35**(4), 399–405 (2018). https://doi.org/10.1002/sres.2540

17. Lamphere, C.: The dawn of a newish era: how AI, robotics, and everything in between shapes our world. Online Searcher **42**(4), 27–30 (2018)

18. Kowalczuk, Z., Czubenko, M., Merta, T.: Interpretation and modeling of emotions in the management of autonomous robots using a control paradigm basedon a scheduling variable. Eng. Appl. Artif. Intell. **91**, 103562 (2020)

19. Griffey, J.: Chapter 1: Introduction. Libr. Technol. Rep. **55**(1), 5–9 (2019)

20. Haenlein, M., Kaplan, A.: A brief history of artificial intelligence: on the past, present, and future of artificial intelligence. Calif. Manage. Rev. **61**(4), 5–14 (2019)

21. https://www.mckinsey.com/featured-insights/artificial-intelligence/global-ai-survey-ai-proves-its-worth-but-few-scale-impact

22. Tambe, P., Cappelli, P., Yakubovich, V.: Artificial intelligence in human resources management: challenges and a path forward. Calif. Manage. Rev. **61**(4), 15–42 (2019)

23. Jia, Q., Guo, Y., Li, R., Li, Y., Chen, Y.: A conceptual artificial intelligence application framework in human resource management. In: Proceedings of the International Conference on Electronic Business, pp. 106–114 (2018

24. Chichester, M.A., Jr., Giffen, J.R.: Recruiting in the robot age: examining potential EEO implications in optimizing recruiting through the use of artificial intelligence. Comput. Internet Lawyer **36**(10), 1–3 (2019)

25. Kulkarni, S.B., Che, X.: Intelligent software tools for recruiting. J. Int. Technol. Inf. Manage. **28**(2), 2–16 (2019)
26. Gelbard, R., Ramon, G.R., Carmeli, A., Bittmann, R.M., Talyansky, R.: Sentiment analysis in organizational work: towards an ontology of people analytics. Expert. Syst. **35**(5), 1 (2018). https://doi.org/10.1111/exsy.12289
27. Jarrahi, M.H.: Artificial intelligence and the future of work: human-AI symbiosis in organizational decision making. Bus. Horiz. **61**(4), 577–586 (2018)
28. Pan, Y.: Heading toward artificial intelligence 2.0. Engineering, **2**(4), 409–413 (2016)
29. Mertens, J.: IBM study: more than half of CHROs see cognitive computing as a disruptive force in the next three years. Workforce Solutions Rev. **8**(3), 27–31 (2017)
30. Looking to the Future: 2020 Insight. KM World, **29**(1), 6–8 (2020)
31. Bingham, T., Galagan, P.: AI is coming for everyone. TD: Talent Dev. **72**(12), 26–30 (2018)
32. Kompella, K.: A guide to emotional AI for business. EContent **42**(3), 36–37 (2019)
33. Krakovsky, M.: Artificial (emotional) intelligence: enabled by advances in computing power and neural networks, machines are getting better at recognizing and dealing with human emotions. Commun. ACM **61**(4), 18–19 (2018). https://doi.org/10.1145/3185521

Feature Selection Using Ensemble Techniques

Yash Kaushik[✉], Muskaan Dixit, Nikhil Sharma, and Monika Garg

Manav Rachna International Institute of Research and Studies, Faridabad, India
`monikagarg.fet@mriu.edu.in`

Abstract. Data used in Machine Learning tasks need to be pre-processed and prepared to improve its quality. Features or variables in data play a major role in the results obtained after applying Machine Learning models. The features which are irrelevant to the domain should be discarded with the objective of improving the accuracy and validity of results. For this purpose, Feature Selection is used. It is a way of reducing the size, the purpose of settling down to the right element from the original elements by removing the negative, redundant or noisy features. Feature selection can often result in better learning performance, such as, lower computational cost, and better model translation. It is very important to shed some light on the nature of feature selection for student performance measurement, because constructive educational approaches can be found in the appropriate set of features. Feature selection plays a major role in refining the quality of the data models. Increased data quality can produce better results and therefore based options for such quality data can increase the quality of education by predicting performance. In the light of the aforementioned fact, it is necessary to carefully stabilize the selection of the algorithm. Feature selection key can directly affect classification accuracy and simplify operation. Several data experiments were performed to demonstrate the effectiveness of the proposed method. Selective bias may also be the term used in data analytics. In this paper, two ensemble techniques namely, Random Forests and Gradient Boosting Machines have been applied on a dataset, for the purpose of Feature Selection. Experimental results show that Gradient Boosting Machines are better at Feature Selection.

Keywords: Feature selection · Random forests · Gradient boosting machines

1 Introduction

Over the past decade, the enthusiasm for using Feature Selection (FS) techniques has shifted from being a model that is proving to be a real catalyst for model building. In order to use machine learning methods effectively, pre-processing the data is essential. Feature selection is one of the most common and important techniques for early data processing, and it has become a very important part of the machine learning process. It is the process of finding the right features and removing inaccurate, unwanted, or noisy data. This process speeds up data mining algorithms, improves the precision of the guesswork, and increases the accuracy. Our interest is concentrated on high quality data. The sheer amount of high-quality data has posed the greatest challenge to existing

© Springer Nature Singapore Pte Ltd. 2021
P. K. Singh et al. (Eds.): FTNCT 2020, CCIS 1395, pp. 288–298, 2021.
https://doi.org/10.1007/978-981-16-1480-4_25

machine operating methods. Depending on the supervised learning, Feature Selection provides a set of features for designers using one of the following methods. One is, specified dimensions for support features that maximize test scope, Another is Overall, the bottom set is the best commitment between size and test score. The method of choice (fs) method has changed dramatically over the last few years and, many papers have found domains with (hundreds to tens of thousands of variables). New approaches are being proposed to deal with these stimulating tasks that include many negative and abnormal variables and often the same few examples of training. 1. We are looking for "variable" variable input variables and, "features" built-in input variables. We use null "variables" and "element" where there is no view in selection algorithms, e.g. Text partitioning problem, represented documents, which is an indication of the size of the terminology consisting of word counting, view and understanding of data, decrease in size and storage requirements, reduce training times and use, reduce the size curse to improve predictive performance. The feature selection problem based on supervised instruction is: Given a set of candidate features that selects a standard set defined by one of three methods. A set-size setup that enables an experimenter with a small size satisfies a specific limit on a test scale and is possible to better understand the results obtained by the inducer, reducing its storage capacity. The indirect feature does not apply to import, but not all relevant features are useful. The selection criteria included are that the time spent in training the model is greatly reduced due to the limited number of parameters used.

Authors of a paper [1] give information about robustness of feature selection techniques which needs importance while analyzing the selected feature subsets. This shows that these techniques are of useful for higher dimensional domains and small sample sizes. In addition, they also investigated the effects of integrating feature selection strategies on categorization, providing a new strategy for model selection.

Another paper [2] lets us consider about the contingency of feature selection, which might provide us with a basic classification in hierarchical system of feature selection techniques, and communicate its use, variety and introduction of a few important applications and future bioinformatics applications. This paper also provides taxonomy of these techniques there were areas of application and their diversification in common and the new coming bioinformatics applications.

This paper is organized as follows: Sect. 1 introduces the concept of Feature Selection. Need of Feature Selection is highlighted in Sect. 2. The various categories of Feature selection techniques are explained in Sect. 3. Section 4 surveys the literature. The methodology adopted in this article is explained in Sect. 5. Experiments performed and results obtained are discussed in Sect. 6. Paper is concluded in Sect. 7.

2 Need of Feature Selection

Feature selection as the name describes is to pick out important features from a specific data set or in simple terms to cut back number of input variables while developing a predictive model and is additionally referred to as variable selection. Nowadays, datasets have abundant information with data which is collected using countless of IoT devices and sensors. Now the times datasets have huge number of attributes in which not all are useful a large number of features make a model bulky, time-taking, high dimensional and harder to implement in production.

Feature selection is vital as there is noisy data which needs to be removed. Lots of low frequent features, multi-type features, too many features compared to samples, complex models, samples in real scenario is non-homogenous with training and test samples. All these points make it very important for data to be cleaned properly. Data cleaning is the most important and tedious work in data mining. If the data is not cleaned and arranged properly it will take much more time to get the desired results. It also reduces the computation time involved to get the model and helps us to focus on what is more important. It reduces the risk of Over-fitting that is also known as curse of dimensionality the dimensionality of the features space increases, number of configurations can grow exponentially which becomes very difficult if we have huge amount of data. It improves Accuracy which leads to less misleading data means and thus improving accuracy, data training time is reduced so that less data means that algorithms train faster. Feature selection also reduce the computational cost of modelling [3].

Seeing all the points we realize how much important it is to select the correct features accurately. One feature may not seem as important but it can be related to some other attribute too. Feature Selection methods helps with these problems by reducing the dimensions, reducing redundancy, reducing noisy data without much loss of the total information. By applying feature selection methods we get to know the significance of each feature in improving the model.

Feature selection can be done manually by data analysts but when the amount of attributes are in enormous amount it is not feasible for a person to do and it might take longer duration of time to complete a given project. Here comes the need for various feature selection methods.

3   Feature Selection Techniques

Feature Selection techniques can be categorized into following categories. Techniques which need to be applied depends upon the type on the type of data whether it is numerical or categorical.

3.1   Filter Methods

Filter methods are not dependent on any learning algorithm, but depend on the complete aspects of the training data. Filter-based feature selection methods [4] use statistical measures to check the correlation or dependency between the given input variables that how much are they dependent on each other that can be filtered to choose the most relevant features. Statistical measures for feature selection must be chosen carefully based on the data type of the input variable and the output or response variable. In filter methods, features are selected by selecting the most relevant attributes without using any machine learning algorithm. Various statistical tests are done like chi square test, ANOVA test, LDA, information gain, fisher score, correlation coefficient, variance threshold etc. and features are selected on the basis of their scores in various statistical tests for their correlation with the outcome variable. Here correlation is considered as a subjective term.

3.2 Wrapper Methods

Wrapper methods use learning algorithms to evaluate the features. Wrapper methods [5] are of various kinds too and we try to use subset of features and train a data from it. These processes have large number of steps and we also need to consider which method is to applied when depending upon our input data and the type of result e get whether it is numerical or categorical data.

3.3 Hybrid Methods

Hybrid methods combine properties of both Filter and Wrapper methods.

3.4 Embedded Methods

There is also another technique referred to as embedded technique of feature selection and is most advanced one. In our paper we have applied two different embedded techniques only. The difference between the filter and wrapper method is that Wrapper methods measure the "usefulness" of features supported on the classifier performance. On the opposite hand, the filter methods focus and acquire the intrinsic properties of the features measured via univariate statistics instead of cross-validation performance. There are different algorithms in java, python, R. Each one has its importance and some disadvantages like few feature selection techniques can be applied only on data having not large number of attributes or in some cases the accuracy is increased if there are larger number of variables.

In this paper, we have applied two Feature selection algorithms, namely Gradient Boosting Machines (GBM) and Random Forests (RF) [6]. These two techniques are described as follows:

3.4.1 Gradient Boosting Machines

In Gradient Boosting [7, 8], additive regression models are built by iteratively fitting a simple base learner to currently updated pseudo-residuals by applying least squares at every further iteration. The objective of this method is to evolve a function F*(x) which maps x to y, so that when the joint distribution of all values (y, x) is taken, the expected value of $\Psi(y, F(x))$ which is some specified loss function is minimized. This relation is depicted in Eq. (1).

Where y is the random output or dependent variable and $x = \{x_1, x2,...x_n\}$ is a set of random input variables.

$$F^*(x) = \arg\min E_{y,x}\Psi(y, F(x)) \tag{1}$$

3.4.2 Random Forests

Random Forests [9–11] were developed as an extension to the popular ensemble technique called Bagging. It is a tree-based ensemble technique where each tree depends on a set of random variables. Random Forests are used for prediction in various domains like Traffic estimation and congestion on roads due to traffic [12].

Equation (2) shows the mean square generalization error in Random Forests for a numeric predictor h(x)

$$E_{X,Y}(Y - h(X))^2 \tag{2}$$

The Random Forest predictor is constructed by taking the mean over k of the trees $\{h(x, \theta_k)\}$.

Equation (3) states the case for infinite numbers of trees in the forest

$$E_{X,Y}(Y - av_k h(X, \theta_k))^2 \rightarrow E_{X,Y}(Y - E_\theta h(X, \theta))^2 \tag{3}$$

4 Literature Survey

This section reviews the work done by some researchers.

This paper [13] introduces a new feature selection algorithm based on the wrapper process using neural networks. An important feature of this algorithm is the automatic determination of neural network structures during the process. Their algorithm uses a constructive approach that incorporates linking information in selecting features and determining neural network structures. The test results show the essence of a constructive approach to selecting features with integrated structure.

In this work [14], a propose a method of selecting a multi-filter element based on an method that includes the issuance of four filtering methods to achieve optimal selection. Then they also conducted a detailed evaluation of our proposed method using a benchmark acquisition dataset for intrusion detection, NSL-KDD and decision-making tree planning. The findings show that our proposed approach can effectively reduce the number of features from 41 to 13 and has a higher level of accuracy and classification accuracy compared to other classification strategies.

Recent advances [4] in computer technology in terms of speed, cost, and acquisition of large amounts of computer power and the ability to process large amounts of data in a timely manner have stimulated interest in increasing data mining requests to extract useful information from data. Machine learning has become one of the most widely used methods in these data mining applications. In this study, the authors examined the various options between classes and selected methods of using distance in relation to their effectiveness in advancing inclusion data to attract decision trees. The results of their research showed that intermediate-stage measures lead to better performance compared to expected measures, in general.

In this paper [15], writers have presented a review of the state of the art approach to the selection of scientific-theoretic features. The concepts of the importance of feature importance and redundancy are well defined, as well as Markov's outfit. The problem with the right feature selection is explained. An integrated theoretical framework has been developed, which can re-establish successful success strategies, reflecting the limitations made in each case. There are many open-ended issues in the field that are also being presented.

The authors in this paper [16] applied three Machine Learning techniques namely- Support Vector Machines, Multilayer Perceptron and Random Forests to predict the residency of teachers in Indian universities related to Information and Communication Technology awareness. Results showed that Random Forests was far better at prediction than other two algorithms with prediction accuracy of 72.8% and prediction time of 0.12 s.

Feature Selection is an important phase in Data Analysis and Machine Learning. In a paper [17], the authors have applied Machine Learning algorithms to analyze few categories of Cyber attacks.

In another paper [18], Feature selection is performed to select genes of Microarray datasets, with the objective of applying it for cancer diagnosis. Then Support vector machines technique is applied for classification purpose.

A paper [19] introduces the concept of variable and Feature selection and its objectives. The article emphasizes on various aspects like Feature construction, Feature ranking, multivariate Feature selection and some assessment methods to validate features.

5   Methodology

The research outline adopted in this paper is defined in Fig. 1. It consists of several phases which are explained as follows.

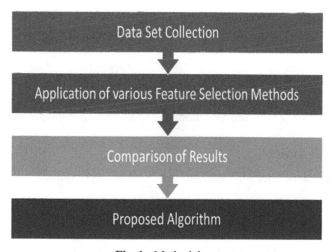

Fig. 1. Methodology

5.1   Dataset Collection

Dataset of store sales was collected and its parameters are described below in Table 1:

Table 1. Dataset Parameter Description

Parameters	Description
Shipping.Cost	This parameter determines the shipping cost used for shipping items to consumers
Order.Quantity	It is the number of units to be added in order to reduce inventory costs
Product.Category	It is all the products offering the same general functionality
Product.Container	This parameter is the art of incorporating or protecting a product for distribution, sale and use
Order.ID	is a unique **number** which you'll need to identify and track your **orders**
Product.Sub.Category	It is with respect to a given category, a sub-category while the category is a group
Ship.Date	Shipping date is the date the order is sent from the merchant or the last store to the customer
Order.Date	Order Date means the date on which the decision and final order of the Decision is issued by the Commission
Ship.Mode	Shipping Mode is a shipment name that defines travel mode
Province	Province is the main division of land or sovereignty
Order.Priority	The term used in fulfilling the practices that place certain submissions before others
Customer.Segment	We divide customers into groups based on general characteristics so that companies can sell to each group effectively and efficiently

5.2 Algorithm Application

As aforementioned, Random Forests and Gradient Boosting Machines were applied on the collected dataset for Feature Selection.

5.3 Results Comparison

The results of feature selection obtained from both the algorithms, RF and GBM were compared.

5.4 Proposed Algorithm

Since the results of GBM are better as compared to Random Forests, we propose GBM for feature selection.

6 Experiments and Results

In this paper, Random Forests and Gradient Boosting Machines were applied on the dataset with the objective of Feature Selection. The experiments have been performed using R Studio. Table 2 shows the results obtained from both algorithms.

Table 2. Feature Importance given by RF and GBM

Random forests	Gradient boosting machines
Order.ID	Shipping.Cost
Order.Date	Order.Quantity
Order.Priority	Product.Category
Order.Quantity	Product.Container
Ship.Mode	Order.ID
Shipping.Cost	Product.Sub.Category
Province	Ship.Date
Customer.Segment	Order.Date
Product.Category	Ship.Mode
Product.Sub.Category	Province
Product.Container	Order.Priority
Ship.Date	Customer.Segment

It is evident from the results shown in Table 2 that GBM is better at feature selection and importance as compared to RF. Therefore, we propose GBM for the purpose of Feature Selection.

Table 2 shows the priority order of the parameters which are responsible for Store sales by both - RF method and GBM method. GBM method is more accurate as compared to RF method. While using GBM method we were able to arrange the data in the order which is based on the priority that the parameter with the maximum value is at the top i.e. Shipping.Cost and the parameter with the least value is placed in the bottom i.e. Customer.Segment. GBM method gives the result with the values and by using these values we are also able to produce the Feature Importance graph. This graph is more visually understandable and we are also able to decide that which parameter is more important and is more responsible for the sales in store.

Table 3 shows the percentage assigned by GBM to each parameter in sequence.

Table 3. Feature importance percentage by GBM

Gradient boosting machines	Percentage
Shipping.Cost	38.81237
Order.Quantity	15.8415
Product.Category	8.672646
Product.Container	7.289848

(continued)

Table 3. (*continued*)

Gradient boosting machines	Percentage
Order.ID	6.758149
Product.Sub.Category	5.424211
Ship.Date	4.711707
Order.Date	4.274776
Ship.Mode	3.511199
Province	2.477245
Order.Priority	1.326632
Customer.Segment	0.899724

Figure 2 shows the various features, ordered as per importance using GBM technique. It clearly states that the parameter Shipping.Cost has the highest value from all other parameters.

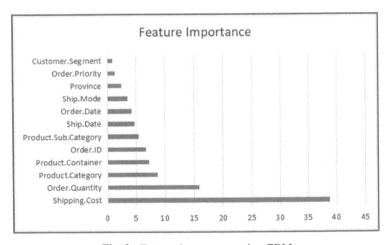

Fig. 2. Feature importance using GBM

7   Conclusion and Future Scope

This paper presents a survey of the feature selection methods expected in the literature. A few popular feature selection methods like Filter method, Wrapper method, Embedded methods were introduced. From embedded feature selection category, Random Forests and Gradient Boosting Machines were applied on a dataset for selecting important features. Experiments were performed in R Studio and the obtained results show that GBM performs better than RF in terms of Feature Selection. In future, other well-known techniques for Feature Selection can be experimented.

References

1. Saeys, Y., Abeel, T., Van de Peer, Y.: Robust feature selection using ensemble feature selection techniques. In: Daelemans, W., Goethals, B., Morik, K. (eds.) ECML PKDD 2008. LNCS (LNAI), vol. 5212, pp. 313–325. Springer, Heidelberg (2008). https://doi.org/10.1007/978-3-540-87481-2_21
2. Saeys, Y., Inza, I., Larrañaga, P.: A review of feature selection techniques in bioinformatics. Bioinformatics 23(19), 2507–2517 (2007)
3. Chandrashekar, G., Sahin, F.: A survey on feature selection methods. Comput. Electr. Eng. 40(1), 16–28 (2014)
4. Osanaiye, O., Cai, H., Choo, K.-K., Dehghantanha, A., Xu, Z., Dlodlo, M.: Ensemble-based multi-filter feature selection method for DDoS detection in cloud computing. EURASIP J. Wirel. Commun. Netw. 2016(1), 1 (2016). https://doi.org/10.1186/s13638-016-0623-3
5. Jović, A., Brkić, K., Bogunović, N.: A review of feature selection methods with applications. In: 38th International Convention on Information and Communication Technology, Electronics and Microelectronics (MIPRO), pp. 1200–1205. IEEE (2015)
6. Goyal, M., Pandey, M.: Towards prediction of energy consumption of HVAC plants using machine learning. In: Batra, U., Roy, N.R., Panda, B. (eds.) REDSET 2019. CCIS, vol. 1229, pp. 254–265. Springer, Singapore (2020). https://doi.org/10.1007/978-981-15-5827-6_22
7. Friedman, J.H.: Stochastic gradient boosting. Comput. Stat. Data Anal. 38(4), 367–378 (2002)
8. Goyal, M., Pandey, M.: Extreme gradient boosting algorithm for energy optimization in buildings pertaining to HVAC plants. EW, EAI (2020). https://doi.org/10.4108/eai.13-7-2018.164562
9. Prasad, A.M., Iverson, L.R., Liaw, A.: Newer classification and regression tree techniques: bagging and random forests for ecological prediction. Ecosystems 9(2), 181–199 (2006)
10. Breiman, L.: Random forests. Mach. Learn. 45(1), 5–32 (2001)
11. Cutler, A., Cutler, D.R., Stevens, J.R.: Random forests. In: Zhang, C., Ma, Y. (eds.) Ensemble Machine Learning. Springer, Boston, MA (2012). https://doi.org/https://doi.org/10.1007/978-1-4419-9326-7_5
12. Khanna, A., Goyal, R., Verma, M., Joshi, D.: Intelligent traffic management system for smart cities. In: Singh, P.K., Paprzycki, M., Bhargava, B., Chhabra, J.K., Kaushal, N.C., Kumar, Y. (eds.) FTNCT 2018. CCIS, vol. 958, pp. 152–164. Springer, Singapore (2019). https://doi.org/10.1007/978-981-13-3804-5_12
13. Kabir, M.M., Islam, M.M., Murase, K.: A new wrapper feature selection approach using neural network. Neurocomputing 73(16–18), 3273–3283 (2010)
14. Piramuthu, S.: Evaluating feature selection methods for learning in data mining applications. Eur. J. Oper. Res. 156(2), 483–494 (2004)
15. Vergara, J.R., Estévez, P.A.: A review of feature selection methods based on mutual information. Neural Comput. Appl. 24(1), 175–186 (2013). https://doi.org/10.1007/s00521-013-1368-0
16. Verma, C., Illés, Z., Stoffová, V.: Predictive modeling to predict the residency of teachers using machine learning for the real-time. In: Singh, P.K., Sood, S., Kumar, Y., Paprzycki, M., Pljonkin, A., Hong, W.-C. (eds.) FTNCT 2019. CCIS, vol. 1206, pp. 592–601. Springer, Singapore (2020). https://doi.org/10.1007/978-981-15-4451-4_47
17. Malhotra, H., Dave, M., Lamba, T.: Security analysis of cyber attacks using machine learning algorithms in eGovernance projects. In: Singh, P.K., Sood, S., Kumar, Y., Paprzycki, M., Pljonkin, A., Hong, W.-C. (eds.) FTNCT 2019. CCIS, vol. 1206, pp. 662–672. Springer, Singapore (2020). https://doi.org/10.1007/978-981-15-4451-4_52
18. García-Nieto, J., Alba, E., Jourdan, L., Talbi, E.: Sensitivity and specificity based multiobjective approach for feature selection: application to cancer diagnosis. Inf. Process. Lett. 109(16), 887–896 (2009)

19. Guyon, I., Elisseeff, A.: An introduction to variable and feature selection. J. Mach. Learn. Res. **3**(Mar), 1157–1182 (2003)
20. Singh, P., Paprzycki, M., Bhargava, B., Chhabra, J., Kaushal, N., Kumar, Y.: Futuristic trends in network and communication technologies. FTNCT 2018. Communications in Computer and Information Science **958**, 141–166 (2018)
21. Singh, P., Sood, S., Kumar, Y., Paprzycki, M., Pljonkin, A., Hong, W.C.: Futuristic trends in networks and computing technologies. FTNCT. Commun. Comput. Inf. Sci. **1206**, 3–707 (2019)

Query Reverse Engineering
in the Context of the Semantic Web:
A State-of-the-Art

Leandro Tabares-Martín[1,2]([⊠]), Nemury Silega-Martínez[1], and Marc Gyssens[2]

[1] University of Informatics Sciences, Havana, Cuba
{ltmartin,nsilega}@uci.cu
[2] Hasselt University, Hasselt, Belgium
{leandro.tabaresmartin,marc.gyssens}@uhasselt.be

Abstract. The Query Reverse Engineering problem tries to discover a query that satisfies a set of examples based on data stored in a data source. Notwithstanding this problem has been an active research field in the relational database's research community during several years, it is starting to be approached in the context of the Semantic Web. This study is the first of its kind providing a systematic review of the state-of-the-art with regard to Query Reverse Engineering in the context of the Semantic Web. Guided by a methodology for conducting systematic mapping studies, this paper provides insights about the existing approaches to the problem, as well as some of the remaining research opportunities in it.

Keywords: Query by example · Query by output · Query reverse engineering · Semantic web

1 Introduction

In its simplest form, the Query Reverse Engineering (QRE) problem can be defined as stated by Tran et al. [27]: "given a database D and a result table T, which is the output of some *known* or *unknown* query Q on D; the goal of QRE is to reverse engineer a query Q' such that the output of query Q' on database D is equal to T". While trying to fill the gap between non-specialized users and database technologies, researchers working in this problem have produced an array of related concepts and subfields which are not immediately easy to distinguish, such as *query-by-example*, *query-by-output*, and *query reverse engineering*, among others [13].

The principal aim of a systematic mapping study such as the one we are presenting here, is to provide an overview of a research field by classifying contributions pertaining to that field [24]. Such studies can help us in getting a significantly better insight in the subject at hand [8,9,11,15].

Such a systematic mapping methodology was developed originally by the "Evidence for Policy and Practice Information and Coordinating Centre" (EPPI) [22,23]. Later, the EPPI mapping methodology was modified by the "Social Care Institute for Excellence" (SCIE). This was motivated on the one hand by a shortage of empirical data necessary for answering certain questions using the

P. K. Singh et al. (Eds.): FTNCT 2020, CCIS 1395, pp. 299–308, 2021.
https://doi.org/10.1007/978-981-16-1480-4_26

systematic review methodology, and on the other hand the need to describe the literature in a broad field of interest [9]. SCIE also introduced the term "systematic mapping methodology". They worked out detailed instructions for reviewers [9]. Currently, these kinds of studies are being used in various domains of knowledge following appropriately adapted methodologies [7,10,16,25].

With regard to Query Reverse Engineering, other systematic studies have been conducted [20]. However, these studies have not been focused on Semantic Web technologies. The aim of the current work is to make a systematic study of published literature about Query Reverse Engineering in the context of the Semantic Web.

The remainder of this paper is organized as follows: Sect. 2 gives some background of related studies in the field. Section 3 explains the methodological design of this study, and Sect. 4 describes our findings. Finally, Sect. 5 summarizes the main conclusions arrived after conducting the current study, as well as promising opportunities for future work.

2   Background and Related Studies

An important precursor to the field of Query Reverse Engineering is "Query By Example" (QBE). In the mid1970s, Zloof [29] introduced this language to facilitate query writing in the relational model. It has been extensively investigated since then (see, e.g., [21], and references therein). The connection with the theme of this paper is that processing QBE has often been described as reverse engineering database queries from representative examples. There are actually two different aspects to this. The first aspect is to determine whether a query satisfying all examples provided actually exists. The second aspect is then finding such a query. These two aspects can be formalized as follows based on the work of [28]:

Suppose we are given a query family Q, a database D, and a set E of examples consisting of pairs of instances over D and corresponding outputs.

- **Problem 1 (Satisfiability).** Determine whether there exists a query in Q that satisfies E.
- **Problem 2 (Learning).** Find a query in Q that satisfies E, if such a query exists.

In the context of the Semantic Web the QRE has been approached by the studies of [5,6,12]. These studies have their roots in previous work for other data models [26].

In spite of the advantages presented by the QBE paradigm for non-specialized users of database technologies, to the best of our knowledge and as reported by [20] there have not been systematic studies approaching this paradigm from a Semantic Web perspective.

3   Method

3.1   Research Questions

In accordance with this work's goal, the following research questions have been formulated:

– *RQ1*: Which approaches have been followed to conduct studies on Query Reverse Engineering in the context of the Semantic Web (QRESW)?

- • RQ1.1: Which papers have been published?
- • RQ1.2: In which manner has the number of publications evolved over time?
- • RQ1.3: In which venues papers about QRESW have been mostly published?

– *RQ2*: How has the QRESW process been performed?

- • RQ2.1: Which algorithmic approaches have been followed?
- • RQ2.2: Which algorithms can be seen as an evolution of previously existing algorithms?
- • RQ2.3: Which are the main technologies used to perform the QRESW process?
- • RQ2.4: Which are the principal datasets employed to validate the developed algorithms?

– *RQ3*: Which are the research opportunities in the existing literature with regard to QRESW?

3.2   Search

Several methodologies for systematic mapping research [18,19,24] agree in the PICO (Population, Intervention, Comparison and Outcomes) structure as key elements that need to be specified. Specifically for the software engineering area and this research in particular, these elements can be defined as follows:

– *Population*: In software engineering experiments, "population" might refer to a specific role, a category of engineers, an area of application, or an industry group. In this study's context, it is referred to papers regarding to Query Reverse Engineering in the context of the Semantic Web.
– *Intervention*: In software engineering, "intervention" might refer to a methodology, tool, technology or procedure addressing a particular issue. In our context it refers to the algorithms, technologies and datasets used to perform the Query Reverse Engineering process.
– *Comparison*: In software engineering, "comparison" might refer to a methodology, tool, technology, or procedure which the intervention (see above) is being compared. We compare the different algorithmic approaches followed to perform the QRESW process, identifying similar aspects and studying their temporal evolution. On the other hand, we make a review of the main tools employed to codify them as computer programs.

– *Outcomes*: In our context, "outcomes" refers to the effort for a user to get a satisfactory query.

The PICO methodology allowed to identify the following keywords: "query reverse engineering", "query by output", "query-by-output", "query by example", "query-by-example", "query inference", "query learning", "SPARQL" and "RDF".

The databases have been selected according to the reports published in [14]. The SCOPUS database omits hyphens so we did not use keywords containing hyphens to search in it. Based on the identified keywords, Table 1 shows the search strings used and Table 2 contains the number of results per database after performing the search.

Table 1. Search strings used per database.

Database	Search
WoS	TS=(("query reverse engineering" OR "query by example" OR "query-by-example" OR "query by output" OR "query-by-output" OR "query inference" OR "query learning") AND ("SPARQL" or "RDF"))
SCOPUS	ALL (("query reverse engineering" OR "query by example" OR "query-by-example" OR "query by output" OR "query-by-output" OR "query inference" OR "query learning") AND ("SPARQL" OR "RDF"))
ACM	[[All: "query reverse engineering"] OR [All: "query by example"] OR [All: "query-by-example"] OR [All: "query by output"] OR [All: "query-by-output"] OR [All: "query inference"] OR [All: "query learning"]] AND [All: "sparql" or "rdf"]
ScienceDirect	(("query reverse engineering" OR "query by example" OR "query-by-example" OR "query by output" OR "query-by-output" OR "query inference" OR "query learning") AND ("SPARQL" or "RDF"))

Table 2. Number of search results per database.

Database	Search results
WoS	10
SCOPUS	354
ACM	102
ScienceDirect	200

3.3   Study Selection

Some articles were excluded on the basis of titles and abstracts, while other articles were required full-text reading and quality assessment. "Backward snowball sampling" [17] was used to identify other studies that has not been previously included. The following inclusion criteria were applied to titles and abstracts:

– Studies in the field of Semantic Web technologies.
– Studies with regard to Query Reverse Engineering.
– Studies published between 2008 (the SPARQL language becomes a recommendation of the World Wide Web Consortium) and 2019 (the current study having been carried out in 2020).

The criteria below were used to exclude studies:

– Studies must present peer-reviewed materials.
– Studies must be presented in English or Spanish.
– Studies must be accessible as full text.
– Studies should not be duplicates of previous studies.

Figure 1 shows the number of articles included in the study at each stage of the selection process.

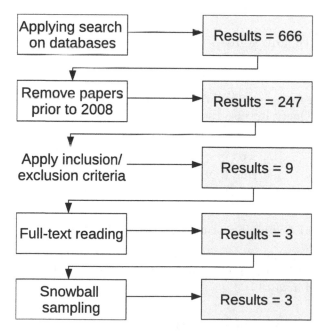

Fig. 1. Number of articles included in the study at each stage of the selection process.

Full-text reading allowed to identify further articles that should be removed as they were out of scope. We note that the remaining articles (3) were then used for "backward snowball sampling" [17]. This allowed us to conclude that there are not other known studies regarding the topic.

3.4   Data Extraction Process

Table 3 shows the developed template to conduct the data extraction from the identified primary studies.

Table 3. Data extraction template.

Item	RQ
Study ID	
Article title	RQ1.1
Authors	
Publication year	RQ1.2
Publication venue	RQ1.3
Algorithmic approach	RQ2.1
Relations among studies	RQ2.2
Technologies used to develop the algorithms	RQ2.3
Datasets used to perform the reverse engineering process	RQ2.4
Remaining gaps in the field	RQ3

4   Results of the Mapping

4.1   Papers with Regard to QRESW (RQ1.1)

During the time frame considered in this study three papers have been published with regard to Query Reverse Engineering in the context of the Semantic Web. Their titles are as follows:

- "Reverse engineering SPARQL queries" [6].
- "SPARQLByE: Querying RDF data by example" [12].
- "Interactive inference of SPARQL queries using provenance" [5].

4.2   Temporal Evolution of the QRESW (RQ1.2)

The temporal evolution of research about QRESW is shown in Fig. 2. It is worthwhile to mention that the first two publications were partial results of a doctoral thesis presented in 2018 [13].

4.3   Publication Venues (RQ1.3)

In this study, we only considered peer-reviewed venues (not only journals, but also peer-reviewed workshops and conferences). In Table 4, it is shown how the articles are distributed over these venues. Some of the main venues in the research field have been selected to publish the studies, emphasizing the high importance of this research.

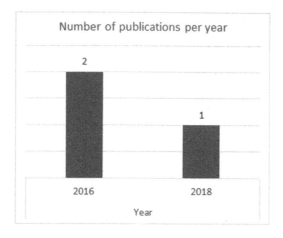

Fig. 2. Temporal evolution of the studies on QRESW.

Table 4. Publication venues.

Venue	Studies
VLDB 2016	[12]
WWW 2016	[6]
ICDE 2018	[5]

4.4   Algorithmic Approaches (RQ2.1)

All the studies on QRESW take a greedy approach to learn the queries. This kind of heuristics make at each stage a locally optimal choice with the intent of finding eventually a global optimum. While this approach allows to solve the problem in a reasonable amount of time, it does not guarantee that a global optimum is found, leaving space to new research with regard to query optimization.

4.5   Algorithmic Evolution (RQ2.2)

Notwithstanding the novelty of the application field and the adaptations made, it could be possible to backtrack some of the ideas involved in the studies of [6,12] to the procedures followed by [26] during the implementation of the FOIL system.

4.6   Technologies (RQ2.3)

While conducting this study, it was noted that the Java language, the Apache Jena framework as well as the Virtuoso Open Source triplestore were involved in the totality of the papers identified. This allows to take them into account as references for future studies.

4.7   Datasets (RQ2.4)

Four main datasets were used in the identified studies. Table 5 shows the relation between the studies and the datasets:

– DBpedia and DBpedia Query Logs are general purpose datasets containing data extracted from Wikipedia. They offer a SPARQL endpoint available for querying [2] and its query logs are available online [3].
– The SP2B dataset is a benchmark [1] for SPARQL performance. It is integrated in the DBLP scenario comprising both a data generator to create DBLP-like queries of arbitrary size, as well as a collection of benchmark queries.
– The "Berlin SPARQL Benchmark" (BSBM) [4] provides a suite of benchmarks to compare performance of such systems across different architectures.

Table 5. Datasets used to conduct the identified studies.

Dataset	Studies
DBpedia	[5]
DBpedia query logs	[6, 12]
SP2B	[5]
BSBM	[5]

4.8   Research Opportunities

This study allowed us to identify the following existing research opportunities in the field:

– Reverse engineering SPARQL queries for a larger fragment of the language (e.g. involving more than the AND, OPTIONAL and FILTER operators).
– Derive instance equivalent queries with an increased load of meaningful information in the derived triple patterns.
– Ranking of the derived patterns to increase the expressiveness of the query.
– Usage of projections to discover queries from entities that are not directly related.
– Proposal of frameworks mixing QRESW with machine learning data completion algorithms to explore both explicitly stated and learnt data.

5   Conclusions and Future Work

Notwithstanding query reverse engineering on relational databases having been an active research field for several years, it has only started recently in the context of the Semantic Web. To the best of our knowledge, only three studies within the time frame considered here have covered this topic in this context. They have been published in some of the top conferences in the fields of Databases and Web Research. These studies have approached the QRESW problem using greedy algorithmic approaches, leaving space for deeper research on query optimization. Moreover, some of the ideas behind these algorithms can be traced back to similar ones from the 1990, adapted to the new context.

In accordance with this new context, the technologies employed to implement the algorithms are Java as programming language, the Apache Jena as framework for semantic SPARQL queries as well as Virtuoso Open Source to store the RDF graphs. Besides that, the main data set used in the different studies to validate the developed algorithms is DBpedia, followed by the SP2B and BSBM data sets.

Query Reverse Engineering in the context of the Semantic Web remains as a promising research field. Among other ones, enlarging the fragments of the SPARQL language considered so far is an interesting area for further exploration.

Acknowledgments. The authors would like to acknowledge to BOF for its support to the current research through the Research Project R-10405.

References

1. http://dbis.informatik.uni-freiburg.de/index.php?project=SP2B/download.php
2. http://dbpedia.org/sparql
3. https://aksw.github.io/LSQ/
4. http://wifo5-03.informatik.uni-mannheim.de/bizer/berlinsparqlbenchmark/
5. Abramovitz, E., Deutch, D., Gilad, A.: Interactive inference of sparql queries using provenance. In: 2018 IEEE 34th International Conference on Data Engineering (ICDE), pp. 581–592. IEEE (2018)
6. Arenas, M., Diaz, G.I., Kostylev, E.V.: Reverse engineering sparql queries. In: Proceedings of the 25th International Conference on World Wide Web, pp. 239–249 (2016)
7. Barreiros, E., Almeida, A., Saraiva, J., Soares, S.: A systematic mapping study on software engineering testbeds. In: 2011 International Symposium on Empirical Software Engineering and Measurement, pp. 107–116. IEEE (2011)
8. Bates, S., Clapton, J., Coren, E.: Systematic maps to support the evidence base in social care. Evid. Policy J. Res. Debate Pract. **3**(4), 539–551 (2007)
9. Clapton, J., Rutter, D., Sharif, N.: SCIE systematic mapping guidance. SCIE, London (2009)
10. Condori-Fernandez, N., Daneva, M., Sikkel, K., Wieringa, R., Dieste, O., Pastor, O.: A systematic mapping study on empirical evaluation of software requirements specifications techniques. In: 2009 3rd International Symposium on Empirical Software Engineering and Measurement, pp. 502–505. IEEE (2009)
11. Coren, E., Fisher, M.: The conduct of systematic research reviews for SCIE knowledge reviews (2006)
12. Diaz, G., Arenas, M., Benedikt, M.: Sparqlbye: querying RDF data by example. Proc. VLDB Endowment **9**(13), 1533–1536 (2016)
13. Diaz-Caceres, G.: Increasing the usability of graph databases by learning SPARQL queries and RDF data. Ph.D. thesis, University of Oxford (2018)

14. Dyba, T., Dingsoyr, T., Hanssen, G.K.: Applying systematic reviews to diverse study types: an experience report. In: First International Symposium on Empirical Software Engineering and Measurement (ESEM 2007), pp. 225–234. IEEE (2007)

15. Grant, M.J., Booth, A.: A typology of reviews: an analysis of 14 review types and associated methodologies. Health Inf. Libr. J. **26**(2), 91–108 (2009)

16. Jalali, S., Wohlin, C.: Agile practices in global software engineering-a systematic map. In: 2010 5th IEEE International Conference on Global Software Engineering, pp. 45–54. IEEE (2010)

17. Jalali, S., Wohlin, C.: Systematic literature studies: database searches vs. backward snowballing. In: Proceedings of the 2012 ACM-IEEE International Symposium on Empirical Software Engineering and Measurement, pp. 29–38. IEEE (2012)

18. James, K.L., Randall, N.P., Haddaway, N.R.: A methodology for systematic mapping in environmental sciences. Environ. Evid. **5**(1), 7 (2016)

19. Kitchenham, B., et al.: Guidelines for performing systematic literature reviews in software engineering. version 2.3. Engineering **45**(4ve), 1051 (2007)

20. Martins, D.M.L.: Reverse engineering database queries from examples: state-of-the-art, challenges, and research opportunities. Inf. Syst. **83**, 89–100 (2019), https://doi.org/10.1016/j.is.2019.03.002

21. Mottin, D., Lissandrini, M., Velegrakis, Y., Palpanas, T.: New trends on exploratory methods for data analytics. Proc. VLDB Endow. **10**(12), 1977–1980 (2017). https://doi.org/10.14778/3137765.3137824

22. Oakley, A., Gough, D., Oliver, S., Thomas, J.: The politics of evidence and methodology: lessons from the eppi-centre. Evid. Policy J. Res. Debate Pract. **1**(1), 5–32 (2005)

23. Peersman, G.: A descriptive mapping of health promotion in young people. University of London (1996)

24. Petersen, K., Vakkalanka, S., Kuzniarz, L.: Guidelines for conducting systematic mapping studies in software engineering: an update. Inf. Softw. Technol. **64**, 1–18 (2015). http://www.sciencedirect.com/science/article/pii/S0950584915000646

25. Qadir, M.M., Usman, M.: Software engineering curriculum: a systematic mapping study. In: 2011 Malaysian Conference in Software Engineering, pp. 269–274. IEEE (2011)

26. Quinlan, J.R.: Learning logical definitions from relations. Mach. Learn. **5**(3), 239–266 (1990)

27. Tran, Q.T., Chan, C.Y., Parthasarathy, S.: Query reverse engineering. VLDB J. **23**(5), 721–746 (2014). https://doi.org/10.1007/s00778-013-0349-3

28. Weiss, Y.Y., Cohen, S.: Reverse engineering spj-queries from examples. In: Proceedings of the 36th ACM SIGMOD-SIGACT-SIGAI Symposium on Principles of Database Systems, PODS 2017, Association for Computing Machinery, New York, NY, USA, pp. 151–166 (2017). https://doi.org/10.1145/3034786.3056112

29. Zloof, M.M.: Query-by-example: the invocation and definition of tables and forms. In: Proceedings of the 1st International Conference on Very Large Data Bases. VLDB 1975, Association for Computing Machinery, New York, NY, USA, pp. 1–24 (1975). https://doi.org/10.1145/1282480.1282482

Time Series Forecasting for Coronavirus (COVID-19)

Priyal Sobti[1], Anand Nayyar[2(✉)], and Preeti Nagrath[1]

[1] Computer Science and Engineering, Bharati Vidyapeeth's College of Engineering,
New Delhi 110063, India
[2] Graduate School, Faculty of Information Technology, Duy Tan University,
Da Nang 550000, Vietnam
anandnayyar@duytan.edu.vn

Abstract. The upsurge of the novel coronavirus has spread to many countries and has been declared a pandemic by WHO. It has shaken the most powerful countries across the world like the USA, UK, and has affected economies of various countries. The coronavirus or the 2019-nCoV causes the disease that has been named COVID-19. This disease transmits by inhaling droplets that are expelled by an infected person. It has been affecting people in different ways and has been found to be threatening for the older population or people with comorbidities. It has been seen that the virus 2019-nCoV spreads faster than the two of its antecedents namely severe acute respiratory syndrome coronavirus (SARS-CoV) and Middle East respiratory syndrome coronavirus (MERS-CoV). No cure or vaccine has been discovered as of now and taking precautions like staying at home are the only possible solutions.

Our study analyzes the current trend of the disease in India and predicts future trends using time series forecasting. The official dataset provided by John Hopkins University through a GitHub repository has been used for the research for the time period of 22 January 2020 to 31 May 2020. The trend in cases, fatalities, and the people who have recovered until the date of 31 May 2020 has been discussed in the paper. It has been seen through the findings that the total number of cases is expected to rise to 2,15,000 by the end of May 2020 i.e. 31 May 2020 as per the AR (Autoregression) model. ARIMA (Autoregressive Integrated Moving Average) model predicts the number of cases to be 2,05,000 until the same date. Actual data has shown that the number of confirmed cases is 1,90,609 as on 31 May 2020 giving a percentage error of 7.57% and 12.85% for ARIMA and AR model respectively. Comparison between the findings of the two models has been shown later in the paper.

Keywords: COVID-19 · Coronavirus · SARS-CoV-2 · Lockdown · Social distancing · Time series forecasting · Time series analysis

1 Introduction

COVID-19 is an infectious disease caused by a novel virus, SARS-CoV-2 or 2019-nCoV. It has symptoms like dry cough, fever, breathing difficulties (Singhal 2020) and

© Springer Nature Singapore Pte Ltd. 2021
P. K. Singh et al. (Eds.): FTNCT 2020, CCIS 1395, pp. 309–320, 2021.
https://doi.org/10.1007/978-981-16-1480-4_27

in severe cases it has been found to be fatal for older people and people with pre-existing medical conditions. The only technique believed to slow the spread of the virus is social distancing and hence, the extended lockdown in India till 17 May 2020. It has infected over 2.2 million people worldwide as of 18 April 2020 and over 1,50,000 fatalities (W.H.O. 2020) have been reported till the same date. It is a highly contagious disease and the only way to protect ourselves is by social distancing and taking care of our personal hygiene like washing our hands for at least 20 s. The virus allows for spread to take place very quickly as it has an incubation period ranging from 7 days to 14 days and in some cases, it has even reached 24 days. The first case of the disease had been reported in India on 30 January 2020. Since then, the number of infections has been on the rise and has recently begun to slow down in some states. The worst affected states remain Maharashtra, Delhi, and Tamil Nadu.

Across the world, the worst affected countries are namely Italy, France, Spain, Britain, the United States of America with New York as the epicenter for the outbreak. The disease has taken a toll on the health care systems of the countries and it goes to show that no country was prepared for the pandemic. The massive fatalities tolls in developed countries are indicative of the overburdened healthcare systems and the fact that the services are not able to reach the people who need them the most.

In our study, we aim to analyze the trend and make predictions for the number of cases, fatalities and recoveries in India using time series forecasting. Time series is a collection of information that is accumulated sequentially over time (Chatfield 2000). Time series forecasting makes predictions using data made up of time series. Time series forecasting makes forecasts using past and present values. Time series forecasting is regularly used in the field of sales forecasting (Ansuj et al. 1996), inventory control, capacity planning, budgeting, financial markets (Tay and Cao 2001) and much more (Chatfield 2000). Time series model provides predictions for the future and this gives us an opportunity to compare the results with the actual observed values. Models namely ARIMA (Benvenuto et al. 2020) (Dehesh et al. 2020) and AR have been used to carry out time series forecasting and make predictions for the number of cases till the end of May 2020. ARIMA techniques have been regularly used due to their accuracy for forecasting as well as time series analysis (Contreras et al. 2014). ARIMA model is a class of models that are used to study the past values of a time series and predict future values. Also, ARIMA is a combination of two processes i.e. an Auto Regressive (AR) process and a Moving Average process and models based on these processes are also available. One of the models namely AR model has also been used in this study.

The objectives of the paper are:

- To use time-series analysis to analyze the trend using the data provided by John Hopkins University (John Hopkins University Dataset 2020 (accessed on May 12, 2020)).
- To use time-series forecasting to predict the trends in cases, fatalities and recoveries using different time series forecasting models like ARIMA.
- To compare the trends and the predictions made by two time series forecasting models namely ARIMA and AR.
- To analyze the results obtained from the two models to understand the situation and draw conclusions from it.

The paper consists of 5 sections. Section 2 highlights the literature review conducted in the domain of research. Section 3 focuses on the methodology used to solve the problem at hand. Section 4 highlights and showcases the results obtained and the analysis of the results. Section 5 contains the conclusion for the paper.

2 Literature Review

The researchers and academicians across the world are carrying out extensive research in this field and some of them are as follows. Arti et al. (2020) have suggested a tree-based model in which some people are quarantined and some are left undetected due to lack of symptoms, hiding travel history, etc. They have shown the effect of lockdown by considering different scenarios and the number of days.

Gupta et al. (2020) have performed exploratory data analysis and have used time-series forecasting to predict future trends. According to one such model used; they have shown that 3 million people may get infected if proper measures are not taken. They had conducted their study when the number of cases in India was 536 and were expected to rise to 7000 as per the ARIMA time series forecasting method.

Baud et al. (2020) have re-estimated the mortality rates. They have obtained the mortality rates by dividing the number of deaths on a given day by the number of patients that have contracted the disease 14 days prior. Their findings have suggested a mortality rate of 5.6% in China and 15.2% outside China.

Deb et al. (2020) went onto show the effect of partial and total lockdown by proposing a time series model.

Petropoulos et al. (2020) showed using forecasting that the number of cases is expected to rise. They have shown the trajectories for the reported cases as well as the recovered cases and have analyzed the same for different time periods since the outbreak.

Healthcare impact due to COVID-19 has been shown by Chatterjee et al. (2020) wherein they have developed a compartmental SEIR model. Aspects like patient hospitalization, the requirement of Intensive Care Units (ICUs) had been modelled using SimVoi software. They have concluded by suggesting that the Indian healthcare might be overwhelmed by the end of May.

Pandey et al. (2004) used two models namely SEIR and Regression models to predict the trend and the changes in trend in the COVID-19 spread. They found that the number of cases till 30 March 2020 will be less than 0.5 per million in India.

Age-related impact of social distancing on the COVID-19 pandemic in India has been discussed by Singh et al. (2020). They went onto suggest a mathematical model of the disease transmission that takes into account both the age and the social contact structure. They have emphasized the fact that while keeping a check on the total number of cases, it is also required to take into account the age group affected. The paper also showed that how the three-week lockdown in India starting from 25 March 2020 is insufficient and also suggested some ways to contain the spread of the virus including extending the lockdown with periodic relaxations.

Roy et al. (2020) have conducted a study to understand the notions and the thoughts of Indian population when it comes to coronavirus. The study shows that people are appropriately aware of preventive measures. However, people have apprehensions regarding their mental health during this time and are predominantly worried about catching the infection.

Drug repurposing is used regularly nowadays where drugs that are originally developed for some other diseases are used to treat other diseases. Muralidharan et al. (2020) have tried to understand the mechanism of the proposed drugs namely lopinavir, oseltamivir and ritonavir which are being used to reduce the virulence in the infected patients.

Sahoo et al. (2020) have also highlighted the mental distress that is being caused by various factors like fear of infection, economic loss, unemployment, lack of social interaction and much more. They have presented two such case studies which had been reported to their medical services.

Tanne et al. (2020) have discussed how doctors and healthcare systems are dealing with the pandemic. They have discussed the impact in various countries like India, the U.S.A, Spain, Japan, South Korea and many more in terms of the number of cases and the subsequent response of the country to tackle the pandemic.

LSTM techniques have been proposed by Tomar et al. (2020) and estimation for the next 30 days for the number of positive cases in India has been provided. Also, the effect of measures like lockdown and social distancing has been discussed.

The use of epidemiological models has been shown by Rajesh Ranjan (2020) for the prediction for COVID-19 outbreak. Susceptible-infected recovered (SIR) and exponential models were used to make predictions using the known data and it has been seen that India will enter equilibrium by the end of May provided there is no community transmission.

Vellingiri et al. (2020) have discussed the symptoms for COVID-19 and how the symptoms are different from SARS, MERS and common flu. Also, drugs available, treatment methodology and ongoing vaccine trials have also been discussed. Some traditional Indian medicinal plants that can provide some therapeutic relief have also been discussed.

Time series analysis and forecasting have been used as the main technique for predicting confirmed cases for COVID-19. Time Series forecasting as defined by Chatfield et al. (2000) is predicting values on the basis of data constituting time series. Gooijer et al. (2006) have assessed the past 25 years of research that have gone into time series forecasting and have reviewed some influential work in this area.

3   Methodology

Time series analysis is the technique to analyze the time-series data to find characteristics and statistics from the data (Chatfield 2000). On the other hand, time series forecasting (Chatfield 2000) is the technique to predict future values from the existing data values.

The first step followed for time series forecasting included data pre-processing. The data has been taken from the official GitHub repository provided by John Hopkins University which is daily updated with the latest numbers. Since the study is focused on cases in India, the relevant row was chosen and the data frame obtained after that was transposed as the dates had to be taken as a column. The data is then converted into a Time Series object with the dates as the index. We can also visualize the time series data using time series decomposition that allows decomposition into three distinct components namely trend, seasonality, and noise.

The model used for time series forecasting includes Autoregression (AR) and Autoregressive Integrated Moving Average (ARIMA). ARIMA is the most commonly used model for time series forecasting and includes parameter selection that shall yield the best possible outcome. After choosing the optimal combination of parameters the model is fit and the corresponding plots are obtained. After analyzing the given trend and preparing the model, appropriate functions like predict() were used to predict the future behavior of the cases, fatalities, and recoveries from 13 May 2020 to 31 May 2020.

Figure 1 represents the steps that are followed in the methodology.

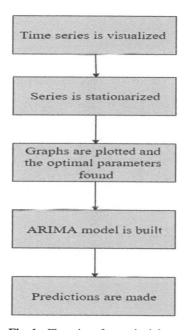

Fig. 1. Flowchart for methodology

4   Experimental Analysis

4.1   Dataset

The dataset provided by John Hopkins University (John Hopkins University Dataset 2020 (accessed on May 12, 2020)) in the form of a GitHub repository has been used. The repository is regularly updated with the latest numbers. The dataset contains the number of confirmed cases, fatalities as well as the number of recoveries for countries globally. This study makes use of numbers for India and the trend in confirmed cases, fatalities and recoveries is visualized.

4.2 Plot Analysis

The time-series data created was first plotted to see the general trend for the number of cases, recoveries, and fatalities. Figure 2 shows the current trend of cases in India. Similar plots can be seen for the number of deaths and recoveries in India through Figs. 3 and 4 respectively.

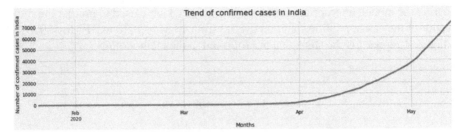

Fig. 2. The trend of confirmed cases in India

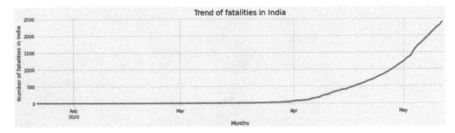

Fig. 3. The trend of the number of fatalities in India

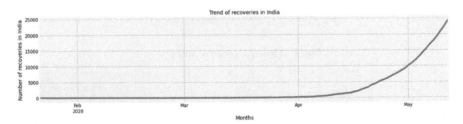

Fig. 4. The trend of the number of recoveries in India

Time series data can be decomposed into three components namely trend, seasonality, and residual with the help of a built-in library function. Any time series can be broken into systematic or non-systematic components where systematic components are the ones that have some form of recurrence while non-systematic components are otherwise. Level, trend, and seasonality are systematic components while noise is a non-systematic component. These components can be either added together called the additive model or they can be multiplied together called the multiplicative model.

Seasonal decompose () is an inbuilt function that allows for automatic time series decomposition by plotting the original data, trend, seasonality, and residual components which is nothing but the time series after the trend and the seasonal component is removed.

Figure 5 shows the decomposition for the time series depicting the number of cases in India. The seasonal component shows the short-term cycle that repeats itself in terms of the number of cases. The residual component shows how the cases had been very less during the initial days of the month but around the end of March and the beginning of April, there had been a spike in the number of cases.

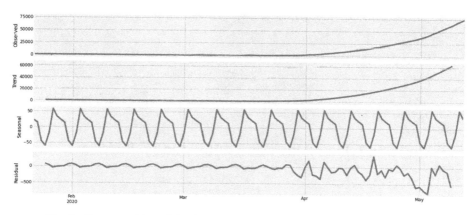

Fig. 5. Decomposition of the time series depicting the number of cases in India

4.3   Results and Discussion

Using the Autoregression (AR) model the future trend has been predicted from 13 May 2020 to 31 May 2020. The plot still shows an upward trend in the number of cases as well as the number of recoveries and fatalities. All these predictions have been made in the mathematical sense and social elements like the fear of the disease, people adhering to lockdown rules have not been taken into consideration. Figure 6 shows the prediction for the number of cases that are still expected to rise. The prediction shows that the number of cases will be as high as 2,15,000 by the end of May 2020 considering the current trend in the number of cases. Figure 7 and Fig. 8 shows the forecast for the number of fatalities and recoveries as per the AR model.

Similarly, the ARIMA model has also been used to do similar predictions as it is considered to be one of the most commonly used models for time series forecasting. Figure 9 shows the plot for the number of confirmed cases as per the ARIMA model. Also, Fig. 10 and Fig. 11 shows the trend for the number of fatalities and the number of recoveries as per the ARIMA model for COVID-19. All the figures that have been obtained for the two models show an exponential increase in the number of confirmed cases as well as the number of recoveries and fatalities for the increasing x-axis which is time.

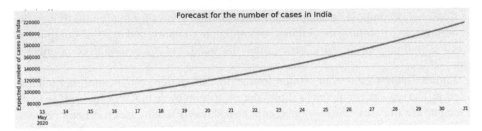

Fig. 6. Forecast for confirmed cases as per the AR model

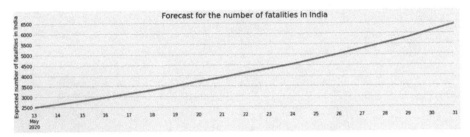

Fig. 7. Forecast for number of fatalities as per the AR model

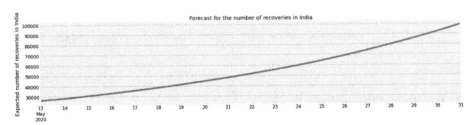

Fig. 8. Forecast for number of recoveries as per the AR model

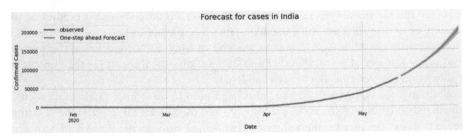

Fig. 9. Forecast for confirmed cases as per the ARIMA model

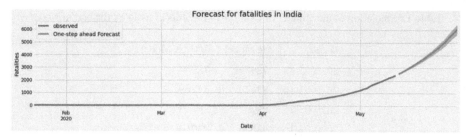

Fig. 10. Forecast for number of fatalities as per the ARIMA model

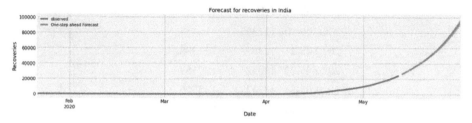

Fig. 11. Forecast for number of recoveries as per the ARIMA model

ARIMA model is a combination of two processes namely an Auto Regressive (AR) process and a Moving Average process and models based on these processes are also available. Equation 1 represents the equation for predicting values using the AR model:

$$Y = \beta_0 + \beta_1 * l_1 + \beta_2 * l_2 + .. + \beta_n * l_n \tag{1}$$

where Y represents the observed value, $\beta_1, \beta_2 \ldots$ are regression betas and $l_1, l_2, \ldots$ represent the lag values. A similar equation can be given for the MA model. Equation 2 represents the equation for predicting values using the MA model:

$$Y = \beta_0 + \beta_1 * e\_l_1 + \beta_2 * e\_l_2 + . . + \beta_n * e\_l_n \tag{2}$$

where e_l_1, e_l_2 and so on represent random residual deviations between the MA model and target variable.

ARIMA (p, d, q) is a non-seasonal ARIMA model where p is number of autoregressive terms, q is the number of forecast errors in the prediction equation and d is the number of nonseasonal differences. Equation 3 represents the general forecasting equation used by the ARIMA model to predict future values.

$$y_t = \mu + \alpha_1 y_{t-1} + \ldots + \alpha_p y_{t-p} - \theta_1 e_{t-1} - \ldots - \theta_q e_{t-q} \tag{3}$$

where y_t represents the data on which ARIMA has to be applied, $\alpha_1, \alpha_2 \ldots$ are AR coefficients and θ_1, θ_2 and so on are MA coefficients.

Table 1 summarizes and compares the predictions that have been made by the two models from 13 May 2020 to 31 May 2020. It can be seen that there is a rise in the total number of cases and both the models go to show that the total number of cases will more than 2,00,000 by the end of May.

Table 1. Prediction of the number of COVID-19 patients in India by the end of May.

Date	AR Model	ARIMA Model
2020-05-13	78989	78944
2020-05-14	83470	83269
2020-05-15	88202	88193
2020-05-16	93646	93704
2020-05-17	99064	99034
2020-05-18	104479	104698
2020-05-19	110845	110525
2020-05-20	117303	116414
2020-05-21	123672	122308
2020-05-22	130924	129153
2020-05-23	138428	135706
2020-05-24	146061	142415
2020-05-25	154542	150172
2020-05-26	163414	157964
2020-05-27	172424	166435
2020-05-28	182315	175950
2020-05-29	192787	185117
2020-05-30	203471	194975
2020-05-31	215028	205039

5   Conclusion and Future Scope

In this study, two time series forecasting models namely AR and ARIMA models were used to analyze and predict the number of confirmed cases for COVID-19 in India. The data provided by John Hopkins University included the data for the COVID-19 pandemic worldwide. Therefore, proper techniques had been applied to extract the data for India and carry out time series fore-casting till the end of May 2020. The data has been analyzed and it has been found out that the number of cases is expected to rise till the end of May 2020. Both the ARIMA and AR model point towards an increasing number of cases as well as an increasing number of fatalities and recoveries. Table 1 shows that the number of confirmed cases in India will cross 2,00,000 by the end of May 2020. The results from this study have been concluded using the data until the 12 May 2020. Actual data has shown that the number of confirmed cases in India are 1,90, 609 as on 31 May 2020 giving a percentage error of 7.57% for the ARIMA model and 12.8% for the AR model. The trend shows an exponential upsurge in the number of cases and this can aggravate due to negligence of individuals or community spread. Furnishing the hospital with proper medical equipment can help tackle the pandemic efficiently.

In the future, other time series forecasting models can be used to accurately predict the trend by taking into consideration other factors like adherence to lockdown rules, people following the required precautions etc. as the results obtained can help medical authorities better prepare for the situation.

References

Ansuj, A.P., Camargo, M., Radharamanan, R., Petry, D.: Sales forecasting using time series and neural networks. Comput. Ind. Eng. **31**(1–2), 421–424 (1996)

Arti, M., Bhatnagar, K.: Modeling and predictions for covid 19 spread in India. ResearchGate (2020)

Baud, D., Qi, X., Nielsen-Saines, K., Musso, D., Pomar, L., Favre, G.: Real estimates of mortality following COVID-19 infection. The Lancet Infectious Diseases (2020)

Benvenuto, D., Giovanetti, M., Vassallo, L., Angeletti, S., Ciccozzi, M.: Application of the arima model on the Covid-2019 epidemic dataset. Data Brief, 105340 (2020)

Chatfield, C.: Time-Series Forecasting. CRC Press, Boca Raton (2000)

Chatterjee, K., Chatterjee, K., Kumar, A., Shankar, S.: Healthcare impact of Covid-19 epidemic in India: a stochastic mathematical model. Med. J. Armed Forces India (2020)

Contreras, J., Espinola, R., Nogales, F.J., Conejo, A.J.: Arima models to predict next-day electricity prices. IEEE Trans. Power Syst. **18**(3), 1014–1020 (2003)

Deb, S., Majumdar, M.: A time series method to analyze incidence pattern and estimate reproduction number of covid-19. arXiv preprint arXiv:2003.10655 (2020)

De Gooijer, J.G., Hyndman, R.J.: 25 years of time series forecasting. Int. J. Forecast. **22**(3), 443–473 (2006)

Dehesh, T., Mardani-Fard, H., Dehesh, P.: Forecasting of covid-19 confirmed cases in different countries with arima models. medRxiv (2020)

Gupta, R., Pal, S.K.: Trend analysis and forecasting of covid19 outbreak in India. medRxiv (2020)

John Hopkins university dataset. (2020). https://github.com/CSSEGISandData/COVID-19. Accessed 12 May 2020

Muralidharan, N., Sakthivel, R., Velmurugan, D., Gromiha, M.M.: Computational studies of drug repurposing and synergism of lopinavir, oseltamivir and ritonavir binding with sars-cov-2 protease against covid-19. J. Biomolecular Struct. Dyn. **56** 1–6 (2020)

Pandey, G., Chaudhary, P., Gupta, R., Pal, S.: Seir and regression model based covid-19 outbreak predictions in India. arXiv preprint arXiv:2004.00958 (2020)

Petropoulos, F., Makridakis, S.: Forecasting the novel coronavirus covid-19. PLoS ONE **15**(3), (2020)

Ranjan, R.: Predictions for covid-19 outbreak in India using epidemiological models. medRxiv (2020)

Roy, D., Tripathy, S., Kar, S.K., Sharma, N., Verma, S.K., Kaushal, V.: Study of knowledge, attitude, anxiety & perceived mental healthcare need in Indian population during covid-19 pandemic. Asian J. Psychiatry, 102083 (2020)

Sahoo, S., et al.: Self-harm and covid-19 pandemic: an emerging concern–a report of 2 cases from India. Asian J. Psychiatry (2020)

Singh, R., Adhikari, R.: Age-structured impact of social distancing on the covid-19 epidemic in India. arXiv preprint arXiv:2003.12055 (2020)

Singhal, T.: A review of coronavirus disease-2019 (covid-19). The Indian J. Pediatrics, 1–6 (2020)

Tanne, J.H., Hayasaki, E., Zastrow, M., Pulla, P., Smith, P., Rada, A.G.: Covid-19: how doctors and healthcare systems are tackling coronavirus worldwide. BMJ, 368 (2020)

Tay, F.E., Cao, L.: Application of support vector machines in financial time series forecasting. Omega, **29**(4), 309–317 (2001)

Tomar, A., Gupta, N.: Prediction for the spread of covid-19 in India and effectiveness of preventive measures. Sci. Total Environ. 138762 (2020)

Vellingiri, B., et al.: Covid-19: a promising cure for the global panic. Sci. Total Environ. 138277 (2020)

W.H.O.: Coronavirus disease 2019 (Covid19): situation report (2020)

Leveraging Artificial Intelligence Tools to Combat the COVID-19 Crisis

Loveleen Gaur, Gurinder Singh, and Vernika Agarwal[✉]

Amity International Business School, Amity University, Noida, Uttar Pradesh, India
{lgaur,gsingh,vagarwal1}@amity.edu

Abstract. The severity of the coronavirus disease (COVID-19) has shaken the world forcefully and sent economies into difficult times. As stated by the World Health Organization on 11 March 2020, the impact of the current unprecedented situation will cause the major cost of lives and financial damage across the globe. The various stakeholders, including scientists, doctors, economists, politicians, are seeking the help of data scientist to explore disruptive technologies which can aid in reducing the pandemic's effects. In these unprecedented times, Artificial Intelligence (AI) has emerged as a promising tool which can play a huge role in various domains. There are several fields where disruptive technologies like AI is utilised to the fight against COVID-19 such as generating real-time warnings and alerts, tracing prediction, interactive dashboards, diagnosing risks, suggesting treatments and cures, facilitating "contactless" deliveries, and social control. The focus of the present study is to analyze the contribution of AI to track and fight against COVID-19.

Keywords: COVID-19 · Pandemic · Artificial intelligence · WHO · Disruptive technologies

1 Introduction

The emergence of global pandemic COVID-19 is attracting the attention of various stakeholders since the start of 2020. A serious issue of the rising number of cases and limited healthcare facilities hit most nations and had a profound impact on the way we see our world and our lives everyday [1]. The alarming rate of infection and pattern of spread threatens the global ecosystem, despite the safety measures put in place to contain the spread of the virus, the containment of the virus is at a nascent stage. Social distancing or refraining from doing what is inherently human, which is to find solace in the company of others, the nations worldwide are unsuccessful in curbing the COVID pandemic. Within this context of global threat, community distancing, as well as the crashing of healthcare services, the role of the Artificial Intelligence (AI) in our healthcare system is to identify and prevent the spread of COVID-19 effectively, is the motivation behind the present study.

The contribution of new data science technologies, specifically AI, can thus, aid in finding the best possible solution to combating this outbreak [2]. The major questions

© Springer Nature Singapore Pte Ltd. 2021
P. K. Singh et al. (Eds.): FTNCT 2020, CCIS 1395, pp. 321–328, 2021.
https://doi.org/10.1007/978-981-16-1480-4_28

for the data scientist across the globe are "How can AI predict the spread of the infection?", "How can we use AI help in medical diagnoses?", "How an AI aid in vaccine development?" and "How can we aid AI methods for community control?"

Despite misleading claims made by the mainstream media, much of what we call AI does not involve any sort of "intelligence", understanding or consciousness per se rather, successful applications of automation (mostly based on software) are conflated with AI. Indeed, we have different interpretations and definitions of AI across the globe, and depending on the industry problems, we are using it to solve. We can simplify its explanations to be the capability and capacity of a computer, or other devices, to do tasks that generally require human intelligence to generate the desired outcomes [3]. Various AI tools can prove to be extremely helpful in tackling the COVID-19 epidemic, triggered by the SARS-Cov-2 virus, ranging from detecting historical disease patterns to predicting the outbreak of the pandemic in the next likely region [4]. AI can be employed for the detection, diagnosing and preventing the spread of the COVID-19.

The World Health Organization (WHO) has immediately advised countries to implement all possible preventive measures to ensure the wellbeing of human lives everywhere. As of the latest COVID-19 outbreak situation (11 June 2020), 7,461,864 cases have been reported as Coronavirus positive, with 419,090 reported deaths across 213 countries worldwide (WHO 2020). The COVID-19 outbreak has not only destroyed civilisation on a mass scale but has severely damaged the global economy and the business community.

The World Economic Forum & WHO has created a platform, the COVID Action Platform, to convene the business community for protecting livelihoods, facilitating work, walk-of-life and mobilising support for COVID-19 responses across various national boundaries. COVID-19 stands as being quite like the SARS outbreak in 2003 with one advantage or potential lay in technological advancements such as Artificial Intelligence that enabled the authorities to control the situation within reasonable limits [5].

A Canadian company, Blue Dot attempted to make predictions regarding the next outbreak for COVID-19 and was reported to be the first organisation to reveal this in late December. Blue Dot is a perfect example of AI being used in producing early warnings and alerts. Many additional applications of Artificial Intelligence have eventually arisen with the outbreak of the pandemic; BenevolentAI and Imperial College London stated that a drug appropriate for treating rheumatoid arthritis, Barictinib, might be operative in preventing the Coronavirus destroying thousands of lives. Insilico Medicine in Hong Kong has also worked on an AI algorithm that has designed six new-found molecules that can prevent viral replications between two bodies [6]. The COVID-19 outbreak has become a significant threat to human life as well as for the global economy, requiring immediate measures to combat crisis scenarios.

The Communicable Diseases Cluster of WHO discussed factors like transmissibility, history of similar infections, gestation timeframe resulting in an increased mortality rate, the nature of the organism and preventive measures against the disease directly affects the public health response to an epidemic and its spread [7].

Moreover, another big issue for the decision-makers and researchers is to deal with is the growing rate of the date, known as big data. The crucial point is handling real-time data emerging out every day in the process of fighting against this virus. AI is a crucial point in this context since the applications of AI towards solving the complex issues in several fields, including engineering, medicine, economy, and psychology has been widely recognised. The use of big data analysis can result in identifying the pattern of viral activity in any country [8]. The study by [9] discusses the benefits that the health care policymakers can get by using AI for early detection and preparation of the nation against the outbreak of COVID-19 to make better decisions. Overall, it can be understood that AI is very useful in medical imaging and image processing to accurately diagnose COVID-19 [10]. Using AI techniques to deal with COVID-19 related issues can fill the void between AI-based methods and medical approaches and treatments. AI specialists' use of AI platforms can help in making connections between various parameters and speed up the processes to obtain optimum results.

2   How Is AI Contributing to Combating COVID-19?

With the focus to foreground the effect of AI applications, we have analysed the most recent AI-related research papers and articles as well as the latest updates on COVID-19.

Amid the entire Crisis during the outbreak of the COVID-19 pandemic, Peter Hotez, Baylor College of Medicine, USA elaborated on how disruptive technologies can be helping in many ways — from predicting the outbreak of the phenomenon to generating real-time warnings and alerts, interactive dashboards, diagnosing risks, suggesting treatments, social control that prevents the destruction of bigger segments of the framework. The study by [11] discusses the use of AI-based approach for screening of compounds which can be used as a potential adjuvant for the COVID-19 vaccine. It can significantly reduce the time that is needed for the development of the vaccine. Also, AI methods can help in the screening of available drugs which will enhance the process of vaccine development. The various algorithms of AI can be trained for identifying the existing drugs that potentially demonstrate efficacy in the treatment of COVID-19 [12].

Whether Artificial intelligence (AI) is something that surpasses human intelligence or not is still a question, but it certainly lends humans a helping hand when they need it the most. The study by [13], found that the significant forefront in which Big data, artificial intelligence and blockchain technology can concretely help is by understanding the fast-changing situation and help drive an effective disaster response. Further, the study by [14], analyses that these new technologies can provide near real-time information about emerging trends and provide early warning into how the virus spreads. It can aid the various government and non-government organisation to monitor the spread of COVID-19 effectively. Governments and private corporations are developing apps that allow users to share their whereabouts and social contacts voluntarily. Hence, many organisations are adopting a multidimensional approach to identify the best solutions or AI tools for combating the COVID-19 outbreak all around the world. As discussed, AI can be used in tracking and making predictions based on past information. This tracing of disease patterns and generating forecasts has eventually resulted in the surfacing of data dashboards that visualise the pandemic. The top panels include those of UpCode, the New York Times, and HealthMap. Microsoft Bing's AI tracker is another dashboard that provides a global overview of the COIVD-19 outbreak. Even Tableau has created a COVID-19 Data Hub, to facilitate the data visualisation of the pandemic.

Moreover, we AI can be used for identification of nearby COVID-19 patients by using real-time location data sourced through mobile communication infrastructure and location services as discussed by [15], in their recent study. Taking these into considerations, several mobile applications have been developed by the government's world over. These applications alert users when they are in close contact with an infected person. The government of the People's Republic of China (PRC) have launched 'close Contact' App 2020 [16]. Furthermore, apps with maps to track the disease also became popular very quickly in Hong Kong, South Korea, India (Arogya Setu App), to name a few countries. In most of these applications, the system residents based on location data analysis.

The paper by [8], discusses the various advantages of using AI-based platforms is to accelerate the process of diagnosis and treatment of the COVID-19 disease.

The various AI tools can also aid in public communication and information providing during these unprecedented times. The research by [17], have carried out the study for the use of AI-enabled chat boxes to provide answers for breast cancer patients. Similar chat boxes can be made for patients who are suffering from COVID-19 or are home quarantined to ease the load on healthcare.

In this health crisis of COVID-19 pandemic, Artificial intelligence has the technology and the necessary speed to check which drugs work for the virus using the internal stimulation of High-tech computers. But this use of AI also highlights the problems that AI faces, it analyses a massive chunk of data and then identifies some underlying existing repeating patterns and makes a decisive action by identifying the past data and then projecting how the future pattern will follow. The algorithm simply fails to analyse or draw a parallel between present and previous conditions. AI works on the assumption that the environment is static and not dynamic, thus sometimes making severe errors in judgment. Humans are lying on the same plan where the algorithm of AI fails, human intelligence requires past data to analyses and judge the present situation, on how to tackle it, and how to minimise the damage.

Human intervention has significance in the entire process because humans have the capabilities of learning from one situation and applying it to innumerable scenarios based on the necessity of the problem. In contrast, AI systems learn from scratch, and any changes in the scene result in reanalysing the pattern. This initial benchmarking for demonstrating the potential of machine learning in COVID-19 is given by the study by [18]. They proposed a hybrid machine learning approach to predict the COVID-19, using data from Hungary.

Neural networks can study and capturing various intricate patterns in the data. Neural Network-Based Models have been successful in multiple domains, like voice recognition and Natural Language Processing (NLP). Recently, the study by [19] has developed COVID-19 detection neural network (COVNet) to help researchers and epidemiologists to understand and create an AI tool for testing the population for COVID-19. COVID-Net is an open access Neural net that works particularly well for image recognition. COVID-Net used training data of chest x-rays using 5,941 images taken from 2,839 of the patients with different lung infections from bacterial to COVID-19 to draw potential conclusions regarding the outbreak of a global pandemic.

Further, [20] suggested in their study, that a deep learning model can accurately detect COVID-19 and differentiate it from community-acquired pneumonia and other lung diseases. The survey by [21], focused on the performance of convolutional neural network architectures for medical image classification. It was concluded that the use of Deep Learning techniques with X-ray imaging might extract significant biomarkers related to the Covid-19 disease. A summary of the various AI tools used in the literature is given in Table 1.

Table 1. Summary of AI tools

S.No	Author	Application area	Methodology
1	[6]	Design six new-found molecules to prevent viral replications between two bodies	AI Algorithm
2	[8]	Identifying the pattern of viral activity in any country	Big Data
3	[9]	Early detection of COVID-19	AI Algorithm
4	[10]	Medical imaging and image processing to accurately diagnose COVID-19	AI Algorithm
5	[11]	Screening of compounds for vaccine development	AI-based approach
6	[12]	Identifying the existing drug for the treatment of COVID-19	AI Algorithm
7	[13]	Disaster response	Big data, artificial intelligence and blockchain technology
8	[14]	Real-time information about emerging trends and provide early warning into how the virus spreads	AI Algorithm
9	[15]	Identification of nearby COVID-19 patients by using real-time location data sourced through mobile communication	AI Algorithm
10	[17]	AI-enabled chat boxes to provide answers for patients	AI Algorithm
11	[18]	Reanalysing the pattern of COVID spread with real time data	Machine learning
12	[19]	COVID-19 detection neural network (COVNet)	AI tool
13	[20]	Detection of COVID-19 and differentiate it from community-acquired pneumonia and other lung diseases	Deep learning model
14	[21]	Medical image classification	Convolutional neural network architectures

From the above discussion and various available researches, it can be said that AI can be employed to help detect, diagnose and prevent the spread of the virus. Various AI tools can help in identifying patterns and anomalies predict the range of COVID-19. It can reduce the time for medical diagnosis. AI is used for understand the epidemiological patterns by surveillance (e.g. WHO Early Warning System, Bluedot). Institutions such as Johns Hopkins University and the OECD (oecd.ai) have made dashboards, which are highly interactive which can track the virus' spread through real-time data.

2.1 Challenges Faced During the Implementation of AI

The book by [22], explains, the importance of such disruptive technologies is seen in such critical times when these help in reducing the burden on the workforce and resources. Human involvement and innovation have a vital role in leveraging what various disruptive technologies can make it possible. One methodology can be implemented by gathering an enormous amount of new data from the current circumstances for human-decisions as well as for AI systems. While, on the other hand, human knowledge and creativity can be used to undertake abstractions that Artificial Intelligence (AI) fails to cover. The primary failure occurs when the testing environment changes even slightly, resulting in re-learning from scratch. From Data scientists to coding AI systems to domain experts for understanding the problem statement, combating pandemics like COVID-19 demands unconventional thinking to see and analyse beyond the boundaries of structured problems to generate unique solutions.

Apart from various AI applications and tools that are being used to combat the COVID-19 outbreak all around the globe, researchers and epidemiologists are continually facing the major obstacle of the inadequacy of the data to understand the patterns and diagnose the COVID-19 pandemic spreading rapidly among more than 200 countries [23]. In addition to the inadequacy of data, another primary concern for the use of AI and other data analysis tools is the use of location data and other (potentially) personally or demographically identifiable data on such scale results in the production of a 'data exhaust' that invariably has consequences. [24], states that protection of data is an essential component and several considerations should be considered to guarantee the lawful processing of personal data.

Designing the high degree of AI in systems or tools that are required for the current outbreak of the COVID-19 pandemic requires in-depth knowledge of computer science as well as medicines and, thus, it becomes difficult to find people who can be trained efficiently for both, especially in the short term.

3 Conclusion

The COVID-19 global pandemic has severely damaged the entire framework of society. Every industry from healthcare to information technology and organizations such as WHO are continually working on tracking the spread of the disease and producing the tools to combat the current crisis scenarios. Data science, however, can be used as a medium to bridge the gap between the present and future of this global imbalance with joint human efforts [25, 26]. AI is the key to the future due to its distinct features and applications ranging from generating real-time warnings and alerts to predicting the outbreak, and in the implementation of effective social control measures to overcome the COVID-19 global pandemic. Human intelligence is more influential in its ability to understand and analyse possible outcomes through abstract thought, and Artificial Intelligence is strong in identifying repetitive patterns by analysing big data. And together they can erect two pillars on which the monument of hope can be established and which in turn presents itself as a symbol of success over the COVID-19 pandemic. These AI technologies could provide a lot of innovative ideas and solution for fighting local and global medical emergencies.

References

1. Settanni, E.: Those who do not move, do not notice their (supply) chains—inconvenient lessons from disruptions related to COVID-19. AI & Society 1 (2020)
2. Kraus, J.L.: Can artificial intelligency revolutionise drug discovery? AI & Society, 1–4 (2019)
3. Forbes 2018, The Key Definitions of Artificial Intelligence (AI) That Explains Its Importance (2018). https://www.forbes.com/sites/bernardmarr/2018/02/14/the-key-definitions-of-artificial-intelligence-ai-that-explain-its-importance/#732eae4f4f5d. Accessed 14 Apr 2020
4. Lai, C.C., Shih, T.P., Ko, W.C., Tang, H.J., Hsueh, P.R.: Severe acute respiratory syndrome coronavirus 2 (SARS-CoV-2) and corona virus disease-2019 (COVID-19): the epidemic and the challenges. Int. J. Antimicrobial Agents, 105924 (2020)
5. Sohrabi, C., et al.: World Health Organization declares global emergency: a review of the 2019 novel coronavirus (COVID-19). Int. J. Surgery (2020)
6. Digimonica 10 March 2020, How Canadian AI start-up BlueDot spotted Coronavirus before anyone else had a clue. https://diginomica.com/how-canadian-ai-start-bluedot-spotted-coronavirus-anyone-else-had-clue. Accessed 12 Apr 2020
7. The Lancet 1 April 2020, COVID-19 and artificial intelligence: protecting healthcare workers and curbing the simple. https://www.thelancet.com/journals/landig/article/PIIS2589-7500(20)300546/fulltext. Accessed 12 Apr 2020
8. Jamshidi, M.B., Lalbakhsh, A., Talla, J., Mohyuddin, W.: Artificial intelligence and COVID-19: deep learning approaches for diagnosis and treatment. In: IEEE Access (2020). https://doi.org/10.1109/access.2020.3001973
9. Ting, D.S.W., Carin, L., Dzau, V., Wong, T.Y.: Digital technology and COVID-19. Nat. Med. 1–3 (2020)
10. Naudé, W.: Artificial Intelligence against COVID-19: an early review (2020)
11. Ahuja, A.S., Reddy, V.P., Marques, O.: Artificial Intelligence and COVID-19: A Multidisciplinary Approach (2020)
12. Smith, M., Smith, J.C.: Repurposing therapeutics for COVID-19: supercomputer-based docking to the SARS-CoV-2 viral spike protein and viral spike protein-human ACE2 interface (2020)
13. Qadir, J., Ali, A., ur Rasool, R., Zwitter, A., Sathiaseelan, A., Crowcroft, J.: Crisis analytics: big data-driven crisis response. J. Int. Human. Action 1(1), 12 (2016)
14. Ali, A., Qadir, J., ur Rasool, R., Zwitter, A., Sathiaseelan, A., Crowcroft, J.: Big data for development: applications and techniques. Big Data Anal. 1(1), 2 (2016)
15. Zwitter, A., Gstrein, O.J.: Big data, privacy and COVID-19–learning from humanitarian expertise in data protection (2020)
16. Mozur, P., Raymond, Z., Aaron, K.: In coronavirus fight, China gives citizens a color code, with red flags. New York Times. sec. Business (2020). https://www.nytimes.com/2020/03/01/business/china-coronavirus-surveillance.html. Accessed 15 June 2020

17. Bibault, J.E., Chaix, B., Guillemassé, A., Cousin, S., Escande, A., Perrin, M., Brouard, B.: A chatbot versus physicians to provide information for patients with breast cancer: blind, randomized controlled noninferiority trial. J. Med. Internet Res. **21**(11), (2019)

18. Pinter, G., Felde, I., Mosavi, A., Ghamisi, P., Gloaguen, R.: COVID-19 pandemic prediction for hungary; a hybrid machine learning approach. Mathematics **8**(6), 890 (2020)

19. Wang, L., Wong, A.: COVID-Net: a tailored deep convolutional neural network design for detection of COVID-19 cases from chest radiography images. arXiv, arXiv-2003 (2020)

20. Li, L., et al.: Artificial intelligence distinguishes COVID-19 from community acquired pneumonia on chest CT. Radiology, **10**, 200905 (2020)

21. Apostolopoulos, I.D., Mpesiana, T.A.: Covid-19: automatic detection from x-ray images utilising transfer learning with convolutional neural networks. Phys. Eng. Sci. Med. **1**, 52 (2020)

22. Huang, R.H., Liu, D.J., Tlili, A., Yang, J.F., Wang, H.H.: Handbook on Facilitating Flexible Learning During Educational Disruption: The Chinese Experience in Maintaining Undisrupted Learning in COVID-19 Outbreak. Smart Learning Institute of Beijing Normal University, Beijing (2020)

23. Naudé, W.: Artificial intelligence vs COVID-19: limitations, constraints and pitfalls. Ai & Society, 1 (2020b)

24. Olbrechts, A.: Statement by the EDPB chair on the processing of personal data in the context of the COVID-19 outbreak. Text. European Data Protection Board - European Data Protection Board (2020). https://edpb.europa.eu/news/news/2020/statement-edpb-chair-processing-personal-data-context-covid-19-outbreak_en

25. Singh, P., Paprzycki, M., Bhargava, B., Chhabra, J., Kaushal, N., Kumar, Y.: Futuristic Trends in Network and Communication Technologies. FTNCT 2018. Communications in Computer and Information Science, vol. 958, pp. 141–166 (2010)

26. Singh, P., Sood, S., Kumar, Y., Paprzycki, M., Pljonkin, A., Hong, W.C.: Futuristic trends in networks and computing technologies. FTNCT. Commun. Comput. Inf. Sci **1206**, 3–707 (2019)

COVID-19 Real Time Impact Analysis
India vs USA

Govind Agarwal[1], Loveleen Gaur[1(✉)], and Ankur Singh Bist[2]

[1] Amity University, Noida, India
lgaur@amity.edu
[2] Quanto-Labs, Jaipur, India

Abstract. This is the time when the whole world is facing a crisis like never before, which has taken the form of a pandemic called the Coronavirus outbreak. The situation is way bigger and tense than it seems. The outbreak of COVID-19 has exposed both the developed and developing nations of the world with an evolving challenge like never before. All the developed nations are witnessing unprecedented collapse of their public healthcare systems and institutions, weak enforcement of laws to prevent the spread of infection and unimpressive crowd management techniques.

We can hear health officials calling for huge drastic & rapid responses in early days when the infected number of people were relatively small. Some people are telling that we are overreacting but that is not true. It was never really fine to begin in such a fashion but if we don't notice the seriousness of this crisis it will be very late. The following research is based on insights & comparisons between India and United States and the reason for choosing the strong & powerful nations are as follows:

- India is still counted as a developing nation whereas, USA is the most developed country in the world.
- The healthcare facilities in USA are way advance as compared to India yet the number of cases there were extremely high.
- India and USA also have a huge difference when it comes to the population and yet the number of cases each day is quite low in India. The number of recovery cases are also higher in India.

So, the question is What went wrong? Why is India in a better place in comparison to the world's super power USA in this pandemic?

Keywords: Coronavirus · Pandemic · Unprecedented

1 Introduction

On December 31, 2019 in WUHAN a city of CHINA that reported the WORLD HEALTH ORGANISATION that a pneumonia from an unknown virus has been detected. The scientist & doctors of World Health Organization worked 24*7 to finally analyses and

© Springer Nature Singapore Pte Ltd. 2021
P. K. Singh et al. (Eds.): FTNCT 2020, CCIS 1395, pp. 329–336, 2021.
https://doi.org/10.1007/978-981-16-1480-4_29

came out with a conclusion that suggested that this disease is called the Coronavirus (COVID-19).

On January 31, 2020 World Health Organisation declared this outbreak as a Public Health Emergency of International Concern. The symptoms of this disease are just similar to a normal flu like cough, fever, and body ache but what makes it fatal is the severe breathing problem (World Health Organisation 2020).

As per the report of World Health Organization Coronavirus is a disease that has affected 216 countries of the world. The total number of confirmed cases are 7,764,621; the total number of recovered persons are 3,982,057 & the number of deaths occurred in the world are 428,740 as of June 13,2020. The top 5 country's having a greater number of people affected from the Coronavirus are "USA, BRAZIL, RUSSIA, INDIA, UK" up till June 12 as per the World Health Organization reports (World Health Organisation 2020).

2 Literature Review

Siddhartha Rastogi the managing director of Ambit Asset Management in his article, "The New Normal: Analysis of COVID-19 Impact on the Indian Economy" wrote about how businesses are going through a transformation phase in the form of digitization & innovation. He also wrote about the various investment strategies being used as a tool to rebuild the economy amid this pandemic (Siddhartha Rastogi 2020).

Ben Hu, Xingyi Ge, Lin-Fa Wang and Zhengli Shi in their research journal titled "Bat origin of human coronaviruses" have mentioned about two viruses mainly Severe Acute Respiratory Syndrome Coronavirus (SARS-CoV) & Middle East Respiratory Syndrome Coronavirus (MERS-CoV). They have also mentioned about the actual origin of these viruses along with their comparison of transmission (Ben Hu 2015).

Siham Amirou, Abdelatif Zerizer, Imane Haddadou and Andre Merlin have discussed about the PLA kit that has been used to discovered this Coronavirus in humans. In their research paper titled "Effects of corona discharge treatment on the mechanical properties of bio-composites from polylactic acid and Algerian date palm fibres", they have clearly discussed about the methods & materials required to produce a tasting kit for accurate results & further treatment (Siham AMIROU 2013).

The Indian Express published an article named "Explained: How Covid-19 has affected the global economy" which discussed about the overall impact of this virus on the global economy (The Indian Express 2020).

David M Patrick, Martin Petric, Danuta M Skowronski have given a detailed study on the Severe Acute Respiratory Syndrome Coronavirus (SARS-CoV) in their research article named "An outbreak of human coronavirus OC43 infection and serological cross-reactivity with SARS coronavirus". In their study they have mentioned that such viruses affect the elderly population the most & hence need to be treated carefully (David M, Patrick MD 2006).

3 Research Objective

Coronavirus takes around 5 days or more to get identified in a human body. Absence of symptoms & delayed response makes it difficult to give a clear picture about the exact number of people being affected by it. Therefore, tools like Time Series & Prophet Model comes to the rescue. These models are not only helpful in identifying the virus but also gives a future projection of the number of confirmed cases that could occur in the days to come. This research focuses on:

1) Examining the spread of Covid-19 in India & USA.
2) And predicts the total number of confirmed cases in the days to come.

4 Methodology

The research paper mainly focuses on the impact of the Covid-19 which has spread across the globe, creating a pandemic. This study is based on descriptive analysis which highlights the number of confirmed cases that are going to happen in both the countries. It has been quantified with the help of a data set taken from the inbuild library of R called the "covid19.analytics". The software used for completing this research is called R-Studio.

5 Results and Findings

While examining & analysing the data it has been observed that models like Times Series & Prophet Model are helpful to get future projections of the confirmed cases in both the countries quite accurately.

5.1 Prediction of Confirmed Cases in India

The latest time series Covid-19 data has been collected from an inbuild library of R called the "covid19.analytics". The raw data obtained from the library was then taken through a lot of cleaning process in order to achieve the required data set for further use.

This data consists of 143 observation with 2 variables i.e. 'Date & Confirmed Cases' (Fig. 1).

It includes the entries of confirmed cases from 22nd January to 12th June 2020. Till mid-April it has been identified that the number of confirmed cases in India were constant but in the later days, the number of confirmed cases started to increase at faster rate. The reason being reopening the economy for the public.

Prediction for the total number of confirmed cases for the next 18 days that is till 30th June has been done using the PROPHET MODEL. This model is best suited with time series that have strong seasonal effect like yearly weekly & daily seasonality in the historical data (Fig. 2).

As on 12th June, the actual number of confirmed cases were 297,535 whereas the prediction done with the help of the above given model for the same date was 288,694. The model gives us the confidence band which clearly states that the predicted values can be slightly higher, lower, or closer to the actual value. These predictions are valid assuming that the current condition of lockdown is continued.

Results as per the forecast say that the numbers of confirmed cases till 30th June which is 161th day will be 0.42 Million.

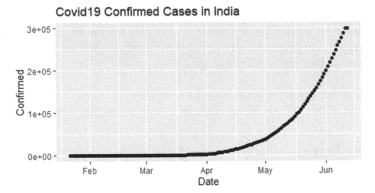

Fig. 1. Graphical representation of Confirmed Cases in India

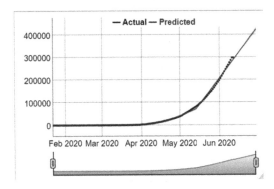

Fig. 2. Graphical Representation of Forecast using DY Plot

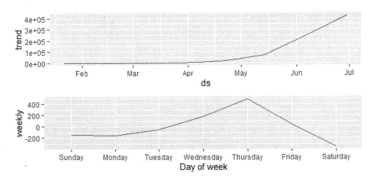

Fig. 3. Graphical Representation of Prophet Plot Components

Components of the forecast which includes the 'trend & weekly report' has been calculated using the 'Prophet Plot Components Model' (Fig. 3).

The confirmed cases are usually higher on Thursdays and lower on Fridays & Saturdays.

In order to check the performance of the model, comparison between the actual & the predicted number of confirmed cases need to be done (Fig. 4).

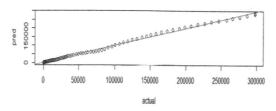

Fig. 4. Comparison of Actual & Predicated Cases

Red Line: Represents the predicated number of confirmed cases.

Circles: Depict the actual number of confirmed cases.

The actual vs predicated plot is linear which states that the prediction is not underestimated or overestimated.

Accuracy of the result can be checked by the following method:

Multiple R-squared: 0.9974

Adjusted R-squared: 0.9974

The Adjusted R-square is 0.9974 which is quite high. This clearly indicates the above given model has a very high confidence, stating that it is statistically significant.

5.2   Prediction of Confirmed Cases in United States

The latest time series Covid-19 data has been collected from an inbuild library of R called the "covid19.analytics". The raw data obtained from the library was then taken through a lot of cleaning process in order to achieve the required data set for further use.

This data consists of 143 observation with 2 variables i.e. 'Date & Confirmed Cases' (Fig. 5).

Fig. 5. Graphical Representation of Confirmed Cases in US

The data includes entries of confirmed cases from 22nd January to 12th June 2020. Till mid-March it has been identified that the number of confirmed cases in United States were constant but in the later days, the number of confirmed cases started to increase at faster rate.

Prediction for the total number of confirmed cases for the next 18 days that is till 30th June has been done using the PROPHET MODEL. This model is best suited with time series that have strong seasonal effect like yearly weekly & daily seasonality in the historical data.

As on 12th June, the actual number of confirmed cases were 2,048,986 whereas the prediction done with the help of the above given model for the same date was 2.05 million. The model gives us the confidence band which clearly states that the predicted values can be slightly higher, lower, or closer to the actual value. These predictions are valid assuming that the current condition is continued. So, this plot also helps us to focus on any specific range of dates (Fig. 6).

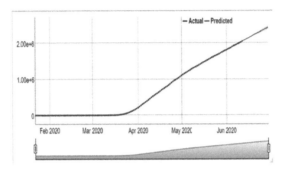

Fig. 6. Graphical Representation of Forecast using DY Plot

Results as per the forecast say that the numbers of confirmed cases till 30th June which is 161st day will be 2.43 million.

Components of the forecast which includes the 'trend & weekly report' has been calculated using the 'Prophet Plot Components Model' (Fig. 7).

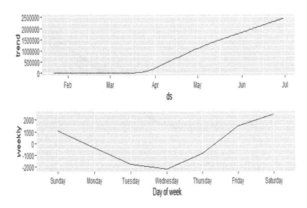

Fig. 7. Graphical Representation of Prophet Plot Components

The confirmed cases are usually higher on Fridays & Saturdays and lower on Wednesdays.

In order to check the performance of the model, comparison between the actual & the predicted number of confirmed cases need to be done (Fig. 8).

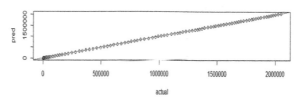

Fig. 8. Comparison of Actual & Predicated Cases

Red Line: Represents the predicated cases.

Circles: Depict the actual number of cases.

The actual vs predicated plot is linear which states that the prediction is not underestimated or overestimated.

Accuracy of the result can be checked by the following method:

Multiple R-squared: 1

Adjusted R-squared: 1

The Adjusted R-square is 1 which is quite high so that means the model has a very high confidence and is statistically significant.

6 Coronavirus Outbreak: Comparison Between India and United States

Basis	India	United States
Confirmed Cases (Till 30th June)	0.42 Million	2.43 Million
Weekly Report	Higher on Thursdays, Lower on Fridays & Saturdays	Higher on Fridays & Saturdays, Lower on Wednesday
Lockdown	Whole Economy	Partial Lockdown in few cities

7 Conclusion

The total number of confirmed cases in India & USA could go up to 0.42 million & 2.43 million respectively till 30th June. The number of confirmed cases in USA are much higher as compared to India. This is because unlike India the American government was not able to anticipate the spread of the virus & announce an immediate Lockdown.

India went into a complete lockdown with all economic activity coming to a standstill in the initial days of this pandemic whereas in United States there were only few major cities which went into a partial lockdown. The numbers of cases are increasing with each passing day and this will only slow down if the lockdown keeps continuing.

This Lockdown will prevent the virus from spreading by means of social distancing & home quarantine of the public. At the moment this virus has created a pandemic situation for everyone world-wide and as a global community we have the potential to stop it only if we take serious measures. This disease has acted as a wake-up call for the humankind to rethink the damages that it has done to the environment & start taking corrective actions to fix those in all walks of life.

8   Research Gape and Future Scope

- There are other techniques & tools of machine learning which can be used for prediction, resulting in higher accuracy.
- This research could be carried out on a global data set instead of doing a comparison between two economies.
- The following study gives a prediction till 30th June; however, the number of days could be increased with the increasing number of cases.
- The following study can also be done from two angles, a) First assumption being that there is complete Lockdown in both the countries and b) Second being there is no restriction in both the countries.

References

World Health Organisation: World Health Organisation Emergiencies (2020). https://www.who.int/emergencies/diseases/novel-coronavirus-2019/events-as-they-happen. Accessed 18 May 2020

World Health Organisation: Worldometer, from COVID-19 CORONAVIRUS PANDEMIC (2020). https://www.worldometers.info/coronavirus/?. Accessed 13 June 2020

Ben Hu, X.G.-F.: Bat origin of human coronaviruses. Virology Journal, Hu et al. Virology Journal (2015). Accessed 18 May 2020

David, M., Patrick, M.D.: An outbreak of human coronavirus OC43 infection and serological cross-reactivity with SARS coronavirus. Research gate, 8 (2006). https://www.researchgate.net/publication/5469347. Accessed 18 May 2020

Siddhartha, R.: The New Normal: Analysis of COVID-19 Impact on the Indian Economy. Making Smalltalk, p. 1 (2020). Accessed 18 May 2020

Siham, A.Z.: Effects of corona discharge treatment on the mechanical properties of biocomposites from polylactic acid and Algerian date palm fibres. Research Gate, vol. 8. https://www.researchgate.net/publication/256733476. Accessed 18 May 2020

The Indian Express: Explained: How Covid-19 has affected the global economy. The Indian Express (2020). https://indianexpress.com/article/explained/explained-how-has-covid-19-affected-the-global-economy-6410494/. Accessed 20 May 2020

Cold Start in Function as a Service: A Systematic Study, Analysis and Evaluation

Ravi Prakash Varshney[✉] and Dilip Kumar Sharma[✉]

GLA University, Mathura, India
ravi_varshney@outlook.com, dilip.sharma@gla.ac.in

Abstract. Function as a Service is one of the most popular and used offerings of cloud paradigm and hence is continuously evolving with both changes in the offering and the implementation. To the service user, it still seems to be a black box completely abstracting the hardware implementation underneath. However, it still suffers from the common pitfalls of virtualization, and the evaluation of these pitfalls becomes inevitable. Particularly, reusing the container for the next call, having minimal idle time to avoid the cost, and meeting the demand or auto-scaling are few of the key stakeholders in controlling the instantiation of new containers. Hence, cold starts within the function call. This study aims to outline the key factors that are mainly responsible for the cold starts and their impact on the duration of the cold start. We conducted a series of AWS Lambda executions with different configurations and dependencies to understand the implications of different cold start factors.

Keywords: Cold Start · Serverless · Function as a Service · Benchmarking · Lambda · Cloud computing

1 Introduction

Serverless computing has proved to be a path-breaking and revolutionary service offered by cloud computing. It lets the development community focus all alone on development without marginally worrying about procurement, maintenance, and up-gradation of the underlying infrastructure. Function as a Service or otherwise commonly known as FaaS is one of the key implementations of Serverless architecture. It allows anyone to build and manage their applications without the complexity of maintaining the underlying infrastructure. Serverless architecture is not a magic spell and does not imply that are no servers involved at all. Serverless architecture relies on containers for its functioning. In the Serverless architecture, the applications run on ephemeral stateless containers [1], set up by the cloud providers. The containers are set up via triggering of events and terminate once the execution is complete.

Function as a Service has been widely accepted and used by the industry across the globe. The features of the FaaS that make it so accessible and fit for use are as follows:

1. Offloading of all infrastructure related operations, maintenance, updates, patches, etc. to the cloud provider

© Springer Nature Singapore Pte Ltd. 2021
P. K. Singh et al. (Eds.): FTNCT 2020, CCIS 1395, pp. 337–349, 2021.
https://doi.org/10.1007/978-981-16-1480-4_30

2. Support for all major programming languages.
3. Auto-scaling of application as load increases
4. Elasticity: Application gets more resources allotted on the increase in the number of requests and auto adjusted when the requests decreases
5. High Availability

Function as a Service paradigm is a well-established paradigm and is supported by all the major cloud providers. All of them have an equivalent offering in the serverless domain. AWS offers AWS Lambda [1]; Microsoft has named it as Azure Function [2], Google calls its offering as Google Cloud Functions [3]. We have few offerings in open source space, like Apache Open Whisk [4] and Kubeless [5]. However, the popularity and adoption of the serverless paradigm has introduced challenges never seen before and a tough task to imbibe balance between performance and task [6]. One of the key reasons for its wide adoption is the ease with which it lets the [7] user decentralize computing away from the traditional data centers and help in cost savings. For this study, we have focused on AWS Lambda.

AWS Lambda offers many features like autoscaling, availability, and still be very cost-effective. The cost-effectiveness of AWS Lambda is attributed to various factors. Firstly, the billing of the function is done in terms of the execution time of the function and is charged in granular multiples of 100 ms. Secondly, the charges or the cost of running is comparatively lower when compared to peers. However, it does not mean that they are no complexities involved with it. The working or the execution model of the AWS Lambda can be classified into two blocks, one at the provider and other, on the user side. First, you need to create and configure the AWS lambda as per your requirement. At this moment, the definition and dependencies of the lambda are stored in an S3 bucket. Once the lambda is invoked or requested for execution, a container is mounted with the required resources as per the lambda configuration. The application code is loaded into the memory for execution. The time spent during this entire process of setting up the container to meet the application requirements and then loading the code and required dependencies for its execution is referred to as the Cold Start [8].

As illustrated in Fig. 1, the cold start time involves both the provider side and as well as some part of the user side. However, the significant chunk of the time is still on the provider side, making it tough for the development community to reduce the cold start time to a greater extent.

It is not mandatory that the AWS lambda always must go through the same set of steps specified earlier. Once the lambda is invoked and hence initialized, it remains active or commonly known as "warm" for a brief period, if another invocation of the lambda or function call happens within this period, then it does not have to go through the initialization steps but can reuse the warm container. This brief period is known as the "Warm call", meaning the containers are not terminated as soon as the lambda execution is complete but are available for a brief period even after the execution of the lambda is complete, making the containers reusable for near future calls. As explained in Fig. 3, the first call of the lambda is responsible for the setting up of the container and initialization of the code (Fig. 2).

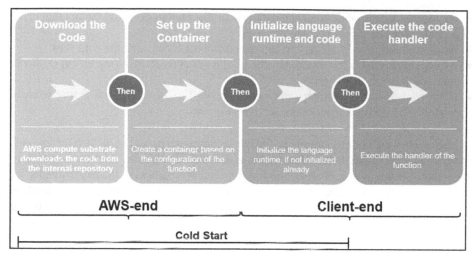

Fig. 1. The life cycle of a typical serverless function

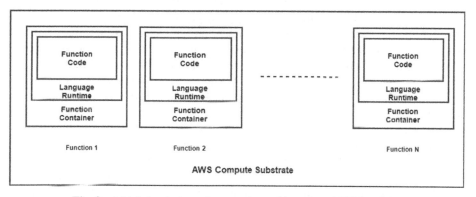

Fig. 2. A high-level view of a container with various AWS Lambdas

However, later calls within the quick interval does not go through the container set up but only through code execution. The only solution to eradicate cold starts in the lambda calls is to keep always the containers warm so that the containers do not have to go through the initialization steps.

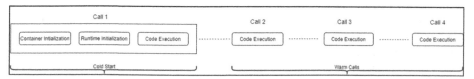

Fig. 3. Timeline of a cold and warm function calls

The main contributions of this paper are as follows.

- We present a systematic study and analysis of the various potential factors that drive the behavior of cold starts in the functions.
- We also illustrate the relationship between different factors and the cold start.
- We benchmark the factors backed by the samples accumulated during the experiments conducted as a part of this study.
- Then, we highlight the existing open issues related to a cold start and future work in progress for the betterment of the serverless model.

After the introduction of the paper, the remainder of the paper is structured as follows. First, Sect. 2 elaborates on the related work in this area. Then, Sect. 3 details the problem statement. Section 4 describes the proposed model by explaining the experiment's set up and the goal of the experiment. Then, in Sect. 5, the results are analyzed based on different factors, and in the last Sect. 6, the work is summarized and points to future work.

2 Related Work

There has been lately proper academic research and study across the Function-as-a-Service paradigm and highlighting the open issues and future work in the area. In the study done by Jorn Kuhlenkamp et al. [9] proposed an experiment design and corresponding toolkit for quantifying elasticity and its associated trade-offs with latency, reliability, and execution costs. [10] Baldini, Ioana, et al. has discussed in their work that scaling to zero helps reduce costs but leads to the problem of cold starts when restarting the containers and plays a role in identifying whether serverless is the appropriate option for the implementation. Also, David Balla et al. [11] studied the dependency of the language runtime on the performance of function as Service applications and presented insights for different workloads. Johannes Manner et al. [12] explained the process of benchmarking the performance and expenditure aspect of the FaaS applications through a set of experiments. They focused on their study more on self-hosted FaaS platforms and have tried to study the impact of load on the scaling offered by FaaS. Another research study by Villamizar et al. [13] was done on function as a Service Platform. They scoped their research around three system architectures: A monolithic architecture, an architecture based on microservices, and lastly, a cloud function or native architecture. They have discussed scenarios where the monolithic system was transformed into a loosely coupled cloud function resulting in a better performing and robust data system. They were also able to show a reduction in cost by decomposing the monolithic system into a set of microservices. This reduction was further enhanced by running the set of microservices on the cloud in a FaaS platform. They demonstrated that they were able to reduce the cost of up to 70%. Another cross-cloud provider study was done by Malawski et al. [14], focusing specifically on interaction via API gateways. They measured the performance on both the client and the provider side. They measured the overhead involved in the calls, including the network latency, platform routing, and scheduling overhead. They did not include cold starts in their study, which we would like to emphasize in this study. Manoj Kumar [15], in his detailed analysis of services offered by different cloud providers, has not only compared and evaluated them but has highlighted the open problems that the different services suffer at the moment and how does the future look for them. In their literature review, Joel Scheuner et al. [16] surveyed different evaluations done on FaaS platforms, identified the gap between academia and industrial research, and then analyzed the performance measurements of FaaS offerings of different platforms. Garrett McGrath et al. [17] have also studied how cold starts while designing the model for a serverless computing platform in.NET. Philipp Leitner et al. [18] in their empirical study of FaaS software development too have highlighted the problems involved with cold starts in applications. To mitigate the cold starts, a workaround of pinging the container to keep it warm helps in reducing the latency but incurs cost and maintenance of the workaround piece of code. Martins H. et al. [19] benchmarked the performance of serverless platforms and evaluated the reuse of containers to study the cold start time. But they have focused on interval between the calls in the entirety only for analyzing the cold start.

We are aiming at identifying the factors that affect the cold start times. These factors than can be considered during design decisions for different types of applications. The study aims at benchmarking the factors backed by the samples accumulated during the experiments conducted as a part of this study.

3   Problem Statement

Solution architects and developers, while designing any application or a program, tend to achieve the non-functional objectives that mainly include the throughput, latency, availability, reliability, running costs, and deployment costs. The feature in the context of the paper has a role to play in some of these objectives. It will affect the throughput as a slight portion of the execution time is consumed by container to be in a state to start processing and do the actual work. Also, the cold start increases the latency of the function as it is the time taken in the process of creating the container to serve requests. Also, the cold start time is included in the billed duration. Thus it affects the running cost too. We aim to study and identify the behavior of a cold start, which can help in design decisions. We try to find the factors that affect the cold start and in what ways. In conclusion, we define our problem statement as follows:

- What is the duration between the function calls or interval between two function calls after a cold start is inevitable?
- Does cold start depend upon the programming language used for implementing the function or is agnostic to the programming language?
- Does cold start also depend upon the memory requirement of the function or is independent of it?
- Does the size of the deployment package or the associated dependencies impact the cold start duration?

4   Proposed Work

In this section, we describe our proposed work based on an experimental design, which includes the setup of the experiment, the goals, the methodology, and the future proposal work. We list in detail the steps of the execution, the results of the experiments, and the insights derived from the results.

4.1 Goal

The goal of the experiments performed in this study is to derive results and conclusions based on the metrics collected during the experiments' process. We aim to collect metrics concerning all the four problem statements that have been outlined earlier. Based on the experiments' metrics, we want to baseline the behavior of cold start concerning different environmental factors.

4.2 Set Up

The study focusses on establishing the relationship between the different factors and the cold starts. To analyze the coupling between the factors and cold start, we require information about the instances when cold start occurred during function invocations over a period. Thus, we have set up an environment in AWS, where we execute lambda functions on different periodic intervals and with different configurations over a duration. To achieve the intended goal, several ways were considered and evaluated for collecting the information on cold starts. We thrive on having accurate results, collecting logs for the detailed analysis, and excluding other factors that resemble noise in the experiment. Henceforth, we opted to use the provider's logs to evaluate the occurrence of cold starts during function invocations. In the case of AWS Lambda, the AWS by itself provides the information in the log referred to as "Init Duration," which is equivalent to the time taken by AWS to initialize the environment for execution of the function. We extract this information from the logs and build a metric on it. The "Init Duration" metric includes time taken to create the container and load the function and its dependencies on the container. We have enlisted programming language, the memory of the program, the frequency or the periodic interval of the execution and the size of the deployment factors as the main factors which will be analyzed in this study to identify their impact on the cold start of the function.

We have created lambda functions in different programming languages. We have chosen languages like python, node, C#, and Java so that we cover all the majority types of language in this study. Also, irrespective of the lambda written in different languages, the core functionality implemented within the lambda is the same in all the cases. We are using the same implementation of the sort algorithm in all the different lambdas with the same set of inputs. The reason for having the same implementation in all the lambdas it to focus on the cold start and avoid other noise in the experiment.

Similarly, we executed the lambdas is a different memory configuration to understand and establish the relationship of memory and CPU with a cold start. The executions logs of all these lambdas are logged in the CloudWatch service provided by AWS. CloudWatch is a service provided by AWS to log and monitor the resources. As a part of all the executions of lambdas, the "Init duration" metric is also logged in CloudWatch in all the function calls where the cold start execution occurred. We are using the logs generated because of the lambda executions and only extract the required metric from the logs to build the result set for the experiment. In case of a cold start, the lambda execution logs contain an entry for "Init Duration" metric. However, since there is no initialization involved in the case of a warm execution, the log does not have any entry for the "Init Duration" metric. Table 1 covers all the different factors that we are analyzing on their relationship with a cold start (Fig. 4).

Table 1. Different dimensions/factors evaluated in the study

Number	Dimensions
1	Programming Language
2	Frequency of function execution
3	Memory/CPU allotted to function
4	Deployment package size

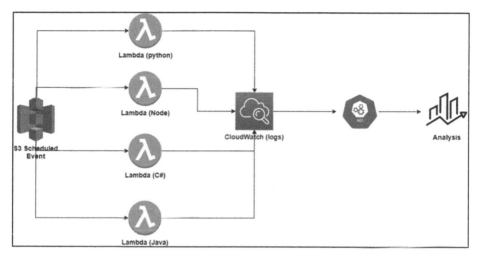

Fig. 4. The architecture of the experiment set up

5   Results

In this section, we explain the series of extensive function calls as a part of the study set up and then later rigorously analyze the data collected to derive insights. The set of experiments or the function calls are executed for each dimension to study the relationship between the dimension and the cold start. The experiment set up varies with each dimension.

5.1   Programming Language

Cloud providers offer many options in programming languages that you can use to write your functions. With reference to AWS, you can write your function logic in many languages that include JavaScript, Python, Nodejs, Java, and C#. The wide array of languages provides flexibility to the users. The set of languages offered do include the compiled languages like Java and C# as they let users perform complex business logic with ease. However, since these languages are compiled based and involve compile and runtime overhead.,Ideally, the set of up containers for executing the compiler-based languages and their runtime would be an extra overhead compared to other languages like

Nodejs or python. We have created the lambda functions with the same functionality in different programming languages. All other configurations for the functions like a periodic interval of execution or the CPU or memory allocated remain the same. The periodic interval for function execution is set to 15 min, and the memory allotted to the function is 512 MB. Each lambda function of different languages was executed around 200 times, and then the cold start time was calculated (Fig. 5).

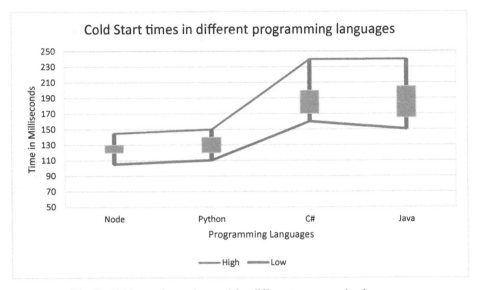

Fig. 5. Cold start times observed for different programming languages

From the results, it is evident that the compiler-based languages like Java and C# have higher cold start times when compared to other languages like NodeJS and Python. The highest cold start time noticed for C# and JAVA was in the range of 225–250 ms, but for NodeJS and Python, the highest cold start time was 150 ms.

5.2 Frequency of Function Execution

Cold starts occur when the containers are not reused for the function executions and need to be recreated and set up again. The cloud providers try to keep the containers up and running for a specific duration despite no new calls, mainly to ensure that the future calls can be served from the same container, and the cold starts are avoided. However, the containers cannot run forever. Running containers forever without any incoming calls will incur the cost and is a non-sustainable solution. It defeats the purpose of a serverless platform that relies on on-demand resource allocation and zero elasticity. We conduct a series of function calls at different frequencies to establish a relation between the occurrence of cold start and the period between two subsequent calls. We have chosen the period from as small as one minute to the extent of 15 min. We then executed the function for over 200 times for each of the different frequencies mentioned to record its relationship with the cold start (Fig. 6).

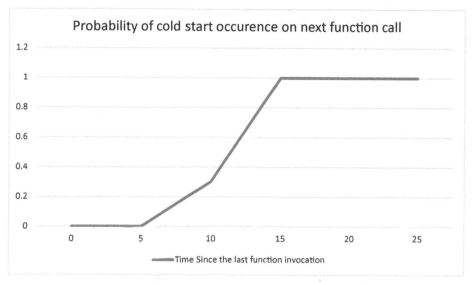

Fig. 6. Probabilities of occurrence of cold function start for different time intervals

As per the results, there was no occurrence of cold start when the periodic interval was less than 5 min. It means that the containers are always warm for each of the languages. However, as the periodic interval between the function calls increased to 10 min, few occurrences of cold starts. Furthermore, once the periodic interval crossed 10 min, the occurrence of cold start executions shoots higher, and after reaching 15 min, every single function execution was a cold start execution.

5.3 Memory

To execute a function in the serverless ecosystem, memory is allocated. During the process of setting up the container and the runtime environment, the process allocates the required memory for the execution of the function. We performed a set of function calls with different memory configurations to evaluate the impact of memory requirements on the cold start. For our study, we have chosen a few memory configurations to evaluate. We have chosen 512 MB, 2048 MB, and 3008 MB. The remaining factors, like programming language and frequency of execution, remain the same for all the different lambdas and hence, removing the noise from the setup (Figs. 7 and 8).

It is visible from the result for both the languages that as the memory allotted to the function is increased, the cold start times have increased too.

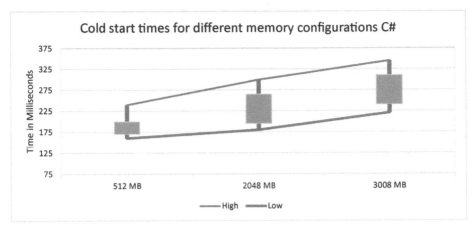

Fig. 7. Cold start time observed for different memory configurations (C#)

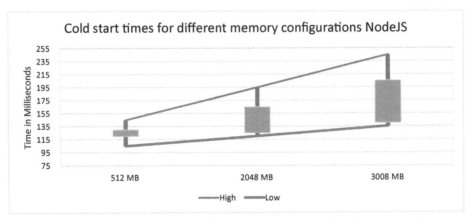

Fig. 8. Cold start time observed for different memory configurations (NodeJS)

5.4 Deployment Package Size

To be able to execute the function for the first time, the function image must be copied over to the container, load into the memory, load the associated dependencies and libraries. So, the increase in the size of the deployment package should result in an increase in the cold start time as well. To evaluate the argument, we executed three different sets of lambdas in each C# and Python. Each of the lambdas has a different package size and a good number of dependencies (Figs. 9 and 10).

From the results obtained, it is crystal clear that as the size of the deployment package increased or, in other terms, the dependencies have increased, the cold start time has gone for a toss as the time required to load the packages and associated dependencies increases with size.

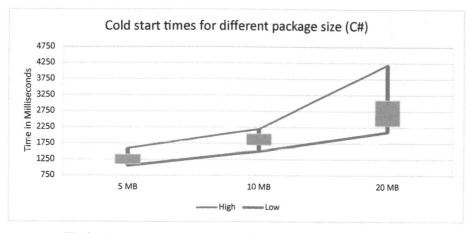

Fig. 9. Cold start time observed for different deployment package (C#)

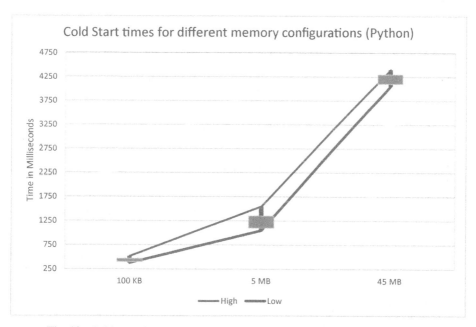

Fig. 10. Cold start time observed for different memory configurations (Python)

6 Conclusion

Our study and the set of experiments were aimed at identifying the key factors and their level of impact on its duration. We outlined a few factors and studied how these factors fared when a series of executions were conducted. Based on the experiments' results, it can be concluded that the duration of cold starts depends on the type of programming language, memory settings, and the size of the function's deployment package. The deployment package size appears to be a critical factor in the study, as it is evident that the duration of the cold start varies a lot with an increase in the size of deployment. The executions of a C# lambda with 2048 MB of memory limit and 1 MB of package size resulted in an average cold start time of around 250 ms but when the same set of executions were repeated but by increasing the size of the deployment package to 20 MB resulted in an increase of cold start to multiple folds to around 2400 ms. It is proven from the study that the type of programming language also plays a crucial role in the cold start where compile-based languages ought to take more cold start duration.

References

1. "Serverless Computing" https://aws.amazon.com/serverless/. Accessed 15 Jun 2020
2. Azure Functions. https://azure.microsoft.com/en-in/services/functions/. Accessed 15 Jun 2020
3. "Cloud Functions". https://cloud.google.com/functions. Accessed 15 Jun 2020
4. "Open Source Serverless Cloud Platform". https://openwhisk.apache.org/. Accessed 15 Jun 2020
5. "The Kubernetes Native Serverless Framework". https://kubeless.io/. Accessed 15 Jun 2020
6. Lin, P.M., Glikson, A.: Mitigating cold starts in serverless platforms: a pool-based approach. arXiv preprint arXiv:1903.12221 (2019)
7. Varghese, B., Buyya, R.: Next generation cloud computing: new trends and research directions. Futur. Gener. Comput. Syst. **79**, 849–861 (2018)
8. "Serverless@re:Invent 2017". https://aws.amazon.com/blogs/compute/serverless-reinvent-2017/. Accessed 17 Jun 2020
9. Kuhlenkamp, J., Werner, S., Borges, M.C., Ernst, D., Wenzel, D.: Benchmarking elasticity of FaaS platforms as a foundation for objective-driven design of serverless applications. In: Proceedings of the 35th Annual ACM Symposium on Applied Computing, pp. 1576–1585, March 2020
10. Baldini, I., et al.: Serverless computing: current trends and open problems. In: Chaudhary, S., Somani, G., Buyya, R. (eds.) Research Advances in Cloud Computing, pp. 1–20. Springer, Singapore (2017)
11. Balla, D., Maliosz, M., Simon, C., Gehberger, D.: Tuning runtimes in open source FaaS. In: Hsu, C.H.., Kallel, S., Lan, K.C., Zheng, Z. (eds.) Internet of Vehicles. Technologies and Services Toward Smart Cities. IOV 2019. Lecture Notes in Computer Science, Jan 2020, vol. 11894. Springer, Cham (2020)
12. Manner, J., Wirtz, G.: Impact of application load in function as a service. In: 13th Symposium and Summer School on Service-Oriented Computing, At Crete, Greece, June 2019
13. Villamizar, M., et al.: Infrastructure cost comparison of running web applications in the cloud using AWS lambda and monolithic and microservice architectures. In: 2016 16th IEEE/ACM International Symposium on Cluster, Cloud and Grid Computing (CCGrid), Cartagena, pp. 179–182 (2016)
14. Malawski, M., Figiela, K., Gajek, A., Zima, A.: Benchmarking heterogeneous cloud functions. In: Heras, D.B., Bougé, L. (eds.) Euro-Par 2017. LNCS, vol. 10659, pp. 415–426. Springer, Cham (2018). https://doi.org/10.1007/978-3-319-75178-8_34
15. Kumar, M.: Serverless architectures review, future trend and the solutions to open problems. Am. J. Software Eng. **6**(1), 1–10 (2019)
16. Scheuner, J., Leitner, P.: The state of research on function-as-a-service performance evaluation: a multivocal literature review. arXiv, pp. arXiv-2004 (2020)

17. McGrath, G., Brenner, P.R.: Serverless computing: Design, implementation, and performance. In 2017 IEEE 37th International Conference on Distributed Computing Systems Workshops (ICDCSW), pp. 405–410. IEEE, June 2017

18. Leitner, P., Wittern, E., Spillner, J., Hummer, W.: A mixed-method empirical study of Function-as-a-Service software development in industrial practice. J. Syst. Softw. **149**, 340–359 (2019)

19. Martins, H., Araujo, F., da Cunha, P.R.: Benchmarking serverless computing platforms. J. Grid Comput. **15**, 1–19 (2020)

Optimization and Performance Measurement Model for Massive Data Streams

Vivek Kumar[1]([✉]) [iD], Dilip K. Sharma[2], and Vinay K. Mishra[3]

[1] Kalam Technical University, Lucknow, Uttar Pradesh, India
[2] GLA University, Lucknow, Uttar Pradesh, India
[3] S.R.M. Group of Professional Colleges, Lucknow, Uttar Pradesh, India

Abstract. Massive Data Stream (MDS) is one research section of Big Data. The data streams which have large velocity are also known as Elephant Flows. The challenges of Velocity, as per Gartner's definition, are addressed. This paper proposes an algorithm that handles and processes Massive Data Streams. The Service Oriented Architecture (SOA) is used to capture and process massive data at higher velocity. Three types of parallel task running strategies are explored for the use in SOA. The error is adjustable according to available memory for getting more accurate results. The results show that 99% confidence is achieved at the cost of hyper-logarithmic space in memory.

Keywords: Massive data stream · Elephant flows · Synopsis data structure · Big data · Event stream analytics

1 Introduction

Big Data always means the size that overwhelms the space and processing power of available architecture. Space-efficient algorithms are required to process big data. Few such algorithms are arising in network traffic monitoring, machine learning, internet search, signal processing, and scientific computing. Processing requires $O(N)$ space and $O(\log^k N)$ poly-logarithmic space. Whenever the approximation factor decreases, space requirement increases (Kumar, Sharma, and Mishra 2020). There are various sampling techniques to sample the stream:

1. Reservoir Sampling
2. Sliding Window
3. Histograms
4. Multi-resolution Methods
5. Sketches

1.1 Background and Motivation

Stream Analytics is used to perform high velocity analysis on voluminous data coming from various devices to processes. The next step is to extract information and find patterns, relationships and trends from data streams to raise alerts or feed information to reporting and visualization tools. Application of Stream Analytics may be:

© Springer Nature Singapore Pte Ltd. 2021
P. K. Singh et al. (Eds.): FTNCT 2020, CCIS 1395, pp. 350–359, 2021.
https://doi.org/10.1007/978-981-16-1480-4_31

- Data Protection
- Identity Protection
- Customer Relationship (CRM)
- Association Mining
- Context Mining

The sketching approaches include compressive sensing, data stream algorithms and dimensionality reduction. Dimensionality reduction is used for reducing data dimension while preserving geometric structure. The popular mathematical models for developing sketching algorithms are given below (University, 2017):

a. Algorithms for big matrices come under Numerical linear algebra which includes regression, matrix completion, low rank approximation, etc.
b. Recovery of signals based on few linear measurements is known as compressed sensing.
c. Fast algorithms for approximately computing the Fourier Transform of signals which are sparse in the frequency domain.

The various Data Processing Algorithms for streams are given as under:

1. Las Vegas: If a randomized algorithm returns the right answer but running time varies, it is known as Las Vegas Algorithm.
2. Monte Carlo: It has bounds on the running time but may not return the correct result.
3. Randomized Algorithms: It is simply as a probability distribution over a set of deterministic algorithms.

  a. Chebychev's Inequality: Let x be a random variable, then: $P(|X - M| > K) <= $ sigma^2/K^2, for any positive number k. It bounds the variance of random variable.
  b. Chernoff Bounds: Its applications are:

    i. Frequent Pattern Mining
    ii. Lossy Counting Algorithm.

1.2 Overview of the Paper and Contributions

Brief rough "sketches" of data has been introduced as a new approach of computing for big data. The difference in size of these sketches as compared to original data is exponentially much lesser. Sketches retain the number of distinct elements in the data set which is significant and valuable. The sketching methods are applied for approximate query processing in databases, data compression in the web, network packet tracing and measurement and signal processing or acquisition.

1.3 More Details and Summary of the Approach

The stream processing platform focuses on real time application which is growing exponentially. Scalability and fault-tolerance are the characteristics that are desired for the stream computing platform. The optimization problem is about using the minimum number of resources to serve the big data stream. Resource allocation depends on the volume and velocity of big data. Modeling of data stream requires deep analysis of big data to optimize the performance.

1.4 Summary of the Results and Conclusions

Azure Event Hub and Azure IoT Hub directly connect to stream analytics for stream data ingestion and Azure Blob for historical data ingestion. The performance of data stream algorithm is measured by the number of passes on stream, the space consumed by algorithm and the time taken by algorithm. Accuracy is the significant key factor in approximation algorithms. Accuracy is often stated as $(\mathcal{E}, \delta)$ approximation. It means that algorithm achieves an error of less than $\mathcal{E}$ with probability $(1 - \delta)$. The proposed model minimizes the number of resources and addresses the memory optimization problem.

1.5 Arrangement of Sections in Article

This article is arranged in five sections. First section discusses the background and prerequisites. Section 2 derives the conclusions made from literature survey and related work. Section 3 proposes the architecture and algorithm. Section 4 shows the experimentation and results. Section 5 derives conclusions based on experiments performed and put some light on future directions.

2   Literature Survey and Research Gap

The architectures proposed so far have their advantages. The architectures get obsolete as the technology changes. Hence revision is needed for coping up with the new challenges. One such architecture, Lambda Architecture (Kreps 2014) beats the CAP theorem as an approach to building stream processing applications. It can be used on top of Storm, MapReduce and other similar systems. The applications also changes according to architectures and new applications with improved algorithms are created. News Recommendation System (NRS) is a complex and asynchronous transformation applications that need to run with low latency use lambda architecture. NRS crawl through various news sources or use single API that provides news from various sources. NRS process and normalize all the inputs rationally (Singh, Tripathi, and Kumar 2019). The lambda architecture's emphasis is on retaining input data intact as it gives advantage while modeling data transformations. On the other hand different code base is required at batch and streaming side to sync which is quite complex (Singh, Sood, Kumar, Paprzycki, Pljonkin, and Hong 2019).

Data Transformations become complex and time-sensitive when the data at source is approaching with an overwhelming speed and there we need probabilistic data structures for analyzing the data on the wire. Probabilistic data structures (PDS) are well suited for unstructured data storage, and fast retrieval. One such PDS, Accommodative Bloom Filter (ABF) (Singh, Garg, Batra, Kumar, and Rodrigues 2018) is suggested for insertion of bulk data. Middleware optimizes massive queries in distributed stream system and uses PubSub (Publish/Subscribe System) to achieve loosely-coupled communication (Zhou, Aberer, and Tan 2008). A distributed stream system is complex in the manner that each data node may generate packets in parallel with overlapping timestamps. A method is proposed for executing query on graph data stream by constructing plurality of synopsis data structure (Corp, 2013). The algorithm uses incremental mesh decimation for reading data from a stream and writing to another stream, in a single pass, using fixed size buffer based on quadratic error metric and edge collapse (Wu and Kobbelt 2003). A static optimization tool, SpinStreams (Mencagli, Dazzi, and Tonci 2018), is a cost model used to detect the efficiency of initial application. Optimizations are suggested by generating code to be run on Stream Processing System (SPS). A survey of recent work on optimizing the system latency and throughput in Data Stream Processing System (DSPS) has been conducted with three directions namely computation optimization, stream I/O optimization, and query deployment (Zhang, Zhang, Wu, He, and Johns 2020). The hardware conscious computing is preferred when there is a fixed set of hardware on which different datasets have to be evaluated, e.g., LHC (Large Hadron Collider) (CERN 2020) whereas this is not the case in heterogeneous computing where hardware varies. The consciousness should me more towards platform-independent parallelism. The most crucial computing resources for big data are memory and parallel hardware (Khanna, Goyal, Verma, and Joshi, 2018). The query deployment uses sketch data structure to answer the query in hyperlog. We have used such deployment to answer the queries in real time or near-real time (Singh, Paprzycki, Bhargava, Chhabra, Kaushal, and Kumar 2018b).

The scope of machine learning in query handling is significant and used for optimizing query. Data mining and machine learning applications focus on maximizing submodular functions under cardinality constraints. Algorithm for $1/2 - \varepsilon$ approximation and $1/3 - \varepsilon$ approximation of the optimum is proposed using sublinear space in window size (Epasto, Lattanzi, Vassilvitskii, and Zadimoghaddam 2017). The sublinear space will not suffice for big data, a step ahead to be taken for making sketch in hyperlog space. Solving a problem in fixed window size is always a priority with desired complexity of log, polylog, or hyperlog space. Large scale optimization problem on massive datasets is solved in a resource efficient manner (Kumar, Sharma, and Mishra 2019) (Assadi 2018). Three types of task running strategies are there in parallel computing listed as Parallel AND, Parallel OR and Probabilistic Fork. The parallel task execution must be sequential (Vakilinia, Zhang, Qiu 2016). We have also optimized massive datasets in a window arrival manner and then used sketch technique in parallel manner which is better than the techniques studied so far. The summary sketch uses the data structure capable of handling count of elements appearing in the window stream.

3 Proposed Work

The stream is ingested for analysis and for answering the questions of type like what happened, when happened, and how happened. The Massive Data Stream Processing Architecture is proposed (see Fig. 1).

The figure shows the steps involved between stream generation and actionable insight with all possible combinations. The answers received from these questions are then used

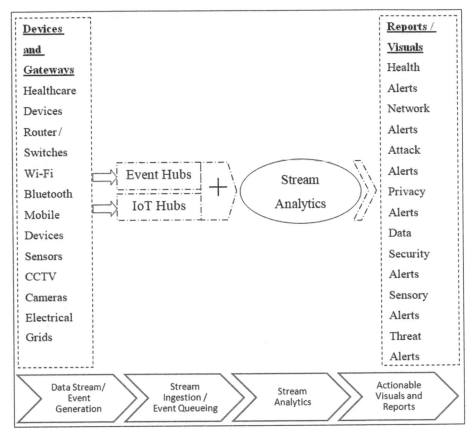

Fig. 1. The proposed massive data stream processing architecture

to answer the new questions like what will happen next, when it will happen again, and how to stop loss. The answers of this step are used to generate notifications and alerts for actions. In response to analysis, one might want to send command or data:

- To switch on alarm
- To change device setting if analytics application has administrative rights
- To power grids for power management like shutting down the grid or transferring load to other grids
- To dashboards for human action
- To ambulance for patient pickup
- To mobile users for data theft or security threat
- To data lakes for storage

3.1 Data Stream

Streams are generated from various devices like sensors, CCTV cameras, healthcare devices, Bluetooth, WiFi etc. Various events are also generated which comes as stream and hence this phase is also known as Event Generation.

3.2 Stream Ingestion

In this phase stream ingestion is performed based on the data sources. Event Hubs and IoT Hubs are used to perform this step.

Event Hubs
This is a data ingestion service for real-time data that is scalable. The sources stream millions of events per second and builds data pipeline to give response to business challenges quickly and in real time.

IoT Hubs
This is a data ingestion service for real-time data from Internet of Things. The sources are embedded devices deployed at various locations geographically. Either each device or a master device streams data in megabytes or sometimes gigabytes per second.

3.3 Stream Analytics

This phase analyzes the data ingested through IoT Hubs and Event Hubs with the help of proposed algorithm which is devised for big data analysis.

3.4 Actionable Visuals

The graphs, plots and dynamic dashboards are generated in this phase for human under-standable visuals. The human may then generate reports or fire an event or alarm manually. We devised an algorithm for the identified problem. Its known to us that memory (Random Access Memory) is hardware and cannot be scaled up or down frequently as per requirement of big data processing applications. Big data may fit into the memory at once or may get flooded. The availability of memory is not possible at times due to other critical programs running in memory. These critical programs lock the memory and thus memory chunks/blocks cannot be swapped. This situation requires a technique that may use disk whenever required as virtual memory. Although the concept of virtual memory already exist but works according to predefined operating system algorithms. There is a requirement of algorithm that can work according to demand of the program and may retain and process big data in memory, with varying velocity, in less than a unit.

3.5 Proposed Algorithm

The processing of data for streams has to be done infinitely but with constant memory and time complexity for a particular model. The algorithm constructs Big Table (ι) in memory and maintains ι_m as five-tuple metadata. The metadata contains η as dataset info, $ч_r$ as number of rows, $ч_c$ as number of columns and ω as width of stride. The big table contains metadata and data approximation (δ). The metadata returns approximate recently used values (ψ) or deep dive into δ. The hash key h_k is generated from a hash function. The value (v) is calculated and updated at h_k for item i in δ. The algorithm devised is stated as follows:

Algorithm
Initialize, $\iota \leftarrow \phi$
$\iota_m \leftarrow (\eta, ч_r, ч_c, \omega, s)$
$\iota \leftarrow (\iota_m, \delta)$
If q in ι_m:
return ψ
    else:
        fork t for each i in δ:
          if $h_k(i)$ in δ_i:
            return $v(h_k)$
          else:
            return ϕ
        join t

Like, if there is a query for k variables/features/columns only, then binary data of those k columns will be loaded and processed. The analysis is done in read only mode and hence does not require any update in already existing pre-processed data residing in memory in the data table.

3.6 Deployment

The issues and steps while deploying streaming application are given below:

1. Prepare a cluster (C) with cluster manager (CM).

2. Configure sufficient memory (SM) capable of handling stream in windows. The size of memory depends on the velocity (f) of the data. If the rate of data is in kilo bits per second (Kbps), and the size of window is Ψ, number of windows to be stored for processing at a time is η, then memory required μ is defined as:

$$\mu \geq \eta\psi \, kb$$

On arrival of new data stream, new window is created and the dated window slides out to either discard or to store in data-lake. The memory requirement, thus, remains same for the lifetime of application.

3. Cluster write-ahead logs are configured for fault tolerance.

4 Experiments and Results

Experiments performed to evaluate the proposed approach and algorithm. The dataset Yelp Review (Kaggle 2019) of 10 GB, is used for logging results. The available memory of the system is 8 GB, out of which 4.5 GB is free for user processes.

The performance of data stream algorithm is measured by the number of passes on stream. Assuming that we are passing the stream only once, the space consumed by algorithm is log (log (n)). The absolute error calculated on data sizes of 10 MB, 100 MB and 1 GB (see Fig. 2).

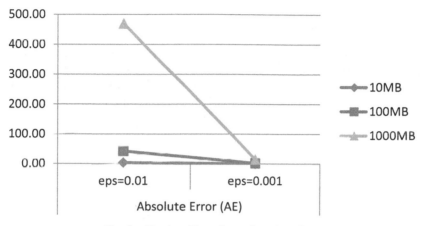

Fig. 2. Absolute Error for various data sizes

The relative error calculated on data sizes of 10 MB, 100 MB and 1 GB (see Fig. 3). It is clearly visible that relative error rapidly decreases with the increase in confidence. The 99.9% accuracy is enough expectation in big data processing because of the exhaustion of computing resources. Appropriate computation is avoided in big data due to volumi-nous data with elephant flows. Big data definition says the size of data that exhaust the resources, no matter how efficient and effective computing resources are there.

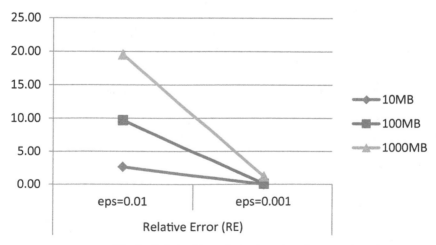

Fig. 3. Relative Error for various data sizes

Accuracy is the significant key factor in approximation algorithms and stated as ($\mathcal{E}$, δ) approximation. The devised algorithm achieves an error of less than $\mathcal{E}$ with probability 0.99. The algorithm optimization does not cover speed up factor rather the focus is on minimization of error and space requirement. The results show significant achievements in these areas.

4.1 Results and Findings

The memory requirement is hyper logarithmic and is better than poly logarithmic for all other algorithms stated so far. The relative error shows that if $\mathcal{E} = 0.01$ then confidence is 99% and at this confidence, the error at 1 GB data is 1.19 which is acceptable in big data computing. Moreover, the use of wisely chosen hashing algorithms has made it possible.

5 Conclusion

The results show that the memory requirement for the high volume data is very less. On arrival of new data stream, new window is created and the dated window slides out to either discard or to store in data-lake. The memory requirement, thus, remains same for the lifetime of application. The algorithm acquires hyper-log space in memory at the confidence of 99%. The execution time may be reduced using GPU. The algorithm will work well for distributed architectures due to its nature of parallelism.

References

Assadi, S.: Combinatorial optimization on massive datasets: streaming, distributed, and massively parallel computation. Ph.D. Thesis, University of Pennsylvania, Philadelphia (2018)

CERN. Retrieved from CERN Accelerating Sciences (2020). https://home.cern/science/accelerators/large-hadron-collider

Corp, I.B.: Patent No. 8,392,398. Washington, DC (2013)

Epasto, A., Lattanzi, S., Vassilvitskii, S., Zadimoghaddam, M.: Submodular optimization over sliding windows. In: 26th International Conference on World Wide Web, p. 421430 (2017)

Kaggle. Yelp Dataset. Retrieved July 24, 2020, from kaggle.com (2019). https://www.kaggle.com/yelp-dataset/yelp-dataset

Khanna, A., Goyal, R., Verma, M., Joshi, D.: Intelligent traffic management system for smart cities. In: Singh, P.K., Paprzycki, M., Bhargava, B., Chhabra, J.K., Kaushal, N.C., Kumar, Y. (eds.) FTNCT 2018. CCIS, vol. 958, pp. 152–164. Springer, Singapore (2019). https://doi.org/10.1007/978-981-13-3804-5_12

Kreps, J.: Retrieved from O'Reilly (2014). https://www.oreilly.com/ideas/questioning-the-lambda-architecture

Kumar, V., Sharma, D.K., Mishra, V.K.: Mille Cheval framework: A GPU-based in-memory high-performance computing framework for accelerated processing of big-data streams. J. Supercomput. (2020). https://doi.org/10.1007/s11227-020-03508-3

Kumar, V., Sharma, D.K., Mishra, V.K.: Predicting manufacturing feasibility using context analysis. In: Elçi, A., Sa, P.K., Modi, C.N., Olague, G., Sahoo, M.N., Bakshi, S. (eds.) Smart Computing Paradigms: New Progresses and Challenges. AISC, vol. 767, pp. 125–130. Springer, Singapore (2020). https://doi.org/10.1007/978-981-13-9680-9_9

Mencagli, G., Dazzi, P., Tonci, N.: Spinstreams: a static optimization tool for data stream processing applications. In: Proceedings of the 19th International Middleware Conference, p. 6679 (2018)

Singh, A., Garg, S., Batra, S., Kumar, N., Rodrigues, J.J.: Bloom filter based optimization scheme for massive data handling in IoT environment. Future Gener. Comput. Syst. **82**, 440–449 (2018)

Singh, N., Tripathi, A., Kumar, V.: Production prediction based on News using sentimental analysis. In: 4th International Conference on Information Systems and Computer Networks (ISCON), p. 3236 (2019)

Singh, P., Paprzycki, M., Bhargava, B., Chhabra, J., Kaushal, N., Kumar, Y.: Futuristic trends in network and communication technologies. Commun. Comput. Inf. Sci. **958**, 141–166 (2018)

Singh, P., Sood, S., Kumar, Y., Paprzycki, M., Pljonkin, A., Hong, W.C.: Futuristic trends in networks and computing technologies. Commun. Comput. Inf. Sci. **1206**, 3–707 (2019)

University, H.: Retrieved from Sketching Algorthms for Big Data (2017). https://www.sketching bigdata.org/fall17/

Vakilinia, S., Zhang, X., Qiu, D.: Analysis and optimization of big-data stream processing. In: IEEE Global Communications Conference (GLOBECOM), p. 16 (2016)

Wu, J., Kobbelt, L.: A stream algorithm for the decimation of massive meshes. Graphics interface **3**, 185–192 (2003)

Zhang, S., Zhang, F., Wu, Y., He, B., Johns, P.: Hardware-conscious stream processing: A survey. ACM SIGMOD Record **48**(4), 18–29 (2020)

Zhou, Y., Aberer, K., Tan, K.L.: Toward massive query optimization in large-scale distributed stream systems. In: Issarny, V., Schantz, R. (eds.) Middleware 2008. Middleware 2008. Lecture Notes in Computer Science, vol 5346. Springer, Heidelberg (2008). https://doi.org/https://doi.org/10.1007/978-3-540-89856-6_17

A Proposal for Early Detection of Heart Disease Using a Classification Model

Sarita Mishra[✉] ⓘ, Manjusha Pandey ⓘ, Siddharth Swarup Rautaray ⓘ, and Mahendra Kumar Gourisaria ⓘ

Kalinga Institute of Industrial Technology (Deemed To Be University), Bhubaneswar, Odisha, India
{1964006,manjushafcs,siddharthfcs}@kiit.ac.in,
mkgourisaria2010@gmail.com

Abstract. The rapid evolution in the human lifestyle, starting from food habits to resting patterns and many others such as drinking, smoking, etc. has paved way for not only the aged people but also the younger ones towards various types of heart diseases. This fact has presented a big challenge in front of health practitioners and also data scientists to handle successfully such enormous amounts of data generated at a rapid rate. In order to face this challenge, the technology is advancing day by day and simultaneously the biological pathology is also improving and becoming more efficient with every passing day. This paper focuses on several features of people such as the age, sex, cp, trestbps, chol, fbs, restecg, thalac, exang, oldpeak, slope, ca, thal, and eventually predicts the patient's health status mentioning preventive measures to avoid any risk of cardiovascular disease (CVD). The Cleveland Heart disease dataset is taken from the UCI Repository for the research purpose of this paper. It presents a comparitive analysis of three different machine learning based algorithms; Logistic Regression, Naïve Bayes, and Random Forest that are implemented with the One-vs-all approach for multiclass classification of the target attribute of the dataset. With the help of this model, data scientists predict the health condition of the person, and the results are notified to the patient and the concerned physician. The output is a multiclass classification which will give values ranging between 0 to 4 with 0 indicating the absence of any heart problem, 1 indicates slight abnormal behaviour in the heart's functioning, and so on with class 4 indicating a critical state. The results of this paper shows that out of the three algorithms used in this research, the Random forest algorithm gives the highest accuracy of 89.13%.

Keywords: CVD · One-vs-All algorithm · Logistic regression · Naïve Bayes · Random Forest

1 Introduction

The heart is a muscular organ whose role is to pump oxygenated blood throughout the entire body. It constitutes the principal element of the body. It accumulates the deoxygenated blood from the body in the left ventricle and transmits it to the lungs

© Springer Nature Singapore Pte Ltd. 2021
P. K. Singh et al. (Eds.): FTNCT 2020, CCIS 1395, pp. 360–367, 2021.
https://doi.org/10.1007/978-981-16-1480-4_32

through the left auricle. The lungs oxygenate the blood and transmit it to the right auricle, which spreads it throughout the body via the right ventricle. The below Fig. 1 depicts this working of the heart.

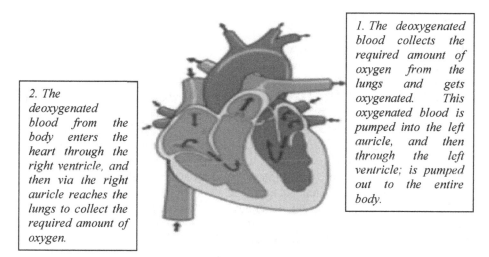

2. The deoxygenated blood from the body enters the heart through the right ventricle, and then via the right auricle reaches the lungs to collect the required amount of oxygen.

1. The deoxygenated blood collects the required amount of oxygen from the lungs and gets oxygenated. This oxygenated blood is pumped into the left auricle, and then through the left ventricle; is pumped out to the entire body.

Fig. 1. Working of the Heart

Heart disease, also known as Cardiovascular Disease (CVD) has become one of the major reasons behind the increasing mortality rate all over the world. According to the World Health Organization (WHO), stroke and heart attack have led to (24%) of death in India [1].

A heart attack generally occurs when the blood flow towards the heart gets blocked due to the presence of a blood clot. In most of the cases, people tend to survive through the first heart attack and continue to live according to their daily lifestyle. But, a heart attack requires a person to make some changes in their lifestyle which affects their food habits, resting patterns and also may include some exercises and medications, if suggested by their physicians. CVD can be stopped from leading to fatal conditions if properly taken care of and taking conscious measures to prevent it. This demands early detection of the chances of a person being affected by heart disease. Such early detection and prediction of CVD demand the efficient health data handling [2] followed by the development and application of various machine learning models.

Many data scientists have researched and come up with several models to predict the same. This paper presents a comparison of Logistic Regression, Naïve Bayes, and Random Forests algorithms with the One-vs-all approach. The results of this research work is presented in terms of the accuracy that each of the algorithm provides in classifying the testing data points of the Cleveland Heart Disease dataset. Accuracy in prediction is defined as the ratio between the number of data points that are correctly classified to the total number of data points that are classified.

The paper is further arranged as follows. Section 2 presents, in brief, the previous works regarding the prediction of heart disease. Section 3 explains working of the model, the dataset used, and the algorithms used in this paper. Section 4 shows the obtained results and the paper finally concludes in Section 5 with Sect. 6 hinting towards the future research works that be done based on this research work.

2   Literature Review

Till date, many researchers have developed multiple classification models for classifying the healthcare data, that have proved to be efficient classifier models. Few of their research works are discussed here.

Kirsi Varpa et al. in 2011 [3], in their paper have compared the One-vs-all and One-vs-one approaches for KNN and SVM algorithms in making predictions about the Otoneurological dataset. Their results show that these two binary classifier methods have performed much better than the multiclass classifiers built from the same algorithms. Also, in their work KNN algorithm has shown the highest accuracy than all other classifiers. Hin Wai Lui et al. in 2018 [4], have build an Myocardial Infaction multiclass classifier combining the convolutional neural network with the recurrent neural network that can be embedded into wearable ECG devices. This model was able to schieve an accuracy of 97.2% and a sensitivity of 92.4%.

Musfiq Ali et al. in 2019 [5], have performed classification on a heart disease dataset with four different machine learning based algorithms and compared their performances based on the accuracies they provided. The four algorithms used were Decision Trees, Random Forest SVM, and Gaussian Naive Bayes. According to their results, Gaussian Naive Bayes and Random Forest gave the highest accuarcy of 91.21% while Decision tree showed the lowest accuracy of 84.62%. Also in 2019, Anurag Kumar Verma et al. [6], categorized skin disease into six classes namely psoriasis, seborrheic dermatitis, lichen planus, pityriasis rosea, chronic dermatitis, and pityriasis rubra. They have used six different machine learning classification algorithms to build their ensembles by bagging, Adaboost, and Gradient Boosting to classify the patients into one of the six categories of skin disease. They were able to observe the significant improvement in the predictive accuracy of the ensembled multiclass classifier when compared with the individual classifiers.

3   Dataset and Algorithms Used

Till date, there has not been too many models developed for the multiclass classification of heart disease patients. This paper is based on a dataset of CVD patients classifying them into five distinct categories. The below Fig. 2 depicts the proposed model's workflow.

As shown in the figure below, the first task in the proposed model is *data collection*. For this paper, the data is collected from the Cleveland Heart disease dataset that is obtained from the UCI Repository. The dataset includes features [7] such as age, sex indicating the age and gender of the patient respectively. The next feature is CP that is the chest pain type. Chest pain can sometimes be considered as a dangerous condition if the pain is accompanied by chest tightness, heaviness, or a crushing sensation or if the pain is followed by weakness, nausea, shortness of breath, sweating, dizziness, or

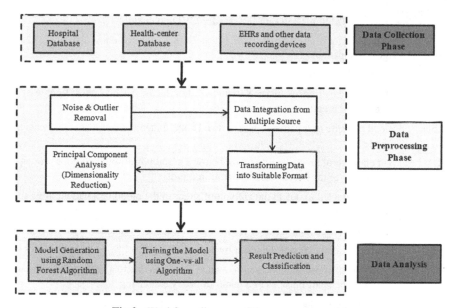

Fig.2. Workflow diagram of the proposed model

fainting. Another feature that is considered is the trestbps that is the blood pressure of a person while at rest. The trestbps value within the range 60 to 100 beats per minute indicates the proper functioning of the heart. The next feature is cholesterol, which when increases beyond a certain threshold value can lead to various obstructions in the proper functioning of the heart. Fasting blood sugar (fbs) is a test conducted to detect the amount of sugar in the blood of a patient after an overnight fast. An fbs value of less than 120 mg/dl can be considered as normal. Restecg and thalach refer to measuring the electrical functionality and maximum heart rate achieved by a person's heart. Exang refers to exercise-induced angina which is caused due to a reduction in blood supply to the heart muscles as a result of heavy exercising. Thalassemia is a disease caused due to lack of haemoglobin in the body. Some other features that are considered in the prediction of heart disease include oldpeak, slope, and ca (number of major blood vessels ranging from 0 to 3). The below Table 1 summarizes the aforementioned features that are taken into consideration while predicting the heart disease status for a patient.

After the reduced dataset is obtained, it is partitioned into two parts. 70% of the dataset is considered as the *training dataset* and the remaining 30% as the *testing dataset.* After the dataset with reduced dimensionality is obtained, we need to *create the model* which will predict the patient's health status and classify him in one of the five categories (0: absence of heart disease, 1: slight problem in normal functioning of the heart, 2: a condition worse than stage 1, but can be handled with proper physical activity and diet, 3: needs proper diagnosis and require medication, and 4: denotes a critical state). This paper proposes the creation of the model using the three different algorithms: Logistic regression, Naïve Bayes, and Random Forest using the One-vs-all approach.

The *Logistic Regression* is a machine learning based algorithm generally used for binary classification. However, it can also be used for multiclass classification with the

Table 1. Relevant features for CVD prediction.

Age	Age of the patient
Sex	Gender of the patient
cp	Chest pain experienced by the patient based on factors such as chest tightness, shortness of breath, sweating, etc.
trestbps	Blood pressure of a patient while at rest. Proper range is from 60 to 100 beats per minute
chol	Bad cholesterol level should remain below a certain threshold value for proper functioning of the heart. (measurement in mg/dl)
fbs	A test conducted to detect the amount of sugar in the blood of a patient after an overnight fast. Normal when less than 120 mg/dl
restecg	Pattern generated as a result of recording the electrical functionality of the heart
Thalach	The maximum heart rate achieved by a person's heart
Exang	It refers to exercise-induced angina which is caused due to a reduction in blood supply to the heart muscles as a result of heavy exercising
Oldpeak	ST depression induced by exercise relative to rest ('ST' relates to positions on the ECG plot.)
Slope	The slope of the peak exercise ST segment
Ca	Number of major vessels (range 0–3)
Thal	Thalassemia is a disease caused due to lack of haemoglobin in the body
Target	Heart disease detection result

One-vs-all approach i.e. by building multiple binary classifier models of the same. The logistic regression algorithm uses a sigmoidal function to predict the probability of a data point belonging to a particular class [8]. The probability can be estimated by.

$$P = 1/\left(1 + e^{-z}\right) \tag{1}$$

where $z = b_0 + bx + bx + \ldots$ that is the linear combination of the independent attributes of the dataset. *Naïve Bayes* is another easy-to-use machine learning based algorithm used for both binary and multiclass classification. It assumes complete independence between every two features of the dataset [9]. This algorithm can be used for large datasets and it follows the Baye's theorem that can be represented as follows:

$$P(\text{label}|\text{features}) = (P(\text{label}) * P(\text{feature}|\text{label}))/P(\text{features}) \tag{2}$$

Where P(label) is the prior probability of label, P(label|features) P(featureslabel) is the prior probability of a data point belonging to a particular label and P(features) is the prior probability that a specific featureset has occurred [10].

Random Forest, as suggested by its name, is a collection of multiple decision trees [10]. This algorithm generates a number of decision trees each having its own subset of features and training data points. Based on these feature subset and training tuples, each tree comes up with its own outcome. But the random forest algorithm chooses the outcome of the tree that gives best prediction by majority voting [11].

One-vs-All approach based multiclass classifier model is developed by building 'n' number of binary classifiers using the above algorithms where 'n' is the number of classes in the target variable of the dataset. For this research work, 'n' is equal to 5. Each of the binary classifier is dedicated to one class, which the classifier considers to be 1 and all other classes to be 0. The binary classifier thus makes predictions about a data point belonging to a particular class. The One-vs-all algorithm is given below.

Algorithm: One-vs-all for multi-class classifier

Inputs: Training algorithm L
Dataset X
Class labels vector y = [1....k]
Main:
1: For i = 1 to k:
(a)   Create a new binary vector y_i for each label where y_i = 1 if it belongs to label i and y_i = 0 otherwise.
Output: Final Prediction

---

4   Results

The results obtained from this research work imply that the Random Forest algorithm gives the highest accuracy of 89.13% with the One-vs-all approach for multiclass classification of the target variable of the Cleveland Heart Disease dataset, followed by Logistic Regression and Naïve Bayes with 86.74% and 85.65% respectively. The below Table 2 gives the accuracies of the algorithms used.

Table 2. Accuracies of the algorithms used

Algorithm	Accuracy (%)
Naïve bayes	85.65217
Logistic regression	86.73913
Random forest	89.13043

The following Figs. 3 and 4 represent the line graph and bar plot comparison of the accuracies obtained by the Naïve Bayes, Logistic Regression, and Random Forest algorithms.

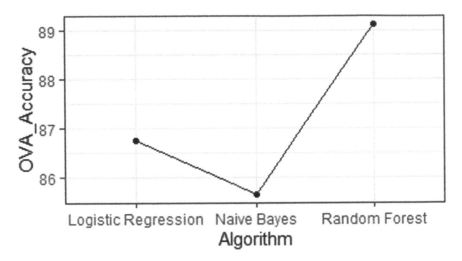

Fig. 3. Line graph of the Accuracies obtained

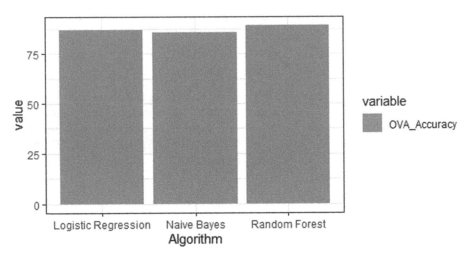

Fig. 4. Bar plot for the Accuracies obtained

5   Conclusion

The rapidly increasing mortality rate throughout the globe due to heart disease patients each year has led to the emergence of developing better models for prediction and identification of CVD symptoms in people and alerting the patient and their physician immediately so that appropriate actions can be taken to prevent the disease or to eradicate it if the person is already a victim. So, in order to serve the purpose, the paper has presented a comparative analysis of three machine learning based models created using the One-vs-all approach to categorize into distinct classes the people who are suffering from heart disease based on the level of criticality in their conditions so that each of them can be provided services by their physicians based on their condition. The results have shown that Random Forest has shown the best performance with an accuarcy of 89.13% followed by Naïve Bayes and Logistic Regression.

6   Future Work

As an extension to this research work, the future data scientists can apply the One-vs-all technique on several other algorithms that could provide better accuracies. Also, the same can be applied on various ensembles of these algorithms that may give even higher accuracy values. Further, different feature engineering techniques can be applied on the dataset to enhance the model's predictive performance.

References

1. Latha, C.B.C., Jeeva, S.C.: Improving the accuracy of prediction of heart disease risk based on ensemble classification techniques. Inform. Med. Unlocked. **16** 100203 (2019). https://doi.org/10.1016/j.imu.2019.100203
2. Baitharu, T.R., Pani, S.K.: Analysis of data mining techniques for healthcare decision support system using liver disorder dataset. Procedia Comput. Sci. **85**, 862–870 (2016)
3. Varpa, K., Joutsijoki, H., Iltanen, K., Juhola, M.: Applying one-vs-one and one-vs-all classifiers in k-nearest neighbour method and support vector machines to an otoneurological multiclass problem. In: Article In Studies In Health Technology And Informatics, pp. 579-583 (2011). 10.3233l978-1-60750-806-9-579
4. Lui, H.W., Chow, K.L.: Multiclass classification of myocardial infarction with convolutional and recurrent neural networks for portable ECG devices. Inform. Med. Unlocked **13**, 26–33 (2018)
5. Ali, M., Khan, M.I., Imran, M.A., Siddiki, M.: Heart disease prediction using machine learning algorithms (2019)
6. Verma, A.K., Pal, S., Kumar, S.: Comparison of skin disease prediction by feature selection using ensemble data mining techniques. Inform. Med. Unlocked **16**, 100202 (2019). https://doi.org/10.1016/j.imu.2019.1002.02
7. Saxena, K., Sharma, R.: Efficient heart disease prediction system. Procedia Comput. Sci. **85,** 962–969 (2016). https://doi.org/10.1016/j.procs.2016.05.288
8. Bagley, S.C., White, H., Golomb, B.A.: Logistic regression in the medical literature:: standards for use and reporting, with particular attention to one medical domain. J. Clin. Epidemiol. **54**(10), 979–985 (2001). https://doi.org/10.1016/s0895-4356(01)00372-9
9. Salmi, N.: Rustam: Z.: Naïve bayes classifier models for predicting the colon cancer. In: IOP Conference Series: Material Science And Engineering vol. 546, p. 052068 (2019). https://doi.org/10.1088/1757-899X/546/5/052068
10. Mishra, S., Pandey, M., Rautaray, S.S., Gourisaria, M.K.: A survey on big data analytical tools and techniques in healthcare sector. Int. J. Emerg. Technol. **11**(3), 554–560 (2020)
11. Lebedev, A.V., Westman, E., Van Westen, G.J.P.: Random Forest ensembles for detection and prediction of Alzheimer's disease with a good between-cohort robustness. NeuroImage: Clinical, 6, 115–125 (2014). https://doi.org/10.1016/j.nicl.2014.08.023

Analysis of Using the Fuzzy Intervals Apparatus for Applied Tasks

Alexander Bozhenyuk$^{(\boxtimes)}$ (ID), Olesiya Kosenko (ID), Evgeny Kosenko (ID), and Margarita Knyazeva (ID)

Southern Federal University, Nekrasovsky str. 44, 347922 Taganrog, Russia

Abstract. This article examines the transport and logistics system and analyzes the methods of assignment the initial data. One of the main parameters when designing a new, or planning the activities of an existing system, is demand. The adequacy of the obtained solution depends on the correct determination of the demand. The paper considers non-deterministic methods for specifying the initial data. It is shown that the apparatus of fuzzy-interval specification of the data of the transport and logistics system is an adequate scheme for solving the problem, taking into account the factors that introduce uncertainty. The application of the extended maximum operation and the operation of adding fuzzy intervals $(L\text{–}R)$–type are considered. The analysis of the feasibility of using each operation for a specific case in determining the demand of the transport and logistics system. A methodology for assessing demand is proposed for the possibility of effective planning of the transport and logistics system.

Keywords: Transport and logistics system · Demand · Non-deterministic value · Probability · Fuzzy set · Fuzzy interval · Fuzzy number

1 Introduction

In a market economy, the main task of enterprises is to increase the competitiveness of products. The level of competitiveness is determined by its quality, the costs of organizing production, which includes such economic indicators as reducing the time for delivering materials and components, determining the optimal volume of their stock, etc. Systemic and methodological approaches to the issues of process management of industrial complexes are closely related to changes in the internal and external environment of organizations operating in the transport and logistics complex.

The main parameters characterizing the transport and logistics system are the cost of transporting a unit of production, the amount of demand for products, the available stock of products, etc. The absence of deficit and surplus of resources are the defining requirements for the parameters in such a system. An effective solution to any problem depends on an adequate interpretation of the input and output data of the system. At the same time, the problem of the formation of the efficient operation of the transport and logistics system refers to the problems of optimization in conditions of uncertainty [1]. To optimize the supply problem, it is necessary to estimate the demand. A realistic

© Springer Nature Singapore Pte Ltd. 2021
P. K. Singh et al. (Eds.): FTNCT 2020, CCIS 1395, pp. 368–378, 2021.
https://doi.org/10.1007/978-981-16-1480-4_33

assessment of demand is complicated by factors that introduce significant uncertainty and fuzziness of the final values, which requires the use of methods that operate on inaccurate data.

For a long time, the uncertainty models used in parameter estimation and identification had a stochastic or probabilistic nature, based on the known distributions of the quantities under consideration. But in many practical situations there is not enough information to consider uncertain factors obeying any probabilistic model, or these factors may not satisfy one or another condition imposed on them by the probabilistic uncertainty model [2]. Such requirements are the requirements for the independence of the initial values or a special form of their distributions, etc.

At present, the interval representation of uncertainty factors is attracting more and more attention of engineers, as the least restrictive and most adequate to many practical formulations of problems [3–9].

2 Setting Demand Parameters Under Uncertainty

An essential attribute of any production activity is the need to make decisions related to the best choice. This problem is relevant when it is impossible to accurately assess the planned demand and, as a consequence, costs. The problem of the best solution arises if the number of alternatives is greater than one. Moreover, the problem of choosing the best solution from the set of feasible ones can be described in terms of the preferences of some solutions over others. Decision-making problems in which the preference relation is described in the form of a utility function are called mathematical programming problems [10]. At the same time, two directions can be distinguished in mathematical programming. The first direction includes problems with deterministic initial data, that is, all the initial information required for a solution is fully defined. The second direction includes problems in which the initial information contains elements of uncertainty. In this case, methods for solving problems in cases where some parameters are random variables with known distribution laws are combined into a class of stochastic programming problems. If the problem statement contains imprecise, indefinite elements, the description of which uses the theory of fuzzy sets, then this is a fuzzy mathematical programming problem. The vagueness in the formulation of such problems can be contained both in the description of the set of alternatives and in the specification of the utility function.

The formal statement of the transport type mathematical programming problem is as follows.

– There are I points of sources (producers) of products, where a_i ($i = 1,2,...,I$) is a set that determines the distribution of products by producers or suppliers, and J points of consumption of these products, where b_j ($j = 1,2,...,J$) is a set that specifies needs, that is, the demand for a certain product. A matrix of costs $C = (c_{ij})$ is given, where c_{ij} is the cost of moving a unit of production from the i-th source to the j-th consumer. The matrix $X = (x_{ij})$ defines the vector of the quantity of products intended for transportation from the i-th source to the j-th consumer. The problem is to find a matrix $X = (x_{ij})$ that minimizes the total cost of transportation:

$$F(X) = \sum_{i=1}^{I} \sum_{j=1}^{J} c_{ij} x_{ij} \rightarrow min, \tag{1}$$

under conditions:

$$\sum_{i=1}^{I} x_{ij} = b_j, \ (j = \overline{1, I}),$$

$$\sum_{i=1}^{I} x_{ij} = a_i, \ (i = \overline{1, I}),$$

$$x_{ij} \geq 0, \ i = \overline{1, I}, \ (j = \overline{1, I}).$$

Demand forecasting includes quantitative methods such as the use of statistically accumulated sales data. As a rule, the apparatus of the theory of probability is used to solve problems with accumulated statistical data. But when defining logistic problems with stochastic demand, it is necessary to correctly take into account the uncertainty of demand, based on information technology for collecting and processing the corresponding real data. For each consumer, demand is a random variable, relative to which the mathematical expectation and variance are statistically determined. When determining the demand for each consumer, taking into account the permissible probabilities of the occurrence of an unsold balance of goods and its shortage, we determine the minimum and maximum values of demand [9]:

$$\int_0^{b_{jmin}} \frac{\Theta}{\sigma_j^2} exp\left\{-\frac{\Theta^2}{2\sigma_j^2}\right\} d\Theta = \alpha, j = 1, 2, \ldots, n,$$

$$\int_{b_{jmax}}^{\infty} \frac{\Theta}{\sigma_j^2} exp\left\{-\frac{\Theta^2}{2\sigma_j^2}\right\} d\Theta = \alpha, j = 1, 2, \ldots, n,$$

where α is some rather small probability (for example, $\alpha = 0.05$); Θ is a random value of the demand parameter.

As a result of solving these equations, we get the minimum and maximum values of demand:

$$b_{jmin} = \sigma_j(-2\ln(1-\alpha))\frac{1}{2}, j = 1, 2, \ldots, n, \ \ b_{jmax} = \sigma_j(-2\ln\alpha)\frac{1}{2}, j = 1, 2, \ldots, n.$$

In this case, the components of the vector $X = (x_1, x_2, \ldots, x_n)$, which determines the plan of transportation of products from suppliers to manufacturers, must satisfy the constraint:

$$b_{jmin} \leq x_j \leq b_{jmax}, j = 1, 2, \ldots, n.$$

In this case, the apparatus of mathematical statistics is used to solve the problem. The obvious disadvantage is that the transport and logistics problem with uncertainty in demand is solved under the assumption that the distribution densities of random demand are known. The vulnerability of this hypothesis is obvious, since real demand is a non-stationary process, the parameters of which depend on many factors (season, day of the week, etc.). Therefore, the application of probability theory in a number of situations is not correct and reasonable enough [11]. The reason for this is the lack of available data, which does not allow us to establish with a sufficient degree of confidence the adequacy of the probabilistic model chosen to describe the situation. In the absence of statistical data, the determination of demand is carried out using expert estimates. In such conditions, there is a need for other, different from probabilistic, approaches to assessing the existing uncertainty. One of these approaches is based on the application of fuzzy set theory.

Fuzzy sets were defined by L. Zadeh in 1965 as a formal apparatus for processing natural language utterances [12]. On the other hand, fuzzy sets provide an expert with great flexibility in evaluating numerical indicators. For example, when answering the question, what will be the expected demand for a particular product, an expert can indicate pessimistic, optimistic and most probable estimates, and the information obtained can be combined in the form of a fuzzy interval.

In the works [13–16], conclusions about the indispensability of the apparatus of fuzzy sets were presented. Making an effective decision depends on the formulation of the problem. In particular, there are tasks in which:

– there are no specific initial data, and you can rely only on the experience and professionalism of the experts involved;
– only some of the characteristics of alternative options for possible situations are known, that is, the problem of making decisions under conditions of partial uncertainty.

By means of the theory of fuzzy sets, it is possible to strictly describe vague, not precisely defined objects, without formalization of which it is impossible to make significant progress in modeling intellectual processes. In this case, the fixation of specific parameter values is subjective. However, for expert methods, the nature of the measurements and the type of scale in which information is obtained from an expert and which determines the permissible type of operations used in expert assessment are important.

Planning technology in reality should take into account that demand is a non-deterministic quantity. In this case, both probabilistic models and the apparatus of fuzzy mathematics can be used to solve the planning problem.

Let the parameters with uncertainty be represented as fuzzy numbers. In this case, it is necessary to indicate that any parameters of the problem can be fuzzy. In a transport-type linear programming problem, function (1) usually determines the total cost of transportation and its components have a natural uncertainty. In vector form, the linear programming problem is written as follows:

$$F(X) = C^T X,$$

where.

$$C = \begin{pmatrix} c_1 \\ c_2 \\ c_n \end{pmatrix}, X = \begin{pmatrix} x_1 \\ x_2 \\ x_n \end{pmatrix}.$$

Let c_{ij} be fuzzy numbers with membership functions, which have the form:

$$\mu_j(c_j) = \exp\left\{ \frac{(c_j - \overline{c_j})^2}{2D_j} \right\}, j = 1, 2, \ldots, n.$$

Then the membership function of the criterion function of the problem under consideration will have the form:

$$\mu(y) = \mu[F(X)] = \exp\left\{ -\frac{(y - m(X))^2}{2D(X)} \right\},$$

here $m(X) = \sum_{j=1}^{n} \overline{c}_j x_j,\ D(X) = \sum_{j=1}^{n} D_j x_j^2.$

Using the procedure of transition from a fuzzy problem to a clear one, described in [9], we choose some fixed value of the membership level $\mu(y) = \alpha$, which corresponds to $y = y^*$, that is:

$$\exp\left\{ \frac{(y^* - m(x))^2}{2D(x)} \right\} = \alpha.$$

This implies: $(y^* - m(x))^2 = -2D(x)ln\alpha$. Choosing the value y^* from the condition:

$$y^*(x) = min\left\{ m(x) - (-2D(x)ln\alpha)^{0.5},\ m(x) + (-2D(x)ln\alpha)^{0.5} \right\},$$

we get:

$$y^*(x) = m(x) - (-2D(x)ln\alpha)^{0.5} = m(x) - D^{0.5}(x)\left(\ln\left(\frac{1}{\alpha^2}\right) \right)^{0.5}$$

$$= m(x) - kD^{0.5}(x) = \sum_{j=1}^{n} \overline{c}_j x_j - k\left(\sum_{j=1}^{n} d_j^2 x_j \right)^{0.5},\ k = \left(\ln\left(\frac{1}{\alpha^2}\right) \right)^{0.5}.$$

Then the original linear programming problem (1) can be reformulated as follows: find a vector $X^T = (x_1, x_2, ..., x_n)$ maximizing $y^*(x)$ on the set of constraints that correspond to the stated transport type problem. The use of this apparatus entails difficulties in solving the problem for newly created transport and logistics systems. This is due to the fact that when planning demand, there is not enough statistical data to determine the law of distribution of the quantity of demand as a fuzzy parameter. At the same time, it is also difficult to compare the relationship between the possible values of the demand value and the corresponding probabilities and to determine the variance of the demand parameters.

Thus, the above-described demand parameters can be specified for each of the product consumers by fuzzy functions with a rectangular membership function:

$$\mu(x_j) = \begin{cases} 1, x_j \in [b_{jmin}, b_{jmax}], \\ 0, x_j \notin [b_{jmin}, b_{jmax}]. \end{cases}$$

An example of such a function is shown in Fig. 1:

An extension of the concept of a fuzzy number is the concept of a fuzzy interval. In the general case, a fuzzy interval is a fuzzy value with a convex membership function [17–19]. This definition is general, which may complicate their practical use. From a computational point of view, it is convenient to use more specific definitions of fuzzy

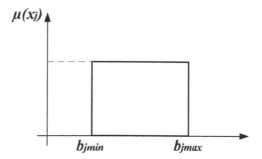

Fig. 1. Interval setting of the demand value

numbers and intervals in the form of analytical approximation using the so-called $(L–R)$ – functions. The resulting fuzzy numbers and intervals in the form $(L–R)$ – functions allow covering a fairly wide class of specific membership functions.

A fuzzy interval $(L\text{-}R)$-type is a fuzzy quantity $B = \{x, \mu_B(x)\}$, the membership function of which can be represented in the form of a composition of some L – function and some R – function as follows [18, 19]:

$$
\mu_B(x) = \begin{cases} L\left(\frac{a-x}{\alpha}\right), x \leq a \\ 1, a \leq x \leq b \\ R\left(\frac{x-b}{\beta}\right), x \geq b, \end{cases} \tag{2}
$$

where α, β – left and right fuzziness coefficients, respectively, determining the specific type of the membership function; a, b – respectively lower and upper modal values of the fuzzy interval.

The membership function (2) of a fuzzy interval $(L–R)$ – type is uniquely determined by the four of its parameters $\langle a, b, \alpha, \beta \rangle$. Fuzzy intervals $(L–R)$ – types are denoted as $B_{LR} = a, b, \alpha, \beta$. If $a = b$, then a fuzzy interval $(L–R)$ – type is a fuzzy number $(L–R)$ – type. Figure 2 shows a fuzzy interval $(L–R)$ – type:

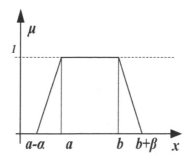

Fig. 2. Example of a fuzzy interval $(L–R)$ – type

Since fuzzy numbers and fuzzy intervals are fuzzy sets, all properties and all operations of interval mathematics and fuzzy sets are valid for them.

3   Mathematical Apparatus for Working with Fuzzy Intervals

The theory of fuzzy sets, in particular, fuzzy numbers, is a step towards the conjugation of classical exact mathematics and the imprecision of the real world. Their obvious incompatibility has led to the need to develop a new theory, a set of concepts in which inaccuracy is perceived as a universal reality of our life. In this case, in the aggregate, a certain complete and consistent system of rules for performing operations on objects of this theory is formed, that is, a special algebra.

When developing algebras over a set of fuzzy numbers, the so-called generalization principle is usually used, which allows one to transfer various mathematical operations from crisp sets to fuzzy ones. Since fuzzy numbers and intervals are fuzzy sets, all properties are true for them and all operations defined for fuzzy sets are feasible [9].

Analysis of transport and logistics systems showed that demand is the main characteristic, which is reflected in all subsystems (production, purchase, warehousing, transportation, sales, etc.) of this system. Demand is an indicator of how interested potential buyers are in a product or are determined to buy it. This value is quite variable and depends on a long list of factors: a specific period of time, purchasing power, economic situation, demographic component, climatic conditions, politics, etc. There are many ways to determine the demand for a product. Expert assessment methods are based on assessments of trends in the development of demand for individual goods in the future. These assessments can be given by highly qualified specialists who have extensive scientific and practical experience. Their main content lies in the rational organization of the expertise of the problem of forecasting demand and in the processing of the results of individual expert assessments.

Let us determine that it is advisable to assess the parameters of demand by experts using a fuzzy-interval apparatus. At the same time, it is proposed to carry out operations on fuzzy intervals in different ways.

Since the total demand is of decisive importance in transport and logistics problems, it is natural to consider the operations of adding fuzzy numbers, union of fuzzy sets, adding fuzzy intervals and the extended maximum operation for fuzzy intervals [18, 19].

Definition 1. The operation of adding fuzzy numbers (intervals), denoted as $\tilde{A} + \tilde{B} = \tilde{C} = \{z, \mu_{\tilde{C}}(z)\}$, where the membership function of the result $\mu_{\tilde{C}}(z)$ will be determined by the formula:

$$\mu_{\tilde{C}}(z) = sup\{min\{\{\mu_{\tilde{A}}(x), \mu_{\tilde{B}}(x)\}\}\}. \tag{3}$$

Definition 2. The union of two fuzzy sets A and B is understood as a fuzzy set C, with membership functions:

$$\mu_{\tilde{C}}(x) = \mu_{\tilde{A}\cup\tilde{B}} = max\{\mu_{\tilde{A}}(x), \mu_{\tilde{B}}(x)\}. \tag{4}$$

Definition 3. Algebraic union (algebraic sum) of two fuzzy sets A and B is called a fuzzy set C, the membership function of which is determined by the formula:

$$\mu_{\tilde{C}}(x) = \mu_{\tilde{A}}(x) + \mu_{\tilde{B}}(x) - \mu_{\tilde{A}}(x) * \mu_{\tilde{B}}(x). \tag{5}$$

The main practical advantage of the apparatus of fuzzy interval mathematics is the ability to carry out direct arithmetic operations with fuzzy interval numbers. Fuzzy interval mathematics can be seen as a generalization of the mathematics of ordinary intervals. At the same time, for practical application (3)−(5), it is necessary to determine the corresponding values to the membership function. For this, it is necessary to perform a study at the level of frequency distributions. In this regard, the problem arises of a reasonable transformation of frequency distributions into the corresponding fuzzy intervals. In the general case, fuzzy-interval mathematics can be reduced to the decomposition of fuzzy intervals into their constituent α-levels and to further operating with them within the framework of interval mathematics [20, 21].

Definition 4. The operation of addition of two fuzzy numbers (L–R) of type A and B is denoted as $A_{LR} + B_{LR} = C_{LR} = \langle a, b, \alpha, \beta \rangle$, here parameters a, b, α, β are defined as follows:

$$a = a_A + a_B, \quad b = b_A + b_B, \quad \alpha = \alpha_A + \alpha_B, \quad \beta = \beta_A + \beta_B. \tag{6}$$

Definition 5. The operation of the extended maximum for fuzzy intervals will make it possible to determine the parameters of the resulting fuzzy interval as:

$$
\begin{aligned}
a &= \max(a_A, a_B), \quad b = \max(b_A, b_B), \\
\alpha &= a - \min(a_A - \alpha_A, a_B - \alpha_B), \\
\beta &= \min(b_A + \beta_A, b_B + \beta_B).
\end{aligned}
\tag{7}
$$

4 Practical Problem Solving

Let a certain area S with three sub-areas of product consumption A, B, C, shown in Fig. 3 [22], be given:

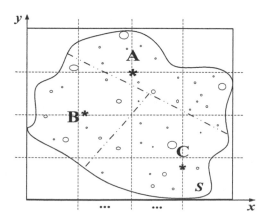

Fig. 3. Demand area example

According to expert estimates, these subareas have the following demand values, given in the form of fuzzy intervals: $A_{LR} = \langle 4, 6, 2, 5 \rangle$, $B_{LR} = \langle 4, 11, 3, 3 \rangle$, $C_{LR} = \langle 6, 8, 4, 2 \rangle$. Let us determine the total demand for area S for the possibility of further planning the activities of the transport and logistics system.

In a graphical interpretation, the demand values of the three sub-areas in the form of fuzzy intervals are shown in Fig. 4:

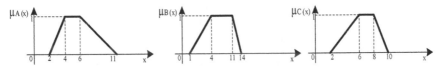

Fig. 4. Setting the demand area

For correct operations on sets according to formulas (3)−(5), it is necessary to split the presented sets into α-levels, which requires additional analysis that is not provided for in the problem. The total demand of the area S as a result of the operation of adding three fuzzy intervals, according to (6), is shown in Fig. 5:

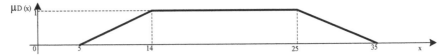

Fig. 5. The result of adding fuzzy intervals

The final result according to (7) is equal to $S_{LR} = A_{LR} + B_{LR} + C_{LR} = \langle 6, 11, 5, 10 \rangle$ and is shown in Fig. 6:

Fig. 6. Extended maximum result for fuzzy intervals

As the analysis of the obtained results shows, it is advisable to apply the extended maximum operation when it is necessary to obtain a general solution to the problem of forecasting the demand for subdomains by experts. In this case, the operation of adding fuzzy intervals (L–R) – type is advisable to use when determining the total demand of the area under consideration.

5   Conclusion

The analysis of the mathematical apparatus proposed for the representation of undefined parameters allows us to draw the following conclusion. The use of probability theory for setting demand parameters and solving problems of building transport and logistics systems is not always correct, since statistical data is required to build an adequate probabilistic model. This condition is not always feasible when designing systems. The most justified setting of the parameters of the considered system in the form of fuzzy intervals. The paper shows that the extended maximum operation takes place when evaluating the decision of expert experts, and it is advisable to calculate the determination of the total demand using the operation of adding two fuzzy numbers $(L–R)$ – type. The operations of addition and algebraic union of fuzzy numbers allow avoiding unreasonable expansion of a fuzzy interval, but they require partitioning the fuzzy set into α-levels, which requires additional analysis of the problem. Thus, the application of the theory of fuzzy sets is based on the possibility of an adequate representation of the parameters of such systems using these sets. In further works, it is planned to present the results of the study of the division of fuzzy intervals into α-levels in order to identify the degree of unreasonable expansion, and the effect of this value on the final result of solving the problem.

Acknowledgments. The reported study was funded by the Russian Foundation for Basic Research according to the research project N 20–01-00197.

References

1. Afanasyeva, H.: Statistical analysis of air traffic in latvian region. In: proceedings of The Second International Conference Simulation, Gaming, Training and Business Process Reengineering in Operations, pp. 125–129, RTU, Riga (2000)
2. Bucciarelli, E., Chen, S.-H., Corchado, J.M. (eds.): DECON 2019. AISC, vol. 1009. Springer, Cham (2020). https://doi.org/10.1007/978-3-030-38227-8
3. Jaulin, L., Kieffer, M., Didrit, O., Walter, É.: Applied Interval Analysis. Springer London, London (2001). https://doi.org/10.1007/978-1-4471-0249-6
4. Ayhan, M.S., Berens, P.: Test-time data augmentation for estimation of heteroscedastic aleatoric uncertainty in deep neural networks. In: 1st Conference on Medical Imaging with Deep Learning (MIDL 2018), Amsterdam, Netherlands (2018)
5. Lo, S.-C., Ma, H.-W., Lo, S.-L.: Quantifying and reducing uncertainty in life cycle assessment using the Bayesian Monte Carlo method. Sci. Total Environ. **340**(1–3), 23–33 (2005)
6. Jøsang, A.: Subjective Logic. Springer International Publishing, Cham (2016)
7. Tannert, C., Elvers, H.-D., Jandrig, B.: The ethics of uncertainty. In the light of possible dangers, research becomes a moral duty. EMBO Rep. **8**(10), 892–896 (2007)
8. Shackley, S., Wynne, B.: Representing uncertainty in global climate change science and policy: boundary-ordering devices and authority. Sci. Technol. Hum. Values **21**(3), 275–302 (1996)
9. Seraya, O.: Mnogomernye modeli logistiki v usloviyah neopredelennosti. FOP Stecenko I.I, Kharkiv (2010)
10. Kulpa, Z.: Diagrammatic representation of interval space in proving theorems about interval relations. Reliable Comput. **3**, 209–217 (1997)
11. Seising, R.: The Fuzzification of Systems: The Genesis of Fuzzy Set Theory and Its Initial Applications. Studies in Fuzziness and Soft Computing, vol. 216, Springer (2007). https://doi.org/10.1007/978-3-540-71795-9

12. Zadeh, L.A., Fu, K.S., Shimura, M. (eds.): Fuzzy Sets and Their Applications. Academic Press, New York, USA (1975)
13. Raskin, L., Sira, O., Karpenko, V.: Transportation management in a distributed logistic consumption system under uncertainty conditions. Eureka: Phys. Eng. **4**, 82–90 (2019)
14. Dubois, D., Prade, H.: Fuzzy Sets and Systems. Academic Press, N.Y. (1980)
15. Shannon, A., Atanassov, K.T.: Intuitionistic fuzzy graphs from α-, β- and (α, b)-levels. Notes Intuitionistic Fuzzy Sets **1**(1), 32–35 (1995)
16. Zhang, H., Liu, D.: Fuzzy Modeling and Fuzzy Control. Birkhäuser, Basel (2006)
17. Muromcev, D.Yu, Shamkin, V.N.: Optimization methods and project decision making. TGTU, Tambov (2015)
18. Bozhenyuk, A.V., Gerasimenko, E.M., Kacprzyk, J., Rozenberg, I.N.: Flows in Networks Under Fuzzy Conditions. Springer International Publishing, Cham (2017)
19. Robert, F.: Neural-Fuzzy Systems. Abo Akademi University, Abo (1995)
20. Zadeh, L.A.: Fuzzy sets. Inf. Control **8**, 338–353 (1965)
21. Sevastjanov, P.V., Róg, P., Venberg, A.V.: A constructive numerical method for the comparison of intervals. In: Wyrzykowski, R., Dongarra, J., Paprzycki, M., Waśniewski, J. (eds.) PPAM 2001. LNCS, vol. 2328, pp. 756–761. Springer, Heidelberg (2002). https://doi.org/10.1007/3-540-48086-2_84
22. Senthilkumar, P., Rajendran, G.: An algorithmic approach to solve fuzzy linear systems. J. Inf. Comput. Sci. **8**, 503–510 (2011)
23. Kosenko, O., Shestova, E., Sinyavskaya, E., Kosenko, E., Nomerchuk, A., Bozhenyuk, A.: Development of information support for the rational placement of intermediate distribution centers of fuel and energy resources under conditions of partial uncertainty In: XX IEEE International Conference on Soft Computing and Measurements (SCM), pp. 224–227 (2017)

Mobile Healthcare Service for Self-organization in Older Populations During a Pandemic

Alexander Pchelkin[✉], Natalia Gusarova, Natalia Dobrenko, and Alexandra Vatyan

ITMO University, Saint-Petersburg 197101, Russia
natfed@list.ru

Abstract. Elderly people make up an increasing part of the population, and they need tools to maintain active longevity, such as diagnostic, monitoring and reference systems. At the same time, the need constantly arises for more and more new support systems specialized for the needs of a specific target group.

One of the most important problems of older people is to record information about emerging health problems. This problem became especially acute during the coronavirus pandemic. Elderly people were isolated and lost the opportunity to attend medical facilities. As a result, many emerging issues are left without due attention. In addition, many older people experience memory problems. If information about the problem is not recorded at the time of its occurrence, the patient may forget important symptoms, their location, strength or duration. This can adversely affect the quality of care that a doctor can provide.

The article discusses the development of mobile health troubles self-fixation service for elderly groups, which allows to eliminate or at least reduce these problems. The main functionality of the application is the creation of medical notes, where the user can specify the symptom and the place of its occurrence, give a detailed text description of the problem, attach a photo or voice record, and also select a specialist to contact with this symptom. In addition, through a pre-trained neural network, the service provides the possibility of a comprehensive analysis of several symptoms and a more accurate choice of a doctor.

Keywords: Active longevity · Health troubles self-fixation · Medical notes

1 Introduction

Elderly people make up an increasing part of the Russian population. According to the Federal State Statistics Service (Rosstat), the number of people, receiving an old-age pension exceeds 37 million people, which is more than 25% of the total population [1]. At the same time, the technical literacy of pensioners is also growing. The first smartphones appeared in Russia in 2000 and since 2007 began to gain immense popularity. Mobile devices and gadgets have become an everyday part of life, even for the elderly.

Along with age, health problems come. Many pensioners are capable of self-provision and self-regulation. Due to the development of the Internet and remote communication, and tools for maintaining active longevity (such as as diagnostic, monitoring

© Springer Nature Singapore Pte Ltd. 2021
P. K. Singh et al. (Eds.): FTNCT 2020, CCIS 1395, pp. 379–390, 2021.
https://doi.org/10.1007/978-981-16-1480-4_34

and reference systems) older people have the opportunity to continue to live an ordinary life.

There are many similar systems in the world, but new systems are constantly required to meet the highly specialized needs of a specific target audience. The elderly in Russia are a prime example of such a target group.

It is often difficult for an elderly patient to provide full symptom information, including exact location, their nature, duration and associated sensations, especially if the patient has a complex of diseases and did not record the data right away.

The problem is even more acute if the patient suffers from dementia, which is just typical for the elderly. However, dementia is also found among younger population groups, in particular, it is characteristic of people suffering from multiple sclerosis. According to the World Health Organization (WHO), there are about 50 million people with dementia worldwide [2] and almost 10 million new cases of the disease occur annually [3]. At the same time, one of the countries with the highest prevalence of the disease is Russia. Often people with Alzheimer's disease, Parkinson's disease, sclerosis, brain abscess are faced with the fact that they cannot rely solely on their memory [4].

An outbreak of coronavirus infection has demonstrated the relevance of this problem. Due to the isolation regime, older people were left alone with their health problems. Under quarantine conditions, elderly can only wait for the removal of restrictive measures to contact specialists. However, the quality of care that doctors will be able to provide them in the future will largely be related to the completeness of the information that patients can provide.

In this regard, the development of an application focused on the realities of Russia, which would allow older people as well as people with memory problems to conveniently and quickly record their notes on their health, is an urgent task.

This article describes the process of collecting application requirements (based on the analysis of articles, existing applications, and survey results), reveals the technical details of project development and feedback from users before and after the outbreak of the pandemic.

2 Background and Related Works

Various applications for mobile health are widely represented in the market and in the literature. They are aimed at solving a wide range of healthcare problems, such as, for example, supporting self-care among population groups with health restrictions, monitoring compliance with treatment regimens and regimens, ensuring two-way communication between patients and clinicians, etc.

The development of such applications requires a thorough analysis of the subject area, future users, as well as competitor applications. The chances of scaring off future users are extremely high. According to statistics, 25% of users refuse applications after the first use [5].

The formation of requirements for the future application began with the analysis of articles on the development of medical applications, the perception of these applications by patients and the identification of the strengths and weaknesses of mobile healthcare.

According to [6], wide accessibility for the population is the main advantage of mobile healthcare, however, in recent years, its serious shortcomings have been manifested, among which there is a lack of confidentiality and data security, as well as a lack of good examples of effectiveness.

The authors [7] claim that users value features that save time compared to existing methods, and find the application useful when it is simple and intuitive to use, provides specific instructions for better management, and communicates with designated people. Article [8] is dedicated to the strengths and weaknesses of mobile medical applications. Strengths include: attracting patients to their services and empowering patients. Among the weaknesses are the reliability, relevance, personalization and accessibility of these tools. In [9], the importance of involving future users in the process of creating mobile medical applications is noted. Focus group surveys allowed authors to improve their prototype platform.

The article [10] discusses specific needs of people with multiple sclerosis. The article emphasizes the importance of the intuitiveness of working with the application at the first start, as well as the need to clearly substantiate the benefits of using the application to the user.

Thus, the analysis shows that there is a wide range of problems that must be considered when developing mobile healthcare application, especially if the application is developed for the elderly and people with impaired memory. Thereby, the authors of this article pose the following tasks:

- Determination of functional requirements and requirements for ease of use of medical applications for older people based on analysis of feedback on competitor applications and survey results;
- Developing a prototype application according to these requirements;
- Testing the prototype and collecting user feedback on their satisfaction with the product and interest in future use.

3   Revealing Requirements for Symptoms Diary Mobile Application

The first step in forming application requirements was the analysis of reviews under medical applications for the elderly. Most often, in negative reviews, users complain about bugs in applications (for example, when applications suddenly stop working, lose data or slow down the gadget too much). Also frequently mentioned are the size of user interface elements, intrusive advertising, lack of flexible settings, and the need for registration.

The second stage of determining the application requirements was a survey of the main audience. The survey involved 68 people in a large city (St. Petersburg) over the age of 55 years. The survey was conducted in polyclinics among elderly people waiting for their turn to receive an appointment.

The survey methodology was a questionnaire [11]. Questionnaire results can be seen in the Table 1.

Table 1. The results of the questionnaire to identify specific requirements

Question	Answer	Result
Do you use mobile devices?	Yes	94%
Do you use a smartphone?	Yes	70%
Do you use apps on smartphones?	Yes	41%
Do you use medical apps on smartphones?	Yes	16%
Have you encountered a situation where you have difficulty describing symptoms to your doctor?	Yes	88%
Do you have memory problems?	Yes	82%
Do you somehow capture information about your symptoms?	Yes	35%
Do you use a smartphone to record information about symptoms?	Yes	3%
What difficulties do you encounter when using mobile apps?	On-screen keyboard input	65%
	Small interface sizes	53%
	Lack of Russian language	50%
	Confusing app navigation	47%
	Mandatory registration	20%
What additional features might interest you when using the symptom diary mobile app?	Voice input	41%
	Ability to attach photos	29%
	Export data from the application	21%
	Specialist recommendations	15%

Questionnaire results confirm the relevance of the development. Smartphones really have a fairly widespread prevalence among the elderly (70%), and the vast majority of respondents (88%) experienced problems with describing symptoms at a doctor's appointment.

Based on the collected information, the following requirements are put forward for the future application:

1. The application can be localized in Russia;
2. The application allows to store notes about symptoms;
3. The application interface is designed for users with minimal experience interacting with mobile applications;
4. The application interface is designed for users with low vision (use large fonts, buttons and icons);
5. When creating a new note, the desired symptom can be selected from the list of symptoms;
6. When creating a note, it is possible to give a detailed text description of the symptom;

7. When creating a note, it is possible to attach an audio file from voice recorder or device with a description of the symptom;
8. When creating a note, it is possible to attach a photo from camera or device to demonstrate the symptom;
9. The system does not collect any information identifying the user or his relatives, medical card numbers and payment data;
10. All application data is stored only on the user's device;
11. The application does not require registration;
12. The system gives recommendations for contacting a specialist (optionally);
13. The system allows to structure and sort stored data;
14. The system allows to export saved data.

In order to finally verify the appropriateness of the development, an analysis was made of similar applications for compliance with the requirements outlined above. To do this, in the official Android application store "Google Play" [12], applications were searched by the combinations of the words "Diary", "Note", "Health" and "Symptom". As a result, the 10 most popular applications were selected and analyzed. The results are presented in the Table 2.

Table 2. Analysis of existing applications for compliance with the specified requirements

Application	Requirements													
	1	2	3	4	5	6	7	8	9	10	11	12	13	14
Updoc [13]		✓			✓	✓		✓	✓	✓			✓	✓
Health log [14]		✓	✓	✓	✓	✓			✓		✓		✓	✓
Medical Diary [15]			✓	✓					✓	✓	✓			✓
Correlation [16]	✓	✓			✓				✓	✓	✓		✓	✓
Health Diary [17]		✓		✓	✓				✓	✓	✓	✓		
Symdir [18]		✓	✓						✓	✓	✓		✓	✓
Manage My Pain [19]	✓	✓	✓	✓	✓	✓			✓	✓	✓		✓	
Symptomate [20]	✓		✓		✓				✓		✓	✓		
Therapist [21]	✓			✓	✓	✓			✓		✓	✓		
My health [22]	✓		✓		✓		✓		✓	✓	✓		✓	

Thus, expert assessments made it possible to determine that the programs currently available on the market for recording notes on symptoms do not satisfy the set of requirements outlined above. Thus, the relevance of continuing development has been confirmed.

4 Proposed Solution

4.1 Application Description

The main idea of the app is to make the process of adding notes about symptoms as simple as possible, and to provide users with useful information based on their records.

The main functionality of the application is creating medical notes. Within the note, the user can indicate the symptom and the place of its occurrence, give a detailed text description of the problem, attach a photo and a voice recorder, and select a specialist associated with this symptom. The application also provides search by notes, sorting notes by a specialist, editing and deleting notes.

The application provides functionality for exporting notes, but it is not presented in the prototype, because work on it is still underway.

The system may provide some support in selecting a specialist according to particular symptom or to symptoms combination. To do this, the system formes an assumption about a possible diagnosis and offers to contact a specialist of the appropriate profile, not disclosing the presumptive diagnosis to the user. This is done in order not to misinform the user in case of an error, and also to exclude situations when the patient begins to self-medicate. At the same time, due to the simultaneous analysis of several symptoms, the chance to get to the right specialist increases. Its implementation of this functionality is described in Sect. 4.5.

4.2 Technology Selection

To create a mobile application, the Apache Cordova PhoneGap framework was used [23]. This technology allows to develop an application using JavaScript, HTML5 and CSS3, and then compile it as an installation package. Such applications are called hybrid, because it does not work directly in the operating system, but through the WebView, which acts as the execution environment [24]. To interact with the camera or microphone, special plugins are used [25, 26]. For the users, the hybrid application is no different from the native one. But for the developer, such a solution allows to save development time, as well as to provide cross-platform application [27].

4.3 Structure

The developed prototype is a Single Page Application (SPA). The structure of the application is shown in the Fig. 1.

The main component of the application is "app", where all the scripts and page templates necessary for work are loaded. Key project pages are: Home Page, Settings Page, Note View Page, Note Add Page, System Information Page.

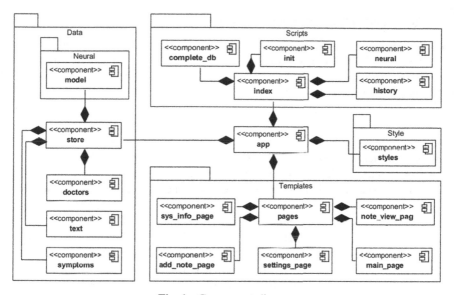

Fig. 1. Component diagram

4.4 Data Storage

All data are stored on the user's device. This decision is related to previously announced security requirements. Data is divided into two groups: data of the application and user data. Symptom notes contain textual information, graphic and audio files.

The application data storage structure is shown in Fig. 2.

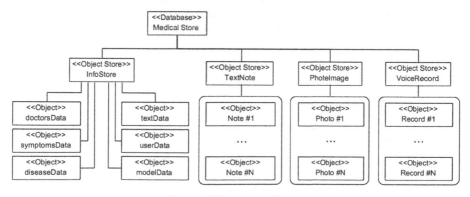

Fig. 2. Object store diagram

IndexedDB [28] is used to store all data. IndexedDB is a NoSQL data store in JSON format inside the browser. Unlike localStorage, this storage allows to store files in the form of blob (Binary Large Object), which is necessary for storing graphic and audio information.

4.5   Functionality of Contacting a Specialist

Some support in choosing a specialist can provide a preliminary analysis of symptoms. Nowadays, machine learning and artificial intelligence are actively used to analyze data in medicine [29]. For example, in the application Your.MD, specially trained artificial intelligence is able to give individual medical advice based on the symptoms of the user [30].

However, the development of such a system is an extremely complex process, requiring the involvement of a large number of third-party specialists. In addition to creating or adapting the network itself, it is required to collect data on the symptoms and diseases characteristic of a specific target audience and region for its training. Therefore, to verify the demand for such functionality by the target audience, a simple neural network was used for the prototype.

The neural network was developed in Python. The disease symptom knowledge base was used to train the network. This data was provided by the Presbyterian hospital in New York [31] and contains information from text summaries of patient extracts.

The neural network consists of three layers and 132 neurons. Our experiments have shown that despite the simplicity of the network, it managed to achieve an accuracy of 86% on the test data.

All complex calculations were performed in advance, so the neural network in the application does not load smartphones too much and remains accessible to users with rather weak smartphone models, which is typical for the target group under consideration.

5   Results and Discussion

5.1   Evaluation of the Effectiveness and Usability of the Developed System

Two surveys were conducted to evaluate the effectiveness and usability of the application.

To assess usability, the System Usability Scale (SUS) was used. In systems engineering, SUS is a simple ten-point Likert scale that provides a global perspective on subjective usability ratings [32]. The usability of the system, as defined by ISO 9241, Part 11, can only be measured taking into account the context of use of the system. In addition, usability measurements have several different aspects:

- effectiveness (can users successfully achieve their goals)
- efficiency (how much effort and resources are spent on achieving these goals)
- satisfaction (was the experience satisfactory).

Before starting the survey, the user was informed about the functionality of the application. After that, the survey participant was provided with a device with an application installed on it. The next few minutes were given to the user to deal with the system, after which they were given a test task that consisted of creating a note about a specific symptom. After the task was completed, a SUS survey was conducted in which users evaluated the usability of the application.

In total, 20 elderly people took part in the experiment. According to the survey, the average SUS score was 78%. This indicates a high usability of the developed system [32].

The second survey was conducted after long-term use of the app. The developed application was installed on the devices of elderly people who agreed to participate in the experiment. After three months, they were contacted by the specified phone numbers and asked a few questions about the app. In total, 12 people participated in the experiment.

This study partially coincided with the beginning of the introduction of the isolation regime. Therefore, it was decided to contact the experiment participants again a month after the introduction of restrictive measures. 11 participants were called, 9 of whom continued to use the app even after the experiment ended. The survey was conducted with them again to assess the changes.

The results of surveys conducted before and after entering isolation mode are presented in Table 3.

Table 3. The results of the questionnaire after three months of using the application

Question	Answer	Before	After
How often have you written notes about the symptoms?	Every day	17%	33%
	Several times a week	75%	67%
	Once a week or less	8%	0%
Have you visited a doctor during the experiment?	Yes	67%	22%
Did you use the information stored in the application when describing the symptoms at the doctor's appointment? (The question was asked only to those who visited the doctor)	Yes	75%	100%
Did the saved data help in describing the symptoms?	Yes	67%	100%
What features did you actively use in the application?	Create notes	100%	100%
	Attaching photos	75%	78%
	Attaching audio files	42%	44%
	Filter notes	33%	44%
	Search by notes	33%	67%
	Analysis of notes	17%	11%
Will you continue using the app in the future?	Yes	67%	89%

The survey results show the importance of development. Many participants in the experiment continued to use the application, even after the end of the study (9 out of 12 participants). Against the background of the coronavirus epidemic, many users began to use the application more actively. Many began to use it more often (every day users: 17% before the outbreak and 33% after). Users also began to use the app's functionality more actively. The only poorly-used function was the analysis of symptoms. The survey showed a rather low (17% before and 11% after) interest of users in this function. At least in the form in which it exists in the application at the moment. For this reason, in further development, first of all, it is necessary to concentrate on the implementation of other functions identified during the collection of requirements, for example, exporting data from an application and encrypting data.

5.2 Application Prototype

The main result of the work was a prototype medical application for creating notes about the symptoms that users experience. Examples of how the app works are shown in Fig. 3.

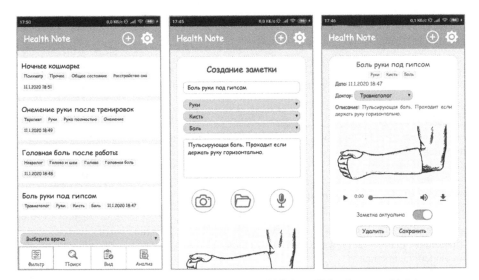

Fig. 3. Main page (left), Creating note (middle), and Viewing note (right).

6 Conclusion

The tasks posed in the article were successfully resolved.

- The functional and practical requirements for medical applications for the elderly and people with memory problems were defined. The requirements were determined based on analysis of similar mobile medical applications, as well as on a survey of the main audience of the application.
- The prototype application was developed according to the collected requirements. The application implements functionality for creating, storing and managing notes, filtering and searching for notes is implemented, the system is trained to analyze symptoms and advise doctors. The application works in several languages, including Russian.
- In order to assess the effectiveness and usability of the developed system several surveys were conducted: usability and after long-term use (conducted before and after the onset of the pandemic). The average point survey for evaluating usability (SUS)

was 78%, which indicates the high convenience and intuitiveness of the use of the developed system. Surveys conducted after long-term use have shown the relevance of development and demand for many of the app's features. According to the results of the survey conducted before the pandemic, many participants claimed that they would continue to use the app even after the end of the experiment. This was confirmed by the results of the survey conducted a month after the introduction of the quarantine.

The data identified during requirements collection can be used later in the development of other applications for this target audience. The developed prototype has a flexible structure, due to which, in the future, it is possible not only to refine and improve the application, but also to create others on its basis, significantly reducing the development time.

The project code is publicly available at: https://github.com/HealthNote/Prototype.

References

1. Rosstat: Population. https://eng.gks.ru/population
2. Medlineplus: Dementia. https://medlineplus.gov/dementia.html
3. World Health Organisation: Dementia. https://www.who.int/news-room/fact-sheets/detail/dementia
4. Global, regional, and national burden of Alzheimer's disease and other dementias, 1990–2016: a systematic analysis for the Global Burden of Disease Study 2016. The Lancet Neurology, v. 18, is. 1, pp.88–106, 01 January 2019
5. Localytics: 25% of Users Abandon Apps After One Use. https://info.localytics.com/blog/25-of-users-abandon-apps-after-one-use
6. Whittaker, R.: Issues in mHealth: findings from key informant interviews. JMIR 14(5) (2012). https://www.jmir.org/2012/5/e129
7. Mendiola, M.F., Kalnicki, M., Lindenauer, S.: Valuable features in mobile health apps for patients and consumers: content analysis of apps and user ratings. JMIR 3(2) (2015). https://mhealth.jmir.org/2015/2/e40
8. Vo, V., Auroy, L., Sarradon-Eck, A.: Patients' perceptions of mHealth apps: meta-ethnographic review of qualitative studies. JMIR Mhealth Uhealth 7(7), e13817 (2019). https://mhealth.jmir.org/2019/7/e13817
9. Bendixen, R.M, Fairman, A.D., Karavolis, M., Sullivan, C., Parmanto, B.: A user-centered approach: understanding client and caregiver needs and preferences in the development of mhealth apps for self-management. JMIR Mhealth Uhealth 5(9) (2017). https://mhealth.jmir.org/2017/9/e141
10. Giunti, G., Kool, J., Romero, O., Zubiete, E.D.: Exploring the specific needs of persons with multiple sclerosis for mhealth solutions for physical activity: mixed-methods study. JMIR 6(2) (2018). https://mhealth.jmir.org/2018/2/e37
11. Research Methodology: Questionnaires. https://research-methodology.net/research-methods/survey-method/questionnaires-2
12. Google Play. https://play.google.com/store
13. Updoc. https://play.google.com/store/apps/details?id=com.updochealth.updochealth
14. Health Log. https://play.google.com/store/apps/details?id=andrew.arproductions.healthlog
15. Medical Diary. https://play.google.com/store/apps/details?id=eu.lifemonitor
16. Correlate. https://play.google.com/store/apps/details?id=symptoms.diary.tracker
17. Health Diary. https://play.google.com/store/apps/details?id=com.decodelab.healthdiarybd

18. Simdir. https://play.google.com/store/apps/details?id=dk.kalorieopslag.symdir
19. Manage My Pain. https://play.google.com/store/apps/details?id=com.lcs.mmp.lite
20. Symptomate. https://play.google.com/store/apps/details?id=com.symptomate.mobile
21. Therapist. https://play.google.com/store/apps/details?id=com.forevolabs.terapevt
22. My Health. https://play.google.com/store/apps/details?id=ru.medsolutions.myhealth
23. Apach Cordova. https://cordova.apache.org
24. Charland, A., Leroux, B., Mobile application development: web vs. native. ACM. https://dl.acm.org/doi/10.1145/1941487.1941504
25. Cordova plugin camera. https://www.npmjs.com/package/cordova-plugin-camera
26. Cordova plugin media capture. https://www.npmjs.com/package/cordova-plugin-media-capture
27. EWeek: PhoneGap Simplifies iPhone, Android, BlackBerry Development. https://www.eweek.com/development/phonegap-simplifies-iphone-android-blackberry-development
28. W3: IndexedDB. https://www.w3.org/TR/IndexedDB
29. Lovis, C.: Unlocking the power of artificial intelligence and big data in medicine. J. Med. Internet Res. **21**(11) (2019)
30. Artificial intelligence in the real world. An Economist Intelligence Unit briefing paper. An Economist Intelligence Unit briefing paper. https://eiuperspectives.economist.com/sites/default/files/Artificial_intelligence_in_the_real_world_1.pdf
31. Disease-Symptom Knowledge Database. https://people.dbmi.columbia.edu/~friedma/Projects/DiseaseSymptomKB/index.html
32. System Usability Scale (SUS). https://www.usability.gov/how-to-and-tools/methods/system-usability-scale.html

Bioinspired Multi-memetic Algorithm

Boris K. Lebedev, Oleg B. Lebedev$^{(\boxtimes)}$, and Ekaterina O. Lebedeva

Southern Federal University, Rostov-on-Don, Russia

Abstract. The paper considers a multi-memetic ant algorithm of discrete optimization. An algorithm has been developed for choosing and appropriate strategies for using a meme from a swarm of available memes. The work of multi-memetic ant algorithm of discrete optimization is illustrated by the example of a partition problem, which is widely used in solving optimization problems: VLSI partitions; clustering, coloring, click highlighting, matching, etc. Given a graph $G(X, U)$. It is necessary to split the set X into subsets X_1 and X_2, $X_1 \cup X_2 = X$, $X_1 \cap X_2 = \emptyset$, $X_i = \emptyset$. To search for a solution to a problem, a complete solution search graph $R(X, E)$ is used. Agent a_k does not construct a route on the $R(X, E)$, but forms subgraph. Multi-memetic ant algorithm by the constructive algorithm (meme), each of the agents a_k forms the set. In all memes, the formation of the set X_{lk} is carried out sequentially (step by step). Agent a_k uses the probabilistic rule for choosing the next vertex to include it in the generated set $X_{lk}(t)$. Each meme uses its own the strategy of forming the set X_{lk}. In the first meme, the partition of the graph $G(X, U)$ is searched for by the geodesic distribution $R(X, E)$, and the pheromone is deposited on the set of edges E. The main difference between the second meme and the first is that the agent searches for a solution on the graph $G(X, U)$. Pheromone is plotted only at the vertices of the graph $G(X, U)$. This leads to a sharp reduction in the number of pheromone points and, consequently, memory. The peculiarity of the third meme M_3 is that on the top x_i of the graph $G(X, U)$ two indicators φ_{i1k} and φ_{i2k} are formed: φ_{i1k} – the total level of the pheromone deposited on x_i only in the cases when x_i was part of $X_{1k}(t)$; φ_{i2k} is the total level of pheromone deposited on only in cases where x_i was not part of $X_{lk}(t)$. The exponent φ_{li} characterizes the preference for the node $X_{lk}(t)$ for the vertex x_i. The fourth meme is characterized in that two sets $X_{1k}(t)$ and $X_{2k}(t)$ are formed in parallel. The fifth meme implements an approach based on the decomposition of the data structure in the formation of the set of vertices and deposition of pheromone. In the modified approach, pheromone deposition is carried out on the graph $R(X, E)$, and the formation of a subset of vertices is carried out on the oriented graph $B(X, V)$. The algorithm based on multi-memetic hybridization has the properties of self-adaptation. By increasing the efficiency of the search, the hybrid algorithm to reduce the number of agents in the system and increases its speed.

Keywords: Meme · Memetic algorithm · Ant algorithm · Multi-memetic hybridization · Adaptation · Swarm of particles · Optimization

© Springer Nature Singapore Pte Ltd. 2021
P. K. Singh et al. (Eds.): FTNCT 2020, CCIS 1395, pp. 391–401, 2021.
https://doi.org/10.1007/978-981-16-1480-4_35

1 Introduction

One of the promising modern directions in the field of evolutionary computing is memetic algorithms (MA) [1]. They are based on the neo-Darwinian principles of evolution and the concept of a meme, proposed by R. Dawkins in 1976 [2].

A meme is a unit of transmitting cultural information that is distributed from one person to another through imitation, learning, etc. The term memetic algorithms were first proposed by P. Moscato in 1989 [3] to denote a class of stochastic global search methods. Memetic algorithms combine the strengths of local search methods focused on specific practical tasks and population-based global search methods. To date, the methods of this class have been successfully used to solve problems of combinatorial, continuous, dynamic and multi-criteria optimization [1–5]. In the context of MA, a meme is an implementation of some local optimization method that refines the solution in the search process. In a number of works, MA is considered as a combination of a population search for a global optimum and procedures for local refinement of solutions, which gives a synergistic effect. The memetic algorithms were successful for solving optimization problems in various fields. As studies have shown [6–9], the choice of memes has a very large effect on the performance of MA. The concept of memetic algorithms provides ample opportunities for the development of various modifications of these algorithms, which may differ in the frequency of performing a local search, the conditions for its completion, and so on [5]. Practically significant modifications of memetic algorithms involve the simultaneous use of various memes. Such algorithms are called multi-memetic. To date, there are a large number of publications showing various options for the hybridization of metaheuristic methods with various local search methods [10]. These algorithms use complex heuristic methods of local search, focused on specific tasks. Despite their high efficiency, they are of limited use, since researchers do not have a priori information about which meme is most optimal for this task. To overcome this drawback, the so-called multi-memes adaptive algorithms were proposed [2, 6, 7]. Using the most effective sets of memes allows you to find the optimal solution in fewer iterations compared to less efficient sets. Known is the strategy of random descent (random descent choice). Here, in the first step, the meme is randomly selected from the swarm M. The selected meme is used until it ceases to provide local refinement of solutions. Then another meme is randomly selected, etc. The greedy strategy methods apply memes to each agent in the population, and then select the meme that shows the best result. The disadvantage of greedy methods is the high cost of computing resources. Also interesting is the direction of studying the mechanism for choosing memes according to several different criteria.

The paper considers the task of constructing a multi-memetic ant algorithm, including the development of 5 memes and the selection of a suitable strategy for using one or another meme from a swarm of available memes M. As criteria for evaluating the effectiveness, the average value of the objective function based on the results of a multi-start is used, as well as the number of iterations, which, given the limit on the number of iterations of the local search, uniquely determines the maximum number of tests.

2   Statement of the Problem

The work of the ant discrete optimization algorithm is illustrated by the example of the problem of graph partitioning into subgraphs, which is widely used in solving problems such as clustering, coloring, highlighting clicks, matching, partitioning VLSI, etc.

Let a graph $G(X, U)$ be given, where X is the set of vertices, $|X| = n$, U is the set of edges. It is necessary to split the set X into two nonempty and disjoint subsets X_1 and X_2, $X_1 \cup X_2 = X, X_1 \cap X_2 = \emptyset, X_i \neq \emptyset$. The following nodes are imposed on the formed nodes (blocks, components): $|X_1| = n_1, |X_2| = n_2, n_1 + n_2 = n$. The optimization criterion is the number (total cost) of bonds $- F$ between X_1 and X_2. The goal: $F \to$ min.

The metaheuristics of the ant algorithm is based on a combination of two techniques: the general scheme is based on the basic method, which includes the built-in procedure. The basic method is to implement an iterative procedure to find the best solution, based on the mechanisms of adaptive behavior of an ant colony. The built-in procedure is a constructive algorithm for constructing by the ant some specific interpretation of the solution [11]. Essentially, an inline routine is a meme. The ant algorithm is actually a hybrid algorithm. It is based on the integration of a basic iterative structure with a meme - a built-in constructive local search procedure.

To find a solution to the problem, we use the complete solution graph $R(X, E)$, where E is the set of all edges of the complete graph connecting the set of vertices X. On the set of edges E we will lay the pheromone. The process of finding solutions by the ant algorithm is iterative. A pheromone is laid out on the set of edges E. An agent constructs a route on the decision search graph $R(X, E)$, which is an interpretation of the solution. In the work, unlike the canonical paradigm, the agent forms the subgraph $R_1(X_1, E_1)$, $R_1 \subset R$.

At first, at all vertices of the graph G, the same (small) amount of pheromone Q/m, where $m = |E|$, is deposited. Each iteration t includes three stages. At the first stage of each iteration, the constructive algorithm considered as a meme is executed. At the second and third stages, the basic iterative procedure is performed. Multi-memetic algorithms use several memes to find the optimum. The decision to choose a meme for a particular individual in a population is very often made dynamically. Moreover, local search methods focused on various tasks compete with each other. As a result, the overall performance of MA remains high despite the fact that there is no predetermined information about the problem being solved.

The work uses five methods of local optimization underlying memes. To select a particular meme at each iteration of the algorithm, a hypereuristics was used when, for each solution formed, an agent randomly selects a meme from a swarm of memes and the probability of choosing each meme does not change during iterations. In all memes, the formation of the set X_{1k} is carried out sequentially. Consider the first meme M_1.

At the first stage of each iteration of the ant algorithm by the constructive algorithm (meme), each of the agents $z_k \in Z = \{z_k | k = 1, 2, \ldots, n\}$ forms the set X_{1k} where k is the number of the agent. A team of agents forms many interpretations of $W = \{W_k | k = 1, 2, \ldots, n\} \cdot W_k = \{X_{1k} \cdot X_{2k}\}$. The search for solutions is carried out in the column for the search for solutions $R(X, E)$. At the second stage, pheromone is removed by agents. The third stage is the evaporation of the pheromone. Pheromones are deposited by agents on the ribs after the complete formation of solutions. The local goal of agent

z_k when searching for a solution is to form the set X_{1k} such that the maximum amount of pheromone is postponed at the vertices of the node X_{1k}.

Agents have their own "memory". Each agent stores in memory a list of the vertices of the graph traversed by it. At each step t, agent z_k has a list of vertices already included in the set being formed $-X_{1k}(t)$ and a list of remaining vertices $X_{ck}(t)$, $X_{1k}(t) \cup X_{ck}(t) = X$. $X_{Ik}(0) = \emptyset_2 \cdot X_{2k}(0) = X$, $X_{ck}(t)$, $X_{2k}(0) = X$. The pheromone distribution over the vertices and edges of the decision graph $R(X, E)$, which functions as a repository of collective evolutionary memory, is stored in memory. At the first step, a priori, each vertex set $X_{1k}(t)$, where $t = 1$, includes a vertex of the graph G, $(\forall i, j)[X_{li}(1) \cap X_{lj}(1) = \emptyset]$. Such a distribution is necessary so that all vertices of the graph G have the same chance of being the starting point in the formation of the node X_1. In modifications of the algorithm, l_n ants were also used, with each group of l ants using the same $X_{1i}(1)$ as the initial one. Agent scans all the vertices $X_{ck}(t)$, that are free at this step t. For each vertex $x_i \in X_{ck}(t)$, two indicators are calculated (Fig. 1):

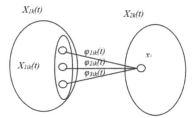

Fig. 1. Index structure φ_{ik}

– φ_{ik} is the total pheromone level on the edges of the graph R connecting x_i with the vertices of the node $X_{1k}(t)$;
– s_{ik} is connections on the graph G between x_i and $X_{1k}(t)$.

By additive convolution of the indicators φ_{ik} and s_{ik}, the potential cost Φ_{ik} of the connections $x_i \in X_{ck}(t)$ with $X_{1k}(t)$ is determined.

$$\Phi_{ik} = \alpha(\varphi_{ik}) + \beta(s_{ik}), \tag{1}$$

where α, β are control parameters that are selected experimentally.

The index Φ_{ik} characterizes the attractiveness (preference) of the inclusion of x_i in $X_{1k}(t)$. Vertex $x_i \in X_{ck}(t)$ in the formed node $X_{1k}(t)$ is determined by the following relation:

$$P_{ik} = \Phi_{ik}/\Sigma_i(\Phi_{ik}). \tag{2}$$

Agent z_k with probability P_{ik} chooses one of the vertices that is included in the set $X_{1k}(t)$ and excluded from the set $X_{ck}(t)$. At the second stage of the iteration, each agent z_k lays the pheromone on the edges of the complete subgraph $R_{1\kappa} \subset R$, built on the vertices of the set X_{1k}, in column R. In this work, we use the ant-cycle method of ant systems. In this case, the pheromone is deposited by agents on the edges of the graph R after the complete formation of solutions. The amount of pheromone $\tau_k(l)$ deposited by agent z_k on each edge of the subgraph $R_{1\kappa} \subset R$ constructed at the l-th iteration is determined as follows:

$$\tau_k(l) = Q/D_k(l), \tag{3}$$

where the l – number of the iteration, Q is the total amount of pheromone deposited by the k-th ant on the edges of the subgraph $R_{1\kappa} \subset R$, $D_k(l)$ is the number of bonds on the graph G between the sets X_{1k} and X_{2k} formed by the k-th ant on the l-th iteration.

The main difference between the second meme and the first one is that the full search graph $R(X, E)$ is excluded from the search process by the agent for the solution. Pheromone, in accordance with formula (3), is delayed only at the vertices of the graph $G(X, U)$. This leads to a sharp reduction in the number of pheromone points and, therefore, memory, since the number of edges of the graph $R(X, E)$ is much greater than the number of vertices.

The potential cost Φ_{ik} of bonds $x_i \in X_{ck}(t)$ with $X_{1k}(t)$ is defined as:

$$\Phi_{ik} = \alpha(\varphi_{ik}) + \beta(s_{ik}), \tag{4}$$

where φ_{ik} is the total pheromone level at the vertex x_i of the graph $G(X, U)$;

s_{ik} is the connections on the graph G between x_i and $X_{1k}(t)$ connecting x_i with the vertices of the node $X_{1k}(t)$.

The peculiarity of the third meme M_3 is that on the vertex x_i of the graph $G(X, U)$ two indicators φ_{i1k} and φ_{i2k} are formed:

– φ_{i1k} is the pheromone deposited on x_i, only in cases where x_i was part of $X_{1k}(t)$;
– φ_{i2k} is the pheromone deposited on x_i only in cases where x_i was not part of $X_{1k}(t)$.

The exponent φ_{1i} characterizes the preference for the node $X_{1k}(t)$ for the vertex x_i.
The exponent φ_{2i} characterizes the preference for the node $X_{2k}(t)$ for the vertex x_i.
The process of deposition of pheromone agent is as follows. Let an agent z_k form a set X_{1k}. The values of the set of exponents φ_{1i} corresponding to the vertices included in X_{1k}, as well as the values of the set of exponents φ_{2i} corresponding to the vertices not included in X_{1k}, increases by the value determined by expression (3).

We introduce the exponent $\theta_i = \varphi_{1i} - \varphi_{2i}$. Among the indicators θ_i with a negative value, the maximum negative value δ is determined: $(\forall i | \theta_i < 0)[\delta \geq |\theta_i|$. To eliminate the negative values of the indicators θ_i, all indicators are assigned a new value $\theta_i + \delta$.

The potential cost Φ_i of bonds $x_i \in X_{ck}(t)$ with $X_{1k}(t)$ is defined as:

$$\Phi_{ik} = \alpha(\theta_{ik}) + \beta(s_{ik}), \tag{5}$$

The probability P_{ik} of the inclusion of the vertex $x_i \in X_{ck}(t)$ in the formed node $X_{1k}(t)$ is determined by relation (3), and the deposition of the pheromone by relation (4).

The fourth meme differs from the third in that the agent forms two sets $X_{1k}(t)$ and $X_{2k}(t)$ in parallel. Let $X_{ck}(t)$ be the set of unassigned vertices. At step t, for each vertex

$x_i \in X_{ck}(t)$, the potential cost Φ_{i1k} of connections $x_i \in X_{ck}(t)$ with $X_{1k}(t)$ and Φ_{i2k} with $X_{2k}(t)$ is determined as:

$$\Phi_{i1k} = \alpha(\varphi_{i1k}) + \beta(s_{i1k}); \; \Phi_{i2k} = \alpha(_{i2k}) + \beta(s_{i2k}) \tag{6}$$

The probability P_{i1k} of the inclusion of the vertex $x_i \in X_{ck}(t)$ in the formed node $X_{1k}(t)$ is determined by the following relation:

$$P_{i1k} = \Phi_{i1k}/(\Phi_{i1k} + \Phi_{i2k}),$$

into the formed node $X_{2k}(t)$

$$\tag{7}$$

$$P_{i2k} = \Phi_{i2k}/(\Phi_{i1k} + \Phi_{i2k}).$$

In the fifth meme, an approach is used based on the decomposition of the data structure in the formation of the set of vertices $X_{1k} \subset X$ and deposition of pheromone [12]. In the meme M_1 considered above, the formation of a subset of the vertices $X_{1k} \subset X$ and the deposition of the pheromone is carried out on the same graph $R(X, E)$. In the modified approach, pheromone is deposited on the graph $R(X, E)$, and the formation of a subset of vertices $X_{1k} \subset X$ will be carried out in the oriented graph $B(X, V)$, where X is the set of vertices, $|X| = n$. The set of oriented edges V is formed as follows. From each vertex $x_i \in X$ there are $(n - i)$ edges that enter the vertices with numbers from $i + 1$ to n.

We arrange the vertices of the graph $B(X, V)$ in a ruler so that all edges are directed from left to right (Fig. 2). We introduce the starting vertex S_t associated with all vertices of the graph $B(X, V)$. The S_t vertex is used for the initial placement of agents and is not part of the formed subset. We call the graph $B(X, V)$ with vertices located in a line (ordered) a pattern of the graph $B(X, V)$.

St $\qquad$ 1 $\qquad\qquad\qquad\qquad\qquad\qquad\qquad\qquad$ n

Fig. 2. Route in column $B(X, V)$

To form a subset X_1 containing n_1 vertices, this means building on the template of the graph $B(X, V)$ an oriented route M_{1k} containing n_1 vertices (Fig. 2). Each of the agents forms its decision by moving from one vertex to another on the template of the solution search graph $B(X, V)$. On the set of edges E we will lay the pheromone. The amount of pheromone on the rib characterizes the advantage of choosing this rib compared to others when moving [12].

The process of constructing the oriented route M_{1k} is step-by-step, starting from the peak S_t. Agent applies the probabilistic rule for choosing the next vertex on the template of the graph $B(X, V)$ to include its generated route M_{1k}. The choice of the next vertex is made taking into account the restriction imposed on the list of candidates, providing the ability to build an oriented route containing a given number of vertices. One of the vertices of the graph template $B(X, V)$ with numbers from 1 to $n - (n_1 - 1)$ can be included in the route M_{1k}. The last $(n_1 - 1)$ vertices in the line of the template for graph $B(X, V)$ (Fig. 3) are reserved so that you can build an oriented route containing n_1 vertices.

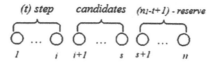

Fig. 3. Route formation

Let t steps be completed. This means that the route M_{1k} includes t vertices of the template of the graph $B(X, V)$. Let the last vertex of the route selected in step t be vertex number i. The candidates for inclusion in the route at step $t + 1$ are the vertices with numbers from $(i + 1)$ to $s = n - (n_1 - t + 1)$. The restrictions imposed on the candidate list reserve $(n_1 - t)$ the latter in the line of vertices of the template for graph $B(X, V)$, starting from $s + 1$, in order to guarantee the possibility of constructing a directed route containing n_1 vertices.

After constructing the route, all the vertices of the route form the set X_1, and all the vertices that are not included in the route form the set X_2. When forming the subset X_1, in the column $R(X, E)$ at the first step, n alternatives are considered, at the second step $(n - 1)$, etc. At the last step $- (n - (n_1 - 1))$ alternatives. In total, when forming a subset containing n_1 vertices, for n_1 steps it is always considered:

$$n + (n - 1) + (n - 2) + \ldots + (n - n_1 + 1) = \{[n + (n - n_1 + 1)]/2\} \cdot n_1 = ((2n - n_1 + 1)/2) \cdot n_1 \text{ alternatives.}$$

When constructing a route in the directed graph $B(X, V)$, the first step always considers $(n - (n_1 - 1) = (n - n_1 + 1)$ alternatives. For $t - 1$ of the previous steps, $t - 1$ could be chosen in the worst case the vertices located in the template of graph $B(X, V)$ at positions 1 through $t - 1$. At the next step t, these vertices in the amount of $t - 1$ can no longer be candidates for inclusion in the route M_{1k}. In addition, from among the candidates at step t, the last vertices in the line of vertices of the template of the graph $B(X, V)$ are excluded for reservation. Thus, at step t we can consider $[(n - (t - 1) - (n_1 - t)] = (n - n_1 + 1)$ alternatives. In total, when forming a subset containing n_1 vertices, for n_1 steps we always consider $[(n - n_1 + 1) + (n - n_1 + 1)]/2) \cdot n1 = [(2n - 2n_1 + 2)]/2) \cdot n1$.

Each agent lays pheromone on the edges of the complete subgraph and then an additional amount of pheromone is laid off on all the edges of the oriented route constructed by the ant. The amount of pheromone added is calculated according to the route estimate.

3 Multi-memetic Hybridization

The results of a number of studies [1–9] indicate that the task of choosing the best meme should be considered as a multi-criteria problem. The main task of constructing such algorithms is the choice of a suitable strategy for using one or another meme from a swarm of available memes. The task belongs to the class of meta-optimization problems [10, 14–19]. The indicated strategy is sometimes called hyperheuristic. The following three categories of hypereuristics used in adaptive multi-memetic hypereuristics are best known: random hypereuristics, greedy hypereuristics, hypereuristics with choice-function. The proposed algorithm uses one of the options for greedy hypereuristics.

Multi-memetic hybridization leads to an algorithm with self-adaptation properties, since memes compete in the search process and the meme that won at this stage of the search is used in subsequent stages.

The following adaptive algorithm is used in the work. At each iteration l, the set of memes $M(l) = \{M_k | k = 1, 2, \ldots, v\}$ is determined, which will be used at this iteration. The population of agents Z is divided into v subpopulations of Z_k of equal power, the number of which is equal to the number of memes used by agents in iteration l. The number of agents in the subpopulation Z_k is proportional to the average value of the objective function $D_k(l-1)$ of the solutions obtained by agents using the M_k meme based on the results of the previous iterations. Next, at iteration l, the procedure corresponding to the first step of the ant algorithm is first performed. Each subpopulation of Z_k agents generates many decisions using the M_k meme. The second stage of the ant algorithm. All agents of all subpopulations lay pheromone on the graphs $R(X, E)$, $G(X, U)$, in accordance with estimates of solutions constructed on iteration l. Then the pheromone evaporates on the graphs $R(X, E)$, $G(X, U)$. Further, based on the results of work at iteration l, for each subpopulation Z_k, the average value of the objective function $D_k(l)$ of solutions obtained by agents using the meme M_k is calculated. A subpopulation of Z_k with the worst value of $D_k(l)$ is determined. The meme M_k is deleted from the set $M(l) : M(l+1) = M(l) \backslash M_k$. The agent population is divided into $v - 1$ subpopulations of Z_k of equal power. At the next iteration, agents work with a set of memes $M(l + 1)$. Several iterations of ant algorithm are performed with one set of memes $M(l)$. In other words, the modification of the set of memes is performed after performing a portion of iterations. The average value of the objective function $D_k(l)$ of the solutions obtained at all iterations by the agents of the subpopulation Z_k using the meme M_k is calculated.

The second approach involves redistributing the quantitative composition of the Z_k subpopulations after each iteration portion. The average value of the objective function D_k of solutions obtained at all iterations by agents of the subpopulation Z_k using the meme M_k is calculated. The minimum estimate D_{min} is determined. $(\forall k)[D_{min.} \leq D_k]$. For each subpopulation Z_k, the estimate $\delta_k = D_k - D_{min}$ is determined. The quantitative composition N_k of the subpopulation Z_k proportional to the estimate δ_k is determined by the formula $N_k \approx \left(\delta_k / \sum_{kk} (\delta_k)\right) \cdot |Z|$. The results of statistical analysis show that the proposed adaptive multi-memetic algorithm using a swarm of memes gives the best result for the same number of iterations as single-mode algorithms. Moreover, the results of statistical tests show that the use of the first approach has increased convergence of the algorithm in the region of a certain local minimum.

4   Experimental Studies

For the experiments, we used the synthesis procedure for control examples with the well-known F_{opt} [13, 20]. To carry out the testing, ten graphs were formed. Examples containing up to 200 vertices were examined ($v_1 = 20$, $v_2 = 40$, $v_3 = 60$, $v_4 = 80$, $v_5 = 100$, $v_6 = 120$, $v_7 = 140$, $v_8 = 160$, $v_9 = 180$, $v_{10} = 200$). The number of edges m in the graph G is on average $n^2/4$. The weight of the vertices was taken to be zero, and the weight of all edges was taken to be one. The graphs were "split" into two subgraphs.

As part of the work, a comparative study of the efficiency of the memetic algorithm was carried out depending on the used local optimization algorithms and their number.

Since the efficiency of the algorithm significantly depends on the random values of free parameters, in all studies, each computational experiment was carried out using the multistart method 100 times. The dimensionless quantity $\xi = F_{opt}/F$ is used as the quality assessment, where F is the average value of the solution estimate obtained using the developed algorithm, based on the multistart results. The parameter NI was fixed — the average number of iterations at which the algorithm converges when the population size is $P = 100$.

At the beginning, tests were carried out for each meme separately. All of the memes provided great results. The best results were obtained using the M_3 and M_5 memes. The algorithm with the M_1 meme completed its work after a small number of iterations, which indicates the premature convergence of the method in the region of a certain local minimum.

The tests were then run using all the memes in a random sequence to solve. Studies have shown that the resulting estimate and the total time for solving the problem are little dependent on the sequence. All memes are most effective for small to medium sized examples. The test results (values of indicators ξ) for 10 examples, Table 1.

Table 1. The results of experimental studies

	v_1	v_2	v_3	v_4	v_5	v_6	v_7	v_8	v_9	v_{10}	NI
M_1	0,94	0,94	0,93	0,94	0,93	0,93	0,93	0,94	0,93	0,93	100
M_2	0,95	0,95	0,94	0,94	0,94	0,95	0,94	0,94	0,94	0,94	105
M_3	0,97	0,97	0,96	0,96	0,97	0,97	0,96	0,96	0,96	0,96	105
M_4	0,95	0,96	0,95	0,95	0,95	0,94	0,95	0,95	0,95	0,95	110
M_5	0,98	0,98	0,98	0,97	0,95	0,95	0,95	0,95	0,95	0,95	110
M_m	0,95	0,95	0,95	0,95	0,95	0,95	0,95	0,95	0,95	0,95	115

The results of statistical analysis show that the proposed adaptive multi-memetic algorithm using a swarm of memes $M_m = \{M_1, M_2, M_3, M_4, M_5\}$ gives the best result for the same number of iterations as single-mode algorithms.

5 Conclusion

The paper presents modifications of the standard built-in constructive procedure of the ant algorithm. It uses double and two-level pheromone deposition, decomposition of the data structure used in the process of constructing a route (forming a subgraph) and for pheromone deposition. In the developed algorithm, the ant is not building a route on the decision search graph $R(X, E)$, but a subgraph. The concept of ant algorithm representation as a hybridization of a meme with a basic iterative structure is considered. Developed a swarm of memes in the amount of 5 pieces. Investigated ant algorithm built on each meme. Analysis of the average number of iterations shows that the use of memes using pheromone deposition at the vertices of the graph allows us to find the optimal solution for a smaller number of iterations. A wide computational experiment was carried out to study the effectiveness of various sets of memes depending on their type and quantity. Two approaches to the construction of an adaptive multi-memetic algorithm using a swarm of memes are proposed. Multi-memetic hybridization leads to an algorithm with self-adaptation properties, since memes compete in the search process and the meme that won at this stage of the search is used in subsequent iterations. The results of the study demonstrate that the multi-memetic method turned out to be the most effective for the selected examples. The presented research results allow us to conclude that the proposed hybridization of the ant algorithm allows not only to increase the probability of localizing the global extremum of the objective function, but also to increase the accuracy of the solution. In addition, by increasing the efficiency of the search, the hybrid algorithm makes it possible to its speed.

Acknowledgements. This research is supported by grants of the Russian Foundation for Basic Research of the Russian Federation, the project № 20-07-00260.

References

1. Karpenko, A.P.: Modern Search Engine Optimization Algorithms. Algorithms Inspired by Nature: A Tutorial. M: Publishing House MSTU (2014). (in Russian). 446 p.
2. Cotta, C., Moscato, P.B.: Handbook of Memetic Algorithms. Springer, Heidelberg (2012). 368p.
3. Moscato, P., Corne, D., Glover, F., Dorigo, M.: Memetic algorithms: a short introduction. In: Book: New Ideas in Optimization. McGraw-Hill, pp. 219–234 (1999)
4. Krasnogor, N.: Studies on the theory and design space of memetic algorithms. Doctorial dissertation. University of the West of England, Bristol (2002). 412 p.
5. Neri, F., Cotta, C.: Memetic algorithms and memetic computing optimization: a literature review. Swarm and Evolutionary Computation, pp. 1–14 (2012)
6. Karpenko, A.P., Sakharov, M.K.: Multimeme global optimization based on the algorithm of the evolution of the mind. 2014 Information Technologies № 7, pp. 23–30 (2014). (in Russian)
7. Karpenko, A.P., Chernobrivchenko, K.A.: Multimeme modification of the hybrid ant algorithm of continuous optimization HCIAC. Electr. Sci. Tech. J. (2012). (in Russian). Email № FS7748211
8. Lebedev, B.K., Lebedev, O.B.: The memetic partition algorithm. Bulletin of the Rostov State University of Railway Engineering. Publishing House of RGUPS, Rostov-on-Don № 2(62), pp. 136–145 (2017). (in Russian)
9. Lebedev, B.K., Lebedev O.B.: A hybrid bio-inspired algorithm based on the integration of the branch and border method and the ant colony method. Bulletin of the Rostov State University of Railway Engineering. Publishing House of RGUPS, Rostov-on-Don № 2(70), pp. 77–88 (2018). (in Russian)
10. Ong, Y.-S., Lim, M.-H., Zhu, N., Wong, K.-W.: Classification of adaptive memetic algorithms: A comparative study. IEEE Trans. Syst. Man Cybern. **36**(1), 141–152 (2006)
11. Dorigo, M., Stützle, T.: Ant Colony Optimization. MIT Press, Cambridge (2004). 345 p.
12. Lebedev, B.K., Lebedev, O.B., Lebedeva, E.M.: Resource allocation based on hybrid swarm intelligence models. Sci. Tech. J. Inf. Technol. Mech. Opt. **17**(6), 1063–1073 (2017). (in Russian)

13. Cong, J., Romesis, M., Xie, M.: Optimality, scalability and stability study of partitioning and placement algorithms. In: Proceedings of the International Symposium on Physical Design, Monterey, CA, pp. 88–94 (2003)

14. Vorobyova, E.Yu., Karpenko, A.P., Seliverstov, E.Yu.: Co-hybridization of particle swarm algorithms. Science and Education. MSTU named after N.E. Bauman. Electronic Journal № 4 (2012). (in Russian)

15. Lebedev, B.K., Lebedev, O.B., Lebedev, V.B.: Hybridization of swarm intelligence and genetic evolution on the example of placement. Electronic Scientific Magazine: Software Products, Systems And Algorithms № 4 (2017). https://doi.org/10.15827/2311-6749.25.280. (in Russian)

16. Cheng, Yu., Sha, D.Y.: A hybrid particle swarm optimization for job shop scheduling problem. Computers & Industrial Engineering, pp. 791–808 (2006)

17. Agasiev, T.A., Karpenko, A.P.: Modern techniques of global optimization. Information Technologies. M: Publishing House of MSTU. N.E. Bauman №6, pp. 370–386 (2018). (in Russian)

18. Clerc, M.: Particle Swarm Optimization. ISTE, London (2006). 246 p.

19. Kureichik, V.M., Lebedev, B.K., Lebedev, O.B.: Partitioning based on modeling the adaptive behavior of biological systems. Neurocomputers: development, application № 2, pp. 28–33 (2010). (in Russian)

20. Ong, Y.S., Keane, A.J.: Meta-Lamarckian learning in memetic algorithms. IEEE Trans. Evol. Comput. **8**(2), 99–110 (2004)

Multimodal Interaction: Taxonomy, Exchange Formats

Artem Ryndin, Ekaterina Pakulova(✉), and Gennady Veselov

Institute of Computer Science and Infomation Security, Southern Federal University,
Taganrog 347900, Russian Federation
epakulova@sfedu.ru
http://ictis.sfedu.ru/

Abstract. Today multimodal approach is relevant in any sphere of our digital life. The technologies aim to suggest the best and the most comfortable way for human-human and human-machine interaction. One of the direction to do that is the usage of multimodal communication. The new possibilities in technology (powerful mobile devices, advanced sensors, new ways of output, etc.) have opened up a new research field of multimodal interaction. In this paper, we define the detailed multimodal taxonomy and consider the exchange format for voice and facial data.

Keywords: Multimodality · Network · Exchange formats · Taxonomy

1 Introduction

Naturally, a human investigates the surrounding world with five senses: sight, touch, listen, taste, and smell. Some researches also distinguish proprioception [23]. All the available senses are employed, both in series and in parallel in a human brain. It organizes in a multimodal way. The human receives information from various resources, processes it and gets the combined result. Traditional human-computer communication is unimodal. The multimodal interaction research goal is to design and develop interfaces, and technologies that eliminate the limitations of HCI and unlock its full potential [4]. The modern human-computer interaction solutions enable the use of various human modalities in the development of multimodal interaction systems.

The term "modality" is complex. Here, in this paper modality may be understood as belonging of the reflected stimulus to the specific sensory system. The sensory is responsible for the perception of particular signals from the environment or internal environment [6, 18]. In the technical field, the term "modality" refers to the concrete combination of an interaction device with an interaction language [22], in a physiological sense it is understood as the possibilities of human perception (sensors) and human action (motor). In our opinion, for multimodal interaction systems modality refers to an information representation of human physical characteristics (human perception) and which are used in some communication environment. Modalities are distinguished between the so-called

© Springer Nature Singapore Pte Ltd. 2021
P. K. Singh et al. (Eds.): FTNCT 2020, CCIS 1395, pp. 402–411, 2021.
https://doi.org/10.1007/978-981-16-1480-4_36

action modalities and perception modalities [22]. Action modalities refer to the available input forms to transmit information from the user to the system. In contrast, perception modalities relate to the transmission of data from the system to the user. In other words, we deal with input and output modalities [9]. For the realization of multimodal HCI the multimodal interfaces [16,21] are developed. They proceed with the information transfer and implement the multimodal interaction.

We consider the system of the multimodal interaction as a client-server framework. A multimodal device measures the characteristics of the user, generates data packets and sends them to the destination side.

Generally, there can be two scenarios: with processing and merging of modalities on the source-side or on the destination-side.

In the first case, on the destination-side, multimodal information is processed, fused and sent to another user or system. Thus, the system transmits a large amount of "raw" heterogeneous information: audio, video, text, photos, etc. This information should not be lost or corrupted, since in this case, the modality parameters can be lost. Therefore, in this scenario, there are high requirements for data transmission and loss reduction. On the other hand, this approach reduces the requirements for the computation capacity of the transmitting device.

In the second case, the processing of multimodal data on the source-side significantly reduces the load on the network, since it substantially reduces the size of the transmitted data. But in this case, the multimodal transmitter must be capable of handling different modalities, extracting their parameters and fusing them.

Modalities may be used for the identification and monitoring of the physiological state of a user. The joint input of information from various sensors and inputs may be done through multimodal interfaces. The multimodal interfaces may adapt to the user's task, conditions and environment.

Various sets of modalities are using for multiple applications. It means that each multimodal application needs a particular set of information for exchanging between user and system during task performance. Thus, for instance, modalities for multimodal authentication system are different than for eHealth application.

Based on the understanding of input and output modalities we may consider the taxonomy. The taxonomy contains two classes: the class of all possible input modalities and the class of all possible output modalities. The input modalities are generated by humans while output modalities are perceived by humans. The quantity of elements in these two classes is not equal. They are asymmetrical [8].

At this time, the researches proposed different taxonomies of the multimodal data. We considered them in section "Related works". However, none of them can cover the full spectrum of interaction that can be possible between human and machines.

The contribution of this paper is to describe the detailed taxonomy for the input multimodal data and provide it with the interchange format. We outline interchange formats for each class of modalities based on the existing approach.

2   Related Works

The issue of the design of multimodal data taxonomy arises since the 1970s. We may outline two tendencies in taxonomy classification: taxonomies based on human senses and taxonomies based on devices that provide capabilities for input to and perceive output from information systems.

On of the first attempt to make classification of input modalities was made in [13]. The authors considered the possible ways for HCI.

In [26], the taxonomy of input/output modalities in the three directions (graphics, acoustics and haptics) is presented.

Authors in [7,8] built up a taxonomy of unimodal input and output modalities with hierarchical levels of abstraction. They distinguished four different classes at the so-called abstract supper level. They are linguistic, analogue, arbitrary, and explicit. The next level is "generic". At this level, static and dynamic representations for graphic, acoustic and haptic communication channels are considered. The last level is the atomic or sub-atomic level. This level concretizes in categories the means of communication channels (for instance, written, spoken, graphs, images etc.)

In [5], the authors considered the taxonomy for five communication channel. They are acoustic, visual, haptic, olfactory and text. The authors outline input and output modalities.

However, one of the common approaches is to build the task-oriented classification of communication channels. For example, in [17], we considered the classification of a user's communication channels for multimodal authentication system.

In [3], the authors made a complication survey about Human-Computer Interaction methods. They considered papers and report from 1974 [13] until 2014 [25]. Their taxonomy is based on human-computer interaction with considering the user's capability to provide the input modality and perceive the output modality.

The authors of [10] considered the HCI from the device capability implementation. They analyzed 510 papers and presented a unified cross-device taxonomy and overview of state of the art.

3   Taxonomy of Multimodal Interaction

Based on the taxonomy proposed in [5], we detailed it with possible modalities parameters (Fig. 1) and defined the exchange format for "raw" information representation. There is no purpose to describe all possible modalities parameters. We aim to show their diversity.

The most informative communication channels are acoustics, visual and proprioception [23].

The acoustic communication channel may be described by paralinguistic and extralinguistic channels. By simple words, the paralinguistic channel presents verbal communication (speech), and the extralinguistic channel transmits the

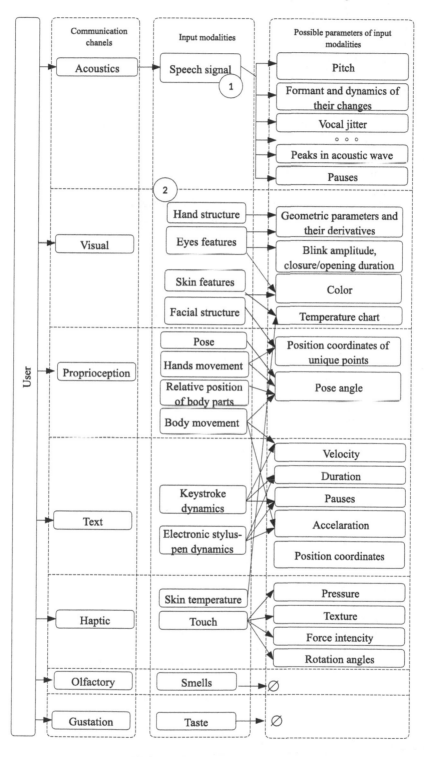

Fig. 1. Taxonomy of multimodal interaction

other relevant to the speech information (cough, laughter, sigh, etc.) [11]. Moreover, the acoustic communication channel may also transmit the information which is not directly related to the act of speech and may be based on it. For example, we made a research on the influence of the heart rate on the speech signal and we show that the heart rate may be extracted from the speech signal [20].

The visual and proprioception communication channels transmit the user appearance and his behavioural characteristics by video and image technical means. The technical devices collect static and dynamic characteristics of the user. Generally, his information is unique for each user. Facial expressions reflect information about emotions, mood, a person's attitude to the situation. They help us to conclude about his/her character, belonging to a social stratum, as well as about age, gender and racial origin. Human emotions generate the typical facial expressions associated with facial muscle activity [5].

Proprioception characterizes the position of a person in space, relative position of body parts and body movements.

The characteristics of haptic modalities are also informative. The nature of the haptic interfaces and haptic modalities are considered in [15]. In [27], the authors considered the characteristics of haptic receptors in skin, muscles and tendons. They also proposed the taxonomy of multimodal haptic devices.

The textual communication channel mainly presented by keystroke and electronic stylus pen dynamics. Keystroke is a behavioural biometric parameter which reflets the unique manner of typing [24].

4   Multimodal Interaction Architecture

Fig. 2. Multimodal data transmission procedure

Various applications of multimodal interactions should be agreed upon Multimodal Architecture and Interfaces specification [12]. The goal of the W3C Multimodal Interaction Architecture (MMI Architecture) is to provide a way to coordinate multiple modalities in a standard way, with standard methods of communication. This standard defines the components of the multimodal system: modality components, interaction manager. The messages between components in the MMI Architecture are referred to as life-cycle events. MMI Architecture defines two types of events. The first one is the generic control events: starting and stopping events and also their acknowledgements. The second type reflects the modality- or application events. These events are used in processing procedures. There are no requirements about a specific format for life-cycle events.

However, the specification describes an XML format. Basically, researchers may define modality component by themselves. However, the life-cycle events of the MMI should be implemented.

On Fig. 2, we consider multimodal data transmission procedure within the modality component. The peculiarity of the proposed procedure is the transmission of obtained modalities through the network. On the source-side modalities are encoding into exchange format and send to the destination-side where they are decoding and process.

In such approach is it necessary to agree with exchange formats for various classes of modalities which are transmitted through the network.

5   Exchange Information Formats

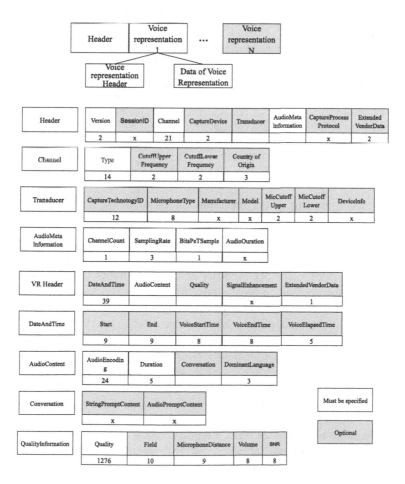

Fig. 3. Record format for voice data

The parameters of user modalities obtain various statistical characteristics. It leads to the assumption that they may have various requirements for Quality of Service. However, they may be used for one application at the same time.

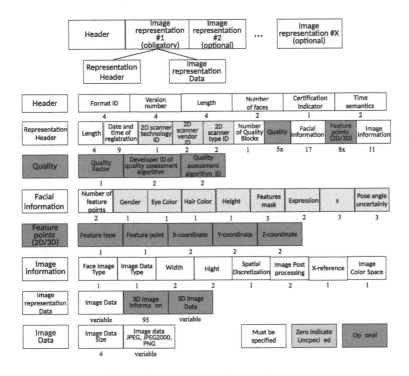

Fig. 4. Record format for facial image

One of the challenge today is the absence of the standard exchange format for various classes of modalities. The Multimodal Architecture and Interfaces specification [12] defines the architecture and requirements to multimodal interaction system. However, it omits the specific formats for the component which handles media for either capture or processing.

We assume that it is possible to use the interchange format of biometric data for multimodal information and formats for video data encoding. Let us consider the possible interchange formats for multimodal biometric information. In [19], the Common Biometric Exchange File Format was proposed (CBEFF). The purpose of CBEFF is to define a common exchange format for biometric data for providing the interoperability of biometric-based applications and systems. The CBEFF defines three main sections in for the exchange format: standard biometric header, biometric specific memory block and signature block. Each section may include optional subsections. It is assumed that CBEFF may be used for the following biometric parameters: Multiple Biometrics Used, Facial Features, Voice, Fingerprint, Iris, Retina, Hand Geometry, Signature Dynamics, Keystroke Dynamics, Lip Movement, Thermal Face Image, Thermal Hand

Image, Gait, Body Odor, DNA, Ear Shape, Finger Geometry, Palm Geometry, Vein Pattern.

The [14] proposed another structure of CBEFF. They define the following possible field for CBEFF: the standard biometric header, the biometric data block, and possibly the optional security block. The standard biometric header includes metadata of specific characteristics of the biometric data (e.g., biometric data format, modality, its creation date). The content of the biometric data block may reflect the biometric data exchange format or some service data (e.g., data by vendors to support their own unique implementation features/processing). The security block may include integrity-related data (e.g., digital signature, HASH or key, etc.).

There are also other attempts to standardized the biometric exchange format. For instance, the ISO standards (19794) may be used for this purpose. In this paper, we consider two of them: the standard for acoustic data [2] and the standard for the format of facial images [1]. The [2] specifies a data exchange format for storing, recording, and transmitting digitized acoustic human voice data (speech). It is supposed that this format is appropriate for a single speaker recorded in a single session. This format is presented on Fig. 3.

The [1] provides the requirements for the four types of face images: basic, frontal, full frontal and token frontal. The considered requirements cover support various specification of the facial image. It includes the image encoding format, degree of rotation, camera position, lighting condition, resolution of the image. The structure of the format is presented on Fig. 4.

Like in other analogues the data in these standards are written in XML format.

6   Conclusion

Today multimodal approach is a very perspective way of development of info-communication systems. In this paper, we detailed the taxonomy for multimodal data. We considered the exchange format for voice and facial modalities. For future work, we are going to define the exchange format for other classes of modalities.

Acknowledgements. The authors would like to thank the anonymous referees for their valuable comments and helpful suggestions. This work is supported by the Russian Foundation For Basic Research (grant 19-37-90129) and Council on grants of the President of the Russian Federation.

References

1. Information technology-biometric data interchange formats-19794-part 5: Face image data (2014)
2. Information technology-biometric data interchange formats-19794-13: Voice data (2018)

3. Augstein, M., Neumayr, T.: A human-centered taxonomy of interaction modalities and devices. Interact. Comput. **31**(1), 27–58 (2019)
4. Baig, M.Z., Kavakli, M.: Multimodal systems: taxonomy, methods, and challenges. arXiv preprint arXiv:2006.03813 (2020)
5. Basov, O., Saitov, I.: The main interpersonal communication channel and their projection on infocommunication systems. SPIIRAS Proc. **7**(30), 122–140 (2013). (in Russian)
6. Basov, O.: Reasoning of the transition to polymodal infocommunicational systems. Trudy **18**, 19–22 (2015)
7. Bernsen, N.O.: A reference model for output information in intelligent multimedia presentation systems. In: Proceedings of the ECAI'96 Workshop on: Towards a Standard Reference Model for Intelligent Multimedia Presentation Systems (1996)
8. Bernsen, N.O.: Multimodality theory. In: Tzovaras, D. (ed.) Multimodal User Interfaces, pp. 5–29. Springer, Heidelberg (2008). https://doi.org/10.1007/978-3-540-78345-9_2
9. Blattner, M.M., Glinert, E.P.: Multimodal integration. IEEE Multimedia **3**(4), 14–24 (1996)
10. Brudy, F., et al.: Cross-device taxonomy: survey, opportunities and challenges of interactions spanning across multiple devices. In: Proceedings of the 2019 CHI Conference on Human Factors in Computing Systems, pp. 1–28 (2019)
11. Campoy-Cubillo, M.C., Querol-Julián, M.: Assessing multimodal listening. B. Crawford, & I. Fortanet-Gómez, Multimodal Analysis in Academic Setting: From Research to Teaching, pp. 193–212 (2015)
12. Dahl, D.A.: The w3c multimodal architecture and interfaces standard. J. Multimodal User Interfaces **7**(3), 171–182 (2013)
13. Foley, J.D., Wallace, V.L.: The art of natural graphic man–machine conversation. Proc. IEEE **62**(4), 462–471 (1974)
14. Herr, F., Podio, F.L.: Common biometric exchange formats framework standardization. Technical report (2015)
15. Kortum, P.: HCI Beyond the GUI: Design for Haptic, Speech, Olfactory, and Other Nontraditional Interfaces. Elsevier, Amsterdam (2008)
16. Oviatt, S.: Mulitmodal interactive maps: designing for human performance. Hum.-Comput. Interact. **12**(1–2), 93–129 (1997)
17. Pakulova, E., Ryndin, A., Basov, O.: Multi-path multimodal authentication system for remote information system. In: Proceedings of the 12th International Conference on Security of Information and Networks, pp. 1–4 (2019)
18. Pakulova, E., Ryndin, A., Basov, O., Struev, D.: Principles of constructing polymodal infocommunication systems for information space user service. In: 2017 IEEE 11th International Conference on Application of Information and Communication Technologies (AICT), pp. 1–5. IEEE (2017)
19. Podio, F.L., Dunn, J.S., Reinert, L., Tilton, C.J., O'Gorman, L.: CBEFF common biometric exchange file format. Technical report, National Inst of Standards And Technology Gaithersburg MD (2001)
20. Poleshenkov, D., Pakulova, E., Basov, O.: Research on dependences of speech pitch parameters on pulse and heartbeat signals. In: Young Scientist's Third International Workshop on Trends in Information Processing, vol. 2500 (2019)
21. Ronzhin, A., Karpov, A.: Multimodal interfaces: main principles and cognitive aspects. Trudy SPIIRAN **3**, 300–319 (2006)
22. Schaffer, S.: Modeling modality selection in multimodal human-computer interaction: extending automated usability evaluation tools for multimodal input. Ph.D. thesis, Technische Universitaet Berlin (Germany) (2016)

23. Schuessel, F.: Multimodal input fusion for companion technology. Ph.D. thesis, Ulm University (2017)
24. Stan, L., Li, Z., Jain, A.K.: Encyclopedia of Biometrics. In: IZ, vol. 1. Springer, Heidelberg (2009)
25. Turk, M.: Multimodal interaction: a review. Pattern Recogn. Lett. **36**, 189–195 (2014)
26. Tzovaras, D.: Multimodal User Interfaces: From Signals to Interaction. Springer, Heidelberg (2008). https://doi.org/10.1007/978-3-540-78345-9
27. Wang, D., Ohnishi, K., Xu, W.: Multimodal haptic display for virtual reality: a survey. IEEE Trans. Industr. Electron. **67**(1), 610–623 (2019)

Development of a Automated Environmental Monitoring System with Forecasting

Elena Volkova, Said Muratchaev[✉], and Alexey Volkov

National Research University of Electronic Technology, Bld. 1, Shokin Square, 124498 Moscow, Russia

Abstract. All environmental and monitoring systems are most often based on the accumulated statistics of various parameters of temperature, harmful emissions, humidity, carbon dioxide. This paper describes methods of implementing machine learning algorithms for forecasting problems within a specifically developed ASMOS system in Russia. The proposed algorithm makes it possible to consider the change in temperature for several hours in advance, as well as days. Later this algorithm can be implemented in the system for assessing hazardous environmental situations, where a comparison of hazardous factors affecting the environment carried out.

Keywords: Forecasting · Environmental monitoring · Sensors · ANN

1 Introduction

Machine learning algorithms widely used in all areas of the IT industry. This is mainly due to an excess of accumulated information in various areas. The accumulated information can be used as the experience, which adjusts the previously "rigid" algorithms by changing their coefficients depending on the problem being solved. From an environmental point of view, the amount of data used in this area is quite large, and as a rule, existing algorithms do not consider the accumulated statistics in various environmental monitoring and control systems.

There is a certain baseline performance level, against which the algorithm is improved through the introduction of accumulated data. After integrating machine learning algorithms, it becomes possible to compare the performance of the improved algorithm with the base one to assess the effectiveness of the proposed solution. As soon as the algorithm is ready and debugged, it becomes necessary to adapt the algorithm to new data which may appear later in the real operation of the system where the algorithm was integrated.

Many manufacturing sectors are weather dependent, such as agriculture. Climate can change dramatically, making old methods of weather forecasting less effective. By implementing machine learning algorithms in weather forecasting, it is possible to achieve an increase in forecast accuracy for several hours/days ahead, which can greatly affect the

The research was supported financially by Center for Scientific and Technical Information «Sensorika» NIU MIET NOTS RTSSS: AAAA-A20-1200130090100-3.

© Springer Nature Singapore Pte Ltd. 2021
P. K. Singh et al. (Eds.): FTNCT 2020, CCIS 1395, pp. 412–421, 2021.
https://doi.org/10.1007/978-981-16-1480-4_37

correct decisions on harvesting, or on preventing various catastrophic situations. Data analysis and machine learning algorithms are used to predict weather conditions, such as random forest classification, time series forecasting, or simply regression analysis.

Machine learning enables systems to learn and improve from their own experience without direct operator intervention. With the introduction of the concept of machine learning, it has become much easier to work with data analysis and forecasting. Machine learning does not require an understanding of the physical processes that govern the atmosphere, but uses accumulated data to predict future situation. Therefore, this process can be used as a weather forecasting method.

In [1], an algorithm for forecasting precipitation is presented based on two NWP (Numerical weather prediction) models: WRF (Weather Research and Forecasting) and MM5 (Fifth Generation Penn State/NCAR Mesoscale). NWP is a method for modeling and predicting the state of the atmosphere using a computer model, and WRF is a set of programs that implement the calculation. The WRF model has a wide variety of meteorological applications and is used on scales from meters to thousands of kilometers. Based on the obtained results of the model operation, it was possible to reach the Root Mean Square Error (RMSE) parameter in the region between 0.756 and 0.668 for 12- and 24-h forecasts. It is assumed that these results can be improved by using machine learning algorithms that will use statistics more effectively.

Preprocessing and the concept of using data arrays in forecasting algorithms is also important. So, in [2] the distributed observation approach is used in assimilation and fore-casting of ensemble data. The work uses the Ensemble of Data Assimilations (EDA) data centering approach, which achieves an 80% reduction in mean square error. The results of this work show a variety of approaches to the problems of forecasting meteorological data.

The article [3] presents a comparative overview and a proposal for using the archi-tecture of the neural network LTSM (Long short-term memory) to solve the problem of forecasting weather data. The basic concepts of the LTSM neural network are ana-lyzed and the results of the algorithm are presented. The results obtained indicate that the algorithm does a good job and the correct prediction is achieved in 85% of cases. However, algorithms based on neural networks require computational power of very different orders of magnitude than classical machine learning algorithms. This fact must be used as a fundamental in the development of a specific system, since this introduces additional computational costs for the system, which it may not cope with.

LSTM models are widely used, as an example in [4], Recurrent Neural Network (RNN) with LSTM is used to predict wind speed. An important factor in forecasting is the accuracy of the measured parameters of wind, humidity, temperature, and so on. Wind measurements were carried out at 5 levels, which made it possible to more accurately measure the wind speed depending on the height of the sensors.

Energy efficient application of prediction algorithms is shown in the article [5]. Using a forecast for 24 h ahead, system can distribute the consumed energy in the sensors, calculate the solar radiation and humidity. All of these factors affect the efficiency of solar panels. The architecture of a neural network for forecasting is considered and the resulting graphs are shown, which show the comparative characteristics of the forecasting algorithms.

The problems of forecasting the state of meteorological data also affect the efficiency of energy distribution. The article [6] presents a comparative and indicative analysis of the various models for forecasting the state of the weather, and also shows a model of the proposed algorithm, which showed results better than the classical forecasting algorithms. The graphs are based on the ANN and SVR algorithms. On the basis of the obtained MRE and RMSE, the proposed method showed the best results.

One of the popular directions in the field of artificial intelligence is also the increase the number of renewable energy sources [7]. Energy sources of this kind are usually intermittent and uncontrolled. The question arises of generation, replacement and increase in the productivity of renewable energy sources through the introduction of forecasting algorithms. The work adapted the SVM algorithm for specific values, which increased the indicators to 27%.

To solve the problem of weather forecasting, algorithms of the ARIMA family are often used, for example, in [8], several varieties of the ARIMA algorithm are given. The parameters MAPE, MaxAPE, and MAE were used to assess the efficiency of these algorithms. These parameters allow to accurately determine the stability and efficiency of forecasts. Wavelet-Based ARIMA algorithm showed good results of parameters, in particular, the MAPE parameter is 0.0039.

As the monitoring systems grow, the information collected from the sensors grows, which is why the implementation of Big Data technologies is an urgent task [9]. The concepts used on large data sets involve finding hidden dependencies that cannot be seen on small data sets. The author uses several algorithms for forecasting at once, namely linear regression and SVM.

Based on the analysis of the Indian dataset, this paper [10] assumes the use of the MLR (Multiple Linear Regression) algorithm, since the input data have many parameters. The algorithm is used to predict rainfall and precipitation. The performance was evaluated using an MSE of 11,9, which is a satisfactory value.

2 Methodology

2.1 System Architecture

Elasticsearch was chosen as the database, as a Kafka queue service, and as a tool for primary data processing - Logstash. There is only one solution to implement visualization when working with the Elasticsearch database - Kibana. Thus, the overall system architecture is shown in Fig. 1. The number of Elasticsearch components according to the Paxos algorithm must be odd to ensure consensus. The number of Logstash components is determined only by the amount of input data, and this component of the system can be automatically scaled out when the Logstash load average threshold is reached.

As you can see from Fig. 1, IoT sensors must write data to Kafka, we will form methods for solving this problem. The first solution is to use the Kafka stream API, but this option requires changing the operating code of the sensor itself, which is not always possible. Also, in cases where there is no way to influence the source code that implements the sensors, you can use specialized lightweight messaging clients such as filebeat, fluentbit. This class of tools is used to send messages from various sources to data storage systems. However, it is not always possible to install a client on the platform

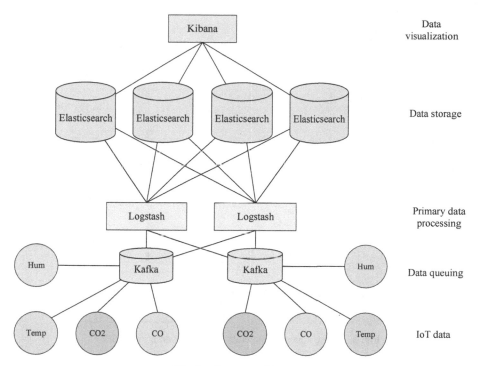

Fig. 1. System architecture

where the IoT sensor is launched; in such cases, Logstash should be used as a system for centralized data collection from some sensors.

The optimal solution is to use libraries that allow you to write a cluster from IoT sensors or data aggregators directly to Kafka, since the use of computing resources will be minimized. Moreover, in the case of using non-JSON data from the IoT, they can be processed at the Logstash - the data processing level.

As shown in Fig. 2, if it is impossible to change the IoT sensor code, you can use the message sender on each aggregator or sensor in order to receive data, preprocess it, and send it to Kafka using the appropriate protocol. This solution minimizes the load on the central processing and visualization system, since some of the operations are carried out on the client side. It should be noted that the implementation of such an architecture does not carry tangible additional loads on the sensors. A small amount of RAM is enough for filebeat to work, and it can also be run in a container to provide isolation from the application in order to minimize errors.

Since it is not always possible to install software on the IoT sensor side and influence the way messages are displayed, an alternative option for collecting message logs was implemented - creating a separate Logstash, the role of which is to collect logs from some of the sensors, as shown in Fig. 3. In this case, some delay, after the event is generated, Logstash will not immediately receive information about it. Also, in such an implementation, Logstash will consume the resources of a centralized cluster, which is more difficult to maintain than in a situation with a decentralized load.

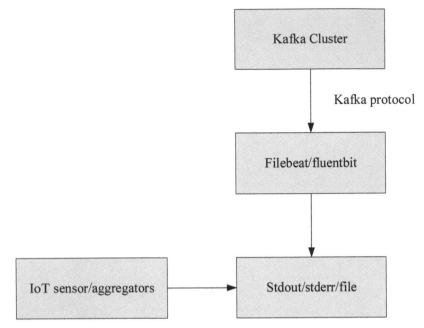

Fig. 2. Using a message sender on sensors or aggregators

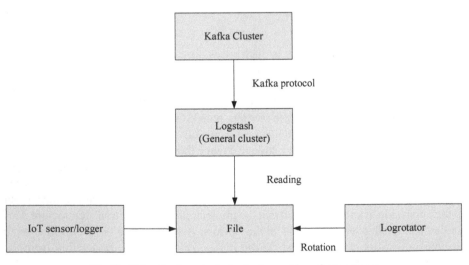

Fig. 3. Using the Logstash cluster to read logs from sensors

According to Elasticsearch storage design data, implementing a production cluster will require separate servers to implement hot, warm, and cold indexes. This will significantly reduce load and use slower disks for read-only indexes. There have been no methods for predicting the performance of a cluster in scientific papers; therefore, the load on the cluster must be increased gradually and scaled horizontally in the event of a lack of resources. This approach should be used until a mathematical model for predicting the performance of the Elasticsearch cluster is implemented.

Another important architectural solution from the point of view of a productive cluster is the use of dedicated control nodes, identified in the theoretical part, so as not to lose control of the cluster when incoming requests increase, as well as the use of Elastic curator for preliminary calculation of some operations, for example, creating indexes.

From an implementation point of view, the management components of the Elasticsearch cluster should not have storage used for user data; therefore, the procedure for deploying, updating and rolling back them will be significantly simplified compared to components that store hot and cold indexes. When creating a cluster, a machine learning modeler should use co-located clusters of 1 or 3 nodes. Thus, the cluster can be deployed on a local developer PC and provide an approximate simulation of the system.

2.2 Sensors Overview

The sensor system is developed on LoRaWAN communication technology. All of them are connected to data aggregators, which are presented as PYNQ-Z2. There is a problem with the hardware implementation of various algorithms such as software development or machine learning. The main solution to this problem is the PYNQ system-on-chip. The PYNQ board is the preferred choice over other boards due to processing power and cost, but the main aspect of board selection is the use of Python to write various programs.

PYNQ is an open source project from Xilinx that makes it easy to design embedded systems using Xilinx Zynq SoCs. This is achieved through the use of a web architecture that is browser agnostic. PYNQ uses the open source Jupyter Notebook framework to run the Interactive Python (IPython) core and web server directly on the ARM processor of the Zynq device. The web server provides kernel access through a set of browser-based tools that provide a toolbar, bash terminal, code editor, and Jupyter notebooks. Browser Tools are implemented using a combination of JavaScript, HTML and CSS and work in any modern browser. Figure 4 shows the PYNQ system-on-chip.

PYNQ uses Python to program both the embedded processors and the board itself. Python is a high-level programming language. The Python language increases the level of program abstraction and programmer productivity. However, this is not a mutually exclusive choice. PYNQ uses CPython, which is written in C and integrates thousands of C libraries and can be extended with optimized code written in C. Wherever appropriate, a more productive Python environment should be used, and whenever efficiency dictates, the code can be used in C language at a lower level.

Using the Python language and libraries, you can take advantage of the programmable logic and microprocessors in Zynq to create more functional and interesting embedded systems. With PYNQ, you can create high-performance embedded applications with parallel hardware execution, process video at high frame rates, accelerate hardware algorithms, process signals in real time, and much more. PYNQ is designed for various equipment design, prototyping, machine learning and data analysis and much more.

The final prototype of the ANN that can be used in this system is shown in Fig. 5. Due to the lack of a distributed network of sensors, implementation of this architecture is postponed until the deployment of the monitoring system. The neural network will be

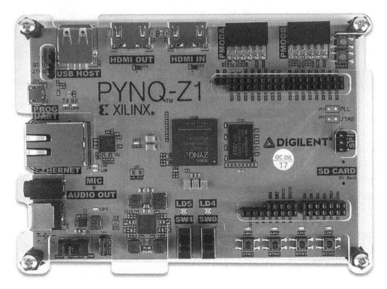

Fig. 4. Pynq-Z2 board

based on the LSTM model, which allows maintaining high rates of correct predictions about the state of the environment.

PYNQ uses the Jupyter Notebook, a popular free interactive environment that uses the Python programming language to combine code, text, images, videos, and diagrams and distribute them to others. Previously, it was called IPython Notebook, but the name has changed in order to emphasize compatibility not only with Python, but also with other programming languages. Jupyter Notebook is a client-server application that allows you to edit and run files through your web browser. The Jupyter Notebook application can run on a local computer and does not require Internet access, or it can be installed on a remote server.

3   Results

The ARIMA model was used as a prediction algorithm, since the performance power of the PYNQ-Z2 board is sufficient to start working in real time. The data array for training the algorithm are temperature measurements and other indicators over the past 5 years. The results of the work are presented in Fig. 6.

The forecasting algorithm model was implemented in Python in the Jupyter Notebook environment. Data for the algorithm was collected in real time and processed through the developed server described earlier in Fig. 1.

$$MAPE = \frac{1}{n}\sum_{t=1}^{n} \frac{AbsoluteError_t}{ActualDemand_t} \times 100 \tag{1}$$

Equation (1) indicates the main measure of the efficiency of various models and algorithms of neural networks. Based on this indicator, one can judge the success of the implemented model. The indicator specifically for this model corresponds to 3,4%.

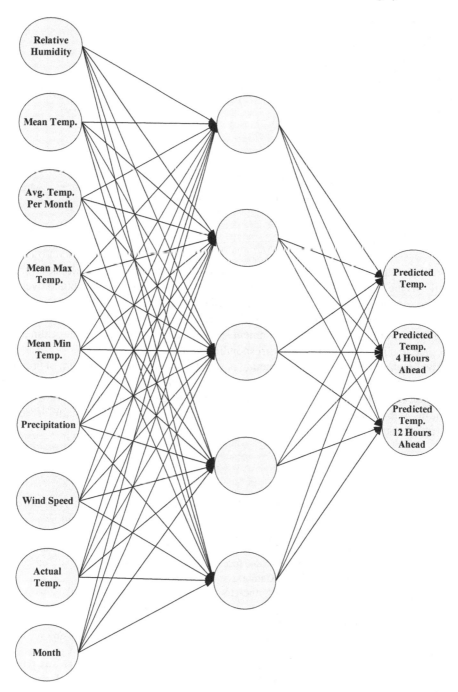

Fig. 5. Neural network architecture

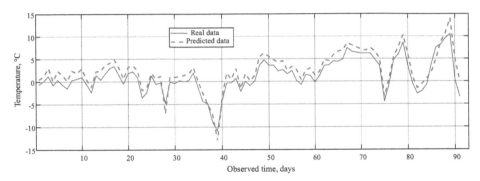

Fig. 6. Results of a related model

4 Conclusion

The monitoring system architecture and neural network model were developed. Subsequently, as the system is implemented, and the network of sensors is distributed over the city area, a neural network will be implemented based on the accumulated statistics.

Presented results indicate the high efficiency of machine learning algorithms in the problems of predicting the environment. MAPE metrics for various algorithms are presented and implemented in the corresponding code.

The graph shows the result of the neural network in relation to the problem of predicting temperature. The root mean square error of this algorithm is 3,4%. The implemented system works and functions as a prototype. Further development of this work is possible in the form of introducing a system of decisions based on collected features; as an algorithm, a neural network can be implemented.

References

1. Wardah, T., Kamil, A.A., Sahol Hamid, A.B., Maisarah, W.W.I.: Statistical verification of numerical weather prediction models for quantitative precipitation forecast. In: 2011 IEEE Colloquium on Humanities, Science and Engineering, Penang, pp. 88–92 (2011)
2. Hólm, E.V., Lang, S.T.K., Fisher, M., Kral, T., Bonavita, M.: Distributed observations in meteorological ensemble data assimilation and forecasting. In: 2018 21st International Conference on Information Fusion (FUSION), Cambridge, pp. 92–99 (2018)
3. Fente, D.N., Kumar Singh, D.: Weather forecasting using artificial neural network. In: 2018 Second International Conference on Inventive Communication and Computational Technologies (ICICCT), Coimbatore, pp. 1757–1761 (2018)
4. Ningsih, F.R., Djamal, E.C., Najmurrakhman, A.: Wind speed forecasting using recurrent neural networks and long short term memory. In: 2019 6th International Conference on Instrumentation, Control, and Automation (ICA), Bandung, Indonesia, pp. 137–141 (2019)
5. Chen, C., Duan, S., Cai, T., Liu, B.: Online 24-h solar power forecasting based on weather type classification using artificial neural network. Solar Energy **85**(11), 2856–2870 (2011)
6. Yang, H.-T., Huang, C.-M., Huang, Y.-C., Pai, Y.-S.: A weather-based hybrid method for 1-day ahead hourly forecasting of PV power output. IEEE Trans. Sustain. Energy **5**(3), 917–926 (2014)

7. Sharma, N., Sharma, P., Irwin, D., Shenoy, P.: Predicting solar generation from weather forecasts using machine learning. In: 2011 IEEE International Conference on Smart Grid Communications (SmartGridComm), Brussels, pp. 528–533 (2011)
8. Narendra Babu, C., Eswara Reddy, B.: Predictive data mining on average global temperature using variants of ARIMA models. In: IEEE-International Conference on Advances in Engineering, Science and Management (ICAESM - 2012), Nagapattinam, Tamil Nadu, pp. 256–260 (2012)
9. Madan, S., Kumar, P., Rawat, S., Choudhury, T.: Analysis of weather prediction using machine learning & big data. In: 2018 International Conference on Advances in Computing and Communication Engineering (ICACCE), Paris, pp. 259–264 (2018)
10. Grace, R.K., Suganya, B.: Machine learning based rainfall prediction. In: 2020 6th International Conference on Advanced Computing and Communication Systems (ICACCS), Coimbatore, India, pp. 227–229 (2020)

Application of Machine Learning Methods in Modeling Hydrolithospheric Processes

Sergey Sizov[1]($\boxtimes$), Tatiana Drovosekova[2]($\boxtimes$), and Ivan Pershin[2]($\boxtimes$)

[1] Southern Federal University, Bolshaya Sadovaya 105/42, 344006 Rostov-na-Donu, Russia
[2] North-Caucasus Federal University, Pushkina 1, 355017 Stavropol, Russia

Abstract. One of the most urgent problems in the study and analysis of hydrolithospheric processes is the construction of verifiable mathematical and computer models that make it possible to predict the behavior of an object under various initial conditions and input influences. Recently, machine learning methods have been increasingly used in geological research. This paper discusses machine learning methods used in geological exploration to automate data analysis, as well as used for neural network information modeling of geological objects.

Keywords: Machine learning · Neural networks · Math modeling · Geologic · System analysis

1 Introduction

The hydrolithosphere is one of the main shells of the biosphere, on the safety of which all living things largely depend. Deterioration of the quality of surface water, the need for high-quality and reliable sources of clean water, an unfavorable situation with surface water, the desire for reliable and high-quality water sources, the disposal of industrial waste, irrational mining of minerals are the main examples of the serious impact on humans on hydrolithospheric processes threatening proportions [1, 19–21].

Lack of drinking resources of the required quality is becoming almost a global environmental disaster today.

The water supply systems are huge and constantly increasing volumes of wastewater, utilization in the Earth's hydrolithosphere leads to an increase in consumption and energy resources, the danger of the environment, and outbreaks of epidemics [2, 15–17]. The main problem of the exploitation of hydrolithospheric resources is their depletion and pollution, disruption of natural biochemical cycles and protected destruction of the biosphere.

Recently, more and more people are talking about the potential of the global water cycle, the consequences of which can be reliably predicted [3, 12, 22].

Therefore, one of the main tasks is the rational and environmentally safe use of natural resources, analysis of the state of the hydrolithosphere, and forecasting the development of technogenic processes and their management.

© Springer Nature Singapore Pte Ltd. 2021
P. K. Singh et al. (Eds.): FTNCT 2020, CCIS 1395, pp. 422–431, 2021.
https://doi.org/10.1007/978-981-16-1480-4_38

Mineral waters are one of the most important natural resources for balneology. The basis of the resort resources of the Caucasian Mineral Waters is mineral waters of various composition. In terms of richness and diversity, the KMV group of mineral springs is a rare phenomenon: here and the Narzan spring in Kislovodsk with its "cold boiling water" seething from carbon dioxide, and the hot waters of Pyatigorsk and Zheleznovodsk, radon (Pyatigorsk), hydrocarbonate-chloride-sodium (Essentuki) others water. Out of 130 mineral springs, 90 are exploited for medicinal purposes [1, 18].

In recent decades, the methods of using modern technologies [2, 13], the threat of penetration of surface water soils, surface waters and radioactive waste [12] into working aquifers [2] has increased.

In connection with the current situation used with the exploitation of mineral water deposits, modeling of hydrolithospheric processes is of great importance.

Until recently, reduced physical and analog types of models were used to study the processes occurring in the hydrolithosphere, but the high complexity, labor and time required to simulate such models limit the limits of their use. In connection with the rapid pace of computer technology, especially the development of computers, in the study of the processes occurring in the hydrolithosphere, there is a massive transition to mathematical and computer modeling. Simultaneously with a decrease in the cost of computing equipment, there is a rapid increase in the speed of equipment and the volume of external and internal memory, which makes it possible to perform a huge amount of calculations and process large amounts of data in a short period of time. The use of mathematical and computer modeling of physical processes increases the range of applicability of this direction, but requires the development of other methodological approaches to modeling.

Modeling a hydrolithospheric object begins with the construction of a diagram of hydrogeological sections of sedimentary rocks. The study is carried out by drilling, and using geophysical and seismic measurements. An example of a geological section of the base of Mount Zheleznaya (Zheleznovodskoe mineral water deposit) is shown in Fig. 1.

Mathematical models of hydrolithospheric objects, as a rule, are described by differential filtration equations and are calculated using numerical methods (for example, the finite difference method) [3, 23]. After that, the model can be converted to discrete form and numerically calculated using a computer.

This approach allows you to build complex three-dimensional models of the processes taking place inside the object. Its advantage is also the high accuracy of modeling in the presence of a large amount of information about the structure of the hydrolithospheric object, filtration coefficients of porous layers, fluid velocity in the layer, hydrodynamic heads, etc.

The main disadvantage of this approach is a sharp increase in computational complexity with an increase in the size of the model and the number of parameters. It is necessary to constantly find a balance between the accuracy of the model and its complexity and size. It should also be noted the complexity of modeling structures with a curvilinear shape [2].

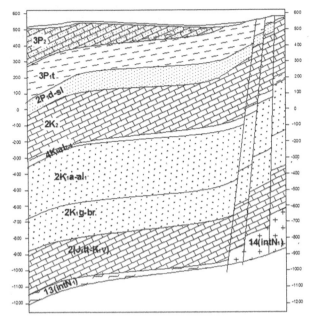

Fig. 1. Geological section.

2 Application of Neural Networks in Hydrolithospheric Research

One of the most promising areas of modeling and control of hydrolithospheric processes is the use of machine learning methods and neural networks (neural networks). A neural network is a mathematical model based on the principles of functioning of a biological neural network. This approach originated in the 1980s, but gained popularity only in the early 2010s due to the increase in the performance of computers capable of performing complex calculations.

A neural network consists of layers on which interconnected units or "neurons" are located, which perform the simplest mathematical calculations, for example, multiplying the results of calculations obtained from previous neurons. The learning process of such an algorithm is an adjustment of each neuron taking into account the maximum quality of the final forecast. Figure 2 shows an example of a three-layer neural network.

The neural network recognizes patterns in data gradually, starting with the analysis of the simplest relationships between the variables of the first neural layers, and ending with complex abstract structures in the last layers. A typical neural network is able to find solutions to problems based on organized quantitative data, for example, tables, specialized networks - to work on images and time sequences.

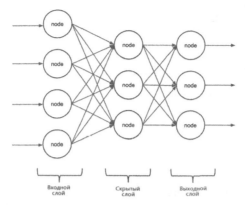

Fig. 2. Three-layer neural network

The main advantages of this approach are the ability to analyze a huge amount of initial empirical data for solving a variety of applied problems and creating complex multivariate models. In contrast to the classical numerical modeling of geolithospheric processes, the introduction of additional parameters makes it possible to increase the accuracy of the model without requiring a large number of changes to the program code.

There are several specialized classes of neural networks such as convolutional neural networks and recurrent neural networks.

Convolutional Neural Networks (CNN) are neural network architecture adapted for image recognition. It mimics some of the features of the visual cortex, which contains simple cells that respond to straight lines at different angles and complex cells that are activated when certain sets of simple cells are activated. Neural networks of this type are usually used for image and voice recognition.

The use of CNN allows to reduce the sensitivity of the forecasts generated by the neural network to changes in scale, displacement, rotation, change of perspective, as well as other changes in the original image [7]. Convolutional neural networks use methods that provide invariance to scaling, rotation and spatial systems [11]:

- local receptor fields;
- general synaptic coefficients;
- hierarchical organization with spatial sub-samples.

Currently, convolutional artificial neural networks and their variations are the best algorithms for the accuracy of recognition and detection of objects in images. For the first time, the quality of object recognition in images by neural networks exceeded the quality of human recognition in 2012 at the ImageNet competition [6].

An example of a convolutional neural network architecture is shown in Fig. 3.

As shown in Fig. 3, CNN consists of various types of layers - convolutional, subsampling and the neural network itself - the perceptron.

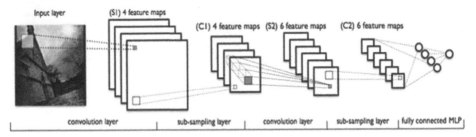

Fig. 3. Topology of CNN

Convolutional and subsampling layers alternate and create an input feature vector for perceptron processing. CNN is a good middle ground between biologically plausible networks and a conventional multilayer perceptron. Now the best results in image recognition are obtained with their help. The average recognition accuracy of such networks exceeds conventional ANNs by 10–15%. SNS is a key technology in Deep Learning [7, 14].

The main strength of CNN is the concept of shared weights. Despite their large size, these networks have few configurable parameters compared to the neocognitron. There are types of CNN (for example, Tiled Convolutional Neural Network), similar to the neocognitron. Such neural networks use partial rejection of associated weights, but the learning algorithm remains the same and is based on back propagation of the error. CNNs can run quickly on a sequential machine and learn quickly by parallelizing the convolution process on each map, and also deconvolution when propagating the error over the network [7].

In application to hydrogeological studies, this type of neural networks is used in seismic exploration to automate the marking of seismic sections. Figure 4 shows an example of an automatically annotated section from the Netherlands Dataset obtained during the study [4] of using machine learning methods to interpret seismic data.

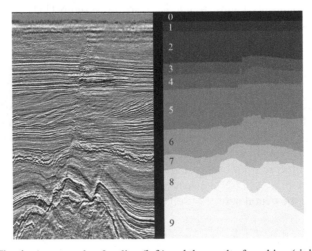

Fig. 4. An example of a slice (left) and the result of marking (right)

Collecting and interpreting geological survey data is a critical task in field development. This is an extremely resource-intensive task for the solution of which convolutional neural networks were used in the study [4]. The array of analyzed data is the Netherlands Offshore F3 Block data freely available in the Open Seismic Repository [8]. The dataset consists of 384 km^2 of time migrated 3D seismic data, with 651 inlines and 951 crosslines, located at the North Sea, Netherlands offshore [4]. This dataset contains tagged data for training the network.

In the course of the study, two neural networks were created, one for classifying the types of rock layers and the other for semantic separation (marking) of seismograms.

The first neural network was based on the Danet FNC architecture (Fig. 5). It is fully CNN capable of distinguishing between pixel-sized fascia [9]. This neural network is trained on datasets marked manually and after that it can create a mask corresponding to the sections of rocks.

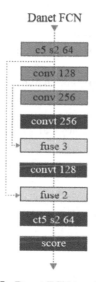

Fig. 5. Danet FCN topology

This model is based on the VGG-FCN topology. Its main difference is converting fully connected layers at the end of the network structure into single convolutions and adding a transposed convolution to discretize its input parameters to the image size. This allows to reduce the used data structures and, as a consequence, the training time of the model [10].

A pre-trained neural network was used to analyze the dataset. As a result of additional training of the model on the data from this set, it was possible to achieve a recognition accuracy of 81.6%.

In the second application, for the semantic classification of the use of pre-trained on geological data CNN. Its topology is shown in Fig. 6 [11].

Fig. 6. CNN topology to semantic classify sesmic data

This network consists of three blocks. The first $5 \times 5 \times 64$ block with local normalization and the next 2×2 join layer. The second block is a $3 \times 3 \times 128$ convolution with local normalization and the next 2×2 join layer. The third block consists of two fully connected layers of 2048 neurons each and a linear classifier [11].

In the case of the marking task, the accuracy ranged from 90 to 95%, depending on the size of the training sample [4]. The result of the network is shown in Fig. 5.

Another type of artificial neural networks that have found their application in geology are recurrent neural networks. Sample of topology shown in Fig. 7.

Recurrent neural networks (RNNs) are a type of neural network in which connections between network elements form a directed sequence. This feature allows you to process sets of events over time. Their difference from standard multilayer neural networks is that they can use internal memory to compute data chains of arbitrary length. Therefore, they are well suited for tasks where something holistic is divided into separate parts, such as tasks such as text recognition, speech recognition, etc. This class of networks is also used in the tasks of analyzing geological data.

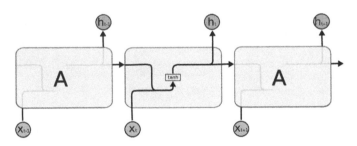

Fig. 7. An example of a fragment of the RNN topology

The paper [5] considers the case of adaptation of a neural network to predict flow rates in wells in the U22 geological layer of the Severo-Vakhskoye field. The following are used as initial parameters for training the model:

1. Time and date of measurement
2. Well numbers
3. Well injectivity
4. Production wells flow rates (oil).
5. Production wells flow rates (water).
6. Selection of liquid (water + oil).
7. Water cut.

8. Well operation time.
9. Depth of immersion of the pump.

The training parameter in this task is simultaneously the flow rates of water and oil or water cut. To train the network, a dataset was used from 01.01.1997 to 01.10.2000. The set of training examples for each well was 58. A group of 9 production and 6 observation wells is used as an object of study. The final training sample consisted of 452 examples and 11 fields [5].

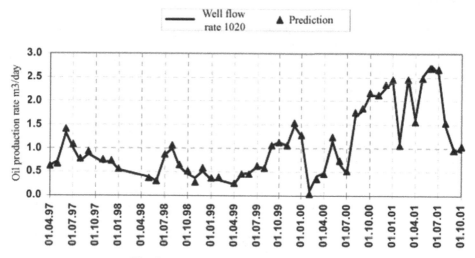

Fig. 8. Neural network model of well 1020

The NeuroPro025 software package was used as a modeling environment. The neural network consisted of 3 layers with 10 neurons in each layer [5]. The correspondence of the model predictions to the initial data is shown in Fig. 8.

The average learning error for this well was 7% and the cumulative production error was 2.3%. For wells with a flow rate of more than 50 m3 per day, the average error was 0.18% and the cumulative production was 0.03%. The model adaptation error for all wells was no more than 1.5% [5].

3   Conclusions

Machine learning methods are increasingly being used in geological research. They are effective in solving repetitive tasks or tasks with a large amount of multidimensional data (good quality and correctly processed).

The objectivity, productivity and adaptability of machine learning algorithms make them ideal solutions for a wide range of problems of various scales.

Machine learning is an innovative area that has already taken an important place in geological research due to the possibility of reducing costs and improving project economics.

This article discusses only a small part of the possible applications of artificial neural networks for the study of hydrolithospheric processes. Promising areas of their use are also: clarification of physical and chemical parameters of layers; intelligent management of field exploitation, etc. These methods allow you to save significant funds when conducting research and describing deposits. The more accurate the models form the basis for the subsequent exploitation of the field, the longer it can exist and the less damage to the environment will be caused.

References

1. Malkov, A.V., Pomelyayko, I.S., Pershin, I.M.: Designing a control system for underground water intakes. IOP Conf. Ser. Earth Environ. Sci. 022–026 (2019)
2. Drovosekova, T.I., Pershin, I.M.: Peculiarities of modelling hydro-lithospheric processes in the region of Kavkazskiye Mineralnye Vody (Caucasus Mineral Springs). In: Proceedings of the 19th International Conference on Soft Computing and Measurements, SCM 2016, pp. 215–217 (2016)
3. Kukharova, T.V., Pershin, I.M.: Conditions of application of distributed systems synthesis methods to multidimensional object. In: International Multi-Conference on Industrial Engineering and Modern Technologies, FarEastCon 2018, pp. 86–90 (2019)
4. Netherlands Dataset: A New Public Dataset for Machine Learning in Seismic Interpretation. https://arxiv.org/pdf/1904.00770v1.pdf. Accessed 20 Aug 2020
5. Ivanenko, B.P.: Nejrosetevoe imitacionnoe modelirovanie neftyanyh mestorozhdenij i gidro-geologicheskih obyektov. Izdatelskij Dom Tomskogo gosudarstvennogo universiteta, Tomsk (2014)
6. Large Scale Visual Recognition Challenge 2012 (ILSVRC2012). https://image-net.org/challenges/LSVRC/2012. Accessed 20 Aug 2020
7. Convolutional neural network, part 1: structure, topology, activation functions and learning set. https://habr.com/ru/post/348000/. Accessed 20 Aug 2020
8. O. S. R. dGB Earth Sciences, "Netherlands offshore f3 block - survey" (2017)
9. Chevitarese, D., Szwarcman, D., Silva, R.M.D., Brazil, E.V.: Seismic facies segmentation using deep learning. In: AAPG ACE (2018)
10. Semantic Segmentation of Seismic Images. https://arxiv.org/pdf/1905.04307.pdf. Accessed 20 Aug 2020
11. Chevitarese, D.S., Szwarcman, D., e Silva, R.M.G., Brazil, E.V.: Deep learning applied to seismic facies classification: a methodology for training. In: EAGE Saint Petersburg (2018)
12. Drovosekova, T.I., Sizov, S.B.: Parallel computations annexed to the problem of physical processes simulation. World Sci. Discov. Ser. B 2(2), 17–22 (2014)
13. Drovosekova, T.I., Zhernosek, I.A.: Modeling of hydrolithospheric processes from the Caucasian Mineralnye Vody region. World Sci. Discov. Ser. B 1(1), 44–52 (2013)
14. Drovosekova, T.I.: Osobennosti modelirovaniya protsessov filtratsii na yazyike Python. Universitetskie chteniya – 2017 Materialyi nauchno-metodicheskih chteniy PGU, pp. 15–21 (2017)
15. Drovosekova, T.I., Pershin, I.M.: Osobennosti modelirovaniya gidrolitosfernyih protsessov regiona Kavkazskih Mineralnyih Vod. Mezhdunarodnaya konferentsiya po myagkim vyichisleniyam i izmereniyam 1(1–3), 229–232 (2016)
16. Tsapleva, V.V., Dushin, S.E.: Razrabotka matematicheskoy modeli vliyaniya g. beshtau na gidrolitosferu regiona g. Lermontova. Izvestiya SPbGETU LETI (1), 53–56 (2011)
17. Martirosyan, A.V., Martirosyan, K.V., Pershin, I.M.: Analysis of the caucasus mineral waters' field's modeling. Mod. Appl. Sci. 9, 204 (2015)

18. Pershin, I.M., Drovosekova, T.I.: Peculiarities of modelling hydro-lithospheric processes in the region of Kavkazskiye Mineralnye Vody (caucasus mineral springs). In: Proceedings of the 19th International Conference on Soft Computing and Measurements, SCM 7519732, pp. 215–217 (2016)

19. Pershin, I.M., Pervukhin, D.A., Ilyushin, Y.V., Afanaseva, O.V.: Design of distributed systems of hydrolithosphere processes management. A synthesis of distributed management systems. IOP Conf. Ser. Earth Environ. Sci. **87**, 032029, 1–7 (2017)

20. Pershin, I.M., Pervukhin, D.A., Ilyushin, Y.V., Afanaseva, O.V.: Design of distributed systems of hydrolithospere processes management. Selection of optimal number of extracting wells. IOP Conf. Ser. Earth Environ. Sci. **87**, 032030, 1–6 (2017)

21. Grigorev, V.V., Byistrov, S.V., Pershin, I.M., Mansurova, O.K., Pershin, M.I.: Kachestvennoe raspredelenie mod v sistemah s raspredelennyimi parametrami. Mehatronika avtomatizatsiya upravlenie **7**, 12–18 (2016)

22. Pershin, I.M., Malkov, A.V., Pershin, M.I.: Operativnoe i strategicheskoe upravlenie rezhimami ekspluatatsii gidrolitosfernyih ob'ektov. Nedropolzovanie XXI vek. Mezhotraslevoy nauchno-tehnicheskiy zhurnal № 6a (44) yanvar 2014, pp. 40–47 (2014)

23. Pershin, I.M., Dubogrey, V.F., Malkov, A.V.: Metodika sinteza raspredelennyih sistem upravleniya rezhimami ekspluatatsii mestorozhdeniy mineralnyih vod. Izvestiya vuzov. Geologiya i razvedka **2**, 74–78 (2012)

Brain Tumor Segmentation Using Unet

Sneha Raina⬛, Abha Khandelwal(✉), Saloni Gupta, and Alka Leekha

Bharati Vidyapeeth's College of Engineering, New Delhi, India

Abstract. We are at the cusp of a massive Bio-medical revolution. Advances in medical engineering have been supplying us enormous amounts of data, such as medical scans, electroencephalography, genome, and protein sequences. Computer vision algorithms show promise in extracting features and learning patterns from this complex data. One such application is the segmentation of Brain Tumors. There have been a number of somewhat successful attempts at the demarcation of brain tumors through simple Convolutional Neural networks (CNN), CNN-Support Vector Machines, DenseNets, Unets, etc. In this paper, we worked with the database consisting of brain Magnetic Resonance images, with each image composed of three channels together with the manually extracted abnormality masks for segmentation. If implemented for real-world applications, this technology can be used to generate semantic segmentation on Brain MR Images in real-time. We have implemented a U-net architecture, a fully connected CNN. We were successful in demarcating the tumors in the brain MR image accurately.

Keywords: Biomedical engineering · Unet · Semantic segmentation · Computer vision

1 Introduction

We have come a long way since the dawn of this decade in terms of technology. Technology has paved the way to greater achievements and helped us explore the depths that weren't thought to be possible a decade ago. Technology is constantly evolving and conquering greater heights. The extent of technological advancement can also be seen in how CNNs and deep learning are being used for detecting diseases in plants [22]. Many implementations of technology have been seen in the medical field which has contributed to saving lives and providing a healthier society.

Our motivations to conduct this research were derived from the fact that the contribution of technology cannot be denied in the field of medical science. Technology can aid medical professionals in saving some precious time which can be crucial in saving a life. More importantly, technology can help develop a better healthcare system for places that lack efficient doctors. To rule out a possible ailment, the doctors often ask questions to know more about the symptoms and then reach a conclusion which is time-consuming. If all the data is directly fed to a machine, it can save a lot of time and provide assistance in health care [23]. The advancement in the field of computer vision technology has opened many new territories to explore. A combination of medical imaging and computer vision

© Springer Nature Singapore Pte Ltd. 2021
P. K. Singh et al. (Eds.): FTNCT 2020, CCIS 1395, pp. 432–443, 2021.
https://doi.org/10.1007/978-981-16-1480-4_39

technology can help achieve a better diagnosis and automate the task of identifying the disease.

The timely detection and treatment can increase the life expectancy of a patient diagnosed with tumors. In this paper, we have built upon a model to detect and quantify the glioma tumor [14] which is indicated through the brain Magnetic Resonance Imaging scan. We started with reading all about the existing work done in this arena. MR images of the brain along with the fluid-attenuated inversion recovery (FLAIR) abnormality masks extracted manually for segmentation were used as the dataset. The images were acquired from The Cancer Imaging Archive (TCIA). In any biomedical image processing task, localization of each pixel is important. Besides the number of images available to train a Machine Learning model is limited. U-net makes up for the limited data using data augmentation on the available samples. U-net has a contracting and a symmetric expanding path both consisting of several convolutional layers, and max pooling layer in contracting path and upsampling layer in expansion path which helps in achieving high resolution features this helping in better localization. Moreover, it helps in cell segmentation tasks to help make distinction between the same class object which are touching by using weighted loss. So, we passed the dataset through the u-net model. The Results that we obtained have been analyzed and concluded in the following sections. Lastly, we also delve upon the future scope of the MRI segmentation technology.

2 Literature Review

The concepts of machine learning and semantic segmentation, in particular, have a great role to play in the field of Biomedical Imaging. In this paper, we take up the case of Brain Tumor identification. In the case of gliomas or any other tumors, not only is it sufficient that models identify the presence or absence of the tumor but the shape, size, and region where it occurs are equally crucial for the prognosis. Every tumor is different and hence we need an approach that will aid the doctors to minutely identify the extent of the tumor. This is the point where instance aware semantic segmentation falls into the frame. Jian Sun et al. [1] came up with a design to achieve the said task using Multi-task Network Cascade (MNC) model which yields a fast and accurate segmentation of instances. The crux was that the network would take an input image of random size, and output semantic segmentation outcomes with the awareness of the instances. There are three steps of this cascade: suggesting box-level occurrences, regression of instances of mask-level, and categorization of each case. These three phases are built so that convolutionary features can be shared. Every stage requires a loss expression, but the later stage loss relies on the performance of the prior stage, meaning that the three-loss terms are not autonomous. A variational Region of Interest (RoI) warping layer was built to compensate for the technical challenges encountered in the loss function. The RoI warping layer was propelled by the differentiable characteristics of overlaying features but was extended to several recommended boxes of significance rather than the whole image. The RoI warping layer had a predefined value of output and an indefinite value of input. This property is advantageous when dealing with diverse kinds of datasets.

An average segmentation architecture consists of a down sampling path that extracts coarse semantic features, an up sampling path that restores the image resolution at the output so that it can be the same as at the input, and an optional post-processing module for refining of the predictions obtained from the model. Simon Jegou et al. [2] extended Densely Connected Convolutional Networks (DenseNet), a recent CNN architecture, to achieve better accuracy in semantic segmentation. The network obtained as a result is very deep. It has from 56 to 103 layers. This network with very few parameters achieves better results for urban scenes understanding datasets like Gatech and CamVid. It doesn't require pre-training, additional post-processing, or temporal information.

Deep CNNs (DCNNs) have been arduously utilized for data segmentation into multiple classes from various modalities and attaining performances that are on par with the state-of-the-art models. However, the computing devices have limited capacity in terms of memory due to which the down sampling or cropping of the input volume which is fed to the deep CNNs becomes necessary which is a problem often encountered when dealing with a large amount of 3D data of high resolution.

Olaf Ronnerberger et al. [4] presented a network and technique for training that depends on the more efficient utilization of the annotated samples available using data augmentation. This network is called U-net. U-net has evolved from a fully convolutional network [5]. The U-net architecture comprises of a shrinking path to acquire context and a symmetric broadening path enabling more accuracy in localization. End-to-end training can be done in U-net from a little number of images and it makes U-net capable of beating the preceding best method which was the sliding-window convolutional network [3].

The crucial change in the architecture of U-net is the great number of feature channels in up sampling, which makes the network capable of transmitting information of the context to the layers of higher resolution. The outcome is the symmetric expansive path to the contracting path and it produces a u-shaped architecture. This technique allows the smooth segmentation of the large input images by an overlaptile strategy (Fig. 1).

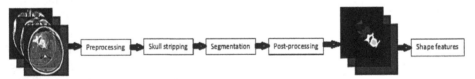

Fig. 1. A schema demonstrating steps of data processing for the inference of molecular subtype from a brain MRI sequence [6].

In another implementation of Unet by Abdelilah ADIBA et al. [7], they proposed a U-net model derived from ResNet-34 which uses transfer learning for automated semantic segmentation building. This model was tested on the INRIA dataset. The results obtained outperformed all the past works done on the INRIA dataset. These outcomes may be attributed to the many methods like discriminative fine-tuning, progressive image resizing and gradual unfreeze used during training. The authors concluded that despite the fact that U-Net has shown pronounced results with respect to constructing segmentation, the latest methodologies can be used to obtain even more improved outcomes and accuracy in problems like Generative Adversarial Networks.

Chengjia Wang et al. [9] developed a two-stage modified U-net framework based on the architecture of the Self-Normalization Network (SNN) and images super-Resolution CNN (SRCNN). This framework learns to determine an RoI within the full volume while simultaneously classifying voxels without any resolution loss. For this, a DCNN framework with two stages was proposed. Such a framework can be obtained by concatenating two U-net like networks. The proposed DCNN model classifies all the voxels within an axial slice based on a predefined neighborhood of axial slices around it. The change in input data size is also accommodated as the two U-Net like DCNNs can be trained separately or end-to-end which provides flexibility to the proposed model. In this study, a four-step training procedure was obtained by conjoining both approaches. A new learning pipeline with multiple stages was used for the training process. This system has an auxiliary output which segments MR data by using non-static RoI abstraction. When training is done with the customized procedure for learning and the dice coefficient which is weighted, segmentation performance better than that of the state-of-the-art Deep CNNs is shown by this framework with advanced similarity metrics.

Now we come to the main purpose of our research which is the segmentation of brain tumors. A successful glioma segmentation has been shown by 3D U-net and its variants, such as the cascade subregions using anisotropic convolutions [18], the ensembled U-net model [17], U-net regularized using autoencoder [19], the dense block with dilated convolutions embedded U-net [21] and No New-net with fine-tuning [20].

Mahmoud-Al-Ayyoub et al. [10] used four classification algorithms viz Tree J48, Artificial Neural Network (ANN), Lazy-IBk, and Naive Bayes, and compared them to find the most accurate algorithm for classifying MR images as images with or without tumor. The images were first preprocessed to make them suitable for use. They were converted to grayscale and the contrast was increased. ImageJ tool was used to define the area of Interest by drawing a circle around it and then compressing the images in .tiff file format. Next, features like mean gray value, circularity, aspect ratio, etc. were extracted using the same tool.

The classifiers were compared on four parameters- correctness, recall value, precision value, and the F measure value. ANN performed the best followed by Lazy- IBk, J48 and Naive Bayes algorithms were the least accurate. The accuracy of these results algorithms can be further be increased by using MRI scans of higher resolution and by using classifier boosting algorithms.

There are two types of brain tumors [13]: malignant (cancerous) and benign (non-cancerous). Ruixuan Lang et al. [8] proposed an approach based on the CNN-SVM model to recognize brain tumors and differentiate between the two types of tumors. This model utilizes the strength of both CNN and SVM. In this model, CNN was employed to extract features from the images of the brain tumor and the SVM classifier was used for the classification of tumors into malignant and benign tumors. This model has shown great results in terms of accurately identifying both tumors distinctly.

Computerized segmentation of the tumor, along with its sub-regions, will be of aid in detecting, controlling, and managing brain cancer treatment. Jing Liu et al. [11] suggested a new 3D U-net model that has a hierarchical adversarial network integrated into it for glioblastoma subregion segmentation, viz tumor enhancement (ET), entire tumor (WT), and tumor center (TC) from various sequences of MRI. An end-to-end training was done in the proposed network as in generative adversarial research. In addition, the MRIs are fed into the proposed neural network after being pre-processed by a bias correction method. The generalization in the vanilla 3D U-net model was improved by the suggested method as proven by 5-fold cross-validation while retaining an adequate segmentation accuracy. However, the authors also noted that the training of this model is time-consuming and memory costly.

A major problem faced in brain tumor segmentation is that useful feature information is often suppressed by too much noise in the images. To tackle this issue, Bin Chen et al. [12] proposed a novel Convolutional Attention Module (CAM), the selectivity of which combined with the feature reusability of Densely connected convolutional Network (DenseNet) will help in emphasizing the more meaningful features. The benefit of using DenseNet over a traditional model can be clearly seen by comparing the different values of the Dice Similarity Coefficient (DSC) given in Table 1. All the models were tested on a multi-modal Brain Tumor Image Segmentation (BRATS 2015) dataset.

Table 1. Comparison of DSC values of different algorithms [12]

Method	DSC		
	Core	Enhancing	Complete
U-net	0.71 ± 0.04	0.61 ± 0.06	0.82 ± 0.03
U-net with CAM	0.71 ± 0.04	0.62 ± 0.06	0.83 ± 0.03
DenseNet	0.71 ± 0.04	0.62 ± 0.06	0.083 ± 0.03
DenseNet with CAM	0.72 ± 0.04	0.63 ± 0.06	0.84 ± 0.03

The improved results are due to the increased reusability in DenseNet as compared to U-net. The results have further improved with the use of CAM as it has two very distinct advantages which give it an edge over traditional methods: 1) it not only emphasizes regions of importance but also suppresses irrelevant areas in the image; 2) fine-grained information can be more selectively recovered from downsampling layers. From the results, it was concluded that the model can indeed be a useful aid for medical professionals.

Recent analysis shows that the different genomic subtypes of the lower grade gliomas can be identified using their shape features. Lower Grade Gliomas (LGG) are grade 2 and grade 3 brain tumors. These tumors, unlike grade 1, are infiltrative and show the tendency of relapsing. Mateusz Buda et al. [6] proposed an automatic way of quantifying the tumor characteristics through its images. A deep learning-based segmentation was used to evaluate if these characteristics can be used to determine the genomic subtypes of the tumor. The U-Net architecture was used to accomplish the goal. The data was collected from 5 institutions that incorporate genomic information of 110 patients. This approach attained 82% and 85% mean and median dice coefficient respectively for tumor segmentation.

Thus, we concluded that Unet architecture can be utilized to segment low-grade gliomas from Brain MRI images.

3 Implementation

3.1 Dataset

The source of the dataset is Kaggle which uses the images acquired from TCIA [25]. This dataset was selected for its ease in training as well as testing and processing as it has binary mask images as labeled data. The dataset has MR images of the brain along with the FLAIR abnormality masks extracted manually for segmentation. They are associated with a hundred and ten patients incorporated in the compilation of lower-grade glioma (LGG) at The Cancer Genome Atlas, with available data on at least FLAIR pattern and genomic conglomeration (Fig. 2).

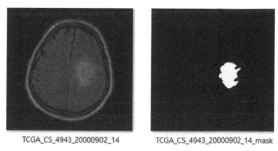

TCGA_CS_4943_20000902_14   TCGA_CS_4943_20000902_14_mask

Fig. 2. Example of an image from the dataset which shows the 3 channel RGB image and mask

The dataset consists of two folders namely: images (PNG format RGB images) and masks (PNG Images of Mask RGB with regions filled with the value of labels). The images in the dataset are in.tif format and every image has 3 channels. For 101 cases, 3 sequences are available, i.e. pre-contrast, FLAIR, post-contrast (in this order of channels). Masks are binary, single-channel images. FLAIR abnormality which exists in the FLAIR sequence is segmented. The dataset is organized into 110 folders named after a case ID that contains information about the source institution.

3.2 Model Used

U-Net is a fully connected CNN which uses data augmentation on the cataloged samples. This leads to improved use of the samples available already. The system comprises a contracting pathway and a symmetric expansive pathway due to which network appears to be shaped like alphabet U. This symmetry allows localization to be more accurate (Fig. 3).

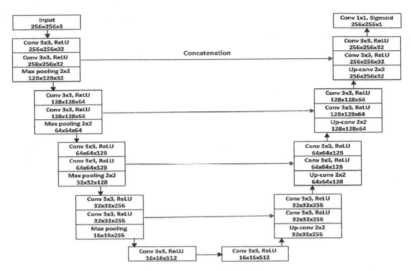

Fig. 3. U-Net architecture used for skull stripping and segmentation [4].

The contracting path adheres to the typical convolutional network architecture. This path adds two repetitively unpadded 3 × 3 convolutions, each accompanied by a 2 × 2-dimension max pooling operation and a rectified linear unit (ReLU) for downsampling. At each move of downsampling the feature channels are doubled. The feature map is up sampled at every step of the expanding course, which is then accompanied by an up-convolution of dimension 2 × 2. This halves the number of feature channels. Also, the expansive path involves two 3 × 3 convolutions, each followed by a ReLU. At the output layer, each vector of the 64-component feature is assigned to the necessary number of classes using a 1 × 1 convolution. 23 convolutional layers make up the network.

3.3 Training Details

During the first step of implementation, the model reads the training images. The training images vary from each other significantly in terms of size for different patients so the images are then preprocessed. The preprocessing consists of selecting a common frame of reference for scaling the images, removing the skull for a focused brain region analysis (skull stripping), normalizing the intensity of tissues by level adjustment and adaptive window, and normalizing z-score of the entire dataset. The training volume is then cropped and padded. The final training dataset is obtained after resizing followed by the normalization of the training volume.

The validation images are read by the model. The validation volume obtained is preprocessed followed by the cropping and padding. The resultant volume is padded and resized and a validation dataset is obtained after the normalization of the validation volume. Then the model calculates val_dsc, val_loss and loss for each individual epoch. At the end it gives us the best val_dsc score out of all along with performing semantic segmentation on the test set Brain MRI images. The images get saved at the path provided.

4 Results

The model when run at various epochs added a mask around the tumors in the test dataset and saved those images in the path provided. For comparing the performance of our model at various epochs, we consider the value of the Dice similarity coefficient which is also known as the F1 score. DSC is a metric which lies between 0 to 1 and tells us the most comprehensive correlation between predicted pixels and real value. The best val_dsc obtained was 0.8913 when the model was run at 75 epochs.

The below image is a snippet from the destination folder, where our model saves the segmented tumors from the MRI Images (Fig. 4).

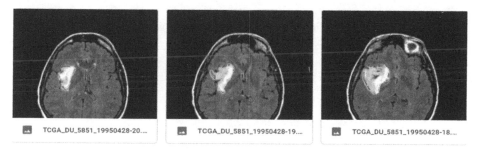

TCGA_DU_5851_19950428-20....   TCGA_DU_5851_19950428-19....   TCGA_DU_5851_19950428-18....

Fig. 4. Images from result

The below graphs represent the val_dsc at 25,50,75 and 100 epochs.
25 Epochs: - Best validation mean DSC was 0.869722 (Fig. 5).

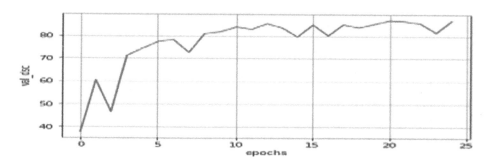

Fig. 5. Plot of val_dsc for 25 epochs

50 Epochs: - Best validation mean dsc: 0.883393 (Fig. 6).

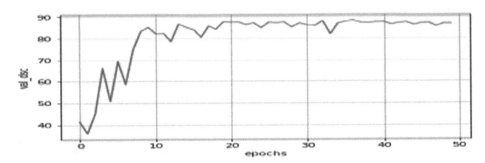

Fig. 6. Plot of val_dsc for 50 epochs

75 Epochs: - Best validation mean DSC: 0.891338 (Fig. 7)

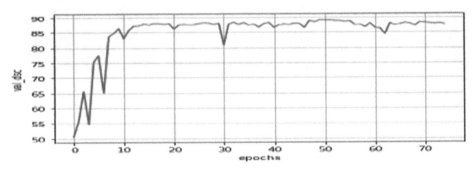

Fig. 7. Plot of val_dsc for 75 epochs

100 Epochs: - Best validation mean DSC: 0.876262 (Fig. 8).

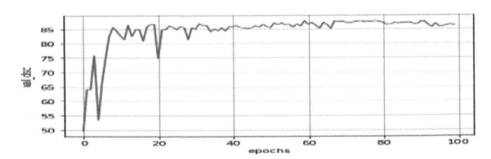

Fig. 8. Plot of val_dsc for 100 epochs

As is evident from the graphs above, the best dsc value was obtained when the model was run at 75 epochs.

5 Conclusion

Biomedical imaging has a long way to go. We have managed to achieve commendable results with the technology available to us. The Unet model was successfully trained to predict the boundary around the tumor. The previous best DSC obtained for the same model by Mateusz Buda [6] was 0.881506 whereas we obtained val_dsc of 0.891338 The results we obtained on the TGIA dataset are very close to the perception of a medical professional. Predicting tumors using Imaging technology is vital today. We are constrained by time and resources, but if precise prototypes are created, they can be integrated in several ways into the standard treatment approach.

6 Future Scope

Recently, 2D and 3D deep convolutional neural networks are increasingly being used for the segmentation task of medical images. This is due to the availability of large labeled datasets from which hierarchical features can be learned. The Downside of 3D network was concluded to be the high cost of computing.

Qiangguo Jin et al. [15] presented RA-UNet to accurately retrieve the volume of interest (VOI) and segment the section of tumors in the liver. The method used a three-dimensional modified attention aware segmentation on a network with a basic structure analogous to a 3-dimensional U-Net. Low-level features maps are coupled with high-level features maps to acquire contextual information. This would be the first research wherein biomedical volumetric images were assessed with residual focus processes. RA-UNet was also broadened to the BraTS2017 and BraTS2018 brain tumor segmentation data sources, and the findings demonstrate that RA-UNet still accomplishes decent performance in the segmentation of brain tumor.

Other models such as PSP-Net [16] or multi-level spatial fusion mechanism as proposed by Ritabrata S. et al. [24] can be experimented with.

The results can be further improved by better extraction of images, enhancing Mask level instances or by working on RoI pooling feature maps. Another alternative is to use different models like the ones proposed above to achieve real-world applications.

References

1. Dai, J., He, K., Sun, J.: Instance-aware semantic segmentation via multi-task network cascades. arXiv:1512.04412v1 (2015)
2. Jegou, S., Drozdzal, M., Vazquez, D., Romero, A., Bengio, Y.: The one hundred layers tiramisu: fully convolutional DenseNets for semantic segmentation. arXiv:1611.09326v3 [cs.CV] (2017)
3. Ciresan, D.C., Gambardella, L.M., Giusti, A., Schmidhuber, J.: Deep neural networks segment neuronal membranes in electron microscopy images. In: NIPS, pp. 2852–2860 (2012)
4. Ronneberger, O., Fischer, P., Brox, T.: U-Net: convolutional networks for biomedical image segmentation. In: Navab, N., Hornegger, J., Wells, W.M., Frangi, A.F. (eds.) MICCAI 2015. LNCS, vol. 9351, pp. 234–241. Springer, Cham (2015). https://doi.org/10.1007/978-3-319-24574-4_28

5. Long, J., Shelhamer, E., Darrell, T.: Fully convolutional networks for semantic segmentation. In: Proceedings of the IEEE Conference on Computer Vision and Pattern Recognition, pp. 3431–3440 (2015)
6. Buda, M., Saha, A., Mazurowski, M.A.: Association of genomic subtypes of lower-grade gliomas with shape features automatically extracted by a deep learning algorithm. Comput. Biol. Med. **109**, 218–225 (2019)
7. Adiba, A., Hajji, H., Maatouk, M.: Transfer learning and U-Net for buildings segmentation. In: SMC 2019: Proceedings of the New Challenges in Data Sciences: Acts of the Second Conference of the Moroccan Classification Society, pp. 1–6 (2019). https://doi.org/10.1145/3314074.3314088
8. Lang, R., Jia, K., Feng, J.: Brain Tumor identification based on CNN-SVM model. In: ICBEB 2018: Proceedings of the 2nd International Conference on Biomedical Engineering and Bioinformatics, pp. 31–35 (2018). https://doi.org/10.1145/3278198.3278209
9. Wang, C., MacGillivray, T., Macnaught, G., Yang, G., Newby, D.: A two-stage 3D Unet framework for multi-class segmentation on full resolution image. arXiv:1804.04341v1 [cs.CV] (2018)
10. Al-Ayyoub, M., Husari, G., Darwish, O., Alabed, A.: Machine learning approach for brain tumor detection. In: ACM International Conference Proceeding Series (2012). https://doi.org/10.1145/2222444.2222467
11. Liu, J., Yin, P., Wang, X., Yang, W., Cheng, K.: Glioma subregions segmentation with a discriminative adversarial regularized 3D Unet. In: ISICDM 2019: Proceedings of the Third International Symposium on Image Computing and Digital Medicine, pp. 269–273 (2019). https://doi.org/10.1145/3364836.3364891
12. Chen, B., Wang, J., Chi, Z.: Improved DenseNet with convolutional attention module for brain tumor segmentation. In: ISICDM 2019: Proceedings of the Third International Symposium on Image Computing and Digital Medicine, pp. 22–26 (2019). https://doi.org/10.1145/3364836.3364841
13. Brazier, Y.: Tumors: Benign, premalignant, and malignant (2019). https://www.medicalnewstoday.com/articles/249141
14. Brain Tumor: Types, Risk Factors, and Symptoms. "https://www.healthline.com/health/brain-tumor".
15. Jin, Q., Meng, Z., Sun, C., Wei, L., Su, R.: RA-UNet: a hybrid deep attention-aware network to extract liver and tumor in CT scans. arXiv:1811.01328v1 [cs.CV] (2018)
16. Zhao, H., Shi, J., Qi, X., Wang, X., Jia, J.: Pyramid scene parsing network. In: Proceedings of the IEEE Conference on Computer Vision and Pattern Recognition, pp. 2881–2890 (2017)
17. Kamnitsas, K., et al.: Ensembles of multiple models and architectures for robust brain tumour segmentation. In: Crimi, A., Bakas, S., Kuijf, H., Menze, B., Reyes, M. (eds.) BrainLes 2017. LNCS, vol. 10670, pp. 450–462. Springer, Cham (2018). https://doi.org/10.1007/978-3-319-75238-9_38
18. Wang, G., Li, W., Ourselin, S., Vercauteren, T.: Automatic brain tumor segmentation using cascaded anisotropic convolutional neural networks. In: Crimi, A., Bakas, S., Kuijf, H., Menze, B., Reyes, M. (eds.) BrainLes 2017. LNCS, vol. 10670, pp. 178–190. Springer, Cham (2018). https://doi.org/10.1007/978-3-319-75238-9_16
19. Myronenko, A.: 3D MRI brain tumor segmentation using autoencoder regularization. In: Crimi, A., Bakas, S., Kuijf, H., Keyvan, F., Reyes, M., van Walsum, T. (eds.) BrainLes 2018. LNCS, vol. 11384, pp. 311–320. Springer, Cham (2019). https://doi.org/10.1007/978-3-030-11726-9_28
20. Isensee, F., Kickingereder, P., Wick, W., Bendszus, M., Maier-Hein, K.: No new-net. In: Crimi, A., Bakas, S., Kuijf, H., Keyvan, F., Reyes, M., van Walsum, T. (eds.) BrainLes 2018. LNCS, vol. 11384, pp. 234–244. Springer, Cham (2019). https://doi.org/10.1007/978-3-030-11726-9_21

21. van Tulder, G., de Bruijne, M.: Learning cross-modality representations from multi-modal images. IEEE Trans. Med. Imaging **38**(2), 638–648 (2018)

22. Leekha, A., Bhardwaj, S., Sarthak: Transfer and residual learning for plant disease detection. J. Multi-Disciplinary Eng. Technol. **13**(1), 22–27 (2019)

23. Beri, R., Dubey, M.K., Gehlot, A., Singh, R.: A study of e-healthcare system for pregnant women. In: Singh, P.K., Sood, S., Kumar, Y., Paprzycki, M., Pljonkin, A., Hong, W.-C. (eds.) FTNCT 2019. CCIS, vol. 1206, pp. 545–556. Springer, Singapore (2020). https://doi.org/10.1007/978-981-15-4451-4_43

24. Sanyal, R., Chakrabarty, K., Reddy, G.D., Sengupta, V.: Carcinoma classification from breast histopathology images using a multi level spatial fusion mechanism of deep convolutional features from differently stain normalized patches. In: Singh, P.K., Sood, S., Kumar, Y., Paprzycki, M., Pljonkin, A., Hong, W.-C. (eds.) FTNCT 2019. CCIS, vol. 1206, pp. 579–591. Springer, Singapore (2020). https://doi.org/10.1007/978-981-15-4451-4_46

25. Pedano, N., Flanders, A.E., Scarpace, L., Mikkelsen, T., Eschbacher, J.M., Hermes, B., Ostrom, Q.: Radiology Data from The Cancer Genome Atlas Low Grade Glioma [TCGA-LGG] collection. The Cancer Imaging Archive (2016). https://doi.org/10.7937/K9/TCIA.2016.L4LTD3TK

Influence of Membership Function Type on the Accuracy of Video Tracking Algorithm

Alexander Bozhenyuk$^{(\boxtimes)}$ (iD) and Kirill Morev (iD)

Southern Federal University, Nekrasovsky Street 44, 347922 Taganrog, Russia
morev-ki@ya.ru

Abstract. The article presents the results of intuitionistic fuzzy sets using in practice, as well as the study of the used belonging and non-belonging functions influence on the result of the video object tracking algorithm work. Fuzzy logic is used for evaluating the degree of assigned correspondences truth between keypoints of the object being followed image and the search window. The algorithm's accuracy estimates are based on synthetically generated data provided with a ground true markup that allows evaluating the degree of calculated correspondences truth. In an effort to obtain objective algorithm estimates, several different metrics are used.

Keywords: Object tracking · Key points of images · Intuitionistic fuzzy sets

1 Introduction

Nowadays computer vision is a high-speed developing area of scientific knowledge. So one of the major way to develop this area is to create and embed new approaches and solutions in latest platforms, requiring computer vision tasks solving.

However, modern tasks are complex and high-performance requirement, so researchers are have to combine robustness, accuracy and low performance cost in their algorithms. In order to obtain high-speed method, we use image key points (KP) to represent images in compact form. A new approach for comparing two KP clouds of different images observed in paper. New approach based on intuitionistic fuzzy sets [1]. We solving object tracking tasks by comparing of KP clouds (KPs of object and KPs of search window) for localize object's center and compute it's bounding box [2]. In other worlds, in proposed approach the object tracking task solved by comparing two KP clouds in order to find true and strong correspondence between the descriptors of KPs neighborhoods (direction of the brightness gradient, brightness histogram, etc.) [3, 4]. In this case correspondence is a true if it's connect points on different images, represented the same point in 3D-space, despite at its spatial shift, brightness or size changes. A false comparison is the opposite of the true. Intuitionistic fuzzy sets using for evaluating the truth of correspondences. We inspired to fuzzy sets using when studying some of the correspondences, estimates often seems like the next: "not quite down", "it would be a little to the right", "a little lower", etc. So, been inspired, we propose a new approach, given in part 2. Approach based on key points matching, using intuitionistic fuzzy sets.

© Springer Nature Singapore Pte Ltd. 2021
P. K. Singh et al. (Eds.): FTNCT 2020, CCIS 1395, pp. 444–453, 2021.
https://doi.org/10.1007/978-981-16-1480-4_40

A short survey of intuitionistic fuzzy sets given in part 1 of the paper. And after new approach presentation, in part 3 we present results of experiments with different membership functions and their influence at proposed approach accuracy and robustness.

2   Survey of Intuitionistic Fuzzy Set

There some difference between classical fuzzy and intuitionistic sets. And the main distinction is a degree of uncertainty, presented in intuitionistic fuzzy set [5]. Of course, degree of membership and non-membership are present in both sets classical and intuitionistic fuzzy.

Intuitionistic fuzzy set can be represented as:

$$\{\langle x, \mu(x), \nu(x), \pi(x)\rangle | x \in E\},$$

in formula above, symbols mean the following: x is an element of E, $\mu(x)$ degree of membership of x to the set A, $\nu(x)$ is the non-membership degree and $\pi(x)$ is the uncertainty degree. Furthermore:

$$\pi(x) = 1 - \mu(x) - \nu(x).$$

The intuitionistic fuzzy set have one very important requirement:

$$\mu(x) + \nu(x) \leq 1,$$

and if $\mu(x) + \nu(x) = 1$, then the intuitionistic fuzzy set lost it's intuitionistic features and becomes a classical fuzzy set. Figure 1 presents an example of an intuitionistic fuzzy set interpretation in triangle form [1, 6]:

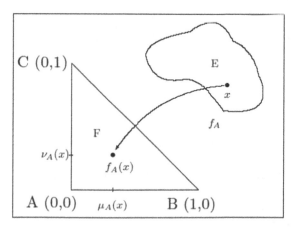

Fig. 1. Intuitionistic fuzzy set geometric interpretation example

3 Our Approach

Now we present an algorithm for solving video object tracking task. Proposed algorithm is robust to the rotation and scale changing. Algorithm based on representing of video frame and object image in KPs form and on tools of intuitionistic fuzzy sets. We shortly present three classical stages of video tracking with KPs process.

First stage is to detect key points on object template and search window images. After KPs are found, second stage is to compute description of founded key points. As part of this work, the analysis of existing methods key point detection and description was done, and the BRISK algorithm [7] was chosen as the most compactable for our work in real time on noisy images. The third stage of our approach is a KPs comparison. In the new method, we are suggest to use structure of the object's image KPs (distances and angles between all KP images) and look for KP in the same structure search window. We consider a quantitative evaluate of descriptors differences for all KP of two images. A ratio threshold filters the tentative matches:

$$f(dif) = 1 - \frac{dif}{des\_len},$$

$$\begin{cases} match = true, \text{ if } f(dif) \geq 0,8 \\ match = false, \text{ if } f(dif) < 0,8 \end{cases},$$

in formula above, symbols mean the following: dif presents difference between descriptions; $desc\_len$ is descriptor length; and $match$ is match trueness we checked.

The difference between point descriptions used to calculate the non-membership degree of points to set of true matches. Non-membership function shown below:

$$v(x) = 1 - \frac{aXORb}{512},$$

where x – evaluated correspondence, a is KP descriptor from object template; b is the descriptor KP in the search box from the same correspondence.

After, matches passed the threshold, used to compute the structure of the correspondences points: some match, taken randomly, assigned as major or main correspondence. Further, from corresponding point of main correspondence to point of template or search window, orientation (angle) and distance (scale) are assigned. The distance is evaluated as Euclidean distance:

$$D = \sqrt[2]{(X_i - X_j)^2 + (Y_i - Y_j)^2},$$

where D is evaluated distance, i and j are indices of different evaluated points of image, and X and Y are coordinate values of KP center in image. To compute angle between points, we calculate angle between two vectors: first vector presented by two points (point of main correspondence and point of estimated correspondence) where point of main correspondence takes as beginning of the vector, and second vector presented by X axis of image.

In Fig. 2 shows the process of key points structure computing. Matches that have passed the ratio threshold filtering are marked as yellow. Structure of key points indicated

Search window **Object**

Fig. 2. Structure of object in template and search window and correspondences between structures (Color figure online)

by red lines. Key points centers are yellow circles. To compute structure, we use reference point (blue star in Fig. 2) and estimate the distance and angles to all other points.

Based on the assumption of geometric transformation similarity, we assume that moving an object in the search window and changing its scale and orientation, all true matches produce a cluster of equally moving in space points. So the structure of the points will similar to template's and, the distances and orientations of true correspondences points will change in direct proportion. So observed only geometric transformations, next equals are true:

$$
\begin{cases}
\frac{M_1 dist_{obj}}{M_1 dist_{win}} = \frac{M_2 dist_{obj}}{M_2 dist_{win}} = \cdots = \frac{M_n dist_{obj}}{M_n dist_{win}} \\
M_1 angle_{obj} - M_1 angle_{win} = \cdots = M_n angle_{obj} - M_n angle_{win}
\end{cases},
$$

where $M_i dist_{obj}$ and $M_i dist_{win}$ are distances from KP of the object or the search box respectively to KP of main correspondence, and $M_i angle_{obj}$ and $M_i angle_{obj}$ are KP orientations.

After evaluating, orientation and distance changes are used to calculate template rotation and scale changes. After tentative correspondences filtered and find true matches, the localization of object center in the search window is not hard task. However, in real-systems it's some noisy presents in data. So, matches will be marked as true if changes in scale and orientation object parameters will be within:

$$
\begin{cases}
\delta_{dist} \pm \sigma_{dist} \\
\delta_{angle} \pm \sigma_{angle}
\end{cases},
$$

where δ is the mean value, and σ is the standard deviation for the distribution of changes in distances (dist) and rotation angle (angle). So, after calculated distances and orientations changes for all tested matches, it's not hard to calculate averages δ and σ for the distribution. We can filter potentiality wrong matches by some threshold of possible change of scale or rotation. If scale or orientation change is more than threshold value, evaluated match is false. Ratio of change value and threshold is degree of belonging. In our case, membership function presented as:

$$\mu(x) = \max\left(1 - \frac{|dist - \delta_{dist}|}{\sigma_{dist}}, 1 - \frac{|angle - \delta_{angle}|}{\sigma_{angle}}\right),$$

where $dist$ is the change in distance KP; $angle$ - change of its rotation angle; δ_{scale} and δ_{rotate} - the average change values of scale and rotation, respectively; σ_{dist} and σ_{angle} are the changes standard deviations.

Now, for every tested match, calculated degrees of membership and non-membership. However, according to one very important requirement from chapter 1, sum of membership and non-membership functions should be smaller one. We use approach, presented by Atanasov K. in [8], which make possible to transform extra big sum of membership and non-membership functions from square from (Fig. 3 on the left) to classical triangular form (Fig. 3 on the right).

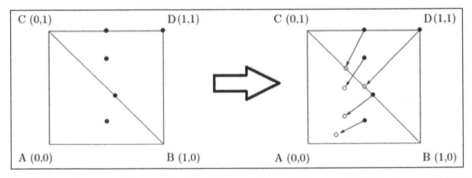

Fig. 3. Transformation. Incorrect intuitive fuzzy set form (left); correct intuitive fuzzy set (right)

The transformation applied by continuous bijective transformation:

$$(n, m) = \begin{cases} < 0,0 >, if\ n = m = 0 \\ < \dfrac{m^2}{m+n}, \dfrac{mn}{m+n} >, if\ n, m \in [0,1]\ \text{и}\ n \geq m\ \text{и}\ n + m \neq 0 \\ < \dfrac{mn}{m+n}, \dfrac{m^2}{m+n} >, if\ n, m \in [0,1]\ \text{и}\ n \leq m\ \text{и}\ n + m \neq 0 \end{cases}$$

Further, applying bijective transformation to obtained values of membership and non-membership degrees, we evaluate matches between the points of template image and search windows. This make possible to find true matches and evaluate changes of object rotation, scale and shift. After, the procedure of deffuzification provide information to divide true and false matches [9, 10]. We introduced following rules to generate decision of our algorithm: a) if $\mu\ (x) > \nu\ (x) + \pi\ (x)$, then the correspondence is true; b) if $\nu\ (x) \geq \mu\ (x) + \pi\ (x)$, then the correspondence is false; c) If $\mu\ (x) + \pi\ (x) > \nu\ (x)$, then required an additional check. If rule "C" is execute, it is necessary to run more complex examination of object neighborhood in search window. In [11], two different cases are present. But short summary is presented here to. Case 1: $\mu(x) + \nu(x) < \pi(x)$ indicate, that structure of KPs is badly broken, but KPs descriptors are very similar. Either much of false matches or strong changes of object shape that violated KPs structure (strong projective transformation), made this situation possible. This uncertainty can be resolved by considering KPs in the radius R = 0.25x (x is largest dimension of the object) around every KPs of true matches in search window. After additional check, if half or more of the KPs consisting inside tested radius, consists in above search window and template images tested radiuses, tested match is true. And case 2: $\mu(x) + \nu(x) > \pi(x)$. Case 2 indicates the preservation of the structure of the object with a difference of neighborhoods of points from the estimated pair. A similar situation occurs when the object occluded (tree crowns, other objects, landscape elements, etc.). In this case, to eliminate the uncertainty, a second search is made for the object point from the estimated pair. The radius of the second search area is assigned R = 0.1m, where m is also the largest size of the object. If a singular point is found in the indicated neighborhood that corresponds to the point of the object by at least 80%, then the point of the object is replaced from the pair being evaluated by a new, just found point. Otherwise, the match is considered false.

4   Experiments and Results

The observed algorithm was implemented on C++ language of programming. Experiments was running to evaluate robustness of proposed algorithm with difference methods of expert's experience interpolation. Learned membership functions was taken from presented expert's experience, we use few interpolation methods: 1 – linear interpolation, 2 – parabolic interpolation and 3 – Lagrange polynomial interpolation. Used expert's experience presented at Figs. 4 and 5.

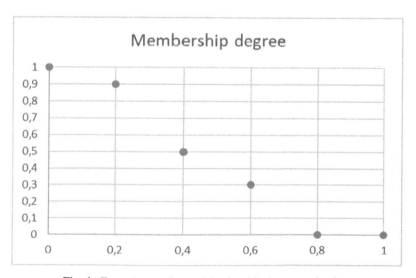

Fig. 4. Expert's experience. Membership degree evaluation.

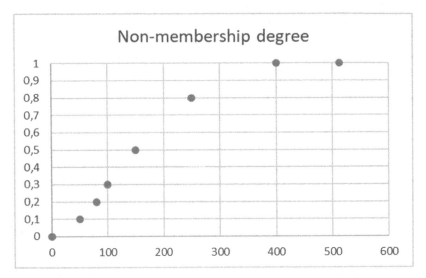

Fig. 5. Expert's experience. Non-membership degree evaluation

Those expert's experience was interpolated by few observed before methods (Fig. 6):

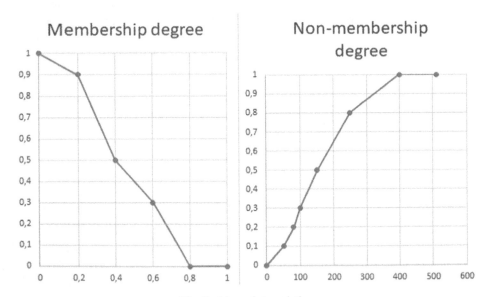

Fig. 6. Linear interpolation.

After parabolic interpolation we have next results (Fig. 7):

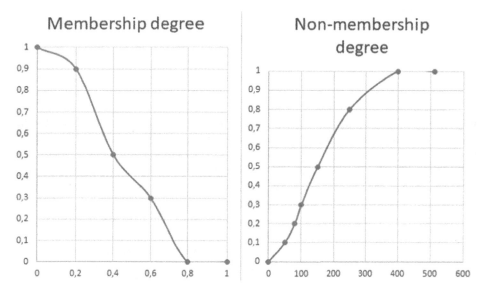

Fig. 7. Parabolic interpolation.

Lagrange interpolation results (Fig. 8):

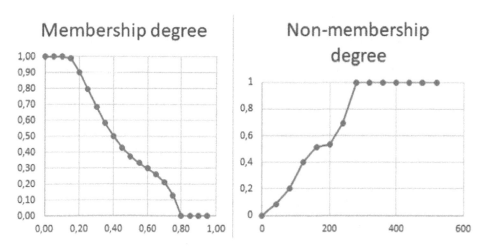

Fig. 8. Lagrange interpolation.

After different interpolation methods use, we got a results of algorithm accuracy and robustness estimates.

The algorithm's accuracy is determined from the analysis of the object area predicted by the algorithm and the real one, and the robustness is based on the number of failures in the video [12]. To calculate the accuracy, use the formula:

$$Acc = \frac{R_t^G \wedge R_t^T}{R_t^G \vee R_t^T},$$

where the divisible is the area of the intersection area of the region predicted by the tracking algorithm and the object's region, and the divisor is the area of the region union area.

A distinctive feature of the metric based on the overlap area analysis is that it takes into account both the location of the object and its size and does not give such large errors when tracking is disrupted, as when using the average and average errors in determining the coordinates of the center. As soon as the algorithm begins to lose the object and smoothly moves to the background, the value of the score approaches 0 and becomes zero when the algorithm completely moves to the background, regardless of how far away from the object the predictions of the tracking algorithm have gone.

The stability of the algorithm is calculated based on the number of failures of object tracking, where the failure is considered to be a decrease in the accuracy metric less than a certain threshold (in this work, the Acc threshold = 0.3). Stability is determined by the formula:

$$Rob = \frac{N_{wr}}{N_{com}},$$

where N_{wr} is the number of failures of the tracking algorithm, and N_{com} is the total number of frames in the video sequence.

Estimates are present in Table 1.

Table 1. Algorithm estimates.

Interpolation	Accuracy	Robustness
Linear	0.484	0.759
Parabolic	0.563	0.796
Lagrange polynomial	0.459	0.762

Results present benefits of parabolic interpolation using with observed videotracking algorithm. Lowest accuracy is shown by membership function given from Lagrange interpolation. Low accuracy can be explained by exaggerated membership estimates at the edges of functions of membership and non-membership. And lowest robustness presented by algorithm version with linear interpolation of expert's experience is justified by rough transitions between points that caused the loss of some information.

In this work intuitionistic fuzzy sets was used in practice and we are intend to study more complex and deeper problems of video tracking algorithm accuracy improvement. Completed study of expert's experience interpolation is very important in intuitionistic fuzzy sets sphere. We can retrieve useful knowledge in a subject area and use them in a novel and strong algorithms. Using the extension of expert's experience we can solve hard tasks in conditions of lack of information or knowledge about environment or local sphere of using. We well be happy to benefit the scientific community with the benefits of our research. Accuracy and robustness metrics in basics taken from [12].

References

1. Atanasov, K.: On Intuitionistic Fuzzy Sets Theory. Springer, Heidelberg (2012). https://doi.org/10.1007/978-3-642-29127-2
2. Tassov, K.L., Bekasov, D.E.: Overlapping solving in tracking tasks. Eng. Mag. Sci. Innov. 6(18), 1–8 (2013)
3. Salahat, E., Qasaimeh, M.: Recent advances in feature extraction and description algorithms: hardware designs and algorithmic derivatives. In: Computer Vision: Concepts, Methodologies, Tools, and Applications, pp. 27–57. IGI Global (2018). https://doi.org/10.4018/978-1-5225-5204-8
4. Bay, H., Tuytelaars, T., Van Gool, L.: SURF: speeded up robust features. In: Leonardis, A., Bischof, H., Pinz, A. (eds.) ECCV 2006. LNCS, vol. 3951, pp. 404–417. Springer, Heidelberg (2006). https://doi.org/10.1007/11744023_32
5. Atanassov, K.: Intuitionistic fuzzy sets. Fuzzy Sets Syst. 20(1), 87–96 (1986)
6. Atanassov, K.: More on intuitionistic fuzzy sets. Fuzzy Sets Syst. 33(1), 37–45 (1989)
7. Leutenegger, S., Chli, M., Siegwart, R.: BRISK: binary robust invariant scalable keypoints. In: IEEE International Conference on Computer Vision (ICCV), pp. 2548–2555 (2011). https://doi.org/10.1109/Fcvpr.2011.5995387
8. Atanassov, K.: Remark on a property of the intuitionistic fuzzy interpretation triangle. Notes Intuit. Fuzzy Sets 8(1), 34–36 (2002)
9. Bian, J., Lin, W.Y., Matsushita, Y., Yeung, S.K., Nguyen, T.D., Cheng, M.M.: GMS: grid-based motion statistics for fast, ultra-robust feature correspondence. In: 2017 IEEE Conference on Computer Vision and Pattern Recognition (CVPR), pp. 2828–2837 (2017)
10. Yang, M., Wu, Y., Hua, G.: Context-aware visual tracking. IEEE Trans. Pattern Anal. Mach. Intell. 31(7), 1195–1209 (2009)
11. Belyakov, S., Bozhenyuk, A., Morev, K., Rozenberg, I.: Comparison of key points clouds of images using intuitionistic fuzzy sets. In: Silhavy, R. (ed.) CSOC 2020. AISC, vol. 1225, pp. 366–374. Springer, Cham (2020). https://doi.org/10.1007/978-3-030-51971-1_30
12. Shchelkunov, A., Kovalev, V., Morev, K., Sidko, I.: The metrics for tracking algorithms evaluation. Izvestiya SFedU. Eng. Sci. 1, 233–245 (2020)

An Approach to the Medical-Type Data Multiobjective Analysis

Nailya S. Asfandiyarova[1], Olga V. Dashkevich[1], Liliya A. Demidova[2],
Natalia V. Doroshina[1(✉)], and Ekaterina I. Suchkova[1]

[1] Ryazan State Medical University named after Academician I.P. Pavlov,
9, Vysokovol'tnaya Street, 390026 Ryazan, Russia
`aprel4@live.ru`
[2] Institute of Information Technologies, MIREA-Russian Technological University,
78, Vernadskogo avenye, 119454 Moscow, Russia
`liliya.demidova@rambler.ru`

Abstract. The problem of analyzing a set of multivariate data of a medical type describing the presence/absence of chronic diseases in 2523 patients without taking into account the time factor is considered. Of particular interest is the study of the influence of a history of type 2 diabetes mellitus on the occurrence of other diseases. To identify and analyze hidden dependencies in medical data sets, it is proposed to use standard Data Mining algorithms for association rules mining, taking into account such indicators (criteria) as support, reliability, lift, and persuasion. The analysis of various algorithms for multi-criteria decision-making is carried out. An approach to multicriteria analysis of medical-type data with the formation of Pareto - the front of optimal decisions, formed from the previously obtained association rules is proposed. Examples are given that confirm the effectiveness of the proposed approach to the analysis of medical data. The ways of searching for further research are outlined.

Keywords: Associative rules · Medical data · Multi-criteria · Optimal decision search

1 Introduction

Medical data, which can be considered as Big Data extracted from medical information systems, are of scientific interest today for analyzing and obtaining an objective assessment and prediction of the patient's condition, as well as identifying new medical knowledge and contributing to more effective clinical decision-making and patient care [1, 2]. For example, many expert systems are known for making medical diagnoses. For the most part, they are created on the basis of rules describing combinations of various symptoms of individual diseases. The goals of intelligent data processing in medicine have a very wide range - discriminant analysis [3], classification [4], cluster analysis [5], association rules mining [1, 2, 6–23, 26], etc. Association rules mining as the task of

© Springer Nature Singapore Pte Ltd. 2021
P. K. Singh et al. (Eds.): FTNCT 2020, CCIS 1395, pp. 454–464, 2021.
https://doi.org/10.1007/978-981-16-1480-4_41

which is to find hidden patterns between related objects in databases is one of the most widespread and promising in medicine [12–14, 17–21, 26].

Some of the notations used below are presented in Table 1.

Table 1. Symbols used

Symbols	Full title
AH	Arterial hypertension
AR	Associative rule
CHF	Chronic heart failure
CVB	Cardiovascular disease
CVD	Cerebrovascular disease
MI	Myocardial infarction
MCO	Multicriteria optimization
MCD	Multiple chronic diseases
OA	Osteoarthritis
T2DM	Type 2 diabetes mellitus

If a patient has two or more diseases, then it is advisable to include him in the list of patients with multiple chronic diseases (MCD). Recently, there has been an increase in the number of patients with MCD, caused primarily by obesity and aging of the population. Diseases of the cardiovascular system, joints, and kidneys prevail in the structure of MCD. There is a gender difference in the prevalence of a number of diseases [24].

Our study is a continuation of work on the search and analysis of associative rules found in the structure of the MCD among 2523 patients. A total of 2254 (89,34%) such patients were identified. Among patients with MCD in all age categories, the prevalence of women was noted (62,71% in general). The list of all diseases consists of 17 items. T2DM occurs in 407 (16,13%) patients, and all of them have MCD [25].

The aim of the study is to develop an approach to multicriteria analysis of multidimensional medical data. At the initial stage, a statistical analysis of the data was carried out to identify the point and interval characteristics of the MCD structure. Further, for ARs mining was carried out using such indicators of AR quality as support, reliability, lift, persuasiveness as criteria. With different indicators of support and reliability 2 327 ARs were obtained. At this stage of the study, a multi-criteria analysis of the initial data is carried out - the identification of AR that dominate others as optimal according to two criteria of maximum support and reliability.

2   Search Aspects of Association Rules for Medical Data

The basic concept in the theory of AR is a transaction - a set of events that occur together. AR consists of two sets of elements (sets), called condition A (*antecedent*) and consequence B (*consequent*), and is written as $\{A\} \rightarrow \{B\}$ - association. AR is formed in the view: "If a condition, then a consequence", i.e. "If A, then B". Moreover, the sets A and B are such that $A \cap B = \emptyset$.

In medicine, such rules can be written as follows:

$\{$disease$\} \rightarrow \{$disease$\}$,
$\{$symptom$\} \rightarrow \{$disease$\}$,
$\{$disease$\} \rightarrow \{$treatment method$\}$, etc.

In our study, diseases, the gender and age of patients (as signs), were considered as sets of elements A and B. At the same time, AR mining with the subsequent quantitative description of the relationship between two or more diseases is of considerable interest. In this case, a transaction can be called a set of diseases in a particular patient.

ARs describe the relationship between sets of elements corresponding to a condition and a consequence. The following dimensionless indicators characterize these relations.

Support is an indicator that determines how often a set of items appears in a dataset:

$$Supp(A \rightarrow B) = \frac{\text{number of transactions containing A and B}}{\text{total number of transactions}} \tag{1}$$

Confidence is an indicator that determines how often a rule is correct:

$$Conf(A \rightarrow B) = \frac{\text{number of transactions containing A and B}}{\text{number of transactions containing only A}} \tag{2}$$

Lift is an indicator that determines the dependence of elements A and B

$$Lift(A \rightarrow B) = \frac{Conf(A \rightarrow B)}{Supp(B)} \tag{3}$$

If this indicator is greater than 1, then the relationship between A and B is positive, if it is less than 1, then it is negative, with the value of the indicator equal to 1, there is no relationship between A and B.

Conviction is a measure of the error rate:

$$Conv(A \rightarrow B) = \frac{1 - Supp(B)}{1 - Conf(A \rightarrow B)} \tag{4}$$

These indicators together indicate the strength of the relationship between cause and effect and the usefulness of a particular AR.

The main advantage of ARs is their easy perception. In [26], ARs are classified into the following three types.

1. Useful AR containing valid information that was previously unknown but has a logical explanation. Such rules can be used to make decisions that are beneficial.
2. Trivial AR containing real and easily explainable information that is already known. Sometimes such AR can be used to check the implementation of decisions made on the basis of previous analysis.

3. Incomprehensible AR containing information that cannot be explained. Such rules can be obtained either on the basis of anomalous values or deeply hidden knowledge. Directly such rules cannot be used for making decisions, since their inexplicability can lead to unpredictable results. Further analysis is required for a better understanding.

The AR mining methodology using frequent sets consists of two steps:

1) search for frequent sets;
2) generation of ARs based on frequent sets that satisfy the conditions of minimum support and confidence.

The most common AR at some minimum thresholds of support and confidence can be found using the well-known Apriori algorithm, first proposed by Rakesh Agrawal, Tomasz Imielinsky and Arun Swami in 1993 [7]. The algorithm has many modifications. Thus, in [22], it was noted that RElim, Apriori TID and FP-Growth are the best AR mining algorithms in terms of performance, memory size, and response time. But nevertheless Apriori is used in many researches [1, 6–8, 11, 13, 15, 17–23, 26].

This algorithm is based on the concept of a frequent set (frequently occurring set) - a subject set with support greater than a given minimum level.

Mathematically, the Apriori algorithm idea is as follows [13]:

$$\forall a_n : supp(\{a_1, a_2, \ldots, a_{n-1}\}) \geq supp(\{a_1, a_2, \ldots, a_n\}) \tag{5}$$

So, we have

$$\forall a_n : supp(\{a_1, a_2, \ldots, a_{n-1}\}) < T \Rightarrow supp(\{u_1, u_2, \ldots, a_n\}) < T, \tag{6}$$

$$supp(\{a_1, a_2, \ldots, a_n\}) \geq T \Rightarrow \forall i \in 1 \ldots n : supp(\{a_1, a_2, \ldots, a_n\}/\{a_i\} \geq T \tag{7}$$

where T is support minimal level.

This algorithm is characterized by a predetermined required number of elements in the found rules. Let us denote this number by M.

General scheme of work:

Step 1. Filtering all a_i and leaving only those elements for which $supp(\{a_i\} \geq T$. Initialization $C_i^1 = \{a_i\}$ for filtered items.

Step 2. At the k-th step, candidates for inclusion in the set of popular sets are generated based on rule (7) using the sets generated at the previous step, if the condition on the right side of condition (7) is satisfied for all k elements of the new candidate, then is calculated $supp(\{a_{l,1}, a_{l,2}, \ldots, a_{l,k}\})$. If this value is greater than the minimum support then $C_l^k = \{a_{l,1}, a_{l,2}, \ldots, a_{l,k}\}$ is initialized.

In addition, the Apriori algorithm uses the anti-monotonicity property: if a subject set A is not frequent, then adding a new item B does not make it more frequent. This property can significantly reduce the search space for ARs.

The algorithm is relatively easy to use, but effective only for small sets, or with a high level of minimal support.

As a rule, at the initial stage of the search, a large number of ARs are identified, which can reach tens of thousands. At the same time, the implementation of a multi-criteria approach to identifying optimal ARs and ARs mining, taking into account the principles of Pareto dominance according to certain criteria, is of significant interest. The implementation of this task will draw the attention of specialists to the most stable ARs.

3   Multi-criteria Association Rules Optimization

In practical research, situations often arise in which the results obtained must be optimized according to several criteria simultaneously. In this case, the problem of multicriteria optimization (MCO) is solved, the formal setting of which is as follows.

Let D be an arbitrary set of feasible solutions (alternatives) and $f_1(x), f_2(x), \ldots, f_n(x)$ be numerical functions (criteria) defined on the set D.

The function $f(x) = (f_1(x), f_2(x), \ldots, f_n(x))$ is the vector criteria.

Then the task $f(x) \rightarrow min \ (max) \ (x \in D)$ is called a multiobjective optimization problem.

Ideal in this problem is to find a solution that belongs to the intersection of the sets of optimal solutions to all problems. But, as a rule, several functions do not reach the extreme at one of the same point simultaneously. The way out is to find some compromise in achieving the set local goals. Pareto dominance relation is the main relation by which the comparison of the found solutions is made.

In the MCO problem a solution $x_0 \in D$ is called Pareto optimal if doesn't exist another solution $x \in D$ which would be prefer than x_0.

The Set of Pareto optimal points (many unimprovable or effective points) form a set Dp. Thus, optimal solutions to the MCO problem should be fight only among the elements of the set Dp.

The Pareto set includes solutions that are not inferior to each other in criterion estimates, that is, solutions of which no one dominates the other.

The variety of methods the Pareto set of optimal solutions constructions indicates the relevance of this problem. A detailed review of such methods can be found, for example, in [14]. These include the grid method, the method based on lexicographic tournament selection, and evolutionary methods based on genetic algorithms. In the latter, the rules for the formation of the fitness function are considered, which ensure the movement of individuals in the population, ultimately, in the direction of the Pareto set.

With respect to extraction of the set of Pareto-ARs can be identified [16]. It uses a genetic algorithm NSGA-II for search Pareto optimal sets of rules for the three-pronged problem of the single-lens optimization and genetic algorithm SOGA to optimize the fitness function of the weighted sum of the three objectives for the comparison of computational experiments.

In the same paper, it was shown that the best rule is the Pareto-optimal rule in relation to support and confidence [16].

ARs in which the support and confidence values exceed a certain predetermined threshold are called strong rules.

In the course of the research, it was decided to use two criteria for searching for the Pareto set: confidence $conf(A \rightarrow B)$ and support $supp(A \rightarrow B)$ under the condition of maximizing both criteria

$$f(x) = \{conf(A \rightarrow B), supp(A \rightarrow B)\} \rightarrow max \qquad (8)$$

The Pareto-optimal set of AR can be found based on the its definition. First, you need to order the rules in descending order of one of the criteria (confidence). Among them, you must choose the one with the highest value of the second criterion - support. Let the first optimal AR be found in this way. Next, you need to select the rules with a lower confidence, but with a support greater than that of the first rule, and then select the rule with the highest confidence among these rules. This will be the second optimal AR. These actions must be repeated until the original list of all ARs is exhausted.

As a result, in the obtained optimal set of ARs, the confidence will decrease with a simultaneous support increase.

4   Experimental Results

In the course of the research, when analyzing the studied set of medical data, standard algorithms were used to process real data. The experimental part included a multicriteria search for association rules taken from Table 2, dominating over others.

Table 2. ARs groups

Support	Confidence	ARs number	Average confidence	Lift < 1
≥0,10	≥0,5	353	0,775	13
≥0,10	≥0,6	329	0,729	11
≥0,05	≥0,5	868	0,771	–
≥0,05	≥0,6	777	0,797	–

For the given boundaries of the five age groups (18–44 years old, 45–59 years old, 60–74 years old, 75–89 years old, 90–99 years old) recommended by World Health Organization, four ARs groups were found at different thresholds of support and reliability (Table 2). The choice of the initial values of support and reliability is taken from the analysis of studies [1, 9, 12, 14, 19, 21]. When searching for association rules, the maximum length of the rule antecedent was taken equal to five elements (diseases).

The role of T2DM in the structure of the MCD was investigated separately. With support of at least 0,10, 75 rules with T2DM were found, and with support of at least 0,05, 90 rules with T2DM were found. In both cases, T2DM was present only in the antecedent of the rule and did not occur in the consequent of any rule.

With support of at least 0,10, the antecedents of the rules consisted of subsets of the set of diseases {T2DM, AH, OA}. With a decrease in support to 0,05, the set of diseases expanded to {T2DM, AH, OA, CHF, CVD, kidney disease}. Also, with a support threshold of 0,1, the identified AR showed a high predisposition to T2DM in women. AR that create associations for the treatment of T2DM in men have not been identified.

In the task of our research, the number of identified ARs turned out to be too large (Table 2), therefore, for their further interpretation and analysis, it is expedient to construct a Pareto set of optimal solutions representing the most significant AR.

For each of the four ARs groups of Table 2, *eight identical sets* of Pareto optimal rules were obtained (Table 3).

Table 3. Pareto-optimal ARs

AR	conf	supp	lift	conv
{Woman, OA, CHF, CVD} → {AH}	1,000	0,155	1,190	159730479,588
{Woman, OA, CVD} → {AH}	0,998	0,187	1,188	75,393
{CHF, CVB, CVD} → {AH}	0,996	0,216	1,186	43,686
{OA, CVD} → {AH}	0,995	0,257	1,185	34,715
{Woman, CVD} → {AH}	0,993	0,272	1,181	22,123
{CVD} → {AH}	0,987	0,409	1,174	11,964
{OA} → {AH}	0,899	0,480	1,070	1,582
{Woman} → {AH}	0,846	0,554	1,007	1,035

In the structure of the MCD, a special place belongs to AH as the most common cardiovascular pathology. Visualization of the resulting set can be represented by a graph (Fig. 1). The thickness of the lines and the indicator near it indicates the frequency of the joint appearance of the disease/symptom with AH in the Pareto set of ARs (the thicker the line, the greater the frequency of the joint appearance of the disease/symptom).

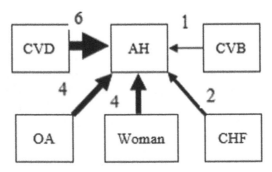

Fig. 1. Visualization of the optimal Pareto set of ARs

The direction of the arrows in our case should not be interpreted so that the presence of CVD, OA, CHF or CVB leads to the occurrence of hypertension. Obtaining AH as a consequent of all Pareto-optimal AR probably indicates that AH acts as a provoking factor in the occurrence of a disease/symptom. For example, the presence of hypertension in a patient can lead to complications such as CVD, OA, CHF, CVB. The rule, {Woman} → {AH}, can be interpreted as the prevalence of AH in women.

Despite the high confidence scores (conf > 0,9) in the first six rules, high conviction scores (e.g. conv = 159730479,588) are quite perplexing for them. This apparently means that such hypotheses need to be subjected to additional analysis. The last two rules with consequential hypertension are probably the most acceptable characteristics.

Thus, our AR obtained in the course of the research balance between the trivial and useful groups [26].

However, these results confirm the Pareto charts constructed for specific cases. A Pareto chart is a graphical reflection of the Pareto law, the cumulative dependence of the distribution of certain resources or results on a large set (sample) of causes. It allows you to show which diseases are most typical (80%) for a selected group of people.

So, for the total number of patients, the Pareto diagram shows that in the structure of the MCD, the dominant diseases are AH, OA, CVD, CHF, CVB, and kidney diseases (Fig. 2).

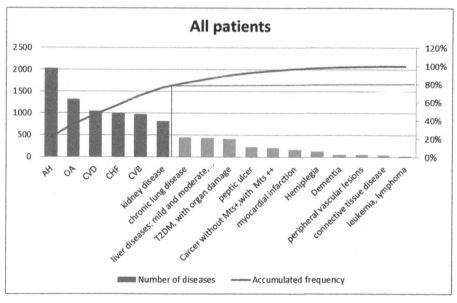

Fig. 2. Pareto chart for all patients (2523 people)

Women (1649 people, 65,4% of the surveyed) of all age categories are characterized by AH, OA, CVD, CHF, kidney disease, CVB. Men (874 people, 34,6% of the surveyed) are characterized by AH, OA, CVD, CHF, kidney disease, chronic lung disease, liver disease of varying severity and CVB. Apparently, the appearance in this set of diseases of the lungs and liver in men is associated with bad habits - smoking and alcohol consumption.

If we consider among all patients, for example, the largest age category 60–74 years (36,0% of the surveyed), then the main diseases here are AH, OA, CVD, CHF, kidney disease, CVB and dementia. Most of these diseases are involved in the construction of the Pareto set for all previously obtained ARs.

5 Discussion/Further Researchs

Initially, the aim of the study was to identify the role of T2DM in the structure of the MCD. T2DM disease was not included in the optimal Pareto set. However, there are researches with the obtained optimal ARs, including diabet [21]. For example, {Diabet} → {Hypertension} (conf: 0,72, lift: 1,11); {CVD} → {Diabet} (conf: 0,92, lift: 1,11); {Hypertension} → {Diabet} (conf: 0,92, lift 1,07); {Acute renal failure} → {Diabet} (conf: 0,94, lift: 1,11). Obviously, research is needed on an extended database (with the addition of symptoms, medical prescriptions) using additional Data Mining algorithms.

It should be noted that, if necessary, an evolutionary optimization algorithm can be used to construct association rules for data sets on patients with MCD with simultaneous division of patients into age groups that are optimal from the point of view of similarity of MCD structure and provide specified threshold values of the main quality indicators of rules.

The results obtained at this stage of the study are intermediate. AR take into account only the facts of joint manifestation of transactions (diseases) and do not take into account the temporal aspect, namely, the sequence of the occurrence of morbidity.

In the future, it is planned to move to the search for sequential patterns - the appearance of certain diseases in time (sequential analysis) and the use of fuzzy algorithms for ARs mining.

6 Conclusion

In this study, standard methods were used to identify association rules from a large database of patients with multiple chronic diseases. The original database is provided by doctors from various clinics and is representative. Further selection of the optimal rules was carried out according to two criteria - support and reliability, which should be maximized simultaneously. For certain thresholds of these parameters, the optimal Pareto set was obtained, including eight ARs, in which the central place is occupied by the disease of AH.

The main conclusion of the study can be considered that the most correlating diseases were AH, OA, CHF, CVD, angina pectoris for all patients. These diseases are usually associated with age-related changes in patients [25]. The interconnection of the MCD available in patients is confirmed by the identification of association rules and the construction of a set of Pareto.

References

1. Aljawarneh, S., Anguera, A., Atwood, J.W., et al.: Particularities of data mining in medicine: lessons learned from patient medical time series data analysis. J. Wirel. Commun. Netw. **2019**, 260 (2019). https://doi.org/10.1186/s13638-019-1582-2

2. Dashkevich, O.V., Nizov, A.A., Lapkin, M.M., Trutnev, E.A., Gershunskaya, V.V.: Metabolic syndrome in the practice of a city polyclinic therapist: the experience of therapy with metformin and a dietary product - seaweed jam, enriched with chromium. Russian Medico-Biological Herald Named After Academician I.P. Pavlov, no. 2, pp. 88–92 (2013)
3. Silkina, U.I., Balandin, V.A.: Discriminant analysis of variational pulsometry parameters. Rossiiskii tekhnologicheskii zhurnal = Russ. Technol. J. **8**(3), 81–91 (2020). https://doi.org/10.32362/2500-316X-2020-8-3-81-91. (in Russian)
4. Demidova, L., Klyueva, I., Pylkin, A.: Hybrid approach to improving the results of the SVM classification using the random forest algorithm. Proc. Comput. Sci. **150**, 455–461 (2019)
5. Sutherland, E.R., Goleva, E., King, T.S., Lehman, E., Stevens, A.D., Jackson, L.P., et al.: Cluster analysis of obesity and asthma phenotypes. PLoS ONE **7**(5), (2012). https://doi.org/10.1371/journal.pone.0036631
6. Parva, E., Boostani, R., Ghahramani, Z., Paydar, Sh: The necessity of data mining in clinical emergency medicine; a narrative review of the current literatrue. Bull. Emerg. Trauma. **5**(2), 90–95 (2017)
7. Agrawal, R., Imielinski, T., Swami, A.: Mining association rules between sets of items in large databases. In: SIGMOD 1993 Proceedings of the 1993 ACM SIGMOD International Conference on Management of Data, pp. 207–216 (1993)
8. Srikant, R., Agrawal, R.: Fast algorithms for Mining Association rules in large database. In: VLDB 1994 Proceedings of the 20th International Conference on Very Large Data Bases, pp. 487–499 (1994)
9. Aggarwal, C.C.: Data Mining. The Textbook. Springer, Cham (2015). https://doi.org/10.1007/978-3-319-14142-8
10. Rauch, J., Šimůnek, M.: Alternative approach to mining association rules. In: FDM 2002, The Foundation of Data Mining and Knowledge Discovery, The Proceedings of the Workshop of ICDM02, pp 157–162 (2002)
11. Aldosari, B., Almodaifer, G., Hafez, A., Mathkour, H.: Constrained association rules for medical data. J. Appl. Sci. **12**, 1792–1800 (2012)
12. Baranov, A., et al.: Methods and tools for complex intellectual analysis of medical data. In: Proceedings of the ISA RAS, vol. 65.2, pp. 81–93 (2015)
13. Kirichenko, D.O., Artemov, M.A.: Optimization of input data in the problem of finding patterns and association rules. Vestnik VSU Ser. Syst. Anal. Inf. Technol. **4**, 63–70 (2014)
14. Karpenko, A.P., Semenikhin, A.S., Mitina, E.V.: Population methods of approximation of the Pareto set in the problem of multicriteria optimization. Overview. Science and Education: Electronic Scientific and Technical Publication, no. 4 (2012). http://technomag.edu.ru/doc/363023.html
15. Dogadina, E.P., Kropotov, Yu.A.: Determination of the Pareto-optimal set for the implementation of work on the example of the application of the genetic algorithm. Control Systems, Communications and Security, no. 3 (2015)
16. Ishibuchi, H., Kuwajima, I., Nojima, Y.: Multiobjective association rule mining. In: PPSN Workshop on Multiobjective Problem Solving from Nature, T. 12 (2006)
17. Ul Huq, S.T., Ravi, V.: Evolutionary Multi-Objective Optimization Framework for Mining Association Rules. https://e.mail.ru/attach/15948407140027385752/0%3B3/?folder-id=0&x-email=ndoroshina%40mail.ru
18. Kumar Soni, H.: Multi-objective Association Rule Mining using Evolutionary Algorithm. https://www.researchgate.net/publication/318542116
19. Billig, V.A., Ivanova, O.V., Tsaregorodtsev, N.A.: Construction of associative rules in the problem of medical diagnostics. Software Products and Systems, no. 2 (114) (2016)
20. Chen, C.-H., Hong, T.-P., Tseng, V.S.: Finding Pareto-front membership functions in fuzzy data mining. Int. J. Comput. Intell. Syst. **5**(2), 343–354 (2012)

21. Tarutin, A.V., Nabatov, A.V.: Application of methods of genetic algorithms for constructing a Pareto set in multiobjective optimization problems. Eng. Bull. Don, no. 4 (2015)

22. Konak, A., Coit, D., Smith, A.: Multi-objective optimization using genetic algorithms: a tutorial. Reliab. Eng. Syst. Safety **91**(9) (2006)

23. Lakshmi, K.Sa, Vadivub, G.: Extracting association rules from medical health records using multi-criteria decision analysis. Proc. Comput. Sci. **115**, 290–295 (2017)

24. Asfandiyarova, N.S., Dashkevich, O.V., Zaikin, E.V., et al.: Gender and age structure of multiple chronic diseases in patients of Ryazan region. Klinitsist. The Clinician **11**(3–4) (2017)

25. Asfandiyarova, N.S., Dashkevich, O.V., Doroshina, N.V., Suchkova, E.I.: Type 2 diabetes mellitus and multiple chronic diseases. Diabetes Mellitus **21**(6), 455–461 (2018). https://doi.org/10.14341/DM9605

26. Matveykin, V.G., Dmitrievsky,, B.S., Lyapin, N.R.: Intelligent Analysis Information Systems. Mechanical Engineering (2008). 92 p.

The Fuzzy Approach for Classification Borrowers of Microfinance Organizations

Valentina Kuznetsova[⊠] [iD]

Astrakhan State University, 20, Tatisheva Street, Astrakhan, Russia
arhelia@bk.ru

Abstract. The evolution of information technology is accompanied by a comprehensive modification of the service sector, including microfinancing. This part of the Russian financial market shows stabilize growth annually. However, the availability of loans for Russians in a symbiosis with low financial literacy and high debt burden led to a large number of debts to MFOs. This, together with the tendency to an increase in the number of cases of license withdrawal from MFOs, leads to the relevance of developing a scoring model that could identify borrowers with high profitability and low probability of default at the stage of applying for a microloan and "cut off" potentially insolvent applicants. Within the framework of this work, a methodology for clustering MFO clients is proposed based on the fuzzy criterion "level of financial responsibility", which is the basis for assessing the effectiveness of microfinance.

Keywords: Microfinance · Fuzzy modeling · Clustering techniques · Risk management · Classification of borrowers

1 Introduction

The development of information technology is accompanied by a complex transformation of the service sector, including the microfinancing, which is undergoing an upsurge in the Russian financial market. According to data published in the "Review of Key Indicators of Microfinance Institutions" by the Central Bank of the Russian Federation [1], in 2019 the aggregate portfolio of microfinance organizations (MFIs) grew to 212 billion rubles (Fig. 1). The volume of micro-loans issued increased by 25% and amounted to 412 billion rubles.

The popularity of microfinance services is primarily due to the fact that, unlike the classical system of bank lending, when making a decision to issue a microloan, only primary verification of the authenticity of the documents provided is carried out, and the average time for consideration of an application does not exceed 30 min.

The transition to modern remote service technologies further increases the availability and popularity of microcredit services. However, against the background of the high debt burden of the Russian population, the availability of microcredit for the majority of residents of the Russian Federation very often leads to lending to persons who are unable to subsequently repay the loan. Financial consumers are unable to adequately assess the

P. K. Singh et al. (Eds.): FTNCT 2020, CCIS 1395, pp. 465–474, 2021.
https://doi.org/10.1007/978-981-16-1480-4_42

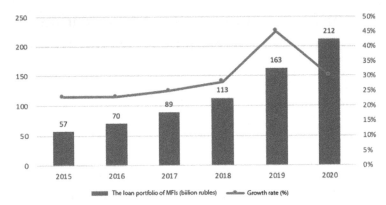

Fig. 1. Change in the size of the loan portfolio of Russian MFIs in 2015–2020.

risks of entering into a microfinance agreement due to the continuing low level of finan-cial literacy. The availability of microcredit for the majority of residents of the Russian Federation very often leads to lending to persons who are unable to subsequently repay the loan [2].

Most likely, the growth in the number of defaulted borrowers, who currently require prompt action, is not sufficiently effective in terms of their maladjustment in the digital economy. As a result, the share of overdue debt on "quick" loans in 2019 alone increased by 7.3% and reached a record figure of 27.3%.

To solve this problem, the state strengthens the regulation of MFIs, and every year makes attempts to tighten their regulatory framework: limiting the maximum debt, maxi-mum interest rate, term of the loan agreement, etc. [3]. Also, the introduction of a unified standard for the collection of overdue debts, as well as the tightening of the regulatory framework for the activities of collection agencies, sharply limited the possibilities of these organizations in the field of debt collection.

Besides according to the Bulletin on Current Trends in the Russian Economy [4], a continuing decline in real disposable incomes of the population is being recorded, which is the most protracted in recent Russian history. In general, over 5 years, the real drop in income was 10.8% from the level of 2013, taking into account the lump sum payment and 10.7% without taking it into account.

The decrease in the marginality of microfinance raises the question of the effec-tiveness of the applied scoring models, which could more accurately identify potential default applicants even at the stage of consideration of the loan application. This, in turn, would make it possible to improve the methods of decision-making on microfinancing and "face-to-face", i.e. borrowers who applied for a loan at the MFI office, and online borrowers who applied the website.

The current scoring models are based on the classical classification of applicants - "good" (the one that will potentially repay the loan) and "bad" (the one that most likely will not repay the loan: the delay exceeds 30 days) [5]. However, there are different types of borrowers among the "good" ones - those who repay the loan on time, those who return after reminders, or as a result of a court order. The available classification does not reflect this specificity of returns, and also does not take into account the degree to which borrowers belong to a particular type. Their affiliation is strictly defined: if the payment is delayed by at least 1 day, the borrower is automatically classified as unreliable.

2   Materials and Methods

Within the framework of this work, it is planned to carry out clustering of borrowers by categories that reflect the profitability of financing each of the applicants, using cluster analysis. To express the degree of belonging to the categories identified as a result of clustering, it was decided to use the theory of fuzzy sets. Fuzzy logic has been successfully applied in many fields of knowledge since Lotfi Zadeh introduced this theory in 1965 [6]. Its applications can be found in medicine, artificial intelligence, decision theory, operations research, and many other scientific fields. Fuzzy logic is used in cases where the meaning of truth can vary from completely true to completely false, which makes it possible to more accurately describe a person's subjective judgment using linguistic variables.

Within the framework of credit scoring, attempts have already been made to use the theory of fuzzy sets, described in the works of scientists from Ghana [7], Morocco [8, 9], where the fuzzy expert system singled out borrowers with "low", "medium" and "high" on the basis of associative rules. creditworthiness, and the parameters of the categories were proposed to be determined by decision makers or experts.

For the analysis, within the framework of this work, statistical data of borrowers of the basic microfinance organization were taken, which was chosen as one of the leading microfinance organizations of the Southern Federal District. An impersonal customer base of 20,000 records for 2017 was taken as a basis. Data collection was additionally carried out through interviews with the organization's management and observation of the firm's financial operations.

3   Results

3.1   Criteria

Statistical analysis included data on the presence and duration of credit delinquency (in days) of borrowers from the base organization (Fig. 2). For visual analysis, a diagram was built that reflects how many borrowers from the analyzed list were overdue and how long it was.

Its construction made it possible to identify characteristic "breaking" points. As a result of a conversation with the head of a microfinance organization, whose client base was used, it was revealed that:

- on the 90th day of delay in the return of the microloan, the case for the return of borrowed funds is transferred to the court at the place of registration of the borrower;
- on the 150th day of delay in the return of the microloan, the right to collect the debt is transferred to the collectors. Compensation for each loan agreement is 30% of the total debt ("body" of the loan + interest for use + late payment interest).

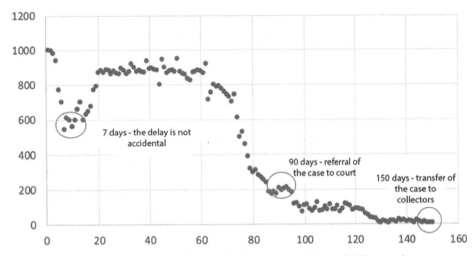

Fig. 2. Diagram which showing the frequency and time of delinquencies.

At the same time, no statistical regularity was found in the 30-day delay period defined in the classical scoring model. Based on the data obtained, a fuzzy criterion "financial responsibility" was formulated, which characterizes the behavior of borrowers when repaying a loan. To determine the fuzzy criterion [10]:

1. Introduced linguistic variable K = "Level of financial responsibility".
2. A term-set of values of the linguistic variable K = {"high", "medium", "low", "default"} has been introduced. This number of values was determined on the basis of the "turning point" dates of delinquencies, which made it possible to further cluster borrowers into 4 categories (K1, K2, K3, K4).
3. Trapezoidal numbers are assigned to the introduced term-set.

For a set with a high level of financial responsibility (K1), a trapezoid is assigned (1):

$$y = \begin{cases} 1, x \leq 0 \\ \frac{15-x}{15}, \end{cases} 0 \leq x \leq 1 \tag{1}$$

For a set with an average level of financial responsibility (K2), a trapezoid is assigned (2):

$$y = \begin{cases} \frac{x}{15}, 0 \leq x < 15 \\ 1; 15 \leq x \leq 60 \\ \frac{90-x}{30}, 60 < x \leq 90 \end{cases} \tag{2}$$

For a set with a low level of financial responsibility (K3), a trapezoid is assigned (3):

$$y = \begin{cases} \frac{x+60}{30}, 60 \leq x < 90 \\ 1; 90 \leq x \leq 135 \\ \frac{150-x}{15}, 135 < x \leq 150 \end{cases} \tag{3}$$

For a set with a default level of financial responsibility (K4), a trapezoid is assigned (4):

$$y = \begin{cases} 1, x \geq 150 \\ \frac{x-135}{15}, \end{cases} 135 \leq x \leq 15 \tag{4}$$

The graphical view of the proposed fuzzy classifier is shown in Fig. 3.

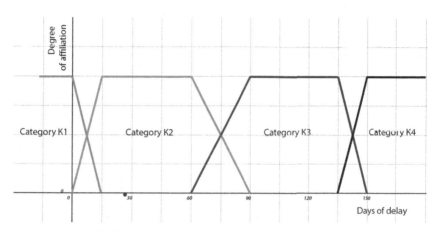

Fig. 3. Graphic view of the proposed fuzzy classifier.

In addition to the amount of delay, the categories of borrowers identified as a result of clustering are characterized by the profit that the microcredit company will receive after the loan is repaid:

- Category K1 - no delay. Profit consists of % use.
- Category K2 - delay from 0 to 90 days. The profit is made up of% use +% for delay.
- Category K3 - delay from 90 to 150 days. Profit: % use +% for delays minus the cost of repaying the loan.
- Category K4 - overdue over 150 days. Loss: 30% of the principal and all accrued interest as a result of the sale of the right of claim under the contract to collectors.

3.2 Classification

Thus, the classification of clients who have previously received a loan is reduced to an analysis of the terms of the previous delay, on the basis of which the borrower is assigned a certain category [5]. However, for primary borrowers, this approach is unacceptable, since they do not have a credit history. The results of the analysis of the set of available parameters in the basic scoring model showed that it is not possible to unambiguously characterize the representatives of each category of borrowers - multivariate statistical analysis showed that all borrowers are evenly distributed across the selected categories. This led to the need to develop its own criterion, reflecting the level of financial responsibility of the applicant. However, for its application, it is necessary to obtain additional personalized information about the applicant, which is absent in the set of parameters of the basic scoring model.

To solve this problem, a method was developed for constructing an extended digital profile of the borrower (EDPB) [12]. It assumes for an offline borrower (applying for a loan personally through the office of MFI) to build an EDPB to analyze his physiological characteristics, appearance, verbal and non-verbal signs (of the i-th borrower) and to identify in his character the so-called. "Radicals" by the method of "7 radicals" Victor Ponomarenko. To build an EDPB for an online borrower (applying for a loan remotely through the MFI website), it is necessary to analyze his page on the social network and identify a set of data characterizing his activity on the Internet. In both cases, over a period of time, a database with a credit history was formed, which formed the basis of the table of precedents.

At the same time, in the table of precedents, on the basis of credit history data, sets $<K^m; \mu^m; K^{m+1}; \mu^{m+1}>$, где K^m and K^{m+1} where K^m и K^{m+1} are "adjacent" categories of borrowers (for example, K^1 and K^2, K^2 and K^3, K^3 and K^4), and μ^m and μ^{m+1} are the degree of belonging of the i-th borrower to the corresponding category K^m и K^{m+1} (according to the graphical version of classifier).

Thus, the EDPB of an offline borrower is a tuple $<B_i; R_i^j; K^m; \mu m; K^{m+1}; \mu m>$, where B_i are the values of the parameters of the basic scoring model.

EDPB of the online borrower: $\left(B_i; DP_i^j; K^m; \mu m; K^{m+1}; \mu m\right)$, where DP_i^j are the values of the information about the borrower's activity on the Internet downloaded from the social network page.

Based on the above, the methodology for classifying borrowers using the precedent approach can be presented in the form of a block diagram (Fig. 4).

It is important to note that if, as a result of calculating the Hemming distance according to the basic scoring model (B_i), there are several precedents, then further calculations are carried out taking into account the risk strategy of the MFI:

– when the decision maker chooses a strategy to minimize the risk of an MFI, the precedent is selected in which the index m in K^m takes the greatest value. In case of equality of indices m, leave the precedent in which the value of μ^m will be minimal.
– when the decision maker chooses the strategy of the greatest loyalty to the borrower, then the precedent is chosen in which the index m in K^m takes the smallest value. In case of equality of indices m, leave the precedent in which μ^m will be the maximum.

4 Discussion

The main criterion for decision makers when making a decision is the rate of return on investment (ROI). General formula for calculating profitability:

$$ROI(N) = \frac{\sum_{i=1}^{N} P_i}{V}, \tag{5}$$

where $P_i = W_i - R_i$, P_i – profit received from the i-th client, W_i – income from the i-th client (net of borrowed funds), R_i – costs associated with the return of the loan through

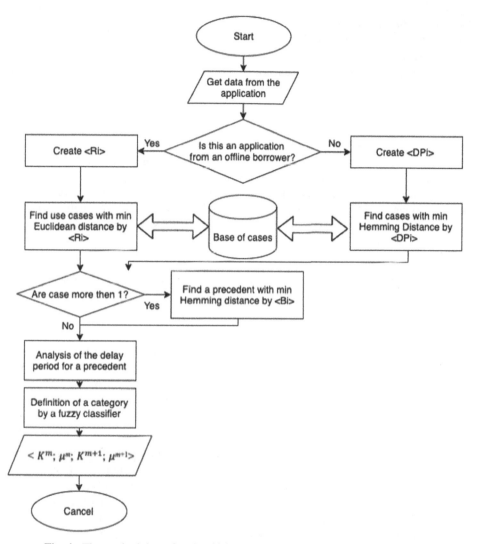

Fig. 4. The methodology for classifying borrowers using a precedent approach

the court in the event of such a need (services of lawyers for the preparation of court documents).

Amount of income W_i from microfinance of the i-th borrower depends on the loan amount, days of use of funds and interest for use. In addition, it should be noted that the value W_i is influenced by the degree of belonging of the borrower to a particular category. There are no legal costs for category K^1, there is no delay in the loan, so the formula for calculating income takes the form:

$$K^1 : W_i = S_i P_i^{use} D_i^{use}, \tag{6}$$

where S_i – the amount of borrowed funds issued to the i-th client; P_i^{use} – percentage for the use of borrowed funds; D_i^{use} – the term for which the loan was issued under the terms of the agreement.

For category K^2 and K^3 when calculating income, it is necessary to additionally take into account the fact of delay by adding the amount of the penalty for delay:

$$K^2, K^3 : W_i = S_i P_i^{use}(D_i^{use} + D_i^{del}) + S_i P_i^{del} D_i^{del}, \tag{7}$$

where P_i^{del} – interest for late repayment of borrowed funds; D_i^{del} – number of days of delay in repayment of borrowed funds. When calculating profit when lending to a borrower category K^3 income will decrease by the amount of expenses R_i.

For category K^4 income is derived from the total debt (including interest for use and delinquency) sold at a discount to collectors. Usually the discount coefficient (q) is 0,7–0,8. So to calculate W_i of customer from category K^4 we have formula:

$$K^4 : W_i = (1 - q) * (S_i P_i^{use}(D_i^{use} + D_i^{del}) + S_i P_i^{del} D_i^{del}). \tag{8}$$

Taking into account formulas 5–8, the total income received from the issuance of a microloan to the i-th applicant is calculated by the formula:

$$W_i = W^m \mu^m + W^{m+1} \mu^{m+1}, \tag{9}$$

where μ^m, μ^{m+1}- degrees of belonging to categories K^m and K^{m+1} respectively.

Thus, to make a decision to issue or refuse to issue a microloan to the next $(N + 1)$-th applicant, it is necessary to calculate $ROI(N)$ and $ROI(N + 1)$. An application for microcredit is approved subject to the following conditions:

$$ROI(N + 1) \geq ROI(N), \tag{10}$$

where $ROI(N + 1)$ – profitability of the loan portfolio in the event that a loan is issued to the $(N + 1)$-th applicant, $ROI(N)$ – the profitability of the loan portfolio before the receipt of the loan application from the $(N + 1)$ th applicant. In this case, the number of days of using the loan, the interest in use and delay, the period for which the loan is issued is determined for the $(N + 1)$-th borrower from his application.

In general, the methodology for making a decision on the issuance of microloans in an MFI can be formulated as follows:

1. The decision maker chooses a risky strategy: minimizing risks or the greatest loyalty to the client;
2. Information about the applicant is downloaded from the loan application.
3. If the borrower applies for the first time:

   - for an offline borrower B_i; R_i^j is determined.
   - for an online borrower DP_i is determined, B_i is taken from the application.

4. The category of the borrower is determined according to the method for determining the primary offline borrower or the method of the primary online borrower, depending on the method of his circulation. If the borrower applies again, the category is

determined by the latest credit service or credit history in a third-party organization from the Bureau of Credit Histories.

5. The profitability of the applicant's loan service is calculated. If the profitability does not decrease, the application is approved. Otherwise, it is rejected.

5 Conclusion

The widespread introduction and intensive growth of information technologies are transforming all areas of financial services, including the Russian microfinance market, which shows steady growth every year. At the same time, with the increase in the number of clients applying for credit services, including remotely, the number of overdue and unpaid loans is growing, which indicates the need to revise the current scoring system of MFIs operating in offline and online modes.

Solving the problem of clustering borrowers using a fuzzy criterion for the level of financial responsibility allowed developing a methodology for classifying potential borrowers based on building their extended digital profile. In addition to standard characteristics (credit history, financial situation, demographic data) [11], such a digital profile takes into account human behavior, including in social networks, which is a direction for further research.

The methodology for making a decision on the issuance of microloans proposed in this article is based on the classification of borrowers by the level of financial responsibility and the profitability of their service in terms of the return on equity of MFIs.

References

1. Overview of key microfinance institutions. Central Bank (2019). https://www.cbr.ru/Content/Document/File/73687/review_mfi_19Q1.pdf. Accessed 6 May 2020
2. Barinov, A.S.: The debt burden of the Russian population in the context of threats to economic security. Natl. Interests Priorities Secur. 7(364), 1270–1286 (2018). https://doi.org/10.24891/ni.14.7.1270. Accessed 6 May 2020
3. Belobabchenko, M.N.: Limitations in the issuance of consumer loans by MFIs. Law Practice. 2, 150–154 (2019)
4. Bulletin on current trends in the Russian economy, February 2020. https://ac.gov.ru/uploads/2-Publications/rus_feb_2020.pdf. Accessed 6 May 2020
5. Dudarkova, O.Yu.: Problems of making investment decisions in the face of uncertainty. Econ. Manage. XXI Century Dev. Trends 33–2, 127–132 (2016)
6. Azhmukhamedov, I.M.: A dynamic fuzzy cognitive model of the influence of threats on the information security of a system. Inf. Technol. Secur. 2, 68–72 (2010)
7. Abdulrahman, U.F.I., Panford, J.K., Hayfron-Acquah., J.B.: Fuzzy logic approach to credit scoring for micro finance in Ghana: a case study of KWIQPLUS money lending. Int. J. Comput. Appl. 94(8), 11–18 (2014). from: http://www.academia.edu/15502256/Fuzzy_Logic_Approach_to_Credit_Scoring_for_Micro_Finance_in_Ghana_A_Case_Study_of_K WIQPLUS_Money_Lending. Accessed 6 May 2020
8. Baesens, B., Van Gestel, T., Viaene, S.: Benchmarking state-of-the-art classification algorithms for credit scoring. J. Oper. Res. Society 54(6), 627–635 (2003)

9. Bennouna, G., Tkiouat, M.: Fuzzy logic approach applied to credit scoring for microfinance in Morocco. https://www.sciencedirect.com/science/article/pii/S1877050918301352. Accessed 6 May 2020
10. Protalinsky, O.M., Azhmukhamedov, I.M.: System analysis and modeling of poorly structured and poorly formalized processes in sociotechnical systems. http://www.ivdon.ru/ru/magazine/archive/n3y2012/916. Accessed 6 May 2020
11. Óskarsdóttira, M., Bravo, C., Sarrautec, C., Vanthienena, J., Baesensa, B.: The value of big data for credit scoring: Enhancing financial inclusion using mobile phone data and social network analytics. https://doi.org/10.1016/j.asoc.2018.10.00.004. Accessed 6 May 2020
12. Kuznetsova, V.Y.: The fuzzy approach for clustering borrowers of microfinance organizations. Model. Opt. Inf. Technol. **8**(2) (2020). https://moit.vivt.ru/wp-content/uploads/2020/05/Kuznetsova_2_20_1.pdf. https://doi.org/10.26102/2310-6018/2020.29.2.031. (in Russian)

Hybrid Movie Recommender System - A Proposed Model

Prajna Paramita Parida[✉] [ORCID], Mahendra Kumar Gourisaria [ORCID], Manjusha Pandey [ORCID], and Siddharth Swarup Rautaray [ORCID]

Kalinga Institute of Industrial Technology (Deemed to be University), Bhubaneswar, Odisha, India
{1964003,manjushafcs,siddharthfcs}@kiit.ac.in,
mkgourisaria2010@gmail.com

Abstract. Recommendation systems are intelligent search systems that predict the preferred information and provide suggestions to users. Traditional ways mainly are of content filtering and collaborative approach. However, these approaches show some demerits like the data sparsity, cold start, scalability, etc. Thus to tackle these demerits, the paper focuses on a system based on a hybrid approach that integrates the approaches of content-based and collaborative, employed with a singular value prediction algorithm. In addition to this, a systematic study and a proposed model is presented along with the machine learning algorithm. The study shows that the cosine similarity indexing, ranking, and the SVD algorithm can achieve better research objectives. The main idea is to investigate the present trends and responses of users. Promising validation results are produced by the experiments done over the public database.

Keywords: Hybrid approach · Recommender system · Matrix factorization · Social media

1 Introduction

Many information-based companies utilize recommendation systems on a wider scale such as Twitter, Google, Netflix, LinkedIn, etc. This area of recommender originated in the mid of the 1990s, along with the invention of Tapestry, the first Recommendation System. Movie recommendation plays a major role in the mobile environment. It carries out the aggregation of reviews and users' preferences to help them for better movies and to maximize profit by minimizing risks. This system provides selective information taking prior user habits and history as inputs. However, it requires both timeliness and accuracy. Researchers studied the application of machine learning algorithms as the field of recommendation developed. Since the late 1950s, artificial intelligence got emerged and then machine learning came into existence. An increase in ML algorithms is experienced such as clustering, k- nearest neighbor, Bayes network, regression, etc. This recommendation framework works for a hybrid approach and analyzes the users' history accompanied by feature extraction. So that the parameters like timeliness and

P. K. Singh et al. (Eds.): FTNCT 2020, CCIS 1395, pp. 475–485, 2021.
https://doi.org/10.1007/978-981-16-1480-4_43

accuracy of the recommender system will be improved [1]. An amalgamation of content-based and collaborative methods is done that is influenced by the social media domain at a great pace [2].

Table 1. Comparison between Content and Collaborative approaches

Recommendation algorithms	Advantages	Disadvantages
Content-based	Results are easily interpretable and intuitive No new item or sparsity issue Classification learning supports this technology No need to access users' history	Feature extraction way limits the model New user issue Classification training requires massive data Scalability issue
Collaborative based	Complex unstructured item are processed such as video, music User can be found out easily No need for expertized knowledge Performance increases by an increase in users	Sparsity issue New item and new user problem; Scalability issue History dataset limits the quality of the model

Thus by the above-given Table1, we can establish the fact that both approaches fail to give optimum results individually. However, the combination of the two techniques will find a better solution to the mentioned flaws and will compensate each other. The hybrid associates the filtering and working mechanism into one framework. Below, Fig. 1 is the illustration by which a hybrid mechanism is employed with the combination of the workings of content-based and collaborative where items as well as user similarity, are taken into consideration.

The remaining paper is demonstrated as given: Sect. 2 describes a survey over the literature part, Sect. 3 illustrates the fetching of dataset and important features, and the proposed model for hybrid system is presented in Sect. 4. The mechanism and algorithm that obtains the working of the proposed model is illustrated in Sect. 5. Evaluation criteria are analyzed by validation in Sect. 6 and then in the last section, the conclusion is drawn.

2   Literature Survey

Different approaches have been proposed for suggesting recommendations. In the field of business applications, Guo et al. [3] suggested a novel recommender system that compares pre-purchase ratings with post-purchase ratings so that preferences can be more accurate. The system procures its instantaneous data from the virtual environment of 3D products. It mainly takes the latent choices of the user. It deploys a new mechanism of collecting pre-purchase emotions from electroencephalogram (EEG) signals that are set on a headset. In this way, these pre and post ratings can boost the overall working of the recommender. Pearson correlation computes the similarities for nearest neighbors and

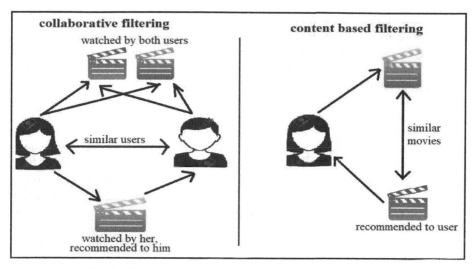

Fig. 1. Combining both techniques for movie recommendation

provides both ratings benefiting e-business. Costin-Gabriel Chiru et al. [4] presented a movie recommender for upgrading a personalized type of recommendation. Various factors like user profile, history preferences, and movie scores are analyzed. A psychological test such as a questionnaire is performed and a similar profile brings out similar choices for genres. Four psychological types such as phlegmatic, choleric, melancholic, and sanguine and their intensity has been estimated. Genres and characteristics are categorized according to these traits. So, in this case, the absence of ratings can be easily dealt with, because the association of user profile with movie probabilities could be considered. But, it fails for accurate value due to the traits evaluation.

Wang et al. [5] present a hybrid recommendation algorithm by taking scores of items based on filtering mechanism and sentimental analysis. The system emphasizes the over score calculation of both positive and negative sentiments. The mechanism works on the Spark platform alleviates flaws of content and collaborative methods and increases accuracy and timeliness. Frangidis et al. [6] comparatively studied between reviewers and movie scripts using Gini-index or SVM approach for increased accurate ratings. The correlation was reflected in the predictions which were carried by sentiment analysis using vector semantic and meta-features. Tools were applied like VADER (Valence Award dictionary) for sentimental analysis and NRC for emotion analysis. A mixture of machine learning algorithms is used such as Multinomial Naive Bayes (MNB), Logistic regression, SVM, Multilayer perceptron. Among these, Multinomial Naive Bayes provided promising results.

Deldjoo *et al.* [7] studied a combination of different features of meta-data and audio-video resources mainly to tackle cold start issues. An extraction from videos constitutes a movie genome is done following the canonical correlation method. This model focuses on items that are combined with interaction taking item content descriptors and making it quite bias-free. Thus works for collaborative enriched content with high coverage as a multimodal recommender system. Soleymani et al. [8] analyzed the movie scenes and its ranking, provided by the emotion of users and features of videos. In this system, physiological signals such as galvanics kin resistance, respiration pattern, electromyograms, body temperature, blood pressure were recorded and stored. The physiological signals were applied to categorize and rank contents of the video to obtain optimal performance with the best features.

Wang *et al.* [9] proposed a recommendation model that works on social content. This system evaluates the user-content matrix and finds out the relevance between video and users for re-sharing suggestions. Based on the user-video matrix, the social content area is constructed to verify relevance. Following the content delivery network, the dynamics of video sharing are high and access patterns are analyzed for matrix modification. R. H. Nidhi et al. [10] experimented on real-time data like tweets for generating a Naive Bayes based classifier. The system is applied on a small train set, providing better accuracy. To improve individual techniques, hybrid systems are composed of combinations of multiple recommendation approaches.

In [11], the authors developed a new hybrid approach named as content-boosted CF, that utilized content-based features in a collaborative model. They overcame the first rater and sparsity problem by building a pseudo matrix of ratings. Then, the model is compared with pure content, collaborative, and naive hybrid systems. Yang et al. [12] referred ratings from page count which are collected from users' data. The measure of likeness of documents by users is demonstrated by the count of read ones. This concept focuses on the cold start issue in CF and utilizes the mean AP correlation method over log information. In this paper, a movie recommendation framework in hybrid form has been suggested by associating the content filtering with collaborative based prediction.

3   Data Collection

The data used in the proposed model has been taken from two sources: the movie database (TMDB) and MovieLens. The dataset from MovieLens is publicly available containing 26 million ratings for 45,000 movies given by 270,000 users. A small dataset is also available containing 100,000 ratings for 9000 movies given by 700 users. One file with TMDB Id of every movie is listed in the MovieLens dataset. Five CSV files are deployed by using the Pandas library on the Jupyter platform. Movies_metadata CSV file contains metadata from TMDB including revenue, genres, date released, etc. Credits CSV file includes director, actor, etc. on credits for a specific movie. The keywords file includes plot keywords for a movie. Links_small file contains a list of movies that are available in the small subset from the MovieLens dataset and the ratings_small file originates from a small dataset of MovieLens having 100,000 ratings. After scraping of data, the stringified features are converted into a form for parsing. Filtering is done multiple times to remove unnecessary attributes and to reduce the dimension of the dataset. The following features being listed in Table 2, are mainly taken into consideration for extraction purposes in the recommendation model. Many attributes or features have to be filtered from the main dataset.

While observing the content based system and collaborative method individually, we conclude that the features for the former technique consist of movie or users' profiles and the latter technique focuses on the interaction pattern of the user with the movie.

Table 2. Feature set for data extraction

Features	Description
rating	Ratings given by specific user
userId	User's identity
movieId	Movie Id for TMDb
title	Official name of the movie
tmdbId, imdbId	Movie Id given on respective platform
Id	Movie Id by TMDb
timestamp	Duration when ratings are given
genre	category of movie
vote_count	No.of votes given by users
vote_average	Average reviews of movie

However, the hybrid recommender engine utilizes both attribute sections and combines all important features. Below Fig. 2 depicts the trend of amalgamation of both ways of feature selection and unification.

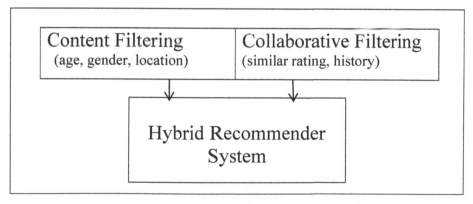

Fig. 2. Feature extraction for hybrid movie recommendation

Due to this, data demands a lot of extraction and preprocessing steps. Noises of the original collected data are eliminated such as emojis, hashtags, repetitive words, punctuations, web-links, special characters, and other irrelevant data. Thus to make the data in a form that it would be easily parsed through the machine, raw data are transformed into clean data. The processed data discovers the pattern and becomes understandable to interpret. The final data accomplish the normalization steps and becomes suitable to be analyzed by the main algorithm.

4   Hybrid Movie RecommendationModule

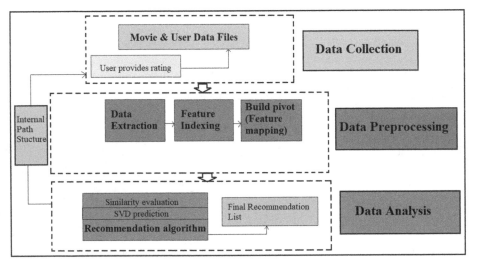

Fig. 3. Framework for proposed movie recommendation system

The procedure of movie recommendation in a stepwise manner is illustrated in Fig. 3 given above, describing three stages of data collection, data preprocessing, and data analysis. The data collection section depicts the retrieval of data from the databases having user-rated movie data and users' profile data. These are the dataset that has to be procured and saved for updating. Users keep on adding their ratings or reviews which are also updated. Data preprocessing includes the feature analysis by filtering and indexing to get pivot data. It filters noises and unnecessary attributes. Normalization provides matrices to estimate similarity for score calculation. The final task is data analysis that calculates scores from cosine similarity matrices and ranking is done. Then the SVD based prediction provides the estimated ratings to finalize the suggestion list according to a user request. There also lies an internal path structure that connects the first section with the last section to update the ratings data. The combined Recommendation Systems [13] over the movies-user experience is an aspect for searching preferred movies by minimizing the searching time, scalability, and cold start issue.

The main idea is to imply SVD prediction as it is a matrix factorization technique for better dimensionality reduction and is used as a collaborative filtering purpose. Matrix factorization follows a structure of associating user entities with movie entities based on ratings. Below Fig. 4 shows the singular value decomposition performed for factorization.

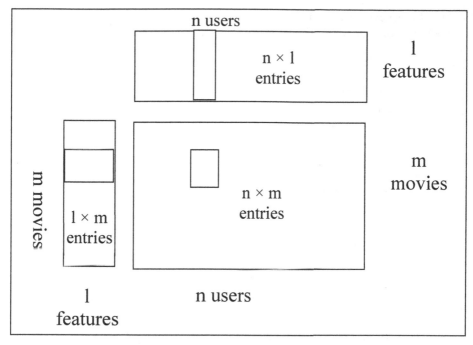

Fig. 4. Matrix Factorization technique

5 Implementation

Data being collected, it requires integration, cleaning, transformation, segmentation, stemming, and removal of noise for the pre-processing phase [14]. The hybrid approach combines the content features of metadata with user interaction of ratings forming a learned model of collaborating SVD predictions. Neighboring users are estimated by similarity dimensions and obtains an integrated weighted ratings named as 'est'. This

	title	vote_count	genre	id	est
368	Hackers	406.0	Crime	10428	3.599223
534	The Glass Shield	9.0	Drama	72031	3.599223
91	Across the Sea of Time	2.0	Adventure	139405	3.599223
494	Eat Drink Man Woman	76.0	Comedy	10451	3.599223
187	The White Balloon	20.0	Drama	46785	3.599223
160	Lawnmower Man 2: Beyond Cyberspace	32.0	Action	11525	3.599223
665	Picture Bride	5.0	Drama	30304	3.599223
49	Money Train	224.0	Action	11517	3.599223
589	Legends of the Fall	636.0	Adventure	4476	3.599223
395	Mallrats	400.0	Comedy	2293	3.599223

Fig. 5. Hybrid preliminary movie recommendation list

could be further extended for different comparisons with other approaches by analyzing accuracy measures on various data. In the end, by creating a recommendation list as shown in Fig. 5, we intend to present the below SVD proposed algorithm in a systematic procedure.

SVD Algorithm for the Proposed Recommender System :

Inputs:
Dataset containing CSV files
Metadata of mean movie rating
Normalized similarity score

Mains:
1. Convert required features into normalized vector forms.
2. Estimate count of the normalized vectors by semantic metrics like TfIdf and CountVectorizer to get count matrix, being retrieved as:

$$\text{TfIdf}_{i,j} = \text{Tf}_{i,j} \times \log\left(\frac{N}{df_i}\right)$$

(1)

where $\text{Tf}_{i,j}$: Total no. of occurrences of i in j,
df_i : Total no. of documents or speeches containing i,
N : No. of documents or speeches
3. Calculate cosine similarities with the help of the count matrix. Mathematically, given as:

$$Similarity(a,b) = \cos(a,b) = \frac{a \cdot b}{\|a\| * \|b\|}$$

(2)

4. Build the pivot user-item matrix by indexing and merging with ratings data.
5. Split the data by KFold metric to get trainset and testset and perform Singular Value decomposition (SVD) prediction on the trainset.
6. Obtain similarity scores in sorted form to be mapped for ranking and apply prediction.
7. Sort estimated ratings (est) and obtain list based on users' given data and movie title.

Outputs:
Preliminary recommendation list
Predicted ratings

---

6 Empirical Analysis

The tests for the recommendation mechanism are available online as well as offline ways. Online test like A/B test analyzes users' behaviour whereas train-test split and K

Fold cross-validation comes under offline tests. We have employed cross-validation that estimates the skill of machine learning models by digging to the training sets and testing sets as a resampling procedure [15, 16]. The algorithm insights are supported by RMSE or MSE optimization which leads to better results minimizing the squared error or loss. Mathematically, described as:

$$RMSE = \sqrt{\frac{\sum_{i=1}^{n} (Predicted_i - Actual_i)^2}{N}} \tag{3}$$

$$MAE = \frac{1}{n} \sum |y - \hat{y}| \tag{4}$$

where n: Total no of data points.
$|y - \hat{y}|$: Absolute value of residual.

Moreover, we can validate the SVD prediction by comparing it with the KNN approach which is one of the nearest neighbor algorithm. Below Figure 6 and 7 shows the evaluation results by Root mean square error (RMSE) and Mean absolute error (MAE) which are optimized to 0.8961 and 0.6905 respectively, whereas the other approach has larger values. As lower the RMSE and MAE values, the better is the proposed algorithm.

```
Evaluating RMSE, MAE of algorithm SVD on 5 split(s).

                 Fold 1  Fold 2  Fold 3  Fold 4  Fold 5  Mean    Std
RMSE (testset)   0.8945  0.9012  0.8940  0.8952  0.8956  0.8961  0.0026
MAE (testset)    0.6913  0.6947  0.6884  0.6874  0.6905  0.6905  0.0025
Fit time         4.52    4.43    4.40    4.37    4.41    4.42    0.05
Test time        0.12    0.12    0.11    0.37    0.11    0.17    0.10
```

Fig. 6. Evaluation results based on SVD algorithm

```
Evaluating RMSE, MAE of algorithm KNNBasic on 5 split(s).


                Fold 1  Fold 2  Fold 3  Fold 4  Fold 5  Mean    Std
RMSE (testset)  0.9632  0.9612  0.9698  0.9621  0.9773  0.9667  0.0061
MAE (testset)   0.7402  0.7386  0.7458  0.7384  0.7523  0.7431  0.0053
Fit time        0.19    0.20    0.20    0.19    0.20    0.20    0.01
Test time       1.43    1.43    1.60    1.42    1.40    1.46    0.07
```

Fig. 7. Evaluation results based on KNNBasic algorithm

7   Conclusion and Future Work

Thus, the movie recommendation framework being proposed searches preferred movies from collaborative based predictions.The objective is to analyze the development of the recommender system that employs a machine learning algorithm and assistance to data mining areas. The main purpose is to provide a better knowledge management system and to improve the accuracy and timeliness compared to previous models. It filters unusable data by delivering personalized ideas. So that, useful movie suggestions will be available to the users readily. The recommendation process is a comprehensive work that involves distinct users along with movies, collected from reviews on social media platforms. The proposed framework could be improved with more datasets and more recent movies and we expect more extraction of information from different social media platforms to improve this system. However, the study of requirements, design, and maintenance suggests more research opportunities to be investigated and could be more explored to work for a dynamic environment.

References

1. Rutkowski, L., Korytkowski, M., Scherer, R., Tadeusiewicz, R., Zadeh, L.A., Zurada, J.M. (eds.): ICAISC 2017. LNCS (LNAI), vol. 10246. Springer, Cham (2017). https://doi.org/10.1007/978-3-319-59060-8
2. Zhang, H.R., Min, F., He, X., Xu, Y.Y.: A hybrid recommender system based on user-recommender interaction. Math. Probl. Eng. (2015)
3. Guo, G., Elgendi, M.: A new recommender system for 3d e-commerce: an EEG based approach. J. Adv. Manage. Sci. 1(1), 61–65 (2013)
4. Chiru, C.G., Dinu, V.N., Preda, C., Macri, M.: Movie recommender system using the user's psychological profile. In: IEEE International Conference on ICCP (2015)
5. Wang, Y., Mingming Wang, M., Xu, W.: A sentiment-enhanced hybrid recommender system for movie recommendation: a big data analytics framework. Wirel. Commun. Mobile Comput., vol. 2018, Article ID 8263704, 9 pages (2018)
6. Frangidis, P., Georgiou, K., Papadopoulos, S.: Sentiment analysis on movie scripts and reviews. In: Maglogiannis, I., Iliadis, L., Pimenidis, E. (eds.) AIAI 2020. IAICT, vol. 583, pp. 430–438. Springer, Cham (2020). https://doi.org/10.1007/978-3-030-49161-1_36

7. Deldjoo, Y., Dacrema, M.F., Constantin, M.G.: Movie genome: alleviating new item cold start in movie recommendation. User Model. User-Adapted Interact. **29**(2), 291–343 (2019)
8. Soleymani, M., Chanel, G., Kierkels, J.J., Pun, T.: Affective ranking of movie scenes using physiological signals and content analysis. In: Second Workshop on Multimedia Semantics, pp. 32–39 (2008)
9. Wang, Z., Sun, L., Zhu, W., Yang, S., Li, H., Wu, D.: 'Joint social and content recommendation for user-generated videos in Online social network.' IEEE Trans. Multimedia **15**(3), 698–709 (2013)
10. Nidhi, R.H., Annappa, B.: Twitter-User recommender system using tweets: a content-based approach. In: International Conference on Computational Intelligence in Data Science (ICCIDS) (2017)
11. Melville, P., Mooney, R.J., Nagarajan, R.: Content-boosted collaborative filtering for improved recommendations. **23**, 187–192 (2002)
12. Wei, B., Wu, J., Yang, C., Zhang, Y., and Zhang, L.: Cares: a ranking-oriented cadal recommender system. In *Ninth Joint Conference on Digital libraries*, pages 203–212. ACM, (2009).
13. Jain, K.N., Kumar, V., Kumar, P., Choudhury, T.: Movie recommendation system: hybrid information filtering system. In: Bhalla, S., Bhateja, V., Chandavale, A.A., Hiwale, A.S., Satapathy, S.C. (eds.) Intelligent Computing and Information and Communication. AISC, vol. 673, pp. 677–686. Springer, Singapore (2018). https://doi.org/10.1007/978-981-10-7245-1_66
14. Kim, T.Y., Pan, S.B., Kim, S.H.: Sentiment digitization modeling for recommendation system. Sustainability **12**(12), 5191 (2020)
15. Srivastava, N., Lamba, T., Agarwal, M.: Comparative analysis of different machine learning techniques. In: Singh, P.K., Sood, S., Kumar, Y., Paprzycki, M., Pljonkin, A., Hong, W.-C. (eds.) FTNCT 2019. CCIS, vol. 1206, pp. 245–255. Springer, Singapore (2020). https://doi.org/10.1007/978-981-15-4451-4_19
16. Handa, N., Sharma, A., Gupta, A.: An inclusive study of several machine learning based non-functional requirements prediction techniques. In: Singh, P.K., Sood, S., Kumar, Y., Paprzycki, M., Pljonkin, A., Hong, W.-C. (eds.) FTNCT 2019. CCIS, vol. 1206, pp. 482–493. Springer, Singapore (2020). https://doi.org/10.1007/978-981-15-4451-4_38

Development of a Text and Speech Enabled Conversational Agent for Students' Activities Planning Using Dialog Flow

Oghenetega Erekata[1], Ambrose Azeta[1], Sanjay Misra[1(✉)], Modupe Odusami[1], and Ravin Ahuja[2]

[1] Covenant University, Ota, Nigeria
{ambrose.azeta,sanjy.misra,
modupe.odusami}@covenantuniversity.edu.ng
[2] Shri Vishwakarma Skill University, Gurgaon, India

Abstract. Conversational agents are now ubiquitous and catching speed as an application of computer communication and are able to respond intelligently like humans. Some of these agents help humans with their everyday tasks. Students perform several activities in school and having to remember all these activities can be stressful thereby increasing lethargy because a user has to surf through multiple pages in order to obtain relevant information. The aim of this project is to automate personal assistants for activities planning most especially for students. This study proposed a machine learning intent classification algorithm provided by Google's Dialog flow API to make seamless conversations with the user. The proposed system makes use of Node.Js for server-side programming, React.Js for building the user interface and Mongo.Db as its database and most especially Dialogflow API for natural language processing. The results showed that the system could be used in real-time by making use of the aforementioned technologies.

Keywords: Chatbots · Conversational agents · Dialog flow · Personal assistant

1 Introduction

Conversational agents are "computer programs that are capable of interpreting and responding to user statements in ordinary natural language [1]. They are software-based – systems designed to interact with humans using natural language [2]. Turing test which describes an agent as being intelligent if it is able to fool a human interrogator [3]. Turing test was limited to text only, the human interrogator is aware of the two participants taking the test in which one is a human being and one is an intelligent agent. Over the years, conversational agents have gone from being simple rule-based pattern matching agents to being natural language processing agents that make use of machine learning. Most of the information available to us today are in form of texts i.e. emails, blogs, reports, tweets, etc. making it easier for these machine learning models to scale [4]. Adoption of chatbots has also increase, especially with the launch of chatbot platforms by Facebook [5, 6]. Chatbots are also being used in various virtual assistant like Siri (Apple),

© Springer Nature Singapore Pte Ltd. 2021
P. K. Singh et al. (Eds.): FTNCT 2020, CCIS 1395, pp. 486–499, 2021.
https://doi.org/10.1007/978-981-16-1480-4_44

Echo (Amazon), Google Now (Google), Cortana (Microsoft) in which these assistants help humans get things done The architectures and information retrieval processes of these chatbots take advantage of advances in machine learning [7]. Others have adopted "generative models" to respond to user inputs; they use Statistical Machine Translation (SMT) techniques to "translate" input phrases into output responses. Seq2Seq models, a variant of generative models that make use of Recurrent Neural Networks like Long Short Term Memory Gated Recurrent Unit to encode and decode input phrases into responses is a current best practice [8, 9]. Generally, the technologies used for the chatbots are computationally intensive [10]. Also, several researchers have argued that Conversational agents need more than technical capabilities to succeed [2]. This study is motivated by the problem of seamless interactions like a friend that will enable students to get things done quickly and also get familiar with their environment in no time.

In this study, we developed a conversational agent and web-based digital assistant that make use of both text and speech. The main contribution of this study is the provision of a text and speech-enabled conversational for student's activities planning that helps students to solve the problem of seamless interactions thereby fostering the development of automatic personal assistant. The remaining part of this paper is sectioned into: Sect. 2 presents literature review. Next, Sect. 3 presents the system analysis and design followed by experimental analysis. Results and Discussion in Sect. 4. Section 6 presents the conclusion and future area of research.

2 Related Works

There are a lot of existing conversational agents out there today. Some being embedded into the operating systems of smartphones, some are added as features on some social networks and some acting as standalone applications. A lot of them being used in various fields like medicine, education, entertainment, finance, etc. but there are only a handful of chatbots that can help students keep their busy life in check. Authors in [11] utilized blink the bee on chat apps like Facebook Messenger and Kik and this helped users create to-do lists and also to switch the order of their tasks and also mark out completed tasks after a list has been created. Authors in [12] presented an artificial conversational agent, called Harlie that runs on a smartphone. Experimental result showed that the proposed model could play a major role in the next generation of speech and communication therapy for people living with many neurological and other conditions. Authors in [13] integrated Computer Assisted Language Learning with chatbots to teach a language without the need for a classroom or a teacher. The proposed model is an improvement in learning outcomes by using chatbot as a conversational partner. Authors in [14] designed a conversational agent called FarmChat to answer farmer queries. Experimental results showed that the proposed model has the potential to effectively meet the information needs of farmers at scale. Authors in [15] utilized Artificial Intelligence Markup Language to build up a conversational agent. The proposed model interacts with user using text and voice responses based on android application chatbot. However, the chatbot could only answer questions that have the answer in its database. Authors in [16] designed a rule-based chatbot called ALICE based on the Artificial Intelligence Markup Language. ALICE did not require a sophisticated natural language analysis or logical inference, but the pattern-template matching rules have to be very large for effective performance [17]. Authors in [18] proposed a chatbot using Artificial Intelligence Markup Language (AIML) and Latent Semantic Analysis (LSA). The proposed model automatically gives immediate responses to the users based on the data set of Frequently Answered Questions. Authors in [19] discussed different approaches used for deploying chatbots based on Artificial Intelligence Markup Language (AIML). It was concluded from their studies that Artificial Intelligence Markup Language-based chatbots are lightweight and easy to implement [19]. Considering the findings from the related studies, chatbot has shown to play a very prominent role as human-computer interfaces. This study thereby leveraged on existing advantages and presented conversational agents using dialogue flow. There are several other related works available on speech technology in education [20, 21].

3   System Analysis and Design

This section focuses on the analysis and design of the proposed system. System analysis decomposes the proposed method into its component pieces to define how well those components interact to accomplish the already established requirements. The proposed system comprises of both functional and non-functional requirements.

3.1   Functional Requirements

Each functional requirement is uniquely identified by an identification number, a title, target user and the priority to indicate the importance given to it—MUST (M), SHOULD (S), COULD (C) and WON'T (W)—as depicted in Table 1.

Table 1. Functional requirements

Req. ID	Requirement description	Target users	Priority
REQ-SYS-001	Login and Logout	User	M
REQ-SYS-002	Sign up (Registration)	User	M
REQ--001	Add to-do item	User	M
REQ--002	Delete to-do item	User	M
REQ--003	Schedule reminder for an assignment or group project	User	M
REQ--004	Display information concerning a particular course	User	M
REQ--005	Display information concerning all pending to-dos and assignments/group projects	User	M
REQ--006	Send push notification regularly to user about pending to-dos and group projects	User	M
REQ--007	Mark an assignment as completed and remove it from pending tasks	User	M
REQ--008	Provide relevant information about itself to the user	User	M
REQ--009	Display information about the lectures the user is currently having and also schedule for a particular day	User	M

3.2 Non-functional Requirements.

This section specifies the non-functional features such as audit, control and security, data requirements, usability requirements, service level targets, user volume, data growth and retention requirements, etc. that the proposed system must possess from a business perspective. The details of the non-functional requirements is depicted in Table 2.

Table 2. Non-functional requirements

Req.ID	Category	Requirement description	Target user	Priority
REQ--001	Control & Security	User password must not be displayed on the screen during user input	User	M
REQ--002	Performance	Response for a particular request shouldn't take more than 15 s	User	M
REQ--003	Performance	Chat history should load in less than a 30 s whenever user opens the chat page	User	M
REQ--004	Control & Security	System must ensure that a particular user is logged in before the chat page can be available for sending requests	User	M
REQ--005	Usability	User interface and interaction should be as simple as possible	User	M
REQ--006	Performance	User password must not be displayed on the screen during user input	User	M
REQ--007	Maintainability	Response for a particular request shouldn't take more than 15 s	Developer	M
REQ--008	Maintainability	User interface and interaction should be as simple as possible	Developer	M

3.3 Architecture Design

This section provides description on the architectural design, including the data and application aspect of the proposed system ranging from very high level to lower levels of abstractions. The application architecture of the proposed system is depicted in Fig. 1.

- The Web Frontend: This component of the application is what allows the user to send a query to the Dialogflow agent. This component can be implemented using various frontend technologies such as HTML, CSS and JavaScript. The proposed system made use of a JavaScript library—React.Js. React.Js is a component-based JavaScript library that implements a browser-independent DOM system responsible for building user interfaces. The components can then be rendered on the DOM, and users can also add styles to these components. The text obtained from the user needs to be processed and sent in a format compatible with what is expected by the Node.Js client. The message is JSON formatted, and then a call is made to the Node.Js client using JavaScript built-in Fetch API which helps in sending the data to the Node.Js client.

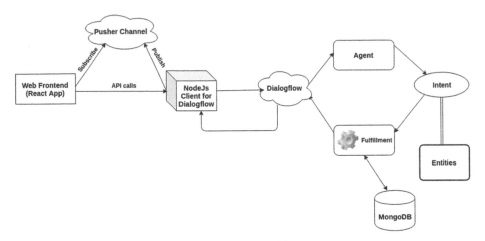

Fig. 1. Application architecture

- Pusher Channel: this provides real-time communication between servers, apps and devices. They are primarily used for notifications, chat, web pages and basically for applications requiring real-time communication. Channel connection is the fundamental means of communicating with Pusher API services. It is a bidirectional connection and can receive messages as well as emit messages from the server. Whenever a user types in a message, React.Js frontend makes a call to the Node.Js client, the processing is then done by the Node.Js client. Pusher then triggers a 'bot-response' event on a 'planner-bot' channel that publishes the message to the Pusher channel. The already subscribed React.Js frontend then realizes that there is a message that has been triggered by the Node.Js client gets the response from the channel, updates the chat history and then displays the response to the user.
- Node.JS Client For Dialog flow: This component consists of a server created using a JavaScript runtime called Node.JS. The Node.Js client is the component used in designing and integrating a conversational agent into any application or device. The server sends the message to the Dialog flow API, receives the intent and the response and then send the result back to the client. A client library called Dialog flow does the major role of communicating with the Dialog flow agent. A session is established to ensure secure communication between the Node.Js clients. In order to develop this connection, a session id is specified. A session id helps Dialog flow API knows what device is establishing such connection and also treats conversations from a particular client as the same.
- Dialog flow API: This API receives a request from the client, processes the request using a machine learning (ML) driven architecture and sends the response back to the client. To determine an appropriate response to the client, specific processes have to be carried out on the client's message. Firstly, we need to know the user's intent. In

essence, an intent is a unit of a conversation that is triggered by a specific phrase the user inputs. This can be a command ("Set a reminder for me", "What is the next course I'm having", "Turn on the light", "What is the name of my CSC 422 lecturer") or a response to a question ("Okay, next tomorrow", "Yes", "Thank you, next"). Secondly, entities need to be detected, and for Dialog flow API to recognize intents, intents needs to undergo a training phase. During the training phase the user enters possible texts, words or phrases that can trigger the intent. In Dialog flow, a keyword or a key phrase is known as an entity. Dialog flow comes with some built-in entities such as date, time, country, location, etc. Thirdly, the context has to be determined. By default, a Dialog flow agent would assume that all intents are the same, invoking any intent that matches the user's input. However, this can trigger the wrong intent. The way Dialog flow solves this problem is by making use of contexts, intents are configured in the form of contexts. Finally, there might be an optional feature called fulfilment created via a webhook. When creating intent, the developer has two options, either have the agent reply with the input given by the user or replying based on the result gotten from a webhook response. Dialogue flow calls the webhook a developer configures with an HTTP POST request containing a JSON body. The JSON object includes information on the user's input, the contexts, any extracted entities, etc. The webhook then does processing on the HTTP request, telling Dialogflow how to respond, which output context to set, etc. The implementation of webhook for the proposed system was done using a Node.Js Dialog flow fulfilment library. A MongoDb database is connected to the webhook, this database contains the data that would be manipulated based on the detected intent.

3.4 System Design

The system design details the design of the various components of the system and their working relationships, to expound on the functions defined in the functional requirements and how it was implemented in the proposed system. This comprises application model and data model. The application model consists of the use case diagram, class diagram, sequence diagram, and activity diagram as depicted in Fig. 2, 3, 4 and Fig. 5. Table 3 depicts the narrative for the use case.

The class diagram shows the various classes in the system, shows some of the methods implemented in those classes and also displays the relationship among the various classes system.

The data model is made up of a logical and physical model. Figure 6 shows the logical data diagram while the description of Logical data entity for the proposed system is depicted in Table 4. The physical data model diagram and the physical data entity description for the proposed system are shown in Fig. 7, respectively.

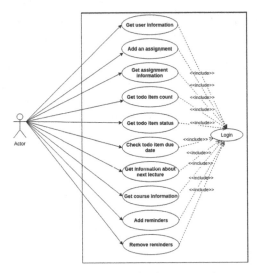

Fig. 2. Use case diagram for the proposed system

Table 3. Use case narrative for adding an assignment

Various use cases	Narrative
Use case 1	User
Goal in content	User should be able to add a new assignment/group work
Priority	High
Preconditions	User must provide the assignment name (course code), the time of submission
Post condition (success end)	Assignment is added to list of assignments for that particular user
Post condition (failure end)	Assignment is not added to assignments list for that particular user
Actor	User
Trigger	A request from the frontend client to add a new assignment
Description (event flow)	Actor action: Types in text that specifying that he/she wants to add an assignment
	System response: Sends a request to Dialogflow API, this extracts the relevant information from the text. If the accurate information is gleaned from the text, it is then saved to the database

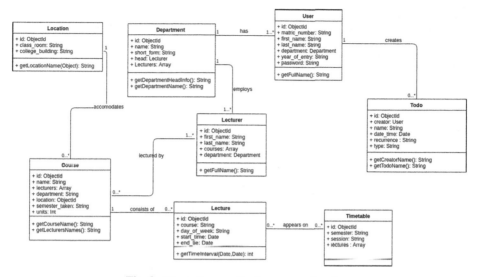

Fig. 3. Class diagram for the proposed system

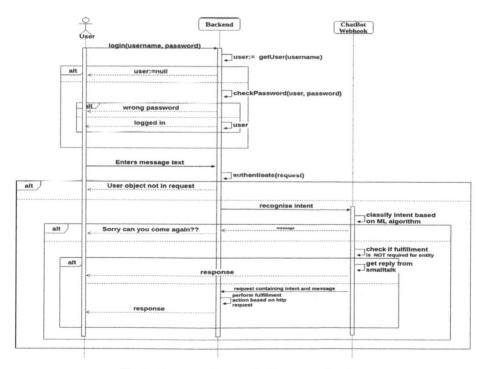

Fig. 4. Sequence diagram for the proposed system

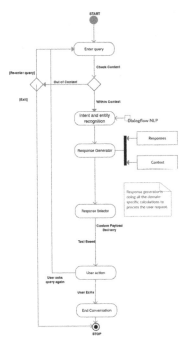

Fig. 5. Activity diagram for the proposed system

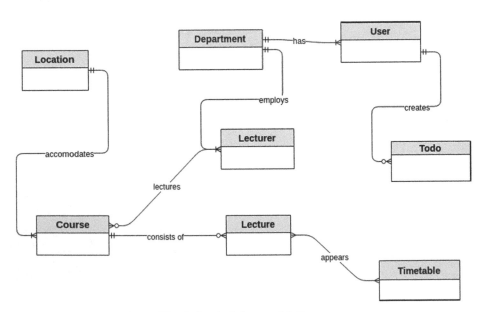

Fig. 6. Logical data model diagram

Table 4. Logical data entity description for the proposed system

Logical data entity	Logical data entity description
User	Includes information about users that registered on the system. User id would be unique for each record
Course	Includes detail about the courses offered by students. Course id would be unique for each record
Department	Includes information about departments. Department id would be unique for each record
Lecturer	Includes information about lecturers in a department. Lecturer id would be unique for each record
Lecture	Includes information about lectures taken in a semester. Lecture id would be unique for each record
Location	Includes information about the lecture location. Location id would be unique for each record
Timetable	Includes information about the timetable for a particular semester. Timetable id would be unique for each record
Todo	Includes information about a particular to-do item. To-do id would be unique for each record

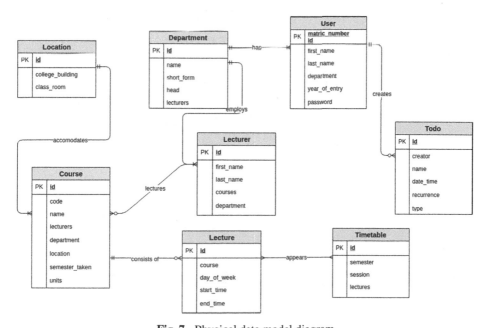

Fig. 7. Physical data model diagram

4 Experimental Analysis

The proposed system in Sect. 3 was implemented using a CPU with minimum requirement of 1.5 GHz or faster processor and 2 GB RAM. Agile methodology was employed because during the course of development, improvements had to be made to the system requirement. User authentication was primarily accomplished using Passport.Js (an authentication middleware for Node.Js). A library express-session handles session generation in Express.Js that is not normally done handled directly. An interface called signup page and login page are derived. Several modules such as small talk module, assignment handling module, reminders handling module, information retrieval module, and speech processing module are also derived. Dialog flow API enables integration of agents with google assistant. Google assistant provides a speech processing module that performs speech-to-text and text-to-speech for a developer without having to write the algorithm from scratch.

The approach presented in this paper provided an automatic personal assistant for activities planning most especially for students. Figure 8 shows how the agent would respond to popular requests from the user. A sample conversation in which the user types in a request and the intent classifier classifies the request as an 'assignment.add' action is depicted in Fig. 9. The user can schedule assignments, set reminders, query for information, make use of smalltalk, etc. via speech as depicted in Fig. 10.

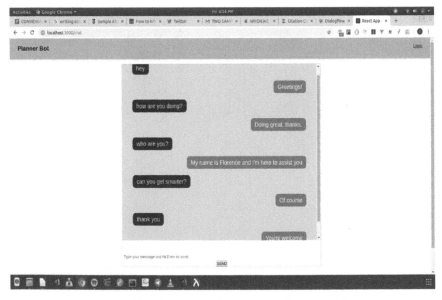

Fig. 8. Sample conversation using small talk module

From Fig. 8, hard coding responses to popular user requests are enabled it on Dialog flow and provided sample responses to popular user requests.

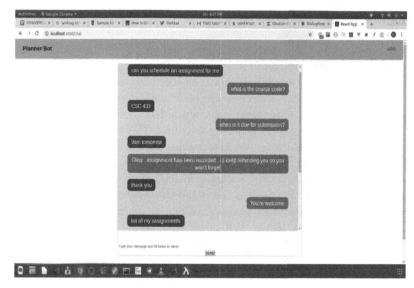

Fig. 9. Assignment scheduling

From Fig. 9, if the user doesn't specify some important data needed for the intent to be fulfilled, the user is prompted to supply the necessary information before any further processing is done.

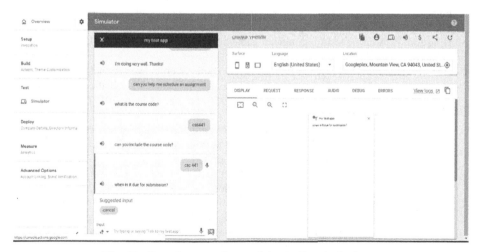

Fig. 10. Speech processing module via Google Assistant

From Fig. 10, the user can schedule assignments, set reminders, query for information, make use of Smalltalk, etc. via speech.

5 Conclusion and Future Work

The solution proposed by this study was a conversational agent for students' activities planning using Dialogflow, Node.Js and Pusher API to make seamless conversations with the user. The system uses natural language processing to analyze chat and extracts intents of the user. This study successfully provides an automatic conversational agent that helps students schedule assignments, save reminders and also glean important information pertaining their major work schedule in school. This study shows that the use of Dialog flow with the other aforementioned technologies was able to achieve an effective web based personal digital assistant that makes use of both text and speech. Future recommendation will be to make use of Socket.io instead of using Pusher API to maintain a bidirectional connection between the client and the server. The purpose of this is to juxtapose the speed of Pusher API with that of Socket.io. Web push notifications can also be integrated into the system so as to allow students opt-in to timely updates from the application to effectively re-engage them with customized, relevant content.

Acknowledgments. We acknowledge the support provided by Covenant University through the Centre for Research, Innovation, and Discovery (CUCRID).

References

1. Rossen, B., Lok, B.: A crowdsourcing method to develop virtual human conversational agents. Int. J. Hum. Comput. Stud. **70**(4), 301–319 (2012)
2. Feine, J., Gnewuch, U., Morana, S., Maedche, A.: A taxonomy of social cues for conversational agents. Int. J. Hum. Comput. Stud. **132**, 138–161 (2019)
3. Hingston, P.: A turing test for computer game bots. IEEE Trans. Comput. Intell. AI Games **1**(3), 169–186 (2009)
4. Hussain, S., Ameri Sianaki, O., Ababneh, N.: A survey on conversational agents/chatbots classification and design techniques. In: Barolli, L., Takizawa, M., Xhafa, F., Enokido, T. (eds.) WAINA 2019. AISC, vol. 927, pp. 946–956. Springer, Cham (2019). https://doi.org/10.1007/978-3-030-15035-8_93
5. Ukpabi, D.C., Aslam, B., Karjaluoto, H.: Chatbot adoption in tourism services: a conceptual exploration. Robots, Artificial Intelligence, and Service Automation in Travel, Tourism and Hospitality, pp. 105–121. Emerald Publishing Limited (2019)
6. Zarouali, B., Van den Broeck, E., Walrave, M., Poels, K.: Predicting consumer responses to a chatbot on Facebook. Cyberpsychol. Behav. Soc. Netw. **21**(8), 491–497 (2018)
7. Bos, S.: Towards Natural Language Understanding using Multimodal Deep Learning (2017)
8. Cahn, J.: CHATBOT: Architecture, design, & development. University of Pennsylvania School of Engg & Applied Science Dept. of Computer and Information Science (2017)
9. Young, T., Hazarika, D., Poria, S., Cambria, E.: Recent trends in deep learning based natural language processing. IEEE Comput. Intell. Mag. **13**(3), 55–75 (2018)
10. Androutsopoulou, A., Karacapilidis, N., Loukis, E., Charalabidis, Y.: Transforming the communication between citizens and government through AI-guided chatbots. Govern. Inf. Quart. **36**(2), 358–367 (2019)
11. Nixon, M., DiPaola, S., Bernardet, U.: An eye gaze model for controlling the display of social status in believable virtual humans. In 2018 IEEE Conference on Computational Intelligence and Games (CIG), pp. 1–8. IEEE (2018)

12. Ireland, D., et al.: Hello harlie: enabling speech monitoring through chatbot conversations. Stud. Health Technol. Inf. **227**, 55–60 (2016)
13. Shawar, B.A : Integrating CALL systems with chatbots as conversational partners. Computación y Sistemas, **21**(4), 615–626 (2017)
14. Jain, M., Kumar, P., Bhansali, I., Liao, Q.V., Truong, K., Patel, S.: FarmChat: a conversational agent to answer farmer queries. In: Proceedings of the ACM on Interactive, Mobile, Wearable and Ubiquitous Technologies, vol. 2, no. 4, pp. 1–22 (2018)
15. Doshi, S.V., Pawar, S.B., Shelar, A.G., Kulkarni, S.S : Artificial intelligence Chatbot in Android system using open source program-O. Int. J. Adv. Res. Comput. Commun. Eng. (2017)
16. AbuShawar, B., Atwell, E.: ALICE chatbot: Trials and outputs. Computación y Sistemas **19**(4), 625–632 (2015)
17. Lokman, A.S., Zain, J.M: One-match and all-match categories for keywords matching in chatbot. Am. J. Appl. Sci. **7**(10), 1406 (2010)
18. Thomas N.T., Vishwa, A.; An E-business Chatbot using AIML and LSA. In: 2016 International Conference on Advances in Computing, Communication and Informatics (ICACCI), 21–24 September (2016)
19. Satu, M.S., Parvez, M.H: Review of integrated applications with AIML based chatbot. In: 2015 International Conference on Computer and Information Engineering, pp. 87–90. IEEE (2015)
20. Azeta, A.A., Azeta, V.I., Misra, S., Ananya, M.: A transition model from web of things to speech of intelligent things in a smart education system. In: Sharma, N., Chakrabarti, A., Balas, V.E. (eds.) Data Management, Analytics and Innovation. AISC, vol. 1042, pp. 673–683. Springer, Singapore (2020). https://doi.org/10.1007/978-981-32-9949-8_47
21. Azeta, A.A., Misra, S., Azeta, V.I., Osamor, V.C.: Determining suitability of speech-enabled examination result management system. Wireless Netw. **25**(6), 3657–3664 (2019). https://doi.org/10.1007/s11276-019-01960-5

Constructing of Semantically Dependent Patterns Based on SpaCy and StanfordNLP Libraries

Valentin P. Okhapkin[1], Elena P. Okhapkina[2,3], Anastasia O. Iskhakova[4], and Andrey Y. Iskhakov[4(✉)]

[1] Center of Expert and Analytical and Information Technologies of Accounts Chamber of the Russian Federation, Moscow, Russian Federation
[2] Bauman Moscow State Technical University, Moscow, Russian Federation
okhapkina.ep@bmstu.ru
[3] Russian State University for the Humanities, Moscow, Russian Federation
[4] V.A. Trapeznikov Institute of Control Sciences of Russian Academy of Sciences, Moscow, Russian Federation
{iao,iay}@ipu.ru

Abstract. The current stage of the tools development for processing Russian-language texts is associated with a weak elaboration of algorithms for identifying entities and dividing sentences into semantic, logically justified parts. In particular, how to determine an actor, actions performed by him/her, and the object(s) over which these actions are performed in a sentence. It is important to understand that the NLP algorithm should be designed in such a way that would identify the listed elements of the sentence not by the principle of a pre-compiled dictionary and the coincidence of parts of the sentence with it, but on the basis of highlighting universal dependencies. To this end, the team of authors have developed and tested algorithms based on the design of patterns universally describing various parts of a sentence: an actor, his/her actions and objects that these actions are directed to. To solve this problem, authors used the tools for parsing sentences into parts of speech and their dependencies (StanfordNLP); processing dependencies and identifying the tree structure of the sentence.

Keywords: Parsing · Semantically dependent patterns · SpaCy · StanfordNLP

1 Introduction

The technological approach to identifying specific phrases (or words) in a sentence during text analysis involves the use of natural language models. In particular it is necessary to use tools that can detect parts of speech, the relations between words within a sentence, the normal form, and so on. Social networks text analysis in the context of negative statements requires labeled data dictionaries, but this condition is still not enough for detecting texts with signs of aggression. A single word or phrase with a negative connotation according to the labeled data dictionary does not allow us to make a clear

© Springer Nature Singapore Pte Ltd. 2021
P. K. Singh et al. (Eds.): FTNCT 2020, CCIS 1395, pp. 500–512, 2021.
https://doi.org/10.1007/978-981-16-1480-4_45

conclusion that the analyzed statement is negative (it has clear signs of aggression). Often words that form a dependency group to a word with a negative marker are its objects. These words allow getting more information about the nature of the statement, and, consequently, increasing the probability of a correct assessment as negative or neutral (including positive). Revealing the semantic boundaries of collocations, phrases, which include a word with a negative marker, is possible by constructing semantically dependent patterns. The pattern contains a scheme of parts of speech and their dependencies in a sentence. Thus, the analysis algorithm identifies all possible collocations and phrases matching the scheme and having a word(s) with a negative marker from the labeled data dictionary.

The task of identifying the boundaries of a phrase with a negative context is not only in the scientific research focus, but also in a focus of private companies. These companies attract text analytics specialists from all over the world, for example, on the Kaggle platform [1].

2   The Methodology of the Research

The sequence of actions in researches devoted to the analysis of Russian-language texts is complicated by the fact that widely used software solutions, with all the advantages in flexibility and accuracy of extracted data, are focused on the English language. For example, this refers to the extraction of entities according to some semantic rules. The StanfordNLP library has the ability to connect the Russian language model, but it does not provide the model with flexible tools for extracting semantic links, individual parts of the dependency tree, the presence of links to the left and right from the analyzed word, the boundaries of these links, and so on. At the same time, the SpaCy library has this set of methods and allows you to expand its capabilities with custom NLP-functions, but does not have a developed the Russian language model: just a model as a part of a multilingual package, for example, to extract only four entities in the Russian language model against eighteen entities for the English language model [2, 3]. In this sense, a researcher and algorithm developer have to perform a number of actions for preprocessing the text in Russian language. To solve the problem of constructing semantically dependent patterns in Russian the following steps are necessary:

a) Select and load the Russian language model, which includes a lemmatizer, a tokenizer, a POS tagger, a model of the dependence of words in a sentence;
b) Select and connect to the text analysis script of a library that can use the language model loaded in stage a). To use in analysis means to be able to form an object that has all the attributes of words: token, part of speech (including punctuation marks), word dependency in a sentence, and attributes for software manipulations, such as converting and comparing words in a sentence, and so on.;
c) Develop and identify patterns according to which a logically complete part of a statement can be extracted from a sentence, reflecting the main information component. For example, in the statement "today it is already obvious to everyone that Moskal'sky (en. Muscovite) imperialism has begun a creeping intervention in the Crimea", the main information component with a negative connotation is the phrase

"imperialism has begun an intervention". Other objects characterize the direction of the verb "begun". Here the pattern is formed around the verb "begun", the nouns "imperialism" and "intervention", which are subordinate to the verb. This subordination binds the phrase together and allows you to refer to it as a lexical unit.

d) Select and connect specialized or generalized (containing both negative and neutral or positive words) dictionaries. To work with Russian-language texts containing negative word labels, it can be use the WordNet-Affect lexical database. The choice of this thesaurus is related to the number of synsets and relationships between concepts (about 3 thousand words and expressions of the Russian language).

The problem of identifying phrases and expressions containing aggression is a stage in a larger task – identifying segments of a social network in which an exchange of this kind of messages (in the public domain) between users took place. At the stage, this part of the study is an overview and represents visualization in the neo4j graph database management system. The choice of this system is due to its full compatibility with the Python language, which was chosen as the development language. Also the system has an ability to create new types of links in the graph from the program code, where the basic text analysis algorithms are executed.

For the analysis we used a database that is a set of messages from the social network "Vkontakte" for the period of 2014. Data was collected using open data from the open communities. The most representative topics in the messages are politics, music, and cinema. On the graph in the neo4j system, we will show an example, written manually, but based on real messaging detected by researchers in the database. Automatic calculation requires the development of a separate algorithm (what the team is currently working on) for converting the source dataset into a graph database and visualization. Manual organization is performed using the internal neo4j Cypher language (the language supports CRUD functionality).

3   Pattern Construction

The semantic structure of the analyzed text can be obtained using the SpaCy [2] and StanfordNLP [3] libraries. These libraries provide quite powerful functionality for processing, extracting and analyzing specific information, for example, labeling sentences or phrases as negative or aggressive statements, and they are specialized libraries for working with text. They include a fairly wide range of models of natural languages of Western and Asian countries. To construct patterns, we will use the SynTagRus model of the Russian language developed in the laboratory of computational linguistics at the Institute for Information Transmission Problems of the Russian Academy of Sciences (Kharkevich Institute) [4]. In 2019 this model had more than 1 million tokens (more than 66 thousand sentences) in a wide range of topics and genres: from fiction to scientific and newspaper articles for the period from 1960 to 2016. First we will configure the Russian language model to work using Python with the StanfordNLP library (see Fig. 1).

● ● ●

```
1 config = {'proceccors': 'tokenize, mwt, pos, lemma, depparse',
2 'use_gpu': False,
3 'lang': 'ru',
4 'tokenize_model_path': '../ru_syntagrus_models/ru_syntagrus_tokenizer.pt',
5 'pos_model_path': '../ru_syntagrus_models/ru_syntagrus_tagger.pt',
6 'pos_pretrain_path': '../ru_syntagrus_models/ru_syntagrus.pretrain.pt',
7 'lemma_model_path': '../ru_syntagrus_models/ru_syntagrus_lemmatizer.pt',
8 'depparse_model_path': '../ru_syntagrus_models/ru_syntagrus_parser.pt',
9 'depparse_pretrain_path': '../ru_syntagrus_models/ru_syntagrus.pretrain.pt'}
```

Fig. 1. Config dictionary for connecting the Russian language model.

Here, the **config** dictionary contains configuration parameters for connecting the Russian language model (tokenizer, lemmatizer, parser, etc.). After that, you need to create a pipeline-processor (or pipeline), so that the analyzed sentence passed through the pipeline gets a number of attributes. The code created by the pipeline is shown in the Fig. 2 below.

● ● ●

```
1 snlp = stanfordnlp.Pipeline(**config)
2 nlp = StanfordNLPLanguage(snlp)
```

Fig. 2. Connecting the Russian language model in StanfordNLP with the SpaCy parser.

The last StanfordNLPLanguage command allows getting a class that, on the one hand, has the Russian language model described above and, on the other hand, has methods for working with the text using the SpaCy library. Semantic analysis of the utterance is performed by a command of the following type (see Figs. 3 and 4).

● ● ●

```
1 doc = nlp("РУССКИЙ МИР. Ватник с воплем 'КРЫМ НАШ' напал с
2 ножом на участника пикета, посвященного депортации
3 крымских татар в Нюене (фото).")
```

Fig. 3. Original social media post in Russian language.

● ● ●

```
1 doc = nlp("RUSSIAN WORLD. Vatnik shouting 'CRIMEA IS OUR' attacked a
2 participant of the picket dedicated to the deportation of Crimean Tatars in Nyuen
3 with a knife (photo).")
```

Fig. 4. Translation of the post to English language (Color figure online).

The doc object has the following important analysis attributes: text – a word in an utterance (sentence), pos_ – part of speech, dep_ – dependency of a word in a sentence, and so on. The output of information about the attributes of this utterance is shown in Table 1.

Table 1. The attributes of the words.

Word	Part of speech tag	Dependence tag
РУССКИЙ (RUSSIAN)	ADJ	amod
МИР (WORLD)	NOUN	root
	PUNCT	punct
Ватник (Vatnik)	NOUN	nsubj
с (with)	ADP	case
воплем (shouting)	NOUN	nmod
"	PUNCT	punct
КРЫМ (CRIMEA)	ADJ	obl
НАШ (OUR)	PROPN	nsubj
"	PUNCT	punct
напал (attacked)	VERB	root
…	…	…

Here, obviously, the key words are "Vatnik" and "attacked" which express the negative connotation of the utterance. However, the utterance is perceived so only by a person who uniquely builds connections between words. Labeling the word "Vatnik" as a trigger, denoting an expression exclusively from the negative side, is not a good approach to the task of identifying aggression. For example, the sentence "Women in vatniks (en. Quilted jackets) who raised our energy industry" contains a separate word "Vatnik" ("Quilted jacket"), but cannot be perceived as negative. In the given example, this statement is rather neutral or positive. Thus, the more additional links in a sentence a word with a negative marker has the more probability that the sentence is characterized correctly from an emotional point of view [5].

There are several ways to act: to identify all the existing connections of a word with a negative label and determine their emotional color according to the labeled data dictionary, or to develop patterns according to which collocations and phrases with negative labels of words in dependencies will be extracted. The second approach is preferable in practice, since it identifies negative entities in the utterance, but not generalizations with the largest number of negative markers. The presence of negative entities is most useful when analyzing social networks from the standpoint of the organization of destructive information influence [6].

Let's give an example of constructing a pattern for a utterance from Table 1. Above, we determined that the word "Vatnik" is perceived negatively when it has a connection with the verb "attack". This is due to the fact that the "Vatnik" (quilted jacket) in the sense of a part of the wardrobe cannot act independently (this is nonsense). Also, the action "attack" is negative when it is directed at a person, for example, a picket participant. Thus, the phrase "to attack someone" significantly increases the probability that there are signs of aggression in the utterance. Then the construction of the pattern may look as shown in Fig. 5.

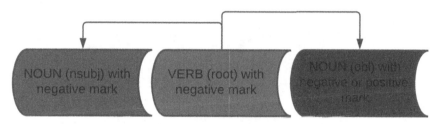

Fig. 5. The pattern for extracting entities with negative labels.

The advantage of patterns using is their universality in relation to various genres and topics of the analyzed texts. In this case, only the dictionary with the negative labeled words requires updating. It is obvious that the development of patterns is a laborious process, but their number is countable and finite. The more patterns we have, the greater is the coverage of extracted collocations and phrases [7].

Let's look at another example with a different pattern (see Fig. 6 and 7).

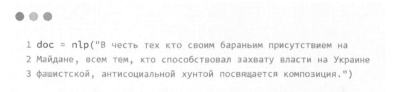

```
1 doc = nlp("В честь тех кто своим бараньим присутствием на
2 Майдане, всем тем, кто способствовал захвату власти на Украине
3 фашистской, антисоциальной хунтой посвящается композиция.")
```

Fig. 6. Original social media post in Russian language.

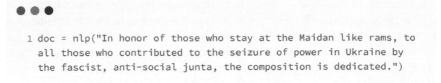

```
1 doc = nlp("In honor of those who stay at the Maidan like rams, to
  all those who contributed to the seizure of power in Ukraine by
  the fascist, anti-social junta, the composition is dedicated.")
```

Fig. 7. Translation of the post to English language.

Here the phrases "contributed to the seizure of power in Ukraine" and "stay at the Maidan like rams" have the greatest emotional color. Separate phrases such as "fascist junta" and "anti-social junta" will not be analyzed due to the fact that they are quite confidently extracted when referring to the dictionary of negative words [8]. The phrases highlighted at the beginning of the paragraph can be extracted using the patterns shown in Fig. 8a and 8b.

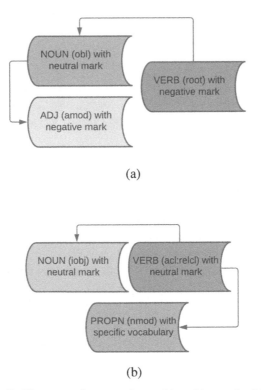

(a)

(b)

Fig. 8. The pattern for extracting entities with negative labels.

Let us emphasize that the number of patterns is a countable and finite set. The main requirement when constructing a pattern is the requirement that the set of extracted phrases should not intersect with sets of phrases of another pattern [9–11].

The database of messages of the social network "VKontakte" has 262.665 messages and 1.127.762 comments written to them. A simple arithmetic calculation will show that for a sentence with an average length of 8–12 words (often there are utterances divided into separate messages – they are considered as a separate sentences), you will need to perform from 24,000 to 36,000 operations (passes with the specified dictionary parameters) to analyze a single message. Thus, a computational experiment to identify messages and comments with signs of aggression in a pattern will amount to ~33 to 50 billion operations (excluding the operations like parsing text, searching for patterns, and writing the result to the database). The technical platform for the experiment: Intel i7 (3.4 GHz, 4 Cores), 6 GB (available free memory with background Windows OS workers). The results of the experiment are presented in Table 2.

Table 2. Statistical information about the execution of the pattern search algorithm.

Word	Value
Number of patterns	20
Extracted with signs of aggression	562.133
The number of negative posts with comment length of more than 10	103.482
The number of "like" marks for all messages (not comments under the message) for which the negative word dictionary pattern applied	630.089

It is important to note that the number of negative messages exceeding the number of messages (262.665 records in the database) is due to the fact that the patterns also worked on the basis of comments. Also, the patterns shown in Fig. 2a and 2b are common forms of utterance formation. This is obvious due to the fact that biggest part of utterances addressed from one person to another contain verbs supplemented with nouns. Indirectly, we can conclude that messages that did not get statistics on the triggering of patterns contain short remarks that characterize the topic about which the comment was made [12–15].

3.1 Syntactic Relations Tree and Ancestors Property

The SpaCy library includes the displacy.render rendering method. The code for dependency tree graphic display is shown in Fig. 9 below.

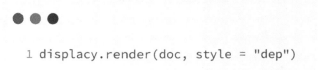

```
1 displacy.render(doc, style = "dep")
```

Fig. 9. The code for dependency tree graphic display with the displacy.render.

Here, the style option indicates that you need to build a dependency tree of words of the sentence. For example, the value "ent" means that you need to output the parsed text labeled with named entities (abbrev. NE). The graphic display of the dependency tree is shown in Fig. 10.

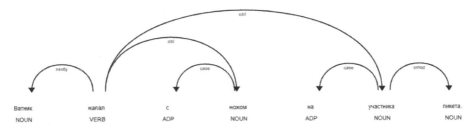

Fig. 10. Rendering a dependency parse tree.

Visualization does not directly solve the problem of identifying patterns with negative labels. However, it allows you to clearly and quickly determine the dependencies between words. To identify relations between words in a sentence there are the "ancestors" property among the attributes of the doc object. This property points to the rightmost token among the dependencies of the analyzed word. In fact using the ancestor property makes it is possible to detect the semantic boundaries of dependent words [16, 17]. In turn this property forms a logically complete part of an utterance or a sentence. The code below allows to define all relations with the root of a sentence on the right. Using the diagram in Fig. 8, it is easy to see that from the right of the root of the sentence – "напал" (en. "attacked") there are two direct connections with the words "ножом" (en. "knife") and "участника" (en. "participant"). These words can be extracted using the code below (see Fig. 11).

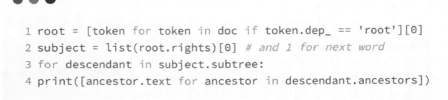

```
1 root = [token for token in doc if token.dep_ == 'root'][0]
2 subject = list(root.rights)[0]  # and 1 for next word
3 for descendant in subject.subtree:
4 print([ancestor.text for ancestor in descendant.ancestors])
```

Fig. 11. Defining relations with the roof of sentence.

The output for this code is represented by a list of words ['ножом', 'участника'] (en. ['knife', 'participant']) that are directly related to the word "напал" (en. "attacked") that are labeled as a negative word. Thus using the SpaCy library in combination with the developed model of the Russian language provides good opportunities for extracting logically complete phrases.

Figure 3 shows that the words included in the pattern shown in Fig. 1 have objects that characterize the verb and nouns: attacked a participant of the picket with a knife. These objects characterize the event and can be used as generalization parameters when analyzing text corpora, for example, a social network segment [18, 19]. The request can be formed in the form of: identify description of all violent actions with the use of cold weapons in messages set. Visualization of this query can be shown in the graph.

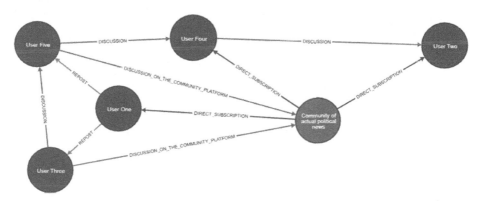

Fig. 12. Rendering a dependency parse tree.

In the graph in Fig. 4, the red arrows labeled DIRECT_SUBSCRIPTION show the propagation of subscription information, such as messages from community administrators. This is a centralized information channel. Users like User Three and User Five are not subscribers to the community of actual political news but they are subscribers to some community users and can repost messages for them, have private discussion with them and discussions on the community platform [8]. Information that we previously identified as containing aggressive content began to circulate.

Syntactically, the graph construction as in Fig. 12 in the neo4j system is reproduced quite simply (see Fig. 13).

Here, lines 1–7 form the nodes of the graph, and lines 9 – 18 form connections between the nodes and their form.

● ● ●

```
 1 create (potential_aggressor:SocialNetworkPublic {title:'Community
   of actual political news', tagline:'Public'})
 2 create (user_one:SocialNetwork {title:'User One',
   tagline:'University student'})
 3 create (user_two:SocialNetwork {title:'User Two', tagline:'Bank
   officer'})
 4 create (user_three:SocialNetwork {title:'User Three',
   tagline:'Government employee'})
 5 create (user_four:SocialNetwork {title:'User Four',
   tagline:'Housewife'})
 6 create (user_five:SocialNetwork {title:'User Five',
   tagline:'Businessperson'})
 7
 8 create
 9 (potential_aggressor)-[:DIRECT_SUBSCRIPTION {roles:'attempt to
   influence'}]->(user_one),
10 (potential_aggressor)-[:DIRECT_SUBSCRIPTION {roles:'attempt to
   influence'}]->(user_two),
11 (potential_aggressor)-[:DIRECT_SUBSCRIPTION {roles:'attempt to
   influence'}]->(user_four),
12 (user_one)-[:REPOST]->(user_three),
13 (user_one)-[:REPOST]->(user_five),
14 (user_three)-[:DISCUSSION]->(user_five),
15 (user_five)-[:DISCUSSION]->(user_four),
16 (user_four)-[:DISCUSSION]->(user_two),
17 (user_three)-[:DISCUSSION_ON_THE_COMMUNITY_PLATFORM]->
   (potential_aggressor),
18 (user_five)-[:DISCUSSION_ON_THE_COMMUNITY_PLATFORM]->
   (potential_aggressor)
19
20 return potential_aggressor
```

Fig. 13. Graph construction of the dependency parse tree.

4 Summary

The estimation of information influence, as well as the methods of its detection, depends, among other things, on the accuracy of settings of algorithms for text processing: how many patterns are available for text processing. In the context of identifying aggressive, destructive information, the labeled data dictionary of negative words plays a key role [20]. It is the combination of "dictionary-pattern" that increases the ability to accurately identify a negative utterance and its semantic boundaries. It is important to note that the construction of patterns requires the fulfillment of the uniqueness condition – the pattern should be focused on extracting collocations and phrases only of a certain morphological construction. For example, an actor, its action, in relation to what or to whom the action is directed [21]. Or there are an action and its objects. Using a dictionary of negative words while working with patterns allows to signal that a particular implementation of the pattern in the form of an extracted phrase has signs of aggression or destructive information, and is not a variant of neutral or positive use of the word.

It would be promising to use the described approach to the analysis of text messages in a small social group, in which the actor is known in advance [9]. And he/she is forming and directing all statements to the group members in such a way as to influence and achieve a given goal. Probably, the sequence of messages of the actor will have some characteristic features that distinguish his/her behavior strategy from other participants in the dialogue.

Acknowledgements. The reported study is funded by RFBR according to the research project No. 18–29-22104 "Development of socio-cyberphysical system of monitoring of diverse Internet-content for counteraction to manifestation of aggression, pressure and other forms of destructive impact on individual and group consciousness of users".

References

1. Tweet Sentiment Extraction. https://www.kaggle.com/c/tweet-sentiment-extraction. Accessed 01 Aug 2020
2. spaCy·Industrial-strength Natural Language Processing in Python. https://spacy.io/. Accessed 15 July 2020
3. Software - The Stanford Natural Language Processing Group. https://nlp.stanford.edu/software/. Accessed 15 July 2020
4. GitHub – UniversalDependencies / UD_Russian-SynTagRus: Russian language. https://github.com/UniversalDependencies/UD_Russian-SynTagRus. Accessed 05 July 2020
5. Iskhakova, A., Iskhakov, A., Meshcheryakov, R.: Research of the estimated emotional components for the content analysis. In: International Conference "Applied mathematics, computational science and mechanics: current problems", AMCSM 2018, Journal of Physics: Conference Series, p. 012065. Institute of Physics Publishing, Voronezh (2018)
6. Iskhakova, A., Iskhakov, A., Meshcheryakov, R.: The problem of formalization of the destructive influence of the user's virtual environment in the problem of malicious content detecting. In: Proceedings of the Second International Scientific Conference "Thinking Models and Integration of Information and Control Systems, pp. 46–50, KBNC RAS publishing house, Nalchik (2018)
7. Iskhakova, A., Meshcheryakov, R.: Automatic search of the malicious messages in the internet of things systems on the example of an intelligent detection of the unnatural agents requests. In: RPC 2017 - Proceedings of the 2nd Russian-Pacific Conference on Computer Technology and Applications, pp. 85–89. Institute of Electrical and Electronics Engineers Inc., Vladivostok (2017)
8. Iskhakova, A.: Processing of big data streams in intelligent electronic data analysis systems. In: Proceedings of the VIth International Workshop 'Critical Infrastructures: Contingency Management, Intelligent, Agent-Based, Cloud Computing and Cyber Security' (IWCI 2019), pp. 14–19. Atlantis Press, Irkutsk (2019)

9. Shumskaya, A.: Using Euclidean and Mahalanobis distances while solving the problem of the text origin identification. In: 11th International Conference Interactive Systems Interactive Systems: Problems of Human - Computer Interaction. Collection of Scientific Papers, pp. 211–217. Ulyanovsk State Technical University, Ulyanovsk (2016)

10. Abramyan, M.E., Litovchenko, D.E.: About some new approaches to text sentiment analysis and toxicity analysis using deep learning methods. In: Proceedings of Eighth China-Russia Conference. Southern Federal University, I.I. Vorovich Institute of Mathematics, Mechanics, and Computer Science, pp. 97–101. Southern Federal University, Rostov-on-Don, Taganrog (2019)

11. Vo, A.-D., Nguyen, Q.-P., Ock, C.-Y.: Semantic and syntactic analysis in learning representation based on a sentiment analysis model. Appl. Intell. **50**(3), 663–680 (2019). https://doi.org/10.1007/s10489-019-01540-2

12. Li, L., Goh, T.-T., Jin, D.: How textual quality of online reviews affect classification performance: a case of deep learning sentiment analysis. Neural Comput. Appl. **32**(9), 4387–4415 (2018). https://doi.org/10.1007/s00521-018-3865-7

13. Zvonarev, A., Bilyi, A.: A comparison of machine learning methods of sentiment analysis based on Russian language twitter data. In: CEUR Workshop Proceedings. 11. "MICSECS 2019 - Proceedings of the 11th Majorov International Conference on Software Engineering and Computer Systems" (2020)

14. Moshkin, V., Yarushkina, N., Andreev, I.: The sentiment analysis of unstructured social network data using the extended ontology SentiWordnet. In: Proceedings - International Conference on Developments in eSystems Engineering, DeSE. 12th International Conference on the Developments in eSystems Engineering, DeSE, pp. 576–580. Institute of Electrical and Electronics Engineers Inc., Kazan (2019)

15. Smetanin, S.: The applications of sentiment analysis for Russian language texts: current challenges and future perspectives. IEEE Access. 110693–110719 (2020)

16. Baymurzina, D.R., Kuznetsov, D.P., Burtsev, M.S.: Language model embeddings improve sentiment analysis in Russian. Komp'juternaja lingvistika i intellektual'nye tehnologii, 53–62 (2019)

17. Tiwari, D., Singh, N.: Ensemble approach for twitter sentiment analysis. Int. J. Inf. Technol. Comput. Sci. **11**(8), 20–26 (2019)

18. Sharma, S., Jain, A.: Role of sentiment analysis in social media security and analytics. Wiley Interdisc. Rev. Data Min. Knowl. Discov. **10**, e1366 (2020)

19. Asif, M., Ishtiaq, A., Ahmad, H., Aljuaid, H., Shah, J.: Sentiment analysis of extremism in social media from textual information. Telematics Inform. **48**, 1013452020 (2020)

20. Sharma, D., Sabharwal, M., Goyal, V., Vij, M.: Sentiment analysis techniques for social media data: a review. Adv. Intell. Syst. Comput. **1045**, 75–90 (2020)

21. Mayer-Schönberger, V., Cukier, K.: Big data: A revolution that will transform how we live, work, and think. Houghton Mifflin Harcourt (2013)

Electronic Medical Records Data Analysis Technologies and Services for the Cardiovascular Diseases Risk Prediction

Alexander A. Zakharov[1]([✉]), Irina G. Zakharova[1], Pavel Y. Gayduk[1],
Dmitry V. Panfilenko[1], Alexander A. Kotelnikov[1], and Yulia S. Reshetnikova[2]

[1] Institute of Mathematics and Computer Science, Tyumen State University, Tyumen, Russia
a.a.zakharov@utmn.ru
[2] Department of Public Health and Health Care, Tyumen State Medical University,
Tyumen, Russia

Abstract. The aim of our research is to develop technologies and methods for data mining of electronic medical records (EHR). We use our approach to create predictive models of the total risk of cardiovascular diseases (CVD) in apparently healthy individuals before taking therapeutic measures. We have developed methods and technologies for extracting valid information from unstructured EHR data, first, patient examination protocols, taking into account the requirements for secure distributed storage and processing of medical information. The developed special services for visualizing the values of objective indicators allow us to determine the appropriate sets of predictors for predictive models for assessing the risk of CVD. Visualization services provide aggregated data for modeling the patient's problem-oriented digital phenotype. In our case, this is an optimal data structure that combines key indicators for predicting the degree of CVD risk from the point of view of criteria (rules) adopted in cardiology with additional features. We determine these features based on the analysis of data extracted from a large array of EHR. The software implementation of the developed technologies allows not only assessing the risk of CVD, but also collecting data for further improving the accuracy of predictive models. The software product may be useful in preventive examinations and mass screenings.

Keywords: Prediction · Cardiovascular risk · Data mining · Electronic medical records · Machine learning

1 Introduction

Diseases of the circulatory system are the leading cause of death and disability. In the structure of total mortality in the Russian Federation in 2019, these diseases account for more than 841 thousand cases, which is 57.3%. Moreover, 52% of the deceased are men 16–59 years old, women 16–54 years old. According to the official statistics of the Russian Federation, in 2018, ischemic heart disease (IHD) accounted for 52.9% of cases, cerebrovascular diseases and myocardial infarction, 30.8% and 6.6%, respectively, of

© Springer Nature Singapore Pte Ltd. 2021
P. K. Singh et al. (Eds.): FTNCT 2020, CCIS 1395, pp. 513–524, 2021.
https://doi.org/10.1007/978-981-16-1480-4_46

the total number of deaths from diseases of the circulatory system. Moreover, 30–40% of patients die at the prehospital stage [1].

In situations involving cardiovascular disease, predicting future events is essential for a range of stakeholders, from the individual patient to healthcare providers and insurance companies. Assessment of cardiovascular risk is also important for prophylactic treatment of patients who are asymptomatic, but the risk of CVD for them can be quite high [2]. A qualitative prediction of CVD risks allows making decisions about the type and intensity of care, as well as assessing the effectiveness and cost of treatment interventions. However, despite the large number of known factors that are significant for the prognosis of the disease, accurate prognosis and stratification of patients according to CVD risk remains a challenge. A special place here is occupied by cases with low or intermediate short-term risk [3]. This determines the relevance of research related to the creation of predictive models, their implementation in the form of IT services for the analysis of CVD risks of a specific population with the possibility of increasing the accuracy of the forecast when new data in the use of IT services.

1.1 Background

To create an effective strategy for early detection of diseases, assessing the severity and predicting side effects, it is necessary to analyze a large amount of clinical data traditionally obtained from the results of comparative randomized medical trials. The main criterion for these clinical experiments results accuracy is the assessment by R. Fischer of individual relationships in a single experiment. At the same time, the competent use of statistical methods allows to increase the clarity, visibility and objectivity of the results' presentation. In 1948, to study the epidemiology of atherosclerosis, the US Public Health Service initiated the longest-running epidemiological study in the history of medicine, the Framingham Heart Study, which laid the foundations for preventive cardiology [4]. Note that the authors of the Framingham scale warned about the problems of extrapolating their results to other populations. For example, a sufficient number of publications [5, 6] indicate that the use of the Framingham risk scale in the European region leads to an overestimation of the real observed risk. In particular, observation of an experimental group of men participating in the British Regional Heart Study for 10 years showed that the use of the Framingham scale led to an overestimation of the absolute risk of coronary death by 47% and the total rate of fatal and non-fatal coronary events - by 57% [7].

In 2003, a group of European, including Russian, cardiologists (State Research Center for Preventive Medicine) presented the SCORE (Systematic Coronary Risk Evaluation) scale, which allows calculating the prior probability of a fatal cardiovascular event in the next 10 years. The scale takes into account local economic, social and health conditions for countries with low and high CVD mortality rates [8]. However, according to L. Getz et al. [9], the use of the SCORE scale for Norway leads to the fact that among 40-year-old Norwegians 22.5% of women fall into the 95% confidence interval (19.3–25.7%) and the vast majority of men (85.9%; 83.2–88.6%) have a high risk of CVD. For the age of 65, 84.0% of women (80.6–87.4%) and 91.6% of men (88.6–94.1%) fall into the high-risk category. And this despite the fact that mortality from CVD in Russia is 8 times higher than in Norway.

The results of a prospective study (Munster, Germany) assessing the risk of coronary artery disease complications (sudden death) in elderly men and in postmenopausal women in the next 8 years led to the PROCAM model (Prospective Cardiovascular Munster Study) development. The model uses three unmodified risk factors (age, history of myocardial infarction, hereditary burden), as well as six modifiable ones (smoking, blood pressure, total cholesterol, triglycerides, high-density lipoprotein cholesterol, diabetes mellitus). The main limitation of the PROCAM model, according to the authors, is that the prediction algorithm uses research data from the German population. The dissemination of this national study results to other populations is impractical, since the population of each country has its own socio-ethnic characteristics [10].

Rahimi K. et al. [11] studied 64 basic risk prediction models and 50 of their modifications in order to identify independent risk predictors in patients with heart failure. The models used data from 48 clinical studies. Of the 64 models, 43 were used to predict death, 10 to predict hospitalization, and 11 to predict death and hospitalization. It is of interest to evaluate the usefulness of the models for making clinical decisions. The discriminatory power of models predicting death was higher than that of models predicting only hospitalization or hospitalization and death. Evaluations also showed that age, renal function, blood pressure, blood sodium level, left ventricular ejection fraction, gender, brain natriuretic peptide level, New York Heart Association functional class, diabetes, index are the most informative predictors of mortality body weight and physical activity. The average number of predictors for the most complete model reported in these studies was nine, and overall they ranged from 3 to 314. The predictive power of the models ranged from 61% to 80%. From a clinical point of view, the analysis showed that a number of risk prediction tools are suitable for use in clinical practice, especially when an outcome such as death is of interest. The combination of modern advances in the field of medical knowledge with methods and technologies for data analysis have led to the development of new prediction methods. The ability to receive digital data from electronic medical records (EHR), including laboratory tests and patient examination protocols, made it possible to use Data Mining technologies [12]. With the help of these technologies, it is possible to create new multifunctional risk prediction models for a specific population, as well as to identify unobvious objective and useful in practice patterns that help to look for answers to key questions of multivariate systems analysis.

We can reformulate these questions in relation to the analysis of EHR data as follows:

- What criteria can be effective to identify groups of patients that differ in the CVD risk degree?
- What features affect the accuracy of predicting the patient's condition for a particular time interval? What is the extent of their influence?
- Is there population and/or temporal variability in selected features that determine the health status of patients, and what are its structural characteristics?
- Changes in what features can lead to systematic causal changes in others?

1.2 Related work

Traditional approaches to predicting cardiovascular risk do not always identify those who benefit from preventive treatment. The use of classification, regression, and other

Data Mining models, due to the higher predicting accuracy, can increase the number of identified patients who benefit from preventive treatment, while avoiding the treatment of those patients who do not need it]. For example, Ahmad T. et al. [13] used clinical data of 378,256 patients without cardiovascular disease in the UK over the previous 10 years to determine significant risk factors. Risk factors were blood pressure, cholesterol, age, smoking, and diabetes mellitus - characteristic of the algorithms for predicting CVD risk used in the ACC/AHA (American College of Heart/American Heart Association). The authors compared the results of machine learning algorithms (random forest, logistic regression, gradient boosting machines, and neural networks) with an algorithm from the ACC/AHA guidelines for predicting the first cardiovascular event within 10 years. In 24,970 patients (6.6%), real cases of cardiac events occurred within 10 years. Depending on the chosen algorithm, the accuracy increased by 1.7%–7.6% compared to the ACC/AHA prediction.

Studying the complex relationships between risk factors using machine learning methods, Weng S. F. et al. [14] assessed the possibilities of improving predicting the risk of cardiovascular diseases. They conducted a study on a large labeled sample containing patient data from the Swedish National Heart Failure Registry with detailed demographic, clinical, laboratory, and therapy data. Machine learning algorithms made it possible to predict the results with good accuracy, and cluster analysis revealed four phenotypes that differed in both results and response to therapy.

Using machine learning methods based on the construction of optimal partitions of the feature space, and recognition methods, Dyuzheva E. V et al. [15] presented the results of a clinical and epidemiological study to identify risk factors for the death of cardiovascular diseases in patients of medical institutions of the penitentiary systems. With high reliability, the authors identified the predictive factors of hospital mortality in a cardiac patient, which were: the use of a strong tonic drink "chifir", age, weight, height, systolic and diastolic blood pressure, hemoglobin level, heart rate, left ventricular ejection fraction, end systolic and the end diastolic size of the left ventricle, the presence of arterial hypertension, as well as the number of convictions.

When creating predictive models, it is necessary to take into account the specifics of modern biomedical data (BMD). To date, electronic archives of medical information systems (MIS) store significant volumes of such data: laboratory test results, indicators and images of electrocardiograms, descriptions and images of ultrasound examinations, patient examination protocols, etc. The use of MIS as systems for accounting for medical services and generating reports allow minimizing routine paper technologies by linking statistical, financial and material accounting with primary medical documents. However, from the point of view of scientific research, BMDs, in the form in which they are stored, are not particularly valuable, since there are no adequate tools for their processing [16].

Distinctive features of BMDs are their diversity and, as a rule, arbitrary structure, duplication and noise. Moreover, patient records often contain redundant text. Unfortunately, this is due, among other things, to the fact that in some cases doctors consider filling out the examination protocol a formal operation, as well as the doctors' habit of copying and pasting text fragments from one protocol to another [17]. BMD processing and analysis, in addition to security and accessibility to the necessary data, require presentation in a form convenient for research. The creation of an information storage that ensures the structuredness, correctness and consistency of the BMD is a prerequisite for a preliminary analysis that makes it possible to identify unobvious connections and patterns. In this context, we distinguish the data of the electronic medical record (EHR) as a patient's digital footprint, or patient's digital phenotype (PDP) [18]. Further, by CVD-PDP, we mean the optimal data structure that combines two categories of features. These are the key indicators for predicting the degree of CVD risk from the point of view of the criteria (rules) accepted in cardiology and additional features extracted from a large set of EHR data. Based on the PDP, it is possible to reveal the patterns of changes in the state of health, the features of the course of diseases and the effectiveness of the prescribed treatment. At the same time, the primary task - the extraction of valid information from unstructured EHR data (primarily, patient examination protocols), does not have universal solutions, since clinical texts in Russian are not standardized [18, 19].

Solving the issues of normalization and standardization of EHR data supplied by various MISs is the focus of research under the SHARP project (The Strategic Health IT Advanced Research Projects) [20]. Critical clinical information is often in the form of unstructured free text, and converting it to a structured format is not a trivial task. In [21], the authors formulated the following two incentives for transforming unstructured data into structured ones - reducing the time required for expert assessment and reusing data for large-scale automated processing. Factors such as the rate of creation of unstructured clinical information, identification of temporal associations, assessment of context-sensitive text, reduction of concepts to a specific terminology, identification of potential adverse drug reactions determine the need for the use of automated solutions that use natural language processing to analyze EHR data.

The creation of appropriate tools is one of the promising areas of application of the methodology of artificial intelligence for information support of biomedical research [22]. The results of works [23–25], showing the features of the integration of predictive logic and expert rules with machine learning approaches for solving applied problems of preventive medicine, are of particular importance in the context of this study.

Thus, there are no universal models for predicting CVD risks suitable for any population. Models should take into account the specific features of not only the country, but also the region where the initial clinical data were taken. Otherwise, the use of models will involve assumptions that can significantly reduce their predictive value. The available experience allows us to choose the best approaches to extracting information from EHR data and developing our own models that are maximally adapted to regional specifics. Information services based on such models will allow decision-makers to predict with sufficient accuracy, including the economic efficiency of preventive measures.

2   Materials and Methods

We carried out this study as part of an interdisciplinary pilot research project "Smart digital phenotype of a patient" aimed at improving the effectiveness of health preservation within the paradigm "5P Medicine" (prevention, prediction, personalization, participation, practicality) [19]. Specifically, the practical goal was to use an IT-service during preventive examinations for personalized CVD risk degree predicting. To train the prediction model embedded in the service, we used "smart" information support - a data set of the problem-oriented patient digital phenotype (CVD-PDP), extracted from a set of EHRs. When used with new data retrieval, the service provides model retraining. This contributes to the continuous improvement of the service predictive capabilities by machine learning technologies.

Initial data included EHRs with records for 2014–2016 from MIS SAP for Healthcare and from 2017 from MIS 1C: Medicine. Polyclinic. As a result, we received a set of raw data: more than 72,000 text files of medical records, including laboratory protocols (47%) and examination protocols (53%). Medical records are stored in separate XML files ranging in size from 0.5 to 3 kilobytes. This data is of three types in terms of structure: tabular, partially structured text, unstructured text.

Tabular files with specific field names - specialized services form them, as a rule, according to the results of laboratory tests (blood tests, urine tests, etc.). The file can contain the results of measurements of several investigated parameters.

Partially structured text files, along with unambiguously definable and mandatory fields (ECG, ultrasound, etc.), contain free form text statements.

Unstructured Text Files - Physicians enter data based on patient examination protocols. They contain unstructured text, in which, along with the conclusion and recommendations, doctors can indicate additional signs: weight, height, smoking, drinking alcoholic beverages, heredity, etc. These files also contain the diagnosis. Unfortunately, doctors, when indicating a diagnosis, usually do not use the International Classification of Diseases ICD-10, but indicate the diagnosis rather arbitrarily (for example, I25, IHD, CHD, chronic ischemic heart disease).

Note that files of all types initially contain personal data presented in full or in abbreviated form. This determined the nontriviality of static depersonalization methods. We depersonalized the patients personal data according to the following algorithm - the full name of the patient receiving medical services was replaced with an identification number, a year was left from the full date of birth, and the address of the place of residence was deleted. We replaced the doctor's personal data with a code from the reference table. We used the patient's identification number only to maintain the connection between the patient's documents during further data processing.

Performing the data analysis, we found 15 forms for recording the name, and 31 forms for recording the date of birth in the source documents. Analysis of the Named Entity Recognition (NER) software for extracting named entities showed that the most suitable libraries for the implementation of the anonymization process are libraries for Python - Yargy-parser and Natasha [26] with a set of ready-made rules for extracting names, surnames and addresses. In addition, we used pymorphy2 [27] for morphological analysis.

A preliminary analysis of the EHR showed that not only examination protocols, but also laboratory data could be represented by various structures. The reason is that the MIS is in commercial operation and is constantly being improved and updated.

As a result, for further analysis, we selected 68,400 documents related to 1,640 patients born in 2000 and older. The documents clearly indicate: the date of the document formation - in all documents, the date of birth - 1280 patients; gender - 1097 patients, the main diagnosis with the ICD code was present in 174 files (of which 103 - I20, 71 - I25). Before extracting data from unstructured texts, we analyzed more than 1000 files in order to identify possible options for doctors to write the date of visit, blood pressure and diagnosis. For each required parameter, we developed a "context set" of pattern expressions, which we used later to compose regular expressions.

As a result, the contextual set of patterns for the date of visit included 71 expressions, and 36 expressions for recording blood pressure in the examination protocols. For a diagnosis related to I20-I25 according to ICD-10, based on the recommendations of experts, we have compiled a list of 17 expressions indicating the presence of certain phrases in the conclusion (for example, "diagnosis of coronary heart disease", "past diseases: ischemic heart disease", "IHD for a long time", etc.).

For the specified parameters, taking into account the content of the context sets, we have developed a class of regular expressions designed to extract data from unstructured texts. A special set of verification tests (filtering by date, consistency of dates, and the presence of control words in a sentence) made it possible to check the correctness of the results. Based on the results of extracting and filling in missing data, we found that the proportion of EHRs for which the missing values were not correctly filled in was less than 5%, with the exception of the exact formulation of the diagnosis in accordance with ICD-10. In the latter case, the share of uncertainty was more than 40%. Previously, we entered into the database as mandatory binary values for I20-I25 as a whole (presence/absence of a diagnosis of ischemic heart disease), and as optional (if present in the EHR records) clarifying diagnoses (angina pectoris, acute myocardial infarction, etc.).

We correlated preliminary data processing with the creation of a three-layer information storage of anonymized, correct and consistent BMDs. On the first layer, the developed functionality provides anonymization of personal information. This allows users to organize a secure exchange of distributed BMDs (including EHRs from medical information systems of various institutions) in their original form. On the second layer (preprocessed data), we organized coherent distributed storage of key metadata of individual records (structure, date of record creation, doctor ID) and EHR as a whole (patient ID, date of birth, gender, etc.).

The third layer stores "smart" data obtained as a result of extracting valid problem-oriented information - the presence or absence of a disease associated with CVD and the values of objective indicators of health status. In addition, we have intended this layer to store problem-oriented knowledge bases: a dictionary of synonyms for diagnoses, generated after extracting relevant information from the patient examination protocols. Smart data is a table of 33 860 rows and 25 columns-features: Patient ID, Date of birth, Gender, Document type, Doctor's specialization, Date of visit, Systolic blood pressure (SBP), Diastolic blood pressure (DBP), Cholesterol, Glucose, Creatinine, AST, ALT, CHD, I20, I21, I22, I23, I24, I25, IHD selection criterion, Height, Weight, Anonymized text of the document. Note. Patients do not always have laboratory tests on the day they visit the doctor. Therefore, to fill in the appropriate fields, we used the results of tests performed on the day closest to the visit to the doctor.

3   Result and Discussion

We have developed a system of information services that ensure the processing of BMD at all levels of the information storage and focused on the interests of various users.

The services of the system allow users to solve both general and specific problems, starting with the key one - the description and interpretation of data. By interpretation, we mean the analysis of data in order to identify their meaning. Therefore, the defining goal of a particular user becomes apparent. However, the common thing here is the demand for a visual representation of aggregated data in comparison with the data of the digital phenotype of an individual patient. The main difficulty in solving interpretation problems is that the initial data may be noisy; the values of the quantities may be absent or incorrect. Therefore, we assumed that in the corresponding services we should place a special emphasis on studying the data characteristics, the distribution of indicator values, and the results visualizing using various kinds of graphs. Next, we demonstrate the capabilities of the related software (Web-services).

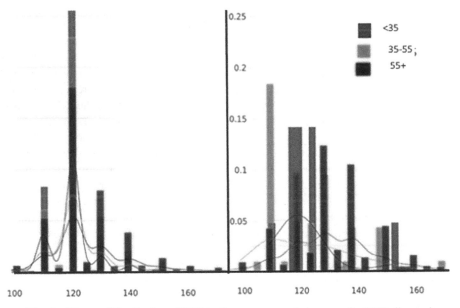

Fig. 1. Women. Distribution of SBP in the presence and absence of a CHD diagnosis

We have developed Web-services for smart data analysis, focusing primarily on the needs of cardiologists. The services provide a visualized representation of the patterns of changes in objective indicators used to predict the CVD risk degree: gender, age, body mass index, systolic and diastolic pressure, laboratory test results, including those taking into account the diagnoses (primary and concomitant diseases). The graph (user interface elements) shown in Fig. 1 illustrate the capabilities of the Web-service for data aggregation and visualization.

At the next stage after the development of services for describing and interpreting data, we started to solve the diagnostic problem. For this purpose, we set and solved the classification problem. For the classifier model, based on the recommendations of doctors and the availability of the necessary data in the EHR, we chose the following features: age, gender, SBP, DBP, cholesterol, glucose, creatinine, AST, ALT, body mass index. The target variable was the binary parameter "presence of coronary heart disease" (CHD).

The analysis of the correlation matrix revealed the following most correlated variables:

AST-ALT. Correlation coefficient	0.78
SBP-DBP. Correlation coefficient	0.62
Age-CHD. Correlation coefficient	0.48.
SBP-CHD. Correlation coefficient	0.37.

To build the classifier, we preliminarily selected four models: a single-class classification, the purpose of which is to detect anomalies, and 3 binary classification models: Logistic Regression (LR), Random Forest (RF), Support Vector Machine (SVM). We divided the dataset for training models and determining the most suitable model into a training (240 records, of which 139 with CHD) and test (139 records, of which 90 with CHD) samples. Of the two variants of the one-class classification Outlier detection and Novelty detection, the best result is accuracy = 0.41. We can explain the low prediction accuracy by characteristic graphs of the distribution function of parameters of healthy patients and patients with coronary artery disease (Fig. 1 and 2). Therefore, to select the model with the highest prediction accuracy, we compared the LR, RF, SVM models. The estimates of the results obtained on the test sample and presented in Table 1 show the advantage of the RF model. The Roc curves shown in Fig. 2 additionally confirms this. Thus, based on the presented estimates, we have chosen the RFmodel for the program implementation of the CVD risk assessment service.

Table 1. Accuracy indicators of LR, RF, SVM models

	Accuracy	Recall/Sensitivity	Specificity	Precision
LR	0.73	0.78	0.68	0.75
RF	0.83	0.90	0.75	0.82
SVM	0.77	0.97	0.51	0.72

We integrated the resulting model in a serialized form into IT service for assessing the risk of coronary heart disease (CHD risk meter), made as a desktop application. The service implements the following data processing pipeline:

1. the user (doctor or paramedic) enters parameter values to determine the risk of coronary heart disease;
2. the service based on the predictive model determines the presence/absence of risk;
3. the user confirms or refutes the obtained result. Finally, the service generates a text file containing data for the model training on a new sample to improve the prediction accuracy.

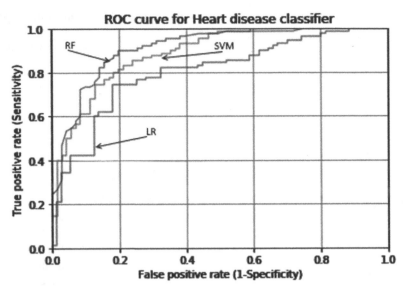

Fig. 2. ROC curves models LR (AUC = 0.88), RF (AUC = 0.91) SVM (AUC = 0.88)

4 Conclusion

In our study, we proceeded, first, from the positive experience of using population models for predicting CVD risks. On the other hand, we tried to expand the training sample and use EHR data for training models. To achieve this goal, we have developed special methods for extracting information from unstructured medical texts. In addition, we have developed Web services designed for experts to select the optimal set of features — the patient's digital phenotype. Healthcare organizations can use the IT service when conducting preventive examinations. We assume that additional predictors will contribute to the increase in its predictive abilities. For example, data from a portable cardiac monitor may be of great importance for improving the accuracy of predicting CVD risks [28]. These important data will make it possible to use IT service in telemedicine systems for remote monitoring of patients' condition. In the present study, we did not address the issues of the adequacy of medical prescriptions for the patient's condition and their compliance with the existing guidelines. We will explore this issue in our future research.

References

1. Federal state statistics service. https://www.gks.ru/folder/12781
2. Vishnevsky, A., Andreev, E., Timoni, S.: Mortality from cardiovascular diseases and life expectancy in Russia. Demogr. Rev. **3**(1), 6–34 (2016)
3. Oganov, R.G., Vaslennikova, G.Ya.: Prevention of cardiovascular diseases - real way to provement of demographic situation in Russia. Kardiologiia **47**(1), 1–8 (2007)
4. Kulikov, V.A.: Fremingham heart research: 65 years of studying the causes of atherosclerosis. Bull. Vitebsk State Med. Univ. **11**(2), 16–24 (2012)

5. Hense, H.W., Schulte, H., Lowel, H., Assmann, G., Keil, U.: Framingham risk function overestimates risk of coronary heart disease in men and women from Germany - results from MONICA Augsburg and the PROCAM cohorts. Eur. Heart J. **24**(10), 937–945 (2003)
6. Thomsen, T.F., McGee, D., Davidsen, M., Jorgensen, T.: A cross-validation of risk-scores for coronary heart disease mortality based on data from the Glostrup Population Studies and Framingham Heart Study. Int. J. Epidemiol. **31**(4), 817–822 (2002). https://doi.org/10.1093/ije/31.4.817
7. Brindle, P., et al.: Predictive accuracy of the Framingham coronary risk score in British men: prospective cohort study. BMJ **29**, 327(7426), 1267 (2003). https://doi.org/10.1136/bmj.327.7426.1267
8. Conroy, R.M., et al., SCORE Project Group: Estimation of ten-year risk of fatal cardiovascular disease in Europe: the SCORE project. Eur. Heart J. **24**(11), 987–1003 (2002). https://doi.org/10.1016/s0195-668x(03)00114-3
9. Getz, L., Sigurdsson, J.A., Hetlevik, I., Kirkengen, A.L., Romundstad, S., Holmen, J.: Estimating the high risk group for cardiovascular disease in the Norwegian HUNT 2 population according to the 2003 European guidelines: modelling study. BMJ **331**(7516), 551 (2005). https://doi.org/10.1136/bmj.38555.648623.8F
10. Matheny, M., McPheeters, M.L., Glasser, A., et al.: Systematic review of cardiovascular disease risk assessment tools. Evid. Synth. 11-05155-EF-1 (2011)
11. Rahimi, K., Bennett, D., Conrad, N., et al.: Risk prediction in patients with heart failure: a systematic review and analysis. JACC Heart Failure **2**(5), 440–446 (2014)
12. Fayyad, U., Piatetsky-Shapiro, G., Smyth, P.: From data mining to knowledge discovery in databases. AI Mag. **17**(3), 37–54 (1996)
13. Ahmad, T., et al.: Machine learning methods improve prognostication, identify clinically distinct phenotypes, and detect heterogeneity in response to therapy in a large cohort of heart failure patients. J. Am. Heart Assoc. **7**(8), e008081 (2018)
14. Weng, S.F., Reps, J., Kai, J., Garibaldi, J.M., Qureshi, N.: Can machine-learning improve cardiovascular risk prediction using routine clinical data? PLoS ONE **12**(4), e0174944 (2017). https://doi.org/10.1371/journal.pone.0174944
15. Dyuzheva, E.V., Kuznetsova, A.V., Senko, O.V.: Determination of risk factors of cardiovascular mortality in institutions of the penitentiary system using the machine learning methods. Inf. Technol. Phys. **2**, 29–45 (2017)
16. Miotto, R., Li, L., Kidd, B.A., Dudley, J.T.: Deep patient: an unsupervised representation to predict the future of patients from the electronic health records. Sci. Rep. **6**, 26094 (2016). https://doi.org/10.1038/srep26094
17. Hirschtick, R.E.: Copy-and-paste. JAMA **295**(20), 2335–2336 (2006). https://doi.org/10.1001/jama.295.20.2335
18. Zakharov, A., Potapov, A., Zakharova, I., Kotelnikov, A., Panfilenko, D.: Infrastructure of the electronic health record data management for digital patient phenotype creating. In: 7th Scientific Conference on Information Technologies for Intelligent Decision-Making Support (ITIDS 2019), pp. 285–289. Atlantis Press (2019). https://doi.org/10.2991/itids-19.2019.51
19. Meystre, S.M., Savova, G.K., Kipper-Schuler, K.C., Hurdle, J.F.: Extracting information from textual documents in the electronic health record: a review of recent research. Yearb. Med. Inform. **17**(01), 128–144 (2008)
20. Pathak, J., Bailey, K.R., Beebe, C.E., Bethard, S., Carrell, D.S., Chen, P.J., et al.: Normalization and standardization of electronic health records for high-throughput phenotyping: the SHARPn consortium. J. Am. Med. Inf. Assoc. **20**(e2), e341–e348 (2013). https://doi.org/10.1136/amiajnl-2013-001939
21. Kreimeyer, K., et al.: Natural language processing systems for capturing and standardizing unstructured clinical information: a systematic review. J. Biomed. Inform. **73**, 14–29 (2017). https://doi.org/10.1016/j.jbi.2017.07.012

22. Weng, S.F., Reps, J., Kai, J., Garibaldi, J.M., Qureshi, N.: Can machine learning improve cardiovascular risk prediction using routine clinical data? PLoS ONE **12**(4), e0174944 (2017). https://doi.org/10.1371/journal.pone.0174944

23. Maksimov, S.A., Tsygankova, D.P., Artamonova, G.V.: Application of regression analysis and classification trees in calculating additional population risk of ischemic heart disease. Health Risk Anal. **3**, 31–39 (2017). https://doi.org/10.21668/health.risk/2017.3.04

24. Chen, J.H., Asch, S.M.: Machine learning and prediction in medicine—beyond the peak of inflated expectations. N. Engl. J. Med. **376**(26), 2507–2509 (2017). https://doi.org/10.1056/NEJMp1702071

25. Steele, A.J., Denaxas, S., Shah, A.D., Hemingway, H., Luscombe, N.M.: Machine learning models in electronic health records can outperform conventional survival models for predicting patient mortality in coronary artery disease. PLoS ONE **13**(8), e0202344 (2018). https://doi.org/10.1371/journal.pone.0202344

26. https://natasha.github.io/ner/

27. https://pymorphy2.readthedocs.io/en/0.2/user/index.html

28. Zakharov, A.A., Potapov, A.P., Zakharova, I.G., Olennikov, E.A.: Telemetric medical system to support cardiological screening. In: 2018 XIV International Scientific-Technical Conference on Actual Problems of Electronics Instrument Engineering (APEIE), pp. 116–120. IEEE (2018)

Application of Genetic Algorithms to the Test Suite Cases Minimization

María Martín-Marín$^{(\boxtimes)}$, Juan José Domínguez-Jiménez$^{(\boxtimes)}$, and Inmaculada Medina-Bulo$^{(\boxtimes)}$

Escuela Superior de Ingeniería, University of Cádiz, Puerto Real, Spain
{maria.martin,juanjose.dominguez,inmaculada.medina}@uca.es

Abstract. Software testing is an important but time-consuming part of the software development life cycle. In fact, it takes almost more than fifty percent of the total cost of development. Organizations spend too much time on testing, so research in this field is necessary to minimize these times and improve the quality of the software projects. In this paper, my colleagues and me present an algorithm to reduce the initial set of test cases and minimize that time cost. Our algorithm eliminates redundant test cases without losing effectiveness applying mutant coverage and genetic algorithms. The results show that with this approach we obtain a minimum test suite with the same effectiveness as the original test suite.

Keywords: Genetic algorithms · Minimization · Software testing · Test automation · Software engineering

1 Introduction

Software testing is a very important topic in *software development*. If we perform good testing, our software will be more reliable. The more we test, the more we can validate the functionality of the software and find possible errors that have not been considered by the developers.

Use of evolutionary approaches for automatic test generation has been for many years an area of interest for a significant number of researchers [1]. Genetic Algorithm (GA) [2] is a type of evolutionary algorithm. This paper presents a way to apply GAs to software testing.

Testing can be very complex in terms of time, so it is necessary to find a way to minimize the set of tests to be tested on a given software, maintaining the same coverage of requirements (assuming that the requirements are the criterion we have chosen to measure the validity of our tests). In other words, we start from a set of tests that, for example, cover all the requirements of the software. Our aim is to reduce redundant test cases from a test data based on a certain criterion, for example the requirements to reduce it and maintain the same coverage of requirements or be very close to it.

In this paper, my colleagues and me will focus on the problem of minimizing the number of mutants generated by mutation tests. Mutation testing is a software testing technique used for evaluating the effectiveness of test suites [6]. We consider only one

© Springer Nature Singapore Pte Ltd. 2021
P. K. Singh et al. (Eds.): FTNCT 2020, CCIS 1395, pp. 525–535, 2021.
https://doi.org/10.1007/978-981-16-1480-4_47

criterion, but there are studies that support the possibility of minimizing sets of test cases by attending to more than one criterion [4], although using other methodologies.

There are already previous works [1, 4, 7–9] that have applied GA to the minimization of test cases. In this research we have determined to use the *Canonical Genetic Algorithm* (CGA]) [10].

The structure of the paper is as follows. Section 2 introduces the basic concepts for understanding how a GA works and defines the concept of mutation testing discussed in this paper. Section 3 defines the problem representation. Section 4 reviews the CGA. Section 5 shows the GA parameters. Section 6 describes the experimental evaluation and discusses the results obtained. Finally, we present the conclusions in Sect. 7 and pending research questions to tackle in the future in Sect. 8.

2 Background

In the section below we will show the main concepts about GAs and mutation testing.

2.1 Genetic Algorithms

A GA is a search heuristic that is inspired by Charles Darwin's theory of natural evolution. An AG is a reflection of the process of natural selection in which the most capable individuals are selected for the reproduction in order to produce offspring of the next generation.

Genetic Algorithms Elements
The Algorithm starts with **a set of solutions** (population) composed of a number of individuals. The solutions of a population are taken and used to form a new population, as we see, this process is very much in relation to the evolution of species. This is motivated by the hope that the new population or offspring will be better than the old one.

Individuals which are selected to build new solutions are chosen in accordance with their fitness score (which tells us how good each individual is according to the nature of the problem), but first we need to generate a new offspring through the **selection, crossing** and **mutation operators** explained in the section below.

Genetic Algorithms Parameters
There are some basic parameters of GA. The section below shows the most important ones to consider.

- *Crossover probability.* Probability of two individuals achieving descendants.
- *Mutation probability.* Probability of mutation of one or more chromosomes.
- *Population size.* Number of individuals in the population
- *Generation number* says how many generations will be created in total.

2.2 Selection Operator

There are different methods to implement the selection operator in the GA, in this paper we opted for the selection by binary tournament.

Tournament selection is a method used to select an individual from a population of individuals in a genetic algorithm. Tournament selection involves holding several "tournaments" between two or more individuals chosen at random from the population. The winner of each tournament (the one with the highest score) is selected for the next generation. The method of selection of individuals is easily adjustable according to the number of individuals participating in the tournament.

In this paper we use a 2-way tournament selection:

- As we are going to hold a binary tournament, two individuals are selected from the population and a tournament is held between them.
- Take the best of both.
- Repeat steps 1 and 2 until the desired population is achieved.

For example, we have these two individuals and the fitness value of each of them:

$$I_1 = \{1001010000\}\, F = 3$$

$$I_2 = \{1000111100\}\, F = 4$$

In this case it would be the I_1 (individual one) who will pass on to the next generation as being the best of both.

2.3 Crossover Operator

In evolutionary computing, the crossover or recombination, is a genetic operator that is applied to combine the genetic information of two parents and thus generate a new offspring. As we know, the genetic information of each individual is stored in an array. There are some methods. In this paper we are implemented the Single-point crossover method. In this method we select two parents. A single point is chosen randomly between the two parents' chromosomes. This point is called the *crossover point*. The chromosomes to the right of that point combine to form the new children. This combination generates two descendants, each of which contains genetic information from both of their parents.

As we can see in (see Fig. 1), we obtain two children from two parents. Once the crossover point is calculated, the first child is created from the chromosomes of Father A to the left of the crossing point, and those of Father B from the right. The second child will be made in an analogous way but starting from Father B.

2.4 Mutation Operator

Mutation can be defined as a small adjustment that is made randomly on one or more chromosomes. This operator is applied to introduce diversity into the population. The

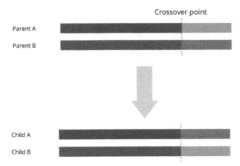

Fig. 1. Crossover operator representation.

mutation is also random, and is much less than the probability of crossover, as even this is the case in natural evolution. If the probability were too high, the AG would be reduced to a random search.

The mutation is essential for the correct performance of the genetic algorithm, since it is essential for the convergence of the algorithm, while the crossover isn't.

There are many mutation operators, in this paper we apply the Bit Flip mutation. One or more bits are selected randomly and their value is changed. Remember that our representation is binary, that is, we change the 0's by 1's and vice-versa.

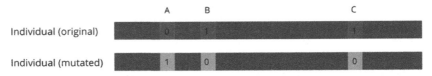

Fig. 2. Mutation operator representation.

As we can see (see Fig. 2) we can see an example. We select three chromosomes at random in the original individual and transmute their value into the final individual.

2.5   Mutation Testing

Is a fault-based software testing technique used for evaluating the effectiveness of test suites. This technique introduces minor modifications in the source code under test, resulting in new programs known as mutants. This is possible to achieve thanks to mutation operators, which are the rules to transform the code and produce new mutants.

A good test case will be able to detect changes, due to the change of functionality of the original program. When a mutant has been detected, it is called a dead mutant. Otherwise, it is an alive mutant. To represent the problem to be minimized, we will use an execution matrix. Next we explain what an execution matrix is:

	m0	m1	m2	m3	m4	m5
t0	0	0	1	1	0	0
t1	1	0	0	0	0	0
t2	1	0	1	1	0	0
t3	0	0	0	0	1	0
t4	1	0	0	1	0	0
t5	0	0	1	0	1	0
t6	0	0	1	0	1	0
t7	0	0	1	0	1	0
t8	0	0	1	0	1	0
t9	0	0	1	0	1	0

In this matrix, the rows represent the test suite cases and the columns represent the total set of mutants, so that, for example, the case where the position [i, j] is equal to 1 means that the test case in row "i" kills the mutant in column "j" and 0 otherwise. Based on these data, we have to find the most appropriate representation to solve the problem of test suites minimization. We discuss this in the next section.

3 Problem Representation

In this section we will explain the representation of the problem in a mathematical way and which has been used to implement the algorithm in C++.

3.1 Introduction to the Test Suites Minimization

Minimization of test cases can be achieved by attending to several criteria [3]. For example, we can minimize a set of test cases so that they cover a significant number of requirements with fewer test cases than the initial set contains. Also, we can minimize those test cases by considering mutation testing, in particular, the mutants that each test case kills, i.e., kill the same number of mutants with a lower set of test cases than the initial set.

This will depend on the nature of the problem to be solved, in our case we will focus the article on the minimization of test cases to be applied to a set of mutants.

3.2 Problem Representation

There are several approaches to representing the problem under study. In this paper, a binary representation has been selected. The initial population will be integrated by a fixed number of individuals that will define a possible solution to the problem, that is, each individual represents a set of test cases.

For example, below we can observe an individual composed of 5 test cases, from T0 to T4. A value equal to "1" in the position "i", means that the test case "Ti" is included in the solution. So, the example below means that the individual "I" is a test cases suite composed by T0 and T3.

$$I = \{10010\}$$

For this reason, a population will be represented in the same way as matrix. Below we display five individuals:

$$I_1 = \{10010\}$$

$$I_2 = \{10001\}$$

$$I_3 = \{01100\}$$

$$I_4 = \{00010\}$$

$$I_5 = \{10010\}$$

This population of five individuals would be represented as a matrix as the one we see below:

$$M_{5,5} = \begin{array}{l} - \ t0 \ t1 \ t2 \ t3 \ t4 \\ I0 \ 1 \ 0 \ 0 \ 1 \ 0 \\ I1 \ 1 \ 0 \ 0 \ 0 \ 1 \\ I2 \ 0 \ 1 \ 1 \ 0 \ 0 \\ I3 \ 0 \ 0 \ 0 \ 1 \ 0 \\ I4 \ 1 \ 0 \ 0 \ 1 \ 0 \end{array}$$

For this case, this will be the population that we will make evolve a certain number of times and we will keep the best possible individual. Which will be the best individual? It will be the one with the least number of test cases, giving the best mutant coverage result. In the following section we see how the fitness function work.

3.3 Fitness Function

The fitness function is one that will provide an evaluation and score for each individual in the population that will indicate how good they are. We know that our goal is to minimize the problem, so we will take the individual or individuals that have a lower score. To evaluate each individual, we go through each of them and with the help of the execution matrix we will know which mutants are covered by each set of test cases (or individual). The aim is to achieve a minimum test suite case that covers the largest number of mutants. In the following Eq. (1) we see how we calculate the fitness:

$$Fitness = t + (mnc * Penalty) \tag{1}$$

- t indicates the number of tests the individual contains (number of 1's) and
- *mnc* is the number of mutants not covered. *Penalty* will be a real value between 1.0 and 2.5.

Further experiments assure us that better results are achieved for penalty values close to 2.5.

4 Proposed Algorithm: Canonical Genetic Algorithm

A basic GA is an evolutionary algorithm based on binary strings, with crossover along with mutation as variation operators, and fitness-proportionate selection. Here we can see the pseudocode of the GA that we propose:

```
BEGIN
    Generate an initial population.
    Computing the evaluation function to each individual in
    the population
    WHILE NOT finished DO
    BEGIN /* Create a new generation. */
        FOR size_population/2 DO
        BEGIN
            1.  Select two individuals for the crossover.
            2.  Cross both individuals with a specified probability and ob-
                tain two descendants.
            3.  Mutate the two descendants with a certain probability.
            4.  Compute the fitness function of the two individuals.
            5.  Add the two mutated individuals for the next offspring.
        END
        IF convergence THEN
            finished:=true
    END
END
```

We will create an initial population that we will evaluate with the fitness function. In the next section we will see the details of each of the operators that we will apply in the algorithm:

- Mutation and crossover operators.
- Selection operator.
- Evaluation or fitness function.

This population will be renewed over a number of generations. Each new population will be generated by applying the crossover and mutation operators, both with a certain probability. If, when assessing the probability, individuals do not cross, the parents will be passed on to the next generation. Always in pairs.

Every time a new generation is generated, we have to evaluate all the individuals with the fitness function, since this function will indicate how good the individuals are and will help us to select the best individuals from the population.

5   Genetic Algorithm Parameters

As we know, GAs are characterized, among other things, by the number of parameters that they can work with. Below is a list of those most relevant and that are used in the implementation (Table 1).

Table 1. GA parameters.

Parameter	Description
SIZE_POPULATION	Total size population
SIZE_GENERATIONS	Number of GA iterations
PENALTY_FACTOR	Penalty applied in the fitness function for mutants not covered
CROSSOVER_RATE	Crossover probability
MUTATION_RATE	Mutation probability

6   Experiments

The GA has been implemented in C++ [10]. The experiments have consisted in applying the algorithm on five execution matrices of different sizes [6], whose optimal cases are well-known, a total of thirty consecutive times. Table 2 identifies each one of these matrices.

Table 2. Detail of the execution matrix of the experiments.

Name	Test	Mutants	Killed	Suite
LA	7	60	53	3
COMBO2	33	890	646	17
TRS	18	213	153	12
MS	36	508	424	8
LAE	94	3647	2877	63

In the first column we see the name of the matrix [6], in the second and third columns respectively, the number of tests and original mutants. In the column labelled "Killed", the number of mutants we can kill in the best case is shown for each matrix, and in the "Suite" column the minimum number of test cases that can kill these mutants.

6.1   Results Achieved

We have applied the GA with the same parameters to each and every one of the matrices that conform this experiment:

- **Size Population**: 100
- **Number of Generations**: 1000
- **Crossover Rate**: 0.95 (95%)
- **Mutation Rate**: 0.09 (9%)
- **Penalty Factor**: 1.5

For each matrix, we will show the result obtained compared to the optimal well-known result.

Experiments with LA Matrix
For this matrix, the optimal test case suite is as follows: $T = \{T1, T3, T7\}$
After running the algorithm, we get the following result: $T = \{T1, T3, T7\}$

Experiments with COMBO2 Matrix
For this matrix, the optimal test case suite is as follows:
 $R = \{T1, T2, T4, T6, T8, T10, T13, T19, T22, T24, T25, T26, T27, T28, T29, T30, T32\}$
After running the algorithm, we get the following result:
 $R = \{T2, T4, T6, T7, T9, T10, T13, T14, T17, T19, T21, T22, T24, T25, T26, T27, T28, T29, T30, T32\}$

Experiments with TRS Matrix
For this matrix, the optimal test case suite is as follows:
 $R = \{T1, T2, T3, T5, T6, T8, T11, T12, T13, T15, T16, T17\}$
After running the algorithm, we get the following result:
 $R = \{T1, T2, T3, T5, T6, T8, T11, T12, T13, T14, T15, T6, T17\}$

Experiments with MS Matrix
For this matrix, the optimal test case suite is as follows:
 $R = \{T1, T4, T7, T21, T27, T33, T34, T35\}$
After running the algorithm, we get the following result:
 $R = \{T3, T4, T6, T7, T8, T9, T18, T19, T22, T28, T31, T33, T34, T35\}$

Experiments with LAE Matrix
After applying the GA to the LAE matrix, of the 63 test cases that compose the minimum optimal suite, the algorithm returns a minimum set of 56 test cases at best.

Overview of Experiments

Table 3 shows the comparative between the results with the optimal test suite and the results with CGA. We can see that:

- In the case of the **LA matrix**, the algorithm has returned the optimal case.
- For the **COMBO2 matrix**, the optimal case requires 17 test cases to kill 646 mutants out of the initial 890 (leaving 60 alive). The GA generates a 20 element test case suite, leaving the same number of mutants alive as in the optimal case.

Table 3. Overview of experiments.

Name	Optimal test suite	Test suite of CGA	Killed mutants with optimal	Killed mutants With CGA
LA	3	3	53	53
COMBO2	17	20	646	646
TRS	12	12	153	153
MS	8	14	424	424
LAE	63	56	2877	2813

- In the case of the **TRS matrix** the optimum case has been achieved, as with the LA matrix.
- In the case of the **MS matrix**, 100% coverage was also achieved, but 6 more test cases were used than in the optimum case.
- Finally, with the **LAE matrix** we obtain the most disparate results. Although the GA generates a lower optimal set (56 test cases), this result has an impact on the number of mutants left alive (64 more than in the optimal case).

As a consequence, more mutants are left uncovered than in the optimal case, because the algorithm leaves 834 mutants uncovered, while the optimal case leaves 770 mutants uncovered. There is a difference of 64 mutants, which, translated to percentages, means that 2% of mutants remain alive.

However, as we have already commented, a percentage of 2% is achieved in terms of the number of living mutants, so we can conclude in this case that, taking into account that the GA are inaccurate algorithms, the result obtained in the LAE matrix is promising.

7 Conclusions

The results obtained in the experimental phase are interpreted below, to subsequently decide which route to take for future work. It is concluded that the results are reasonably promising and that there is value in further research into the application of genetic algorithms to the problem of test case minimization.

8 Future Work

Several improvements to the GA are proposed as future work, including.

- improving the fitness function to assess the relative importance of each individual test.
- improve the selection function by implementing other more complex methods that increase the diversity of the population.

In addition, the implementation of another GA is proposed, whose structure will essentially be the same as that of the CGA. What will change will be the representation, which will be based on permutations. The idea is to approach a solution that is capable of covering 100% of mutants as long as the initial configuration of the execution matrix allows it.

Finally, we would proceed to a comparison in time and cost of the results obtained with the GA designed against those obtained by other strategies used to solve the problem of minimizing test cases.

Acknowledgments. *"It is not possible to write a paper without the assistance and encouragement of other people. This one is certainly no exception"*

I am ineffably indebted to Prof. Francisco Palomo-Lozano for conscientious guidance and encouragement to accomplish this paper. To Dr. Pedro Delgado-Pérez for contributing his brilliant ideas every time we found a stone in the way and his valuable guidance and support. I also acknowledge to Dra. Antonia Estero-Botaro for giving me the opportunity to work with such a brilliant team.

The work was partially funded by the European Commission (FEDER), the Spanish Ministry of Science, Innovation and Universities [projects RTI2018-093608-BC33 and RED2018-102472-T].

References

1. Sharma, C., Sabharwal, S., Sibal, R.: A survey on software testing techniques using genetic algorithm. IJCSI Int. J. Comput. Sci. Issues 381–393 (2013)
2. Goldberg, D.E.: Genetic Algorithms in Search, Optimization and Machine Learning. Addison-Wesley Longman Publishing Co., Inc., Boston (1989)
3. Kiran, A., Butt, W.H., Anwar, M.W., Azam, F., Maqbool, N.: A compreensive investigation of modern test suite optimization trends, tools and techniques. IEEE Access **7**, 25 (2019)
4. Yoo, S., Harman, M.: Regression testing minimization, selection and priorization: a survey. Softw. Test. Verif. Reliab. **22**, 67–120 (2010)
5. Lin, J.-W., Jabbarvand, R., Garcia, J., Malek, S.: Nemo: multi-criteria test-suite mimimization with integer nonlinear programming. In: Proceedings of ICSE 2018: 40th International Conference on Software Engineering, 11 p. (2018)
6. Palomo-Lozano, F., Estero-Botaro, A., Medina-Bulo, I., Núñez, M.: Test suite minimization for mutation testing of WS-BPEL compositions. In: GECCO 2018 July, pp. 1427–1434 (2018)
7. Awan, S.A., Mateen, A., Nazir, M.: Optimization of test case generation using genetic algorithm (GA). Int. J. Comput. Appl. **151**, 6–14 (2016)
8. Akour, M., Abuwardih, L.A., Alhindawi, N., Alshboul, A.: Test case minimization using genetic algorithm: pilot study. In: 2018 28th International Conference on Computer Science and Information Technology (CSIT), pp. 66–70 (2018)
9. Lamichhane, A., Gandhi, P., Goyal, S., Mishra, P.: Software test case optimization using genetic algorithms. Int. J. Sci. Eng. Sci. **1**, 66–70 (2018)
10. Illyes, L.: Canonical Genetic Algorithm; Model, Implementation and Framework (2020)
11. Brownlee, J.: Clever Algorithms: Nature Inspired Programming Recipes, 1st edn. Lulu 2011, Melbourne - Australia (2011)

Ensemble Based Plant Species Recognition System Using Fusion of Hog and Kaze Approach

Sandeep Rathor$^{(\boxtimes)}$

Department of Computer Engineering and Applications, GLA University, Mathura, India
sandeep.rathor@gla.ac.in

Abstract. Recognition of plant species based on images of leaves has been one of the important challenges faced in the field of machine learning. In this paper, we propose a machine learning-based model which can automatically extract relevant features like edges, shape, etc. using two feature extraction algorithms: Histogram of Oriented Gradients and Kaze. The feature vectors are combined to form a final vector which is then fed into 3 classification algorithms, Support Vector Machine (SVM), K-Nearest Neighbors (KNN), and Random Forest algorithm. The result of these classifiers is used to create an ensemble, based on the probabilistic voting approach. The accuracy of our proposed system is more than any single classifier i.e. 92.30%.

Keywords: Plant recognition · Ensemble based machine learning system · KNN · SVM · Hog and Kaze approach

1 Introduction

Plants are significant for the planet earth and every living creature [1]. It gives natural air to inhale or helping in decreasing the contamination level by taking carbon dioxide and giving out oxygen. From being the essential wellspring of nourishment for a few feathered creatures, creatures, and different life forms to giving woods which are a wellspring of furniture and shelter to many organisms. This paper aims to propose a model that can be used to identify the species family and genus of plants based on the leaves. This can prove to be useful in many sectors of society which includes the conservation-related purpose of biodiversity. We know that it is impossible to talk about life without plants because of their importance to the ecological balance. However, with the advent of the 21st century which has brought population explosion along with its greedy needs, people have started altering and often degrading their environment up to such level that now it has resulted in various climatic calamities such as global warming, climate change, melting of glaciers, depletion of ozone layers, etc. Despite the vast benefits of plants to living beings, they are being destroyed at alarming rates. So it is very important to take necessary steps towards the conservation of plants and thus biodiversity. One such step would be to identify plant species.

© Springer Nature Singapore Pte Ltd. 2021
P. K. Singh et al. (Eds.): FTNCT 2020, CCIS 1395, pp. 536–545, 2021.
https://doi.org/10.1007/978-981-16-1480-4_48

One of the most common hazards in the forest is wildfire. They pose a great threat not only to the forest wealth but also to the entire region of flora and fauna, seriously disturbing the biodiversity, ecology, and environment of a region. These forest fires are pushing some species of flora on the verge of extinction. These plants or trees can be identified and then further be re-cultivated in the lab by identifying the species of plant leaves that maybe got left (if any) in fires. The other important significance of the system can be in Ayurveda. Since we know that Ayurveda is the most ancient form of medicinal treatment of various chronic diseases. Ayurveda treatment is done using some special types of plants called herbs. The parts of these herbs like flower, leaf, root, bark, and fruits are mainly used in the preparation of medicines. Also, our system can be useful to farmers, gardeners, or plantsman to get enough knowledge about the plants so that they can take proper care of. Both of these instances required plants to be identified. Currently, the plants are being recognized manually by professionals such as botanists or taxonomists, which are sometimes prone to human errors in many cases. To avoid these human errors, this paper proposes a methodology to identify and recognize the species and genus of plants which makes use of an image of a leaf as an input and a classification of a plant as an output.

Automatic plant species recognition by using leaves has many challenges. However, the leaf of a plant carries some fairly distinguishable characteristics of a plant, certain leaves show similar patterns, colour, and texture. There have been many pieces of research done which includes finding various morphological and statistical features of a leaf that requires a lot of image pre-processing techniques to be done before, eventually increasing the complexity of the system. In contrast, we propose a model that is divided into various steps the first step involves image acquisition which can be done either directly giving an image or by using a camera. The second step is to do some basic digital image processing. The next step is to extract features which will be required to train the model. We have used histogram of oriented gradients feature extraction technique.

2 Related Work

In this section, we will discuss the related work in this context. Plant species recognition has been one of the most challenging and interesting tasks among the researchers in the domain of computer vision and machine learning techniques. Many researchers have been done in this field using various machine learning algorithms, image processing morphological handcrafted techniques, Computer Vision Techniques, Artificial Neural Network, and Dense Neural Network, etc.

One such work was done by Mads Dyrmann et al. [1], in which a deep convolutional neural network was designed to identify the species of seedlings. The proposed classifier system was trained and tested on a data set containing images of 22 plant species which resulted in an overall accuracy of 86.2 %. Meet P. Shah et al. [2], introduces a new modified version of CNN called the dual-path deep convolutional neural network to learn joint feature representations for leaf images. The proposed CNN model was compared against a pre-trained classifier such as the Vanilla CNN classifier and employees a popular handcrafted shape feature which is called a marginalized shape context for feature extraction. Pushpa BR et al. [3], proposed an efficient methodology for Ayurveda plant species recognition using various statistical parameters extracted from leaf images viz. Mean, standard deviation convex-hull ratio isoperimetric quotient, eccentricity, and entropy. Further leaf factor of the input leaf is calculated using the extracted feature values and then on comparing it with the trained values stored in the database. Automatic plant classification using ANN was proposed by Luciano D. S. Pacifico et al. [4]. In this paper, the author used a multilayer perceptron (MLP) ANN trained with a backpropagation algorithm which was then compared with Friedman/Nemenyi test.

A very unique methodology of leaf classification and identification was proposed by Adil Salman et al. [5], using the Canny Edge detector and SVM classifier. They considered the shape of the leaf as the major characteristics to classify plants and thus Canny Edge detector was employed which extracted 15 features from the leaf and then with the help of the SVM classifier they succeeded in classifying 22 different kinds of plants. Research on leaf classification is proposed by Tiagrajah et al. [6]. In this paper, feature extraction of leaf images was done using the combination of Local Binary Pattern (LBP) and Histogram Oriented Gradients (HOG). Two very prominent data sets: Flavia dataset and Swedish dataset were selected to experiment. In this paper, an SVM classifier was used to classify leaf images. Pradip Salve et al. [7] use VIS leaf data set to carry out their research on plant identification. In this paper, the author used Zernike moments and Histogram Oriented Gradients method as a shape descriptor which resulted in 84.66 and 92.67% accuracy.

Classification with leaf shape features using a feed-forward back propagation neural network model is proposed by Amlekar et al. [8]. In this paper, the proposed method gets the leaf image as an input and after image processing, it produces the pattern and features of leaf shape. The new technique based on finding the arrangement of veins on the leaf called the Venation detection technique was proposed by Hoshang Kolivand et al. [9], for which they use a canny edge detection algorithm. The experiment was carried out on 32 images of Malaysian plant leaves which was analyzed and evaluated with two different data sets viz. Flavia and Acer. The average accuracy obtained using Flavia was 98.6% and 89.8 3% for the Acer dataset. For extracting image features efficiently HOG descriptor can be used [10]. It can be utilized for face recognition as well as plant recognition.

3   Proposed Methodology

The proposed method performs classification of plant species in the following five steps: image acquisition, image pre-processing, feature extraction, feature combination, and then classification. The flow of the system is illustrated in Fig 1.

I. **Image acquisition:** The data set used in the proposed model is one of the well-known and reliable data set among researchers working in this domain, which is Leafsnap dataset [11]. This data set consists of leaf images of 185 tree species from the Northeastern United States.

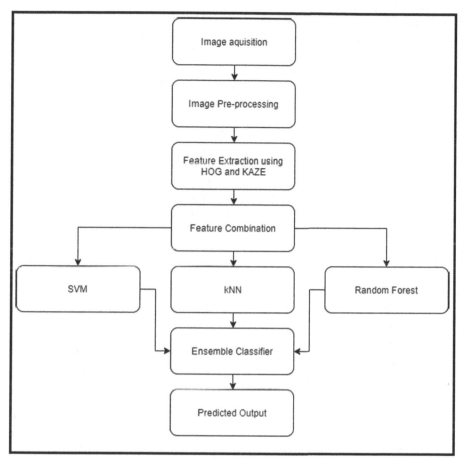

Fig. 1. Proposed model for plant species recognition

In this paper, we have worked with 1000 field images which consist of the following species counts as shown in Table 1.

II. **Image pre-processing**: Image pre-processing is a very crucial step before training the model. It is done to remove any unwanted distortions and to enhance some important distinguishable image features so that our classifier can easily work on the data. The data set consists of images of varying dimensions. So they need to be reshaped into a common dimension to make everything run in a smooth and error freeway. All the input images are then smoothened using the high pass and low pass filters to make the feature extraction phase easier.

III. **Feature extraction**: Basically, there are two types of features that are extracted from the images based: global and local features. Global features are generally used for the classification and detection of objects while local features are used for the recognition of objects. For this paper, we have used a combination of global and local features so that we can get better accuracy by learning both the outer and inner features. In the proposed model histogram oriented gradients (HOG) is used to count the occurrences of gradient orientation in localised portion of an image. This is done by extracting the gradient and orientation of the edges. The complete image is broken down into smaller regions and for each region, the gradients and orientation is calculated. Finally, the HOG generates a Histogram for each of these regions separately using the gradients and orientations of the pixel values. In the proposed model, KAZE is also used for feature extraction purposes [12][13]. It blurs the image, thus reducing the noise but retaining edges with superior localization accuracy and distinctiveness.

IV. **Feature Combination:** Now after extracting feature vectors of each image from HOG andSURF, we combined both of them into a new feature vector, which is considered as the final vector.

V. **Classification:** The proposed model uses an ensemble learning approach which is a combination of three classification algorithms: Support Vector Machine (SVM), K-Nearest Neighbors (KNN) and Random Forest. This ensemble model is based on the probabilistic voting approach. The output of the ensemble model is based on the highest probability of predicted output from individual algorithms. The dataset is split into training and testing dataset in the ratio of 3:1 i.e. 75% of the images are used for training and the rest 25% for testing.

Table 1. Different Images with species counts (taken from Leafsnap dataset)

S. No	Plant species	Count
1	Abies	100
2	Acer	100
3	Betula	100
4	Carya	100
5	Castanea	100
6	Cornus	100
7	Crataegus	100
8	Crytomeria	100
9	Diospyros	100
10	Eucommia	100
	Total	1000

4   Result and Discussion

For the evaluation of the proposed model, we have taken 10 species of trees, each of which contains 100 images as shown in Table 1. Below are the experimental results of 1000 images taken from the leafsnap dataset which are passed into different machine learning classifiers, which eventually will give results based on the aggregate of each of the output of the classifiers.

Figure 2 shows the confusion matrix using the SVM classifier [14]. The serial number used in the Table 1 taken as plant species. It gives 86.2% accuracy. If the same data is passed to the KNN classifier then the results are shown in Fig. 3.

A		Predicted Output									
c	S.No	1	2	3	4	5	6	7	8	9	10
t	1	88	3	2	1	1	1	0	1	2	1
u	2	2	86	4	3	0	1	1	0	0	2
a	3	4	1	84	2	3	2	1	0	2	1
l	4	3	4	1	87	1	0	1	1	1	1
O	5	1	3	1	1	89	2	1	1	0	1
u	6	3	2	2	1	1	85	2	1	1	2
t	7	1	2	1	3	1	2	84	3	2	1
p	8	3	4	2	1	1	1	1	87	0	0
u	9	3	1	3	2	3	0	2	1	85	0
t	10	1	0	1	1	1	1	1	2	5	87

Fig. 2. Confusion Matrix using SVM Classifier

Figure 3 shows the confusion matrix using KNN classifier. Proposed model runs with an accuracy of 70.7% with k = 2.

| A | | | | | | Predicted Output | | | | |
	S.No	1	2	3	4	5	6	7	8	9	10
c											
t	1	80	3	2	2	3	2	4	1	2	1
u	2	3	76	4	3	4	3	2	2	1	2
a	3	2	2	72	4	3	2	5	3	3	4
l	4	3	4	4	67	6	3	2	4	1	6
O	5	1	3	6	1	69	4	6	2	5	3
u	6	5	6	4	3	1	70	2	3	4	2
t	7	2	3	3	3	4	2	74	3	2	4
p	8	2	5	2	4	6	5	9	57	8	6
u	9	1	2	5	3	4	6	4	3	65	7
t	10	3	6	2	1	1	1	2	2	5	77

Fig. 3. Confusion Matrix using KNN Classifier

Figure 4 shows the confusion matrix using the Random Forest classifier. This model runs with an accuracy of 66.5% taking 10 decision trees for each data point. By Figs. 2, 3 and 4, it is clear that if we change the classifier then the prediction result will be changed. Therefore, we proposed an ensemble based [15] plant species recognition and the result of the proposed model is represented in Fig. 5.

$$Accuracy = \frac{\sum True \text{ Predictions}}{Total \text{ Instances}} \tag{1}$$

By using the Eq. (1), accuracy of the proposed model is 92.3%.

Table 2 shows the comparison of different existing machine learning methods to the proposed ensemble-based model. The same is also represented by Fig. 6. So, by the Table 2 and Fig. 6, it is clear that the proposed model is better than any of the other existing methods.

A		Predicted Output									
c	S.No	1	2	3	4	5	6	7	8	9	10
t	1	65	1	2	3	7	4	5	4	5	4
u	2	4	67	2	3	3	6	3	6	3	3
a	3	2	2	71	5	3	2	5	3	3	4
l	4	3	3	4	64	6	3	2	4	5	6
O	5	3	3	6	1	67	4	6	2	5	3
u	6	5	6	4	3	1	70	2	3	4	2
t	7	4	3	3	3	4	2	72	3	2	4
p	8	1	5	2	4	2	5	3	67	5	6
u	9	4	4	5	9	4	3	4	5	55	7
t	10	2	5	3	4	6	6	1	3	3	67

Fig. 4. Confusion Matrix using Random Forest Classifier.

	Predicted Output									
S.No	1	2	3	4	5	6	7	8	9	10
1	93	1	2	1	0	0	1	2	0	0
2	2	90	1	1	2	2	0	0	1	1
3	0	1	92	2	1	1	1	2	0	0
4	0	1	0	95	1	1	0	0	2	0
5	1	1	1	1	91	1	0	1	1	2
6	0	1	0	0	1	92	2	1	1	2
7	2	0	1	1	0	2	92	0	1	1
8	1	1	0	0	2	0	2	91	0	3
9	0	1	0	0	0	3	1	1	93	1
10	0	0	1	1	1	1	1	0	1	94

Fig. 5. Confusion Matrix of the proposed Ensemble Model.

Table 2. Comparision of different existing methods with our proposed method.

Method	Accuracy
SVM	86.2%
KNN	70.7%
Random Forest	66.5%
Mads Dyrmann et al.	86.2%
Proposed Ensemble Based Model	92.3%

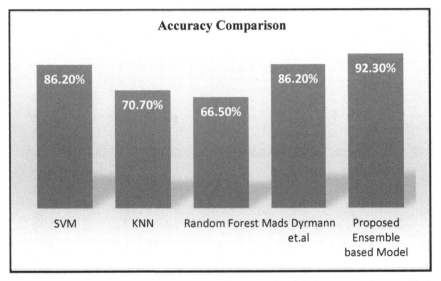

Fig. 6. Accuracy comparison of different existing methods with the proposed ensemble-based model.

5   Conclusion and Future Scope

The proposed ensemble-based plant species recognition system is very helpful for the society to recognize the plants and its species. Every plant has its features that are very useful for human being. Therefore, after the recognition of plant, we can utilize it in our daily life. The proposed model can also be utilized to recognize the Ayurveda plants. It will be helpful to the society for medical purpose. For future perspective, we will focus on a high volume of data set with minimum computation time or overheads.

References

1. Dyrmann, M., Karstoft, H., Midtiby, H.S.: Plant species classification using deep convolutional neural network. Biosys. Eng. **151**, 72–80 (2016)

2. Shah, M. P., Singha, S., Awate, S.P.: Leaf classification using marginalized shape context and shape+ texture dual-path deep convolutional neural network. In: 2017 IEEE International Conference on Image Processing (ICIP), pp. 860–864 (2017)
3. Pushpa, B.R., Anand, C., Nambiar, P.M.: Ayurvedic plant species recognition using statistical parameters on leaf images. Int. J. Appl. Eng. Res. 11(7), 5142–5147 (2016)
4. Pacifico, L. D., Macario, V., Oliveira, J.F.: Plant classification using artificial neural networks. In: 2018 International Joint Conference on Neural Networks (IJCNN), pp. 1–6 (2018)
5. Salman, A., Semwal, A., Bhatt, U., Thakkar, V.M.: Leaf classification and identification using Canny Edge Detector and SVM classifier. In: 2017 International Conference on Inventive Systems and Control (ICISC), pp. 1–4 (2017)
6. Janahiraman, T.V., Yee, L.K., Der, C.S., Aris, H.: Leaf Classification using Local Binary Pattern and Histogram of Oriented Gradients. In: 2019 7th International Conference on Smart Computing & Communications (ICSCC), pp. 1–5 (2019)
7. Salve, P., Sardesai, M., Manza, R., Yannawar, P.: Identification of the plants based on leaf shape descriptors. In: In: Satapathy, S., Raju, K., Mandal, J., Bhateja, V. (eds.) Advances in Intelligent Systems and Computing, vol. 379, pp. 85–101. Springer, New Delhi (2016).https://doi.org/10.1007/978-81-322-2517-1_10
8. Amlekar, M.M., Gaikwad, A.T.: Plant classification using image processing and neural network. In: Balas, V.E., Sharma, N., Chakrabarti, A. (eds.) Data Management, Analytics and Innovation. AISC, vol. 839, pp. 375–384. Springer, Singapore (2019). https://doi.org/10.1007/978-981-13-1274-8_29
9. Kolivand, H., Fern, B.M., Saba, T., Rahim, M.S.M., Rehman, A.: A new leaf venation detection technique for plant species classification. Arab. J. Sci. Eng. 44(4), 3315–3327 (2019)
10. Nassih, B., Amine, A., Ngadi, M., Hmina, N.: DCT and HOG feature sets combined with BPNN for efficient face classification. Procedia Comput. Sci. 148, 116–125 (2019)
11. Kumar, N., et al.: Leafsnap: A computer vision system for automatic plant species identification. In: Fitzgibbon, A., Lazebnik, S., Perona, P., Sato, Y., Schmid, C. (eds.) ECCV 2012. LNCS, vol. 7573, pp. 502–516. Springer, Heidelberg (2012). https://doi.org/10.1007/978-3-642-33709-3_3
12. Singh, P., et al.: Futuristic trends in network and communication technologies. In: Singh, P.K., et al. (eds.) FTNCT 2018. CCIS, vol. 958, pp. 141–166. Springer, Singapore (2018). https://doi.org/10.1007/978-981-13-3804-5
13. Singh, P., Sood, S., Kumar, Y., Paprzycki, M., Pljonkin, A., Hong, W.C.: Futuristic trends in networks and computing technologies. In: Singh, P.K., et al. (eds.) FTNCT 219. CCIS, vol. 1206, pp. 3–707. Springer (2019). https://doi.org/10.1007/978-981-15-4451-4
14. Rathor, S., Jadon, R.S.: The art of domain classification and recognition for text conversation using support vector classifier. Int. J. Arts Technol. 11(3), 309–324 (2019)
15. Rathor, S., Jadon, R.S.: Acoustic domain classification and recognition through ensemble based multilevel classification. J. Ambient Intell. Hum. Comput. 10(9), 3617–3627 (2018). https://doi.org/10.1007/s12652-018-1087-6

Mutative ABC Based Load Balancing in Cloud Environment

Saurabh Singhal$^{(\boxtimes)}$ and Deepak Mangal

Department of Computer Engineering and Applications, GLA University, Mathura, India
{saurabh.singhal,deepak.mangal}@gla.ac.in

Abstract. Cloud computing provides its users with adjustable, on-demand virtual resources over the Internet with pay-per-use models. Due to the cost-benefits, a large number of individuals and organizations have moved their business on the cloud. The services offered by service providers range from software to infrastructure. To accommodate such a large number of users, it becomes vital for the service providers to use the resources efficiently. Thus, load balancing becomes one of the major concerns for service providers. Load balancing in the cloud environment is an NP-hard problem and where researchers have proposed different meta-heuristic solutions for it. To utilize resources efficiently and reducing makespan time of the submitted jobs, the paper proposes an algorithm based on the foraging behavior of honey bees, a mutative artificial bee colony algorithm. The proposed algorithm reduces makespan time as well as improves the fitness function. Through experiments implemented in CloudSim, the results verify that the proposed algorithm reduces makespan when compared with algorithms in literature.

Keywords: ABC · ABC-M · Cloud computing · Load balancing

1 Introduction

In today's scenario, every business like social media, IT industries, and other applications are moving on Cloud computing. Cloud computing is one of the high-performance mechanisms to share resources on the internet by user demand. The maximum use of the utilization of resources is important and it increases system-level performance. For all these reasons, various companies are offering online services with high-level systems. However, people choose one cloud service and send a request to process the task. In cloud computing, the request for execution has to be transferred to any virtual machine by the algorithm. Several virtual machines are supporting this kind of system but problem is, how, where, and on which machine the request has to be sent. For example, if all the requests have been sent to one or two machines and the other machines are free then overall system performance will be down. Therefore, the load balancing term arrives in cloud computing to enhance the overall system performance which is a big challenge for the industry and researcher.

© Springer Nature Singapore Pte Ltd. 2021
P. K. Singh et al. (Eds.): FTNCT 2020, CCIS 1395, pp. 546–555, 2021.
https://doi.org/10.1007/978-981-16-1480-4_49

To distribute various incoming requests to many virtual nodes in such a way that all requests will have a minimum waiting time can be defined as load balancing. There are several static and dynamic load balancing algorithm that has been implemented and suggested as state-of-the-art methods. The static algorithms are easy and easily work in a homogeneous environment but cannot support the changes in parameters at run time [13]. The dynamic algorithms are more efficient and adjust execution according to the changes in parameters as per request. These algorithms work in a heterogeneous environment. However, acceptance of changes in attributes is more complex in all types of algorithms. The limitation of the static and dynamic algorithm of the load balancing algorithm gives a way to research this area.

1.1 Key Motivation

The purposes of carrying out this research are:

- It increases cloud performance and by minimizing the latency of the virtual machine.
- Measurement of all functional requirements and non-functional parameters.
- Maintain scalability in terms of number of users.
- And main issue is minimum service cost as cloud service.

1.2 Metrics of Load Balancing

There are various QoS parameters that are used to measure the performance of load balancing algorithm in cloud environment. Some of them are:

Throughput: Throughput is the number of jobs executed per unit of time. The value of throughput should be for maximum to increase the efficiency of environment [11].

Overhead: Overhead defines the operation cost during execution of a job. For better performance of the algorithm, overhead needs to be minimum.

Fault tolerance The fault tolerance discuss the continuity of execution of job in case of any breakdown/failure of machine. The algorithm must be able to change machine if a failure occurs.

Transfer time: Transfer time is the sum of the time required to allocated resources to the job from one node to other. For better efficacy of system, transfer time should be minimum.

Resource utilization: Utilization is the effective use of the resources in cloud environment. To minimize cost for end users, the resource utilization should be maximum.

Makespan: Makespan defines the total time required for executing all the submitted jobs. The values of makespan time should be minimum in order to complete jobs in the deadline.

The research work is organized as follows: the literature survey of state-of-the art methods for load balancing described in Sect. 2, the proposed framework and algorithm figure out and explain in Sect. 3, Sect. 4 consists experimental results and analysis with traditional methods. Section 5 explores conclusion and future work to extend the research.

2 Related Work

The load balancing algorithms can be classified on the basis of state of the system and process initiation. They are classified into Static and Dynamic on the basis of state and Sender-Initiated, Receiver-Initiated and Symmetric on the basis of process initiation. The taxonomy is depicted in Fig. 1.

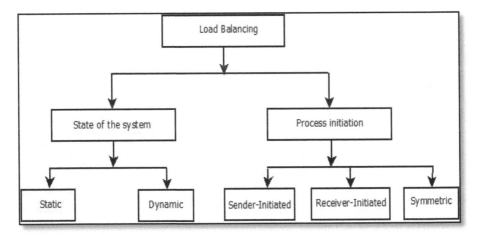

Fig. 1. Taxonomy of load balancing algorithm

There are many challenges and issues in the load balancing algorithm. Such as tolerance of high delays [2] because of the distance between nodes, network bandwidth, etc. It is a location-based issue. Sometimes high storage is required in case of a full replication algorithm. The replication of data at various nodes increases the cost [3]. So, the algorithm is required to increase the level as to manage cost. In terms of operation complexity, load balancing algorithm operation complexity must be minimum. The negative performance occurs with high complexity [5]. Similarly, delay creates a problem in large data communication [14]. Another challenge is POF (point of failure. A central node-based topology would fail if the controller node fails. This distributed system algorithm provides a new way to solve this POF issue.

In 2008, a famous algorithm which was mostly used in the various application was implemented by authors in [17]. An improved version in 2010 with the name central load balancing decision model (CLBDM) has been suggested by the authors in [12]. They worked on application layer session switching. In CLBDB, connection time has been calculated, they have used threshold value and if time exceeded the threshold value then the connection switches to the next node.

In 2012, ant behavior has been taken into consideration in [10, 20] to solve the load balancing problem. As we know, the ant's having a good habit to collect information in a fast way, same used by authors in [10]. As there is no central node, the problem of a single point of failure is avoided. Another advantage of this research is that it searches under-loaded nodes faster.

To solve the load balancing problem, map-reduce is also used. But it takes high processing time [6]. They have also not considered the reduction in tasks. The reliable connection method proposed by [9] in VM mapping. But they have not measured node capabilities and network load. To solve the load balancing problem many researchers have been proposed a dynamic algorithm. However, the results of static algorithms were highly useful but dynamic algorithm having their benefits.

In 2012, Index Name Server algorithm (INS) in [19] was proposed. In INS they have measured the location of the server, hash code, node performance, and path parameter to optimize the selection of access points. The INS having high implementation complexity and network overhead. The authors in [15] extend the WLC algorithm with the name ESWLC. It is a fast algorithm as compared to the existing algorithm. They used a time series with several connections at the node to find node capacity. After several algorithms proposed by researchers such as DDFTP as dual direction downloading algorithm from FTP servers in [1], LBMM as Load Balancing Min-Min in [18], ANT colony, etc. In comparison to all DDFTP is the best algorithm in terms of low complexity and no network overhead.

For more improvement in load balancing genetic algorithms such as ACO, ABC, and PCO in [4]. ALO stands for Ant Lion optimizer is based on the latent period and claimed better result as compared to all. In [4] proposed a dynamic load balancing algorithm in a distributed system. They considered various parameters to achieve better results but did not include a pattern of difficulties.

A review and classification of the load balancing algorithm has been done in [8]. The load balancing algorithms are classified into two classes' namely hybrid and dynamic. They developed a more effective load balancing algorithm. In which they minimize the use of resources and power consumption. But in all, cluster-based and task-based consumption is missing.

The authors [7] used the foraging strategy of the honey bee and proposed an algorithm for cloud load balancing. They worked on response time and tried to improvise cloud services. The suggested algorithm finds an overloaded virtual machine with a threshold value which equals average processing time.

In 2020, [16] proposed MPSO mutation-based PSO as a modified algorithm. This algorithm worked on data centers to utilize the services of servers in the cloud. They propagate tasks at various data centers with division in sub-task as an individual job. They select the appropriate data center for the allocation of subtask as per their availability.

3 Proposed Work

Figure 2 depicts the architecture for Load Balancing Algorithm. The job is submitted by the user via Internet to the cloud broker. Using load balancer, broker distributes the job on servers considering the load on each server. If every server is highly loaded, then the node that has executed similar job is chosen by the balancer.

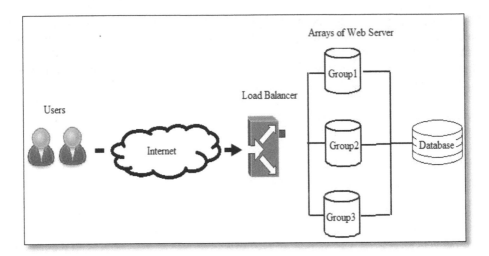

Fig. 2. Architecture of Load Balancing Algorithm

In this paper, a new modified artificial bee colony (ABC), called ABC-Mutative (ABC-M) is described. There are many servers which are under-utilized and available at the data centers level. So, there is appropriate searching process required for such server which is mainly focused in the proposed algorithm. For using the resources on the cloud, the users use the Internet for sending their job requests. Cloud Service Provider ensures that each submitted resource is allocated to some VM for execution. For this, the submitted task may move from one data center to another looking for an under-utilized resource. The submitted task is further divided in pieces commonly termed as job in each turn on these data centers. The data centers search for the under-utilized resources in the data centers for allocating the jobs to them. The proposed algorithm is able to minimize the makespan time of the jobs by assigning it to the available under-utilized data centers.

Artificial Bee Colony-Mutative: Whenever positions of bee is changed then value of fitness function is calculated for each piece of task. The flow of the algorithm is shown in Fig. 3.

As the value of t_{best} improves, the entire population of bee gets better. If the mutation is applied to this value of t_{best} the system will convert the value of the G_{best} value and hence the overall value of G_{best} can improve. The value of G_{best} will be accepted only if the value improves. A Gaussian mutation is applied as the mutation technique on the search space to improve value of G_{best}.

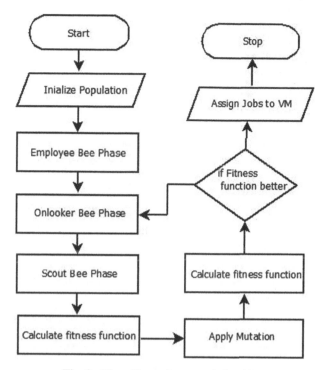

Fig. 3. Flow Chart of proposed algorithm

4 Results

This section discusses the result obtained after comparing the proposed algorithm with other algorithms in literature.

4.1 Implementation Environment

To implement the proposed algorithm, CloudSim 3.0.3 simulator is used. The Eclipse tool is required to be configured with CloudSim, the researchers can model power aware and energy aware cloud solution. The improved value of fitness function is used by proposed algorithm to minimize the utilization time as makespan time.

4.2 Parameters Setting

Total time required to execute all the tasks that are submitted to the environment is termed as makespan time. In cloud computing, it defines the maximum time for executing cloudlets running on different data centers. Makespan time has been considered as the parameter for measuring the performance of proposed algorithm. The proposed algorithm is compared with other nature inspired algorithms like ACO and PSO. The parameters that have been considered for experimental setup are shown in Table 1.

Table 1. Experimental setup.

Entity	Parameters	Values
User	Number of Cloudlets	50–300
Cloudlets	Length	500–10000
	Number of Hosts	2
Host	RAM	4 GB
	Storage	20 GB
	Numbers of VMs	8
	RAM	1 GB
VM	Operating System	Windows
	Numbers of CPUs	1
Data Center	Numbers of CPUs	5–20

4.3 Experimental Result**

Figure 4, 5, and 6 for the value of data centers 5, 10 and 15 respectively. It has been observed the proposed algorithm gives a better value of makespan time. So, it shows that the result of proposed algorithm is better as compared to traditional approaches discussed in literature. Whenever, the proposed algorithm runs with a number of data centers and cloudlets with different set of tasks, the results are improved in the range of 5%-15%. The results in Fig. 7 show the average of makespan time of the algorithms with other algorithms.

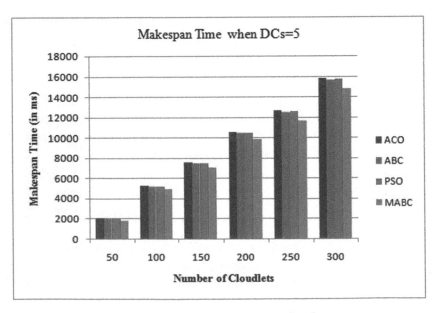

Fig. 4. Makespan Time when DC = 5

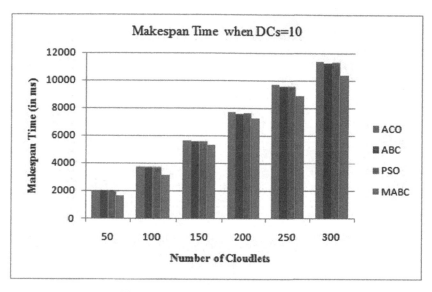

Fig. 5. Makespan Time when DC = 10

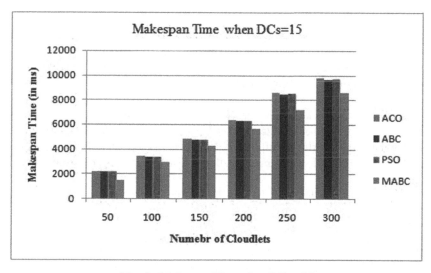

Fig. 6. Makespan Time when DC = 15

We have calculated the makespan time of each virtual machine by varying the data centers and keeping the number of jobs fixed with varying job length from 500–10000 million instructions. As the number of data centers increases the number of machines available to execute jobs is more thus reducing the makespan time. This is evident from Fig. 4, 5 and 6.

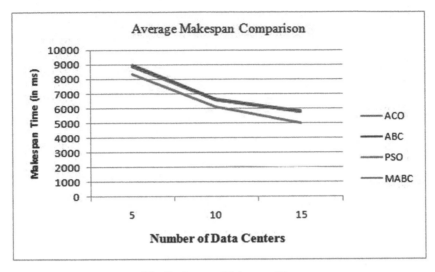

Fig. 7. Average Makespan Time

5   Conclusion

Load balancing in cloud computing is a significant issue as the cloud service providers needs to deal with countless assignment and clients in nature. The appearance pace of jobs varies rapidly therefore load balancing turns out to be all more challenging. In this paper we have examined the issue of load balancing in cloud and have attempted to propose an answer. The proposed load balancing calculation ABC-M lessens the general makespan time and improves the fitness function. This calculation oversees assets successfully dispersed over huge number of data centers. The proposed calculation shows improved outcome in the two scenarios of differing data centers and number of jobs. In future, we can search for various different parameters that help in estimating the exhibition of load balancing.

References

1. Al-Jaroodi, J., Mohamed, N.: Ddftp: dual-direction ftp. In: 2011 11th IEEE/ACM International Symposium on Cluster, Cloud and Grid Computing, pp. 504–513. IEEE (2011)
2. Buyya, R., Ranjan, R., Calheiros, R.N.: Intercloud: Utility-oriented federation of cloud computing environments for scaling of application services. In: Hsu, C.H., Yang, L.T., Park, J.H., Yeo, S.S. (eds.) ICA3PP 2010. LNCS, vol. 6081, pp. 13–31. Springer, Berlin, Heidelberg (2010). https://doi.org/10.1007/978-3-642-13119-6_2
3. Foster, I., Zhao, Y., Raicu, I., Lu, S.: Cloud computing and grid computing 360- degree compared. In: 2008 Grid Computing Environments Workshop, pp. 1–10. IEEE (2008)
4. Gamal, M., Rizk, R., Mahdi, H., Elnaghi, B.E.: Osmotic bio-inspired load balancing algorithm in cloud computing. IEEE Access **7**, 42735–42744 (2019)
5. Grosu, D., Chronopoulos, A.T., Leung, M.Y.: Cooperative load balancing in distributed systems. Concurr. Comput. Pract. Exper. **20**(16), 1953–1976 (2008)

6. Gunarathne, T., Wu, T.L., Qiu, J., Fox, G.: Mapreduce in the clouds for science. In: 2010 IEEE Second International Conference on Cloud Computing Technology and Science, pp. 565–572. IEEE (2010)
7. Hashem, W., Nashaat, H., Rizk, R.: Honey bee based load balancing in cloud computing. KSII Trans. Internet Inf. Syst. **11**(12) (2017)
8. Navimipour, N.J., Charband, Y.: Knowledge sharing mechanisms and techniques in project teams: literature review, classification, and current trends. Comput. Hum. Behav. **62**, 730–742 (2016)
9. Ni, J., Huang, Y., Luan, Z., Zhang, J., Qian, D.: Virtual machine mapping policy based on load balancing in private cloud environment. In: 2011 International Conference on Cloud and Service Computing, pp. 292–295. IEEE (2011)
10. Nishant, K., et al.: Load balancing of nodes in cloud using ant colony optimization. In: 2012 UKSim 14th International Conference on Computer Modeling and Simulation, pp. 3–8. IEEE (2012)
11. Nwobodo, I.: Cloud computing: a detailed relationship to grid and cluster computing. Int. J. Future Comput. Commun. **4**(2), 82 (2015)
12. Radojevi, C.B., Zagar, M.: Analysis of issues with load balancing algorithms in hosted (cloud) environments. In: 2011 Proceedings of the 34th International Convention MIPRO, pp. 416–420. IEEE (2011)
13. Randles, M., Lamb, D., Taleb-Bendiab, A.: A comparative study into distributed load balancing algorithms for cloud computing. In: 2010 IEEE 24th International Conference on Advanced Information Networking and Applications Workshops, pp. 551–556. IEEE (2010)
14. Ranjan, R., Zhao, L., Wu, X., Liu, A., Quiroz, A., Parashar, M.: Peer-to-peer cloud provisioning: Service discovery and load-balancing. In: Antonopoulos, N., Gillam, L. (eds) Cloud Computing. CCN, pp. 195–217. Springer, London (2010). https://doi.org/10.1007/978-1-84996-241-4_12
15. Ren, X., Lin, R., Zou, H.: A dynamic load balancing strategy for cloud computing platform based on exponential smoothing forecast. In: 2011 IEEE International Conference on Cloud Computing and Intelligence Systems, pp. 220–224. IEEE (2011)
16. Singhal, S., Sharma, A.: Load balancing algorithm in cloud computing using mutation based pso algorithm. In: Singh, M., Gupta, P., Tyagi, V., Flusser, J., Ören, T., Valentino, G. (eds.) ICACDS 2020. CCIS, vol. 1244, pp. 224–233. Springer, Singapore (2020). https://doi.org/10.1007/978-981-15-6634-9_21
17. Sotomayor, B., Montero, R.S., Llorente, I.M., Foster, I.: Virtual infrastructure management in private and hybrid clouds. IEEE Internet Comput. **13**(5), 14–22 (2009)
18. Wang, S.C., Yan, K.Q., Liao, W.P., Wang, S.S.: Towards a load balancing in a three-level cloud computing network. In: 2010 3rd International Conference on Computer Science and Information Technology, vol. 1, pp. 108–113. IEEE (2010)
19. Wu, T.Y., et al.: Dynamic load balancing mechanism based on cloud storage. In: 2012 Computing, Communications and Applications Conference, pp. 102–106. IEEE (2012)
20. Zhang, Z., Zhang, X.: A load balancing mechanism based on ant colony and complex network theory in open cloud computing federation. In: 2010 The 2nd International Conference on Industrial Mechatronics and Automation, vol. 2, pp. 240–243. IEEE (2010)

Story Point Based Effort Estimation Model with Machine Learning Techniques in Healthcare

Shanu Verma[1], Rashmi Popli[1], Harish Kumar[1], and Rohit Tanwar[2(✉)]

[1] J.C. Bose University of Science and Technology, Faridabad, India
[2] University of Petroleum and Energy Studies, Dehradun, India

Abstract. Healthcare diseases diagnoses projects often exceed schedules and budgets due to the complication and their large size. Project planning and estimation are exclusively challenging in large and globally distributed projects. Agile with machine learning techniques can overcome these challenges of healthcare projects largely. The purpose of this study is to estimate efforts in large-scale healthcare projects using user story point with machine learning technique. Will be using user stories to estimates the size of Healthcare projects. The templates of user stories: As a [user or destination], I [want to some goal] so that [the goal can be achieved]. According to Bill Wake a good user story must have INVEST acronym. To predict accuracy of machine learning algorithms such as Naïve Bayes, Decision Tree, Logistic Regression cancer patient dataset has used. Writing user stories for healthcare is an easy way to maintain the requirements for an agile project. Agile model in healthcare has used to maintain the effectiveness by adopting the frequently changing demand of the customers. This research paper work on cancer diseases and will provide accuracy, precision, recall using machine learning algorithms such as naïve Bayes, logistic regression, Decision Tree.

Keywords: Agile · Cancer · Decision tree · Effort estimation · Machine learning algorithm · Naïve Bayes · Random forest · Story pointing

1 Introduction

In order to make a healthcare system successful and visible for a longer period, the right care must be provide to the patient and at the right point of time, which can only be achieved, with the use of technology. However, our healthcare system is often unable to meet the exact demands of the patients and the end customers [4]. There is inherent and intense demand viability that makes this whole process of synchronization quite difficult to be maintain and delivered for a considerable period. The mismatch between the demands and the providers have led to many negative effects such as an increase in the cost of the healthcare [10], unexpected rise in the rate of admission. It has linked to the unplanned patient readmission, and the failure to maintain desired patients and provider ratio that have linked to the increased mortality of the patients. Variability in the demand could be the biggest problem that the healthcare industry is facing in current times. For

© Springer Nature Singapore Pte Ltd. 2021
P. K. Singh et al. (Eds.): FTNCT 2020, CCIS 1395, pp. 556–570, 2021.
https://doi.org/10.1007/978-981-16-1480-4_50

multiple healthcare delivery, has a phenomenon that moves from surgery to in-patient recovery, to emergency departments [16], where it has led to performance degradation, reduced resource availability and are more likely to exceed desired provider utilization and occupancy rates.

Now a days increasing healthcare cost is one of the world's most important problem as healthcare is an essential part of our ecosystem [15]. This problem must minimized to meet the needs of health services, for the dynamic, uncertain demand and constantly changing requirements of the customer. As per the latest medicine report, 80% of health care projects fail due to not having an accurate cost estimate. The healthcare sector in India has expected to increase significantly due to current covid-19 pandemic. The healthcare delivery often defined by the concept that a network of clinicians rather than an individual clinician who offers the care for the patients. The failure or the success of the modern healthcare system is determined by the ability of these clinicians [1]. As the complexity within the domain of healthcare increases the varying process and also the clinician gets more difficult to be managed and also aligned that has resulted in increased risk for the patients and improper use of the available resources [1].

Many machine-learning techniques are using for prediction and classification tasks. Using these techniques, several methods for disease diagnosis have developed and evaluated using public datasets. The classification of these studies based on agile machine learning techniques is an important task to reduce the estimates of various types of diseases, which is the aim of this research [2].

The rest of the paper is as follows. In Sect. 2, presented the related work based on machine learning technique using Agile in healthcare. In Sect. 3, discussed the current methods. In Sect. 4, provided the result of related work on disease diagnosis.And the Conclusion and future work presented in Sect. 5.

2 Literature Work

In this section, we are providing an overview of our previous research that is most relevant to our work can be categorized into Machine Learning Algorithm in Healthcare and Agile in Healthcare. Within each category, researchers have investigated different health problems and predictions using different ways these problems are more detailed here. The machine learning algorithm mainly extracts the characteristics of healthcare data such as the patient's age, symptoms, and medical outcome. Researchers predict health-related diseases using different machine learning algorithms that are discussed here. The Agile in Healthcare review of literature mainly emphasized on the Healthcare using agile software development. Referring to the research already done by various researchers helps to find any gaps when the corresponding field is present. Literature review helps motivates researchers to identify critical knowledge gaps and close it breech.

Bhatia et al. (2020) paper predicts urinary infection using the technology of Internet of Things using smart healthcare application. The paper creates a framework in IoT to predict urinary infections and work on four-layer architecture. The paper worked on real scenario and conduct test on four persons for sixty days to monitor their activity. In future, the paper will work on energy efficient system.

Tov et al. (2020) studies and diagnoses three types of cancer based on self-identification of illness. People who sought to diagnose one of the three types of cancer has shown ads on Bing and Google advertising systems. The result of the paper is that modern advertising systems has used to predict people who suffer from serious medical conditions. The questionnaire method is used to collect the data for predict cancer disease. The limitation of this study was questionnaire availability. In future the paper develop questionnaire for new disease.

Raoof et al. (2020) survey paper predicts lung cancer using machine-learning algorithm. Numerous machine learning algorithm are used to predict lung cancer such as Naïve Bayes, Support Vector Machine, Logistic Regression, and Artificial Neural network. The paper also used deep learning algorithm such as Deep Belief Network (DBN), Convolution Neural Network (CNN), and Fully Connected Convolution Networks (FCN). The survey paper discusses causes and symptoms of lung cancer in India and across the globe. The paper will help researchers to see insights in various ML Technology for the detection of lung cancer and in future, the paper uses deep learning techniques to predict lung cancer.

Morbid et al. (2019) paper predict healthcare cost using method such as Artificial Neural Network, Ridge regression model, gradient boosting, SVM, Elastic Net, Lasso, M5, Linear Regression, Random Forest, Bagging and Cart. It calculates using MAPE and R2.The strength of this paper combined both empirical evaluation and systematic literature review. The future studies would be use advanced supervised learning method to improve the performance of cost prediction methods.

Kavitha et al. (2019) study software engineering which has been used by consultants and software vendors in the application of healthcare that range from electronic medical systems, patient record management applications to medical middleware devices. Focusing on a systematic software development process leads to flaws in implementation, leading to loss of quality, cost, and trust. The survey paper analyze software models in the field of software engineering and describe the best Software development life cycle model in smart healthcare that focus on improvement of quality The survey also includes identifying the research challenges of software engineering for smart applications [17]. In addition to these analyzed papers, machine learning based models and its applications in healthcare is taken into account [20–22].

3 Problem Statement

As studied in the literature there are some problems in health care which are budget and doctors. Some costs may be very high while treating the disease and patients cannot afford that fee. According to W.H.O., less than one doctor (0.8) assigned to 1000 patient so doctor's fees are too high. This problem will overcome by using agile in Healthcare and creates a framework for the development of home based system, self-managed. Agile model in healthcare used to remove the ineffectiveness due to frequently changing demand of the customer and patient. Using the Story Point method would projected to cost healthcare.

The problem statement is to estimate whether the patient has cancerous disease or not, with the help of a supervised machine learning algorithm [14]. Supervised machine learning algorithms such as logistic regression, naive Bayes, decision tree have used in this research to predict the cancer disease in patients [3]. A significant number of people in the world suffers from undiagnosed or misdiagnosed cancer diseases. The death toll due to cancer diseases from 2007 to 2020 is 15.7% among males and 8.1% among females. Below is the estimate of new cases and deaths due to cancer diseases in 2020 on gender basis. Used supervised machine learning algorithms such as naïve Bayes, logistic regression, decision trees to find an accurate solution to this problem (Figs. 1 and 2).

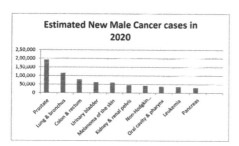

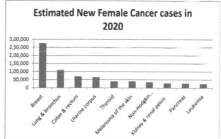

Fig. 1. Estimation new male cancer cases in 2020

Fig. 2. Estimation new female cancer cases in 2020

4 Proposed Solution

The proposed approach includes the number of modules such as Dataset, pre-processing the data, training the models, testing the models, comparison of results and the prediction of cancer disease (Fig. 3).

4.1 Dataset

The Dataset used in this research has collected from several resources as follows:

4.1.1 Classification of Cancer Disease and Dataset I

In low to middle income countries 606,520 people die due to cancer in united states [6]. The patients have different cancer diseases with the most being breast cancer, thyroid cancer, uterine cancer in women and liver, bladder, kidney cancer in men. The cancer Dataset has collected from the American Cancer society (WHO) [5] the features of cancer dataset shown in this Table 1 [8, 9].

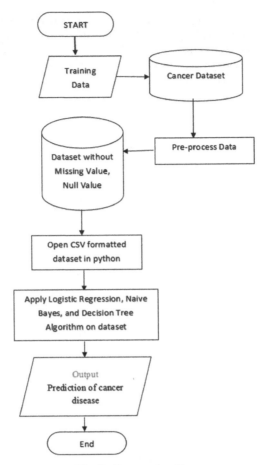

Fig. 3. Proposed outline

Table 1. Feature of cancer dataset

Feature name	Categories	Feature name	Categories
Age	Numeric	Fatigue	Numeric
Gender	Numeric	Cough	Numeric
Smoke	Numeric	Diabetes	Numeric
Alcohol	Numeric	Urine	Numeric
Clump Thickness	Numeric	Blood in stool	Numeric
Cell Size	Numeric	Coughing up blood	Numeric
Cell Shape	Numeric	Vomiting	Numeric

(continued)

Story Point Based Effort Estimation Model561

Table 1. (*continued*)

Feature name	Categories	Feature name	Categories
Radius mean	Numeric	Difficulty Eating	Numeric
Area mean	Numeric	Pelvic Pain	Categorical
Smoothness mean	Numeric	Back Pain	Categorical
Compactness mean	Numeric	Chest Pain	Categorical
Year	Numeric	Skin Type	Categorical
Diagnosis	Numeric	Target class	Categorical
Genes	Numeric		

4.1.2 Data Pre-processing

The term pre-processing used to convert to lean data from raw data. The preprocessing steps of data include cleaning the data, transforming the data, removal of missing fields and outliers, normalize the database [12]. The purpose of normalization is to normalize data in a single type [11]. The purpose of doing this is that the dataset has different digits; some have one digit, two digits and so on. In data, preprocessing data has split into two parts - training data and testing data. The Training and testing models described as below.

4.1.3 Training the Models

Training a model means training the machine with examples. Training data must contain the precise answer, known as a target or target attribute. To train the model machine learning algorithms used to find the relationship between labels and features. These three machine-learning techniques have been trained using different method. For logistic regression, the main step of the training is to search for significant features and calculate their individual p-values. As a judicial rule, if it is below 0.05, only the attribute is significant. The first step to training for Naïve Bayes is to find important features by calculating their probability values. For decision trees, a node partition criterion is required. The best segmentation is that which divides the data into separate groups. Accuracy is a measurement that used to evaluate potential segmentation. A division that divides a feature into two distinct classes is the purest.

4.1.4 Testing the Models

Next section in this research is testing the module with testing data and give result.

Data between the testing and training phases split approximately 40%–60% in this dataset. Under supervised learning algorithms such as Naive Bayes, logistic regression, decision tree, Python divides the dataset into training data and test data in ML (Figs. 4 and 5).

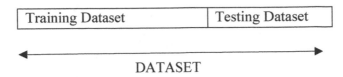

Fig. 4. Train model and test model in Python ML

```
from sklearn.model_selection import train_test_split

cr_x_train, cr_x_test , cr_y_train , cr_y_test = train_test_split(cr_x, cr_y , test_size = .4)
```

Fig. 5. Split the dataset using Python

4.2 Materials and Methods

This section discusses the methodology for estimating efforts using agile machine learning. The objective of this study is to estimate efforts in healthcare using user story point with machine learning technique. To achieve this objective various machine learning algorithms are used such as Logistic Regression, Decision Tree, Naïve Bayes, Hierarchical clustering [11]. In projects developed with Scrum, the software cost estimation differs from traditional estimation model [10]. Story point values used to determine the cost of software developed with the scrum method. Some machine learning algorithms such as Logistic Regression, Decision Tree, K-Near Neighbours, and Naïve Bayes used to find story point values in software developed with Scrum. The following process used for effort estimation using story point [13] (Fig. 6).

Story points used as a unit of measurement in user stories to calculate effort estimation to assess the effort involved in an issue [12]. Typically, story points follow Fibonacci like a sequence; 0,1,1,2,3,5,8,13,21,34,55,89,144, ..

The error rate of our story point-based inference model is better the others to display an empirical evaluation [18]. The user stories has written in very common language where everyone can be competent to understanding. The stories largely fit into agile framework such as scrum and extreme programming. User stories break a large project into a series of steps.

In Simple sentence

"As [destination or user], I [want to do some work], so that [the goal can be achieved]."

Example As researcher I want to estimate on healthcare disease so that it can help in rural areas Here is an example to estimate time and cost using user stories in this Table 2.

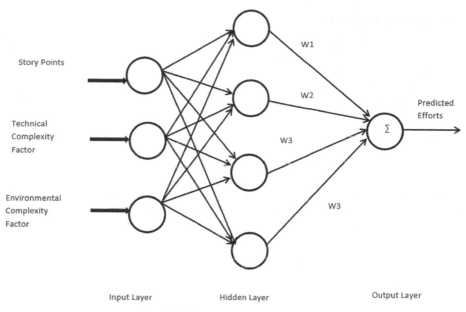

Fig. 6. Using story point predict effort

Table 2. User stories

Total user stories	30
15 of them can be measured in 3 Story Points each	15 * 3 = 45
Remaining can be measured in 5 Story Points each	15 * 5 = 75
Total Story Points	45 + 75 = 120
Velocity	10
Total number of sprints (Total story points/Velocity)	120/10 = 12
Each sprint may take	4 weeks
Estimated time for development	32 weeks
Each sprint cost	40,000
Estimated cost for development	12 * 40,000 = 840,000

4.3 Machine Learning Algorithm in Healthcare

Machine learning algorithm such as Naïve Bayes, Decision Tree, K-nearest neighbour, Logistic Regression, Random forest, Clustering are presented and compared in healthcare. Data of chronic diseases such as lung cancer, cervical cancer, breast cancer, thyroid cancer has obtained from UCI machine learning repositories and Kaggle to test and evaluate the proposed model [10].

4.3.1 Logistic Regression

Logistic regression is simple supervised machine learning algorithm that has used to analyze data and estimate target variables or output variable. Logistic regression estimates the probability that the attainment of the output variable belongs to the appropriate category or not [19]. It has used to predict whether the patient has cancer or not. It is a statistical method used by data scientist to predict whether the patient readmitted or not. The purpose of this algorithm is to examine the correlation between attribute and outcome.

$$\text{Logistic }(n) = a + b1x1 + \ldots \ldots + b_p X_p$$

Where n is the probability of an event. The main assumption for logistic regression is that the events are independent. Logistic Regression has used when the number of events has two groups either X1 or X2 [12]. It used to solve such type of questions "Is age a predictor of cancer, allowing for the other covariates?".

4.3.2 Naïve Bayes

The naïve algorithm defined as the probability method used to classify a dataset based on the famous Bayes theorem of probability and another term is "Probabilistic Classifiers". The Nave Bayes algorithm used to make predictions in real time. Let us consider a dataset that describes whether the patient has certain disease or not. In Naïve Bayes, the dataset has divided into two parts feature matrix and response vector. Feature matrix contains the value of dependent features and response vector consists the value of class variable. The Bayes theorem has the following general equation (Fig. 7):

$$P(A|B) = \frac{P(B|A)P(A)}{P(B)}$$

Where the terms

P denotes the probability.
P (A|B) denotes that probability of event A occurring given that event B has occurred.
P (B|A) denotes that probability of event B occurring given that event A has occurred.
P (A) = the probability of event B has occur.
P (B) = the probability of event A has occur.

Algorithm1 Naïve Bayes Algorithm
---
1 Scan the dataset
2 Calculate the probability of each attribute value (N,N_C,M,P)
3 Apply the formula
  P(attribute value(ai)/subject value(vj)=(N_C + MP)/(N+M)
4 Multiply the probabilities by p.
5 Compare the values and classify the attribute value to one of the predefined set of class.

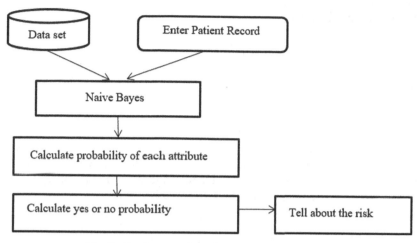

Fig. 7. Implementation of Naïve Bayes Algorithm

4.3.3 Decision Tree Algorithm

The decision tree is the most frequently used machine-learning algorithms to train the dataset for classification and regression analysis [7]. The decision tree algorithm has two parts tests and nodes. The decision tree algorithm used as trees, nodes divided into two categories to detect cancerous disease such as malignant or benign. The decision tree algorithm work on both categorical variable and continuous variable. In this research, the dataset has split into 60% training set and 40% testing set (Fig. 8).

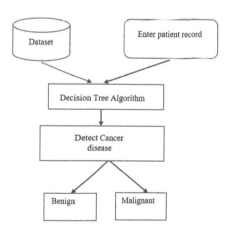

Fig. 8. Implementation of decision tree algorithm

5 Evaluation Metrics

The performance measures, such as precision, recall, F1-score, and accuracy used to evaluate the performance of the proposed model [10].

5.1 Precision

It refers to the rate at which samples are positively classified which is why it is also called positive predictive value (PPV) [7]. Precision is a measure that describes proportion of patients we have diagnosed diseases, whether or not they were actually having the diseases [10]. This returns a percentage of the relevant result. The purpose of precision is to assess 'true positive' with respect to 'false negative' [11].

$$\text{Precision} = \frac{True\ Positive}{True\ Positive + False\ Positive} \times 100$$

5.2 Recall

This refers to the rate at which positive samples detected and another term is sensitivity [7]. It correctly classified by your algorithm refers to the percentage of total relevant results. The purpose of recall is to assess the 'true positive' in relation to the false negative [11].

$$Recall = \frac{True\ Positive}{True\ Positive + False\ Negative} \times 100$$

5.3 F1-Score

The F1-score maintains a balance between the two indicators when they contradict each other [7]. F1-score gives average recall and accuracy [11]. Another term for the F1-score is the F-measure.

$$\text{F1-Score} = \frac{2 \times Recall \times Precision}{Recall + Precision}$$

5.4 Accuracy

The term Accuracy means correct prediction. It used to calculate the true positive and true negative divided by the total number of disease data set [10].

$$Accuracy = \frac{True\ Positive + True\ Negative}{True\ Positive + False\ Positive + True\ Negative + False\ Negative}$$

6   Results and Analysis

This research estimate cancer disease with the help of machine learning algorithms and found out the most accurate, recall, F-score and accuracy of these algorithms. This research uses Python version 3.7.6 and Windows operating system to find accurate, recall, F1-score accuracy. Therefore, the main objective of this research is to find accuracy among this three classification algorithms. The confusion matrix used to find this objective among the algorithms.

Table 3. Prediction using logistic regression algorithm

Class	Precision	Recall	F1-score	Accuracy
Lung cancer	92%	100%	96%	96%
Breast cancer	64%	100%	78%	61%
Cervical cancer	42%	89%	48%	32%

This logistic regression Table 3 predicts precision, recall, F1-score, accuracy for cancerous disease such as lung cancer, breast cancer, and cervical cancer.

Table 4. Prediction using decision tree algorithm

Class	Precision	Recall	F1-score	Accuracy
Lung cancer	100%	69%	82%	83%
Breast cancer	94%	91%	92%	91%
Cervical cancer	33%	96%	49%	33%

This Decision Tree Table 4 predicts precision, recall, F1-score, accuracy for cancerous disease such as lung cancer, breast cancer, and cervical cancer.

Table 5. Prediction using Naïve Bayes Algorithm

Class	Precision	Recall	F1-score	Accuracy
Lung cancer	88%	100%	93%	93%
Breast cancer	81%	95%	87%	82%
Cervical cancer	33%	95%	49%	32%

This Table 5 predicts precision, recall, F1-score, accuracy for cancerous disease such as lung cancer, breast cancer, and cervical cancer.

Table 6. Final analysis result

Class	Precision	Recall	F1-Score	Accuracy
Logistic Regression	66%	96%	74%	64%
Decision tree	76%	85%	74%	69%
Naïve Bayes	67%	97%	76%	69%

This Table 6 shown the final analysis result. This table discuss the average rate of precision, recall, F1-score.

Accuracy and enable us to take the final decision. The average rate of accuracy of Logistic Regression here is 64%. Decision Tree has an average rate of 69% and for Naïve Bayes it is 69%.The average rate of precision of Logistic Regression here is 66%. Decision Tree has an average rate of 76% and for Naïve Bayes it is 67%. The average rate of recall of Logistic Regression here is 96%. Decision Tree has an average rate of 85% and for Naïve Bayes it is 97%. The average rate of F1-score of Logistic Regression here is 74%. Decision Tree has an average rate of 74% and for Naïve Bayes it is 76%.

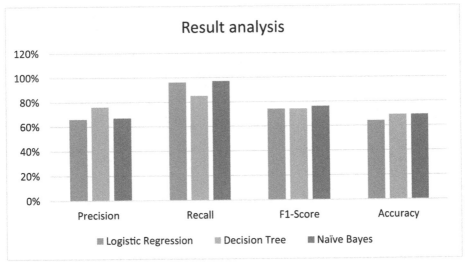

Fig. 9. Prediction of result analysis in supervised machine learning algorithm

This Fig. 9 represent accuracy among Logistic Regression, Decision Tree, and Naive Bayes. From this, it is clear that Decision Tree and Naïve Bayes gives better accuracy result. Therefore, here Decision Tree and Naive Bayes both are performing best than other two classification algorithms.

Logistic Regression < Decision Tree = Naive Bayes

7   Conclusion and Future Work

Nowadays Software plays a very important part of our life. Yet, improvement procedure of software is yet developing and continually experiencing changes with time. Strategy of new development are being refined and evolved. Both Government and Public Hospitals are in shortage of staff. Agile techniques used to create software in healthcare organization and remove the problem of documentation and meet the patient demands. The conclusion of this research shows that agile software model used in healthcare management and improves the service of healthcare delivery system.

In conclusion, as identified through related work, combination and models that are more complex needed to increase the accuracy of early onset of cancer diseases. This paper proposes a framework using a combination of naïve Bayes, decision trees, and logistic regression accurately predict cancer disease. Using the Kaggle and UCI databases, this paper provides guidelines for training and testing the system and thus achieves the most efficient model of multiple rule combinations. Furthermore, this paper proposes a comparative study of several results, including sensitivity, specificity, and accuracy.

Future work may also include the development of a tool to predict the patient's risk of cancer diseases. The framework can extended for use on other models such as unsupervised machine learning, deep learning, etc.

References

1. Carrion, J.: Improving the patient-clinician interface of clinical trials through health informatics technologies. J. Med. Syst. **42**(7), 1–6 (2018). https://doi.org/10.1007/s10916-018-0973-y
2. Hussein, A., Djandji, M., Mahmoud, R.A., Dhaybi, M., Hajj, H.: Augmenting DL with adversarial training for robust prediction of epilepsy seizures. ACM Trans. Comput. Healthcare **1**(3), 1–18 (2020). https://doi.org/10.1145/3386580
3. Thambawita, V., et al.: An extensive study on cross-dataset bias and evaluation metrics interpretation for machine learning applied to gastrointestinal tract abnormality classification. ACM Trans. Comput. Healthcare **1**(3), 1–29 (2020). https://doi.org/10.1145/3386295
4. Meyer, J., Kay, J., Epstein, D., Eslambolchilar, P., Tang, L.: A life of data: characteristics and challenges of very long term self-tracking for health and wellness. ACM Trans. Comput. Healthcare **1**(2), 1–4 (2020). https://doi.org/10.1145/3373719
5. World Cancer Day: Facts about the deadly disease killing one person every 8 minutes. https://www.indiatoday.in/science/story/worldcan-day-2019-cancer-causes-cures-treatments-myths-1446568-2019-02-04
6. https://www.cancer.org/research/cancer-facts-statistics/all-cancer-facts-figures/cancer-facts-figures-2020.html
7. Lu, J., Song, E., Ghoneim, A., Alrashoud, M.: Machine learning for assisting cervical cancer diagnosis: an ensemble approach. Future Gener. Comput. Syst. **106**, 199–205 (2020). https://doi.org/10.1016/j.future.2019.12.033
8. Maliha, S.K.: Cancer disease prediction using Naive Bayes, K-nearest neighbor and J48 algorithm. IEEE – 45670 (2019)
9. Rahmat, T.: Chest X-ray image classification using faster R-CNN. Malaysian J. Comput. **4**(1), 225–236 (2019)

10. Bazila Banu, A., Thirumalaikolundusubramanian, P.: Comparison of Bayes classifiers for breast cancer classification. Asian Pacific J. Cancer Prev. APJCP **19**(10), 2917 (2018). https://doi.org/10.22034/APJCP.2018.19.10.2917

11. Song, R., Zhang, L., Zhu, C., Liu, J., Yang, J., Zhang, T.: Thyroid nodule ultrasound image classification through hybrid feature cropping network. IEEE Access **8**, 64064–64074 (2020). https://doi.org/10.1109/ACCESS.2020.2982767

12. Kurnia, R.: Software Metrics Classification for Agile Scrum Process: A Literature Review (2018)

13. Rathi, M., Singh, A.K.: Breast cancer prediction using Naïve Bayes classifier. Int. J. Inf. Technol. Syst. **1**(2), 77–80 (2012)

14. Duggal, P.: Prediction of Thyroid Disorders Using Advanced Machine Learning Techniques (2020). 978-1-7281–27910/20/$31.00 ©2020 IEEE

15. Shruthi, S.: Prediction of Cancer Diseases Using Navie Bayes Classification (2015)

16. Velayutham, K., Selvan, S.S.A., Unnikrishnan, A.G.: Prevalence of thyroid dysfunction among young females in a South Indian population. Indian J. Endocrinol. Metab. **19**(6), 781 (2015). https://doi.org/10.4103/2230-8210.167546

17. Polit, D., Beck, C.: Nursing Research: Principles and Methods, 7th edn. Lippincott, Williams and Wilkins, Philadelphia (2003)

18. Jamot, M., Pettersson, M.: Agile challenges within regulated healthcare environments. J. Adv. Nurs. **48**(5), 454–462 (2016)

19. Gultekin, M., Kalipsiz, O.: Story point-based effort estimation model with machine learning techniques. Int. J. Softw. Eng. Knowl. Eng. **30**(01), 43–66 (2020). https://doi.org/10.1142/S0218194020500035

20. Polkowski, Z., Vora, J., Tanwar, S., Tyagi, S., Singh, P.K., Singh, Y.: Machine learning-based software effort estimation: an analysis. In: 2019 11th International Conference on Electronics, Computers and Artificial Intelligence (ECAI), Pitesti, Romania, pp. 1–6 (2019). https://doi.org/10.1109/ECAI46879.2019.9042031

21. Bangotra, D.K., Singh, Y., Selwal, A., Kumar, N., Singh, P.K., Hong, W.-C.: An Intelligent opportunistic routing algorithm for wireless sensor networks and its application towards e-healthcare. Sensors **20**(14), 3887 (2020). https://doi.org/10.3390/s20143887

22. Tanwar, S., Bhatia, Q., Patel, P., Kumari, A., Singh, P.K., Hong, W.: Machine learning adoption in blockchain-based smart applications: the challenges, and a way forward. IEEE Access **8**, 474–488 (2020). https://doi.org/10.1109/ACCESS.2019.2961372

Author Index

Printed in the United States
by Baker & Taylor Publisher Services